# PRAISE FOR THE SECOND EDITION OF
## *THE ART OF ASSEMBLY LANGUAGE*

"The previous edition of Hyde's book has been my go-to book for assembly language for years, and there's little doubt that this edition will be similarly long-lived."
—SOFTWARE DEVELOPER TIMES

"This book is a very good read and effectively introduces the reader to this fascinating topic."
—THE ETHICAL HACKER NETWORK

"A welcome addition to the bookshelf of any programmer."
—DR. DOBB'S

"I highly recommend this book for programmers."
—HEX BLOG

"If you want to try assembly language, here is a great new book to help you out."
—SCIENCEBLOGS.COM

"Readers will be comfortable writing in programs using HLA and have a new understanding of how computers operate."
—YYZTECH.CA

"If you have always wanted to learn assembly language then this book might be just what you have been looking for."
—I PROGRAMMER

# THE ART OF ASSEMBLY LANGUAGE, 2ND EDITION

# THE ART OF
# ASSEMBLY LANGUAGE
## 2ND EDITION

## by Randall Hyde

**no starch
press**

San Francisco

18 17 16 15    2 3 4 5 6 7 8 9

Printed in USA


ISBN-10: 1-59327-207-3
ISBN-13: 978-1-59327-207-4

Publisher: William Pollock
Production Editor: Riley Hoffman
Cover and Interior Design: Octopod Studios
Developmental Editor: William Pollock
Technical Reviewer: Nathan Baker
Copyeditor: Linda Recktenwald
Compositor: Susan Glinert Stevens
Proofreader: Nancy Bell

For information on book distributors or translations, please contact No Starch Press, Inc. directly:

No Starch Press, Inc.
245 8th Street, Suite 250, San Francisco, CA 94103
phone: 415.863.9900; info@nostarch.com; www.nostarch.com

*Library of Congress Cataloging-in-Publication Data*

Hyde, Randall.
  The art of Assembly language / by Randall Hyde. -- 2nd ed.
      p. cm.
  ISBN 978-1-59327-207-4 (pbk.)
1.  Assembler language (Computer program language) 2.  Programming languages (Electronic computers)  I. Title.
QA76.73.A8H97 2010
 005.13'6--dc22
                                              2009040777

# BRIEF CONTENTS

# CONTENTS IN DETAIL

# 2
## DATA REPRESENTATION        53

# 3
## MEMORY ACCESS AND ORGANIZATION      111

# 4
# CONSTANTS, VARIABLES, AND DATA TYPES       155

# 5
# PROCEDURES AND UNITS
**255**

# 6
# ARITHMETIC

# 7
# LOW-LEVEL CONTROL STRUCTURES

# 8
# ADVANCED ARITHMETIC

# 9
# MACROS AND THE HLA COMPILE-TIME LANGUAGE     551

## 10
## BIT MANIPULATION

**599**

## 11
## THE STRING INSTRUCTIONS

**633**

# 12
# CLASSES AND OBJECTS                                              651

# ACKNOWLEDGMENTS

## First Edition

This book has literally taken over a decade to create. It started out as "How to Program the IBM PC, Using 8088 Assembly Language" way back in 1989. I originally wrote this book for the students in my assembly language course at Cal Poly Pomona and UC Riverside. Over the years, hundreds of students have made small and large contributions (it's amazing how a little extra credit can motivate some students). I've also received thousands of comments via the Internet after placing an early, 16-bit edition of this book on my website at UC Riverside. I owe everyone who has contributed to this effort my gratitude.

I would also like to specifically thank Mary Phillips, who spent several months helping me proofread much of the 16-bit edition upon which I've based this book. Mary is a wonderful person and a great friend.

I also owe a deep debt of gratitude to William Pollock at No Starch Press, who rescued this book from obscurity. He is the one responsible for convincing me to spend some time beating on this book to create a publishable entity from it. I would also like to thank Karol Jurado for shepherding this project from its inception—it's been a long, hard road. Thanks, Karol.

## Second Edition

I would like to thank the many thousands of readers who've made the first edition of *The Art of Assembly Language* so successful. Your comments, suggestions, and corrections have been a big help in the creation of this second edition. Thank you for purchasing this book and keeping assembly language alive and well.

When I first began work on this second edition, my original plan was to make the necessary changes and get the book out as quickly as possible. However, the kind folks at No Starch Press have spent countless hours improving the readability, consistency, and accuracy of this book. The second edition you hold in your hands is a huge improvement over the first edition and a large part of the credit belongs to No Starch. In particular, the following No Starch personnel are responsible for improving this book: Bill Pollock, Alison Peterson, Ansel Staton, Riley Hoffman, Megan Dunchak, Linda Recktenwald, Susan Glinert Stevens, and Nancy Bell. Special thanks goes out to Nathan Baker who was the technical reader for this book; you did a great job, Nate.

I'd also like to thank Sevag Krikorian, who developed the HIDE integrated development environment for HLA and has tirelessly promoted the HLA language, as well as all the contributors to the Yahoo AoAProgramming group; you've all provided great support for this book.

As I didn't mention her in the acknowledgments to the first edition, let me dedicate this book to my wife Mandy. It's been a great 30 years and I'm looking forward to another 30. Thanks for giving me the time to work on this project.

# 1

## HELLO, WORLD OF ASSEMBLY LANGUAGE

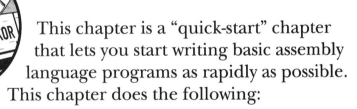 This chapter is a "quick-start" chapter that lets you start writing basic assembly language programs as rapidly as possible. This chapter does the following:

- Presents the basic syntax of an HLA (High Level Assembly) program
- Introduces you to the Intel CPU architecture
- Provides a handful of data declarations, machine instructions, and high-level control statements
- Describes some utility routines you can call in the HLA Standard Library
- Shows you how to write some simple assembly language programs

By the conclusion of this chapter, you should understand the basic syntax of an HLA program and should understand the prerequisites that are needed to start learning new assembly language features in the chapters that follow.

## 1.1 The Anatomy of an HLA Program

A typical HLA program takes the form shown in Figure 1-1.

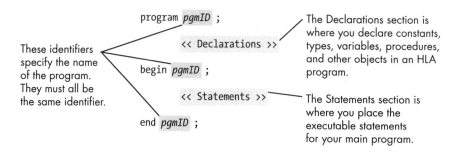

program, begin, and end are HLA reserved words that delineate the program. Note the placement of the semicolons in this program.

*Figure 1-1: Basic HLA program*

*pgmID* in the template above is a user-defined program identifier. You must pick an appropriate descriptive name for your program. In particular, *pgmID* would be a horrible choice for any real program. If you are writing programs as part of a course assignment, your instructor will probably give you the name to use for your main program. If you are writing your own HLA program, you will have to choose an appropriate name for your project.

Identifiers in HLA are very similar to identifiers in most high-level languages. HLA identifiers may begin with an underscore or an alphabetic character and may be followed by zero or more alphanumeric or underscore characters. HLA's identifiers are *case neutral.* This means that the identifiers are case sensitive insofar as you must always spell an identifier exactly the same way in your program (even with respect to upper- and lowercase). However, unlike in case-sensitive languages such as C/C++, you may not declare two identifiers in the program whose name differs only by alphabetic case.

A traditional first program people write, popularized by Kernighan and Ritchie's *The C Programming Language,* is the "Hello, world!" program. This program makes an excellent concrete example for someone who is learning a new language. Listing 1-1 presents the HLA *helloWorld* program.

```
program helloWorld;
#include( "stdlib.hhf" );

begin helloWorld;

    stdout.put( "Hello, World of Assembly Language", nl );

end helloWorld;
```

*Listing 1-1: The helloWorld program*

The #include statement in this program tells the HLA compiler to include a set of declarations from the *stdlib.hhf* (standard library, HLA Header File). Among other things, this file contains the declaration of the stdout.put code that this program uses.

The stdout.put statement is the print statement for the HLA language. You use it to write data to the standard output device (generally the console). To anyone familiar with I/O statements in a high-level language, it should be obvious that this statement prints the phrase Hello, World of Assembly Language. The nl appearing at the end of this statement is a constant, also defined in *stdlib.hhf,* that corresponds to the newline sequence.

Note that semicolons follow the program, begin, stdout.put, and end statements. Technically speaking, a semicolon does not follow the #include statement. It is possible to create include files that generate an error if a semicolon follows the #include statement, so you may want to get in the habit of not putting a semicolon here.

The #include is your first introduction to HLA declarations. The #include itself isn't actually a declaration, but it does tell the HLA compiler to substitute the file *stdlib.hhf* in place of the #include directive, thus inserting several declarations at this point in your program. Most HLA programs you will write will need to include one or more of the HLA Standard Library header files (*stdlib.hhf* actually includes all the standard library definitions into your program).

Compiling this program produces a *console* application. Running this program in a command window prints the specified string, and then control returns to the command-line interpreter (or *shell* in Unix terminology).

HLA is a free-format language. Therefore, you may split statements across multiple lines if this helps to make your programs more readable. For example, you could write the stdout.put statement in the *helloWorld* program as follows:

```
stdout.put
(
    "Hello, World of Assembly Language",
    nl
);
```

Another construction you'll see appearing in example code throughout this text is that HLA automatically concatenates any adjacent string constants it finds in your source file. Therefore, the statement above is also equivalent to

```
stdout.put
(
    "Hello, "
    "World of Assembly Language",
    nl
);
```

Indeed, nl (the newline) is really nothing more than a string constant, so (technically) the comma between the nl and the preceding string isn't necessary. You'll often see the above written as

```
stdout.put( "Hello, World of Assembly Language" nl );
```

Notice the lack of a comma between the string constant and nl; this turns out to be legal in HLA, though it applies only to certain constants; you may not, in general, drop the comma. Chapter 4 explains in detail how this works. This discussion appears here because you'll probably see this "trick" employed by sample code prior to the formal explanation.

## 1.2 Running Your First HLA Program

The whole purpose of the "Hello, world!" program is to provide a simple example by which someone who is learning a new programming language can figure out how to use the tools needed to compile and run programs in that language. True, the *helloWorld* program in Section 1.1 helps demonstrate the format and syntax of a simple HLA program, but the real purpose behind a program like *helloWorld* is to learn how to create and run a program from beginning to end. Although the previous section presents the layout of an HLA program, it did not discuss how to edit, compile, and run that program. This section will briefly cover those details.

All of the software you need to compile and run HLA programs can be found at *http://www.artofasm.com/* or at *http://webster.cs.ucr.edu/*. Select **High Level Assembly** from the Quick Navigation Panel and then the Download HLA link from that page. HLA is currently available for Windows, Mac OS X, Linux, and FreeBSD. Download the appropriate version of the HLA software for your system. From the Download HLA web page, you will also be able to download all the software associated with this book. If the HLA download doesn't include them, you will probably want to download the HLA reference manual and the HLA Standard Library reference manual along with HLA and the software for this book. This text does not describe the entire HLA language, nor does it describe the entire HLA Standard Library. You'll want to have these reference manuals handy as you learn assembly language using HLA.

This section will not describe how to install and set up the HLA system because those instructions change over time. The HLA download page for each of the operating systems describes how to install and use HLA. Please consult those instructions for the exact installation procedure.

Creating, compiling, and running an HLA program is very similar to the process you'd use when creating, compiling, or running a program in any computer language. First, because HLA is not an *integrated development environment (IDE)* that allows you to edit, compile, test and debug, and run your application all from within the same program, you'll create and edit HLA programs using a text editor.[1]

---

[1] HIDE (HLA Integrated Development Environment) is an IDE available for Windows users. See the High Level Assembly web page for details on downloading HIDE.

Windows, Mac OS X, Linux, and FreeBSD offer many text editor options. You can even use the text editor provided with other IDEs to create and edit HLA programs (such as those found in Visual C++, Borland's Delphi, Apple's Xcode, and similar languages). The only restriction is that HLA expects ASCII text files, so the editor you use must be capable of manipulating and saving text files. Under Windows you can always use Notepad to create HLA programs. If you're working under Linux and FreeBSD you can use joe, vi, or emacs. Under Mac OS X you can use XCode or Text Wrangler or another editor of your preference.

The HLA compiler[2] is a traditional *command-line compiler*, which means that you need to run it from a Windows *command-line prompt* or a Linux/FreeBSD/Mac OS X *shell*. To do so, enter something like the following into the command-line prompt or shell window:

```
hla hw.hla
```

This command tells HLA to compile the *hw.hla* (*helloWorld*) program to an executable file. Assuming there are no errors, you can run the resulting program by typing the following command into your command prompt window (Windows):

```
hw
```

or into the shell interpreter window (Linux/FreeBSD/Mac OS X):

```
./hw
```

If you're having problems getting the program to compile and run properly, please see the HLA installation instructions on the HLA download page. These instructions describe in great detail how to install, set up, and use HLA.

## 1.3  Some Basic HLA Data Declarations

HLA provides a wide variety of constant, type, and data declaration statements. Later chapters will cover the declaration sections in more detail, but it's important to know how to declare a few simple variables in an HLA program.

HLA predefines several different signed integer types including int8, int16, and int32, corresponding to 8-bit (1-byte) signed integers, 16-bit (2-byte) signed integers, and 32-bit (4-byte) signed integers, respectively.[3] Typical variable declarations occur in the HLA *static variable section*. A typical set of variable declarations takes the form shown in Figure 1-2.

---

[2] Traditionally, programmers have always called translators for assembly languages *assemblers* rather than *compilers*. However, because of HLA's high-level features, it is more proper to call HLA a compiler rather than an assembler.

[3] A discussion of bits and bytes will appear in Chapter 2 for those who are unfamiliar with these terms.

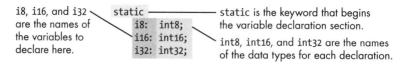

Figure 1-2: Static variable declarations

Those who are familiar with the Pascal language should be comfortable with this declaration syntax. This example demonstrates how to declare three separate integers: i8, i16, and i32. Of course, in a real program you should use variable names that are more descriptive. While names like *i8* and *i32* describe the type of the object, they do not describe its purpose. Variable names should describe the purpose of the object.

In the *static declaration section*, you can also give a variable an initial value that the operating system will assign to the variable when it loads the program into memory. Figure 1-3 provides the syntax for this.

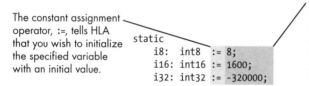

Figure 1-3: Static variable initialization

It is important to realize that the expression following the assignment operator (:=) must be a constant expression. You cannot assign the values of other variables within a static variable declaration.

Those familiar with other high-level languages (especially Pascal) should note that you can declare only one variable per statement. That is, HLA does not allow a comma-delimited list of variable names followed by a colon and a type identifier. Each variable declaration consists of a single identifier, a colon, a type ID, and a semicolon.

Listing 1-2 provides a simple HLA program that demonstrates the use of variables within an HLA program.

```
Program DemoVars;
#include( "stdlib.hhf" )

static
    InitDemo:        int32 := 5;
    NotInitialized: int32;

begin DemoVars;

    // Display the value of the pre-initialized variable:

    stdout.put( "InitDemo's value is ", InitDemo, nl );

    // Input an integer value from the user and display that value:
```

```
        stdout.put( "Enter an integer value: " );
        stdin.get( NotInitialized );
        stdout.put( "You entered: ", NotInitialized, nl );

end DemoVars;
```

*Listing 1-2: Variable declaration and use*

In addition to static variable declarations, this example introduces three new concepts. First, the stdout.put statement allows multiple parameters. If you specify an integer value, stdout.put will convert that value to its string representation on output.

The second new feature introduced in Listing 1-2 is the stdin.get statement. This statement reads a value from the standard input device (usually the keyboard), converts the value to an integer, and stores the integer value into the NotInitialized variable. Finally, Listing 1-2 also introduces the syntax for (one form of) HLA comments. The HLA compiler ignores all text from the // sequence to the end of the current line. (Those familiar with Java, C++, and Delphi should recognize these comments.)

# 1.4   Boolean Values

HLA and the HLA Standard Library provide limited support for boolean objects. You can declare boolean variables, use boolean literal constants, use boolean variables in boolean expressions, and you can print the values of boolean variables.

Boolean literal constants consist of the two predefined identifiers true and false. Internally, HLA represents the value true using the numeric value 1; HLA represents false using the value 0. Most programs treat 0 as false and anything else as true, so HLA's representations for true and false should prove sufficient.

To declare a boolean variable, you use the boolean data type. HLA uses a single byte (the least amount of memory it can allocate) to represent boolean values. The following example demonstrates some typical declarations:

```
static
    BoolVar:     boolean;
    HasClass:    boolean := false;
    IsClear:     boolean := true;
```

As this example demonstrates, you can initialize boolean variables if you desire.

Because boolean variables are byte objects, you can manipulate them using any instructions that operate directly on 8-bit values. Furthermore, as long as you ensure that your boolean variables only contain 0 and 1 (for false and true, respectively), you can use the 80x86 and, or, xor, and not instructions to manipulate these boolean values (these instructions are covered in Chapter 2).

You can print boolean values by making a call to the stdout.put routine. For example:

```
stdout.put( BoolVar )
```

This routine prints the text true or false depending upon the value of the boolean parameter (0 is false; anything else is true). Note that the HLA Standard Library does not allow you to read boolean values via stdin.get.

## 1.5 Character Values

HLA lets you declare 1-byte ASCII character objects using the char data type. You may initialize character variables with a literal character value by surrounding the character with a pair of apostrophes. The following example demonstrates how to declare and initialize character variables in HLA:

```
static
    c: char;
    LetterA: char := 'A';
```

You can print character variables use the stdout.put routine, and you can read character variables using the stdin.get procedure call.

## 1.6 An Introduction to the Intel 80x86 CPU Family

Thus far, you've seen a couple of HLA programs that will actually compile and run. However, all the statements appearing in programs to this point have been either data declarations or calls to HLA Standard Library routines. There hasn't been any *real* assembly language. Before we can progress any further and learn some real assembly language, a detour is necessary; unless you understand the basic structure of the Intel 80x86 CPU family, the machine instructions will make little sense.

The Intel CPU family is generally classified as a *Von Neumann Architecture Machine.* Von Neumann computer systems contain three main building blocks: the *central processing unit (CPU), memory,* and *input/output (I/O) devices.* These three components are interconnected using the *system bus* (consisting of the address, data, and control buses). The block diagram in Figure 1-4 shows this relationship.

The CPU communicates with memory and I/O devices by placing a numeric value on the address bus to select one of the memory locations or I/O device port locations, each of which has a unique binary numeric *address.* Then the CPU, memory, and I/O devices pass data among themselves by placing the data on the data bus. The control bus contains signals that determine the direction of the data transfer (to/from memory and to/from an I/O device).

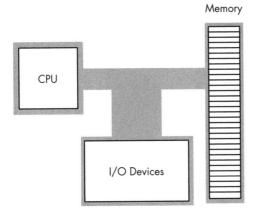

*Figure 1-4: Von Neumann computer system block
diagram*

The 80x86 CPU registers can be broken down into four categories: general-purpose registers, special-purpose application-accessible registers, segment registers, and special-purpose kernel-mode registers. Because the segment registers aren't used much in modern 32-bit operating systems (such as Windows, Mac OS X, FreeBSD, and Linux) and because this text is geared to writing programs written for 32-bit operating systems, there is little need to discuss the segment registers. The special-purpose kernel-mode registers are intended for writing operating systems, debuggers, and other system-level tools. Such software construction is well beyond the scope of this text.

The 80x86 (Intel family) CPUs provide several general-purpose registers for application use. These include eight 32-bit registers that have the following names: EAX, EBX, ECX, EDX, ESI, EDI, EBP, and ESP.

The *E* prefix on each name stands for *extended*. This prefix differentiates the 32-bit registers from the eight 16-bit registers that have the following names: AX, BX, CX, DX, SI, DI, BP, and SP.

Finally, the 80x86 CPUs provide eight 8-bit registers that have the following names: AL, AH, BL, BH, CL, CH, DL, and DH.

Unfortunately, these are not all separate registers. That is, the 80x86 does not provide 24 independent registers. Instead, the 80x86 overlays the 32-bit registers with the 16-bit registers, and it overlays the 16-bit registers with the 8-bit registers. Figure 1-5 shows this relationship.

The most important thing to note about the general-purpose registers is that they are not independent. Modifying one register may modify as many as three other registers. For example, modification of the EAX register may very well modify the AL, AH, and AX registers. This fact cannot be overemphasized here. A very common mistake in programs written by beginning assembly language programmers is register value corruption because the programmer did not completely understand the ramifications of the relationship shown in Figure 1-5.

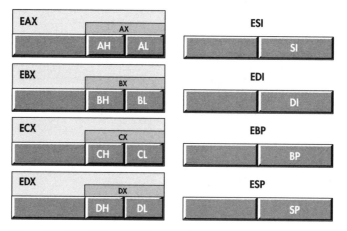

Figure 1-5: 80x86 (Intel CPU) general-purpose registers

The EFLAGS register is a 32-bit register that encapsulates several single-bit boolean (true/false) values. Most of the bits in the EFLAGS register are either reserved for kernel mode (operating system) functions or are of little interest to the application programmer. Eight of these bits (or *flags*) are of interest to application programmers writing assembly language programs. These are the overflow, direction, interrupt disable,[4] sign, zero, auxiliary carry, parity, and carry flags. Figure 1-6 shows the layout of the flags within the lower 16 bits of the EFLAGS register.

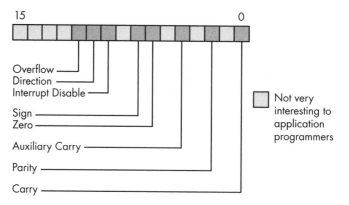

Figure 1-6: Layout of the FLAGS register (lower 16 bits of EFLAGS)

Of the eight flags that are of interest to application programmers, four flags in particular are extremely valuable: the overflow, carry, sign, and zero flags. Collectively, we will call these four flags the *condition codes*.[5] The state of these flags lets you test the result of previous computations. For example, after comparing two values, the condition code flags will tell you whether one value is less than, equal to, or greater than a second value.

---

[4] Application programs cannot modify the interrupt flag, but we'll look at this flag in Chapter 2; hence the discussion of this flag here.

[5] Technically the parity flag is also a condition code, but we will not use that flag in this text.

One important fact that comes as a surprise to those just learning assembly language is that almost all calculations on the 80x86 CPU involve a register. For example, to add two variables together, storing the sum into a third variable, you must load one of the variables into a register, add the second operand to the value in the register, and then store the register away in the destination variable. Registers are a middleman in nearly every calculation. Therefore, registers are very important in 80x86 assembly language programs.

Another thing you should be aware of is that although the registers have the name "general purpose," you should not infer that you can use any register for any purpose. All the 80x86 registers have their own special purposes that limit their use in certain contexts. The SP/ESP register pair, for example, has a very special purpose that effectively prevents you from using it for anything else (it's the *stack pointer*). Likewise, the BP/EBP register has a special purpose that limits its usefulness as a general-purpose register. For the time being, you should avoid the use of the ESP and EBP registers for generic calculations; also, keep in mind that the remaining registers are not completely interchangeable in your programs.

## 1.7 The Memory Subsystem

A typical 80x86 processor running a modern 32-bit OS can access a maximum of $2^{32}$ different memory locations, or just over 4 billion bytes. A few years ago, 4 gigabytes of memory would have seemed like infinity; modern machines, however, exceed this limit. Nevertheless, because the 80x86 architecture supports a maximum 4GB address space when using a 32-bit operating system like Windows, Mac OS X, FreeBSD, or Linux, the following discussion will assume the 4GB limit.

Of course, the first question you should ask is, "What exactly is a memory location?" The 80x86 supports *byte-addressable memory*. Therefore, the basic memory unit is a byte, which is sufficient to hold a single character or a (very) small integer value (we'll talk more about that in Chapter 2).

Think of memory as a linear array of bytes. The address of the first byte is 0 and the address of the last byte is $2^{32}-1$. For an 80x86 processor, the following pseudo-Pascal array declaration is a good approximation of memory:

```
Memory: array [0..4294967295] of byte;
```

C/C++ and Java users might prefer the following syntax:

```
byte Memory[4294967296];
```

To execute the equivalent of the Pascal statement Memory [125] := 0; the CPU places the value 0 on the data bus, places the address 125 on the address bus, and asserts the write line (this generally involves setting that line to 0), as shown in Figure 1-7.

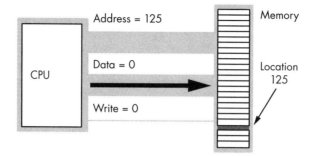

*Figure 1-7: Memory write operation*

To execute the equivalent of CPU := Memory [125]; the CPU places the address 125 on the address bus, asserts the read line (because the CPU is reading data from memory), and then reads the resulting data from the data bus (see Figure 1-8).

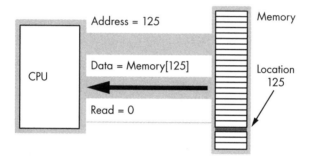

*Figure 1-8: Memory read operation*

This discussion applies *only* when accessing a single byte in memory. So what happens when the processor accesses a word or a double word? Because memory consists of an array of bytes, how can we possibly deal with values larger than a single byte? Easy—to store larger values, the 80x86 uses a sequence of consecutive memory locations. Figure 1-9 shows how the 80x86 stores bytes, words (2 bytes), and double words (4 bytes) in memory. The memory address of each of these objects is the address of the first byte of each object (that is, the lowest address).

Modern 80x86 processors don't actually connect directly to memory. Instead, there is a special memory buffer on the CPU known as the *cache* (pronounced "cash") that acts as a high-speed intermediary between the CPU and main memory. Although the cache handles the details automatically for you, one fact you should know is that accessing data objects in memory is sometimes more efficient if the address of the object is an even multiple of the object's size. Therefore, it's a good idea to *align* 4-byte objects (double words) on addresses that are multiples of 4. Likewise, it's most efficient to align 2-byte objects on even addresses. You can efficiently access single-byte objects at any address. You'll see how to set the alignment of memory objects in Section 3.4.

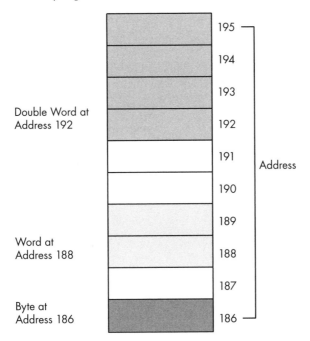

Figure 1-9: Byte, word, and double-word storage in memory

Before leaving this discussion of memory objects, it's important to understand the correspondence between memory and HLA variables. One of the nice things about using an assembler/compiler like HLA is that you don't have to worry about numeric memory addresses. All you need to do is declare a variable in HLA, and HLA takes care of associating that variable with some unique set of memory addresses. For example, if you have the following declaration section:

```
static
    i8          :int8;
    i16         :int16;
    i32         :int32;
```

HLA will find some unused 8-bit byte in memory and associate it with the i8 variable; it will find a pair of consecutive unused bytes and associate i16 with them; finally, HLA will find 4 consecutive unused bytes and associate the value of i32 with those 4 bytes (32 bits). You'll always refer to these variables by their name. You generally don't have to concern yourself with their numeric address. Still, you should be aware that HLA is doing this for you behind your back.

## 1.8 Some Basic Machine Instructions

The 80x86 CPU family provides from just over a hundred to many thousands of different machine instructions, depending on how you define a machine instruction. Even at the low end of the count (greater than 100), it appears as though there are far too many machine instructions to learn in a short time. Fortunately, you don't need to know all the machine instructions. In fact, most assembly language programs probably use around 30 different machine instructions.[6] Indeed, you can certainly write several meaningful programs with only a few machine instructions. The purpose of this section is to provide a small handful of machine instructions so you can start writing simple HLA assembly language programs right away.

Without question, the mov instruction is the most oft-used assembly language statement. In a typical program, anywhere from 25 percent to 40 percent of the instructions are mov instructions. As its name suggests, this instruction moves data from one location to another.[7] The HLA syntax for this instruction is:

```
mov( source_operand, destination_operand );
```

The source_operand can be a register, a memory variable, or a constant. The destination_operand may be a register or a memory variable. Technically the 80x86 instruction set does not allow both operands to be memory variables. HLA, however, will automatically translate a mov instruction with two-word or double-word memory operands into a pair of instructions that will copy the data from one location to another. In a high-level language like Pascal or C/C++, the mov instruction is roughly equivalent to the following assignment statement:

```
destination_operand = source_operand ;
```

Perhaps the major restriction on the mov instruction's operands is that they must both be the same size. That is, you can move data between a pair of byte (8-bit) objects, word (16-bit) objects, or double-word (32-bit) objects; you may not, however, mix the sizes of the operands. Table 1-1 lists all the legal combinations for the mov instruction.

You should study this table carefully because most of the general-purpose 80x86 instructions use this syntax.

---

[6] Different programs may use a different set of 30 instructions, but few programs use more than 30 distinct instructions.

[7] Technically, mov actually copies data from one location to another. It does not destroy the original data in the source operand. Perhaps a better name for this instruction would have been copy. Alas, it's too late to change it now.

**Table 1-1:** Legal 80x86 mov Instruction Operands

| Source | Destination |
|---|---|
| $Reg_8$* | $Reg_8$ |
| $Reg_8$ | $Mem_8$ |
| $Mem_8$ | $Reg_8$ |
| Constant[†] | $Reg_8$ |
| Constant | $Mem_8$ |
| $Reg_{16}$ | $Reg_{16}$ |
| $Reg_{16}$ | $Mem_{16}$ |
| $Mem_{16}$ | $Reg_{16}$ |
| Constant | $Reg_{16}$ |
| Constant | $Mem_{16}$ |
| $Reg_{32}$ | $Reg_{32}$ |
| $Reg_{32}$ | $Mem_{32}$ |
| $Mem_{32}$ | $Reg_{32}$ |
| Constant | $Reg_{32}$ |
| Constant | $Mem_{32}$ |

* The suffix denotes the size of the register or memory location.

† The constant must be small enough to fit in the specified destination operand.

The 80x86 add and sub instructions let you add and subtract two operands. Their syntax is nearly identical to the mov instruction:

```
add( source_operand, destination_operand );
sub( source_operand, destination_operand );
```

The add and sub operands take the same form as the mov instruction.[8] The add instruction does the following:

```
destination_operand = destination_operand + source_operand ;
destination_operand += source_operand;   // For those who prefer C syntax.
```

The sub instruction does the calculation:

```
destination_operand = destination_operand - source_operand ;
destination_operand -= source_operand ;   // For C fans.
```

With nothing more than these three instructions, plus the HLA control structures that the next section discusses, you can actually write some sophisticated programs. Listing 1-3 provides a sample HLA program that demonstrates these three instructions.

---

[8] Remember, though, that add and sub do not support memory-to-memory operations.

```
program DemoMOVaddSUB;

#include( "stdlib.hhf" )

static
    i8:     int8    := -8;
    i16:    int16   := -16;
    i32:    int32   := -32;

begin DemoMOVaddSUB;

    // First, print the initial values
    // of our variables.

    stdout.put
    (
        nl,
        "Initialized values: i8=", i8,
        ", i16=", i16,
        ", i32=", i32,
        nl
    );

    // Compute the absolute value of the
    // three different variables and
    // print the result.
    // Note: Because all the numbers are
    // negative, we have to negate them.
    // Using only the mov, add, and sub
    // instructions, we can negate a value
    // by subtracting it from zero.

    mov( 0, al );    // Compute i8 := -i8;
    sub( i8, al );
    mov( al, i8 );

    mov( 0, ax );    // Compute i16 := -i16;
    sub( i16, ax );
    mov( ax, i16 );

    mov( 0, eax );   // Compute i32 := -i32;
    sub( i32, eax );
    mov( eax, i32 );

    // Display the absolute values:

    stdout.put
    (
        nl,
        "After negation: i8=", i8,
        ", i16=", i16,
        ", i32=", i32,
        nl
```

```
    );

    // Demonstrate add and constant-to-memory
    // operations:

    add( 32323200, i32 );
    stdout.put( nl, "After add: i32=", i32, nl );


end DemoMOVaddSUB;
```

*Listing 1-3: Demonstration of the mov, add, and sub instructions*

## 1.9 Some Basic HLA Control Structures

The mov, add, and sub instructions, while valuable, aren't sufficient to let you write meaningful programs. You will need to complement these instructions with the ability to make decisions and create loops in your HLA programs before you can write anything other than a simple program. HLA provides several high-level control structures that are very similar to control structures found in high-level languages. These include if..then..elseif..else..endif, while..endwhile, repeat..until, and so on. By learning these statements you will be armed and ready to write some real programs.

Before discussing these high-level control structures, it's important to point out that these are not real 80x86 assembly language statements. HLA compiles these statements into a sequence of one or more real assembly language statements for you. In Chapter 7, you'll learn how HLA compiles the statements, and you'll learn how to write pure assembly language code that doesn't use them. However, there is a lot to learn before you get to that point, so we'll stick with these high-level language statements for now.

Another important fact to mention is that HLA's high-level control structures are *not* as high level as they first appear. The purpose behind HLA's high-level control structures is to let you start writing assembly language programs as quickly as possible, not to let you avoid the use of assembly language altogether. You will soon discover that these statements have some severe restrictions associated with them, and you will quickly outgrow their capabilities. This is intentional. Once you reach a certain level of comfort with HLA's high-level control structures and decide you need more power than they have to offer, it's time to move on and learn the real 80x86 instructions behind these statements.

Do not let the presence of high-level-like statements in HLA confuse you. Many people, after learning about the presence of these statements in the HLA language, erroneously come to the conclusion that HLA is just some special high-level language and not a true assembly language. This isn't true. HLA is a full low-level assembly language. HLA supports all the same machine instructions as any other 80x86 assembler. The difference is that HLA has some *extra* statements that allow you to do *more* than is possible with those other 80x86 assemblers. Once you learn 80x86 assembly language with HLA, you may elect to ignore all these extra (high-level) statements and write only low-level 80x86 assembly language code if this is your desire.

The following sections assume that you're familiar with at least one high-level language. They present the HLA control statements from that perspective without bothering to explain how you actually use these statements to accomplish something in a program. One prerequisite this text assumes is that you already know how to use these generic control statements in a high-level language; you'll use them in HLA programs in an identical manner.

### 1.9.1 Boolean Expressions in HLA Statements

Several HLA statements require a boolean (true or false) expression to control their execution. Examples include the if, while, and repeat..until statements. The syntax for these boolean expressions represents the greatest limitation of the HLA high-level control structures. This is one area where your familiarity with a high-level language will work against you—you'll want to use the fancy expressions you use in a high-level language, yet HLA supports only some basic forms.

HLA boolean expressions take the following forms:[9]

```
flag_specification
!flag_specification
register
!register
Boolean_variable
!Boolean_variable
mem_reg relop mem_reg_const
register in LowConst..HiConst
register not in LowConst..HiConst
```

A flag_specification may be one of the symbols that are described in Table 1-2.

**Table 1-2:** Symbols for flag_specification

| Symbol | Meaning | Explanation |
| --- | --- | --- |
| @c | Carry | True if the carry is set (1); false if the carry is clear (0). |
| @nc | No carry | True if the carry is clear (0); false if the carry is set (1). |
| @z | Zero | True if the zero flag is set; false if it is clear. |
| @nz | Not zero | True if the zero flag is clear; false if it is set. |
| @o | Overflow | True if the overflow flag is set; false if it is clear. |
| @no | No overflow | True if the overflow flag is clear; false if it is set. |
| @s | Sign | True if the sign flag is set; false if it is clear. |
| @ns | No sign | True if the sign flag is clear; false if it is set. |

---

[9] There are a few additional forms that we'll cover in Chapter 6.

The use of the flag values in a boolean expression is somewhat advanced. You will begin to see how to use these boolean expression operands in the next chapter.

A register operand can be any of the 8-bit, 16-bit, or 32-bit general-purpose registers. The expression evaluates false if the register contains a zero; it evaluates true if the register contains a nonzero value.

If you specify a boolean variable as the expression, the program tests it for zero (false) or nonzero (true). Because HLA uses the values zero and one to represent false and true, respectively, the test works in an intuitive fashion. Note that HLA requires such variables be of type boolean. HLA rejects other data types. If you want to test some other type against zero/not zero, then use the general boolean expression discussed next.

The most general form of an HLA boolean expression has two operands and a relational operator. Table 1-3 lists the legal combinations.

**Table 1-3:** Legal Boolean Expressions

| Left Operand | Relational Operator | Right Operand |
|---|---|---|
| Memory variable or register | = or == <br> <> or != <br> < <br> <= <br> > <br> >= | Variable, register, or constant |

Note that both operands cannot be memory operands. In fact, if you think of the *right operand* as the source operand and the *left operand* as the destination operand, then the two operands must be the same that add and sub allow.

Also like the add and sub instructions, the two operands must be the same size. That is, they must both be byte operands, they must both be word operands, or they must both be double-word operands. If the right operand is a constant, its value must be in the range that is compatible with the left operand.

There is one other issue: if the left operand is a register and the right operand is a positive constant or another register, HLA uses an *unsigned* comparison. The next chapter will discuss the ramifications of this; for the time being, do not compare negative values in a register against a constant or another register. You may not get an intuitive result.

The in and not in operators let you test a register to see if it is within a specified range. For example, the expression eax in 2000..2099 evaluates true if the value in the EAX register is between 2,000 and 2,099 (inclusive). The not in (two words) operator checks to see if the value in a register is outside the specified range. For example, al not in 'a'..'z' evaluates true if the character in the AL register is not a lowercase alphabetic character.

Here are some examples of legal boolean expressions in HLA:

```
@c
Bool_var
al
esi
eax < ebx
ebx > 5
i32 < -2
i8 > 128
al < i8
eax in 1..100
ch not in 'a'..'z'
```

## 1.9.2   The HLA if..then..elseif..else..endif Statement

The HLA if statement uses the syntax shown in Figure 1-10.

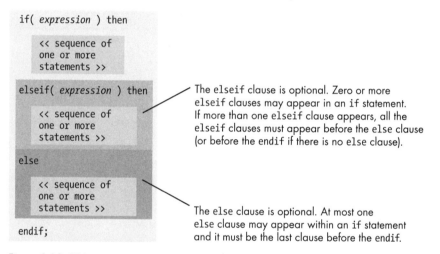

```
if( expression ) then

    << sequence of
    one or more
    statements >>

elseif( expression ) then

    << sequence of
    one or more
    statements >>

else

    << sequence of
    one or more
    statements >>

endif;
```

The elseif clause is optional. Zero or more elseif clauses may appear in an if statement. If more than one elseif clause appears, all the elseif clauses must appear before the else clause (or before the endif if there is no else clause).

The else clause is optional. At most one else clause may appear within an if statement and it must be the last clause before the endif.

Figure 1-10: HLA if statement syntax

The expressions appearing in an if statement must take one of the forms from the previous section. If the boolean expression is true, the code after the then executes; otherwise control transfers to the next elseif or else clause in the statement.

Because the elseif and else clauses are optional, an if statement could take the form of a single if..then clause, followed by a sequence of statements and a closing endif clause. The following is such a statement:

```
if( eax = 0 ) then

    stdout.put( "error: NULL value", nl );

endif;
```

If, during program execution, the expression evaluates true, then the code between the then and the endif executes. If the expression evaluates false, then the program skips over the code between the then and the endif.

Another common form of the if statement has a single else clause. The following is an example of an if statement with an optional else clause:

```
if( eax = 0 ) then

    stdout.put( "error: NULL pointer encountered", nl );

else

    stdout.put( "Pointer is valid", nl );

endif;
```

If the expression evaluates true, the code between the then and the else executes; otherwise the code between the else and the endif clauses executes.

You can create sophisticated decision-making logic by incorporating the elseif clause into an if statement. For example, if the CH register contains a character value, you can select from a menu of items using code like the following:

```
if( ch = 'a' ) then

    stdout.put( "You selected the 'a' menu item", nl );

elseif( ch = 'b' ) then

    stdout.put( "You selected the 'b' menu item", nl );

elseif( ch = 'c' ) then

    stdout.put( "You selected the 'c' menu item", nl );

else

    stdout.put( "Error: illegal menu item selection", nl );

endif;
```

Although this simple example doesn't demonstrate it, HLA does not require an else clause at the end of a sequence of elseif clauses. However, when making multiway decisions, it's always a good idea to provide an else clause just in case an error arises. Even if you think it's impossible for the else clause to execute, just keep in mind that future modifications to the code could void this assertion, so it's a good idea to have error-reporting statements in your code.

## 1.9.3   Conjunction, Disjunction, and Negation in Boolean Expressions

Some obvious omissions in the list of operators in the previous sections are the conjunction (logical and), disjunction (logical or), and negation (logical not) operators. This section describes their use in boolean expressions (the discussion had to wait until after describing the if statement in order to present realistic examples).

HLA uses the && operator to denote logical and in a runtime boolean expression. This is a dyadic (two-operand) operator, and the two operands must be legal runtime boolean expressions. This operator evaluates to true if both operands evaluate to true. For example:

```
if( eax > 0 && ch = 'a' ) then

    mov( eax, ebx );
    mov( ' ', ch );

endif;
```

The two mov statements above execute only if EAX is greater than zero *and* CH is equal to the character *a*. If either of these conditions is false, then program execution skips over these mov instructions.

Note that the expressions on either side of the && operator may be any legal boolean expressions; these expressions don't have to be comparisons using the relational operators. For example, the following are all legal expressions:

```
@z && al in 5..10
al in 'a'..'z' && ebx
boolVar && !eax
```

HLA uses *short-circuit evaluation* when compiling the && operator. If the leftmost operand evaluates false, then the code that HLA generates does not bother evaluating the second operand (because the whole expression must be false at that point). Therefore, in the last expression above, the code will not check EAX against zero if boolVar evaluates false.

Note that an expression like eax < 10 && ebx <> eax is itself a legal boolean expression and, therefore, may appear as the left or right operand of the && operator. Therefore, expressions like the following are perfectly legal:

```
eax < 0  &&  ebx <> eax    &&    !ecx
```

The && operator is left associative, so the code that HLA generates evaluates the expression above in a left-to-right fashion. If EAX is less than zero, the CPU will not test either of the remaining expressions. Likewise, if EAX is not less than zero but EBX is equal to EAX, this code will not evaluate the third expression because the whole expression is false regardless of ECX's value.

HLA uses the || operator to denote disjunction (logical or) in a runtime boolean expression. Like the && operator, this operator expects two legal runtime boolean expressions as operands. This operator evaluates true if either (or both) operands evaluate true. Like the && operator, the disjunction operator uses short-circuit evaluation. If the left operand evaluates true, then the code that HLA generates doesn't bother to test the value of the second operand. Instead, the code will transfer to the location that handles the situation when the boolean expression evaluates true. Here are some examples of legal expressions using the || operator:

```
@z || al = 10
al in 'a'..'z' || ebx
!boolVar || eax
```

Like the && operator, the disjunction operator is left associative, so multiple instances of the || operator may appear within the same expression. Should this be the case, the code that HLA generates will evaluate the expressions from left to right. For example:

```
eax < 0  ||  ebx <> eax  ||  !ecx
```

The code above evaluates to true if EAX is less than zero, EBX does not equal EAX, or ECX is zero. Note that if the first comparison is true, the code doesn't bother testing the other conditions. Likewise, if the first comparison is false and the second is true, the code doesn't bother checking to see if ECX is zero. The check for ECX equal to zero occurs only if the first two comparisons are false.

If both the conjunction and disjunction operators appear in the same expression, then the && operator takes precedence over the || operator. Consider the following expression:

```
eax < 0 || ebx <> eax && !ecx
```

The machine code HLA generates evaluates this as

```
eax < 0 || (ebx <> eax && !ecx)
```

If EAX is less than zero, then the code HLA generates does not bother to check the remainder of the expression, and the entire expression evaluates true. However, if EAX is not less than zero, then both of the following conditions must evaluate true in order for the overall expression to evaluate true.

HLA allows you to use parentheses to surround subexpressions involving && and || if you need to adjust the precedence of the operators. Consider the following expression:

```
(eax < 0 || ebx <> eax) && !ecx
```

For this expression to evaluate true, ECX must contain zero and either EAX must be less than zero or EBX must not equal EAX. Contrast this to the result the expression produces without the parentheses.

HLA uses the ! operator to denote logical negation. However, the ! operator may only prefix a register or boolean variable; you may not use it as part of a larger expression (e.g., !eax < 0). To achieve logical negative of an existing boolean expression, you must surround that expression with parentheses and prefix the parentheses with the ! operator. For example:

```
!( eax < 0 )
```

This expression evaluates true if EAX is not less than zero.

The logical not operator is primarily useful for surrounding complex expressions involving the conjunction and disjunction operators. While it is occasionally useful for short expressions like the one above, it's usually easier (and more readable) to simply state the logic directly rather than convolute it with the logical not operator.

Note that HLA also provides the | and & operators, but they are distinct from || and && and have completely different meanings. See the HLA reference manual for more details on these (compile-time) operators.

### 1.9.4    The while..endwhile Statement

The while statement uses the basic syntax shown in Figure 1-11.

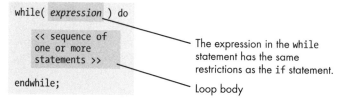
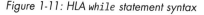

Figure 1-11: HLA while statement syntax

This statement evaluates the boolean expression. If it is false, control immediately transfers to the first statement following the endwhile clause. If the value of the expression is true, then the CPU executes the body of the loop. After the loop body executes, control transfers back to the top of the loop, where the while statement retests the loop control expression. This process repeats until the expression evaluates false.

Note that the while loop, like its high-level-language counterpart, tests for loop termination at the top of the loop. Therefore, it is quite possible that the statements in the body of the loop will not execute (if the expression is false when the code first executes the while statement). Also note that the body of the while loop must, at some point, modify the value of the boolean expression or an infinite loop will result.

Here's an example of an HLA while loop:

```
mov( 0, i );
while( i < 10 ) do

    stdout.put( "i=", i, nl );
    add( 1, i );

endwhile;
```

## 1.9.5   The for..endfor Statement

The HLA for loop takes the following general form:

```
for( Initial_Stmt; Termination_Expression; Post_Body_Statement ) do

    << Loop body >>

endfor;
```

This is equivalent to the following while statement:

```
Initial_Stmt;
while( Termination_Expression ) do

    << Loop body >>

    Post_Body_Statement;

endwhile;
```

Initial_Stmt can be any single HLA/80x86 instruction. Generally this statement initializes a register or memory location (the loop counter) with zero or some other initial value. Termination_Expression is an HLA boolean expression (same format that while allows). This expression determines whether the loop body executes. Post_Body_Statement executes at the bottom of the loop (as shown in the while example above). This is a single HLA statement. Usually an instruction like add modifies the value of the loop control variable.

The following gives a complete example:

```
for( mov( 0, i ); i < 10; add(1, i )) do

    stdout.put( "i=", i, nl );

endfor;
```

The above, rewritten as a while loop, becomes:

```
mov( 0, i );
while( i < 10 ) do

    stdout.put( "i=", i, nl );

    add( 1, i );

endwhile;
```

## 1.9.6 The repeat..until Statement

The HLA repeat..until statement uses the syntax shown in Figure 1-12.
C/C++/C# and Java users should note that the repeat..until statement is
very similar to the do..while statement.

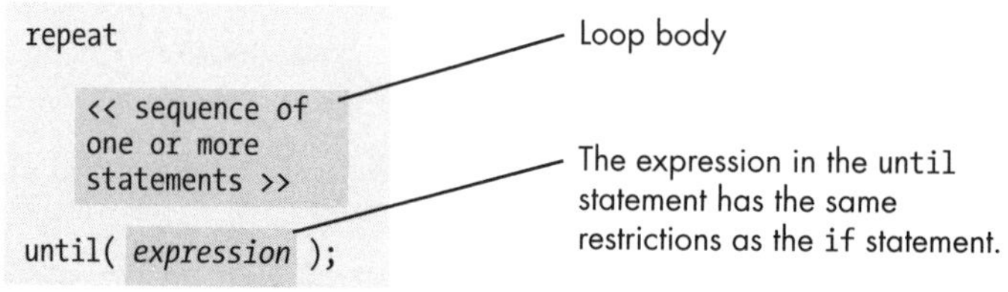

```
repeat                                    ── Loop body

    << sequence of
    one or more
    statements >>                         ── The expression in the until
                                              statement has the same
    until( expression );                      restrictions as the if statement.
```

*Figure 1-12: HLA repeat..until statement syntax*

The HLA repeat..until statement tests for loop termination at the
bottom of the loop. Therefore, the statements in the loop body always
execute at least once. Upon encountering the until clause, the program
will evaluate the expression and repeat the loop if the expression is false
(that is, it repeats while false). If the expression evaluates true, the control
transfers to the first statement following the until clause.
The following simple example demonstrates the repeat..until statement:

```
mov( 10, ecx );
repeat

    stdout.put( "ecx = ", ecx, nl );
    sub( 1, ecx );

until( ecx = 0 );
```

If the loop body will always execute at least once, then it is usually more
efficient to use a repeat..until loop rather than a while loop.

### 1.9.7 The break and breakif Statements

The break and breakif statements provide the ability to prematurely exit from a loop. Figure 1-13 shows the syntax for these two statements.

break;
breakif( *expression* );

The expression in the breakif statement has the same restrictions as the if statement.

Figure 1-13: HLA break and breakif syntax

The break statement exits the loop that immediately contains the break. The breakif statement evaluates the boolean expression and exits the containing loop if the expression evaluates true.

Note that the break and breakif statements do not allow you to break out of more than one nested loop. HLA does provide statements that do this, the begin..end block and the exit/exitif statements. Please consult the HLA reference manual for more details. HLA also provides the continue/continueif pair that lets you repeat a loop body. Again, see the HLA reference manual for more details.

### 1.9.8 The forever..endfor Statement

Figure 1-14 shows the syntax for the forever statement.

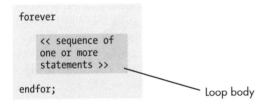

```
forever

    << sequence of
    one or more
    statements >>

endfor;
```

Loop body

Figure 1-14: HLA forever loop syntax

This statement creates an infinite loop. You may also use the break and breakif statements along with forever..endfor to create a loop that tests for loop termination in the middle of the loop. Indeed, this is probably the most common use of this loop, as the following example demonstrates:

```
forever

    stdout.put( "Enter an integer less than 10: " );
    stdin.get( i );
    breakif( i < 10 );
    stdout.put( "The value needs to be less than 10!", nl );

endfor;
```

### 1.9.9 The try..exception..endtry Statement

The HLA try..exception..endtry statement provides very powerful *exception handling* capabilities. The syntax for this statement appears in Figure 1-15.

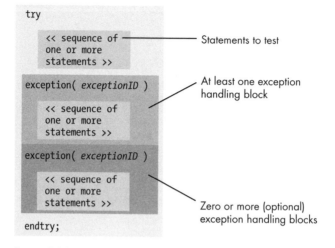

Figure 1-15: HLA try..exception..endtry statement syntax

The try..endtry statement protects a block of statements during execution. If the statements between the try clause and the first exception clause (the *protected block*), execute without incident, control transfers to the first statement after the endtry immediately after executing the last statement in the protected block. If an error (exception) occurs, then the program interrupts control at the point of the exception (that is, the program *raises* an exception). Each exception has an unsigned integer constant associated with it, known as the *exception ID*. The *excepts.hhf* header file in the HLA Standard Library predefines several exception IDs, although you may create new ones for your own purposes. When an exception occurs, the system compares the exception ID against the values appearing in each of the exception clauses following the protected code. If the current exception ID matches one of the exception values, control continues with the block of statements immediately following that exception. After the exception-handling code completes execution, control transfers to the first statement following the endtry.

If an exception occurs and there is no active try..endtry statement, or the active try..endtry statements do not handle the specific exception, the program will abort with an error message.

The following code fragment demonstrates how to use the try..endtry statement to protect the program from bad user input:

```
repeat

    mov( false, GoodInteger );    // Note: GoodInteger must be a boolean var.
    try

        stdout.put( "Enter an integer: " );
```

```
            stdin.get( i );
            mov( true, GoodInteger );

        exception( ex.ConversionError );

            stdout.put( "Illegal numeric value, please re-enter", nl );

        exception( ex.ValueOutOfRange );

            stdout.put( "Value is out of range, please re-enter", nl );

        endtry;

until( GoodInteger );
```

The repeat..until loop repeats this code as long as there is an error during input. Should an exception occur because of bad input, control transfers to the exception clauses to see if a conversion error (e.g., illegal characters in the number) or a numeric overflow occurs. If either of these exceptions occur, then they print the appropriate message, control falls out of the try..endtry statement, and the repeat..until loop repeats because the code will not have set GoodInteger to true. If a different exception occurs (one that is not handled in this code), then the program aborts with the specified error message.[10]

Table 1-4 lists the exceptions provided in the *excepts.hhf* header file at the time this was being written. See the *excepts.hhf* header file provided with HLA for the most current list of exceptions.

**Table 1-4:** Exceptions Provided in *excepts.hhf*

| Exception | Description |
| --- | --- |
| ex.StringOverflow | Attempt to store a string that is too large into a string variable. |
| ex.StringIndexError | Attempt to access a character that is not present in a string. |
| ex.StringOverlap | Attempt to copy a string onto itself. |
| ex.StringMetaData | Corrupted string value. |
| ex.StringAlignment | Attempt to store a string an at unaligned address. |
| ex.StringUnderflow | Attempt to extract "negative" characters from a string. |
| ex.IllegalStringOperation | Operation not permitted on string data. |
| ex.ValueOutOfRange | Value is too large for the current operation. |
| ex.IllegalChar | Operation encountered a character code whose ASCII code is not in the range 0..127. |
| ex.TooManyCmdLnParms | Command line contains too many program parameters. |
| ex.BadObjPtr | Pointer to class object is illegal. |
| | *(continued)* |

---

[10] An experienced programmer may wonder why this code uses a boolean variable rather than a breakif statement to exit the repeat..until loop. There are some technical reasons for this that you will learn about in Section 1.11.

**Table 1-4:** Exceptions Provided in *excepts.hhf* (continued)

| Exception | Description |
| --- | --- |
| ex.InvalidAlignment | Argument was not aligned on a proper memory address. |
| ex.InvalidArgument | Function call (generally OS API call) contains an invalid argument value. |
| ex.BufferOverflow | Buffer or blob object exceeded declared size. |
| ex.BufferUnderflow | Attempt to retrieve nonexistent data from a blob or buffer. |
| ex.IllegalSize | Argument's data size is incorrect. |
| ex.ConversionError | String-to-numeric conversion operation contains illegal (nonnumeric) characters. |
| ex.BadFileHandle | Program attempted a file access using an invalid file handle value. |
| ex.FileNotFound | Program attempted to access a nonexistent file. |
| ex.FileOpenFailure | Operating system could not open the file (file not found). |
| ex.FileCloseError | Operating system could not close the file. |
| ex.FileWriteError | Error writing data to a file. |
| ex.FileReadError | Error reading data from a file. |
| ex.FileSeekError | Attempted to seek to a nonexistent position in a file. |
| ex.DiskFullError | Attempted to write data to a full disk. |
| ex.AccessDenied | User does not have sufficient priviledges to access file data. |
| ex.EndOfFile | Program attempted to read beyond the end of file. |
| ex.CannotCreateDir | Attempt to create a directory failed. |
| ex.CannotRemoveDir | Attempt to delete a directory failed. |
| ex.CannotRemoveFile | Attempt to delete a file failed. |
| ex.CDFailed | Attempt to change to a new directory failed. |
| ex.CannotRenameFile | Attempt to rename a file failed. |
| ex.MemoryAllocationFailure | Insufficient system memory for allocation request. |
| ex.MemoryFreeFailure | Could not free the specified memory block (corrupted memory management system). |
| ex.MemoryAllocationCorruption | Corrupted memory management system. |
| ex.AttemptToFreeNULL | Caller attempted to free a NULL pointer. |
| ex.AttemptToDerefNULL | Program attempted to access data indirectly using a NULL pointer. |
| ex.BlockAlreadyFree | Caller attempted to free a block that was already freed. |
| ex.CannotFreeMemory | Memory free operation failure. |
| ex.PointerNotInHeap | Caller attempted to free a block of memory that was not allocated on the heap. |
| ex.WidthTooBig | Format width for numeric to string conversion was too large. |
| ex.FractionTooBig | Format size for fractional portion in floating-point-to-string conversion was too large. |
| ex.ArrayShapeViolation | Attempted operation on two arrays whose dimensions don't match. |

**Table 1-4:** Exceptions Provided in *excepts.hhf* (continued)

| Exception | Description |
|---|---|
| ex.ArrayBounds | Attempted to access an element of an array, but the index was out of bounds. |
| ex.InvalidDate | Attempted date operation with an illegal date. |
| ex.InvalidDateFormat | Conversion from string to date contains illegal characters. |
| ex.TimeOverflow | Overflow during time arithmetic. |
| ex.InvalidTime | Attempted time operation with an illegal time. |
| ex.InvalidTimeFormat | Conversion from string to time contains illegal characters. |
| ex.SocketError | Network communication failure. |
| ex.ThreadError | Generic thread (multitasking) error. |
| ex.AssertionFailed | assert statement encountered a failed assertion. |
| ex.ExecutedAbstract | Attempt to execute an abstract class method. |
| ex.AccessViolation | Attempt to access an illegal memory location. |
| ex.InPageError | OS memory access error. |
| ex.NoMemory | OS memory failure. |
| ex.InvalidHandle | Bad handle passed to OS API call. |
| ex.ControlC | CTRL-C was pressed on system console (functionality is OS specific). |
| ex.Breakpoint | Program executed a breakpoint instruction (INT 3). |
| ex.SingleStep | Program is operating with the trace flag set. |
| ex.PrivInstr | Program attempted to execute a kernel-only instruction. |
| ex.IllegalInstr | Program attempted to execute an illegal machine instruction. |
| ex.BoundInstr | Bound instruction execution with "out of bounds" value. |
| ex.IntoInstr | Into instruction execution with the overflow flag set. |
| ex.DivideError | Program attempted division by zero or other divide error. |
| ex.fDenormal | Floating point exception (see Chapter 6). |
| ex.fDivByZero | Floating point exception (see Chapter 6). |
| ex.fInexactResult | Floating point exception (see Chapter 6). |
| ex.fInvalidOperation | Floating point exception (see Chapter 6). |
| ex.fOverflow | Floating point exception (see Chapter 6). |
| ex.fStackCheck | Floating point exception (see Chapter 6). |
| ex.fUnderflow | Floating point exception (see Chapter 6). |
| ex.InvalidHandle | OS reported an invalid handle for some operation. |

Most of these exceptions occur in situations that are well beyond the scope of this chapter. Their appearance here is strictly for completeness. See the HLA reference manual, the HLA Standard Library documentation, and the HLA Standard Library source code for more details concerning these exceptions. The ex.ConversionError, ex.ValueOutOfRange, and ex.StringOverflow exceptions are the ones you'll most commonly use.

We'll return to the discussion of the try..endtry statement in Section 1.11. First, however, we need to cover a little more material.

## 1.10 Introduction to the HLA Standard Library

There are two reasons HLA is much easier to learn and use than standard assembly language. The first reason is HLA's high-level syntax for declarations and control structures. This leverages your high-level language knowledge, allowing you to learn assembly language more efficiently. The other half of the equation is the HLA Standard Library. The HLA Standard Library provides many common, easy-to-use, assembly language routines that you can call without having to write this code yourself (and, more importantly, having to learn how to write yourself). This eliminates one of the larger stumbling blocks many people have when learning assembly language: the need for sophisticated I/O and support code in order to write basic statements. Prior to the advent of a standardized assembly language library, it often took considerable study before a new assembly language programmer could do as much as print a string to the display. With the HLA Standard Library, this roadblock is removed, and you can concentrate on learning assembly language concepts rather than learning low-level I/O details that are specific to a given operating system.

A wide variety of library routines is only part of HLA's support. After all, assembly language libraries have been around for quite some time.[11] HLA's Standard Library complements HLA by providing a high-level language interface to these routines. Indeed, the HLA language itself was originally designed specifically to allow the creation of a high-level set of library routines. This high-level interface, combined with the high-level nature of many of the routines in the library, packs a surprising amount of power in an easy-to-use package.

The HLA Standard Library consists of several modules organized by category. Table 1-5 lists many of the modules that are available.[12]

**Table 1-5:** HLA Standard Library Modules

| Name | Description |
|------|-------------|
| args | Command-line parameter-parsing support routines. |
| arrays | Array declarations and operations. |
| bits | Bit-manipulation functions. |
| blobs | Binary large objects—operations on large blocks of binary data. |
| bsd | OS API calls for FreeBSD (HLA FreeBSD version only). |
| chars | Operations on character data. |
| console | Portable console (text screen) operations (cursor movement, screen clears, etc.). |
| conv | Various conversions between strings and other values. |
| coroutines | Support for coroutines ("cooperative multitasking"). |
| cset | Character set functions. |
| DateTime | Calendar, date, and time functions. |

---

[11] For example, see the UCR Standard Library for 80x86 Assembly Language Programmers.

[12] Because the HLA Standard Library is expanding, this list is probably out of date. See the HLA documentation for a current list of Standard Library modules.

**Table 1-5:** HLA Standard Library Modules (continued)

| Name | Description |
| --- | --- |
| env | Access to OS environment variables. |
| excepts | Exception-handling routines. |
| fileclass | Object-oriented file input and output. |
| fileio | File input and output routines. |
| filesys | Access to the OS file system. |
| hla | Special HLA constants and other values. |
| Linux | Linux system calls (HLA Linux version only). |
| lists | An HLA class for manipulating linked lists. |
| mac | OS API calls for Mac OS X (HLA Mac OS X version only). |
| math | Extended-precision arithmetic, transcendental functions, and other mathematical functions. |
| memmap | Memory-mapped file operations. |
| memory | Memory allocation, deallocation, and support code. |
| patterns | The HLA pattern-matching library. |
| random | Pseudo-random number generators and support code. |
| sockets | A set of network communication functions and classes. |
| stderr | Provides user output and several other support functions. |
| stdin | User input routines. |
| stdio | A support module for stderr, stdin, and stdout. |
| stdout | Provides user output and several other support routines. |
| strings | HLA's powerful string library. |
| tables | Table (associative array) support routines. |
| threads | Support for multithreaded applications and process synchronization. |
| timers | Support for timing events in an application. |
| win32 | Constants used in Windows calls (HLA Windows version only). |
| x86 | Constants and other items specific to the 80x86 CPU. |

Later sections of this text will explain many of these modules in greater detail. This section will concentrate on the most important routines (at least to beginning HLA programmers), the stdio library.

### 1.10.1 Predefined Constants in the stdio Module

Perhaps the first place to start is with a description of some common constants that the stdio module defines for you. Consider the following (typical) example:

```
stdout.put( "Hello World", nl );
```

The nl appearing at the end of this statement stands for *newline*. The nl identifier is not a special HLA reserved word, nor is it specific to the stdout.put statement. Instead, it's simply a predefined constant that corresponds to the string containing the standard end-of-line sequence (a carriage return/line feed pair under Windows or just a line feed under Linux, FreeBSD, and Mac OS X).

In addition to the nl constant, the HLA standard I/O library module defines several other useful character constants, as listed in Table 1-6.

**Table 1-6:** Character Constants Defined by the HLA Standard I/O Library

| Character | Definition |
| --- | --- |
| stdio.bell | The ASCII bell character; beeps the speaker when printed |
| stdio.bs | The ASCII backspace character |
| stdio.tab | The ASCII tab character |
| stdio.lf | The ASCII linefeed character |
| stdio.cr | The ASCII carriage return character |

Except for nl, these characters appear in the stdio namespace[13] (and therefore require the stdio. prefix). The placement of these ASCII constants within the stdio namespace helps avoid naming conflicts with your own variables. The nl name does not appear within a namespace because you will use it very often, and typing stdio.nl would get tiresome very quickly.

### 1.10.2   Standard In and Standard Out

Many of the HLA I/O routines have a stdin or stdout prefix. Technically, this means that the standard library defines these names in a namespace. In practice, this prefix suggests where the input is coming from (the standard input device) or going to (the standard output device). By default, the standard input device is the system keyboard. Likewise, the default standard output device is the console display. So, in general, statements that have stdin or stdout prefixes will read and write data on the console device.

When you run a program from the command-line window (or shell), you have the option of *redirecting* the standard input and/or standard output devices. A command-line parameter of the form >outfile redirects the standard output device to the specified file (outfile). A command-line parameter of the form <infile redirects the standard input so that its data comes from the specified input file (infile). The following examples demonstrate how to use these parameters when running a program named *testpgm* in the command window:[14]

```
testpgm <input.data
testpgm >output.txt
testpgm <in.txt >output.txt
```

---

[13] Namespaces are the subject of Chapter 5.

[14] For Linux, FreeBSD, and Mac OS X users, depending on how your system is set up, you may need to type ./ in front of the program's name to actually execute the program (e.g., ./testpgm <input.data).

### 1.10.3  The stdout.newln Routine

The stdout.newln procedure prints a newline sequence to the standard output device. This is functionally equivalent to saying stdout.put( nl );. The call to stdout.newln is sometimes a little more convenient. For example:

```
stdout.newln();
```

### 1.10.4  The stdout.putiX Routines

The stdout.puti8, stdout.puti16, and stdout.puti32 library routines print a single parameter (one byte, two bytes, or four bytes, respectively) as a signed integer value. The parameter may be a constant, a register, or a memory variable, as long as the size of the actual parameter is the same as the size of the formal parameter.

These routines print the value of their specified parameter to the standard output device. These routines will print the value using the minimum number of print positions possible. If the number is negative, these routines will print a leading minus sign. Here are some examples of calls to these routines:

```
stdout.puti8( 123 );
stdout.puti16( dx );
stdout.puti32( i32Var );
```

### 1.10.5  The stdout.putiX Size Routines

The stdout.puti8Size, stdout.puti16Size, and stdout.puti32Size routines output signed integer values to the standard output, just like the stdout.putiX routines. These routines, however, provide more control over the output; they let you specify the (minimum) number of print positions the value will require on output. These routines also let you specify a padding character should the print field be larger than the minimum needed to display the value. These routines require the following parameters:

```
stdout.puti8Size( Value8, width, padchar );
stdout.puti16Size( Value16, width, padchar );
stdout.puti32Size( Value32, width, padchar );
```

The Value* parameter can be a constant, a register, or a memory location of the specified size. The width parameter can be any signed integer constant that is between −256 and +256; this parameter may be a constant, register (32-bit), or memory location (32-bit). The padchar parameter should be a single-character value.

Like the stdout.putiX routines, these routines print the specified value as a signed integer constant to the standard output device. These routines, however, let you specify the *field width* for the value. The field width is the minimum number of print positions these routines will use when printing the value. The width parameter specifies the minimum field width. If the number would require more print positions (e.g., if you attempt to print 1234 with a field width of 2), then these routines will print however many characters are necessary to properly display the value. On the other hand, if the *width* parameter is greater than the number of character positions required to display the value, then these routines will print some extra padding characters to ensure that the output has at least *width* character positions. If the *width* value is negative, the number is left justified in the print field; if the *width* value is positive, the number is right justified in the print field.

If the absolute value of the *width* parameter is greater than the minimum number of print positions, then these stdout.putiXSize routines will print a padding character before or after the number. The *padchar* parameter specifies which character these routines will print. Most of the time you would specify a space as the pad character; for special cases, you might specify some other character. Remember, the *padchar* parameter is a character value; in HLA character constants are surrounded by apostrophes, not quotation marks. You may also specify an 8-bit register as this parameter.

Listing 1-4 provides a short HLA program that demonstrates the use of the stdout.puti32Size routine to display a list of values in tabular form.

```
program NumsInColumns;

#include( "stdlib.hhf" )

var
        i32:    int32;
        ColCnt: int8;

begin NumsInColumns;

        mov( 96, i32 );
        mov( 0, ColCnt );
        while( i32 > 0 ) do

            if( ColCnt = 8 ) then

                stdout.newln();
                mov( 0, ColCnt );

            endif;
            stdout.puti32Size( i32, 5, ' ' );
            sub( 1, i32 );
            add( 1, ColCnt );

        endwhile;
        stdout.newln();

end NumsInColumns;
```

*Listing 1-4: Tabular output demonstration using* stdio.Puti32Size

## 1.10.6  The stdout.put Routine

The stdout.put routine[15] is the one of the most flexible output routines in the standard output library module. It combines most of the other output routines into a single, easy-to-use procedure.

The generic form for the stdout.put routine is the following:

```
stdout.put( list_of_values_to_output );
```

The stdout.put parameter list consists of one or more constants, registers, or memory variables, each separated by a comma. This routine displays the value associated with each parameter appearing in the list. Because we've already been using this routine throughout this chapter, you've already seen many examples of this routine's basic form. It is worth pointing out that this routine has several additional features not apparent in the examples appearing in this chapter. In particular, each parameter can take one of the following two forms:

```
value
value:width
```

The *value* may be any legal constant, register, or memory variable object. In this chapter, you've seen string constants and memory variables appearing in the stdout.put parameter list. These parameters correspond to the first form above. The second parameter form above lets you specify a minimum field width, similar to the stdout.putiXSize routines.[16] The program in Listing 1-5 produces the same output as the program in Listing 1-4; however, Listing 1-5 uses stdout.put rather than stdout.puti32Size.

```
program NumsInColumns2;

#include( "stdlib.hhf" )

var
    i32:    int32;
    ColCnt: int8;

begin NumsInColumns2;

    mov( 96, i32 );
    mov( 0, ColCnt );
    while( i32 > 0 ) do

        if( ColCnt = 8 ) then
```

---

[15] stdout.put is actually a macro, not a procedure. The distinction between the two is beyond the scope of this chapter. Chapter 9 describes their differences.

[16] Note that you cannot specify a padding character when using the stdout.put routine; the padding character defaults to the space character. If you need to use a different padding character, call the stdout.putiXSize routines.

```
            stdout.newln();
            mov( 0, ColCnt );

        endif;
        stdout.put( i32:5 );
        sub( 1, i32 );
        add( 1, ColCnt );

    endwhile;
    stdout.put( nl );

end NumsInColumns2;
```

Listing 1-5: Demonstration of the stdout.put field width specification

The stdout.put routine is capable of much more than the few attributes this section describes. This text will introduce those additional capabilities as appropriate.

## 1.10.7 The stdin.getc Routine

The stdin.getc routine reads the next available character from the standard input device's input buffer.[17] It returns this character in the CPU's AL register. The program in Listing 1-6 demonstrates a simple use of this routine.

```
program charInput;

#include( "stdlib.hhf" )

var
    counter: int32;

begin charInput;

    // The following repeats as long as the user
    // confirms the repetition.

    repeat

        // Print out 14 values.

        mov( 14, counter );
        while( counter > 0 ) do

            stdout.put( counter:3 );
            sub( 1, counter );

        endwhile;

        // Wait until the user enters 'y' or 'n'.
```

---

[17] *Buffer* is just a fancy term for an array.

```
        stdout.put( nl, nl, "Do you wish to see it again? (y/n):" );
        forever

            stdin.readLn();
            stdin.getc();
            breakif( al = 'n' );
            breakif( al = 'y' );
            stdout.put( "Error, please enter only 'y' or 'n': " );

        endfor;
        stdout.newln();

    until( al = 'n' );

end charInput;
```

*Listing 1-6: Demonstration of the stdin.getc() routine*

This program uses the stdin.ReadLn routine to force a new line of input from the user. A description of stdin.ReadLn appears in Section 1.10.9.

## 1.10.8  The stdin.getiX Routines

The stdin.geti8, stdin.geti16, and stdin.geti32 routines read 8-, 16-, and 32-bit signed integer values from the standard input device. These routines return their values in the AL, AX, or EAX register, respectively. They provide the standard mechanism for reading signed integer values from the user in HLA.

Like the stdin.getc routine, these routines read a sequence of characters from the standard input buffer. They begin by skipping over any whitespace characters (spaces, tabs, and so on) and then convert the following stream of decimal digits (with an optional leading minus sign) into the corresponding integer. These routines raise an exception (that you can trap with the try..endtry statement) if the input sequence is not a valid integer string or if the user input is too large to fit in the specified integer size. Note that values read by stdin.geti8 must be in the range −128..+127; values read by stdin.geti16 must be in the range −32,768..+32,767; and values read by stdin.geti32 must be in the range −2,147,483,648..+2,147,483,647.

The sample program in Listing 1-7 demonstrates the use of these routines.

```
program intInput;

#include( "stdlib.hhf" )

var
    i8:     int8;
    i16:    int16;
    i32:    int32;

begin intInput;
```

```
// Read integers of varying sizes from the user:

stdout.put( "Enter a small integer between -128 and +127: " );
stdin.geti8();
mov( al, i8 );

stdout.put( "Enter a small integer between -32768 and +32767: " );
stdin.geti16();
mov( ax, i16 );

stdout.put( "Enter an integer between +/- 2 billion: " );
stdin.geti32();
mov( eax, i32 );

// Display the input values.

stdout.put
(
    nl,
    "Here are the numbers you entered:", nl, nl,
    "Eight-bit integer: ", i8:12, nl,
    "16-bit integer:    ", i16:12, nl,
    "32-bit integer:    ", i32:12, nl
);
```

```
end intInput;
```

*Listing 1-7: stdin.getiX example code*

You should compile and run this program and then test what happens when you enter a value that is out of range or enter an illegal string of characters.

## 1.10.9   The stdin.readLn and stdin.flushInput Routines

Whenever you call an input routine like stdin.getc or stdin.geti32, the program does not necessarily read the value from the user at that moment. Instead, the HLA Standard Library buffers the input by reading a whole line of text from the user. Calls to input routines will fetch data from this input buffer until the buffer is empty. While this buffering scheme is efficient and convenient, sometimes it can be confusing. Consider the following code sequence:

```
stdout.put( "Enter a small integer between -128 and +127: " );
stdin.geti8();
mov( al, i8 );

stdout.put( "Enter a small integer between -32768 and +32767: " );
stdin.geti16();
mov( ax, i16 );
```

Intuitively, you would expect the program to print the first prompt message, wait for user input, print the second prompt message, and wait for the second user input. However, this isn't exactly what happens. For example, if you run this code (from the sample program in the previous section) and enter the text **123 456** in response to the first prompt, the program will not stop for additional user input at the second prompt. Instead, it will read the second integer (456) from the input buffer read during the execution of the `stdin.geti16` call.

In general, the `stdin` routines read text from the user only when the input buffer is empty. As long as the input buffer contains additional characters, the input routines will attempt to read their data from the buffer. You can take advantage of this behavior by writing code sequences such as the following:

```
stdout.put( "Enter two integer values: " );
stdin.geti32();
mov( eax, intval );
stdin.geti32();
mov( eax, AnotherIntVal );
```

This sequence allows the user to enter both values on the same line (separated by one or more whitespace characters), thus preserving space on the screen. So the input buffer behavior is desirable every now and then. The buffered behavior of the input routines can be counterintuitive at other times.

Fortunately, the HLA Standard Library provides two routines, `stdin.readLn` and `stdin.flushInput`, that let you control the standard input buffer. The `stdin.readLn` routine discards everything that is in the input buffer and immediately requires the user to enter a new line of text. The `stdin.flushInput` routine simply discards everything that is in the buffer. The next time an input routine executes, the system will require a new line of input from the user. You would typically call `stdin.readLn` immediately before some standard input routine; you would normally call `stdin.flushInput` immediately after a call to a standard input routine.

**NOTE**   *If you are calling `stdin.readLn` and you find that you are having to input your data twice, this is a good indication that you should be calling `stdin.flushInput` rather than `stdin.readLn`. In general, you should always be able to call `stdin.flushInput` to flush the input buffer and read a new line of data on the next input call. The `stdin.readLn` routine is rarely necessary, so you should use `stdin.flushInput` unless you really need to immediately force the input of a new line of text.*

### 1.10.10   The stdin.get Routine

The `stdin.get` routine combines many of the standard input routines into a single call, just as the `stdout.put` combines all of the output routines into a single call. Actually, `stdin.get` is a bit easier to use than `stdout.put` because the only parameters to this routine are a list of variable names.

Let's rewrite the example given in the previous section:

```
stdout.put( "Enter two integer values: " );
stdin.geti32();
mov( eax, intval );
stdin.geti32();
mov( eax, AnotherIntVal );
```

Using the stdin.get routine, we could rewrite this code as:

```
stdout.put( "Enter two integer values: " );
stdin.get( intval, AnotherIntVal );
```

As you can see, the stdin.get routine is a little more convenient to use.

Note that stdin.get stores the input values directly into the memory variables you specify in the parameter list; it does not return the values in a register unless you actually specify a register as a parameter. The stdin.get parameters must all be variables or registers.

## 1.11 Additional Details About try..endtry

As you may recall, the try..endtry statement surrounds a block of statements in order to capture any exceptions that occur during the execution of those statements. The system raises exceptions in one of three ways: through a hardware fault (such as a divide-by-zero error), through an operating system–generated exception, or through the execution of the HLA raise statement. You can write an exception handler to intercept specific exceptions using the exception clause. The program in Listing 1-8 provides a typical example of the use of this statement.

```
program testBadInput;
#include( "stdlib.hhf" )

static
    u:        int32;


begin testBadInput;

    try

        stdout.put( "Enter a signed integer:" );
        stdin.get( u );
        stdout.put( "You entered: ", u, nl );

      exception( ex.ConversionError )

        stdout.put( "Your input contained illegal characters" nl );

      exception( ex.ValueOutOfRange )
```

```
        stdout.put( "The value was too large" nl );

    endtry;


end testBadInput;
```

*Listing 1-8: try..endtry example*

HLA refers to the statements between the try clause and the first exception clause as the *protected* statements. If an exception occurs within the protected statements, then the program will scan through each of the exceptions and compare the value of the current exception against the value in the parentheses after each of the exception clauses.[18] This exception value is simply a 32-bit value. The value in the parentheses after each exception clause, therefore, must be a 32-bit value. The HLA *excepts.hhf* header file predefines several exception constants. Although it would be an incredibly bad style violation, you could substitute the numeric values for the two exception clauses above.

## 1.11.1  *Nesting try..endtry Statements*

If the program scans through all the exception clauses in a try..endtry statement and does not match the current exception value, then the program searches through the exception clauses of a *dynamically nested* try..endtry block in an attempt to find an appropriate exception handler. For example, consider the code in Listing 1-9.

```
program testBadInput2;
#include( "stdlib.hhf" )

static
        u:      int32;

begin testBadInput2;

    try

        try

            stdout.put( "Enter a signed integer: " );
            stdin.get( u );
            stdout.put( "You entered: ", u, nl );

        exception( ex.ConversionError )

            stdout.put( "Your input contained illegal characters" nl );

        endtry;
```

---

[18] Note that HLA loads this value into the EAX register. So upon entry into an exception clause, EAX contains the exception number.

```
        stdout.put( "Input did not fail due to a value out of range" nl );


    exception( ex.ValueOutOfRange )

        stdout.put( "The value was too large" nl );

    endtry;

end testBadInput2;
```

*Listing 1-9: Nested try..endtry statements*

In Listing 1-9 one try statement is nested inside another. During the execution of the stdin.get statement, if the user enters a value greater than four billion and some change, then stdin.get will raise the ex.ValueOutOfRange exception. When the HLA runtime system receives this exception, it first searches through all the exception clauses in the try..endtry statement immediately surrounding the statement that raised the exception (this would be the nested try..endtry in the example above). If the HLA runtime system fails to locate an exception handler for ex.ValueOutOfRange, then it checks to see if the current try..endtry is nested inside another try..endtry (as is the case in Listing 1-9). If so, the HLA runtime system searches for the appropriate exception clause in the outer try..endtry statement. Within the try..endtry block appearing in Listing 1-9 the program finds an appropriate exception handler, so control transfers to the statements after the exception( ex.ValueOutOfRange ) clause.

After leaving a try..endtry block, the HLA runtime system no longer considers that block active and will not search through its list of exceptions when the program raises an exception.[19] This allows you to handle the same exception differently in other parts of the program.

If two try..endtry statements handle the same exception, and one of the try..endtry blocks is nested inside the protected section of the other try..endtry statement, and the program raises an exception while executing in the innermost try..endtry sequence, then HLA transfers control directly to the exception handler provided by the innermost try..endtry block. HLA does not automatically transfer control to the exception handler provided by the outer try..endtry sequence.

In the previous example (Listing 1-9) the second try..endtry statement was statically nested inside the enclosing try..endtry statement.[20] As mentioned without comment earlier, if the most recently activated try..endtry statement does not handle a specific exception, the program will search through the exception clauses of any dynamically nesting try..endtry blocks. Dynamic nesting does not require the nested try..endtry block to physically appear within the enclosing try..endtry statement. Instead, control could transfer

---

[19] Unless, of course, the program re-enters the try..endtry block via a loop or other control structure.

[20] *Statically nested* means that one statement is physically nested within another in the source code. When we say one statement is nested within another, this typically means that the statement is statically nested within the other statement.

from inside the enclosing try..endtry protected block to some other point in the program. Execution of a try..endtry statement at that other point dynamically nests the two try statements. Although there are many ways to dynamically nest code, there is one method you are probably familiar with from your high-level language experience: the procedure call. In Chapter 5, when you learn how to write procedures (functions) in assembly language, you should keep in mind that any call to a procedure within the protected section of a try..endtry block can create a dynamically nested try..endtry if the program executes a try..endtry within that procedure.

### 1.11.2   The unprotected Clause in a try..endtry Statement

Whenever a program executes the try clause, it preserves the current exception environment and sets up the system to transfer control to the exception clauses within that try..endtry statement should an exception occur. If the program successfully completes the execution of a try..endtry protected block, the program restores the original exception environment and control transfers to the first statement beyond the endtry clause. This last step, restoring the execution environment, is very important. If the program skips this step, any future exceptions will transfer control to this try..endtry statement even though the program has already left the try..endtry block. Listing 1-10 demonstrates this problem.

```
program testBadInput3;
#include( "stdlib.hhf" )

static
    input:  int32;

begin testBadInput3;

    // This forever loop repeats until the user enters
    // a good integer and the break statement below
    // exits the loop.

    forever

        try

            stdout.put( "Enter an integer value: " );
            stdin.get( input );
            stdout.put( "The first input value was: ", input, nl );
            break;

        exception( ex.ValueOutOfRange )

            stdout.put( "The value was too large, re-enter." nl );

        exception( ex.ConversionError )

            stdout.put( "The input contained illegal characters, re-enter." nl );
```

```
        endtry;

    endfor;

    // Note that the following code is outside the loop and there
    // is no try..endtry statement protecting this code.

    stdout.put( "Enter another number: " );
    stdin.get( input );
    stdout.put( "The new number is: ", input, nl );

end testBadInput3;
```

*Listing 1-10: Improperly exiting a try..endtry statement*

This example attempts to create a robust input system by putting a loop around the try..endtry statement and forcing the user to reenter the data if the stdin.get routine raises an exception (because of bad input data). While this is a good idea, there is a big problem with this implementation: the break statement immediately exits the forever..endfor loop without first restoring the exception environment. Therefore, when the program executes the second stdin.get statement, at the bottom of the program, the HLA exception-handling code still thinks that it's inside the try..endtry block. If an exception occurs, HLA transfers control back into the try..endtry statement looking for an appropriate exception handler. Assuming the exception was ex.ValueOutOfRange or ex.ConversionError, the program in Listing 1-10 will print an appropriate error message *and then force the user to re-enter the first value.* This isn't desirable.

Transferring control to the wrong try..endtry exception handlers is only part of the problem. Another big problem with the code in Listing 1-10 has to do with the way HLA preserves and restores the exception environment: specifically, HLA saves the old execution environment information in a special region of memory known as the *stack.* If you exit a try..endtry without restoring the exception environment, this leaves the old execution environment information on the stack, and this extra data on could cause your program to malfunction.

Although this discussion makes it quite clear that a program should not exit from a try..endtry statement in the manner that Listing 1-10 uses, it would be nice if you could use a loop around a try..endtry block to force the reentry of bad data as this program attempts to do. To allow for this, HLA's try..endtry statement provides an unprotected section. Consider the code in Listing 1-11.

```
program testBadInput4;
#include( "stdlib.hhf" )

static
    input:  int32;

begin testBadInput4;
```

```
// This forever loop repeats until the user enters
// a good integer and the break statement below
// exits the loop. Note that the break statement
// appears in an unprotected section of the try..endtry
// statement.

forever

    try

        stdout.put( "Enter an integer value: " );
        stdin.get( input );
        stdout.put( "The first input value was: ", input, nl );

      unprotected

        break;

      exception( ex.ValueOutOfRange )

        stdout.put( "The value was too large, re-enter." nl );

      exception( ex.ConversionError )

        stdout.put( "The input contained illegal characters, re-enter." nl );

    endtry;

endfor;

// Note that the following code is outside the loop and there
// is no try..endtry statement protecting this code.

stdout.put( "Enter another number: " );
stdin.get( input );
stdout.put( "The new number is: ", input, nl );

end testBadInput4;
```

*Listing 1-11: The try..endtry unprotected section*

Whenever the try..endtry statement hits the unprotected clause, it immediately restores the exception environment. As the phrase suggests, the execution of statements in the unprotected section is no longer protected by that try..endtry block (note, however, that any dynamically nesting try..endtry statements will still be active; unprotected turns off only the exception handling of the try..endtry statement containing the unprotected clause). Because the break statement in Listing 1-11 appears inside the unprotected section, it can safely transfer control out of the try..endtry block without "executing" the endtry because the program has already restored the former exception environment.

Note that the unprotected keyword must appear in the try..endtry statement immediately after the protected block. That is, it must precede all exception keywords.

If an exception occurs during the execution of a try..endtry sequence, HLA automatically restores the execution environment. Therefore, you may execute a break statement (or any other instruction that transfers control out of the try..endtry block) within an exception clause.

Because the program restores the exception environment upon encountering an unprotected block or an exception block, an exception that occurs within one of these areas immediately transfers control to the previous (dynamically nesting) active try..endtry sequence. If there is no nesting try..endtry sequence, the program aborts with an appropriate error message.

### 1.11.3    The anyexception Clause in a try..endtry Statement

In a typical situation, you will use a try..endtry statement with a set of exception clauses that will handle all possible exceptions that can occur in the protected section of the try..endtry sequence. Often, it is important to ensure that a try..endtry statement handles all possible exceptions to prevent the program from prematurely aborting due to an unhandled exception. If you have written all the code in the protected section, you will know the exceptions it can raise, so you can handle all possible exceptions. However, if you are calling a library routine (especially a third-party library routine), making a OS API call, or otherwise executing code that you have no control over, it may not be possible for you to anticipate all possible exceptions this code could raise (especially when considering past, present, and future versions of the code). If that code raises an exception for which you do not have an exception clause, this could cause your program to fail. Fortunately, HLA's try..endtry statement provides the anyexception clause that will automatically trap any exception the existing exception clauses do not handle.

The anyexception clause is similar to the exception clause except it does not require an exception number parameter (because it handles any exception). If the anyexception clause appears in a try..endtry statement with other exception sections, the anyexception section must be the last exception handler in the try..endtry statement. An anyexception section may be the only exception handler in a try..endtry statement.

If an otherwise unhandled exception transfers control to an anyexception section, the EAX register will contain the exception number. Your code in the anyexception block can test this value to determine the cause of the exception.

### 1.11.4    Registers and the try..endtry Statement

The try..endtry statement preserves several bytes of data whenever you enter a try..endtry statement. Upon leaving the try..endtry block (or hitting the unprotected clause), the program restores the exception environment. As long as no exception occurs, the try..endtry statement does not affect the values of any registers upon entry to or upon exit from the `try..endtry` statement. However, this claim is not true if an exception occurs during the execution of the protected statements.

Upon entry into an exception clause, the EAX register contains the exception number, but the values of all other general-purpose registers are undefined. Because the operating system may have raised the exception in response to a hardware error (and, therefore, has played around with the registers), you can't even assume that the general-purpose registers contain whatever values they happened to contain at the point of the exception. The underlying code that HLA generates for exceptions is subject to change in different versions of the compiler, and certainly it changes across operating systems, so it is never a good idea to experimentally determine what values registers contain in an exception handler and depend on those values in your code.

Because entry into an exception handler can scramble the register values, you must ensure that you reload important registers if the code following your endtry clause assumes that the registers contain certain values (i.e., values set in the protected section or values set prior to executing the `try..endtry` statement). Failure to do so will introduce some nasty defects into your program (and these defects may be very intermittent and difficult to detect because exceptions rarely occur and may not always destroy the value in a particular register). The following code fragment provides a typical example of this problem and its solution:

```
static
    sum: int32;
        .
        .
        .
    mov( 0, sum );
    for( mov( 0, ebx ); ebx < 8; inc( ebx )) do

        push( ebx );  // Must preserve ebx in case there is an exception.
        forever
            try

                stdin.geti32();
                unprotected break;

            exception( ex.ConversionError )

                stdout.put( "Illegal input, please re-enter value: " );

            endtry;
        endfor;
        pop( ebx );  // Restore ebx's value.
        add( ebx, eax );
        add( eax, sum );

    endfor;
```

Because the HLA exception-handling mechanism messes with the registers, and because exception handling is a relatively inefficient process, you should never use the try..endtry statement as a generic control structure (e.g., using it to simulate a switch/case statement by raising an integer exception value and using the exception clauses as the cases to process). Doing so will have a very negative impact on the performance of your program and may introduce subtle defects because exceptions scramble the registers.

For proper operation, the try..endtry statement assumes that you use the EBP register only to point at *activation records* (Chapter 5 discusses activation records). By default, HLA programs automatically use EBP for this purpose; as long as you do not modify the value in EBP, your programs will automatically use EBP to maintain a pointer to the current activation record. If you attempt to use the EBP register as a general-purpose register to hold values and compute arithmetic results, HLA's exception-handling capabilities will no longer function properly (along with other possible problems). Therefore, you should never use the EBP register as a general-purpose register. Of course, this same discussion applies to the ESP register.

# 1.12 High-Level Assembly Language vs. Low-Level Assembly Language

Before concluding this chapter, it's important to remind you that none of the control statements appearing in this chapter are "real" assembly language. The 80x86 CPU does not support machine instructions like if, while, repeat, for, break, breakif, and try. Whenever HLA encounters these statements, it *compiles* them into a sequence of one or more true machine instructions that do the operation as the high-level statements you've used. While these statements are convenient to use, and in many cases just as efficient as the sequence of low-level machine instructions into which HLA translates them, don't lose sight of the fact that they are not true machine instructions.

The purpose of this text is to teach you low-level assembly language programming; these high-level control structures are simply a means to that end. Remember, learning the HLA high-level control structures allows you to leverage your high-level language knowledge early on in the educational process so you don't have to learn everything about assembly language all at once. By using high-level control structures that you're already comfortable with, this text can put off the discussion of the actual machine instructions you'd normally use for control flow until much later. By doing so, this text can regulate how much material it presents, so, hopefully, you'll find learning assembly language to be much more pleasant. However, you must always remember that these high-level control statements are just a pedagogical tool to help you learn assembly language. Though you're free to use them in your assembly programs once you master the real control-flow statements, you really must learn the low-level control statements if you want to learn assembly language programming. Since, presumably, that's why you're reading this book, don't allow the high-level control structures to become a crutch. When you get to the point where you learn how to really write low-level control statements, embrace and use them (exclusively). As you gain experience with the low-level control statements and learn their advantages and disadvantages, you'll be in a good position to decide whether a high-level or low-level code sequence is most appropriate for a given application. However, until you gain considerable experience with the low-level control structures, you'll not be able to make an educated decision. Remember, you can't really call yourself an assembly language programmer unless you've mastered the low-level statements.

Another thing to keep in mind is that the HLA Standard Library functions are not part of the assembly *language*. They're just some convenient functions that have been prewritten for you. Although there is nothing wrong with calling these functions, always remember that they are not machine instructions and that there is nothing special about these routines; as you gain experience writing assembly language code, you can write your own versions of each of these routines (and even write them more efficiently).

If you're learning assembly language because you want to write the most efficient programs possible (either the fastest or the smallest code), you need to understand that you won't achieve this goal completely if you're using high-level control statements and making a lot of calls to the HLA Standard Library. HLA's code generator and the HLA Standard Library aren't *horribly* inefficient, but the only true way to write efficient programs in assembly language is to *think* in assembly language. HLA's high-level control statements and many of the routines in the HLA Standard Library are great because they let you *avoid* thinking in assembly language. While this is great while you're first learning assembly, if your ultimate goal is to write efficient code, then you have to learn to think in assembly language. This text will get you to that point (and will do so much more rapidly because it uses HLA's high-level features), but don't forget that your ultimate goal is to give up these high-level features in favor of low-level coding.

## 1.13 For More Information

This chapter has covered a lot of ground! While you still have a lot to learn about assembly language programming, this chapter, combined with your knowledge of high-level languages, provides just enough information to let you start writing real assembly language programs.

Although this chapter has covered many different topics, the three primary topics of interest are the 80x86 CPU architecture, the syntax for simple HLA programs, and the HLA Standard Library. For additional topics on this subject, please consult the (unabridged) electronic version of this text, the HLA reference manual, and the HLA Standard Library manual. All three are available at *http://www.artofasm.com/* and *http://webster.cs.ucr.edu/*.

# 2

## DATA REPRESENTATION

 A major stumbling block many beginners encounter when attempting to learn assembly language is the common use of the binary and hexadecimal numbering systems. Although hexadecimal numbers are a little strange, their advantages outweigh their disadvantages by a large margin. Understanding the binary and hexadecimal numbering systems is important because their use simplifies the discussion of other topics, including bit operations, signed numeric representation, character codes, and packed data.

This chapter discusses several important concepts, including:

- The binary and hexadecimal numbering systems
- Binary data organization (bits, nibbles, bytes, words, and double words)
- Signed and unsigned numbering systems

- Arithmetic, logical, shift, and rotate operations on binary values
- Bit fields and packed data

This is basic material, and the remainder of this text depends on your understanding these concepts. If you are already familiar with these terms from other courses or study, you should at least skim this material before proceeding to the next chapter. If you are unfamiliar with this material, or only vaguely familiar with it, you should study it carefully before proceeding. *All of the material in this chapter is important!* Do not skip over any material.

## 2.1 Numbering Systems

Most modern computer systems do not represent numeric values using the decimal (base-10) system. Instead, they typically use a binary or two's complement numbering system.

### 2.1.1 A Review of the Decimal System

You've been using the decimal numbering system for so long that you probably take it for granted. When you see a number like *123*, you don't think about the value 123; rather, you generate a mental image of how many items this value represents. In reality, however, the number 123 represents:

$$1*10^2 + 2*10^1 + 3*10^0$$

or

$$100 + 20 + 3$$

In a decimal positional numbering system, each digit appearing to the left of the decimal point represents a value between 0 and 9 times an increasing power of 10. Digits appearing to the right of the decimal point represent a value between 0 and 9 times an increasing negative power of 10. For example, the value 123.456 means:

$$1*10^2 + 2*10^1 + 3*10^0 + 4*10^{-1} + 5*10^{-2} + 6*10^{-3}$$

or

$$100 + 20 + 3 + 0.4 + 0.05 + 0.006$$

### 2.1.2 The Binary Numbering System

Most modern computer systems operate using binary logic. The computer represents values using two voltage levels (usually 0v and +2.4..5v). Two such levels can represent exactly two unique values. These could be any two different values, but they typically represent the values 0 and 1. These values, coincidentally, correspond to the two digits in the binary numbering system.

The binary numbering system works just like the decimal numbering system, with two exceptions: Binary allows only the digits 0 and 1 (rather than 0..9), and binary uses powers of 2 rather than powers of 10. Therefore, it is very easy to convert a binary number to decimal. For each 1 in the binary string, add in $2^n$ where $n$ is the zero-based position of the binary digit. For example, the binary value $11001010_2$ represents:

$$1*2^7 + 1*2^6 + 0*2^5 + 0*2^4 + 1*2^3 + 0*2^2 + 1*2^1 + 0*2^0$$

$$=$$

$$128 + 64 + 8 + 2$$

$$=$$

$$202_{10}$$

To convert decimal to binary is slightly more difficult. You must find those powers of 2 that, when added together, produce the decimal result.

A simple way to convert decimal to binary is the *even/odd - divide by two* algorithm. This algorithm uses the following steps:

1. If the number is even, emit a 0. If the number is odd, emit a 1.
2. Divide the number by 2 and throw away any fractional component or remainder.
3. If the quotient is 0, the algorithm is complete.
4. If the quotient is not 0 and is odd, insert a 1 before the current string; if the number is even, prefix your binary string with 0.
5. Go back to step 2 and repeat.

Binary numbers, although they have little importance in high-level languages, appear everywhere in assembly language programs. So you should be somewhat comfortable with them.

## 2.1.3 Binary Formats

In the purest sense, every binary number contains an infinite number of digits (or *bits*, which is short for *binary digits*). For example, we can represent the number 5 by any of the following:

101      00000101      0000000000101      ...000000000000101

Any number of leading zero digits may precede the binary number without changing its value.

We will adopt the convention of ignoring any leading zeros present in a value. For example, $101_2$ represents the number 5 but because the 80x86 typically works with groups of 8 bits, we'll find it much easier to zero extend all binary numbers to some multiple of 4 or 8 bits. Therefore, following this convention, we'd represent the number 5 as $0101_2$ or $00000101_2$.

In the United States, most people separate every three digits with a comma to make larger numbers easier to read. For example, 1,023,435,208 is much easier to read and comprehend than 1023435208. We'll adopt a similar convention in this text for binary numbers. We will separate each group of four binary bits with an underscore. For example, we will write the binary value 1010111110110010 as 1010_1111_1011_0010.

We'll number each bit as follows:

1.  The rightmost bit in a binary number is bit position 0.
2.  Each bit to the left is given the next successive bit number.

An 8-bit binary value uses bits 0..7:

$$X_7\ X_6\ X_5\ X_4\ X_3\ X_2\ X_1\ X_0$$

A 16-bit binary value uses bit positions 0..15:

$$X_{15}\ X_{14}\ X_{13}\ X_{12}\ X_{11}\ X_{10}\ X_9\ X_8\ X_7\ X_6\ X_5\ X_4\ X_3\ X_2\ X_1\ X_0$$

A 32-bit binary value uses bit positions 0..31, and so on.

Bit 0 is the *low-order (L.O.)* bit (some refer to this as the *least significant bit*). The leftmost bit is called the *high-order (H.O.)* bit (or the *most significant bit*). We'll refer to the intermediate bits by their respective bit numbers.

## 2.2  The Hexadecimal Numbering System

Unfortunately, binary numbers are verbose. To represent the value $202_{10}$ requires eight binary digits. The decimal version requires only three decimal digits and thus represents numbers much more compactly than in binary. This fact is not lost on the engineers who design binary computer systems. When dealing with large values, binary numbers quickly become unwieldy. Unfortunately, the computer "thinks" in binary, so most of the time it is convenient to use the binary numbering system. Although we can convert between decimal and binary, the conversion is not a trivial task. The hexadecimal (base 16) numbering system solves many of the problems inherent in the binary system. Hexadecimal numbers offer the two features we're looking for: They're very compact, and it's simple to convert them to binary and vice versa. For this reason, most engineers use the hexadecimal numbering system.

Because the radix (base) of a hexadecimal number is 16, each hexadecimal digit to the left of the hexadecimal point represents some value times a successive power of 16. For example, the number $1234_{16}$ is equal to:

$$1*16^3 + 2*16^2 + 3*16^1 + 4*16^0$$

or

$$4096 + 512 + 48 + 4 = 4660_{10}$$

Each hexadecimal digit can represent one of 16 values between 0 and $15_{10}$. Because there are only 10 decimal digits, we need to invent 6 additional digits to represent the values in the range $10_{10}..15_{10}$. Rather than create new symbols for these digits, we'll use the letters A..F. The following are all examples of valid hexadecimal numbers:

$$1234_{16} \quad DEAD_{16} \quad BEEF_{16} \quad 0AFB_{16} \quad FEED_{16} \quad DEAF_{16}$$

Because we'll often need to enter hexadecimal numbers into the computer system, we'll need a different mechanism for representing hexadecimal numbers. After all, on most computer systems you cannot enter a subscript to denote the radix of the associated value. We'll adopt the following conventions:

- All hexadecimal values begin with a $ character; for example, $123A4.
- All binary values begin with a percent sign (%).
- Decimal numbers do not have a prefix character.
- If the radix is clear from the context, this book may drop the leading $ or % character.

Here are some examples of valid hexadecimal numbers:

$1234 $DEAD $BEEF $AFB $FEED $DEAF

As you can see, hexadecimal numbers are compact and easy to read. In addition, you can easily convert between hexadecimal and binary. Consider Table 2-1. This table provides all the information you'll ever need to convert any hexadecimal number into a binary number or vice versa.

**Table 2-1:** Binary/Hexadecimal Conversion

| Binary | Hexadecimal |
| --- | --- |
| %0000 | $0 |
| %0001 | $1 |
| %0010 | $2 |
| %0011 | $3 |
| %0100 | $4 |
| %0101 | $5 |
| %0110 | $6 |
| %0111 | $7 |
| %1000 | $8 |
| %1001 | $9 |
| %1010 | $A |
| %1011 | $B |
| %1100 | $C |
| %1101 | $D |
| %1110 | $E |
| %1111 | $F |

To convert a hexadecimal number into a binary number, simply substitute the corresponding 4 bits for each hexadecimal digit in the number. For example, to convert $ABCD into a binary value, simply convert each hexadecimal digit according to Table 2-1, as shown here:

| A | B | C | D | Hexadecimal |
|------|------|------|------|-------------|
| 1010 | 1011 | 1100 | 1101 | Binary |

To convert a binary number into hexadecimal format is almost as easy. The first step is to pad the binary number with zeros to make sure that there is a multiple of 4 bits in the number. For example, given the binary number 1011001010, the first step would be to add 2 bits to the left of the number so that it contains 12 bits. The converted binary value is 001011001010. The next step is to separate the binary value into groups of 4 bits, for example, 0010_1100_1010. Finally, look up these binary values in Table 2-1 and substitute the appropriate hexadecimal digits, that is, $2CA. Contrast this with the difficulty of conversion between decimal and binary or decimal and hexadecimal!

Because converting between hexadecimal and binary is an operation you will need to perform over and over again, you should take a few minutes and memorize the conversion table. Even if you have a calculator that will do the conversion for you, you'll find manual conversion to be a lot faster and more convenient when converting between binary and hex.

## 2.3   Data Organization

In pure mathematics a value's representation may take require an arbitrary number of bits. Computers, on the other hand, generally work with some specific number of bits. Common collections are single bits, groups of 4 bits (called *nibbles*), groups of 8 bits (*bytes*), groups of 16 bits (*words*), groups of 32 bits (*double words* or *dwords*), groups of 64 bits (*quad words* or *qwords*), groups of 128 bits (*long words* or *lwords*), and more. The sizes are not arbitrary. There is a good reason for these particular values. This section will describe the bit groups commonly used on the Intel 80x86 chips.

### 2.3.1   Bits

The smallest unit of data on a binary computer is a single bit. With a single bit, you can represent any two distinct items. Examples include 0 or 1, true or false, on or off, male or female, and right or wrong. However, you are *not* limited to representing binary data types (that is, those objects that have only two distinct values). You could use a single bit to represent the numbers 723 and 1,245 or, perhaps, the values 6,254 and 5. You could also use a single bit to represent the colors red and blue. You could even represent two unrelated objects with a single bit. For example, you could represent the color red and the number 3,256 with a single bit. You can represent *any two* different values with a single bit. However, you can represent *only two* different values with a single bit.

To confuse things even more, different bits can represent different things. For example, you could use one bit to represent the values 0 and 1, while a different bit could represent the values true and false. How can you tell by looking at the bits? The answer, of course, is that you can't. But this illustrates the whole idea behind computer data structures: *data is what you define it to be.* If you use a bit to represent a boolean (true/false) value, then that bit (by your definition) represents true or false. For the bit to have any real meaning, you must be consistent. If you're using a bit to represent true or false at one point in your program, you shouldn't use that value to represent red or blue later.

Because most items you'll be trying to model require more than two different values, single-bit values aren't the most popular data type you'll use. However, because everything else consists of groups of bits, bits will play an important role in your programs. Of course, there are several data types that require two distinct values, so it would seem that bits are important by themselves. However, you will soon see that individual bits are difficult to manipulate, so we'll often use other data types to represent two-state values.

## 2.3.2 Nibbles

A *nibble* is a collection of 4 bits. It wouldn't be a particularly interesting data structure except for two facts: *binary-coded decimal (BCD)* numbers[1] and hexadecimal numbers. It takes 4 bits to represent a single BCD or hexadecimal digit. With a nibble, we can represent up to 16 distinct values because there are 16 unique combinations of a string of 4 bits:

```
0000
0001
0010
0011
0100
0101
0110
0111
1000
1001
1010
1011
1100
1101
1110
1111
```

In the case of hexadecimal numbers, the values 0, 1, 2, 3, 4, 5, 6, 7, 8, 9, A, B, C, D, E, and F are represented with 4 bits. BCD uses 10 different digits (0, 1, 2, 3, 4, 5, 6, 7, 8, 9) and requires also 4 bits (because we can only represent 8 different values with 3 bits, the additional 6 values we can represent

---

[1] Binary-coded decimal is a numeric scheme used to represent decimal numbers using 4 bits for each decimal digit.

with 4 bits are never used in BCD representation). In fact, any 16 distinct values can be represented with a nibble, though hexadecimal and BCD digits are the primary items we can represent with a single nibble.

### 2.3.3 Bytes

Without question, the most important data structure used by the 80x86 microprocessor is the byte, which consists of 8 bits. Main memory and I/O addresses on the 80x86 are all byte addresses. This means that the smallest item that can be individually accessed by an 80x86 program is an 8-bit value. To access anything smaller requires that we read the byte containing the data and eliminate the unwanted bits. The bits in a byte are normally numbered from 0 to 7, as shown in Figure 2-1.

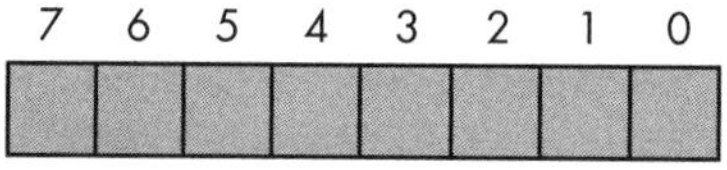

```
7   6   5   4   3   2   1   0
```

Figure 2-1: Bit numbering

Bit 0 is the *low-order bit* or *least significant bit*, and bit 7 is the *high-order bit* or *most significant bit* of the byte. We'll refer to all other bits by their number. Note that a byte also contains exactly two nibbles (see Figure 2-2).

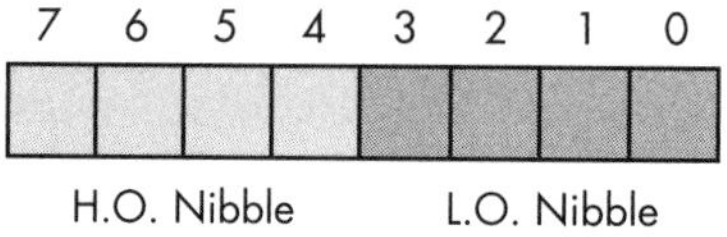

```
7   6   5   4   3   2   1   0
```

H.O. Nibble        L.O. Nibble

Figure 2-2: The two nibbles in a byte

Bits 0..3 compose the *low-order nibble*, and bits 4..7 form the *high-order nibble*. Because a byte contains exactly two nibbles, byte values require two hexadecimal digits.

Because a byte contains 8 bits, it can represent $2^8$ (256) different values. Generally, we'll use a byte to represent numeric values in the range 0..255, signed numbers in the range −128..+127 (see Section 2.8), ASCII/IBM character codes, and other special data types requiring no more than 256 different values. Many data types have fewer than 256 items, so 8 bits is usually sufficient.

Because the 80x86 is a byte-addressable machine, it turns out to be more efficient to manipulate a whole byte than an individual bit or nibble. For this reason, most programmers use a whole byte to represent data types that require no more than 256 items, even if fewer than 8 bits would suffice. For example, we'll often represent the boolean values true and false by $00000001_2$ and $00000000_2$, respectively.

Probably the most important use for a byte is holding a character value. Characters typed at the keyboard, displayed on the screen, and printed on the printer all have numeric values. To communicate with the rest of the world, PCs typically use a variant of the *ASCII character set*. There are 128 defined codes in the ASCII character set.

Because bytes are the smallest unit of storage in the 80x86 memory space, bytes also happen to be the smallest variable you can create in an HLA program. As you saw in the last chapter, you can declare an 8-bit signed integer variable using the int8 data type. Because int8 objects are signed, you can represent values in the range −128..+127 using an int8 variable. You should only store signed values into int8 variables; if you want to create an arbitrary byte variable, you should use the byte data type, as follows:

```
static
        byteVar: byte;
```

The byte data type is a partially untyped data type. The only type information associated with a byte object is its size (1 byte). You may store any 8-bit value (small signed integers, small unsigned integers, characters, and the like) into a byte variable. It is up to you to keep track of the type of object you've put into a byte variable.

### 2.3.4 Words

A word is a group of 16 bits. We'll number the bits in a word from 0 to 15, as Figure 2-3 shows. Like the byte, bit 0 is the low-order bit. For words, bit 15 is the high-order bit. When referencing the other bits in a word, we'll use their bit position number.

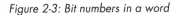
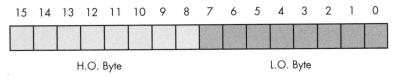

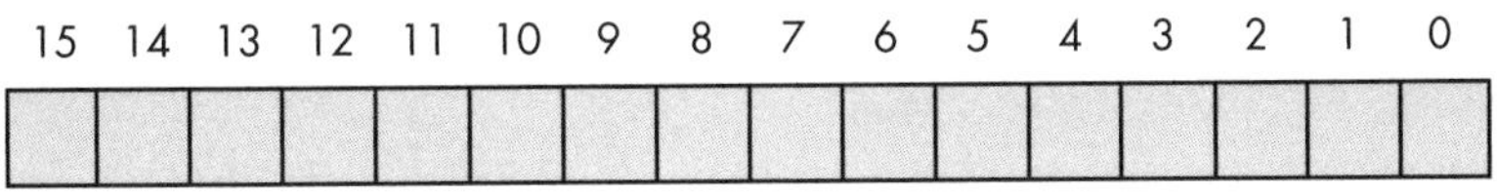

Figure 2-3: Bit numbers in a word

Notice that a word contains exactly 2 bytes. Bits 0..7 form the low-order byte, and bits 8..15 form the high-order byte (see Figure 2-4).

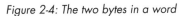

H.O. Byte             L.O. Byte

Figure 2-4: The two bytes in a word

Of course, a word may be further broken down into four nibbles, as shown in Figure 2-5. Nibble 0 is the low-order nibble in the word, and nibble 3 is the high-order nibble of the word. We'll simply refer to the other two nibbles as *nibble 1* or *nibble 2*.

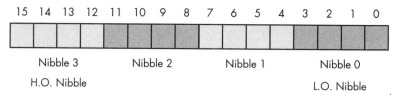

Figure 2-5: Nibbles in a word

With 16 bits, you can represent $2^{16}$ (65,536) different values. These could be the values in the range 0..65,535 or, as is usually the case, the signed values −32,768..+32,767, or any other data type with no more than 65,536 values. The three major uses for words are short signed integer values, short unsigned integer values, and Unicode characters.

Words can represent integer values in the range 0..65,535 or −32,768..32,767. Unsigned numeric values are represented by the binary value corresponding to the bits in the word. Signed numeric values use the two's complement form for numeric values (see Section 2.8). As Unicode characters, words can represent up to 65,536 different characters, allowing the use of non-Roman character sets in a computer program. Unicode is an international standard, like ASCII, that allows computers to process non-Roman characters such as Asian, Greek, and Russian characters.

As with bytes, you can also create word variables in an HLA program. Of course, in the last chapter you saw how to create 16-bit signed integer variables using the int16 data type. To create an arbitrary word variable, just use the word data type, as follows:

```
static
        w: word;
```

## 2.3.5   Double Words

A double word is exactly what its name implies, a pair of words. Therefore, a double-word quantity is 32 bits long, as shown in Figure 2-6.

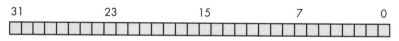

Figure 2-6: Bit numbers in a double word

Naturally, this double word can be divided into a high-order word and a low-order word, four different bytes, or eight different nibbles (see Figure 2-7).

Double words (dwords) can represent all kinds of different things. A common item you will represent with a double word is a 32-bit integer value (that allows unsigned numbers in the range 0..4,294,967,295 or signed numbers in the range −2,147,483,648..2,147,483,647). 32-bit floating-point values also fit into a double word. Another common use for double-word objects is to store pointer values.

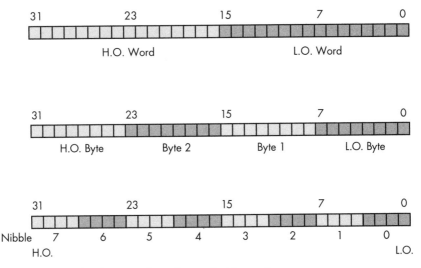

Figure 2-7: Nibbles, bytes, and words in a double word

In Chapter 1, you saw how to create 32-bit signed integer variables using the int32 data type. You can also create an arbitrary double-word variable using the dword data type, as the following example demonstrates:

```
static
        d: dword;
```

## 2.3.6 Quad Words and Long Words

Obviously, we can keep on defining larger and larger word sizes. However, the 80x86 supports only certain native sizes, so there is little reason to keep on defining terms for larger and larger objects. Although bytes, words, and double words are the most common sizes you'll find in 80x86 programs, quad word (64-bit) values are also important because certain floating-point data types require 64 bits. Likewise, the SSE/MMX instruction set of modern 80x86 processors can manipulate 64-bit values. In a similar vein, long-word (128-bit) values are also important because the SSE instruction set on later 80x86 processors can manipulate 128-bit values. HLA allows the declaration of 64- and 128-bit values using the qword and lword types, as follows:

```
static
    q       :qword;
    l       :lword;
```

Note that you may also define 64-bit and 128-bit integer values using HLA declarations like the following:

```
static
    i64         :int64;
    i128        :int128;
```

However, you may not directly manipulate 64-bit and 128-bit integer objects using standard instructions like mov, add, and sub because the standard 80x86 integer registers process only 32 bits at a time. In Chapter 8, you will see how to manipulate these *extended-precision* values.

## 2.4 Arithmetic Operations on Binary and Hexadecimal Numbers

There are several operations we can perform on binary and hexadecimal numbers. For example, we can add, subtract, multiply, divide, and perform other arithmetic operations. Although you needn't become an expert at it, you should be able to, in a pinch, perform these operations manually using a piece of paper and a pencil. Having just said that you should be able to perform these operations manually, the correct way to perform such arithmetic operations is to have a calculator that does them for you. There are several such calculators on the market; the following list shows some of the manufacturers of hexadecimal calculators (in 2010):

- Casio
- Hewlett-Packard
- Sharp
- Texas Instruments

This list is by no means exhaustive. Other calculator manufacturers probably produce these devices as well. The Hewlett-Packard devices are arguably the best of the bunch. However, they are more expensive than the others. Sharp and Casio produce units that sell for well under fifty dollars. If you plan on doing any assembly language programming at all, owning one of these calculators is essential.

To understand why you should spend the money on a calculator, consider the following arithmetic problem:

```
  $9
+ $1
----
```

You're probably tempted to write in the answer $10 as the solution to this problem. But that is not correct! The correct answer is 10, which is $A, not 16, which is $10. A similar problem exists with the following subtraction problem:

```
  $10
- $1
----
```

You're probably tempted to answer $9 even though the correct answer is $F. Remember, this problem is asking, "What is the difference between 16 and 1?" The answer, of course, is 15, which is $F.

Even if these two problems don't bother you, in a stressful situation your brain will switch back into decimal while you're thinking about something else and you'll produce the incorrect result. Moral of the story—if you must do an arithmetic computation using hexadecimal numbers by hand, take your time and be careful about it. Either that, or convert the numbers to decimal, perform the operation in decimal, and convert them back to hexadecimal.

## 2.5   A Note About Numbers vs. Representation

Many people confuse numbers and their representation. A common question beginning assembly language students ask is, "I have a binary number in the EAX register; how do I convert that to a hexadecimal number in the EAX register?" The answer is, "You don't." Although a strong argument could be made that numbers in memory or in registers are represented in binary, it's best to view values in memory or in a register as *abstract numeric quantities*. Strings of symbols like 128, $80, or %1000_0000 are not different numbers; they are simply different representations for the same abstract quantity that we refer to as "one hundred twenty-eight." Inside the computer, a number is a number regardless of representation; the only time representation matters is when you input or output the value in a human-readable form.

Human-readable forms of numeric quantities are always strings of characters. To print the value 128 in human-readable form, you must convert the numeric value 128 to the three-character sequence 1 followed by 2 followed by 8. This would provide the decimal representation of the numeric quantity. If you prefer, you could convert the numeric value 128 to the three-character sequence $80. It's the same number, but we've converted it to a different sequence of characters because (presumably) we wanted to view the number using hexadecimal representation rather than decimal. Likewise, if we want to see the number in binary, then we must convert this numeric value to a string containing a 1 followed by seven 0s.

By default, HLA displays all byte, word, dword, qword, and lword variables using the hexadecimal numbering system when using the stdout.put routine. Likewise, HLA's stdout.put routine will display all register values in hexadecimal form. Consider the program in Listing 2-1, which converts values input as decimal numbers to their hexadecimal equivalents.

```
program ConvertToHex;
#include( "stdlib.hhf" )
static
    value: int32;

begin ConvertToHex;

    stdout.put( "Input a decimal value:" );
    stdin.get( value );
    mov( value, eax );
    stdout.put( "The value ", value, " converted to hex is $", eax, nl );

end ConvertToHex;
```

*Listing 2-1: Decimal-to-hexadecimal conversion program*

In a similar fashion, the default input base is also hexadecimal for registers and byte, word, dword, qword, or lword variables. The program in Listing 2-2 is the converse of the one in Listing 2-1; it inputs a hexadecimal value and outputs it as decimal.

```
program ConvertToDecimal;
#include( "stdlib.hhf" )
static
    value: int32;

begin ConvertToDecimal;

    stdout.put( "Input a hexadecimal value: " );
    stdin.get( ebx );
    mov( ebx, value );
    stdout.put( "The value $", ebx, " converted to decimal is ", value, nl );

end ConvertToDecimal;
```

Listing 2-2: Hexadecimal-to-decimal conversion program

Just because the HLA stdout.put routine chooses decimal as the default output base for int8, int16, and int32 variables doesn't mean that these variables hold decimal numbers. Remember, memory and registers hold numeric values, not hexadecimal or decimal values. The stdout.put routine converts these numeric values to strings and prints the resulting strings. The choice of hexadecimal versus decimal output was a design choice in the HLA language, nothing more. You could very easily modify HLA so that it outputs registers and byte, word, dword, qword, or lword variables as decimal values rather than as hexadecimal. If you need to print the value of a register or byte, word, or dword variable as a decimal value, simply call one of the putiX routines to do this. The stdout.puti8 routine will output its parameter as an 8-bit signed integer. Any 8-bit parameter will work. So you could pass an 8-bit register, an int8 variable, or a byte variable as the parameter to stdout.puti8 and the result will always be decimal. The stdout.puti16 and stdout.puti32 routines provide the same capabilities for 16-bit and 32-bit objects. The program in Listing 2-3 demonstrates the decimal conversion program (Listing 2-2) using only the EBX register (that is, it does not use the variable iValue).

```
program ConvertToDecimal2;
#include( "stdlib.hhf" )
begin ConvertToDecimal2;

    stdout.put( "Input a hexadecimal value: " );
    stdin.get( ebx );
    stdout.put( "The value $", ebx, " converted to decimal is " );
    stdout.puti32( ebx );
    stdout.newln();

end ConvertToDecimal2;
```

Listing 2-3: Variable-less hexadecimal-to-decimal converter

Note that HLA's stdin.get routine uses the same default base for input as stdout.put uses for output. That is, if you attempt to read an int8, int16, or int32 variable, the default input base is decimal. If you attempt to read a register or byte, word, dword, qword, or lword variable, the default input base is hexadecimal. If you want to change the default input base to decimal when reading a register or a byte, word, dword, qword, or lword variable, then you can use stdin.geti8, stdin.geti16, stdin.geti32, stdin.geti64, or stdin.geti128.

If you want to go in the opposite direction, that is you want to input or output an int8, int16, int32, int64, or int128 variable as a hexadecimal value, you can call the stdout.puth8, stdout.puth16, stdout.puth32, stdout.puth64, stdout.puth128, stdin.geth8, stdin.geth16, stdin.geth32, stdin.geth64, or stdin.geth128 routines. The stdout.puth8, stdout.puth16, stdout.puth32, stdout.puth64, and stdout.puth128 routines write 8-bit, 16-bit, 32-bit, 64-bit, or 128-bit objects as hexadecimal values. The stdin.geth8, stdin.geth16, stdin.geth32, stdin.geth64, and stdin.geth128 routines read 8-, 16-, 32-, 64-, and 128-bit values, respectively; they return their results in the AL, AX, or EAX registers (or in a parameter location for 64-bit and 128-bit values). The program in Listing 2-4 demonstrates the use of a few of these routines:

```
program HexIO;

#include( "stdlib.hhf" )

static
    i32: int32;

begin HexIO;

    stdout.put( "Enter a hexadecimal value: " );
    stdin.geth32();
    mov( eax, i32 );
    stdout.put( "The value you entered was $" );
    stdout.puth32( i32 );
    stdout.newln();

end HexIO;
```

Listing 2-4: Demonstration of stdin.geth32 and stdout.puth32

## 2.6   Logical Operations on Bits

There are four primary logical operations we'll do with hexadecimal and binary numbers: and, or, xor (exclusive-or), and not. Unlike for the arithmetic operations, a hexadecimal calculator isn't necessary to perform these operations. It is often easier to do them by hand than to use an electronic device to compute them. The logical and operation is a dyadic[2] operation (meaning

---

[2] Many texts call this a binary operation. The term *dyadic* means the same thing and avoids the confusion with the binary numbering system.

it accepts exactly two operands). These operands are individual binary bits. The and operation is:

```
0 and 0 = 0
0 and 1 = 0
1 and 0 = 0
1 and 1 = 1
```

A compact way to represent the logical and operation is with a truth table. A truth table takes the form shown in Table 2-2.

**Table 2-2:** and Truth Table

| and | 0 | 1 |
| --- | --- | --- |
| 0 | 0 | 0 |
| 1 | 0 | 1 |

This is just like the multiplication tables you've encountered in school. The values in the left column correspond to the leftmost operand of the and operation. The values in the top row correspond to the rightmost operand of the and operation. The value located at the intersection of the row and column (for a particular pair of input values) is the result of logically anding those two values together.

In English, the logical and operation is, "If the first operand is 1 and the second operand is 1, the result is 1; otherwise the result is 0." We could also state this as, "If either or both operands are 0, the result is 0."

One important fact to note about the logical and operation is that you can use it to force a 0 result. If one of the operands is 0, the result is always 0 regardless of the other operand. In the truth table above, for example, the row labeled with a 0 input contains only 0s, and the column labeled with a 0 contains only 0 results. Conversely, if one operand contains a 1, the result is exactly the value of the second operand. These results of the and operation are very important, particularly when we want to force bits to 0. We will investigate these uses of the logical and operation in the next section.

The logical or operation is also a dyadic operation. Its definition is:

```
0 or 0 = 0
0 or 1 = 1
1 or 0 = 1
1 or 1 = 1
```

The truth table for the or operation takes the form appearing in Table 2-3.

**Table 2-3:** or Truth Table

| or | 0 | 1 |
| --- | --- | --- |
| 0 | 0 | 1 |
| 1 | 1 | 1 |

Colloquially, the logical or operation is, "If the first operand or the second operand (or both) is 1, the result is 1; otherwise the result is 0." This is also known as the *inclusive-or* operation.

If one of the operands to the logical or operation is a 1, the result is always 1 regardless of the second operand's value. If one operand is 0, the result is always the value of the second operand. Like the logical and operation, this is an important side effect of the logical or operation that will prove quite useful.

Note that there is a difference between this form of the inclusive logical or operation and the standard English meaning. Consider the phrase "I am going to the store *or* I am going to the park." Such a statement implies that the speaker is going to the store or to the park but not to both places. Therefore, the English version of logical or is slightly different from the inclusive-or operation; indeed, this is the definition of the *exclusive-or* operation.

The logical xor (exclusive-or) operation is also a dyadic operation. Its definition follows:

```
0 xor 0 = 0
0 xor 1 = 1
1 xor 0 = 1
1 xor 1 = 0
```

The truth table for the xor operation takes the form shown in Table 2-4.

**Table 2-4:** xor Truth Table

| xor | 0 | 1 |
| --- | --- | --- |
| 0 | 0 | 1 |
| 1 | 1 | 0 |

In English, the logical xor operation is, "If the first operand or the second operand, but not both, is 1, the result is 1; otherwise the result is 0." Note that the exclusive-or operation is closer to the English meaning of the word *or* than is the logical or operation.

If one of the operands to the logical exclusive-or operation is a 1, the result is always the *inverse* of the other operand; that is, if one operand is 1, the result is 0 if the other operand is 1, and the result is 1 if the other operand is 0. If the first operand contains a 0, then the result is exactly the value of the second operand. This feature lets you selectively invert bits in a bit string.

The logical not operation is a monadic operation (meaning it accepts only one operand):

```
not 0 = 1
not 1 = 0
```

The truth table for the not operation appears in Table 2-5.

**Table 2-5:** not Truth Table

| not | 0 | 1 |
|-----|---|---|
|     | 1 | 0 |

## 2.7 Logical Operations on Binary Numbers and Bit Strings

The previous section defines the logical functions for single-bit operands. Because the 80x86 uses groups of 8, 16, or 32 bits, we need to extend the definition of these functions to deal with more than 2 bits. Logical functions on the 80x86 operate on a *bit-by-bit* (or *bitwise*) basis. Given two values, these functions operate on bit 0, producing bit 0 of the result. They operate on bit 1 of the input values, producing bit 1 of the result, and so on. For example, if you want to compute the logical and of the following two 8-bit numbers, you would perform the logical and operation on each column independently of the others:

```
%1011_0101
%1110_1110
----------
%1010_0100
```

You may apply this bit-by-bit calculation to the other logical functions as well.

Because we've defined logical operations in terms of binary values, you'll find it much easier to perform logical operations on binary values than on other representations. Therefore, if you want to perform a logical operation on two hexadecimal numbers, you should convert them to binary first. This applies to most of the basic logical operations on binary numbers (e.g., and, or, xor, etc.).

The ability to force bits to 0 or 1 using the logical and/or operations and the ability to invert bits using the logical xor operation are very important when working with strings of bits (e.g., binary numbers). These operations let you selectively manipulate certain bits within some bit string while leaving other bits unaffected. For example, if you have an 8-bit binary value $X$ and you want to guarantee that bits 4..7 contain 0s, you could logically and the value $X$ with the binary value %0000_1111. This bitwise logical and operation would force the H.O. 4 bits to 0 and pass the L.O. 4 bits of $X$ unchanged. Likewise, you could force the L.O. bit of $X$ to 1 and invert bit 2 of $X$ by logically oring $X$ with %0000_0001 and logically exclusive-oring $X$ with %0000_0100, respectively. Using the logical and, or, and xor operations to manipulate bit strings in this fashion is known as *masking* bit strings. We use the term *masking* because we can use certain values (1 for and, 0 for or/xor) to mask out or mask in certain bits from the operation when forcing bits to 0, 1, or their inverse.

The 80x86 CPUs support four instructions that apply these bitwise logical operations to their operands. The instructions are and, or, xor, and not.

The and, or, and xor instructions use the same syntax as the add and sub instructions:

```
and( source, dest );
 or( source, dest );
xor( source, dest );
```

These operands have the same limitations as the add operands. Specifically, the *source* operand has to be a constant, memory, or register operand, and the *dest* operand must be a memory or register operand. Also, the operands must be the same size and they cannot both be memory operands. These instructions compute the obvious bitwise logical operation via the following equation:

```
dest = dest operator source
```

The 80x86 logical not instruction, because it has only a single operand, uses a slightly different syntax. This instruction takes the following form:

```
not( dest );
```

This instruction computes the following result:

```
dest = not( dest )
```

The *dest* operand must be a register or memory operand. This instruction inverts all the bits in the specified destination operand.

The program in Listing 2-5 inputs two hexadecimal values from the user and calculates their logical and, or, xor, and not:

```
program LogicalOp;
#include( "stdlib.hhf" )
begin LogicalOp;

    stdout.put( "Input left operand: " );
    stdin.get( eax );
    stdout.put( "Input right operand: " );
    stdin.get( ebx );

    mov( eax, ecx );
    and( ebx, ecx );
    stdout.put( "$", eax, " and $", ebx, " = $", ecx, nl );

    mov( eax, ecx );
    or( ebx, ecx );
    stdout.put( "$", eax, " or $", ebx, " = $", ecx, nl );

    mov( eax, ecx );
    xor( ebx, ecx );
    stdout.put( "$", eax, " xor $", ebx, " = $", ecx, nl );

    mov( eax, ecx );
```

```
    not( ecx );
    stdout.put( "not $", eax, " = $", ecx, nl );

    mov( ebx, ecx );
    not( ecx );
    stdout.put( "not $", ebx, " = $", ecx, nl );

end LogicalOp;
```

*Listing 2-5: and, or, xor, and not example*

## 2.8   Signed and Unsigned Numbers

Thus far, we've treated binary numbers as unsigned values. The binary
number ...00000 represents 0, ...00001 represents 1, ...00010 represents 2,
and so on toward infinity. What about negative numbers? Signed values have
been tossed around in previous sections, and we've mentioned the two's
complement numbering system, but we haven't discussed how to represent
negative numbers using the binary numbering system. Now it is time to
describe the two's complement numbering system.

To represent signed numbers using the binary numbering system, we
have to place a restriction on our numbers: They must have a finite and fixed
number of bits. For our purposes, we're going to severely limit the number
of bits to 8, 16, 32, 64, 128, or some other small number of bits.

With a fixed number of bits we can represent only a certain number of
objects. For example, with 8 bits we can represent only 256 different values.
Negative values are objects in their own right, just like positive numbers and
0; therefore, we'll have to use some of the 256 different 8-bit values to represent negative numbers. In other words, we have to use up some of the bit
combinations to represent negative numbers. To make things fair, we'll
assign half of the possible combinations to the negative values and half to the
positive values and 0. So we can represent the negative values −128..−1 and the
nonnegative values 0..127 with a single 8-bit byte. With a 16-bit word we can
represent values in the range −32,768..+32,767. With a 32-bit double word we
can represent values in the range −2,147,483,648..+2,147,483,647. In general,
with $n$ bits we can represent the signed values in the range $-2^{n-1}$ to $+2^{n-1}-1$.

Okay, so we can represent negative values. Exactly how do we do it?
Well, there are many possible ways, but the 80x86 microprocessor uses
the two's complement notation, so it makes sense to study that method.
In the two's complement system, the H.O. bit of a number is a *sign bit*. If
the H.O. bit is 0, the number is positive; if the H.O. bit is 1, the number is
negative. Following are some examples.

For 16-bit numbers:

```
$8000 is negative because the H.O. bit is 1.
$100 is positive because the H.O. bit is 0.
$7FFF is positive.
$FFFF is negative.
$FFF ($0FFF) is positive.
```

If the H.O. bit is 0, then the number is positive and uses the standard binary format. If the H.O. bit is 1, then the number is negative and uses the two's complement form. To convert a positive number to its negative, two's complement form, you use the following algorithm:

1. Invert all the bits in the number; that is, apply the logical not function.
2. Add 1 to the inverted result and ignore any overflow out of the H.O. bit.

For example, to compute the 8-bit equivalent of –5:

| | |
|---|---|
| %0000_0101 | 5 (in binary). |
| %1111_1010 | Invert all the bits. |
| %1111_1011 | Add 1 to obtain result. |

If we take –5 and perform the two's complement operation on it, we get our original value, %0000_0101, back again, just as we expect:

| | |
|---|---|
| %1111_1011 | Two's complement for -5. |
| %0000_0100 | Invert all the bits. |
| %0000_0101 | Add 1 to obtain result (+5). |

The following examples provide some positive and negative 16-bit signed values:

| |
|---|
| $7FFF: +32767, the largest 16-bit positive number. |
| $8000: -32768, the smallest 16-bit negative number. |
| $4000: +16384. |

To convert the numbers above to their negative counterpart (that is, to negate them), do the following:

| $7FFF: | %0111_1111_1111_1111 | +32,767 |
|---|---|---|
| | %1000_0000_0000_0000 | Invert all the bits (8000h) |
| | %1000_0000_0000_0001 | Add 1 (8001h or -32,767) |
| 4000h: | %0100_0000_0000_0000 | 16,384 |
| | %1011_1111_1111_1111 | Invert all the bits ($BFFF) |
| | %1100_0000_0000_0000 | Add 1 ($C000 or -16,384) |
| $8000: | %1000_0000_0000_0000 | -32,768 |
| | %0111_1111_1111_1111 | Invert all the bits ($7FFF) |
| | %1000_0000_0000_0000 | Add one (8000h or -32,768) |

$8000 inverted becomes $7FFF. After adding 1 we obtain $8000! Wait, what's going on here? –(–32,768) is –32,768? Of course not. But the value +32,768 cannot be represented with a 16-bit signed number, so we cannot negate the smallest negative value.

Why bother with such a miserable numbering system? Why not use the H.O. bit as a sign flag, storing the positive equivalent of the number in the remaining bits? (This, by the way, is known as the *one's complement numbering system.*) The answer lies in the hardware. As it turns out, negating values is the only tedious job. With the two's complement system, most other operations are as easy as the binary system. For example, suppose you were to perform the addition $5 + (-5)$. The result is 0. Consider what happens when we add these two values in the two's complement system:

```
%   0000_0101
%   1111_1011
------------
%1_0000_0000
```

We end up with a carry into the ninth bit, and all other bits are 0. As it turns out, if we ignore the carry out of the H.O. bit, adding two signed values always produces the correct result when using the two's complement numbering system. This means we can use the same hardware for signed and unsigned addition and subtraction. This wouldn't be the case with other numbering systems.

Usually, you will not need to perform the two's complement operation by hand. The 80x86 microprocessor provides an instruction, neg (negate), that performs this operation for you. Furthermore, hexadecimal calculators perform this operation by pressing the change sign key (+/- or CHS). Nevertheless, manually computing the two's complement is easy, and you should know how to do it.

Remember that the data represented by a set of binary bits depends entirely on the context. The 8-bit binary value %1100_0000 could represent a character, it could represent the unsigned decimal value 192, or it could represent the signed decimal value -64. As the programmer, it is your responsibility to define the data's format and then use the data consistently.

The 80x86 negate instruction, neg, uses the same syntax as the not instruction; that is, it takes a single destination operand:

```
neg( dest );
```

This instruction computes *dest* = *-dest*; and the operand has the same limitations as for not (it must be a memory location or a register). neg operates on byte-, word-, and dword-sized objects. Because this is a signed integer operation, it only makes sense to operate on signed integer values. The program in Listing 2-6 demonstrates the two's complement operation by using the neg instruction:

```
program twosComplement;
#include( "stdlib.hhf" )

static
    PosValue:    int8;
    NegValue:    int8;

begin twosComplement;
```

```
        stdout.put( "Enter an integer between 0 and 127: " );
        stdin.get( PosValue );

        stdout.put( nl, "Value in hexadecimal: $" );
        stdout.puth8( PosValue );

        mov( PosValue, al );
        not( al );
        stdout.put( nl, "Invert all the bits: $", al, nl );
        add( 1, al );
        stdout.put( "Add one: $", al, nl );
        mov( al, NegValue );
        stdout.put( "Result in decimal: ", NegValue, nl );

        stdout.put
        (
            nl,
            "Now do the same thing with the NEG instruction: ",
            nl
        );
        mov( PosValue, al );
        neg( al );
        mov( al, NegValue );
        stdout.put( "Hex result = $", al, nl );
        stdout.put( "Decimal result = ", NegValue, nl );

end twosComplement;
```

*Listing 2-6: twosComplement example*

As you've seen previously, you use the int8, int16, int32, int64, and int128 data types to reserve storage for signed integer variables. You've also seen routines like stdout.puti8 and stdin.geti32 that read and write signed integer values. Because this section has made it abundantly clear that you must differentiate signed and unsigned calculations in your programs, you should probably be asking yourself, "How do I declare and use unsigned integer variables?"

The first part of the question, "How do I declare unsigned integer variables," is the easiest to answer. You simply use the uns8, uns16, uns32, uns64, and uns128 data types when declaring the variables. For example:

```
static
    u8:         uns8;
    u16:        uns16;
    u32:        uns32;
    u64:        uns64;
    u128:       uns128;
```

As for using these unsigned variables, the HLA Standard Library provides a complementary set of input/output routines for reading and displaying unsigned variables. As you can probably guess, these routines include stdout.putu8, stdout.putu16, stdout.putu32, stdout.putu64, stdout.putu128, stdout.putu8Size, stdout.putu16Size, stdout.putu32Size, stdout.putu64Size, stdout.putu128Size, stdin.getu8, stdin.getu16, stdin.getu32, stdin.getu64, and stdin.getu128. You use these routines just as you would use their signed integer counterparts except you get to use the full range of the unsigned values with these routines. The source code in Listing 2-7 demonstrates unsigned I/O as well as demonstrates what can happen if you mix signed and unsigned operations in the same calculation.

```
program UnsExample;
#include( "stdlib.hhf" )

static
    UnsValue:    uns16;

begin UnsExample;

    stdout.put( "Enter an integer between 32,768 and 65,535: " );
    stdin.getu16();
    mov( ax, UnsValue );

    stdout.put
    (
        "You entered ",
        UnsValue,
        ".  If you treat this as a signed integer, it is "
    );
    stdout.puti16( UnsValue );
    stdout.newln();

end UnsExample;
```

*Listing 2-7: Unsigned I/O*

## 2.9 Sign Extension, Zero Extension, Contraction, and Saturation

Because two's complement format integers have a fixed length, a small problem develops. What happens if you need to convert an 8-bit two's complement value to 16 bits? This problem and its converse (converting a 16-bit value to 8 bits) can be accomplished via *sign extension* and *contraction* operations.

Consider the value −64. The 8-bit two's complement value for this number is $C0. The 16-bit equivalent of this number is $FFC0. Now consider the value +64. The 8- and 16-bit versions of this value are $40 and $0040, respectively. The difference between the 8- and 16-bit numbers can be described by the rule, "If the number is negative, the H.O. byte of the 16-bit number contains $FF; if the number is positive, the H.O. byte of the 16-bit quantity is 0."

To extend a signed value from some number of bits to a greater number of bits is easy; just copy the sign bit into all the additional bits in the new format. For example, to sign extend an 8-bit number to a 16-bit number, simply copy bit 7 of the 8-bit number into bits 8..15 of the 16-bit number. To sign extend a 16-bit number to a double word, simply copy bit 15 into bits 16..31 of the double word.

You must use sign extension when manipulating signed values of varying lengths. Often you'll need to add a byte quantity to a word quantity. You must sign extend the byte quantity to a word before the operation takes place. Other operations (multiplication and division, in particular) may require a sign extension to 32 bits:

```
Sign Extension:
8 Bits      16 Bits       32 Bits

$80         $FF80         $FFFF_FF80
$28         $0028         $0000_0028
$9A         $FF9A         $FFFF_FF9A
$7F         $007F         $0000_007F
            $1020         $0000_1020
            $8086         $FFFF_8086
```

To extend an unsigned value to a larger one, you must zero extend the value. Zero extension is very easy—just store a 0 into the H.O. byte(s) of the larger operand. For example, to zero extend the 8-bit value $82 to 16 bits, you simply add a 0 to the H.O. byte, yielding $0082.

```
Zero Extension:
8 Bits      16 Bits       32 Bits

$80         $0080         $0000_0080
$28         $0028         $0000_0028
$9A         $009A         $0000_009A
$7F         $007F         $0000_007F
            $1020         $0000_1020
            $8086         $0000_8086
```

The 80x86 provides several instructions that will let you sign or zero extend a smaller number to a larger number. Table 2-6 lists a group of instructions that will sign extend the AL, AX, or EAX register.

**Table 2-6:** Instructions for Extending AL, AX, and EAX

| Instruction | Explanation |
|---|---|
| cbw(); | Converts the byte in AL to a word in AX via sign extension. |
| cwd(); | Converts the word in AX to a double word in DX:AX via sign extension. |
| cdq(); | Converts the double word in EAX to the quad word in EDX:EAX via sign extension. |
| cwde(); | Converts the word in AX to a double word in EAX via sign extension. |

Note that the cwd (convert word to double word) instruction does not sign extend the word in AX to the double word in EAX. Instead, it stores the

H.O. word of the sign extension into the DX register (the notation DX:AX tells you that you have a double-word value with DX containing the upper 16 bits and AX containing the lower 16 bits of the value). If you want the sign extension of AX to go into EAX, you should use the cwde (convert word to double word, extended) instruction.

The four instructions above are unusual in the sense that these are the first instructions you've seen that do not have any operands. These instructions' operands are *implied* by the instructions themselves.

Within a few chapters you will discover just how important these instructions are and why the cwd and cdq instructions involve the DX and EDX registers. However, for simple sign extension operations, these instructions have a few major drawbacks—you do not get to specify the source and destination operands, and the operands must be registers.

For general sign extension operations, the 80x86 provides an extension of the mov instruction, movsx (move with sign extension), that copies data and sign extends the data while copying it. The movsx instruction's syntax is very similar to the mov instruction:

---

```
movsx( source, dest );
```

---

The big difference in syntax between this instruction and the mov instruction is the fact that the destination operand must be larger than the source operand. That is, if the source operand is a byte, the destination operand must be a word or a double word. Likewise, if the source operand is a word, the destination operand must be a double word. Another difference is that the destination operand has to be a register; the source operand, however, can be a memory location.[3] The movsx instruction does not allow constant operands.

To zero extend a value, you can use the movzx instruction. It has the same syntax and restrictions as the movsx instruction. Zero extending certain 8-bit registers (AL, BL, CL, and DL) into their corresponding 16-bit registers is easily accomplished without using movzx by loading the complementary H.O. register (AH, BH, CH, or DH) with 0. Obviously, to zero extend AX into DX:AX or EAX into EDX:EAX, all you need to do is load DX or EDX with 0.[4]

The sample program in Listing 2-8 demonstrates the use of the sign extension instructions.

---

```
program signExtension;
#include( "stdlib.hhf" )

static
    i8:     int8;
    i16:    int16;
    i32:    int32;
```

---

[3] This doesn't turn out to be much of a limitation because sign extension almost always precedes an arithmetic operation that must take place in a register.

[4] Zero extending into DX:AX or EDX:EAX is just as necessary as the CWD and CDQ instructions, as you will eventually see.

```
begin signExtension;

    stdout.put( "Enter a small negative number: " );
    stdin.get( i8 );

    stdout.put( nl, "Sign extension using CBW and CWDE:", nl, nl );

    mov( i8, al );
    stdout.put( "You entered ", i8, " ($", al, ")", nl );

    cbw();
    mov( ax, i16 );
    stdout.put( "16-bit sign extension: ", i16, " ($", ax, ")", nl );

    cwde();
    mov( eax, i32 );
    stdout.put( "32-bit sign extension: ", i32, " ($", eax, ")", nl );

    stdout.put( nl, "Sign extension using MOVSX:", nl, nl );

    movsx( i8, ax );
    mov( ax, i16 );
    stdout.put( "16-bit sign extension: ", i16, " ($", ax, ")", nl );

    movsx( i8, eax );
    mov( eax, i32 );
    stdout.put( "32-bit sign extension: ", i32, " ($", eax, ")", nl );

end signExtension;
```

*Listing 2-8: Sign extension instructions*

Sign *contraction*, converting a value with some number of bits to the
identical value with a fewer number of bits, is a little more troublesome. Sign
extension never fails. Given an $m$-bit signed value, you can always convert it
to an $n$-bit number (where $n > m$) using sign extension. Unfortunately, given
an $n$-bit number, you cannot always convert it to an $m$-bit number if $m < n$.
For example, consider the value −448. As a 16-bit signed number, its hexadecimal representation is $FE40. Unfortunately, the magnitude of this number
is too large for an 8-bit value, so you cannot sign contract it to 8 bits. This is
an example of an overflow condition that occurs upon conversion.

To properly sign contract a value, you must look at the H.O. byte(s) that
you want to discard. The H.O. bytes must all contain either 0 or $FF. If you
encounter any other values, you cannot contract it without overflow. Finally,
the H.O. bit of your resulting value must match *every* bit you've removed
from the number. Here are some examples (16 bits to 8 bits):

```
$FF80 can be sign contracted to $80.
$0040 can be sign contracted to $40.
$FE40 cannot be sign contracted to 8 bits.
$0100 cannot be sign contracted to 8 bits.
```

Another way to reduce the size of an integer is by *saturation*. Saturation is useful in situations where you must convert a larger object to a smaller object, and you're willing to live with possible loss of precision. To convert a value via saturation you simply copy the larger value to the smaller value if it is not outside the range of the smaller object. If the larger value is outside the range of the smaller value, then you *clip* the value by setting it to the largest (or smallest) value within the range of the smaller object.

For example, when converting a 16-bit signed integer to an 8-bit signed integer, if the 16-bit value is in the range −128..+127, you simply copy the L.O. byte of the 16-bit object to the 8-bit object. If the 16-bit signed value is greater than +127, then you clip the value to +127 and store +127 into the 8-bit object. Likewise, if the value is less than −128, you clip the final 8-bit object to −128. Saturation works the same way when clipping 32-bit values to smaller values. If the larger value is outside the range of the smaller value, then you simply set the smaller value to the value closest to the out-of-range value that you can represent with the smaller value.

Obviously, if the larger value is outside the range of the smaller value, then there will be a loss of precision during the conversion. While clipping the value to the limits the smaller object imposes is never desirable, sometimes this is acceptable because the alternative is to raise an exception or otherwise reject the calculation. For many applications, such as audio or video processing, the clipped result is still recognizable, so this is a reasonable conversion.

## 2.10  Shifts and Rotates

Another set of logical operations that apply to bit strings is the *shift* and *rotate* operations. These two categories can be further broken down into *left shifts, left rotates, right shifts,* and *right rotates.* These operations turn out to be extremely useful.

The left-shift operation moves each bit in a bit string one position to the left (Figure 2-8 provides an example of an 8-bit shift).

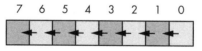

*Figure 2-8: Shift-left operation*

Bit 0 moves into bit position 1, the previous value in bit position 1 moves into bit position 2, and so on. There are, of course, two questions that naturally arise: "What goes into bit 0?" and "Where does the high-order bit go?" We'll shift a 0 into bit 0, and the previous value of the high-order bit will become the *carry* out of this operation.

The 80x86 provides a shift-left instruction, shl, that performs this useful operation. The syntax for the shl instruction is:

```
shl( count, dest );
```

The *count* operand is either CL or a constant in the range 0..*n*, where *n* is one less than the number of bits in the destination operand (for example, $n = 7$ for 8-bit operands, $n = 15$ for 16-bit operands, and $n = 31$ for 32-bit operands). The *dest* operand is a typical destination operand. It can be either a memory location or a register.

When the *count* operand is the constant 1, the shl instruction does the operation shown in Figure 2-9.

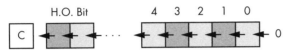

Figure 2-9: Shift-left operation

In Figure 2-9, the *C* represents the carry flag. That is, the H.O. bit shifted out of the operand moves into the carry flag. Therefore, you can test for overflow after a shl( 1, *dest* ); instruction by testing the carry flag immediately after executing the instruction (e.g., by using if( @c ) then... or if( @nc ) then...).

Intel's literature suggests that the state of the carry flag is undefined if the shift count is a value other than 1. Usually, the carry flag contains the last bit shifted out of the destination operand, but Intel doesn't seem to guarantee this.

Note that shifting a value to the left is the same thing as multiplying it by its radix. For example, shifting a decimal number one position to the left (adding a 0 to the right of the number) effectively multiplies it by 10 (the radix):

---

```
1234 shl 1 = 12340
```

---

(shl 1 means shift one digit position to the left.)

Because the radix of a binary number is 2, shifting it left multiplies it by 2. If you shift a binary value to the left twice, you multiply it by 2 twice (that is, you multiply it by 4). If you shift a binary value to the left three times, you multiply it by 8 (2*2*2). In general, if you shift a value to the left *n* times, you multiply that value by $2^n$.

A right-shift operation works the same way, except we're moving the data in the opposite direction. For a byte value, bit 7 moves into bit 6, bit 6 moves into bit 5, bit 5 moves into bit 4, and so on. During a right shift, we'll move a 0 into bit 7, and bit 0 will be the carry out of the operation (see Figure 2-10).

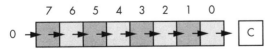

Figure 2-10: Shift-right operation

As you would probably expect, the 80x86 provides a shr instruction that will shift the bits to the right in a destination operand. The syntax is the same as the shl instruction except, of course, you specify shr rather than shl:

---

```
shr( count, dest );
```

---

This instruction shifts a 0 into the H.O. bit of the destination operand, it shifts the other bits one place to the right (that is, from a higher bit number to a lower bit number). Finally, bit 0 is shifted into the carry flag. If you specify a count of 1, the shr instruction does the operation shown in Figure 2-11.

Figure 2-11: Shift-right operation

Once again, Intel's documents suggest that shifts of more than 1 bit leave the carry in an undefined state.

Because a left shift is equivalent to a multiplication by 2, it should come as no surprise that a right shift is roughly comparable to a division by 2 (or, in general, a division by the radix of the number). If you perform $n$ right shifts, you will divide that number by $2^n$.

There is one problem with shift rights with respect to division: A shift right is only equivalent to an *unsigned* division by 2. For example, if you shift the unsigned representation of 254 ($FE) one place to the right, you get 127 ($7F), exactly what you would expect. However, if you shift the binary representation of −2 ($FE) to the right one position, you get 127 ($7F), which is *not* correct. This problem occurs because we're shifting a 0 into bit 7. If bit 7 previously contained a 1, we're changing it from a negative to a positive number. Not a good thing to do when dividing by 2.

To use the shift right as a division operator, we must define a third shift operation: arithmetic shift right.[5] An arithmetic shift right works just like the normal shift-right operation (a logical shift right) with one exception: Instead of shifting a 0 into the high-order bit, an arithmetic shift-right operation copies the high-order bit back into itself; that is, during the shift operation it does not modify the high-order bit, as Figure 2-12 shows.

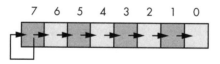

Figure 2-12: Arithmetic shift-right operation

An arithmetic shift right generally produces the result you expect. For example, if you perform the arithmetic shift-right operation on −2 ($FE), you get −1 ($FF). Keep one thing in mind about arithmetic shift right, however. This operation always rounds the numbers to the closest integer that is *less than or equal to the actual result*. Based on experiences with high-level programming languages and the standard rules of integer truncation, most people assume this means that a division always truncates toward 0. But this simply isn't the case. For example, if you apply the arithmetic shift-right operation on −1 ($FF), the result is −1, not 0. Because −1 is less than 0,

---

[5] There is no need for an arithmetic shift left. The standard shift-left operation works for both signed and unsigned numbers, assuming no overflow occurs.

the arithmetic shift-right operation rounds toward −1. This is not a bug in the arithmetic shift-right operation; it just uses a different (though valid) definition of integer division.

The 80x86 provides an arithmetic shift-right instruction, sar (shift arithmetic right). This instruction's syntax is nearly identical to shl and shr. The syntax is:

```
sar( count, dest );
```

The usual limitations on the count and destination operands apply. This instruction operates as shown in Figure 2-13 if the count is 1.

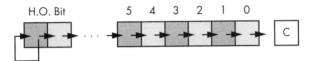

*Figure 2-13: sar( 1, dest ) operation*

Once again, Intel's documents suggest that shifts of more than 1 bit leave the carry in an undefined state.

Another pair of useful operations are *rotate left* and *rotate right*. These operations behave like the shift-left and shift-right operations with one major difference: The bit shifted out from one end is shifted back in at the other end. Figure 2-14 diagrams these operations.

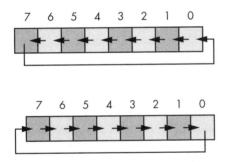

*Figure 2-14: Rotate-left and rotate-right operations*

The 80x86 provides rol (rotate left) and ror (rotate right) instructions that do these basic operations on their operands. The syntax for these two instructions is similar to the shift instructions:

```
rol( count, dest );
ror( count, dest );
```

Once again, these instructions provide a special behavior if the shift count is 1. Under this condition these two instructions also copy the bit shifted out of the destination operand into the carry flag as Figures 2-15 and 2-16 show.

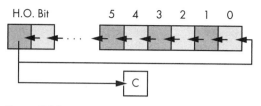

Figure 2-15: rol( 1, dest ) operation

Note that Intel's documents suggest that rotates of more than 1 bit leave the carry in an undefined state.

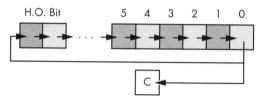

Figure 2-16: ror( 1, dest ) operation

It is often more convenient for the rotate operation to shift the output bit through the carry and shift the previous carry value back into the input bit of the shift operation. The 80x86 rcl (rotate through carry left) and rcr (rotate through carry right) instructions achieve this for you. These instructions use the following syntax:

```
rcl( count, dest );
rcr( count, dest );
```

As is true for the other shift and rotate instructions, the *count* operand is either a constant or the CL register, and the *dest* operand is a memory location or register. The *count* operand must be a value that is less than the number of bits in the *dest* operand. For a count value of 1, these two instructions do the rotation shown in Figure 2-17.

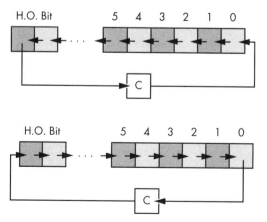

Figure 2-17: rcl( 1, dest ) and rcr( 1, dest ) operations

Again, Intel's documents suggest that rotates of more than 1 bit leave the carry in an undefined state.

## 2.11    Bit Fields and Packed Data

Although the 80x86 operates most efficiently on byte, word, and dword data types, occasionally you'll need to work with a data type that uses some number of bits other than 8, 16, or 32. For example, consider a date of the form 04/02/01. It takes three numeric values to represent this date: month, day, and year values. Months, of course, take on the values 1..12. It will require at least 4 bits (maximum of 16 different values) to represent the month. Days range between 1 and 31. So it will take 5 bits (maximum of 32 different values) to represent the day entry. The year value, assuming that we're working with values in the range 0..99, requires 7 bits (that can be used to represent up to 128 different values). $4 + 5 + 7 = 16$ bits, or 2 bytes. In other words, we can pack our date data into 2 bytes rather than the 3 that would be required if we used a separate byte for each of the month, day, and year values. This saves 1 byte of memory for each date stored, which could be a substantial saving if you need to store many dates. The bits could be arranged as shown in Figure 2-18.

| 15 | 14 | 13 | 12 | 11 | 10 | 9 | 8 | 7 | 6 | 5 | 4 | 3 | 2 | 1 | 0 |
|---|---|---|---|---|---|---|---|---|---|---|---|---|---|---|---|
| M | M | M | M | D | D | D | D | D | Y | Y | Y | Y | Y | Y | Y |

Figure 2-18: Short packed date format (2 bytes)

MMMM represents the 4 bits making up the month value, DDDDD represents the 5 bits making up the day, and YYYYYYY is the 7 bits composing the year. Each collection of bits representing a data item is a *bit field*. For example, April 2, 2001, would be represented as $4101:

| 0100 | 00010 | 0000001 | = %0100_0001_0000_0001 or $4101 |
|---|---|---|---|
| 4 | 2 | 01 | |

Although packed values are *space efficient* (that is, very efficient in terms of memory usage), they are computationally *inefficient* (slow!). The reason? It takes extra instructions to unpack the data packed into the various bit fields. These extra instructions take additional time to execute (and additional bytes to hold the instructions); hence, you must carefully consider whether packed data fields will save you anything. The sample program in Listing 2-9 demonstrates the effort that must go into packing and unpacking this 16-bit date format.

```
program dateDemo;

#include( "stdlib.hhf" )

static
```

```
day:          uns8;
month:        uns8;
year:         uns8;

packedDate: word;

begin dateDemo;

    stdout.put( "Enter the current month, day, and year: " );
    stdin.get( month, day, year );

    // Pack the data into the following bits:
    //
    // 15 14 13 12 11 10  9  8  7  6  5  4  3  2  1  0
    //  m  m  m  m  m  d  d  d  d  d  y  y  y  y  y  y  y

    mov( 0, ax );
    mov( ax, packedDate );  // Just in case there is an error.
    if( month > 12 ) then

        stdout.put( "Month value is too large", nl );

    elseif( month = 0 ) then

        stdout.put( "Month value must be in the range 1..12", nl );

    elseif( day > 31 ) then

        stdout.put( "Day value is too large", nl );

    elseif( day = 0 ) then

        stdout.put( "Day value must be in the range 1..31", nl );

    elseif( year > 99 ) then

        stdout.put( "Year value must be in the range 0..99", nl );

    else

        mov( month, al );
        shl( 5, ax );
        or( day, al );
        shl( 7, ax );
        or( year, al );
        mov( ax, packedDate );

    endif;

    // Okay, display the packed value:

    stdout.put( "Packed data = $", packedDate, nl );
```

```
// Unpack the date:

mov( packedDate, ax );
and( $7f, al );          // Retrieve the year value.
mov( al, year );

mov( packedDate, ax );   // Retrieve the day value.
shr( 7, ax );
and( %1_1111, al );
mov( al, day );

mov( packedDate, ax );   // Retrieve the month value.
rol( 4, ax );
and( %1111, al );
mov( al, month );

stdout.put( "The date is ", month, "/", day, "/", year, nl );


end dateDemo;
```

*Listing 2-9: Packing and unpacking date data*

Of course, having gone through the problems with Y2K (Year 2000), you know that using a date format that limits you to 100 years (or even 127 years) would be quite foolish at this time. If you are concerned about your software running 100 years from now, perhaps it would be wise to use a 3-byte date format rather than a 2-byte format. As you will see in the chapter on arrays, however, you should always try to create data objects whose length is an even power of 2 (1 byte, 2 bytes, 4 bytes, 8 bytes, and so on) or you will pay a performance penalty. Hence, it is probably wise to go ahead and use 4 bytes and pack this data into a double-word variable. Figure 2-19 shows one possible data organization for a 4-byte date.

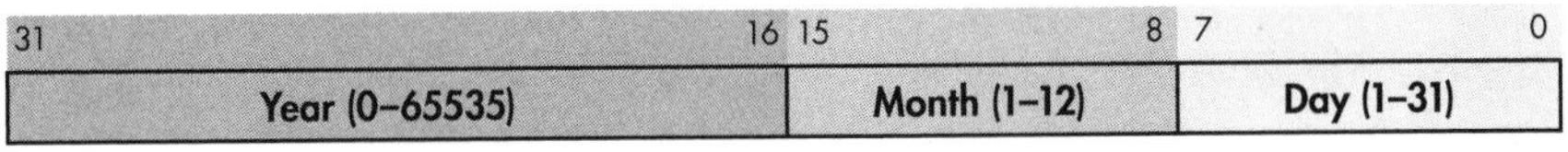

| 31 | | 16 | 15 | | 8 | 7 | | 0 |
|---|---|---|---|---|---|---|---|---|
| | Year (0–65535) | | | Month (1–12) | | | Day (1–31) | |

*Figure 2-19: Long packed date format (4 bytes)*

In this long packed date format we made several changes beyond simply extending the number of bits associated with the year. First, because there are extra bits in a 32-bit double-word variable, this format allocates extra bits to the month and day fields. Because these two fields now consist of 8 bits each, they can be easily extracted as a byte object from the double word. This leaves fewer bits for the year, but 65,536 years is probably sufficient; you can probably assume without too much concern that your software will not still be in use 63,000 years from now when this date format will no longer work.

Of course, you could argue that this is no longer a packed date format. After all, we needed three numeric values, two of which fit just nicely into 1 byte each and one that should probably have at least 2 bytes. Because this "packed" date format consumes the same 4 bytes as the unpacked version, what is so special about this format? Well, another difference you will note between this long packed date format and the short date format appearing in Figure 2-18 is the fact that this long date format rearranges the bits so the Year field is in the H.O. bit positions, the Month field is in the middle bit positions, and the Day field is in the L.O. bit positions. This is important because it allows you to very easily compare two dates to see if one date is less than, equal to, or greater than another date. Consider the following code:

```
mov( Date1, eax );        // Assume Date1 and Date2 are dword variables
if( eax > Date2 ) then    // using the Long Packed Date format.

    << Do something if Date1 > Date2 >>

endif;
```

Had you kept the different date fields in separate variables, or organized the fields differently, you would not have been able to compare Date1 and Date2 in such an easy fashion. Therefore, this example demonstrates another reason for packing data even if you don't realize any space savings—it can make certain computations more convenient or even more efficient (contrary to what normally happens when you pack data).

Examples of practical packed data types abound. You could pack eight boolean values into a single byte, you could pack two BCD digits into a byte, and so on. Of course, a classic example of packed data is the EFLAGS register (see Figure 2-20). This register packs nine important boolean objects (along with seven important system flags) into a single 16-bit register. You will commonly need to access many of these flags. For this reason, the 80x86 instruction set provides many ways to manipulate the individual bits in the EFLAGS register. Of course, you can test many of the condition code flags using the HLA pseudo-boolean variables such as @c, @nc, @z, and @nz in an if statement or other statement using a boolean expression.

In addition to the condition codes, the 80x86 provides instructions that directly affect certain flags (Table 2-7).

**Table 2-7:** Instructions That Affect Certain Flags

| Instruction | Explanation |
| --- | --- |
| cld(); | Clears (sets to 0) the direction flag. |
| std(); | Sets (to 1) the direction flag. |
| cli(); | Clears the interrupt disable flag. |
| sti(); | Sets the interrupt disable flag. |
| clc(); | Clears the carry flag. |
| stc(); | Sets the carry flag. |
| cmc(); | Complements (inverts) the carry flag. |
| sahf(); | Stores the AH register into the L.O. 8 bits of the EFLAGS register. |
| lahf(); | Loads AH from the L.O. 8 bits of the EFLAGS register. |

There are other instructions that affect the EFLAGS register as well; these instructions, however, demonstrate how to access several of the packed boolean values in the EFLAGS register. The lahf and sahf instructions, in particular, provide a convenient way to access the L.O. 8 bits of the EFLAGS register as an 8-bit byte (rather than as eight separate 1-bit values). See Figure 2-20 for a layout of the EFLAGS register.

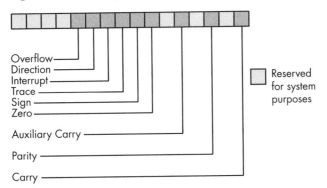

Figure 2-20: EFLAGS register as packed boolean data

The lahf (load AH with the L.O. 8 bits of the EFLAGS register) and the sahf (store AH into the L.O. byte of the EFLAGS register) use the following syntax:

```
lahf();
sahf();
```

## 2.12  An Introduction to Floating-Point Arithmetic

Integer arithmetic does not let you represent fractional numeric values. There-fore, modern CPUs support an approximation of *real* arithmetic: floating-point arithmetic. A big problem with floating-point arithmetic is that it does not follow the standard rules of algebra. Nevertheless, many programmers apply normal algebraic rules when using floating-point arithmetic. This is a source of defects in many programs. One of the primary goals of this section is to describe the limitations of floating-point arithmetic so you will understand how to use it properly.

Normal algebraic rules apply only to *infinite precision* arithmetic. Consider the simple statement $x := x + 1$, where $x$ is an integer. On any modern computer this statement follows the normal rules of algebra *as long as overflow does not occur.* That is, this statement is valid only for certain values of $x$ (*minint* <= $x$ < *maxint*). Most programmers do not have a problem with this because they are well aware of the fact that integers in a program do not follow the standard algebraic rules (e.g., 5/2 does not equal 2.5).

Integers do not follow the standard rules of algebra because the com-puter represents them with a finite number of bits. You cannot represent any of the (integer) values above the maximum integer or below the minimum integer. Floating-point values suffer from this same problem, only worse. After all, the integers are a subset of the real numbers. Therefore, the floating-point values must represent the same infinite set of integers. However, there are an infinite number of real values between any two integer values, so this problem is infinitely worse. Therefore, as well as having to limit your values between a maximum and minimum range, you cannot represent all the values between those two ranges either.

To represent real numbers, most floating-point formats employ scientific notation and use some number of bits to represent a *mantissa* and a smaller number of bits to represent an *exponent*. The end result is that floating-point numbers can only represent numbers with a specific number of *significant* digits. This has a big impact on how floating-point arithmetic operates. To easily see the impact of limited precision arithmetic, we will adopt a simplified decimal floating-point format for our examples. Our floating-point format will provide a mantissa with three significant digits and a decimal exponent with two digits. The mantissa and exponents are both signed values, as shown in Figure 2-21.

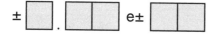

*Figure 2-21: A floating-point format*

When adding and subtracting two numbers in scientific notation, we must adjust the two values so that their exponents are the same. For example, when adding 1.23e1 and 4.56e0, we must adjust the values so they have the same exponent. One way to do this is to convert 4.56e0 to 0.456e1 and then add. This produces 1.686e1. Unfortunately, the result does not fit into three significant digits, so we must either *round* or *truncate* the result to three significant digits. Rounding generally produces the most accurate result, so let's round the result to obtain 1.69e1. As you can see, the lack of *precision* (the number of digits or bits we maintain in a computation) affects the accuracy (the correctness of the computation).

In the previous example, we were able to round the result because we maintained *four* significant digits *during* the calculation. If our floating-point calculation had been limited to three significant digits *during* computation, we would have had to truncate the last digit of the smaller number, obtaining 1.68e1, a value that is even less accurate. To improve the accuracy of floating-point calculations, it is necessary to add extra digits for use during the calculation. Extra digits available during a computation are known as *guard digits* (or *guard bits* in the case of a binary format). They greatly enhance accuracy during a long chain of computations.

The accuracy loss during a single computation usually isn't enough to worry about unless you are greatly concerned about the accuracy of your computations. However, if you compute a value that is the result of a sequence of floating-point operations, the error can *accumulate* and greatly affect the computation itself. For example, suppose we were to add 1.23e3 to 1.00e0. Adjusting the numbers so their exponents are the same before the addition produces 1.23e3 + 0.001e3. The sum of these two values, even after rounding, is 1.23e3. This might seem perfectly reasonable to you; after all, we can maintain only three significant digits, so adding in a small value shouldn't affect the result at all. However, suppose we were to add 1.00e0 to 1.23e3 *ten times.* The first time we add 1.00e0 to 1.23e3 we get 1.23e3. Likewise, we get this same result the second, third, fourth . . . and tenth times we add 1.00e0 to 1.23e3. On the other hand, had we added 1.00e0 to itself 10 times, then added the result (1.00e1) to 1.23e3, we would have gotten a different result, 1.24e3. This is an important thing to know about limited-precision arithmetic:

**The order of evaluation can affect the accuracy of the result.**

You will get more accurate results if the relative magnitudes (that is, the exponents) are close to one another when adding and subtracting floating-point values. If you are performing a chain calculation involving addition and subtraction, you should attempt to group the values appropriately.

Another problem with addition and subtraction is that you can wind up with *false precision.* Consider the computation 1.23e0 − 1.22e0. This produces 0.01e0. Although this is mathematically equivalent to $1.00e-2$, this latter form suggests that the last two digits are exactly 0. Unfortunately, we have only a single significant digit at this time. Indeed, some floating-point unit (FPU) software packages might actually insert random digits (or bits) into the L.O. positions. This brings up a second important rule concerning limited precision arithmetic:

**When subtracting two numbers with the same signs or adding two numbers with different signs, the accuracy of the result may be less than the precision available in the floating-point format.**

Multiplication and division do not suffer from the same problems as addition and subtraction because you do not have to adjust the exponents before the operation; all you need to do is add the exponents and multiply the mantissas (or subtract the exponents and divide the mantissas). By themselves, multiplication and division do not produce particularly poor results. However, they tend to multiply any error that already exists in a value. For example, if you multiply 1.23e0 by 2, when you should be multiplying 1.24e0 by 2, the result is even less accurate. This brings up a third important rule when working with limited-precision arithmetic:

**When performing a chain of calculations involving addition, subtraction, multiplication, and division, try to perform the multiplication and division operations first.**

Often, by applying normal algebraic transformations, you can arrange a calculation so the multiply and divide operations occur first. For example, suppose you want to compute $x * (y + z)$. Normally you would add $y$ and $z$ together and multiply their sum by $x$. However, you will get a little more accuracy if you transform $x * (y + z)$ to get $x * y + x * z$ and compute the result by performing the multiplications first.[6]

---

[6] Of course, the drawback is that you must now perform two multiplications rather than one, so the result may be slower.

Multiplication and division are not without their own problems. When multiplying two very large or very small numbers, it is quite possible for *overflow* or *underflow* to occur. The same situation occurs when dividing a small number by a large number or dividing a large number by a small number. This brings up a fourth rule you should attempt to follow when multiplying or dividing values:

**When multiplying and dividing sets of numbers, try to arrange the multiplications so that they multiply large and small numbers together; likewise, try to divide numbers that have the same relative magnitudes.**

Comparing floating-point numbers is very dangerous. Given the inaccuracies present in any computation (including converting an input string to a floating-point value), you should *never* compare two floating-point values to see if they are equal. In a binary floating-point format, different computations that produce the same (mathematical) result may differ in their least significant bits. For example, 1.31e0 + 1.69e0 should produce 3.00e0. Likewise, 1.50e0 + 1.50e0 should produce 3.00e0. However, if you were to compare (1.31e0 + 1.69e0) against (1.50e0 + 1.50e0), you might find out that these sums are *not* equal to one another. The test for equality succeeds if and only if all bits (or digits) in the two operands are exactly the same. Because this is not necessarily true after two different floating-point computations that should produce the same result, a straight test for equality may not work.

The standard way to test for equality between floating-point numbers is to determine how much error (or tolerance) you will allow in a comparison and check to see if one value is within this error range of the other. The usual way to do this is to use a test like the following:

```
if Value1 >= (Value2-error) and Value1 <= (Value2+error) then ...
```

Another common way to handle this same comparison is to use a statement of the form

```
if abs(Value1-Value2) <= error then ...
```

You must exercise care when choosing the value for *error*. This should be a value slightly greater than the largest amount of error that will creep into your computations. The exact value will depend upon the particular floating-point format you use, but more on that a little later. Here is the final rule we will state in this section:

**When comparing two floating-point numbers, always compare one value to see if it is in the range given by the second value plus or minus some small error value.**

There are many other little problems that can occur when using floating-point values. This text can only point out some of the major problems and make you aware of the fact that you cannot treat floating-point arithmetic like real arithmetic—the inaccuracies present in limited-precision arithmetic can get you into trouble if you are not careful. A good text on numerical analysis or even scientific computing can help fill in the details that are beyond the scope of this text. If you are going to be working with floating-point arithmetic, *in any language,* you should take the time to study the effects of limited-precision arithmetic on your computations.

HLA's if statement does not support boolean expressions involving floating-point operands. Therefore, you cannot use statements like if( x < 3.141) then... in your programs. Chapter 6 will teach you how to do floating-point comparisons.

## 2.12.1    IEEE Floating-Point Formats

When Intel planned to introduce a floating-point unit for its new 8086 microprocessor, it was smart enough to realize that the electrical engineers and solid-state physicists who design chips were probably not the best people to pick the best possible binary representation for a floating-point format. So Intel went out and hired the best numerical analyst it could find to design a floating-point format for its 8087 FPU. That person then hired two other experts in the field, and the three of them (Kahn, Coonan, and Stone) designed Intel's floating-point format. They did such a good job designing the KCS Floating-Point Standard that the IEEE organization adopted this format for the IEEE floating-point format.[7]

To handle a wide range of performance and accuracy requirements, Intel actually introduced *three* floating-point formats: single-precision, double-precision, and extended-precision. The single- and double-precision formats corresponded to C's float and double types or FORTRAN's real and double-precision types. Intel intended to use extended-precision for long chains of computations. Extended-precision contains 16 extra bits that the calculations could use as guard bits before rounding down to a double-precision value when storing the result.

The single-precision format uses a *one's complement 24-bit mantissa* and an *8-bit excess-127 exponent.* The mantissa usually represents a value from 1.0 to just under 2.0. The H.O. bit of the mantissa is always assumed to be 1 and represents a value just to the left of the *binary point.*[8] The remaining 23 mantissa bits appear to the right of the binary point. Therefore, the mantissa represents the value

---

1.mmmmmmm mmmmmmmm mmmmmmmm

---

The mmmm characters represent the 23 bits of the mantissa. Keep in mind that we are working with binary numbers here. Therefore, each position to the right of the binary point represents a value (0 or 1) times a successive negative power of 2. The implied 1 bit is always multiplied by $2^0$, which is 1. This is why the mantissa is always greater than or equal to 1. Even if the other

---

[7] There were some minor changes to the way certain degenerate operations were handled, but the bit representation remained essentially unchanged.

[8] The binary point is the same thing as the decimal point except it appears in binary numbers rather than decimal numbers.

mantissa bits are all 0, the implied 1 bit always gives us the value 1[9]. Of course, even if we had an almost infinite number of 1 bits after the binary point, they still would not add up to 2. This is why the mantissa can represent values in the range 1 to just under 2.

Although there are an infinite number of values between 1 and 2, we can only represent 8 million of them because we use a 23-bit mantissa (the 24th bit is always 1). This is the reason for inaccuracy in floating-point arithmetic—we are limited to 23 bits of precision in computations involving single-precision floating-point values.

The mantissa uses a one's complement format rather than two's complement. This means that the 24-bit value of the mantissa is simply an unsigned binary number, and the sign bit determines whether that value is positive or negative. One's complement numbers have the unusual property that there are two representations for 0 (with the sign bit set or clear). Generally, this is important only to the person designing the floating-point software or hardware system. We will assume that the value 0 always has the sign bit clear.

To represent values outside the range 1.0 to just under 2.0, the exponent portion of the floating-point format comes into play. The floating-point format raises 2 to the power specified by the exponent and then multiplies the mantissa by this value. The exponent is 8 bits and is stored in an *excess-127* format. In excess-127 format, the exponent $2^0$ is represented by the value 127 ($7F). Therefore, to convert an exponent to excess-127 format, simply add 127 to the exponent value. The use of excess-127 format makes it easier to compare floating-point values. The single-precision floating-point format takes the form shown in Figure 2-22.

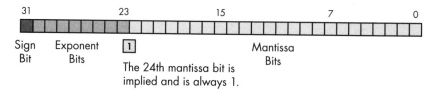

*Figure 2-22: Single-precision (32-bit) floating-point format*

With a 24-bit mantissa, you will get approximately 6 ½ digits of precision (½ digit of precision means that the first six digits can all be in the range 0..9, but the seventh digit can only be in the range 0..*x*, where *x* < 9 and is generally close to 5). With an 8-bit excess-127 exponent, the dynamic range of single-precision floating-point numbers is approximately 2 ± 128 or about 10 ± 38.

Although single-precision floating-point numbers are perfectly suitable for many applications, the dynamic range is somewhat limited and is unsuitable for many financial, scientific, and other applications. Furthermore, during long chains of computations, the limited accuracy of the single-precision format may introduce serious error.

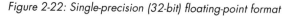

[9] Actually, this isn't necessarily true. The IEEE floating-point format supports *denormalized* values where the H.O. bit is not 0. However, we will ignore denormalized values in our discussion.

The double-precision format helps overcome the problems of single-precision floating-point. Using twice the space, the double-precision format has an 11-bit excess-1023 exponent and a 53-bit mantissa (with an implied H.O. bit of 1) plus a sign bit. This provides a dynamic range of about $10^{\pm308}$ and 14 ½ digits of precision, sufficient for most applications. Double-precision floating-point values take the form shown in Figure 2-23.

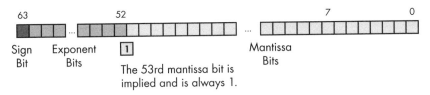

Sign Bit     Exponent Bits     $\boxed{1}$     Mantissa Bits

The 53rd mantissa bit is implied and is always 1.

*Figure 2-23: 64-bit double-precision floating-point format*

In order to help ensure accuracy during long chains of computations involving double-precision floating-point numbers, Intel designed the extended-precision format. The extended-precision format uses 80 bits. Twelve of the additional 16 bits are appended to the mantissa and four of the additional bits are appended to the end of the exponent. Unlike the single- and double-precision values, the extended-precision format's mantissa does not have an implied H.O. bit, which is always 1. Therefore, the extended-precision format provides a 64-bit mantissa, a 15-bit excess-16383 exponent, and a 1-bit sign. The format for the extended-precision floating-point value is shown in Figure 2-24.

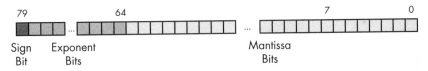

Sign Bit     Exponent Bits     Mantissa Bits

*Figure 2-24: 80-bit extended-precision floating-point format*

On the FPUs all computations are done using the extended-precision format. Whenever you load a single or double-precision value, the FPU automatically converts it to an extended-precision value. Likewise, when you store a single or double-precision value to memory, the FPU automatically rounds the value down to the appropriate size before storing it. By always working with the extended-precision format, Intel guarantees a large number of guard bits are present to ensure the accuracy of your computations.

To maintain maximum precision during computation, most computations use *normalized* values. A normalized floating-point value is one whose H.O. mantissa bit contains 1. Almost any nonnormalized value can be normalized; shift the mantissa bits to the left and decrement the exponent until a 1 appears in the H.O. bit of the mantissa. Remember, the exponent is a binary exponent. Each time you increment the exponent, you multiply the floating-point value by 2. Likewise, whenever you decrement the exponent, you divide the floating-point value by 2. By the same token, shifting the mantissa to the left one bit position multiplies the floating-point value by 2; likewise, shifting the mantissa to the right divides the floating-point value by 2. Therefore, shifting the mantissa to the left one position *and* decrementing the exponent does not change the value of the floating-point number at all.

Keeping floating-point numbers normalized is beneficial because it maintains the maximum number of bits of precision for a computation. If the H.O. bits of the mantissa are all 0, the mantissa has that many fewer bits of precision available for computation. Therefore, a floating-point computation will be more accurate if it involves only normalized values.

There are two important cases where a floating-point number cannot be normalized. Zero is one of these special cases. Obviously it cannot be normalized because the floating-point representation for 0 has no 1 bits in the mantissa. This, however, is not a problem because we can exactly represent the value 0 with only a single bit.

The second case is when we have some H.O. bits in the mantissa that are 0 but the biased exponent is also 0 (and we cannot decrement it to normalize the mantissa). Rather than disallow certain small values, whose H.O. mantissa bits and biased exponent are 0 (the most negative exponent possible), the IEEE standard allows special *denormalized* values to represent these smaller values.[10] Although the use of denormalized values allows IEEE floating-point computations to produce better results than if underflow occurred, keep in mind that denormalized values offer less bits of precision.

### 2.12.2   HLA Support for Floating-Point Values

HLA provides several data types and library routines to support the use of floating-point data in your assembly language programs. These include built-in types to declare floating-point variables as well as routines that provide floating-point input, output, and conversion.

Perhaps the best place to start when discussing HLA's floating-point facilities is with a description of floating-point literal constants. HLA floating-point constants allow the following syntax:

- An optional + or - symbol, denoting the sign of the mantissa (if this is not present, HLA assumes that the mantissa is positive)

- Followed by one or more decimal digits

- Optionally followed by a decimal point and one or more decimal digits

- Optionally followed by an e or E, optionally followed by a sign (+ or -) and one or more decimal digits

Note that the decimal point or the e/E must be present in order to differentiate this value from an integer or unsigned literal constant. Here are some examples of legal literal floating-point constants:

```
1.234   3.75e2   -1.0   1.1e-1   1e+4   0.1   -123.456e+789   +25e0
```

---

[10] The alternative would be to underflow the values to 0.

Notice that a floating-point literal constant cannot begin with a decimal point; it must begin with a decimal digit, so you must use 0.1 to represent .1 in your programs.

HLA also allows you to place an underscore character (_) between any two consecutive decimal digits in a floating-point literal constant. You may use the underscore character in place of a comma (or other language-specific separator character) to help make your large floating-point numbers easier to read. Here are some examples:

---

    1_234_837.25   1_000.00   789_934.99   9_999.99

---

To declare a floating-point variable you use the real32, real64, or real80 data types. Like their integer and unsigned brethren, the number at the end of these data type declarations specifies the number of bits used for each type's binary representation. Therefore, you use real32 to declare single-precision real values, real64 to declare double-precision floating-point values, and real80 to declare extended-precision floating-point values. Other than the fact that you use these types to declare floating-point variables rather than integers, their use is nearly identical to that for int8, int16, int32, and so on. The following examples demonstrate these declarations and their syntax:

---

```
static

        fltVar1:        real32;
        fltVar1a:       real32 := 2.7;
        pi:             real32 := 3.14159;
        DblVar:         real64;
        DblVar2:        real64 := 1.23456789e+10;
        XPVar:          real80;
        XPVar2:         real80 := -1.0e-104;
```

---

To output a floating-point variable in ASCII form, you would use one of the stdout.putr32, stdout.putr64, or stdout.putr80 routines. These procedures display a number in decimal notation, that is, a string of digits, an optional decimal point, and a closing string of digits. Other than their names, these three routines use exactly the same calling sequence. Here are the calls and parameters for each of these routines:

---

```
stdout.putr80( r:real80; width:uns32; decpts:uns32 );
stdout.putr64( r:real64; width:uns32; decpts:uns32 );
stdout.putr32( r:real32; width:uns32; decpts:uns32 );
```

---

The first parameter to these procedures is the floating-point value you wish to print. The size of this parameter must match the procedure's name (e.g., the r parameter must be an 80-bit extended-precision floating-point variable when calling the stdout.putr80 routine). The second parameter specifies the field width for the output text; this is the number of print positions the number will require when the procedure displays it. Note that this width must include print positions for the sign of the number and the decimal point. The third parameter specifies the number of print positions after the decimal point. For example:

```
stdout.putr32( pi, 10, 4 );
```

displays the value

```
_ _ _ _ 3.1416
```

(underscores represent leading spaces in this example).

Of course, if the number is very large or very small, you will want to use scientific notation rather than decimal notation for your floating-point numeric output. The HLA Standard Library stdout.pute32, stdout.pute64, and stdout.pute80 routines provide this facility. These routines use the following procedure prototypes:

```
stdout.pute80( r:real80; width:uns32 );
stdout.pute64( r:real64; width:uns32 );
stdout.pute32( r:real32; width:uns32 );
```

Unlike the decimal output routines, these scientific notation output routines do not require a third parameter specifying the number of digits after the decimal point to display. The width parameter indirectly specifies this value because all but one of the mantissa digits always appear to the right of the decimal point. These routines output their values in decimal notation, similar to the following:

```
1.23456789e+10  -1.0e-104  1e+2
```

You can also output floating-point values using the HLA Standard Library stdout.put routine. If you specify the name of a floating-point variable in the stdout.put parameter list, the stdout.put code will output the value using scientific notation. The actual field width varies depending on the size of the floating-point variable (the stdout.put routine attempts to output as many significant digits as possible, in this case). Here's an example:

```
stdout.put( "XPVar2 = ", XPVar2 );
```

If you specify a field width, by using a colon followed by a signed integer value, then the stdout.put routine will use the appropriate stdout.puteXX routine to display the value. That is, the number will still appear in scientific notation, but you get to control the field width of the output value. Like the field width for integer and unsigned values, a positive field width right justifies the number in the specified field, and a negative number left justifies the value.

Here is an example that prints the XPVar2 variable using 10 print positions:

```
stdout.put( "XPVar2 = ", XPVar2:10 );
```

If you wish to use stdout.put to print a floating-point value in decimal notation, you need to use the following syntax:

```
Variable_Name : Width : DecPts
```

Note that the DecPts field must be a nonnegative integer value.

When stdout.put contains a parameter of this form, it calls the corresponding stdout.putrXX routine to display the specified floating-point value. As an example, consider the following call:

```
stdout.put( "Pi = ", pi:5:3 );
```

The corresponding output is:

```
3.142
```

The HLA Standard Library provides several other useful routines you can use when outputting floating-point values. Consult the HLA Standard Library reference manual for more information on these routines.

The HLA Standard Library provides several routines to let you display floating-point values in a wide variety of formats. In contrast, the HLA Standard Library provides only two routines to support floating-point input: stdin.getf() and stdin.get(). The stdin.getf() routine requires the use of the 80x86 FPU stack, a hardware component that this chapter doesn't cover. Therefore, we'll defer the discussion of the stdin.getf() routine until Chapter 6. Because the stdin.get() routine provides all the capabilities of the stdin.getf() routine, this deferral will not be a problem.

You've already seen the syntax for the stdin.get() routine; its parameter list simply contains a list of variable names. The stdin.get() function reads appropriate values for the user for each of the variables appearing in the parameter list. If you specify the name of a floating-point variable, the stdin.get() routine automatically reads a floating-point value from the user and stores the result into the specified variable. The following example demonstrates the use of this routine:

```
stdout.put( "Input a double-precision floating-point value: " );
stdin.get( DblVar );
```

**WARNING**    *This section discussed how you would declare floating-point variables and how you would input and output them. It did not discuss arithmetic. Floating-point arithmetic is different from integer arithmetic; you cannot use the 80x86 add and sub instructions to operate on floating-point values. Floating-point arithmetic will be the subject of Chapter 6.*

## 2.13 Binary-Coded Decimal Representation

Although the integer and floating-point formats cover most of the numeric needs of an average program, there are some special cases where other numeric representations are convenient. In this section we'll discuss the binary-coded decimal format because the 80x86 CPU provides a small amount of hardware support for this data representation.

BCD values are a sequence of nibbles, with each nibble representing a value in the range 0..9. Of course you can represent values in the range 0..15 using a nibble; the BCD format, however, uses only 10 of the possible 16 different values for each nibble.

Each nibble in a BCD value represents a single decimal digit. Therefore, with a single byte (i.e., two digits) we can represent values containing two decimal digits, or values in the range 0..99 (see Figure 2-25). With a word, we can represent values having four decimal digits, or values in the range 0..9,999. Likewise, with a double word we can represent values with up to eight decimal digits (because there are eight nibbles in a double-word value).

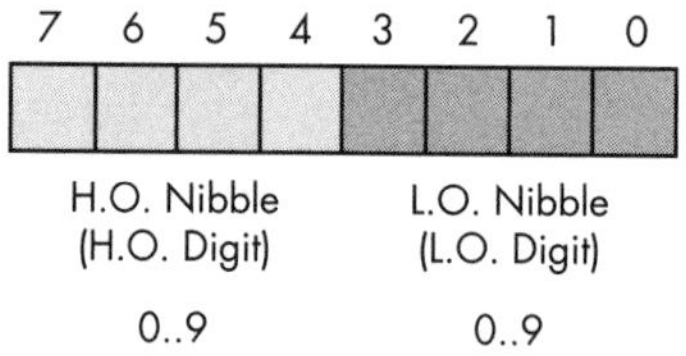

Figure 2-25: CD data representation in memory

As you can see, BCD storage isn't particularly memory efficient. For example, an 8-bit BCD variable can represent values in the range 0..99 while that same 8 bits, when holding a binary value, can represent values in the range 0..255. Likewise, a 16-bit binary value can represent values in the range 0..65,535, while a 16-bit BCD value can represent only about one-sixth of those values (0..9,999). Inefficient storage isn't the only problem. BCD calculations tend to be slower than binary calculations.

At this point, you're probably wondering why anyone would ever use the BCD format. The BCD format does have two saving graces: It's very easy to convert BCD values between the internal numeric representation and their string representation; also, it's very easy to encode multidigit decimal values in hardware (e.g., using a thumb wheel or dial) using BCD. For these two reasons, you're likely to see people using BCD in embedded systems (such as toaster ovens, alarm clocks, and nuclear reactors) but rarely in general-purpose computer software.

A few decades ago people mistakenly thought that calculations involving BCD (or just decimal) arithmetic were more accurate than binary calculations. Therefore, they would often perform important calculations, like those involving dollars and cents (or other monetary units) using decimal-based arithmetic. While it is true that certain calculations can produce more accurate results in BCD, this statement is not true in general. Indeed, for most calculations (even those involving fixed-point decimal arithmetic), the binary representation is more accurate. For this reason, most modern computer programs represent all values in a binary form. For example, the Intel 80x86 floating-point unit supports a pair of instructions for loading and storing BCD values. Internally, however, the FPU converts these BCD values to binary and performs all calculations in binary. It uses BCD only as an external data format (external to the FPU, that is). This generally produces more accurate results and requires far less silicon than having a separate coprocessor that supports decimal arithmetic.

## 2.14  Characters

Perhaps the most important data type on a personal computer is the character data type. The term *character* refers to a human or machine-readable symbol that is typically a nonnumeric entity. In general, the term *character* refers to any symbol that you can normally type on a keyboard (including some symbols that may require multiple key presses to produce) or display on a video display. Many beginners often confuse the terms *character* and *alphabetic character*. These terms are not the same. Punctuation symbols, numeric digits, spaces, tabs, carriage returns (enter), other control characters, and other special symbols are also characters. When this text uses the term *character* it refers to any of these characters, not just the alphabetic characters. When this text refers to alphabetic characters, it will use phrases like "alphabetic characters," "uppercase characters," or "lowercase characters."

Another common problem beginners have when they first encounter the character data type is differentiating between numeric characters and numbers. The character 1 is different from the value 1. The computer (generally) uses two different internal representations for numeric characters (0, 1, ..., 9) versus the numeric values 0..9. You must take care not to confuse the two.

Most computer systems use a 1- or 2-byte sequence to encode the various characters in binary form. Windows, Mac OS X, FreeBSD, and Linux certainly fall into this category, using either the ASCII or Unicode encodings for characters. This section will discuss the ASCII character set and the character declaration facilities that HLA provides.

### 2.14.1  The ASCII Character Encoding

The ASCII (American Standard Code for Information Interchange) character set maps 128 textual characters to the unsigned integer values 0..127 ($0..$7F). Internally, of course, the computer represents everything using binary numbers, so it should come as no surprise that the computer also uses binary values to represent nonnumeric entities such as characters. Although the exact mapping of characters to numeric values is arbitrary and unimportant, it is important to use a standardized code for this mapping because you will need to communicate with other programs and peripheral devices and you need to talk the same "language" as these other programs and devices. This is where the ASCII code comes into play; it is a standardized code that nearly everyone has agreed on. Therefore, if you use the

ASCII code 65 to represent the character 'A', then you know that some peripheral device (such as a printer) will correctly interpret this value as the character 'A' whenever you transmit data to that device.

You should not get the impression that ASCII is the only character set in use on computer systems. IBM uses the EBCDIC character set family on many of its mainframe computer systems. Another common character set in use is the Unicode character set. Unicode is an extension to the ASCII character set that uses 16 bits rather than 7 bits to represent characters. This allows the use of 65,536 different characters in the character set, allowing the inclusion of most symbols in the world's different languages into a single unified character set.

Because the ASCII character set provides only 128 different characters and a byte can represent 256 different values, an interesting question arises: "What do we do with the values 128..255 that one could store into a byte?" One answer is to ignore those extra values. That will be the primary approach of this text. Another possibility is to extend the ASCII character set and add an additional 128 characters to it. Of course, this would tend to defeat the whole purpose of having a standardized character set unless you could get everyone to agree on the extensions. That is a difficult task.

When IBM first created its IBM-PC, it defined these extra 128 character codes to contain various non-English alphabetic characters, some line-drawing graphics characters, some mathematical symbols, and several other special characters. Because IBM's PC was the foundation for what we typically call a PC today, that character set has become a pseudo-standard on all IBM-PC compatible machines. Even on modern machines, which are not IBM-PC compatible and cannot run early PC software, the IBM extended character set survives. Note, however, that this PC character set (an extension of the ASCII character set) is not universal. Most printers will not print the extended characters when using native fonts, and many programs (particularly in non-English-speaking countries) do not use those characters for the upper 128 codes in an 8-bit value. For these reasons, this text will generally stick to the standard 128-character ASCII character set.

Despite the fact that it is a standard, simply encoding your data using standard ASCII characters does not guarantee compatibility across systems. While it's true that an 'A' on one machine is most likely an 'A' on another machine, there is very little standardization across machines with respect to the use of the control characters. Indeed, of the 32 control codes plus delete, there are only four control codes commonly supported—backspace (BS), tab, carriage return (CR), and line feed (LF). Worse still, different machines often use these control codes in different ways. *End of line* is a particularly troublesome example. Windows, MS-DOS, CP/M, and other systems mark end of line by the two-character sequence CR/LF. Older Apple Macintosh computers (Mac OS 9 and earlier) and many other systems mark the end of a line by a single CR character. Linux, Mac OS X, FreeBSD, and other Unix systems mark the end of a line with a single LF character. Needless to say, attempting to exchange simple text files between such systems can be an experience in frustration. Even if you use standard ASCII characters in all your files on these systems, you will still need to convert the data when exchanging files between them. Fortunately, such conversions are rather simple.

Despite some major shortcomings, ASCII data is *the* standard for data interchange across computer systems and programs. Most programs can accept ASCII data; likewise most programs can produce ASCII data. Because you will be dealing with ASCII characters in assembly language, it would be wise to study the layout of the character set and memorize a few key ASCII codes (e.g., for '0', 'A', 'a', etc.).

The ASCII character set is divided into four groups of 32 characters. The first 32 characters, ASCII codes 0..$1F (31), form a special set of nonprinting characters, the *control characters*. We call them control characters because they perform various printer/display control operations rather than display symbols. Examples include *carriage return*, which positions the cursor to the left side of the current line of characters;[11] line feed, which moves the cursor down one line on the output device; and backspace, which moves the cursor back one position to the left. Unfortunately, different control characters perform different operations on different output devices. There is very little standardization among output devices. To find out exactly how a control character affects a particular device, you will need to consult its manual.

The second group of 32 ASCII character codes contains various punctuation symbols, special characters, and the numeric digits. The most notable characters in this group include the space character (ASCII code $20) and the numeric digits (ASCII codes $30..$39).

The third group of 32 ASCII characters contains the uppercase alphabetic characters. The ASCII codes for the characters 'A'..'Z' lie in the range $41..$5A (65..90). Because there are only 26 different alphabetic characters, the remaining 6 codes hold various special symbols.

The fourth, and final, group of 32 ASCII character codes represents the lowercase alphabetic symbols, 5 additional special symbols, and another control character (delete). Note that the lowercase character symbols use the ASCII codes $61..$7A. If you convert the codes for the upper- and lowercase characters to binary, you will notice that the uppercase symbols differ from their lowercase equivalents in exactly one bit position. For example, consider the character codes for 'E' and 'e' appearing in Figure 2-26.

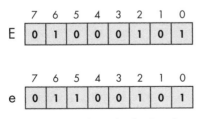

*Figure 2-26: ASCII codes for E and e*

---

[11] Historically, carriage return refers to the *paper carriage* used on typewriters. A carriage return consisted of physically moving the carriage all the way to the right so that the next character typed would appear at the left-hand side of the paper.

The only place these two codes differ is in bit 5. Uppercase characters always contain a 0 in bit 5; lowercase alphabetic characters always contain a 1 in bit 5. You can use this fact to quickly convert between upper- and lowercase. If you have an uppercase character, you can force it to lowercase by setting bit 5 to 1. If you have a lowercase character and you wish to force it to uppercase, you can do so by setting bit 5 to 0. You can toggle an alphabetic character between upper- and lowercase by simply inverting bit 5.

Indeed, bits 5 and 6 determine which of the four groups in the ASCII character set you're in, as Table 2-8 shows.

Table 2-8: ASCII Groups

| Bit 6 | Bit 5 | Group |
|-------|-------|-------|
| 0 | 0 | Control characters |
| 0 | 1 | Digits and punctuation |
| 1 | 0 | Uppercase and special |
| 1 | 1 | Lowercase and special |

So you could, for instance, convert any upper- or lowercase (or corresponding special) character to its equivalent control character by setting bits 5 and 6 to 0.

Consider, for a moment, the ASCII codes of the numeric digit characters appearing in Table 2-9.

Table 2-9: ASCII Codes for Numeric Digits

| Character | Decimal | Hexadecimal |
|-----------|---------|-------------|
| 0 | 48 | $30 |
| 1 | 49 | $31 |
| 2 | 50 | $32 |
| 3 | 51 | $33 |
| 4 | 52 | $34 |
| 5 | 53 | $35 |
| 6 | 54 | $36 |
| 7 | 55 | $37 |
| 8 | 56 | $38 |
| 9 | 57 | $39 |

The decimal representations of these ASCII codes are not very enlightening. However, the hexadecimal representation of these ASCII codes reveals something very important—the L.O. nibble of the ASCII code is the binary equivalent of the represented number. By stripping away (i.e., setting to 0) the H.O. nibble of a numeric character, you can convert that character code to the corresponding binary representation. Conversely, you can convert a binary value in the range 0..9 to its ASCII character representation by simply setting the H.O. nibble to 3. Note that you can use the logical and operation to force the H.O. bits to 0; likewise, you can use the logical or operation to force the H.O. bits to %0011 (3).

Note that you *cannot* convert a string of numeric characters to their equivalent binary representation by simply stripping the H.O. nibble from each digit in the string. Converting 123 ($31 $32 $33) in this fashion yields 3 bytes: $010203; the correct value for 123 is $7B. Converting a string of digits to an integer requires more sophistication than this; the conversion above works only for single digits.

## 2.14.2  HLA Support for ASCII Characters

Although you could easily store character values in byte variables and use the corresponding numeric equivalent ASCII code when using a character literal in your program, such agony is unnecessary. HLA provides support for character variables and literals in your assembly language programs.

Character literal constants in HLA take one of two forms: a single character surrounded by apostrophes or a hash mark (#) followed by a numeric constant in the range 0..127 (specifying the ASCII code of the character). Here are some examples:

---

    'A'    #65    #$41    #%0100_0001

---

Note that these examples all represent the same character ('A') because the ASCII code of 'A' is 65.

With one exception, only a single character may appear between the apostrophes in a literal character constant. That single exception is the apostrophe character itself. If you wish to create an apostrophe literal constant, place four apostrophes in a row (i.e., double up the apostrophe inside the surrounding apostrophes):

---

    ''''

---

The hash mark operator (#) must precede a legal HLA numeric constant (either decimal, hexadecimal, or binary, as the examples above indicate). In particular, the hash mark is not a generic character conversion function; it cannot precede registers or variable names, only constants.

As a general rule, you should always use the apostrophe form of the character literal constant for graphic characters (that is, those that are printable or displayable). Use the hash mark form for control characters (that are invisible or do funny things when you print them) or for extended ASCII characters that may not display or print properly within your source code.

Notice the difference between a character literal constant and a string literal constant in your programs. Strings are sequences of zero or more characters surrounded by quotation marks; characters are surrounded by apostrophes.

It is especially important to realize that

---

    'A' ≠ "A"

---

The character constant 'A' and the string containing the single character A have two completely different internal representations. If you attempt to use a string containing a single character where HLA expects a character constant, HLA will report an error. Strings and string constants are the subject of Chapter 4.

To declare a character variable in an HLA program, you use the char data type. For example, the following declaration demonstrates how to declare a variable named UserInput:

```
static
    UserInput:          char;
```

This declaration reserves 1 byte of storage that you could use to store any character value (including 8-bit extended ASCII characters). You can also initialize character variables as the following example demonstrates:

```
static

    TheCharA:          char := 'A';
    ExtendedChar:      char := #128;
```

Because character variables are 8-bit objects, you can manipulate them using 8-bit registers. You can move character variables into 8-bit registers, and you can store the value of an 8-bit register into a character variable.

The HLA Standard Library provides a handful of routines that you can use for character I/O and manipulation; these include stdout.putc, stdout.putcSize, stdout.put, stdin.getc, and stdin.get.

The stdout.putc routine uses the following calling sequence:

```
    stdout.putc( charvar );
```

This procedure outputs the single-character parameter passed to it as a character to the standard output device. The parameter may be any char constant or variable, or a byte variable or register.[12]

The stdout.putcSize routine provides output width control when displaying character variables. The calling sequence for this procedure is

```
    stdout.putcSize( charvar, widthInt32, fillchar );
```

This routine prints the specified character (parameter c) using at least widthInt32 print positions.[13] If the absolute value of widthInt32 is greater than 1, then stdout.putcSize prints the fillchar character as padding. If the value of widthInt32 is positive, then stdout.putcSize prints the character right justified

---

[12] If you specify a byte variable or a byte-sized register as the parameter, the stdout.putc routine will output the character whose ASCII code appears in the variable or register.

[13] The only time stdout.putcSize uses more print positions than you specify is when you specify 0 as the width; then this routine uses exactly one print position.

in the print field; if *widthInt32* is negative, then stdout.putcSize prints the character left justified in the print field. Because character output is usually left justified in a field, the *widthInt32* value will normally be negative for this call. The space character is the most common *fillchar* value.

You can also print character values using the generic stdout.put routine. If a character variable appears in the stdout.put parameter list, then stdout.put will automatically print it as a character value. For example:

```
stdout.put( "Character c = '", c, "'", nl );
```

You can read characters from the standard input using the stdin.getc and stdin.get routines. The stdin.getc routine does not have any parameters. It reads a single character from the standard input buffer and returns this character in the AL register. You may then store the character value away or otherwise manipulate the character in the AL register. The program in Listing 2-10 reads a single character from the user, converts it to uppercase if it is a lowercase character, and then displays the character.

```
program charInputDemo;
#include( "stdlib.hhf" )
begin charInputDemo;

    stdout.put( "Enter a character: " );
    stdin.getc();
    if( al >= 'a' ) then

        if( al <= 'z' ) then

            and( $5f, al );

        endif;

    endif;
    stdout.put
    (
        "The character you entered, possibly ", nl,
        "converted to uppercase, was '"
    );
    stdout.putc( al );
    stdout.put( "'", nl );

end charInputDemo;
```

*Listing 2-10: Character input sample*

You can also use the generic stdin.get routine to read character variables from the user. If a stdin.get parameter is a character variable, then the stdin.get routine will read a character from the user and store the character value into the specified variable. Listing 2-11 is a rewrite of Listing 2-10 using the stdin.get routine.

```
program charInputDemo2;
#include( "stdlib.hhf" )
static
    c:char;

begin charInputDemo2;

    stdout.put( "Enter a character: " );
    stdin.get(c);
    if( c >= 'a' ) then

        if( c <= 'z' ) then

            and( $5f, c );

        endif;

    endif;
    stdout.put
    (
        "The character you entered, possibly ", nl,
        "converted to uppercase, was '",
        c,
        "'", nl
    );

end charInputDemo2;
```

*Listing 2-11: stdin.get character input sample*

As you may recall from the last chapter, the HLA Standard Library buffers its input. Whenever you read a character from the standard input using stdin.getc or stdin.get, the library routines read the next available character from the buffer; if the buffer is empty, then the program reads a new line of text from the user and returns the first character from that line. If you want to guarantee that the program reads a new line of text from the user when you read a character variable, you should call the stdin.flushInput routine before attempting to read the character. This will flush the current input buffer and force the input of a new line of text on the next input (probably a stdin.getc or stdin.get call).

The end of line is problematic. Different operating systems handle the end of line differently on output versus input. From the console device, pressing the ENTER key signals the end of a line; however, when reading data from a file, you get an end-of-line sequence that is a linefeed or a carriage return/line feed pair (under Windows) or just a line feed (under Linux/ Mac OS X/FreeBSD). To help solve this problem, HLA's Standard Library provides an "end of line" function. This procedure returns true (1) in the AL register if all the current input characters have been exhausted; it returns false (0) otherwise. The sample program in Listing 2-12 demonstrates the stdin.eoln function.

```
program eolnDemo;
#include( "stdlib.hhf" )
begin eolnDemo;

    stdout.put( "Enter a short line of text: " );
    stdin.flushInput();
    repeat

        stdin.getc();
        stdout.putc( al );
        stdout.put( "=$", al, nl );

    until( stdin.eoln() );

end eolnDemo;
```

*Listing 2-12: Testing for end of line using* `stdin.eoln`

The HLA language and the HLA Standard Library provide many other procedures and additional support for character objects. Chapters 4 and 11, as well as the HLA reference documentation, describe how to use these features.

## 2.15  The Unicode Character Set

Although the ASCII character set is, unquestionably, the most popular character representation on computers, it is certainly not the only format around. For example, IBM uses the EBCDIC code on many of its mainframe and mini-computer lines. Because EBCDIC appears mainly on IBM's big iron and you'll rarely encounter it on personal computer systems, we will not consider that character set in this text. Another character representation that is becoming popular on small computer systems (and large ones, for that matter) is the Unicode character set. Unicode overcomes two of ASCII's greatest limitations: the limited character space (i.e., a maximum of 128/256 characters in an 8-bit byte) and the lack of international (beyond the United States) characters.

Unicode uses a 16-bit word to represent a single character. Therefore, Unicode supports up to 65,536 different character codes. This is obviously a huge advance over the 256 possible codes we can represent with an 8-bit byte. Unicode is upward compatible from ASCII. Specifically, if the H.O. 9 bits of a Unicode character contain 0, then the L.O. 7 bits represent the same character as the ASCII character with the same character code. If the H.O. 9 bits contain some nonzero value, then the character represents some other value. If you're wondering why so many different character codes are necessary, simply note that certain Asian character sets contain 4,096 characters (at least their Unicode subset does).

This text will stick to the ASCII character set except for a few brief mentions of Unicode here and there. Eventually, this text may have to eliminate the discussion of ASCII in favor of Unicode because many new operating systems are using Unicode internally (and converting to ASCII as necessary). Unfortunately, many string algorithms are not as conveniently written for Unicode as for ASCII (especially character set functions), so we'll stick with ASCII in this text as long as possible.

## 2.16 For More Information

The electronic edition of this book (on Webster at *http://webster.cs.ucr.edu/* or *http://artofasm.com/*) contains some additional information on data representation you may find useful. For general information about data representation, you should consider reading my book *Write Great Code, Volume 1* (No Starch Press, 2004), or a textbook on data structures and algorithms (available at any bookstore).

# 3

## MEMORY ACCESS AND ORGANIZATION

Chapters 1 and 2 show you how to declare and access simple variables in an assembly language program. This chapter fully explains 80x86 memory access. You will learn how to efficiently organize your variable declarations to speed up access to their data. This chapter will teach you about the 80x86 stack and how to manipulate data on the stack. Finally, this chapter will teach you about dynamic memory allocation and the *heap*.

This chapter discusses several important concepts, including:

- 80x86 memory addressing modes
- Indexed and scaled-indexed addressing modes
- Memory organization
- Memory allocation by program
- Data type coercion

- The 80x86 stack
- Dynamic memory allocation

This chapter will teach to you make efficient use of your computer's memory resources.

# 3.1 The 80x86 Addressing Modes

The 80x86 processors let you access memory in many different ways. Until now, you've seen only a single way to access a variable, the so-called *displacement-only* addressing mode. In this section you'll see some additional ways your programs can access memory using 80x86 *memory addressing modes*. The 80x86 memory addressing modes provide flexible access to memory, allowing you to easily access variables, arrays, records, pointers, and other complex data types. Mastery of the 80x86 addressing modes is the first step toward mastering 80x86 assembly language.

When Intel designed the original 8086 processor, it provided the processor with a flexible, though limited, set of memory addressing modes. Intel added several new addressing modes when it introduced the 80386 microprocessor. However, in 32-bit environments like Windows, Mac OS X, FreeBSD, and Linux, these earlier addressing modes are not very useful; indeed, HLA doesn't even support the use of these older, 16-bit-only addressing modes. Fortunately, anything you can do with the older addressing modes can be done with the new addressing modes. Therefore, you won't need to bother learning the old 16-bit addressing modes when writing code for today's high-performance operating systems. Do keep in mind, however, that if you intend to work under MS-DOS or some other 16-bit operating system, you will need to study up on those old addressing modes (see the 16-bit edition of this book at *http://webster.cs.ucr.edu/* for details).

## 3.1.1 80x86 Register Addressing Modes

Most 80x86 instructions can operate on the 80x86's general-purpose register set. By specifying the name of the register as an operand to the instruction, you can access the contents of that register. Consider the 80x86 mov (move) instruction:

```
mov( source, destination );
```

This instruction copies the data from the *source* operand to the *destination* operand. The 8-bit, 16-bit, and 32-bit registers are certainly valid operands for this instruction. The only restriction is that both operands must be the same size. Now let's look at some actual 80x86 mov instructions:

```
mov( bx, ax );       // Copies the value from bx into ax
mov( al, dl );       // Copies the value from al into dl
mov( edx, esi );     // Copies the value from edx into esi
```

```
mov( bp, sp );        // Copies the value from bp into sp
mov( cl, dh );        // Copies the value from cl into dh
mov( ax, ax );        // Yes, this is legal!
```

The registers are the best place to keep variables. Instructions using the registers are shorter and faster than those that access memory. Of course, most computations require at least one register operand, so the register addressing mode is very popular in 80x86 assembly code.

## 3.1.2  80x86 32-Bit Memory Addressing Modes

The 80x86 provides hundreds of different ways to access memory. This may seem like quite a lot at first, but fortunately most of the addressing modes are simple variants of one another, so they're very easy to learn. And learn them you should! The key to good assembly language programming is the proper use of memory addressing modes.

The addressing modes provided by the 80x86 family include displacement-only, base, displacement plus base, base plus indexed, and displacement plus base plus indexed. Variations on these five forms provide all the different addressing modes on the 80x86. See, from hundreds down to five. It's not so bad after all!

### 3.1.2.1  The Displacement-Only Addressing Mode

The most common addressing mode, and the one that's easiest to understand, is the *displacement-only* (or *direct*) addressing mode. The displacement-only addressing mode consists of a 32-bit constant that specifies the address of the target location. Assuming that variable j is an int8 variable appearing at address $8088, the instruction mov( j, al ); loads the AL register with a copy of the byte at memory location $8088. Likewise, if int8 variable k is at address $1234 in memory, then the instruction mov( dl, k ); stores the value in the DL register to memory location $1234 (see Figure 3-1).

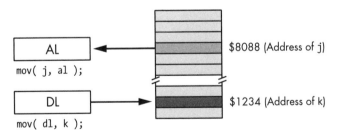

Figure 3-1: Displacement-only (direct) addressing mode

The displacement-only addressing mode is perfect for accessing simple scalar variables. This is named the displacement-only addressing mode because a 32-bit constant (displacement) follows the mov opcode in memory. On the 80x86 processors, this displacement is an offset from the beginning of memory (that is, address 0). The examples in this chapter often access bytes in memory. Don't forget, however, that you can also access words and double words on the 80x86 processors by specifying the address of their first byte (see Figure 3-2).

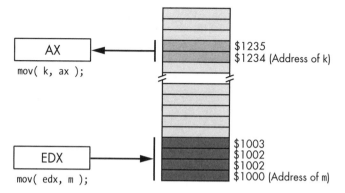

Figure 3-2: Accessing a word or dword using the displacement-only addressing mode

### 3.1.2.2 The Register-Indirect Addressing Modes

The 80x86 CPUs let you access memory indirectly through a register using the *register-indirect* addressing modes. The term *indirect* means that the operand is not the actual address, but rather the operand's value specifies the memory address to use. In the case of the register-indirect addressing modes, the value held in the register is the address of the memory location to access. For example, the instruction mov( eax, [ebx] ); tells the CPU to store EAX's value at the location whose address is in EBX (the square brackets around EBX tell HLA to use the register-indirect addressing mode).

There are eight forms of this addressing mode on the 80x86. The following instructions are examples of these eight forms:

```
mov( [eax], al );
mov( [ebx], al );
mov( [ecx], al );
mov( [edx], al );
mov( [edi], al );
mov( [esi], al );
mov( [ebp], al );
mov( [esp], al );
```

These eight addressing modes reference the memory location at the offset found in the register enclosed by brackets (EAX, EBX, ECX, EDX, EDI, ESI, EBP, or ESP, respectively).

Note that the register-indirect addressing modes require a 32-bit register. You cannot specify a 16-bit or 8-bit register when using an indirect addressing mode.[1] Technically, you could load a 32-bit register with an

---

[1] Actually, the 80x86 does support addressing modes involving certain 16-bit registers, as mentioned earlier. However, HLA does not support these modes and they are not useful under 32-bit operating systems.

arbitrary numeric value and access that location indirectly using the register-indirect addressing mode:

```
mov( $1234_5678, ebx );
mov( [ebx], al );      // Attempts to access location $1234_5678.
```

Unfortunately (or fortunately, depending on how you look at it), this will probably cause the operating system to generate a protection fault because it's not always legal to access arbitrary memory locations. As it turns out, there are better ways to load the address of some object into a register; you'll see how to do this shortly.

The register-indirect addressing modes have many uses. You can use them to access data referenced by a pointer, you can use them to step through array data, and, in general, you can use them whenever you need to modify the address of a variable while your program is running.

The register-indirect addressing mode provides an example of an *anonymous* variable. When using a register-indirect addressing mode, you refer to the value of a variable by its numeric memory address (e.g., the value you load into a register) rather than by the name of the variable—hence the phrase *anonymous variable.*

HLA provides a simple operator that you can use to take the address of a static variable and put this address into a 32-bit register. This is the & (address-of) operator (note that this is the same symbol that C/C++ uses for the address-of operator). The following example loads the address of variable j into EBX and then stores EAX's current value into j using a register-indirect addressing mode:

```
mov( &j, ebx );          // Load address of j into ebx.
mov( eax, [ebx] );       // Store eax into j.
```

Of course, it would have been easier to store EAX's value directly into j rather than using two instructions to do this indirectly. However, you can easily imagine a code sequence where the program loads one of several different addresses into EBX prior to the execution of the mov( eax, [ebx]); statement, thus storing EAX into one of several different locations depending on the execution path of the program.

**WARNING** *The & (address-of) operator is not a general address-of operator like the & operator in C/C++. You may apply this operator only to static variables.[2] You cannot apply it to generic address expressions or other types of variables. In Section 3.13, you will learn about the* load effective address *instruction that provides a general solution for obtaining the address of some variable in memory.*

---

[2] The term *static* here indicates a static, readonly, or storage object.

### 3.1.2.3 Indexed Addressing Modes

The indexed addressing modes use the following syntax:

```
mov( VarName[ eax ], al );
mov( VarName[ ebx ], al );
mov( VarName[ ecx ], al );
mov( VarName[ edx ], al );
mov( VarName[ edi ], al );
mov( VarName[ esi ], al );
mov( VarName[ ebp ], al );
mov( VarName[ esp ], al );
```

*VarName* is the name of some variable in your program.

The indexed addressing modes compute an effective address[3] by adding the address of the variable to the value of the 32-bit register appearing inside the square brackets. Their sum is the actual memory address the instruction accesses. So if *VarName* is at address $1100 in memory and EBX contains 8, then mov(*VarName*[ ebx ], al); loads the byte at address $1108 into the AL register (see Figure 3-3).

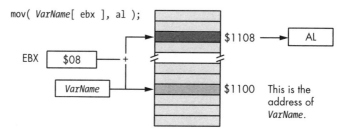

*Figure 3-3: Indexed addressing mode*

The indexed addressing modes are really handy for accessing elements of arrays. You will see how to use these addressing modes for that purpose in Chapter 4.

### 3.1.2.4 Variations on the Indexed Addressing Mode

There are two important syntactical variations of the indexed addressing mode. Both forms generate the same basic machine instructions, but their syntax suggests other uses for these variants.

The first variant uses the following syntax:

```
mov( [ ebx + constant ], al );
mov( [ ebx - constant ], al );
```

These examples use only the EBX register. However, you can use any of the other 32-bit general-purpose registers in place of EBX. This form computes its effective address by adding the value in EBX to the specified constant or subtracting the specified constant from EBX (see Figures 3-4 and 3-5).

---

[3] The effective address is the ultimate address in memory that an instruction will access, once all the address calculations are complete.

```
mov( [ ebx + constant ], al );
```

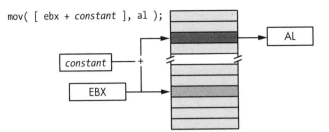

Figure 3-4: Indexed addressing mode using a register plus a constant

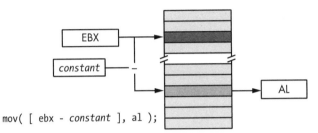

```
mov( [ ebx - constant ], al );
```

Figure 3-5: Indexed addressing mode using a register minus a constant

This particular variant of the addressing mode is useful if a 32-bit register contains the base address of a multibyte object and you wish to access a memory location some number of bytes before or after that location. One important use of this addressing mode is accessing fields of a record (or structure) when you have a pointer to the record data. This addressing mode is also invaluable for accessing automatic (local) variables in procedures (see Chapter 5 for more details).

The second variant of the indexed addressing mode is actually a combination of the previous two forms. The syntax for this version is the following:

```
mov( VarName[ ebx + constant ], al );
mov( VarName[ ebx - constant ], al );
```

Once again, this example uses only the EBX register. You may substitute any of the 32-bit general-purpose registers in lieu of EBX in these two examples. This particular form is useful when accessing elements of an array of records (structures) in an assembly language program (more on that in Chapter 4).

These instructions compute their effective address by adding or subtracting the constant value from VarName's address and then adding the value in EBX to this result. Note that HLA, not the CPU, computes the sum or difference of VarName's address and constant. The actual machine instructions above contain a single constant value that the instructions add to the value in EBX at runtime. Because HLA substitutes a constant for VarName, it can reduce an instruction of the form

```
mov( VarName[ ebx + constant], al );
```

to an instruction of the form

```
mov( constant1[ ebx + constant2], al );
```

Because of the way these addressing modes work, this is semantically equivalent to

```
mov( [ebx + (constant1 + constant2)], al );
```

HLA will add the two constants together at compile time, effectively producing the following instruction:

```
mov( [ebx + constant_sum], al );
```

Of course, there is nothing special about subtraction. You can easily convert the addressing mode involving subtraction to addition by simply taking the two's complement of the 32-bit constant and then adding this complemented value (rather than subtracting the original value).

### 3.1.2.5 Scaled-Indexed Addressing Modes

The scaled-indexed addressing modes are similar to the indexed addressing modes with two differences: (1) The scaled-indexed addressing modes allow you to combine two registers plus a displacement, and (2) the scaled-indexed addressing modes let you multiply the index register by a (scaling) factor of 1, 2, 4, or 8. The syntax for these addressing modes is

```
VarName[ IndexReg32*scale ]
VarName[ IndexReg32*scale + displacement ]
VarName[ IndexReg32*scale - displacement ]

[ BaseReg32 + IndexReg32*scale ]
[ BaseReg32 + IndexReg32*scale + displacement ]
[ BaseReg32 + IndexReg32*scale - displacement ]

VarName[ BaseReg32 + IndexReg32*scale ]
VarName[ BaseReg32 + IndexReg32*scale + displacement ]
VarName[ BaseReg32 + IndexReg32*scale - displacement ]
```

In these examples, BaseReg32 represents any general-purpose 32-bit register, IndexReg32 represents any general-purpose 32-bit register except ESP, and scale must be one of the constants 1, 2, 4, or 8.

The primary difference between the scaled-indexed addressing modes and the indexed addressing modes is the inclusion of the IndexReg32*scale component. These modes compute the effective address by adding in the value of this new register multiplied by the specified scaling factor (see Figure 3-6 for an example involving EBX as the base register and ESI as the index register).

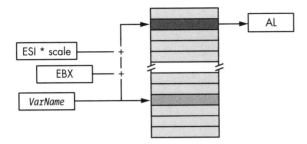

```
mov( VarName[ ebx + esi*scale ], al );
```

*Figure 3-6: Scaled-indexed addressing mode*

In Figure 3-6, suppose that EBX contains $100, ESI contains $20, and VarName is at base address $2000 in memory; then the following instruction

```
mov( VarName[ ebx + esi*4 + 4 ], al );
```

will move the byte at address $2184 ($100 + $20*4 + 4) into the AL register.

The scaled-indexed addressing modes are useful for accessing elements of arrays whose elements are 2, 4, or 8 bytes each. These addressing modes are also useful for access elements of an array when you have a pointer to the beginning of the array.

### 3.1.2.6 Addressing Mode Wrap-up

Well, believe it or not, you've just learned several hundred addressing modes! That wasn't hard now, was it? If you're wondering where all these modes came from, just note that the register-indirect addressing mode isn't a single addressing mode but eight different addressing modes (involving the eight different registers). Combinations of registers, constant sizes, and other factors multiply the number of possible addressing modes on the system. In fact, you need only memorize about two dozen forms and you've got it made. In practice, you'll use less than half the available addressing modes in any given program (and many addressing modes you may never use at all). So learning all these addressing modes is actually much easier than it sounds.

## 3.2  Runtime Memory Organization

An operating system like Mac OS X, FreeBSD, Linux, or Windows tends to put different types of data into different sections (or segments) of memory. Although it is possible to reconfigure memory to your choice by running the linker and specifying various parameters, by default Windows loads an HLA program into memory using the organization appearing in Figure 3-7 (Linux, Mac OS X, and FreeBSD are similar, though they rearrange some of the sections).

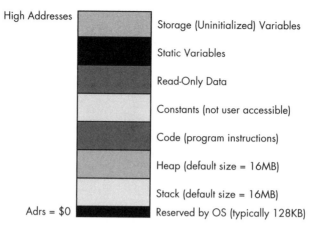

High Addresses

Storage (Uninitialized) Variables

Static Variables

Read-Only Data

Constants (not user accessible)

Code (program instructions)

Heap (default size = 16MB)

Stack (default size = 16MB)

Adrs = $0

Reserved by OS (typically 128KB)

*Figure 3-7: HLA typical runtime memory organization*

The operating system reserves the lowest memory addresses. Generally, your application cannot access data (or execute instructions) at these low addresses. One reason the operating system reserves this space is to help trap NULL pointer references. If you attempt to access memory location 0, the operating system will generate a general protection fault, meaning you've accessed a memory location that doesn't contain valid data. Because programmers often initialize pointers to NULL (0) to indicate that the pointer is not pointing anywhere, an access of location 0 typically means that the programmer has made a mistake and has not properly initialized a pointer to a legal (non-NULL) value.

The remaining six areas in the memory map hold different types of data associated with your program. These sections of memory include the stack section, the heap section, the code section, the readonly section, the static section, and the storage section. Each of these memory sections correspond to some type of data you can create in your HLA programs. Each section is discussed in detail below.

### 3.2.1 The code Section

The code section contains the machine instructions that appear in an HLA program. HLA translates each machine instruction you write into a sequence of one or more byte values. The CPU interprets these byte values as machine instructions during program execution.

By default, when HLA links your program it tells the system that your program can execute instructions in the code segment and you can read data from the code segment. Note, specifically, that you cannot write data to the code segment. The operating system will generate a general protection fault if you attempt to store any data into the code segment.

Remember, machine instructions are nothing more than data bytes. In theory, you could write a program that stores data values into memory and then transfers control to the data it just wrote, thereby producing a program that writes itself as it executes. This possibility produces romantic visions of *Artificial Intelligence* programs that modify themselves to produce some desired result. In real life, the effect is somewhat less glamorous. Generally, self-modifying programs are very difficult to debug because the instructions are constantly changing behind the programmer's back. Because most modern operating systems make it very difficult to write self-modifying programs, we will not consider them any further in this text.

HLA automatically stores the data associated with your machine code into the code section. In addition to machine instructions, you can also store data into the code section by using the following pseudo-opcodes:[4]

| | |
|---|---|
| byte | int8 |
| word | int16 |
| dword | in32 |
| uns8 | boolean |
| uns16 | char |
| uns32 | |

The following byte statement exemplifies the syntax for each of these pseudo-opcodes:

---

byte *comma_separated_list_of_byte_constants* ;

---

Here are some examples:

---

| | |
|---|---|
| boolean | true; |
| char | 'A'; |
| byte | 0, 1, 2; |
| byte | "Hello", 0 |
| word | 0, 2; |
| int8 | -5; |
| uns32 | 356789, 0; |

---

If more than one value appears in the list of values after the pseudo-opcode, HLA emits each successive value to the code stream. So the first byte statement above emits 3 bytes to the code stream, the values 0, 1, and 2. If a string appears within a byte statement, HLA emits 1 byte of data for each character in the string. Therefore, the second byte statement above emits 6 bytes: the characters H, e, 1, 1, and o, followed by a 0 byte.

Keep in mind that the CPU will attempt to treat data you emit to the code stream as machine instructions unless you take special care not to allow the execution of the data. For example, if you write something like the following:

---

```
mov( 0, ax );
byte 0,1,2,3;
add( bx, cx );
```

---

[4] This isn't a complete list. HLA generally allows you to use any scalar data type name as a statement to reserve storage in the code section. You'll learn more about the available data types in Chapter 4.

your program will attempt to execute the 0, 1, 2, and 3 byte values as machine instructions after executing the mov. Unless you know the machine code for a particular instruction sequence, sticking such data values into the middle of your code will generally crash your program. Typically when you place such data in your programs, you'll execute some code that transfers control around the data.

### 3.2.2 The static Section

The static section is where you will typically declare your variables. Although the static section syntactically appears as part of a program or procedure, keep in mind that HLA moves all static variables to the static section in memory. Therefore, HLA does not sandwich the variables you declare in the static section between procedures in the code section.

In addition to declaring static variables, you can also embed lists of data into the static declaration section. You use the same technique to embed data into your static section that you use to embed data into the code section: You use the byte, word, dword, uns32, and so on pseudo-opcodes. Consider the following example:

```
static
    b:    byte := 0;
          byte 1,2,3;

    u:    uns32 := 1;
          uns32 5,2,10;

    c:    char;
          char 'a', 'b', 'c', 'd', 'e', 'f';

    bn:   boolean;
          boolean true;
```

Data that HLA writes to the static memory segment using these pseudo-opcodes is written to the segment after the preceding variables. For example, the byte values 1, 2, and 3 are emitted to the static section after b's 0 byte. Because there aren't any labels associated with these values, you do not have direct access to these values in your program. You can use the indexed addressing modes to access these extra values (examples appear in Chapter 4).

In the examples above, note that the c and bn variables do not have an (explicit) initial value. However, if you don't provide an initial value, HLA will initialize the variables in the static section to all 0 bits, so HLA assigns the NUL character (ASCII code 0) to c as its initial value. Likewise, HLA assigns false as the initial value for bn. In particular, you should note that your variable declarations in the static section always consume memory, even if you haven't assigned them an initial value.

### 3.2.3 The readonly Data Section

The readonly data section holds constants, tables, and other data that your program cannot change during execution. You create read-only objects by declaring them in the readonly declaration section. The readonly section is very similar to the static section with three primary differences:

- The readonly section begins with the reserved word readonly rather than static.
- All declarations in the readonly section generally have an initializer.
- The system does not allow you to store data into a readonly object while the program is running.

Here's an example:

```
readonly
    pi:          real32 := 3.14159;
    e:           real32 := 2.71;
    MaxU16:      uns16 := 65_535;
    MaxI16:      int16 := 32_767;
```

All readonly object declarations must have an initializer because you cannot initialize the value under program control.[5] For all intents and purposes, you can think of readonly objects as constants. However, these constants consume memory, and other than the fact that you cannot write data to readonly objects, they behave like static variables. Because they behave like static objects, you cannot use a readonly object everywhere a constant is allowed; in particular, readonly objects are memory objects, so you cannot supply a readonly object (which you are treating like a constant) and some other memory object as the operands to an instruction.

As with the static section, you may embed data values in the readonly section using the byte, word, dword, and so on data declarations. For example:

```
readonly
    roArray: byte := 0;
             byte 1, 2, 3, 4, 5;
    qwVal:   qword := 1;
             qword 0;
```

### 3.2.4 The storage Section

The readonly section requires that you initialize all objects you declare. The static section lets you optionally initialize objects (or leave them uninitialized, in which case they have the default initial value of 0). The storage section completes the initialization coverage: you use it to declare variables

---

[5] There is one exception you'll see in Chapter 5.

that are always uninitialized when the program begins running. The storage section begins with the storage reserved word and contains variable declarations without initializers. Here is an example:

```
storage
    UninitUns32:    uns32;
    i:              int32;
    character:      char;
    b:              byte;
```

Linux, FreeBSD, Mac OS X, and Windows will initialize all storage objects to 0 when they load your program into memory. However, it's probably not a good idea to depend on this implicit initialization. If you need an object initialized with 0, declare it in a static section and explicitly set it to 0.

Variables you declare in the storage section may consume less disk space in the executable file for the program. This is because HLA writes out initial values for readonly and static objects to the executable file, but it may use a compact representation for uninitialized variables you declare in the storage section; note, however, that this behavior is OS- and object-module-format dependent.

Because the storage section does not allow initialized values, you *cannot* put unlabeled values in the storage section using the byte, word, dword, and so on pseudo-opcodes.

### 3.2.5   The @nostorage Attribute

The @nostorage attribute lets you declare variables in the static data declaration sections (i.e., static, readonly, and storage) without actually allocating memory for the variable. The @nostorage option tells HLA to assign the current address in a declaration section to a variable but not to allocate any storage for the object. That variable will share the same memory address as the next object appearing in the variable declaration section. Here is the syntax for the @nostorage option:

```
    variableName: varType; @nostorage;
```

Note that you follow the type name with @nostorage; rather than some initial value or just a semicolon. The following code sequence provides an example of using the @nostorage option in the readonly section:

```
readonly
    abcd: dword; nostorage;
            byte 'a', 'b', 'c', 'd';
```

In this example, abcd is a double word whose L.O. byte contains 97 ('a'), byte 1 contains 98 ('b'), byte 2 contains 99 ('c'), and the H.O. byte contains 100 ('d'). HLA does not reserve storage for the abcd variable, so HLA associates the following 4 bytes in memory (allocated by the byte directive) with abcd.

Note that the @nostorage attribute is legal only in the static, storage, and readonly sections (the so-called *static* declarations sections). HLA does not allow its use in the var section that you'll read about next.

### 3.2.6 The var Section

HLA provides another variable declaration section, the var section, that you can use to create *automatic* variables. Your program will allocate storage for automatic variables whenever a program unit (i.e., main program or procedure) begins execution, and it will deallocate storage for automatic variables when that program unit returns to its caller. Of course, any automatic variables you declare in your main program have the same *lifetime*[6] as all the static, readonly, and storage objects, so the automatic allocation feature of the var section is wasted in the main program. In general, you should use automatic objects only in procedures (see Chapter 5 for details). HLA allows them in your main program's declaration section as a generalization.

Because variables you declare in the var section are created at runtime, HLA does not allow initializers on variables you declare in this section. So the syntax for the var section is nearly identical to that for the storage section; the only real difference in the syntax between the two is the use of the var reserved word rather than the storage reserved word.[7] The following example illustrates this:

```
var
    vInt:       int32;
    vChar:      char;
```

HLA allocates variables you declare within the var section within the stack memory section. HLA does not allocate var objects at fixed locations; instead, it allocates these variables in an activation record associated with the current program unit. Chapter 5 discusses activation records in greater detail; for now it is important only to realize that HLA programs use the EBP register as a pointer to the current activation record. Therefore, whenever you access a var object, HLA automatically replaces the variable name with [EBP±*displacement*]. Displacement is the offset of the object within the activation record. This means that you cannot use the full scaled-indexed addressing mode (a base register plus a scaled index register) with var objects because var objects already use the EBP register as their base register. Although you will not directly use the two register addressing modes often, the fact that the var section has this limitation is a good reason to avoid using the var section in your main program.

---

[6] The lifetime of a variable is the point from which memory is first allocated to the point the memory is deallocated for that variable.

[7] Actually, there are a few other, minor, differences, but we won't deal with those differences in this text. See the HLA language reference manual for more details.

### 3.2.7  Organization of Declaration Sections Within Your Programs

The static, readonly, storage, and var sections may appear zero or more times between the program header and the associated begin for the main program. Between these two points in your program, the declaration sections may appear in any order, as the following example demonstrates:

```
program demoDeclarations;

static
      i_static:      int32;

var
      i_auto:        int32;

storage
      i_uninit:      int32;

readonly
      i_readonly:    int32 := 5;

static
      j:             uns32;

var
      k:             char;

readonly
      i2:            uns8 := 9;

storage
      c:             char;

storage
      d:             dword;

begin demoDeclarations;

      << Code goes here. >>

end demoDeclarations;
```

In addition to demonstrating that the sections may appear in an arbitrary order, this section also demonstrates that a given declaration section may appear more than once in your program. When multiple declaration sections of the same type (for example, the three storage sections above) appear in a declaration section of your program, HLA combines them into a single group.

## 3.3 How HLA Allocates Memory for Variables

As you've seen, the 80x86 CPU doesn't deal with variables that have names like I, Profits, and LineCnt. The CPU deals strictly with numeric addresses it can place on the address bus like $1234_5678, $0400_1000, and $8000_CC00. HLA, on the other hand, does not force to you refer to variable objects by their addresses (which is nice, because names are so much easier to remember). This is good, but it does obscure what is really going on. In this section, we'll take a look at how HLA associates numeric addresses with your variables so you'll understand (and appreciate) the process that is taking place behind your back.

Take another look at Figure 3-7. As you can see, the various memory sections tend to be adjacent to one another. Therefore, if the size of one memory section changes, then this affects the starting address of all the following sections in memory. For example, if you add a few additional machine instructions to your program and increase the size of the code section, this may affect the starting address of the static section in memory, thus changing the addresses of all your static variables. Keeping track of variables by their numeric address (rather than by their names) is difficult enough; imagine how much worse it would be if the addresses are constantly shifting around as you add and remove machine instructions in your program! Fortunately, you don't have to keep track of variable addresses; HLA does that bookkeeping for you.

HLA associates a current *location counter* with each of the three static declaration sections (static, readonly, and storage). These location counters initially contain 0, and whenever you declare a variable in one of the static sections, HLA associates the current value of that section's location counter with the variable; HLA also bumps up the value of that location counter by the size of the object you're declaring. As an example, assume that the following is the only static declaration section in a program:

```
static
     b     :byte;           // Location counter = 0, size = 1
     w     :word;           // Location counter = 1, size = 2
     d     :dword;          // Location counter = 3, size = 4
     q     :qword;          // Location counter = 7, size = 8
     l     :lword;          // Location counter = 15, size = 16
                            // Location counter is now 31.
```

Of course, the runtime address of each of these variables is not the value of the location counter. First of all, HLA adds in the base address of the static memory section to each of these location counter values (which we call *displacements* or *offsets*). Second, there may be other static objects in modules that you link with your program (e.g., from the HLA Standard Library) or even additional static sections in the same source file, and the linker has to merge the static sections together. Hence, these offsets may have very little bearing on the final address of these variables in memory.

Nevertheless, one important fact remains: HLA allocates variables you declare in a single static declaration section in contiguous memory locations. That is, given the declaration above, w will immediately follow b in memory, d will immediately follow w in memory, q will immediately follow d, and so on. Generally, it's not good coding style to assume that the system allocates variables this way, but sometimes it's convenient to do so.

Note that HLA allocates memory objects you declare in readonly, static, and storage sections in completely different regions of memory. Therefore, you cannot assume that the following three memory objects appear in adjacent memory locations (indeed, they probably will not):

```
static
    b       :byte;
readonly
    w       :word := $1234;
storage
    d       :dword;
```

In fact, HLA will not even guarantee that variables you declare in separate static (or whatever) sections are adjacent in memory, even if there is nothing between the declarations in your code (for example, you cannot assume that b, w, and d are in adjacent memory locations in the following declarations, nor can you assume that they *won't* be adjacent in memory):

```
static
    b       :byte;
static
    w       :word := $1234;
static
    d       :dword;
```

If your code requires these variables to consume adjacent memory locations, you must declare them in the same static section.

Note that HLA handles variables you declare in the var section a little differently than the variables you declare in one of the static sections. We'll discuss the allocation of offsets to var objects in Chapter 5.

## 3.4  HLA Support for Data Alignment

In order to write fast programs, you need to ensure that you properly align data objects in memory. Proper alignment means that the starting address for an object is a multiple of some size, usually the size of an object if the object's size is a power of 2 for values up to 16 bytes in length. For objects greater than 16 bytes, aligning the object on an 8-byte or 16-byte address boundary is probably sufficient. For objects less than 16 bytes, aligning the object at an address that is the next power of 2 greater than the object's size is usually fine. Accessing data that is not aligned at an appropriate address may require extra time; so if you want to ensure that your program runs as rapidly as possible, you should try to align data objects according to their size.

Data becomes misaligned whenever you allocate storage for different-sized objects in adjacent memory locations. For example, if you declare a byte variable, it will consume 1 byte of storage, and the next variable you declare in that declaration section will have the address of that byte object plus 1. If the byte variable's address happens to be an even address, then the variable following that byte will start at an odd address. If that following variable is a word or double-word object, then its starting address will not be optimal. In this section, we'll explore ways to ensure that a variable is aligned at an appropriate starting address based on that object's size.

Consider the following HLA variable declarations:

```
static
    dw:     dword;
    b:      byte;
    w:      word;
    dw2:    dword;
    w2:     word;
    b2:     byte;
    dw3:    dword;
```

The first static declaration in a program (running under Windows, Mac OS X, FreeBSD, Linux, and most 32-bit operating systems) places its variables at an address that is an even multiple of 4,096 bytes. Whatever variable first appears in the static declaration is guaranteed to be aligned on a reasonable address. Each successive variable is allocated at an address that is the sum of the sizes of all the preceding variables plus the starting address of that static section. Therefore, assuming HLA allocates the variables in the previous example at a starting address of 4096, HLA will allocate them at the following addresses:

|       |        | // | Start Adrs | Length |
|-------|--------|----|------------|--------|
| dw:   | dword; | // | 4096       | 4      |
| b:    | byte;  | // | 4100       | 1      |
| w:    | word;  | // | 4101       | 2      |
| dw2:  | dword; | // | 4103       | 4      |
| w2:   | word;  | // | 4107       | 2      |
| b2:   | byte;  | // | 4109       | 1      |
| dw3:  | dword; | // | 4110       | 4      |

With the exception of the first variable (which is aligned on a 4KB boundary) and the byte variables (whose alignment doesn't matter), all of these variables are misaligned. The w, w2, and dw2 variables start at odd addresses, and the dw3 variable is aligned on an even address that is not a multiple of 4.

An easy way to guarantee that your variables are aligned properly is to put all the double-word variables first, the word variables second, and the byte variables last in the declaration, as shown here:

```
static
    dw:     dword;
```

```
dw2:    dword;
dw3:    dword;
w:      word;
w2:     word;
b:      byte;
b2:     byte;
```

This organization produces the following addresses in memory:

```
                     // Start Adrs        Length
dw:     dword;       //    4096             4
dw2:    dword;       //    4100             4
dw3:    dword;       //    4104             4
w:      word;        //    4108             2
w2:     word;        //    4110             2
b:      byte;        //    4112             1
b2:     byte;        //    4113             1
```

As you can see, these variables are all aligned at reasonable addresses.

Unfortunately, it is rarely possible for you to arrange your variables in this manner. While there are many technical reasons that make this alignment impossible, a good practical reason for not doing this is that it doesn't let you organize your variable declarations by logical function (that is, you probably want to keep related variables next to one another regardless of their size).

To resolve this problem, HLA provides the align directive. The align directive uses the following syntax:

```
align( integer_constant );
```

The integer constant must be one of the following small unsigned integer values: 1, 2, 4, 8, or 16. If HLA encounters the align directive in a static section, it will align the very next variable on an address that is an even multiple of the specified alignment constant. The previous example could be rewritten, using the align directive, as follows:

```
static
    align( 4 );
    dw:     dword;
    b:      byte;
    align( 2 );
    w:      word;
    align( 4 );
    dw2:    dword;
    w2:     word;
    b2:     byte;
    align( 4 );
    dw3:    dword;
```

If you're wondering how the align directive works, it's really quite simple. If HLA determines that the current address (location counter value) is not an even multiple of the specified value, HLA will quietly emit extra bytes of padding after the previous variable declaration until the current address in the static section is an even multiple of the specified value. This has the effect of making your program slightly larger (by a few bytes) in exchange for faster access to your data. Given that your program will grow by only a few bytes when you use this feature, this is probably a good trade-off.

As a general rule, if you want the fastest possible access, you should choose an alignment value that is equal to the size of the object you want to align. That is, you should align words to even boundaries using an align(2); statement, double words to 4-byte boundaries using align(4);, quad words to 8-byte boundaries using align(8);, and so on. If the object's size is not a power of 2, align it to the next higher power of 2 (up to a maximum of 16 bytes). Note, however, that you need only align real80 (and tbyte) objects on an 8-byte boundary.

Note that data alignment isn't always necessary. The cache architecture of modern 80x86 CPUs actually handles most misaligned data. Therefore, you should use the alignment directives only with variables for which speedy access is absolutely critical. This is a reasonable space/speed trade-off.

## 3.5 Address Expressions

Earlier, this chapter points out that addressing modes take a couple generic forms, including the following:

```
VarName[ Reg32 ]
VarName[ Reg32 + offset ]
VarName[ RegNotESP32*scale ]
VarName[ Reg32 + RegNotESP32*scale ]
VarName[ RegNotESP32*scale + offset ]
VarName[ Reg32 + RegNotESP32*scale + offset ]
```

Another legal form, which isn't actually a new addressing mode but simply an extension of the displacement-only addressing mode, is:

```
VarName[ offset ]
```

This latter example computes its effective address by adding the constant offset within the brackets to the variable's address. For example, the instruction mov(Address[3], al); loads the AL register with the byte in memory that is 3 bytes beyond the Address object (see Figure 3-8).

Always remember that the *offset* value in these examples must be a constant. If Index is an int32 variable, then Variable[Index] is not a legal address expression. If you wish to specify an index that varies at runtime, then you must use one of the indexed or scaled-indexed addressing modes.

Another important thing to remember is that the offset in Address[*offset*] is a byte address. Despite the fact that this syntax is reminiscent of array indexing in a high-level language like C/C++ or Pascal, this does not properly index into an array of objects unless Address is an array of bytes.

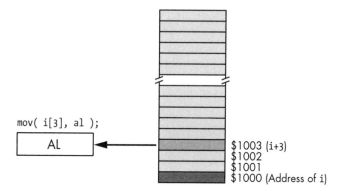

mov( i[3], al );

$1003 (i+3)
$1002
$1001
$1000 (Address of i)

Figure 3-8: Using an address expression to access data beyond a variable

This text will consider an *address expression* to be any legal 80x86 addressing mode that includes a displacement (i.e., variable name) or an offset. In addition to the above forms, the following are also address expressions:

```
[ Reg32 + offset ]
[ Reg32 + RegNotESP32*scale + offset ]
```

This book will *not* consider the following to be address expressions because they do not involve a displacement or offset component:

```
[ Reg32 ]
[ Reg32 + RegNotESP32*scale ]
```

Address expressions are special because those instructions containing an address expression always encode a displacement constant as part of the machine instruction. That is, the machine instruction contains some number of bits (usually 8 or 32) that hold a numeric constant. That constant is the sum of the displacement (i.e., the address or offset of the variable) plus the offset. Note that HLA automatically adds these two values together for you (or subtracts the offset if you use the - rather than + operator in the addressing mode).

Until this point, the offset in all the addressing mode examples has always been a single numeric constant. However, HLA also allows a *constant expression* anywhere an offset is legal. A constant expression consists of one or more constant terms manipulated by operators such as addition, subtraction, multiplication, division, modulo, and a wide variety of others. Most address expressions, however, will involve only addition, subtraction, multiplication, and sometimes division. Consider the following example:

```
mov( X[ 2*4+1 ], al );
```

This instruction will move the byte at address X+9 into the AL register.

The value of an address expression is always computed at compile time, never while the program is running. When HLA encounters the instruction above, it calculates 2 * 4 + 1 on the spot and adds this result to the base address of X in memory. HLA encodes this single sum (base address of X plus 9) as part of the instruction; HLA does not emit extra instructions to compute this sum for you at runtime (which is good, because doing so would be less efficient). Because HLA computes the value of address expressions at compile time, all components of the expression must be constants because HLA cannot know the runtime value of a variable while it is compiling the program.

Address expressions are useful for accessing the data in memory beyond a variable, particularly when you've used the byte, word, dword, and so on statements in a static or readonly section to tack on additional bytes after a data declaration. For example, consider the program in Listing 3-1.

```
program adrsExpressions;
#include( "stdlib.hhf" )
static
  i: int8; @nostorage;
      byte 0, 1, 2, 3;

begin adrsExpressions;

  stdout.put
  (
    "i[0]=", i[0], nl,
    "i[1]=", i[1], nl,
    "i[2]=", i[2], nl,
    "i[3]=", i[3], nl
  );

end adrsExpressions;
```

*Listing 3-1: Demonstration of address expressions*

The program in Listing 3-1 will display the four values 0, 1, 2, and 3 as though they were array elements. This is because the value at the address of i is 0 (this program declares i using the @nostorage option, so i is the address of the next object in the static section, which just happens to be the value 0 appearing as part of the byte statement). The address expression i[1] tells HLA to fetch the byte appearing at i's address plus 1. This is the value 1, because the byte statement in this program emits the value 1 to the static segment immediately after the value 0. Likewise for i[2] and i[3], this program displays the values 2 and 3.

## 3.6 Type Coercion

Although HLA is fairly loose when it comes to type checking, HLA does ensure that you specify appropriate operand sizes to an instruction. For example, consider the following (incorrect) program:

```
program hasErrors;
static
```

```
        i8:     int8;
        i16:    int16;
        i32:    int32;
begin hasErrors;

        mov( i8, eax );
        mov( i16, al );
        mov( i32, ax );

end hasErrors;
```

HLA will generate errors for these three mov instructions. This is because the operand sizes are incompatible. The first instruction attempts to move a byte into EAX, the second instruction attempts to move a word into AL, and the third instruction attempts to move a double word into AX. The mov instruction, of course, requires both operands to be the same size.

While this is a good feature in HLA,[8] there are times when it gets in the way. Consider the following code fragments:

```
static
      byte_values: byte; @nostorage;
                   byte  0, 1;

      . . .

            mov( byte_values, ax );
```

In this example let's assume that the programmer really wants to load the word starting at the address of byte_values into the AX register because she wants to load AL with 0 and AH with 1 using a single instruction (note that 0 is held in the L.O. memory byte and 1 is held in the H.O. memory byte). HLA will refuse, claiming there is a type mismatch error (because byte_values is a byte object and AX is a word object). The programmer could break this into two instructions, one to load AL with the byte at address byte_values and the other to load AH with the byte at address byte_values[1]. Unfortunately, this decomposition makes the program slightly less efficient (which was probably the reason for using the single mov instruction in the first place). Somehow, it would be nice if we could tell HLA that we know what we're doing and we want to treat the byte_values variable as a word object. HLA's type coercion facilities provide this capability.

*Type coercion*[9] is the process of telling HLA that you want to treat an object as an explicit type, regardless of its actual type. To coerce the type of a variable, you use the following syntax:

```
(type newTypeName addressExpression)
```

---

[8] After all, if the two operand sizes are different this usually indicates an error in the program.

[9] This is also called *type casting* in some languages.

The *newTypeName* item is the new type you wish to associate with the memory location specified by *addressExpression*. You may use this coercion operator anywhere a memory address is legal. To correct the previous example, so HLA doesn't complain about type mismatches, you would use the following statement:

```
mov( (type word byte_values), ax );
```

This instruction tells HLA to load the AX register with the word starting at address *byte_values* in memory. Assuming *byte_values* still contains its initial values, this instruction will load 0 into AL and 1 into AH.

Type coercion is necessary when you specify an anonymous variable as the operand to an instruction that directly modifies memory (e.g., neg, shl, not, and so on). Consider the following statement:

```
not( [ebx] );
```

HLA will generate an error on this instruction because it cannot determine the size of the memory operand. The instruction does not supply sufficient information to determine whether the program should invert the bits in the byte pointed at by EBX, the word pointed at by EBX, or the double word pointed at by EBX. You must use type coercion to explicitly specify the size of anonymous references with these types of instructions:

```
not( (type byte [ebx]) );
not( (type dword [ebx]) );
```

**WARNING**    *Do not use the type coercion operator unless you know exactly what you are doing and fully understand the effect it has on your program. Beginning assembly language programmers often use type coercion as a tool to quiet the compiler when it complains about type mismatches without solving the underlying problem.*

Consider the following statement (where *byteVar* is an 8-bit variable):

```
mov( eax, (type dword byteVar) );
```

Without the type coercion operator, HLA complains about this instruction because it attempts to store a 32-bit register in an 8-bit memory location. A beginning programmer, wanting his program to compile, may take a shortcut and use the type coercion operator, as shown in this instruction; this certainly quiets the compiler—it will no longer complain about a type mismatch—so the beginning programmer is happy. However, the program is still incorrect; the only difference is that HLA no longer warns you about your error. The type coercion operator does not fix the problem of attempting to store a 32-bit value into an 8-bit memory location—it simply allows the instruction to store a 32-bit value *starting at the address specified by the 8-bit variable*. The program still stores 4 bytes, overwriting the 3 bytes following *byteVar* in memory. This often produces unexpected results, including the phantom modification of variables in your program.[10] Another, rarer possibility is for the program to abort with a general protection fault. This can occur if the 3 bytes following *byteVar* are not allocated in real memory or if those bytes just happen to fall in a read-only segment in memory. The important thing to remember about the type coercion operator is this: If you cannot exactly state the effect this operator has, don't use it.

Also keep in mind that the type coercion operator does not perform any translation of the data in memory. It simply tells the compiler to treat the bits in memory as a different type. It will not automatically extend an 8-bit value to 32 bits, nor will it convert an integer to a floating-point value. It simply tells the compiler to treat the bit pattern of the memory operand as a different type.

## 3.7  Register Type Coercion

You can also cast a register to a specific type using the type coercion operator. By default, the 8-bit registers are of type byte, the 16-bit registers are of type word, and the 32-bit registers are of type dword. With type coercion, you can cast a register as a different type *as long as the size of the new type agrees with the size of the register.* This is an important restriction that does not exist when applying type coercion to a memory variable.

Most of the time you do not need to coerce a register to a different type. As byte, word, and dword objects, registers are already compatible with all 1-, 2-, and 4-byte objects. However, there are a few instances where register type coercion is handy, if not downright necessary. Two examples include boolean expressions in HLA high-level language statements (e.g., if and while) and register I/O in the stdout.put and stdin.get (and related) statements.

In boolean expressions, HLA always treats byte, word, and dword objects as unsigned values. Therefore, without type coercion, the following if statement always evaluates false (because there is no unsigned value less than 0):

```
if( eax < 0 ) then

    stdout.put( "EAX is negative!", nl );

endif;
```

You can overcome this limitation by casting EAX as an int32 value:

```
if( (type int32 eax) < 0 ) then

    stdout.put( "EAX is negative!", nl );

endif;
```

---

[10] If you have a variable immediately following *byteVar* in this example, the mov instruction will surely overwrite the value of that variable, whether or not you intend for this to happen.

In a similar vein, the HLA Standard Library stdout.put routine always outputs byte, word, and dword values as hexadecimal numbers. Therefore, if you attempt to print a register, the stdout.put routine will print it as a hex value. If you would like to print the value as some other type, you can use register type coercion to achieve this:

```
stdout.put( "AL printed as a char = '", (type char al), "'", nl );
```

The same is true for the stdin.get routine. It will always read a hexadecimal value for a register unless you coerce its type to something other than byte, word, or dword.

## 3.8  The stack Segment and the push and pop Instructions

This chapter mentions that all variables you declare in the var section wind up in the stack memory segment. However, var objects are not the only things in the stack memory section; your programs manipulate data in the stack segment in many different ways. This section describes the stack and introduces the push and pop instructions that manipulate data in the stack section.

The stack segment in memory is where the 80x86 maintains the stack. The *stack* is a dynamic data structure that grows and shrinks according to certain needs of the program. The stack also stores important information about the program including local variables, subroutine information, and temporary data.

The 80x86 controls its stack via the ESP (stack pointer) register. When your program begins execution, the operating system initializes ESP with the address of the last memory location in the stack memory segment. Data is written to the stack segment by "pushing" data onto the stack and "popping" data off the stack.

### 3.8.1  The Basic push Instruction

Consider the syntax for the 80x86 push instruction:

```
push( reg16 );
push( reg32 );
push( memory16 );
push( memory32 );
pushw( constant );
pushd( constant );
```

These six forms allow you to push word or dword registers, memory locations, and constants. You should specifically note that you cannot push byte values onto the stack.

The push instruction does the following:

```
ESP := ESP - Size_of_Register_or_Memory_Operand (2 or 4)
[ESP] := Operand's_Value
```

The pushw and pushd operands are always 2- and 4-byte constants, respectively.

Assuming that ESP contains $00FF_FFE8, then the instruction push( eax ); will set ESP to $00FF_FFE4 and store the current value of EAX into memory location $00FF_FFE4, as Figures 3-9 and 3-10 show.

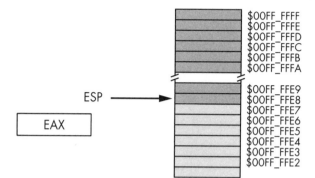

Figure 3-9: Stack segment before the push( eax ); operation

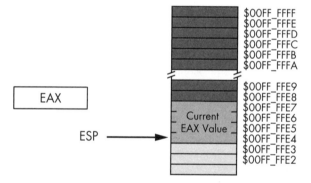

Figure 3-10: Stack segment after the push( eax ); operation

Note that the push( eax ); instruction does not affect the value of the EAX register.

Although the 80x86 supports 16-bit push operations, their primary use in is 16-bit environments such as MS-DOS. For maximum performance, the stack pointer's value should always be an even multiple of 4; indeed, your program may malfunction under a 32-bit OS if ESP contains a value that is not a multiple of 4. The only practical reason for pushing less than 4 bytes at a time on the stack is to build up a double word via two successive word pushes.

### 3.8.2   The Basic pop Instruction

To retrieve data you've pushed onto the stack, you use the pop instruction. The basic pop instruction allows the following forms.

```
pop( reg16 );
pop( reg32 );
```

```
pop( memory16 );
pop( memory32 );
```

Like the push instruction, the pop instruction supports only 16-bit and 32-bit operands; you cannot pop an 8-bit value from the stack. As with the push instruction, you should avoid popping 16-bit values (unless you do two 16-bit pops in a row) because 16-bit pops may leave the ESP register containing a value that is not an even multiple of 4. One major difference between push and pop is that you cannot pop a constant value (which makes sense, because the operand for push is a source operand, while the operand for pop is a destination operand).

Formally, here's what the pop instruction does:

```
Operand := [ESP]
ESP := ESP + Size_of_Operand (2 or 4)
```

As you can see, the pop operation is the converse of the push operation. Note that the pop instruction copies the data from memory location [ESP] before adjusting the value in ESP. See Figures 3-11 and 3-12 for details on this operation.

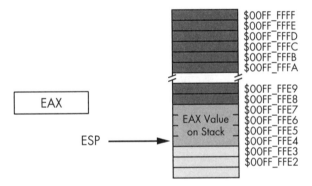

Figure 3-11: Memory before a pop( eax ); operation

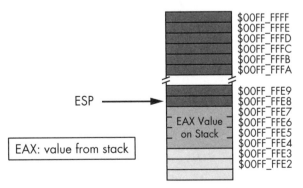

Figure 3-12: Memory after the pop( eax ); instruction

Note that the value popped from the stack is still present in memory. Popping a value does not erase the value in memory; it just adjusts the stack pointer so that it points at the next value above the popped value. However, you should never attempt to access a value you've popped off the stack. The next time something is pushed onto the stack, the popped value will be obliterated. Because your code isn't the only thing that uses the stack (for example, the operating system uses the stack as do subroutines), you cannot rely on data remaining in stack memory once you've popped it off the stack.

### 3.8.3 Preserving Registers with the push and pop Instructions

Perhaps the most common use of the push and pop instructions is to save register values during intermediate calculations. A problem with the 80x86 architecture is that it provides very few general-purpose registers. Because registers are the best place to hold temporary values, and registers are also needed for the various addressing modes, it is very easy to run out of registers when writing code that performs complex calculations. The push and pop instructions can come to your rescue when this happens.

Consider the following program outline:

```
<< Some sequence of instructions that use the eax register >>

<< Some sequence of instructions that need to use eax, for a
        different purpose than the above instructions >>

<< Some sequence of instructions that need the original value in eax >>
```

The push and pop instructions are perfect for this situation. By inserting a push instruction before the middle sequence and a pop instruction after the middle sequence above, you can preserve the value in EAX across those calculations:

```
<< Some sequence of instructions that use the eax register >>
push( eax );
<< Some sequence of instructions that need to use eax, for a
        different purpose than the above instructions >>
pop( eax );
<< Some sequence of instructions that need the original value in eax >>
```

The push instruction above copies the data computed in the first sequence of instructions onto the stack. Now the middle sequence of instructions can use EAX for any purpose it chooses. After the middle sequence of instructions finishes, the pop instruction restores the value in EAX so the last sequence of instructions can use the original value in EAX.

## 3.9 The Stack Is a LIFO Data Structure

You can push more than one value onto the stack without first popping previous values off the stack. However, the stack is a *last-in, first-out (LIFO)* data structure, so you must be careful how you push and pop multiple values.

For example, suppose you want to preserve EAX and EBX across some block of instructions; the following code demonstrates the obvious way to handle this:

```
push( eax );
push( ebx );
<< Code that uses eax and ebx goes here. >>
pop( eax );
pop( ebx );
```

Unfortunately, this code will not work properly! Figures 3-13 through 3-16 show the problem. Because this code pushes EAX first and EBX second, the stack pointer is left pointing at EBX's value on the stack. When the pop( eax ); instruction comes along, it removes the value that was originally in EBX from the stack and places it in EAX! Likewise, the pop( ebx ); instruction pops the value that was originally in EAX into the EBX register. The end result is that this code manages to swap the values in the registers by popping them in the same order that it pushes them.

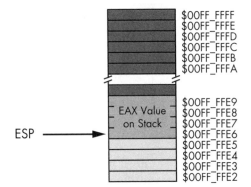

Figure 3-13: Stack after pushing EAX

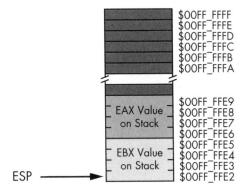

Figure 3-14: Stack after pushing EBX

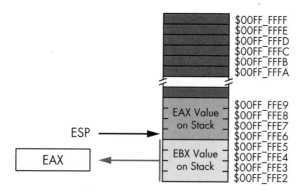

Figure 3-15: Stack after popping EAX

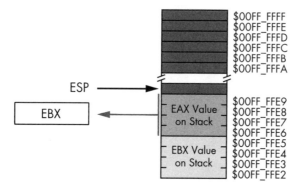

Figure 3-16: Stack after popping EBX

To rectify this problem, you must note that the stack is a last-in, first-out data structure, so the first thing you must pop is the last thing you push onto the stack. Therefore, you must always observe the following maxim:

**Always pop values in the reverse order that you push them.**

The correction to the previous code is:

```
push( eax );
push( ebx );
<< Code that uses eax and ebx goes here. >>
pop( ebx );
pop( eax );
```

Another important maxim to remember is:

**Always pop exactly the same number of bytes that you push.**

This generally means that the number of pushes and pops must exactly agree. If you have too few pops, you will leave data on the stack, which may confuse the running program. If you have too many pops, you will accidentally remove previously pushed data, often with disastrous results.

A corollary to the maxim above is, "Be careful when pushing and popping data within a loop." Often it is quite easy to put the pushes in a loop and leave the pops outside the loop (or vice versa), creating an inconsistent stack. Remember, it is the execution of the push and pop instructions that matters, not the number of push and pop instructions that appear in your program. At runtime, the number (and order) of the push instructions the program executes must match the number (and reverse order) of the pop instructions.

### 3.9.1   Other push and pop Instructions

The 80x86 provides several additional push and pop instructions in addition to the basic push/pop instructions. These instructions include the following:

| | |
|---|---|
| pusha | popa |
| pushad | popad |
| pushf | popf |
| pushfd | popfd |

The pusha instruction pushes all the general-purpose 16-bit registers onto the stack. This instruction exists primarily for older 16-bit operating systems like MS-DOS. In general, you will have very little need for this instruction. The pusha instruction pushes the registers onto the stack in the following order:

---

ax
cx
dx
bx
sp
bp
si
di

---

The pushad instruction pushes all the 32-bit (double-word) registers onto the stack. It pushes the registers onto the stack in the following order:

---

eax
ecx
edx
ebx
esp
ebp
esi
edi

---

Because the pusha and pushad instructions inherently modify the SP/ESP register, you may wonder why Intel bothered to push this register at all. It was probably easier in the hardware to go ahead and push SP/ESP rather than make a special case out of it. In any case, these instructions do push SP or ESP, so don't worry about it too much—there is nothing you can do about it.

The popa and popad instructions provide the corresponding "pop all" operation to the pusha and pushad instructions. This will pop the registers pushed by pusha or pushad in the appropriate order (that is, popa and popad will properly restore the register values by popping them in the reverse order that pusha or pushad pushed them).

Although the pusha/popa and pushad/popad sequences are short and convenient, they are actually slower than the corresponding sequence of push/pop instructions, this is especially true when you consider that you rarely need to push a majority, much less all, of the registers.[11] So if you're looking for maximum speed, you should carefully consider whether to use the pusha(d)/popa(d) instructions.

The pushf, pushfd, popf, and popfd instructions push and pop the EFLAGS register. These instructions allow you to preserve condition code and other flag settings across the execution of some sequence of instructions. Unfortunately, unless you go to a lot of trouble, it is difficult to preserve individual flags. When using the pushf(d) and popf(d) instructions, it's an all-or-nothing proposition—you preserve all the flags when you push them; you restore all the flags when you pop them.

Like the pushad and popad instructions, you should really use the pushfd and popfd instructions to push the full 32-bit version of the EFLAGS register. Although the extra 16 bits you push and pop are essentially ignored when writing applications, you still want to keep the stack aligned by pushing and popping only double words.

### 3.9.2 Removing Data from the Stack Without Popping It

Once in a while you may discover that you've pushed data onto the stack that you no longer need. Although you could pop the data into an unused register or memory location, there is an easier way to remove unwanted data from the stack—simply adjust the value in the ESP register to skip over the unwanted data on the stack.

Consider the following dilemma:

```
        push( eax );
        push( ebx );

        << Some code that winds up computing some values we want to keep
            into eax and ebx >>

        if( Calculation_was_performed ) then

            // Whoops, we don't want to pop eax and ebx!
            // What to do here?

        else
```

---

[11] For example, it is extremely rare for you to need to push and pop the ESP register with the pushad/popad instruction sequence.

```
    // No calculation, so restore eax, ebx.

    pop( ebx );
    pop( eax );

endif;
```

Within the then section of the if statement, this code wants to remove the old values of EAX and EBX without otherwise affecting any registers or memory locations. How can we do this?

Because the ESP register contains the memory address of the item on the top of the stack, we can remove the item from the top of stack by adding the size of that item to the ESP register. In the preceding example, we wanted to remove two double-word items from the top of stack. We can easily accomplish this by adding 8 to the stack pointer (see Figures 3-17 and 3-18 for the details):

```
push( eax );
push( ebx );

<< Some code that winds up computing some values we want to keep
        into eax and ebx >>

if( Calculation_was_performed ) then

    add( 8, ESP ); // Remove unneeded eax/ebx values from the stack.

else

    // No calculation, so restore eax, ebx.

    pop( ebx );
    pop( eax );

endif;
```

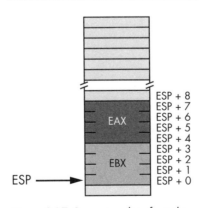

Figure 3-17: Removing data from the stack, before add( 8, esp );

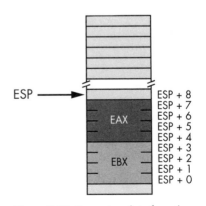

Figure 3-18: Removing data from the stack, after add( 8, esp );

Effectively, this code pops the data off the stack without moving it anywhere. Also note that this code is faster than two dummy pop instructions because it can remove any number of bytes from the stack with a single add instruction.

**WARNING** *Remember to keep the stack aligned on a double-word boundary. Therefore, you should always add a constant that is a multiple of 4 to ESP when removing data from the stack.*

## 3.10 Accessing Data You've Pushed onto the Stack Without Popping It

Once in a while you will push data onto the stack and you will want to get a copy of that data's value, or perhaps you will want to change that data's value without actually popping the data off the stack (that is, you wish to pop the data off the stack at a later time). The 80x86 [reg32 + offset] addressing mode provides the mechanism for this.

Consider the stack after the execution of the following two instructions (see Figure 3-19):

```
push( eax );
push( ebx );
```

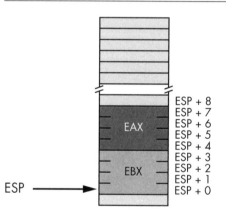

Figure 3-19: Stack after pushing EAX and EBX

If you wanted to access the original EBX value without removing it from the stack, you could cheat and pop the value and then immediately push it again. Suppose, however, that you wish to access EAX's old value or some other value even farther up the stack. Popping all the intermediate values and then pushing them back onto the stack is problematic at best, impossible at worst. However, as you will notice from Figure 3-19, each of the values pushed on the stack is at some offset from the ESP register in memory. Therefore, we can use the [ESP + offset] addressing mode to gain direct access to the value we are interested in. In the example above, you can reload EAX with its original value by using the single instruction

```
mov( [esp+4], eax );
```

This code copies the 4 bytes starting at memory address ESP+4 into the EAX register. This value just happens to be the previous value of EAX that was pushed onto the stack. You can use this same technique to access other data values you've pushed onto the stack.

**WARNING** *Don't forget that the offsets of values from ESP into the stack change every time you push or pop data. Abusing this feature can create code that is hard to modify; if you use this feature throughout your code, it will make it difficult to push and pop other data items between the point where you first push data onto the stack and the point where you decide to access that data again using the [ESP + offset] memory addressing mode.*

The previous section pointed out how to remove data from the stack by adding a constant to the ESP register. That code example could probably be written more safely as this:

```
push( eax );
push( ebx );

<< Some code that winds up computing some values we want to keep
   into eax and ebx >>

if( Calculation_was_performed ) then

    << Overwrite saved values on stack with new eax/ebx values
       (so the pops that follow won't change the values in eax/ebx). >>

    mov( eax, [esp+4] );
    mov( ebx, [esp] );

endif;
pop( ebx );
pop( eax );
```

In this code sequence, the calculated result was stored over the top of the values saved on the stack. Later on, when the program pops the values, it loads these calculated values into EAX and EBX.

## 3.11 Dynamic Memory Allocation and the Heap Segment

Although static and automatic variables are all that simple programs may need, more sophisticated programs need the ability to allocate and deallocate storage dynamically (at runtime) under program control. In the C language, you would use the malloc and free functions for this purpose. C++ provides the new and delete operators. Pascal uses new and dispose. Other languages provide comparable facilities. These memory-allocation routines have a couple of things in common: They let the programmer request how many bytes of storage to allocate, they return a *pointer* to the newly allocated storage, and they provide a facility for returning the storage to the system so the system can reuse it in a future allocation call. As you've probably guessed, HLA also provides a set of routines in the HLA Standard Library that handle memory allocation and deallocation.

The HLA Standard Library mem.alloc and mem.free routines handle the memory allocation and deallocation chores (respectively). The mem.alloc routine uses the following calling sequence:

```
mem.alloc( Number_of_Bytes_Requested );
```

The single parameter is a dword value specifying the number of bytes of storage you need. This procedure allocates storage in the heap segment in memory. The HLA mem.alloc function locates an unused block of memory of the size you specify in the heap segment and marks the block as "in use" so that future calls to mem.alloc will not allocate this same storage. After marking the block as "in use," the mem.alloc routine returns a pointer to the first byte of this storage in the EAX register.

For many objects, you will know the number of bytes that you need in order to represent that object in memory. For example, if you wish to allocate storage for an uns32 variable, you could use the following call to the mem.alloc routine:

```
mem.alloc( 4 );
```

Although you can specify a literal constant as this example suggests, it's generally a poor idea to do so when allocating storage for a specific data type. Instead, use the HLA built-in *compile-time function*[12] @size to compute the size of some data type. The @size function uses the following syntax:

```
@size( variable_or_type_name )
```

The @size function returns an unsigned integer constant that is the size of its parameter in bytes. So you should rewrite the previous call to mem.alloc as follows:

```
mem.alloc( @size( uns32 ));
```

This call will properly allocate a sufficient amount of storage for the specified object, regardless of its type. While it is unlikely that the number of bytes required by an uns32 object will ever change, this is not necessarily

---

[12] A compile-time function is one that HLA evaluates during the compilation of your program rather than at runtime.

true for other data types; so you should always use @size rather than a literal constant in these calls.

Upon return from the mem.alloc routine, the EAX register contains the address of the storage you have requested (see Figure 3-20).

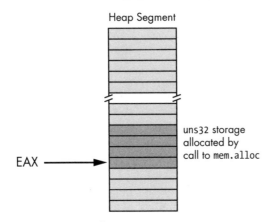

Heap Segment

EAX

uns32 storage
allocated by
call to mem.alloc

Figure 3-20: A call to mem.alloc returns a pointer in the EAX register.

To access the storage mem.alloc allocates, you must use a register-indirect addressing mode. The following code sequence demonstrates how to assign the value 1234 to the uns32 variable mem.alloc creates:

```
mem.alloc( @size( uns32 ));
mov( 1234, (type uns32 [eax]));
```

Note the use of the type coercion operator. This is necessary in this example because anonymous variables don't have a type associated with them and the constant 1234 could be a word or dword value. The type coercion operator eliminates the ambiguity.

The mem.alloc routine may not always succeed. If there isn't a single contiguous block of free memory in the heap segment that is large enough to satisfy the request, then the mem.alloc routine will raise an ex.MemoryAllocationFailure exception. If you do not provide a try..exception..endtry handler to deal with this situation, a memory allocation failure will cause your program to stop. Because most programs do not allocate massive amounts of dynamic storage using mem.alloc, this exception rarely occurs. However, you should never assume that the memory allocation will always occur without error.

When you have finished using a value that mem.alloc allocates on the heap, you can release the storage (that is, mark it as "no longer in use") by calling the mem.free procedure. The mem.free routine requires a single parameter that must be an address returned by a previous call to mem.alloc (that you have not already freed). The following code fragment demonstrates the nature of the `mem.alloc`/`mem.free` pairing:

```
mem.alloc( @size( uns32));

        << Use the storage pointed at by eax. >>
        << Note: This code must not modify eax. >>

mem.free( eax );
```

This code demonstrates a very important point: In order to properly free the storage that `mem.alloc` allocates, you must preserve the value that `mem.alloc` returns. There are several ways to do this if you need to use EAX for some other purpose; you could save the pointer value on the stack using push and pop instructions or you could save EAX's value in a variable until you need to free it.

Storage you release is available for reuse by future calls to the `mem.alloc` routine. The ability to allocate storage when you need it and then free the storage for other use when you have finished with it improves the memory efficiency of your program. By deallocating storage once you have finished with it, your program can reuse that storage for other purposes, allowing your program to operate with less memory than it would if you statically allocated storage for the individual objects.

Several problems can occur when you use pointers. You should be aware of a couple of common errors that beginning programmers make when using dynamic storage allocation routines like `mem.alloc` and `mem.free`:

• Mistake 1: Continuing to refer to storage after you free it. Once you return storage to the system via the call to `mem.free`, you should no longer access that storage. Doing so may cause a protection fault or, worse yet, corrupt other data in your program without indicating an error.

• Mistake 2: Calling `mem.free` twice to release a single block of storage. Doing so may accidentally free some other storage that you did not intend to release or, worse yet, it may corrupt the system memory management tables.

Chapter 4 discusses some additional problems you will typically encounter when dealing with dynamically allocated storage.

The examples thus far in this section have all allocated storage for a single unsigned 32-bit object. Obviously you can allocate storage for any data type using a call to `mem.alloc` by simply specifying the size of that object as `mem.alloc`'s parameter. It is also possible to allocate storage for a sequence of contiguous objects in memory when calling `mem.alloc`. For example, the following code will allocate storage for a sequence of eight characters:

```
mem.alloc( @size( char ) * 8 );
```

Note the use of the constant expression to compute the number of bytes required by an eight-character sequence. Because @size(char) always returns a constant value (1 in this case), the compiler can compute the value of the expression @size(char) * 8 without generating any extra machine instructions.

Calls to mem.alloc always allocate multiple bytes of storage in contiguous memory locations. Hence the former call to mem.alloc produces the sequence appearing in Figure 3-21.

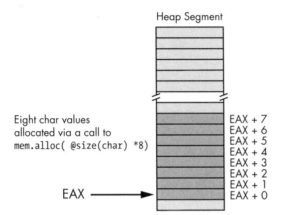

Figure 3-21: Allocating a sequence of eight character objects using mem.alloc

To access these extra character values you use an offset from the base address (contained in EAX upon return from mem.alloc). For example, mov( ch, [eax + 2] ); stores the character found in CH into the third byte that mem.alloc allocates. You can also use an addressing mode like [eax + ebx] to step through each of the allocated objects under program control. For example, the following code will set all the characters in a block of 128 bytes to the NUL character (#0):

```
        mem.alloc( 128 );
        for( mov( 0, ebx ); ebx < 128; add( 1, ebx ) ) do

            mov( 0, (type byte [eax+ebx]) );

        endfor;
```

Chapter 4 discusses composite data structures (including arrays) and describes additional ways to deal with blocks of memory.

You should note that a call to mem.alloc actually allocates slightly more memory than you request. For one thing, memory allocation requests are generally of some minimum size (often a power of 2 between 4 and 16, though this is OS dependent). Furthermore, mem.alloc requests also require a few bytes of overhead for each request (generally around 16 to 32 bytes) to keep track of allocated and free blocks. Therefore, it is not efficient to allocate a large number of small objects with individual calls to mem.alloc. The overhead for each allocation may be greater than the storage you actually use. Typically, you'll use mem.alloc to allocate storage for arrays or large records (structures) rather than small objects.

## 3.12  The inc and dec Instructions

As the example in the previous section indicates—indeed, as several examples up to this point have indicated—adding or subtracting 1 from a register or memory location is a very common operation. In fact, these operations are so common that Intel's engineers included a pair of instructions to perform these specific operations: the inc (increment) and dec (decrement) instructions.

The inc and dec instructions use the following syntax:

```
inc( mem/reg );
dec( mem/reg );
```

The single operand can be any legal 8-bit, 16-bit, or 32-bit register or memory operand. The inc instruction will add 1 to the specified operand, and the dec instruction will subtract 1 from the specified operand.

These two instructions are slightly shorter than the corresponding add or sub instructions (that is, their encoding uses fewer bytes). There is also one slight difference between these two instructions and the corresponding add or sub instructions: They do not affect the carry flag.

As an example of the inc instruction, consider the example from the previous section, recoded to use inc rather than add:

```
    mem.alloc( 128 );
    for( mov( 0, ebx ); ebx < 128; inc( ebx ) ) do

        mov( 0, (type byte [eax+ebx]) );

    endfor;
```

## 3.13  Obtaining the Address of a Memory Object

Section 3.1.2.2 discusses how to use the address-of operator, &, to take the address of a static variable.[13] Unfortunately, you cannot use the address-of operator to take the address of an automatic variable (one you declare in the var section), you cannot use it to compute the address of an anonymous variable, and you cannot use it to take the address of a memory reference that uses an indexed or scaled-indexed addressing mode (even if a static variable is part of the address expression). You may use the address-of operator only to take the address of a simple static object. Often, you will

---

[13] A static variable is one that you declare in the static, readonly, or storage section of your program.

need to take the address of other memory objects as well; fortunately, the 80x86 provides the *load effective address* instruction, lea, to give you this capability.

The lea instruction uses the following syntax:

```
lea( reg32, Memory_operand );
```

The first operand must be a 32-bit register; the second operand can be any legal memory reference using any valid memory addressing mode. This instruction will load the address of the specified memory location into the register. This instruction does not access or modify the value of the memory operand in any way.

Once you load the effective address of a memory location into a 32-bit general-purpose register, you can use the register-indirect, indexed, or scaled-indexed addressing mode to access the data at the specified memory address. Consider the following code fragment:

```
static
    b:byte; @nostorage;
        byte 7, 0, 6, 1, 5, 2, 4, 3;
        .
        .
        .
    lea( ebx, b );
    for( mov( 0, ecx ); ecx < 8; inc( ecx )) do

        stdout.put( "[ebx+ecx] = ", (type byte [ebx+ecx]), nl );

    endfor;
```

This code steps through each of the 8 bytes following the b label in the static section and prints their values. Note the use of the [ebx+ecx] addressing mode. The EBX register holds the base address of the list (that is, the address of the first item in the list), and ECX contains the byte index into the list.

## 3.14  For More Information

An older, 16-bit version of *The Art of Assembly Language Programming* can be found at *http://webster.cs.ucr.edu/*. In that text you will find information about the 80x86's 16-bit addressing modes and segmentation. More information about the HLA Standard Library mem.alloc and mem.free functions can be found in the HLA Standard Library reference manual, also on Webster at *http://webster.cs.ucr.edu/* or at *http://artofasm.com/*. Of course, the Intel x86 documentation (found at *http://www.intel.com/*) provides complete information on 80x86 address modes and machine instruction encoding.

# 4

## CONSTANTS, VARIABLES, AND DATA TYPES

Chapter 2 discussed the basic format for data in memory. Chapter 3 covered how a computer system physically organizes that data in memory. This chapter finishes the discussion by connecting the concept of *data representation* to its actual physical representation. As the title implies, this chapter concerns itself with three main topics: constants, variables, and data structures. This chapter does not assume that you've had a formal course in data structures, though such experience would be useful.

This chapter discusses how to declare and use constants, scalar variables, integers, data types, pointers, arrays, records/structures, unions, and namespaces. You must master these subjects before going on to the next chapter. Declaring and accessing arrays, in particular, seems to present a multitude of problems to beginning assembly language programmers. However, the rest of this text depends on your understanding of these data structures and their memory representation. Do not try to skim over this material with the expectation that you will pick it up as you need it later. You will need it right away, and trying to learn this material along with later material will only confuse you more.

## 4.1 Some Additional Instructions: intmul, bound, into

This chapter introduces arrays and other concepts that will require the expansion of your 80x86 instruction set knowledge. In particular, you will need to learn how to multiply two values; hence the first instruction we will look at is the intmul (integer multiply) instruction. Another common task when accessing arrays is to check to see if an array index is within bounds. The 80x86 bound instruction provides a convenient way to check a register's value to see if it is within some range. Finally, the into (interrupt on overflow) instruction provides a quick check for signed arithmetic overflow. Although into isn't really necessary for array (or other data type) access, its function is very similar to bound; hence the presentation of it at this point.

The intmul instruction takes one of the following forms:

```
// The following compute destreg = destreg * constant

        intmul( constant, destreg16 );
        intmul( constant, destreg32 );

        // The following compute dest = src * constant

        intmul( constant, srcreg16, destreg16 );
        intmul( constant, srcmem16, destreg16 );

        intmul( constant, srcreg32, destreg32 );
        intmul( constant, srcmem32, destreg32 );

        // The following compute dest = src * constant

        intmul( srcreg16, destreg16 );
        intmul( srcmem16, destreg16 );
        intmul( srcreg32, destreg32 );
        intmul( srcmem32, destreg32 );
```

Note that the syntax of the intmul instruction is different from that of the add and sub instructions. In particular, the destination operand must be a register (add and sub both allow a memory operand as a destination). Also note that intmul allows three operands when the first operand is a constant. Another important difference is that the intmul instruction allows only 16-bit and 32-bit operands; it does not multiply 8-bit operands.

intmul computes the product of its specified operands and stores the result into the destination register. If an overflow occurs (which is always a signed overflow, because intmul multiplies only signed integer values), then this instruction sets both the carry and overflow flags. intmul leaves the other condition code flags undefined (so, for example, you cannot meaningfully check the sign flag or the zero flag after executing intmul).

The bound instruction checks a 16-bit or 32-bit register to see if it is between two values. If the value is outside this range, the program raises an exception and aborts. This instruction is particularly useful for checking to see if an array index is within a given range. The bound instruction takes one of the following forms:

```
bound( reg16, LBconstant, UBconstant );
bound( reg32, LBconstant, UBconstant );

bound( reg16, Mem16[2] );
bound( reg32, Mem32[2] );
```

The bound instruction compares its register operand against an unsigned lower bound value and an unsigned upper bound value to ensure that the register is in the range:

```
lower_bound <= register <= upper_bound
```

The form of the bound instruction with three operands compares the register against the second and third parameters (the lower bound and upper bound, respectively).[1] The bound instruction with two operands checks the register against one of the following ranges:

```
Mem16[0] <= register16 <= Mem16[2]
Mem32[0] <= register32 <= Mem32[4]
```

If the specified register is not within the given range, then the 80x86 raises an exception. You can trap this exception using the HLA try..endtry exception-handling statement. The *excepts.hhf* header file defines an exception, ex.BoundInstr, specifically for this purpose. The program in Listing 4-1 demonstrates how to use the bound instruction to check some user input.

```
program BoundDemo;
#include( "stdlib.hhf" );

static
    InputValue:int32;
    GoodInput:boolean;

begin BoundDemo;

    // Repeat until the user enters a good value:

    repeat

        // Assume the user enters a bad value.
```

---

[1] This form isn't a true 80x86 instruction. HLA converts this form of the bound instruction to the two-operand form by creating two readonly memory variables initialized with the specified constants.

```
    mov( false, GoodInput );

    // Catch bad numeric input via the try..endtry statement.

    try

        stdout.put( "Enter an integer between 1 and 10: " );
        stdin.flushInput();
        stdin.geti32();

        mov( eax, InputValue );

        // Use the BOUND instruction to verify that the
        // value is in the range 1..10.

        bound( eax, 1, 10 );

        // If we get to this point, the value was in the
        // range 1..10, so set the boolean GoodInput
        // flag to true so we can exit the loop.

        mov( true, GoodInput );


        // Handle inputs that are not legal integers.

    exception( ex.ConversionError )

      stdout.put( "Illegal numeric format, re-enter", nl );


        // Handle integer inputs that don't fit into an int32.

    exception( ex.ValueOutOfRange )

      stdout.put( "Value is *way* too big, re-enter", nl );


        // Handle values outside the range 1..10 (BOUND instruction).

    exception( ex.BoundInstr )

      stdout.put
      (
          "Value was ",
          InputValue,
          ", it must be between 1 and 10, re-enter",
          nl
      );


    endtry;
```

```
    until( GoodInput );
    stdout.put( "The value you entered, ", InputValue, " is valid.", nl );

end BoundDemo;
```

*Listing 4-1: Demonstration of the bound instruction*

The into instruction, like bound, also generates an exception under certain conditions. Specifically, into generates an exception if the overflow flag is set. Normally, you would use into immediately after a signed arithmetic operation (e.g., intmul) to see if an overflow occurs. If the overflow flag is not set, the system ignores into; however, if the overflow flag is set, then the into instruction raises the ex.IntoInstr exception. The program in Listing 4-2 demonstrates the use of the into instruction.

```
program INTOdemo;
#include( "stdlib.hhf" );

static
    LOperand:int8;
    ResultOp:int8;

begin INTOdemo;

    // The following try..endtry checks for bad numeric
    // input and handles the integer overflow check:

    try

        // Get the first of two operands:

        stdout.put( "Enter a small integer value (-128..+127):" );
        stdin.geti8();
        mov( al, LOperand );

        // Get the second operand:

        stdout.put( "Enter a second small integer value (-128..+127):" );
        stdin.geti8();

        // Produce their sum and check for overflow:

        add( LOperand, al );
        into();

        // Display the sum:

        stdout.put( "The eight-bit sum is ", (type int8 al), nl );


        // Handle bad input here:

    exception( ex.ConversionError )
```

```
                stdout.put( "You entered illegal characters in the number", nl );


            // Handle values that don't fit in a byte here:

        exception( ex.ValueOutOfRange )

            stdout.put( "The value must be in the range -128..+127", nl );


            // Handle integer overflow here:

        exception( ex.IntoInstr )

            stdout.put
            (
                "The sum of the two values is outside the range -128..+127",
                nl
            );


        endtry;

    end INTOdemo;
```

*Listing 4-2: Demonstration of the into instruction*

## 4.2   HLA Constant and Value Declarations

HLA's const and val sections let you declare symbolic constants. The const section lets you declare identifiers whose value is constant throughout compilation and runtime; the val section lets you declare symbolic constants whose values can change at compile time but whose values are constant at runtime (that is, the same name can have a different value at several points in the source code, but the value of a val symbol at a given point in the program cannot change while the program is running).

The const section appears in the same area of your program as the static, readonly, storage, and var sections. It begins with the const reserved word and has a syntax that is nearly identical to the readonly section; that is, the const section contains a list of identifiers followed by a type and a constant expression. The following example will give you an idea of what the const section looks like:

```
const
    pi:              real32   := 3.14159;
    MaxIndex:        uns32    := 15;
    Delimiter:       char     := '/';
    BitMask:         byte     := $F0;
    DebugActive:     boolean  := true;
```

Once you declare these constants in this manner, you may use the symbolic identifiers anywhere the corresponding literal constant is legal. These constants are known as manifest constants. A *manifest constant* is a symbolic representation of a constant that allows you to substitute the literal value for the symbol anywhere in the program. Contrast this with readonly variables; a readonly variable is certainly a constant value because you cannot change such values at runtime. However, there is a memory location associated with readonly variables, and the operating system, not the HLA compiler, enforces the read-only attribute. Although it will certainly crash your program when it runs, it is perfectly legal to write an instruction like mov( eax, ReadOnlyVar );. On the other hand, it is no more legal to write mov( eax, MaxIndex ); (using the declaration above) than it is to write mov( eax, 15 );. In fact, both of these statements are equivalent because the compiler substitutes 15 for MaxIndex whenever it encounters this manifest constant.

If there is absolutely no ambiguity about a constant's type, then you may declare a constant by specifying only the name and the constant's value, omitting the type specification. In the example earlier, the pi, Delimiter, MaxIndex, and DebugActive constants could use the following declarations:

```
const
    pi              := 3.14159;    // Default type is real80.
    MaxIndex        := 15;         // Default type is uns32.
    Delimiter       := '/';        // Default type is char.
    DebugActive     := true;       // Default type is boolean.
```

Symbol constants that have an integer literal constant are always given the smallest possible unsigned type if the constant is zero or positive, or the smallest possible integer type (int8, int16, and so on) if the value is negative.

Constant declarations are great for defining "magic" numbers that might possibly change during program modification. The program in Listing 4-3 provides an example of using constants to parameterize "magic" values in the program. In this particular case, the program defines manifest constants for the amount of memory to allocate for the test, the (mis)alignment, and the number of loop and data repetitions. This program demonstrates the performance reduction that occurs on misaligned data accesses. Adjust the MainRepetitions constant if the program is too fast or too slow.

```
program ConstDemo;
#include( "stdlib.hhf" );

const
    MemToAllocate    := 4_000_000;
    NumDWords        := MemToAllocate div 4;
    MisalignBy       := 62;

    MainRepetitions := 10000;
    DataRepetitions := 999_900;

    CacheLineSize    := 16;
```

```
begin ConstDemo;

    //console.cls();
    stdout.put
    (
        "Memory Alignment Exercise",nl,
        nl,
        "Using a watch (preferably a stopwatch), time the execution of", nl
        "the following code to determine how many seconds it takes to", nl
        "execute.", nl
        nl
        "Press Enter to begin timing the code:"
    );


    // Allocate enough dynamic memory to ensure that it does not
    // all fit inside the cache. Note: The machine had better have
    // at least 4 megabytes mem.free or virtual memory will kick in
    // and invalidate the timing.

    mem.alloc( MemToAllocate );

    // Zero out the memory (this loop really exists just to
    // ensure that all memory is mapped in by the OS).

    mov( NumDWords, ecx );
    repeat

        dec( ecx );
        mov( 0, (type dword [eax+ecx*4]));

    until( !ecx );  // Repeat until ecx = 0.


    // Okay, wait for the user to press the Enter key.

    stdin.readLn();

    // Note: As processors get faster and faster, you may
    // want to increase the size of the following constant.
    // Execution time for this loop should be approximately
    // 10-30 seconds.

    mov( MainRepetitions, edx );
    add( MisalignBy, eax );      // Force misalignment of data.

    repeat

        mov( DataRepetitions, ecx );
        align( CacheLineSize );
```

```
    repeat

        sub( 4, ecx );
        mov( [eax+ecx*4], ebx );
        mov( [eax+ecx*4], ebx );
        mov( [eax+ecx*4], ebx );
        mov( [eax+ecx*4], ebx );

    until( !ecx );
    dec( edx );

until( !edx ); // Repeat until eax is zero.

stdout.put( stdio.bell, "Stop timing and record time spent", nl, nl );


// Okay, time the aligned access.

stdout.put
(
    "Press Enter again to begin timing access to aligned variable:"
);
stdin.readLn();

// Note: If you change the constant above, be sure to change
// this one, too!

mov( MainRepetitions, edx );
sub( MisalignBy, eax );      // Realign the data.
repeat

    mov( DataRepetitions, ecx );
    align( CacheLineSize );
    repeat

        sub( 4, ecx );
        mov( [eax+ecx*4], ebx );
        mov( [eax+ecx*4], ebx );
        mov( [eax+ecx*4], ebx );
        mov( [eax+ecx*4], ebx );

    until( !ecx );
    dec( edx );

until( !edx ); // Repeat until eax is zero.

stdout.put( stdio.bell, "Stop timing and record time spent", nl, nl );
mem.free( eax );


end ConstDemo;
```

*Listing 4-3: Data alignment program rewritten using const definitions*

### 4.2.1 Constant Types

Manifest constants can be any of the HLA primitive types plus a few of the composite types this chapter discusses. Chapters 1, 2, and 3 discussed most of the primitive types; the primitive types include the following:[2]

- boolean constants (true or false)
- uns8 constants (0..255)
- uns16 constants (0..65,535)
- uns32 constants (0..4,294,967,295)
- int8 constants (−128..+127)
- int16 constants (−32,768..+32,767)
- int32 constants (−2,147,483,648..+2,147,483,647)
- char constants (any ASCII character with a character code in the range 0..255)
- byte constants (any 8-bit value including integers, booleans, and characters)
- word constants (any 16-bit value)
- dword constants (any 32-bit value)
- real32 constants (floating-point values)
- real64 constants (floating-point values)
- real80 constants (floating-point values)

In addition to the constant types appearing above, the const section supports six additional constant types:

- string constants
- text constants
- Enumerated constant values
- Array constants
- Record/Union constants
- Character set constants

These data types are the subject of this chapter, and the discussion of most of them appears a little later. However, the string and text constants are sufficiently important to warrant an early discussion of these constant types.

---

[2] This is not a complete list. HLA also supports 64-bit and 128-bit data types. We'll discuss those in Chapter 8.

## 4.2.2   String and Character Literal Constants

HLA, like most programming languages, draws a distinction between a sequence of characters, a *string*, and a single character. This distinction is present both in the type declarations and in the syntax for literal character and string constants. Until now, this text has not drawn a fine distinction between character and string literal constants; now is the time to do so.

String literal constants consist of a sequence of zero or more characters surrounded by ASCII quote characters. The following are examples of legal literal string constants:

```
"This is a string"      // String with 16 characters.
""                      // Zero length string.
"a"                     // String with a single character.
"123"                   // String of length 3.
```

A string of length 1 is not the same thing as a character constant. HLA uses two completely different internal representations for character and string values. Hence, "a" is not a character; it is a string that just happens to contain a single character.

Character literal constants take a couple forms, but the most common form consists of a single character surrounded by ASCII apostrophe characters:

```
'2'         // Character constant equivalent to ASCII code $32.
'a'         // Character constant for lowercase 'A'.
```

As this section notes earlier, "a" and 'a' are not equivalent.

Those who are familiar with C, C++, or Java probably recognize these literal constant forms, because they are similar to the character and string constants in C/C++/Java. In fact, this text has made a tacit assumption to this point that you are somewhat familiar with C/C++ insofar as examples appearing up to this point use character and string constants without an explicit definition of them.

Another similarity between C/C++ strings and HLA's is the automatic concatenation of adjacent literal string constants within your program. For example, HLA concatenates the two string constants

```
"First part of string, "     "second part of string"
```

to form the single-string constant

```
"First part of string, second part of string"
```

Beyond these few similarities, however, HLA strings and C/C++ strings differ. For example, C/C++ strings let you specify special character values using the escape character sequence consisting of a backslash character followed by one or more special characters; HLA does not use this escape character mechanism. HLA does provide, however, several other ways to insert special characters into a string or character constant.

Because HLA does not allow escape character sequences in literal string and character constants, the first question you might ask is, "How does one embed quote characters in string constants and apostrophe characters in character constants?" To solve this problem, HLA uses the same technique as Pascal and many other languages: You insert two quotes in a string constant to represent a single quote, or you place two apostrophes in a character constant to represent a single apostrophe character. For example:

```
"He wrote a "" Hello World"" program as an example."
```

The above is equivalent to:

```
He wrote a "Hello World" program as an example.
```

As Chapter 1 pointed out, to create a single apostrophe character constant, you place two adjacent apostrophes within a pair of apostrophes:

```
''''
```

HLA provides a couple of other features that eliminate the need for escape characters. In addition to concatenating two adjacent string constants to form a longer string constant, HLA will also concatenate any combination of adjacent character and string constants to form a single string constant:

```
'1' '2' '3'                    // Equivalent to "123"
"He wrote a "  '"' "Hello World"  '"' " program as an example."
```

Note that the two *He wrote* strings in the previous examples are identical in HLA.

HLA provides a second way to specify character constants that handles all the other C/C++ escape character sequences: the ASCII code literal character constant. This literal character constant form uses the syntax:

```
#integer_constant
```

This form creates a character constant whose value is the ASCII code specified by integer_constant. The numeric constant can be a decimal, hexadecimal, or binary value. For example:

```
#13          #$d          #%1101    // All three are the same
                                    // character, a carriage return.
```

Because you may concatenate character literals with strings, and the #constant form is a character literal, the following are all legal strings:

```
"Hello World" #13 #10        // #13 #10 is the Windows newline sequence
                             // (carriage return followed by line feed).

"Error: Bad Value" #7        // #7 is the bell character.
"He wrote a " #$22 "Hello World" #$22 " program as an example."
```

Because $22 is the ASCII code for the quote character, this last example is yet a third form of the *He wrote* string literal.

### 4.2.3   String and Text Constants in the const Section

String and text constants in the const section use the following declaration syntax:

```
const
     AStringConst:     string := "123";
     ATextConst:       text   := "123";
```

Other than the data type of these two constants, their declarations are identical. However, their behavior in an HLA program is quite different.

Whenever HLA encounters a symbolic string constant within your program, it substitutes the string literal constant in place of the string name. So a statement like stdout.put( AStringConst ); prints the string 123 to the display. No real surprise here.

Whenever HLA encounters a symbolic text constant within your program, it substitutes the text of that string (rather than the string literal constant) for the identifier. That is, HLA substitutes the characters between the delimiting quotes in place of the symbolic text constant. Therefore, the following statement is perfectly legal given the declarations above:

```
mov( ATextConst, al );        // Equivalent to mov( 123, al );
```

Note that substituting AStringConst for ATextConst in this example is illegal:

```
mov( AStringConst, al );      // Equivalent to mov( "123", al );
```

This latter example is illegal because you cannot move a string literal constant into the AL register.

Whenever HLA encounters a symbolic text constant in your program, it immediately substitutes the value of the text constant's string for that text constant and continues the compilation as though you had written the text constant's value rather than the symbolic identifier in your program. This can save some typing and help make your programs a little more readable if you often enter some sequence of text in your program. For example, consider the nl (newline) text constant declaration found in the HLA *stdio.hhf* library header file:

```
const
    nl: text := "#$d #$a";     // Windows version.

const
    nl:  text := " """" #$a";  // Linux, FreeBSD, and Mac OS X version.
```

Whenever HLA encounters the symbol nl, it immediately substitutes the value of the string "#$d #$a" for the nl identifier. When HLA sees the #$d (carriage return) character constant followed by the #$a (line feed) character constants, it concatenates the two to form the string containing the Windows newline sequence (a carriage return followed by a line feed). Consider the following two statements:

```
        stdout.put( "Hello World", nl );
        stdout.put( "Hello World"  nl );
```

(Notice that the second statement above does not separate the string literal and the nl symbol with a comma.) In the first example, HLA emits code that prints the string Hello World and then emits some additional code that prints a newline sequence. In the second example, HLA expands the nl symbol as follows:

```
        stdout.put( "Hello World" #$d #$a );
```

Now HLA sees a string literal constant (Hello World) followed by two character constants. It concatenates the three of them together to form a single string and then prints this string with a single call. Therefore, leaving off the comma between the string literal and the nl symbol produces slightly more efficient code. Keep in mind that this works only with string literal constants. You cannot concatenate string variables, or a string variable with a string literal, by using this technique.

Linux, FreeBSD, and Mac OS X users should note that the Unix end-of-line sequence is just a single line-feed character. Therefore, the declaration for nl is slightly different in those operating systems (to always guarantee that nl expands to a string constant rather than a character constant).

In the constant section, if you specify only a constant identifier and a string constant (that is, you do not supply a type), HLA defaults to type string. If you want to declare a text constant, you must explicitly supply the type.

```
const
    AStrConst := "String Constant";
    ATextConst: text := "mov( 0, eax );";
```

## 4.2.4  Constant Expressions

Thus far, this chapter has given the impression that a symbolic constant definition consists of an identifier, an optional type, and a literal constant. Actually, HLA constant declarations can be a lot more sophisticated than this because HLA allows the assignment of a constant expression, not just a literal constant, to a symbolic constant. The generic constant declaration takes one of the following two forms:

```
Identifier : typeName := constant_expression ;
Identifier := constant_expression ;
```

Constant expressions take the familiar form you're used to in high-level languages like C/C++ and Pascal. They may contain literal constant values, previously declared symbolic constants, and various arithmetic operators. Table 4-1 lists some of the operations possible in a constant expression.

The constant expression operators follow standard precedence rules; you may use the parentheses to override the precedence if necessary. See the HLA reference at *http://webster.cs.ucr.edu/* or *http://artofasm.com/* for the exact precedence relationships. In general, if the precedence isn't obvious, use parentheses to exactly state the order of evaluation. HLA actually provides a few more operators than these, though the ones above are the ones you will most commonly use; the HLA documentation provides a complete list of constant expression operators.

**Table 4-1:** Operations Allowed in Constant Expressions

| Arithmetic Operators | |
| --- | --- |
| - (unary negation) | Negates the expression immediately following "-". |
| * | Multiplies the integer or real values around the asterisk. |
| div | Divides the left integer operand by the right integer operand, producing an integer (truncated) result. |
| mod | Divides the left integer operand by the right integer operand, producing an integer remainder. |
| / | Divides the left numeric operand by the second numeric operand, producing a floating point result. |
| + | Adds the left and right numeric operands. |
| - | Subtracts the right numeric operand from the left numeric operand. |
| **Comparison Operators** | |
| =, == | Compares left operand with right operand. Returns true if equal. |
| <>, != | Compares left operand with right operand. Returns true if not equal. |
| < | Returns true if left operand is less than right operand. |
| <= | Returns true if left operand is <= right operand. |
| > | Returns true if left operand is greater than right operand. |
| >= | Returns true if left operand is >= right operand. |

*(continued)*

**Table 4-1:** Operations Allowed in Constant Expressions (continued)

| Logical Operators[*] | |
| --- | --- |
| & | For boolean operands, returns the logical and of the two operands. |
| \| | For boolean operands, returns the logical or of the two operands. |
| ^ | For boolean operands, returns the logical exclusive-or. |
| ! | Returns the logical not of the single operand following "!". |

| Bitwise Logical Operators | |
| --- | --- |
| & | For integer numeric operands, returns bitwise and of the operands. |
| \| | For integer numeric operands, returns bitwise or of the operands. |
| ^ | For integer numeric operands, returns bitwise xor of the operands. |
| ! | For an integer numeric operand, returns bitwise not of the operand. |

| String Operators | |
| --- | --- |
| '+' | Returns the concatenation of the left and right string operands. |

[*] Note to C/C++ and Java users: HLA's constant expressions use complete boolean evaluation rather than short-circuit boolean evaluation. Hence, HLA constant expressions do not behave identically to C/C++/Java expressions.

If an identifier appears in a constant expression, that identifier must be a constant identifier that you have previously defined in your program in a const or val section. You may not use variable identifiers in a constant expression; their values are not defined at compile time when HLA evaluates the constant expression. Also, don't confuse compile-time and runtime operations:

```
// Constant expression, computed while HLA is compiling your program:

const
        x           := 5;
        y           := 6;
        Sum         := x + y;


// Runtime calculation, computed while your program is running, long after
// HLA has compiled it:

    mov( x, al );
    add( y, al );
```

HLA directly interprets the value of a constant expression during compilation. It does not emit any machine instructions to compute x + y in the constant expression above. Instead, it directly computes the sum of these two constant values. From that point forward in the program, HLA associates the value 11 with the constant Sum just as if the program had contained the statement Sum := 11; rather than Sum := x + y;. On the other hand, HLA does not precompute the value 11 in AL for the mov and add instructions above; it faithfully emits the object code for these two instructions and the 80x86 computes their sum when the program is run (sometime after the compilation is complete).

In general, constant expressions don't get very sophisticated in assembly language programs. Usually, you're adding, subtracting, or multiplying two integer values. For example, the following const section defines a set of constants that have consecutive values:

```
const
      TapeDAT              :=      0;
      Tape8mm              :=      TapeDAT + 1;
      TapeQIC80            :=      Tape8mm + 1;
      TapeTravan           :=      TapeQIC80 + 1;
      TapeDLT              :=      TapeTravan + 1;
```

The constants above have the following values: TapeDAT=0, Tape8mm=1, TapeQIC80=2, TapeTravan=3, and TapeDLT=4.

## 4.2.5    Multiple const Sections and Their Order in an HLA Program

Although const sections must appear in the declaration section of an HLA program (for example, between the program pgmname; header and the corresponding begin pgmname; statement), they do not have to appear before or after any other items in the declaration section. In fact, like the variable declaration sections, you can place multiple const sections in a declaration section. The only restriction on HLA constant declarations is that you must declare any constant symbol before you use it in your program.

Some C/C++ programmers, for example, are more comfortable writing their constant declarations as follows (because this is closer to C/C++'s syntax for declaring constants):

```
const      TapeDAT              :=      0;
const      Tape8mm              :=      TapeDAT + 1;
const      TapeQIC80            :=      Tape8mm + 1;
const      TapeTravan           :=      TapeQIC80 + 1;
const      TapeDLT              :=      TapeTravan + 1;
```

The placement of the const section in a program seems to be a personal issue among programmers. Other than the requirement of defining all constants before you use them, you may feel free to insert the const declaration section anywhere in the declaration section.

## 4.2.6 The HLA val Section

You cannot change the value of a constant you define in the const section. While this seems perfectly reasonable (constants after all, are supposed to be, well, constant), there are different ways we can define the term *constant*, and const objects follow the rules of only one specific definition. HLA's val section lets you define constant objects that follow slightly different rules. This section discusses the val section and the difference between val constants and const constants.

The concept of "const-ness" can exist at two different times: while HLA is compiling your program and later when your program executes (and HLA is no longer running). All reasonable definitions of a constant require that a value not change while the program is running. Whether or not the value of a "constant" can change during compilation is a separate issue. The difference between HLA const objects and HLA val objects is whether the value can change during compilation.

Once you define a constant in the const section, the value of that constant is immutable from that point forward *both at runtime and while HLA is compiling your program*. Therefore, an instruction like mov( SymbolicCONST, eax ); always moves the same value into EAX, regardless of where this instruction appears in the HLA main program. Once you define the symbol SymbolicCONST in the const section, this symbol has the same value from that point forward.

The HLA val section lets you declare symbolic constants, just like the const section. However, HLA val constants can change their value throughout the source code in your program. The following HLA declarations are perfectly legal:

```
val     InitialValue    := 0;
const   SomeVal         := InitialValue + 1;     // = 1
const   AnotherVal      := InitialValue + 2;     // = 2

val     InitialValue    := 100;
const   ALargerVal      := InitialValue;         // = 100
const   LargeValTwo     := InitialValue*2;       // = 200
```

All of the symbols appearing in the const sections use the symbolic value InitialValue as part of the definition. Note, however, that InitialValue has different values at various points in this code sequence; at the beginning of the code sequence InitialValue has the value 0, while later it has the value 100.

Remember, at runtime a val object is not a variable; it is still a manifest constant and HLA will substitute the current value of a val identifier for that identifier.[3] Statements like mov( 25, InitialValue ); are no more legal than mov( 25, 0 ); or mov( 25, 100 );.

---

[3] In this context, *current* means the value last assigned to a val object looking backward in the source code.

## 4.2.7  Modifying val Objects at Arbitrary Points in Your Programs

If you declare all your val objects in the declaration section, it would seem that you would not be able to change the value of a val object between the begin and end statements of your program. After all, the val section must appear in the declaration section of the program, and the declaration section ends before the begin statement. In Chapter 9, you will learn that most val object modifications occur between the begin and end statements; hence, HLA must provide some way to change the value of a val object outside the declaration section. The mechanism to do this is the ? operator. Not only does HLA allow you to change the value of a val object outside the declaration section, but it also allows you to change the value of a val object almost *anywhere* in the program. Anywhere a space is allowed inside an HLA program, you can insert a statement of the form

```
? ValIdentifier := constant_expression;
```

This means that you could write a short program like the one appearing in Listing 4-4.

```
program VALdemo;
#include( "stdlib.hhf" )

val
    NotSoConstant := 0;

begin VALdemo;

    mov( NotSoConstant, eax );
    stdout.put( "EAX = ", (type uns32 eax ), nl );

    ?NotSoConstant := 10;
    mov( NotSoConstant, eax );
    stdout.put( "EAX = ", (type uns32 eax ), nl );

    ?NotSoConstant := 20;
    mov( NotSoConstant, eax );
    stdout.put( "EAX = ", (type uns32 eax ), nl );

    ?NotSoConstant := 30;
    mov( NotSoConstant, eax );
    stdout.put( "EAX = ", (type uns32 eax ), nl );

end VALdemo;
```

Listing 4-4: Demonstration of val redefinition using the ? operator

## 4.3  The HLA Type Section

Let's say that you simply do not like the names that HLA uses for declaring byte, word, dword, real, and other variables. Let's say that you prefer Pascal's naming convention or perhaps C's naming convention. You want to use terms like integer, float, double, or whatever. If HLA were Pascal, you could redefine the names in the type section of the program. With C you could use a #define or a typedef statement to accomplish the task. Well, HLA, like Pascal, has its own type statement that also lets you create aliases of these names. The following example demonstrates how to set up some C/C++/Pascal–compatible names in your HLA programs:

```
type
        integer:               int32;
        float:                 real32;
        double:                real64;
        colors:                byte;
```

Now you can declare your variables with more meaningful statements like these:

```
static
        i:                     integer;
        x:                     float;
        HouseColor:            colors;
```

If you program in Ada, C/C++, or FORTRAN (or any other language, for that matter), you can pick type names you're more comfortable with. Of course, this doesn't change how the 80x86 or HLA reacts to these variables one iota, but it does let you create programs that are easier to read and understand because the type names are more indicative of the actual underlying types. One warning for C/C++ programmers: don't get too excited and go off and define an int data type. Unfortunately, int is an 80x86 machine instruction (interrupt), and therefore this is a reserved word in HLA.

The type section is useful for much more than creating type isomorphism (that is, giving a new name to an existing type). The following sections demonstrate many of the possible things you can do in the type section.

## 4.4   enum and HLA Enumerated Data Types

In a previous section discussing constants and constant expressions, you saw the following example:

```
const        TapeDAT        :=    0;
const        Tape8mm        :=    TapeDAT + 1;
const        TapeQIC80      :=    Tape8mm + 1;
const        TapeTravan     :=    TapeQIC80 + 1;
const        TapeDLT        :=    TapeTravan + 1;
```

This example demonstrates how to use constant expressions to develop a set of constants that contain unique, consecutive values. There are, however, a couple of problems with this approach. First, it involves a lot of typing (and extra reading when reviewing this program). Second, it's very easy to make a mistake when creating long lists of unique constants and reuse or skip some values. The HLA enum type provides a better way to create a list of constants with unique values.

enum is an HLA type declaration that lets you associate a list of names with a new type. HLA associates a unique value with each name (that is, it *enumerates* the list). The enum keyword typically appears in the type section, and you use it as follows:

```
type
    enumTypeID:             enum { comma_separated_list_of_names };
```

The symbol *enumTypeID* becomes a new type whose values are specified by a list of names. As a concrete example, consider the data type TapeDrives and a corresponding variable declaration of type TapeDrives:

```
type
    TapeDrives: enum{ TapeDAT, Tape8mm, TapeQIC80, TapeTravan, TapeDLT};

static
    BackupUnit:         TapeDrives := TapeDAT;

        .

        .

        .

    mov( BackupUnit, al );
    if( al = Tape8mm ) then

        ...

    endif;

    // etc.
```

By default, HLA reserves 1 byte of storage for enumerated data types. So the BackupUnit variable will consume 1 byte of memory, and you would typically use an 8-bit register to access it.[4] As for the constants, HLA associates consecutive uns8 constant values starting at 0 with each of the enumerated identifiers. In the TapeDrives example, the tape drive identifiers would have the values TapeDAT=0, Tape8mm=1, TapeQIC80=2, TapeTravan=3, and TapeDLT=4. You may use these constants exactly as though you had defined them with these values in a const section.

## 4.5  Pointer Data Types

You've probably experienced pointers firsthand in the Pascal, C, or Ada programming languages, and you're probably getting worried right now. Almost everyone has a bad experience when they first encounter pointers in

---

[4] HLA provides a mechanism by which you can specify that enumerated data types consume 2 or 4 bytes of memory. See the HLA documentation for more details.

a high-level language. Well, fear not! Pointers are actually *easier* to deal with in assembly language than in high-level languages. Besides, most of the problems you had with pointers probably had nothing to do with pointers but rather with the linked list and tree data structures you were trying to implement with them. Pointers, on the other hand, have many uses in assembly language that have nothing to do with linked lists, trees, and other scary data structures. Indeed, simple data structures like arrays and records often involve the use of pointers. So if you have some deep-rooted fear about pointers, forget everything you know about them. You're going to learn how *great* pointers really are.

Probably the best place to start is with the definition of a pointer. Just exactly what is a pointer, anyway? Unfortunately, high-level languages like Pascal tend to hide the simplicity of pointers behind a wall of abstraction. This added complexity (which exists for good reason, by the way) tends to frighten programmers because *they don't understand what's going on.*

If you're afraid of pointers, let's just ignore them for the time being and work with an array. Consider the following array declaration in Pascal:

```
M: array [0..1023] of integer;
```

Even if you don't know Pascal, the concept here is pretty easy to understand. M is an array with 1,024 integers in it, indexed from M[0] to M[1023]. Each one of these array elements can hold an integer value that is independent of all the others. In other words, this array gives you 1,024 different integer variables, each of which you refer to by number (the array index) rather than by name.

If you encounter a program that has the statement M[0]:=100;, you probably won't have to think at all about what is happening with this statement. It is storing the value 100 into the first element of the array M. Now consider the following two statements:

```
i := 0; (* Assume "i" is an integer variable. *)
M [i] := 100;
```

You should agree, without too much hesitation, that these two statements perform the same operation as M[0]:=100;. Indeed, you're probably willing to agree that you can use any integer expression in the range 0..1,023 as an index into this array. The following statements still perform the same operation as our single assignment to index 0:

```
i := 5;                 (* Assume all variables are integers.*)
j := 10;
k := 50;
m [i*j-k] := 100;
```

"Okay, so what's the point?" you're probably thinking. "Anything that produces an integer in the range 0..1,023 is legal. So what?" Okay, how about the following:

```
M [1] := 0;
M [ M [1] ] := 100;
```

Whoa! Now that takes a few moments to digest. However, if you take it slowly, it makes sense and you'll discover that these two instructions perform the exact same operation you've been doing all along. The first statement stores 0 into array element M[1]. The second statement fetches the value of M[1], which is an integer so you can use it as an array index into M, and uses that value (0) to control where it stores the value 100.

If you're willing to accept the above as reasonable, perhaps bizarre, but usable nonetheless, then you'll have no problems with pointers. *Because M[1] is a pointer!* Well, not really, but if you were to change M to "memory" and treat this array as all of memory, this is the exact definition of a pointer. A pointer is simply a memory location whose value is the address (or index, if you prefer) of some other memory location. Pointers are very easy to declare and use in an assembly language program. You don't even have to worry about array indices or anything like that.

### 4.5.1   Using Pointers in Assembly Language

An HLA pointer is a 32-bit value that may contain the address of some other variable. If you have a dword variable p that contains $1000_0000, then p "points" at memory location $1000_0000. To access the dword that p points at, you could use code like the following:

```
mov( p, ebx );          // Load ebx with the value of pointer p.
mov( [ebx], eax );      // Fetch the data that p points at.
```

By loading the value of p into EBX, this code loads the value $1000_0000 into EBX (assuming p contains $1000_0000 and, therefore, points at memory location $1000_0000). The second instruction above loads the EAX register with the dword starting at the location whose offset appears in EBX. Because EBX now contains $1000_0000, this will load EAX from locations $1000_0000 through $1000_0003.

Why not just load EAX directly from location $1000_0000 using an instruction like mov( mem, eax ); (assuming mem is at address $1000_0000)? Well, there are a lot of reasons. But the primary reason is that this mov instruction always loads EAX from location mem. You cannot change the address from where it loads EAX. The former instructions, however, always load EAX from the location where p is pointing. This is very easy to change under program control. In fact, the simple instruction mov( &mem2, p ); will cause those same two instructions above to load EAX from mem2 the next time they execute. Consider the following instruction sequence:

```
mov( &i, p );           // Assume all variables are STATIC variables.
    .
    .
    .
if( some_expression ) then

    mov( &j, p );       // Assume the code above skips this instruction
        .               // and you get to the next instruction by
        .               // jumping to this point from somewhere else.
        .

endif;
mov( p, ebx );          // Assume both of the above code paths wind up
mov( [ebx], eax );      // down here.
```

This short example demonstrates two execution paths through the program. The first path loads the variable p with the address of the variable i. The second path through the code loads p with the address of the variable j. Both execution paths converge on the last two mov instructions that load EAX with i or j depending upon which execution path was taken. In many respects, this is like a *parameter* to a procedure in a high-level language like Pascal. Executing the same instructions accesses different variables depending on whose address (i or j) winds up in p.

### 4.5.2 Declaring Pointers in HLA

Because pointers are 32-bits long, you could simply use the dword type to allocate storage for your pointers. However, there is a much better way to do this: HLA provides the pointer to phrase specifically for declaring pointer variables. Consider the following example:

```
static
    b:          byte;
    d:          dword;
    pByteVar:   pointer to byte := &b;
    pDWordVar:  pointer to dword := &d;
```

This example demonstrates that it is possible to initialize as well as declare pointer variables in HLA. Note that you may only take addresses of static variables (static, readonly, and storage objects) with the address-of operator, so you can only initialize pointer variables with the addresses of static objects.

You can also define your own pointer types in the type section of an HLA program. For example, if you often use pointers to characters, you'll probably want to use a type declaration like the one in the following example.

```
type
     ptrChar:      pointer to char;

static
     cString:      ptrChar;
```

### 4.5.3  Pointer Constants and Pointer Constant Expressions

HLA allows two literal pointer constant forms: the address-of operator
followed by the name of a static variable or the constant NULL. In addition
to these two literal pointer constants, HLA also supports simple pointer
constant expressions.

The NULL pointer is the constant 0. Zero is an illegal address that will
raise an exception if you try to access it under modern operating systems.
Programs typically initialize pointers with NULL to indicate that a pointer has
explicitly *not* been initialized with a valid address.

In addition to simple address literals and the value 0, HLA allows very
simple constant expressions wherever a pointer constant is legal. Pointer
constant expressions take one of the three following forms:

```
&StaticVarName [ PureConstantExpression ]
&StaticVarName + PureConstantExpression
&StaticVarName - PureConstantExpression
```

The *PureConstantExpression* term is a numeric constant expression that
does not involve any pointer constants. This type of expression produces a
memory address that is the specified number of bytes before or after (- or +,
respectively) the *StaticVarName* variable in memory. Note that the first two
forms above are semantically equivalent; they both return a pointer constant
whose address is the sum of the static variable and the constant expression.

Because you can create pointer constant expressions, it should come as
no surprise to discover that HLA lets you define manifest pointer constants
in the const section. The program in Listing 4-5 demonstrates how you can
do this.

```
program PtrConstDemo;
#include( "stdlib.hhf" );

static
     b:  byte := 0;
         byte    1, 2, 3, 4, 5, 6, 7;

const
     pb := &b + 1;
```

```
begin PtrConstDemo;

    mov( pb, ebx );
    mov( [ebx], al );
    stdout.put( "Value at address pb = $", al, nl );

end PtrConstDemo;
```

*Listing 4-5: Pointer constant expressions in an HLA program*

Upon execution, this program prints the value of the byte just beyond b in memory (which contains the value $01).

### 4.5.4 Pointer Variables and Dynamic Memory Allocation

Pointer variables are the perfect place to store the return result from the HLA Standard Library mem.alloc function. The mem.alloc function returns the address of the storage it allocates in the EAX register; therefore, you can store the address directly into a pointer variable with a single mov instruction immediately after a call to mem.alloc:

```
type
    bytePtr:      pointer to byte;

var
    bPtr: bytePtr;

        .
        .
        .

    mem.alloc( 1024 );      // Allocate a block of 1,024 bytes.
    mov( eax, bPtr );       // Store address of block in bPtr.
        .
        .
        .

    mem.free( bPtr );       // Free the allocated block when done using it.
        .
        .
        .
```

### 4.5.5 Common Pointer Problems

Programmers encounter five common problems when using pointers. Some of these errors will cause your programs to immediately stop with a diagnostic message; other problems are more subtle, yielding incorrect results without otherwise reporting an error or simply affecting the performance of your program without displaying an error. These five problems are:

- Using an uninitialized pointer
- Using a pointer that contains an illegal value (e.g., NULL)

- Continuing to use mem.alloc'd storage after that storage has been freed
- Failing to mem.free storage once the program is finished using it
- Accessing indirect data using the wrong data type

The first problem above is using a pointer variable before you have assigned a valid memory address to the pointer. Beginning programmers often don't realize that declaring a pointer variable reserves storage only for the pointer itself; it does not reserve storage for the data that the pointer references. The short program in Listing 4-6 demonstrates this problem.

```
// Program to demonstrate use of
// an uninitialized pointer. Note
// that this program should terminate
// with a Memory Access Violation exception.

program UninitPtrDemo;
#include( "stdlib.hhf" );

static

    // Note: By default, variables in the
    // static section are initialized with
    // zero (NULL) hence the following
    // is actually initialized with NULL,
    // but that will still cause our program
    // to fail because we haven't initialized
    // the pointer with a valid memory address.

    Uninitialized: pointer to byte;

begin UninitPtrDemo;

    mov( Uninitialized, ebx );
    mov( [ebx], al );
    stdout.put( "Value at address Uninitialized: = $", al, nl );

end UninitPtrDemo;
```

*Listing 4-6: Uninitialized pointer demonstration*

Although variables you declare in the static section are, technically, initialized, static initialization still doesn't initialize the pointer in this program with a valid address (it initializes them with 0, which is NULL).

Of course, there is no such thing as a truly uninitialized variable on the 80x86. What you really have are variables that you've explicitly given an initial value and variables that just happen to inherit whatever bit pattern was in memory when storage for the variable was allocated. Much of the time, these garbage bit patterns lying around in memory don't correspond to a valid memory address. Attempting to *dereference* such a pointer (that is, access the data in memory at which it points) typically raises a *Memory Access Violation* exception.

Sometimes, however, those random bits in memory just happen to correspond to a valid memory location you can access. In this situation, the CPU will access the specified memory location without aborting the program. Although to a naive programmer this situation may seem preferable to stopping the program, in reality this is far worse because your defective program continues to run without alerting you to the problem. If you store data through an uninitialized pointer, you may very well overwrite the values of other important variables in memory. This defect can produce some very difficult-to-locate problems in your program.

The second problem programmers have with pointers is storing invalid address values into a pointer. The first problem above is actually a special case of this second problem (with garbage bits in memory supplying the invalid address rather than you producing it via a miscalculation). The effects are the same; if you attempt to dereference a pointer containing an invalid address either you will get a Memory Access Violation exception or you will access an unexpected memory location.

The third problem listed above is also known as the dangling pointer problem. To understand this problem, consider the following code fragment:

```
mem.alloc( 256 );   // Allocate some storage.
mov( eax, ptr );    // Save address away in a pointer variable.
     .
     .              // Code that uses the pointer variable ptr.
     .
mem.free( ptr );    // Free the storage associated with ptr.
     .
     .              // Code that does not change the value in ptr.
     .
mov( ptr, ebx );
mov( al, [ebx] );
```

In this example you will note that the program allocates 256 bytes of storage and saves the address of that storage in the ptr variable. Then the code uses this block of 256 bytes for a while and frees the storage, returning it to the system for other uses. Note that calling mem.free does not change the value of ptr in any way; ptr still points at the block of memory allocated by mem.alloc earlier. Indeed, mem.free does not change any data in this block, so upon return from mem.free, ptr still points at the data stored into the block by this code. However, note that the call to mem.free tells the system that the program no longer needs this 256-byte block of memory and the system can use this region of memory for other purposes. The mem.free function cannot enforce the fact that you will never access this data again; you are simply promising that you won't. Of course, the code fragment above breaks this promise; as you can see in the last two instructions above, the program fetches the value in ptr and accesses the data it points at in memory.

The biggest problem with dangling pointers is that you can get away with using them a good part of the time. As long as the system doesn't reuse the storage you've freed, using a dangling pointer produces no ill effects in your program. However, with each new call to mem.alloc, the system may decide to reuse the memory released by that previous call to mem.free. When this happens, any attempt to dereference the dangling pointer may produce some unintended consequences. The problems range from reading data that has been overwritten (by the new, legal use of the data storage), to overwriting the new data, to (the worst case) overwriting system heap management pointers (doing so will probably cause your program to crash). The solution is clear: *Never use a pointer value once you free the storage associated with that pointer.*

Of all the problems, the fourth (failing to free allocated storage) will probably have the least impact on the proper operation of your program. The following code fragment demonstrates this problem:

```
mem.alloc( 256 );
mov( eax, ptr );
        .           // Code that uses the data where ptr is pointing.
        .           // This code does not free up the storage
        .           // associated with ptr.
mem.alloc( 512 );
mov( eax, ptr );

// At this point, there is no way to reference the original
// block of 256 bytes pointed at by ptr.
```

In this example the program allocates 256 bytes of storage and references this storage using the ptr variable. At some later time the program allocates another block of bytes and overwrites the value in ptr with the address of this new block. Note that the former value in ptr is lost. Because the program no longer has this address value, there is no way to call mem.free to return the storage for later use. As a result, this memory is no longer available to your program. While making 256 bytes of memory inaccessible to your program may not seem like a big deal, imagine that this code is in a loop that repeats over and over again. With each execution of the loop the program loses another 256 bytes of memory. After a sufficient number of loop iterations, the program will exhaust the memory available on the heap. This problem is often called a *memory leak* because the effect is the same as though the memory bits were leaking out of your computer (yielding less and less available storage) during program execution.

Memory leaks are far less damaging than dangling pointers. Indeed, there are only two problems with memory leaks: the danger of running out of heap space (which, ultimately, may cause the program to abort, though this is rare) and performance problems due to virtual memory page swapping. Nevertheless, you should get in the habit of always freeing all storage once you have finished using it. When your program quits, the operating system reclaims all storage, including the data lost via memory leaks. Therefore, memory lost via a leak is lost only to your program, not the whole system.

The last problem with pointers is the lack of type-safe access. This can occur because HLA cannot and does not enforce pointer type checking. F example, consider the program in Listing 4-7.

```
// Program to demonstrate use of
// lack of type checking in pointer
// accesses.

program BadTypePtrDemo;
#include("stdlib.hhf" );

static
        ptr:    pointer to char;
        cnt:    uns32;

begin BadTypePtrDemo;

        // Allocate sufficient characters
        // to hold a line of text input
        // by the user:

        mem.alloc( 256 );
        mov( eax, ptr );


        // Okay, read the text a character
        // at a time by the user:

        stdout.put( "Enter a line of text: " );
        stdin.flushInput();
        mov( 0, cnt );
        mov( ptr, ebx );
        repeat

            stdin.getc();           // Read a character from the user.
            mov( al, [ebx] );       // Store the character away.
            inc( cnt );             // Bump up count of characters.
            inc( ebx );             // Point at next position in memory.

        until( stdin.eoln());


        // Okay, we've read a line of text from the user,
        // now display the data:

        mov( ptr, ebx );
        for( mov( cnt, ecx ); ecx > 0; dec( ecx )) do
```

```
            mov( [ebx], eax );
            stdout.put( "Current value is $", eax, nl );
            inc( ebx );

        endfor;
        mem.free( ptr );


end BadTypePtrDemo;
```

*Listing 4-7: Type-unsafe pointer access example*

This program reads in data from the user as character values and then displays the data as double-word hexadecimal values. While a powerful feature of assembly language is that it lets you ignore data types at will and automatically coerce the data without any effort, this power is a two-edged sword. If you make a mistake and access indirect data using the wrong data type, HLA and the 80x86 may not catch the mistake and your program may produce inaccurate results. Therefore, you need to take care when using pointers and indirection in your programs that you use the data consistently with respect to data type.

## 4.6  Composite Data Types

Composite data types, also known as *aggregate* data types, are those that are built up from other (generally scalar) data types. This chapter covers several of the more important composite data types—character strings, character sets, arrays, records, and unions. A string is a good example of a composite data type; it is a data structure built up from a sequence of individual characters and some other data.

## 4.7  Character Strings

After integer values, character strings are probably the most common data type that modern programs use. The 80x86 does support a handful of string instructions, but these instructions are really intended for block memory operations, not a specific implementation of a character string. Therefore, this section will concentrate mainly on the HLA definition of character strings and will also discuss the string-handling routines available in the HLA Standard Library.

In general, a character string is a sequence of ASCII characters that possesses two main attributes: a *length* and some *character data*. Different languages use different data structures to represent strings. To better understand the reasoning behind the design of HLA strings, it is probably instructive to look at two different string representations popularized by various high-level languages.

Without question, *zero-terminated strings* are probably the most commo string representation in use today because this is the native string format C, C++, C#, Java, and other languages. A zero-terminated string consists o sequence of zero or more ASCII characters ending with a 0 byte. For exampl in C/C++, the string "abc" requires 4 bytes: the three characters 'a', 'b', a 'c' followed by a 0. As you'll soon see, HLA character strings are upward compatible with zero-terminated strings, but in the meantime you shoul note that it is very easy to create zero-terminated strings in HLA. The easi place to do this is in the static section using code like the following:

```
static
        zeroTerminatedString:      char; @nostorage;
                                   byte "This is the zero-terminated string", 0
```

Remember, when using the @nostorage option, HLA doesn't reserve ar space for the variable, so the zeroTerminatedString variable's address in memo corresponds to the first character in the following byte directive. Whenever a character string appears in the byte directive as it does here, HLA emits ea character in the string to successive memory locations. The 0 value at the e of the string terminates this string.

HLA supports a zstring data type. However, those objects are double wo pointers that contain the address of a zstring, not the zero-terminated strin itself. Here is an example of a zstring declaration (and static initialization)

```
static
        zeroTerminatedString:      char; @nostorage;
                                   byte "This is the zero-terminated string", 0;
        zstrVar:                   zstring := &zeroTerminatedString;
```

Zero-terminated strings have two principal attributes: They are very simp to implement, and the strings can be any length. On the other hand, zero-terminated strings have a few drawbacks. First, though not usually importa zero-terminated strings cannot contain the NUL character (whose ASCII co is 0). Generally, this isn't a problem, but it does create havoc once in a whil The second problem with zero-terminated strings is that many operations them are somewhat inefficient. For example, to compute the length of a zero-terminated string, you must scan the entire string looking for that 0 by (counting characters up to the 0). The following program fragment demon-strates how to compute the length of the string above:

```
        mov( &zeroTerminatedString, ebx );
        mov( 0, eax );
        while( (type byte [ebx+eax]) <> 0 ) do

            inc( eax );

        endwhile;

        // String length is now in eax.
```

As you can see from this code, the time it takes to compute the length of the string is proportional to the length of the string; as the string gets longer, it takes longer to compute its length.

A second string format, *length-prefixed strings*, overcomes some of the problems with zero-terminated strings. Length-prefixed strings are common in languages like Pascal; they generally consist of a length byte followed by zero or more character values. The first byte specifies the string length, and the following bytes (up to the specified length) are the character data. In a length-prefixed scheme, the string abc would consist of the 4 bytes $03 (the string length) followed by a, b, and c. You can create length-prefixed strings in HLA using code like the following:

```
static
    lengthPrefixedString:char; @nostorage;
                    byte 3, "abc";
```

Counting the characters ahead of time and inserting them into the byte statement, as was done here, may seem like a major pain. Fortunately, there are ways to have HLA automatically compute the string length for you.

Length-prefixed strings solve the two major problems associated with zero-terminated strings. It is possible to include the NUL character in length-prefixed strings, and those operations on zero-terminated strings that are relatively inefficient (e.g., string length) are more efficient when using length-prefixed strings. However, length-prefixed strings have their own drawbacks. The principal drawback is that they are limited to a maximum of 255 characters in length (assuming a 1-byte length prefix).

HLA uses an expanded scheme for strings that is upward compatible with both zero-terminated and length-prefixed strings. HLA strings enjoy the advantages of both zero-terminated and length-prefixed strings without the disadvantages. In fact, the only drawback to HLA strings over these other formats is that HLA strings consume a few additional bytes (the overhead for an HLA string is 9 to 12 bytes compared to 1 byte for zero-terminated or length-prefixed strings, the overhead being the number of bytes needed above and beyond the actual characters in the string).

An HLA string value consists of four components. The first element is a double-word value that specifies the maximum number of characters that the string can hold. The second element is a double-word value specifying the current length of the string. The third component is the sequence of characters in the string. The final component is a zero-terminating byte. You could create an HLA-compatible string in the static section using code like the following:[5]

```
static
        align(4);
        dword 11;
        dword 11;
```

---

[5] Actually, there are some restrictions on the placement of HLA strings in memory. This text will not cover those issues. See the HLA documentation for more details.

```
TheString: char; @nostorage;
        byte "Hello there";
        byte 0;
```

Note that the address associated with the HLA string is the address of t
first character, not the maximum or current length values.

"So what is the difference between the current and maximum string
lengths?" you're probably wondering. In a literal string they are usually th
same. However, when you allocate storage for a string variable at runtim
you will normally specify the maximum number of characters that can g
into the string. When you store actual string data into the string, the numb
of characters you store must be less than or equal to this maximum value.
The HLA Standard Library string routines will raise an exception if you attem
to exceed this maximum length (something the C/C++ and Pascal format
can't do).

The terminating 0 byte at the end of the HLA string lets you treat an
HLA string as a zero-terminated string if it is more efficient or more convenie
to do so. For example, most calls to Windows, Mac OS X, FreeBSD, and Linu
require zero-terminated strings for their string parameters. Placing a 0 at t
end of an HLA string ensures compatibility with the operating system and
other library modules that use zero-terminated strings.

## 4.8 HLA Strings

As the previous section notes, HLA strings consist of four components: a
maximum length, a current string length, character data, and a zero-terminati
byte. However, HLA never requires you to create string data by manually
emitting these components yourself. HLA is smart enough to automaticall
construct this data for you whenever it sees a string literal constant. So if yc
use a string constant like the following, understand that somewhere HLA i
creating the four-component string in memory for you:

```
stdout.put( "This gets converted to a four-component string by HLA" );
```

HLA doesn't actually work directly with the string data described in th
previous section. Instead, when HLA sees a string object, it always works wi
a *pointer* to that object rather than working directly with the object. Withou
question, this is the most important fact to know about HLA strings and is t
biggest source of problems beginning HLA programmers have with strings in
HLA: *Strings are pointers!* A string variable consumes exactly 4 bytes, the san
as a pointer (because it is a pointer!). Having said all that, let's look at a simpl
string variable declaration in HLA:

```
static
        StrVariable:    string;
```

Because a string variable is a pointer, you must initialize it before you can use it. There are three general ways you may initialize a string variable with a legal string address: using static initializers, using the str.alloc routine, or calling some other HLA Standard Library function that initializes a string or returns a pointer to a string.

In one of the static declaration sections that allow initialized variables (static and readonly) you can initialize a string variable using the standard initialization syntax. For example:

```
static
    InitializedString: string := "This is my string";
```

Note that this does not initialize the string variable with the string data. Instead, HLA creates the string data structure (see Section 4.7) in a special, hidden, memory segment and initializes the InitializedString variable with the address of the first character in this string (the T in This). *Remember, strings are pointers!* The HLA compiler places the actual string data in a read-only memory segment. Therefore, you cannot modify the characters of this string literal at runtime. However, because the string variable (a pointer, remember) is in the static section, you can change the string variable so that it points at different string data.

Because string variables are pointers, you can load the value of a string variable into a 32-bit register. The pointer itself points at the first character position of the string. You can find the current string length in the double-word 4 bytes prior to this address, and you can find the maximum string length in the double-word 8 bytes prior to this address. The program in Listing 4-8 demonstrates one way to access this data.[6]

```
// Program to demonstrate accessing Length and Maxlength fields of a string.

program StrDemo;
#include( "stdlib.hhf" );

static
    theString:string := "String of length 19";

begin StrDemo;

    mov( theString, ebx );  // Get pointer to the string.

    mov( [ebx-4], eax );    // Get current length.
    mov( [ebx-8], ecx );    // Get maximum length.

    stdout.put
    (
```

---

[6] Note that this scheme is not recommended. If you need to extract the length information from a string, use the routines provided in the HLA string library for this purpose.

```
                    "theString = '", theString, "'", nl,
                    "length( theString )= ", (type uns32 eax ), nl,
                    "maxLength( theString )= ", (type uns32 ecx ), nl
            );

end StrDemo;
```

*Listing 4-8: Accessing the length and maximum length fields of a string*

When accessing the various fields of a string variable, it is not wise to access them using fixed numeric offsets as done in Listing 4-8. In the future the definition of an HLA string may change slightly. In particular, the offset to the maximum length and length fields are subject to change. A safer way to access string data is to coerce your string pointer using the str.strRec data type. The str.strRec data type is a record data type (see Section 4.25) that defines symbolic names for the offsets of the length and maximum length fields in the string data type. If the offsets to the length and maximum length fields were to change in a future version of HLA, then the definition in str.strRec would also change. So if you use str.strRec, then recompiling your program would automatically make any necessary changes to your program.

To use the str.strRec data type properly, you must first load the string pointer into a 32-bit register; for example, mov( SomeString, ebx );. Once the pointer to the string data is in a register, you can coerce that register to the str.strRec data type using the HLA construct (type str.strRec [ebx]) Finally, to access the length or maximum length fields, you would use either (type str.strRec [ebx]).length or (type str.strRec [ebx]).maxlen (respectively). Although there is a little more typing involved (versus using simple offsets like −4 or −8), these forms are far more descriptive and much safer than straight numeric offsets. The program in Listing 4-9 corrects the example in Listing 4-8 by using the str.strRec data type.

```
// Program to demonstrate accessing length and maxlen fields of a string

program LenMaxlenDemo;
#include( "stdlib.hhf" );

static
    theString:string := "String of length 19";

begin LenMaxlenDemo;

    mov( theString, ebx );  // Get pointer to the string.

    mov( (type str.strRec [ebx]).length, eax );  // Get current length.
    mov( (type str.strRec [ebx]).maxlen, ecx );  // Get maximum length.
```

```
    stdout.put
    (
        "theString = ", theString, "'", nl,
        "length( theString )= ", (type uns32 eax ), nl,
        "maxLength( theString )= ", (type uns32 ecx ), nl
    );

end LenMaxlenDemo;
```

*Listing 4-9: Correct way to access the* length *and* maxlen *fields of a string*

A second way to manipulate strings in HLA is to allocate storage on the heap to hold string data. Because strings can't directly use pointers returned by mem.alloc (string operations access the 8 bytes prior to the address), you shouldn't use mem.alloc to allocate storage for string data. Fortunately, the HLA Standard Library memory module provides a memory allocation routine specifically designed to allocate storage for strings: str.alloc. Like mem.alloc, str.alloc expects a single double-word parameter. This value specifies the maximum number of characters allowed in the string. The str.alloc routine will allocate the specified number of bytes of memory, plus between 9 and 13 additional bytes to hold the extra string information.[7]

The str.alloc routine will allocate storage for a string, initialize the maximum length to the value passed as the str.alloc parameter, initialize the current length to 0, and store a zero-terminating byte in the first character position of the string. After this, str.alloc returns the address of the zero-terminating byte (that is, the address of the first character element) in the EAX register.

Once you've allocated storage for a string, you can call various string-manipulation routines in the HLA Standard Library to manipulate the string. The next section discusses a few of the HLA string routines in detail; this section introduces a couple of string-related routines for the sake of example. The first such routine is the stdin.gets( *strvar* );. This routine reads a string from the user and stores the string data into the string storage pointed at by the string parameter (*strvar* in this case). If the user attempts to enter more characters than the maximum the string allows, then stdin.gets raises the ex.StringOverflow exception. The program in Listing 4-10 demonstrates the use of str.alloc.

```
// Program to demonstrate str.alloc and stdin.gets

program strallocDemo;
#include( "stdlib.hhf" );

static
    theString:string;

begin strallocDemo;
```

---

[7] str.alloc may allocate more than 9 bytes for the overhead data because the memory allocated to an HLA string must always be double-word aligned, and the total length of the data structure must be a multiple of 4.

```
    str.alloc( 16 );            // Allocate storage for the string and store
    mov( eax, theString );   // the pointer into the string variable.

    // Prompt the user and read the string from the user:

    stdout.put( "Enter a line of text (16 chars, max): " );
    stdin.flushInput();
    stdin.gets( theString );

    // Echo the string back to the user:

    stdout.put( "The string you entered was: ", theString, nl );

end strallocDemo;
```

*Listing 4-10: Reading a string from the user*

If you look closely, you'll see a slight defect in the program above. It allocates storage for the string by calling str.alloc, but it never frees the storag
allocated. Even though the program immediately exits after the last use o
the string variable, and the operating system will deallocate the storage, it
always a good idea to explicitly free up any storage you allocate. Doing s
keeps you in the habit of freeing allocated storage (so you don't forget to
it when it's important); also, programs have a way of growing such that an
innocent defect that doesn't affect anything in today's program becomes a
show-stopping defect in tomorrow's version.

To free storage you allocate via str.alloc, you must call the str.free routin
passing the string pointer as the single parameter. The program in Listing 4-1
a correction of the program Listing 4-10 with this defect corrected.

```
// Program to demonstrate str.alloc, str.free, and stdin.gets

program strfreeDemo;
#include( "stdlib.hhf" );

static
    theString:string;

begin strfreeDemo;

    str.alloc( 16 );            // Allocate storage for the string and store
    mov( eax, theString );   // the pointer into the string variable.

    // Prompt the user and read the string from the user:

    stdout.put( "Enter a line of text (16 chars, max): " );
    stdin.flushInput();
    stdin.gets( theString );
```

```
    // Echo the string back to the user:

    stdout.put( "The string you entered was: ", theString, nl );

    // Free up the storage allocated by str.alloc:

    str.free( theString );

end strfreeDemo;
```

*Listing 4-11: Corrected program that reads a string from the user*

When looking at this corrected program, please take note that the stdin.gets routine expects you to pass it a string parameter that points at an allocated string object. Without question, one of the most common mistakes beginning HLA programmers make is to call stdin.gets and pass it a string variable that they have not initialized. This may be getting old now, but keep in mind that *strings are pointers!* Like pointers, if you do not initialize a string with a valid address, your program will probably crash when you attempt to manipulate that string object. The call to str.alloc and the following mov instruction is how the programs above initialize the string pointer. If you are going to use string variables in your programs, you must ensure that you allocate storage for the string data prior to writing data to the string object.

Allocating storage for a string is such a common operation that many HLA Standard Library routines will automatically allocate the storage for you. Generally, such routines have an a_ prefix as part of their name. For example, the stdin.a_gets combines a call to str.alloc and stdin.gets into the same routine. This routine, which doesn't have any parameters, reads a line of text from the user, allocates a string object to hold the input data, and then returns a pointer to the string in the EAX register. Listing 4-12 presents an adaptation of the two programs in Listings 4-10 and 4-11 that uses stdin.a_gets.

```
// Program to demonstrate str.free and stdin.a_gets

program strfreeDemo2;
#include( "stdlib.hhf" );

static
    theString:string;

begin strfreeDemo2;


    // Prompt the user and read the string from the user:

    stdout.put( "Enter a line of text: " );
    stdin.flushInput();
    stdin.a_gets();
    mov( eax, theString );
```

```
    // Echo the string back to the user:

    stdout.put( "The string you entered was: ", theString, nl );

    // Free up the storage allocated by stdin.a_gets:

    str.free( theString );

end strfreeDemo2;
```

*Listing 4-12: Reading a string from the user with stdin.a_gets*

Note that, as before, you must still free up the storage stdin.a_gets alloca
by calling the str.free routine. One big difference between this routine a
the previous two is the fact that HLA will automatically allocate exactly enou
space for the string read from the user. In the previous programs, the cal
str.alloc allocates only 16 bytes. If the user types more than 16 characte
then the program raises an exception and quits. If the user types fewer
than 16 characters, then some space at the end of the string is wasted. T
stdin.a_gets routine, on the other hand, always allocates the minimum neces
space for the string read from the user. Because it allocates the storage, th
is little chance of overflow.[8]

## 4.9 Accessing the Characters Within a String

Extracting individual characters from a string is a very common task. It is
easy that HLA doesn't provide any specific procedure or language syntax
accomplish this—you simply use machine instructions to accomplish th
Once you have a pointer to the string data, a simple indexed addressing mod
will do the rest of the work for you.

Of course, the most important thing to keep in mind is that *strings ar
pointers*. Therefore, you cannot apply an indexed addressing mode directl
a string variable and expect to extract characters from the string. That is,
is a string variable, then mov( s[ebx], al ); does not fetch the character
position EBX in string s and place it in the AL register. Remember, s is ju
pointer variable; an addressing mode like s[ebx] will simply fetch the byte
offset EBX in memory starting at the address of s (see Figure 4-1).

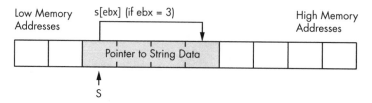

*Figure 4-1: Incorrectly indexing off a string variable*

---

[8] Actually, there are limits on the maximum number of characters that stdin.a_gets will allocate.
This is typically between 1,024 bytes and 4,096 bytes. See the HLA Standard Library source
listings and your operating system documentation for the exact value.

In Figure 4-1, assuming EBX contains 3, s[ebx] does not access the fourth character in the string s; instead it fetches the fourth byte of the pointer to the string data. It is very unlikely that this is what you would want. Figure 4-2 shows the operation that is necessary to fetch a character from the string, assuming EBX contains the value of s.

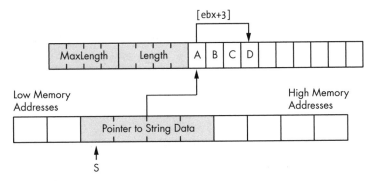

Figure 4-2: Correctly indexing off the value of a string variable

In Figure 4-2 EBX contains the value of string s. The value of s is a pointer to the actual string data in memory. Therefore, EBX will point at the first character of the string when you load the value of s into EBX. The following code demonstrates how to access the fourth character of string s in this fashion:

```
mov( s, ebx );        // Get pointer to string data into ebx.
mov( [ebx+3], al );   // Fetch the fourth character of the string.
```

If you want to load the character at a variable, rather than fixed, offset into the string, then you can use one of the 80x86's scaled indexed addressing modes to fetch the character. For example, if an uns32 variable index contains the desired offset into the string, you could use the following code to access the character at s[index]:

```
mov( s, ebx );          // Get address of string data into ebx.
mov( index, ecx );      // Get desired offset into string.
mov( [ebx+ecx], al );   // Get the desired character into al.
```

There is only one problem with the code above—it does not check to ensure that the character at offset index actually exists. If index is greater than the current length of the string, then this code will fetch a garbage byte from memory. Unless you can a priori determine that index is always less than the length of the string, code like this is dangerous to use. A better solution is to check the index against the string's current length before attempting to access the character. The following code provides one way to do this:

```
mov( s, ebx );
mov( index, ecx );
if( ecx < (type str.strRec [ebx]).length ) then
```

```
        mov( [ebx+ecx], al );

    else

        << Code that handles out-of-bounds string index >>

    endif;
```

In the else portion of this if statement you could take corrective action print an error message, or raise an exception. If you want to explicitly raise an exception, you can use the HLA raise statement to accomplish this. The syntax for the raise statement is

```
raise( integer_constant );
raise( reg32 );
```

The value of the *integer_constant* or 32-bit register must be an exception number. Usually, this is one of the predefined constants in the *excepts.hhf* header file. An appropriate exception to raise when a string index is greater than the length of the string is ex.StringIndexError. The following code demon strates raising this exception if the string index is out of bounds:

```
    mov( s, ebx );
    mov( index, ecx );
    if( ecx < (type str.strRec [ebx]).length ) then

        mov( [ebx+ecx], al );

    else

        raise( ex.StringIndexError );

    endif;
```

## 4.10   The HLA String Module and Other String-Related Routines

Although HLA provides a powerful definition for string data, the real power behind HLA's string capabilities lies in the HLA Standard Library, not in the definition of HLA string data. HLA provides hundreds of string-manipulation routines that far exceed the capabilities found in standard high-level languages like C/C++, Java, or Pascal; indeed, HLA's string-handling capabilities rival those in string-processing languages like Icon or SNOBOL4. This chapter discusses several of the string functions that the HLA Standard Library provides

Perhaps the most basic string operation you will need is to assign one string to another. There are three different ways to assign strings in HLA: by reference, by copying a string, and by duplicating a string. Of these, assignment by reference is the fastest and easiest. If you have two strings and you wish to assign one string to the other, a simple and fast way to do this is to copy the string pointer. The following code fragment demonstrates this:

```
static
        string1:                string  := "Some String Data";
        string2:                string;
            .
            .
            .
        mov( string1, eax );
        mov( eax, string2 );
            .
            .
            .
```

String assignment by reference is very efficient because it involves only two simple mov instructions regardless of the string length. Assignment by reference works great if you never modify the string data after the assignment operation. Do keep in mind, though, that both string variables (string1 and string2 in the example above) *wind up pointing at the same data.* So if you make a change to the data pointed at by one string variable, you will change the string data pointed at by the second string object because both objects point at the same data. Listing 4-13 provides a program that demonstrates this problem.

```
// Program to demonstrate the problem with string assignment by reference

program strRefAssignDemo;
#include( "stdlib.hhf" );

static
    string1:    string;
    string2:    string;

begin strRefAssignDemo;

    // Get a value into string1.

    forever

        stdout.put( "Enter a string with at least three characters: " );
        stdin.a_gets();
        mov( eax, string1 );

        breakif( (type str.strRec [eax]).length >= 3 );

        stdout.put( "Please enter a string with at least three chars:" nl );
```

```
    endfor;

    stdout.put( "You entered: '", string1, "'" nl );

    // Do the string assignment by copying the pointer.

    mov( string1, ebx );
    mov( ebx, string2 );

    stdout.put( "String1= '", string1, "'" nl );
    stdout.put( ""String2= '", string2, "'" nl );

    // Okay, modify the data in string1 by overwriting
    // the first three characters of the string (note that
    // a string pointer always points at the first character
    // position in the string and we know we've got at least
    // three characters here).

    mov( 'a', (type char [ebx]) );
    mov( 'b', (type char [ebx+1]) );
    mov( 'c', (type char [ebx+2]) );

    // Okay, demonstrate the problem with assignment via
    // pointer copy.

    stdout.put
    (
        "After assigning 'abc' to the first three characters in string1:"
        nl
        nl
    );
    stdout.put( "String1= '", string1, "'" nl );
    stdout.put( "String2= '", string2, "'" nl );

    str.free( string1 );      // Don't free string2 as well!


end strRefAssignDemo;
```

*Listing 4-13: Problem with string assignment by copying pointers*

Because both string1 and string2 point at the same string data in this example, any change you make to one string is reflected in the other. Wh: this is sometimes acceptable, most programmers expect assignment to produ‍ a different copy of a string; that is, they expect the semantics of string assignme‍ to produce two unique copies of the string data.

An important point to remember when using *copy by reference* (this ter‍ means copying a pointer) is that you have created an alias of the string da‍ The term *alias* means that you have two names for the same object in memor‍ (for example, in the program above, string1 and string2 are two different names for the same string data). When you read a program, it is reasonab‍ to expect that different variables refer to different memory objects. Aliase‍ violate this rule, thus making your program harder to read and understan‍

because you have to remember that aliases do not refer to different objects in memory. Failing to keep this in mind can lead to subtle bugs in your program. For instance, in the example above you have to remember that string1 and string2 are aliases so as not to free both objects at the end of the program. Worse still, you have to remember that string1 and string2 are aliases so that you don't continue to use string2 after freeing string1 because string2 would be a dangling reference at that point.

Because using copy by reference makes your programs harder to read and increases the possibility that you might introduce subtle defects into your programs, you might wonder why someone would use copy by reference at all. There are two reasons for this: First, copy by reference is very efficient; it involves only the execution of two mov instructions. Second, some algorithms actually depend on copy-by-reference semantics. Nevertheless, before using this technique you should carefully consider whether copying string pointers is the appropriate way to do a string assignment in your program.

The second way to assign one string to another is to copy the string data. The HLA Standard Library str.cpy routine provides this capability. A call to the str.cpy procedure uses the following call syntax:[9]

```
str.cpy( source_string, destination_string );
```

The source and destination strings must be string variables (pointers) or 32-bit registers containing the addresses of the string data in memory.

The str.cpy routine first checks the maximum length field of the destination string to ensure that it is at least as big as the source string's current length. If it is not, then str.cpy raises the ex.StringOverflow exception. If the destination string's maximum length is large enough, then str.cpy copies the string length, the characters, and the zero-terminating byte from the source string to the destination string. When this process is complete, the two strings point at identical data, but they do not point at the same data in memory.[10] The program in Listing 4-14 is a rework of the example in Listing 4-13 using str.cpy rather than copy by reference.

```
// Program to demonstrate string assignment using str.cpy

program strcpyDemo;
#include( "stdlib.hhf" );

static
    string1:    string;
    string2:    string;
```

---

[9] Warning to C/C++ users: note that the order of the operands is opposite that of the C Standard Library strcpy function.

[10] Unless, of course, both string pointers contained the same address to begin with, in which case str.cpy copies the string data over itself.

```
begin strcpyDemo;

    // Allocate storage for string2:

    str.alloc( 64 );
    mov( eax, string2 );

    // Get a value into string1.

    forever

        stdout.put( "Enter a string with at least three characters: " );
        stdin.a_gets();
        mov( eax, string1 );

        breakif( (type str.strRec [eax]).length >= 3 );

        stdout.put( "Please enter a string with at least three chars:" nl )

    endfor;


    // Do the string assignment via str.cpy.

    str.cpy( string1, string2 );

    stdout.put( "String1= '", string1, "'" nl );
    stdout.put( "String2= '", string2, "'" nl );

    // Okay, modify the data in string1 by overwriting
    // the first three characters of the string (note that
    // a string pointer always points at the first character
    // position in the string and we know we've got at least
    // three characters here).

    mov( string1, ebx );
    mov( 'a', (type char [ebx]) );
    mov( 'b', (type char [ebx+1]) );
    mov( 'c', (type char [ebx+2]) );

    // Okay, demonstrate that we have two different strings
    // because we used str.cpy to copy the data:

    stdout.put
    (
        "After assigning 'abc' to the first three characters in string1:"
        nl
        nl
    );
    stdout.put( "String1= '", string1, "'" nl );
    stdout.put( "String2= '", string2, "'" nl );
```

```
    // Note that we have to free the data associated with both
    // strings because they are not aliases of one another.

    str.free( string1 );
    str.free( string2 );


end strcpyDemo;
```

*Listing 4-14: Copying strings using str.cpy*

There are two important things to note about the program in Listing 4-14. First, note that this program begins by allocating storage for string2. Remember, the str.cpy routine does not allocate storage for the destination string; it assumes that the destination string already has storage allocated. Keep in mind that str.cpy does not initialize string2; it only copies data to the location where string2 is pointing. It is the program's responsibility to initialize the string by allocating sufficient memory before calling str.cpy. The second thing to notice here is that the program calls str.free to free up the storage for both string1 and string2 before the program quits.

Allocating storage for a string variable prior to calling str.cpy is so common that the HLA Standard Library provides a routine that allocates and copies the string: str.a_cpy. This routine uses the following call syntax:

```
str.a_cpy( source_string );
```

Note that there is no destination string. This routine looks at the length of the source string, allocates sufficient storage, makes a copy of the string, and then returns a pointer to the new string in the EAX register. The program in Listing 4-15 demonstrates how to do the same thing as the program in Listing 4-14 using the str.a_cpy procedure.

```
// Program to demonstrate string assignment using str.a_cpy

program stra_cpyDemo;
#include( "stdlib.hhf" );

static
    string1:    string;
    string2:    string;

begin stra_cpyDemo;


    // Get a value into string1.

    forever

        stdout.put( "Enter a string with at least three characters: " );
        stdin.a_gets();
        mov( eax, string1 );
```

```
                breakif( (type str.strRec [eax]).length >= 3 );

            stdout.put( "Please enter a string with at least three chars:" nl )

        endfor;


        // Do the string assignment via str.a_cpy.

        str.a_cpy( string1 );
        mov( eax, string2 );

        stdout.put( "String1= '", string1, "'" nl );
        stdout.put( "String2= '", string2, "'" nl );

        // Okay, modify the data in string1 by overwriting
        // the first three characters of the string (note that
        // a string pointer always points at the first character
        // position in the string and we know we've got at least
        // three characters here).

        mov( string1, ebx );
        mov( 'a', (type char [ebx]) );
        mov( 'b', (type char [ebx+1]) );
        mov( 'c', (type char [ebx+2]) );

        // Okay, demonstrate that we have two different strings
        // because we used str.cpy to copy the data:

        stdout.put
        (
            "After assigning 'abc' to the first three characters in string1:"
            nl
            nl
        );
        stdout.put( "String1= '", string1, "'" nl );
        stdout.put( "String2= '", string2, "'" nl );


        // Note that we have to free the data associated with both
        // strings because they are not aliases of one another.

        str.free( string1 );
        str.free( string2 );


end stra_cpyDemo;
```

*Listing 4-15: Copying strings using str.a_cpy*

*Whenever you use copy by reference or* str.a_cpy *to assign a string, don't forget to free the storage associated with the string when you have (completely) finished with that string's data. Failure to do so may produce a memory leak if you do not have another pointer to the previous string data lying around.*

Obtaining the length of a character string is so common that the HLA Standard Library provides a str.length routine specifically for this purpose. Of course, you can fetch the length by using the str.strRec data type to access the length field directly, but constant use of this mechanism can be tiring because it involves a lot of typing. The str.length routine provides a more compact and convenient way to fetch the length information. You call str.length using one of the following two formats:

```
str.length( Reg32 );
str.length( string_variable );
```

This routine returns the current string length in the EAX register.

Another pair of useful string routines is the str.cat and str.a_cat procedures. They use the following syntax:

```
str.cat( srcRStr, destLStr );
str.a_cat( srcLStr, srcRStr );
```

These two routines concatenate two strings (that is, they create a new string by joining the two strings together). The str.cat procedure concatenates the source string to the end of the destination string. Before the concatenation actually takes place, str.cat checks to make sure that the destination string is large enough to hold the concatenated result, and it raises the ex.StringOverflow exception if the destination string's maximum length is too small.

The str.a_cat routine, as its name suggests, allocates storage for the resulting string before doing the concatenation. This routine will allocate sufficient storage to hold the concatenated result, then it will copy the srcLStr to the allocated storage, next it will append the string data pointed at by srcRStr to the end of this new string, and then it will return a pointer to the new string in the EAX register.

*Note a potential source of confusion. The* str.cat *procedure concatenates its first operand to the end of the second operand. Therefore,* str.cat *follows the standard (src, dest) operand format present in many HLA statements. The* str.a_cat *routine, on the other hand, has two source operands rather than a source operand and a destination operand. The* str.a_cat *routine concatenates its two operands in an intuitive left-to-right fashion. This is the opposite of* str.cat. *Keep this in mind when using these two routines.*

Listing 4-16 demonstrates the use of the str.cat and str.a_cat routines.

```
// Program to demonstrate str.cat and str.a_cat

program strcatDemo;
#include( "stdlib.hhf" );

static
    UserName:   string;
    Hello:      string;
    a_Hello:    string;

begin strcatDemo;

    // Allocate storage for the concatenated result:

    str.alloc( 1024 );
    mov( eax, Hello );

    // Get some user input to use in this example:

    stdout.put( "Enter your name: " );
    stdin.flushInput();
    stdin.a_gets();
    mov( eax, UserName );

    // Use str.cat to combine the two strings:

    str.cpy( "Hello ", Hello );
    str.cat( UserName, Hello );

    // Use str.a_cat to combine the string strings:

    str.a_cat( "Hello ", UserName );
    mov( eax, a_Hello );

    stdout.put( "Concatenated string #1 is '", Hello, "'" nl );
    stdout.put( "Concatenated string #2 is '", a_Hello, "'" nl );

    str.free( UserName );
    str.free( a_Hello );
    str.free( Hello );

end strcatDemo;
```

Listing 4-16: Demonstration of str.cat and str.a_cat routines

The str.insert and str.a_insert routines are similar to the string-concatenation procedures. However, the str.insert and str.a_insert routines let you insert one string anywhere into another string, not just at the end of the string. The calling sequences for these two routines are:

```
str.insert( src, dest, index );
str.a_insert( src, dest, index );
```

These two routines insert the source string (*src*) into the destination string (*dest*) starting at character position *index*. The str.insert routine inserts the source string directly into the destination string; if the destination string is not large enough to hold both strings, str.insert raises an ex.StringOverflow exception. The str.a_insert routine first allocates storage for a new string on the heap, copies the destination string (*src*) to the new string, and then inserts the source string (*dest*) into this new string at the specified offset; str.a_insert returns a pointer to the new string in the EAX register.

Indexes into a string are zero based. This means that if you supply the value 0 as the index in str.insert or str.a_insert, then these routines will insert the source string before the first character of the destination string. Likewise, if the *index* is equal to the length of the string, then these routines will simply concatenate the source string to the end of the destination string.

**WARNING**    *If the index is greater than the length of the string, the* str.insert *and* str.a_insert *procedures will not raise an exception; instead, they will simply append the source string to the end of the destination string.*

The str.delete and str.a_delete routines let you remove characters from a string. They use the following calling sequence:

```
str.delete( strng, StartIndex, Length );
str.a_delete( strng, StartIndex, Length );
```

Both routines delete *Length* characters starting at character position *StartIndex* in string *strng*. The difference between the two is that str.delete deletes the characters directly from *strng*, whereas str.a_delete first allocates storage and copies *strng* and then deletes the characters from the new string (leaving *strng* untouched). The str.a_delete routine returns a pointer to the new string in the EAX register.

The str.delete and str.a_delete routines are very forgiving with respect to the values you pass in *StartIndex* and *Length*. If *StartIndex* is greater than the current length of the string, these routines do not delete any characters from the string. If *StartIndex* is less than the current length of the string, but *StartIndex+Length* is greater than the length of the string, then these routines will delete all characters from *StartIndex* to the end of the string.

Another very common string operation is the need to copy a portion of a string to another string without otherwise affecting the source string. The str.substr and str.a_substr routines provide this capability. These routines use the following syntax:

```
str.substr( src, dest, StartIndex, Length );
str.a_substr( src, StartIndex, Length );
```

The str.substr routine copies *Length* characters, starting at position *StartIndex*, from the *src* string to the *dest* string. The dest string must have sufficient storage to hold the new string or str.substr will raise an ex.StringOverflow exception. If the *StartIndex* value is greater than the length of the string, then `str.substr` will raise an `ex.StringIndexError` exception. If *StartIndex+Length* is greater than the length of the source string, but *StartInd* is less than the length of the string, then `str.substr` will extract only thos characters from *StartIndex* to the end of the string.

The `str.a_substr` procedure behaves in a fashion nearly identical to `str.substr`, except it allocates storage on the heap for the destination strin `str.a_substr` handles exceptions identically to `str.substr`, except it never raises a string overflow exception because this will never occur.[11] As you c probably guess by now, `str.a_substr` returns a pointer to the newly allocate string in the EAX register.

After you have been working with string data for a little while, the nee will invariably arise to compare two strings. A first attempt at string compariso using the standard HLA relational operators, will compile but not necessarily produce the desired result:

```
mov( s1, eax );
if( eax = s2 ) then

    << Code to execute if the strings are equal >>

else

    << Code to execute if the strings are not equal >>

endif;
```

Remember, *strings are pointers.* This code compares the two pointers to see if they are equal. If they are equal, clearly the two strings are equal (becau both s1 and s2 point at the exact same string data). However, the fact that t two pointers are different doesn't necessarily mean that the strings are no equivalent. Both s1 and s2 could contain different values (that is, they poi at different addresses in memory), yet the string data at those two address could be identical. Most programmers expect a string comparison for equality be true if the data for the two strings is the same. Clearly a pointer compariso does not provide this type of comparison. To overcome this problem, the HLA Standard Library provides a set of string-comparison routines that wi compare the string data, not just their pointers. These routines use the followi calling sequences:

```
str.eq( src1, src2 );
str.ne( src1, src2 );
str.lt( src1, src2 );
str.le( src1, src2 );
str.gt( src1, src2 );
str.ge( src1, src2 );
```

[11] Technically, `str.a_substr`, like all routines that call `mem.alloc` to allocate storage, can raise a `ex.MemoryAllocationFailure` exception, but this is very unlikely to occur.

Each of these routines compares the *src1* string to the *src2* string and returns true (1) or false (0) in the EAX register depending on the comparison. For example, str.eq( s1, s2 ); returns true in EAX if s1 is equal to s2. HLA provides a small extension that allows you to use the string-comparison routines within an if statement.[12] The following code demonstrates the use of some of these comparison routines within an if statement:

```
stdout.put( "Enter a single word: " );
stdin.a_gets();
if( str.eq( eax, "Hello" )) then

    stdout.put( "You entered 'Hello'", nl );

endif;
str.free( eax );
```

Note that the string the user enters in this example must exactly match Hello, including the use of an uppercase *H* at the beginning of the string. When processing user input, it is best to ignore alphabetic case in string comparisons because different users have different ideas about when they should be pressing the SHIFT key on the keyboard. An easy solution is to use the HLA case-insensitive string-comparison functions. These routines compare two strings, ignoring any differences in alphabetic case. These routines use the following calling sequences:

```
str.ieq( src1, src2 );
str.ine( src1, src2 );
str.ilt( src1, src2 );
str.ile( src1, src2 );
str.igt( src1, src2 );
str.ige( src1, src2 );
```

Other than they treat uppercase characters the same as their lowercase equivalents, these routines behave exactly like the former routines, returning true or false in EAX depending on the result of the comparison.

Like most high-level languages, HLA compares strings using *lexicographical ordering*. This means that two strings are equal if and only if their lengths are the same and the corresponding characters in the two strings are exactly the same. For less-than or greater-than comparisons, lexicographical ordering corresponds to the way words appear in a dictionary. That is, a is less than b is less than c, and so on. Actually, HLA compares the strings using the ASCII numeric codes for the characters, so if you are unsure whether a is less than a period, simply consult the ASCII character chart (incidentally, a is greater than a period in the ASCII character set, just in case you were wondering).

If two strings have different lengths, lexicographical ordering worries about the length only if the two strings exactly match through the length of the shorter string. If this is the case, then the longer string is greater than the

[12] This extension is actually a little more general than this section describes. Chapter 7 explains it fully.

shorter string (and, conversely, the shorter string is less than the longer string. Note, however, that if the characters in the two strings do not match at all then HLA's string-comparison routines ignore the length of the string; for example, z is always greater than aaaaa, even though it is shorter.

The str.eq routine checks to see if two strings are equal. Sometimes, however, you might want to know whether one string *contains* another string. For example, you may want to know if some string contains the substring north or south to determine some action to take in a game. The HLA str.index routine lets you check to see if one string is contained as a substring of another. The str.index routine uses the following calling sequence:

---

str.index( StrToSearch, SubstrToSearchFor );

---

This function returns, in EAX, the offset into *StrToSearch* where *SubstrToSearchFor* appears. This routine returns −1 in EAX if *SubstrToSearchFor* is not present in *StrToSearch*. Note that str.index will do a case-sensitive search. Therefore, the strings must exactly match. There is no case-insensitive variant of str.index you can use.[13]

The HLA strings module contains hundreds of routines besides those appearing in this section. Space limitations and prerequisite knowledge prevent the presentation of all those functions here; however, this does not mean that the remaining string functions are unimportant. You should definitely take a look at the HLA Standard Library documentation to learn everything you can about the powerful HLA string library routines.

## 4.11 In-Memory Conversions

The HLA Standard Library's string module contains dozens of routines for converting between strings and other data formats. Although it's a little premature in this text to present a complete description of those functions, would be rather criminal not to discuss at least one of the available functions, the str.put routine. This routine encapsulates the capabilities of many of the other string-conversion functions, so if you learn how to use this one, you'll have most of the capabilities of those other routines at your disposal.

You use the str.put routine in a manner very similar to the stdout.put routine. The only difference is that the str.put routine "writes" its data to a string instead of the standard output device. A call to str.put has the following syntax:

---

str.put( destString, values_to_convert );

---

Here's an example of a call to str.put:

---

str.put( destString, "I =", i:4, " J= ", j, " s=", s );

---

---

[13] However, HLA does provide routines that will convert all the characters in a string to one case or another. So you can make copies of the strings, convert all the characters in both copies to lowercase, and then search using these converted strings. This will achieve the same result.

*Generally, you would not put a newline character sequence at the end of the string as you would if you were printing the string to the standard output device.*

The *destString* parameter at the beginning of the str.put parameter list must be a string variable, and it must already have storage associated with it. If str.put attempts to store more characters than allowed into the *destString* parameter, then this function raises the ex.StringOverflow exception.

Most of the time you won't know the length of the string that str.put will produce. In those instances, you should allocate storage for a very large string, one that is much larger than you expect, and use this string object as the first parameter of the str.put call. This will prevent an exception from crashing your program. Generally, if you expect to produce about one screen line of text, then you should probably allocate at least 256 characters for the destination string. If you're creating longer strings, you should probably use a default of 1,024 characters (or more, if you're going to produce *really* large strings).

Here's an example:

```
static
    s: string;
        .
        .
        .
    str.alloc( 256 );
    mov( eax, s );
        .
        .
        .
    str.put( s, "R: ", r:16:4, " strval: '", strval:-10, "'" );
```

You can use the str.put routine to convert any data to a string that you can print using stdout.put. You will probably find this routine invaluable for common value-to-string conversions.

## 4.12  Character Sets

Character sets are another composite data type, like strings, built upon the character data type. A character set is a mathematical set of characters with the most important attribute being membership. That is, a character is either a member of a set or it is not a member of a set. The concept of sequence (for example, whether one character comes before another, as in a string) doesn't apply to character sets. Also, membership is a binary relation; a character is either in the set or it is not in the set; you cannot have multiple copies of the same character in a character set. Various operations are possible on character sets, including the mathematical set operations of union, intersection, difference, and membership test.

HLA implements a restricted form of character sets that allows set members to be any of the 128 standard ASCII characters (that is, HLA's character set facilities do not support extended character codes in the range 128..255). Despite this restriction, HLA's character set facilities are very powerful and are handy when writing programs that work with string data. The following sections describe the implementation and use of HLA's character set facilities you may take advantage of character sets in your own programs.

## 4.13 Character Set Implementation in HLA

There are many different ways to represent character sets in an assembly language program. HLA implements character sets using an array of 128 boolean values. Each boolean value determines whether the corresponding character is a member of the character set; that is, a true boolean value indicates that the corresponding character is a member of the set, whereas a false value indicates that the character is not a member of the set. To conserve memory HLA allocates only a single bit for each character in the set; therefore, HLA character sets consume 16 bytes of memory because there are 128 bits in bytes. This array of 128 bits is organized in memory as shown in Figure 4-3.

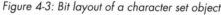

Byte 15 Byte 0

*Figure 4-3: Bit layout of a character set object*

Bit 0 of byte 0 corresponds to ASCII code 0 (the NUL character). If the bit is 1, then the character set contains the NUL character; if this bit contains false, then the character set does not contain the NUL character. Likewise bit 0 of byte 1 (the ninth bit in the 128-bit array) corresponds to the backspace character (ASCII code is 8). Bit 1 of byte 8 corresponds to ASCII code 65, uppercase A. Bit 65 will contain a 1 if A is a current member of the character set; it will contain 0 if A is not a member of the set.

While there are other possible ways to implement character sets, with this bit-vector implementation it is very easy to implement set operations such as union, intersection, difference comparison, and membership tests.

HLA supports character set variables using the cset data type. To declare a character set variable, you would use a declaration like the following:

```
static
    CharSetVar: cset;
```

This declaration will reserve 16 bytes of storage to hold the 128 bits needed to represent a set of ASCII characters.

Although it is possible to manipulate the bits in a character set using instructions like and, or, xor, and so on, the 80x86 instruction set includes several bit test, set, reset, and complement instructions that are nearly perfect for manipulating character sets. The bt (bit test) instruction, for example, will copy a single bit in memory to the carry flag. The bt instruction allows the following syntactical forms.

```
bt( BitNumber, BitsToTest );

bt( reg16, reg16 );
bt( reg32, reg32 );
bt( constant, reg16 );
bt( constant, reg32 );

bt( reg16, mem16 );
bt( reg32, mem32 );     // HLA treats cset objects as dwords within bt.
bt( constant, mem16 );
bt( constant, mem32 );  // HLA treats cset objects as dwords within bt.
```

The first operand holds a bit number, and the second operand specifies a register or memory location whose bit should be copied into the carry flag. If the second operand is a register, the first operand must contain a value in the range $0..n-1$, where $n$ is the number of bits in the second operand. If the first operand is a constant and the second operand is a memory location, the constant must be in the range 0..255. Here are some examples of these instructions:

```
bt( 7, ax );          // Copies bit 7 of ax into the carry flag (CF).
mov( 20, eax );
bt( eax, ebx );       // Copies bit 20 of ebx into CF.

// Copies bit 0 of the byte at CharSetVar+3 into CF.

bt( 24, CharSetVar );

// Copies bit 4 of the byte at DWmem+2 into CF.

bt( eax, DWmem);
```

The bt instruction turns out to be quite useful for testing set membership. For example, to see if the character A is a member of a character set, you could use a code sequence like the following:

```
bt( 'A', CharSetVar );
if( @c ) then

    << Do something if 'A' is a member of the set. >>

endif;
```

The bts (bit test and set), btr (bit test and reset), and btc (bit test and complement) instructions are also useful for manipulating character set variables. Like the bt instruction, these instructions copy the specified bit into the carry flag; after copying the specified bit, these instructions will set (bts), reset/clear (btr), or complement/invert (btc) the specified bit. Therefore, you can use the bts instruction to add a character to a character set via set union (that is, it adds a character to the set if the character was not already a member of the set; otherwise the set is unaffected). You can use the b instruction to remove a character from a character set via set intersectic (that is, it removes a character from the set if and only if it was previously the set; otherwise it has no effect on the set). The btc instruction lets you a character to the set if it wasn't previously in the set; it removes the charac from the set if it was previously a member (that is, it toggles the members of that character in the set).

## 4.14 HLA Character Set Constants and Character Set Expressions

HLA supports literal character set constants. These cset constants make i easy to initialize cset variables at compile time and allow you to easily pass character set constants as procedure parameters. An HLA character set const takes the following form:

```
{ Comma_separated_list_of_characters_and_character_ranges }
```

The following is an example of a simple character set holding the nume digit characters:

```
{ '0', '1', '2', '3', '4', '5', '6', '7', '8', '9' }
```

When specifying a character set literal that has several contiguous valu HLA lets you concisely specify the values using only the starting and endi values of the range thusly:

```
{ '0'..'9' }
```

You may combine characters and various ranges within the same charact set constant. For example, the following character set constant is all the alphanumeric characters:

```
{ '0'..'9', 'a'..'z', 'A'..'Z' }
```

You can use these cset literal constants as initializers in the const and sections. The following example demonstrates how to create the symbolic constant AlphaNumeric using the character set above:

```
const
    AlphaNumeric: cset := {'0'..'9', 'a'..'z', 'A'..'Z' };
```

After the above declaration, you can use the identifier AlphaNumeric anywh the character set literal is legal.

You can also use character set literals (and, of course, character set symbolic constants) as the initializer field for a static or readonly variable. The following code fragment demonstrates this:

```
static
    Alphabetic: cset := { 'a'..'z', 'A'..'Z' };
```

Anywhere you can use a character set literal constant, a character set constant expression is also legal. Table 4-2 shows the operators that HLA supports in character set constant expressions.

**Table 4-2:** HLA Character Set Operators

| Operator | Description |
| --- | --- |
| CSetConst1 + CSetConst2 | Computes the union of the two sets. The set union is the set of all characters that are in either set. |
| CSetConst1 * CSetConst2 | Computes the intersection of the two sets. The set intersection is the set of all characters that appear in both operand sets. |
| CSetConst1 - CSetConst2 | Computes the set difference of the two sets. The set difference is the set of characters that appear in the first set but do not appear in the second set. |
| -CSetConst | Computes the set complement. The set complement is the set of all characters not in the set. |

Note that these operators produce only compile-time results. That is, the expressions above are computed by the compiler during compilation; they do not emit any machine code. If you want to perform these operations on two different sets while your program is running, the HLA Standard Library provides routines you can call to achieve the results you desire. HLA also provides other compile-time character set operators.

# 4.15  Character Set Support in the HLA Standard Library

The HLA Standard Library provides several character set routines you may find useful. The character set support routines fall into four categories: standard character set functions, character set tests, character set conversions, and character set I/O. This section describes these routines in the HLA Standard Library.

To begin with, let's consider the Standard Library routines that help you construct character sets. These routines include cs.empty, cs.cpy, cs.charToCset, cs.unionChar, cs.removeChar, cs.rangeChar, cs.strToCset, and cs.unionStr. These procedures let you build up character sets at runtime using character and string objects.

The cs.empty procedure initializes a character set variable with the empty set by setting all the bits in the character set to 0. This procedure call uses the following syntax (CSvar is a character set variable):

```
cs.empty( CSvar );
```

The cs.cpy procedure copies one character set to another, replacing data previously held by the destination character set. The syntax for cs.cpy

```
cs.cpy( srcCsetValue, destCsetVar );
```

The cs.cpy source character set can be either a character set constant a character set variable. The destination character set must be a character variable.

The cs.unionChar procedure adds a character to a character set. It uses the following calling sequence:

```
cs.unionChar( CharVar, CSvar );
```

This call will add the first parameter, a character, to the set via set unic Note that you could use the bts instruction to achieve this same result; howev the cs.unionChar call is often more convenient. The character value must b in the range #0..#127.

The cs.charToCset function creates a singleton set (a set containing a sing character). The calling format for this function is:

```
cs.charToCset( CharValue, CSvar );
```

The first operand, the character value CharValue, can be an 8-bit registe a constant, or a character variable that holds a value in the range #0..#127 The second operand (CSvar) must be a character set variable. This functio clears the destination character set to all zeros and then unions the specifi character into the character set.

The cs.removeChar procedure lets you remove a single character from a character set without affecting the other characters in the set. This functic uses the same syntax as cs.charToCset, and the parameters have the same attributes. The calling sequence is:

```
cs.removeChar( CharValue, CSvar );
```

Note that if the character was not in the CSVar set to begin with, cs.removeCh will not affect the set. This function roughly corresponds to the btr instructior

The cs.rangeChar constructs a character set containing all the characte: between two characters you pass as parameters. This function sets all bits outside the range of these two characters to 0. The calling sequence is:

```
cs.rangeChar( LowerBoundChar, UpperBoundChar, CSVar );
```

The LowerBoundChar and UpperBoundChar parameters can be constants, registers, or character variables. The values held in LowerBoundChar and UpperBoundChar must be in the range #0..#127. CSVar, the destination character set, must be a cset variable.

The cs.strToCset procedure creates a new character set containing the union of all the characters in a character string. This procedure begins by setting the destination character set to the empty set, and then it unions in the characters in the string one by one until it exhausts all characters in the string. The calling sequence is:

```
cs.strToCset( StringValue, CSVar );
```

Technically, the *StringValue* parameter can be a string constant as well as a string variable; however, it doesn't make any sense to call cs.strToCset this way because cs.cpy is a much more efficient way to initialize a character set with a constant set of characters. As usual, the destination character set must be a cset variable. Typically, you'd use this function to create a character set based on a string input by the user.

The cs.unionStr procedure will add the characters in a string to an existing character set. Like cs.strToCset, you'd normally use this function to union characters into a set based on a string input by the user. The calling sequence for this is:

```
cs.unionStr( StringValue, CSVar );
```

Standard set operations include union, intersection, and set difference. The HLA Standard Library routines cs.setunion, cs.intersection, and cs.difference provide these operations, respectively.[14] These routines all use the same calling sequence:

```
cs.setunion( srcCset, destCset );
cs.intersection( srcCset, destCset );
cs.difference( srcCset, destCset );
```

The first parameter can be a character set constant or a character set variable. The second parameter must be a character set variable. These procedures compute *destCset := destCset op srcCset* where *op* represents set union, intersection, or difference, depending on the function call.

The third category of character set routines test character sets in various ways. They typically return a boolean value indicating the result of the test. The HLA character set routines in this category include cs.IsEmpty, cs.member, cs.subset, cs.psubset, cs.superset, cs.psuperset, cs.eq, and cs.ne.

The cs.IsEmpty function tests a character set to see if it is the empty set. The function returns true or false in the EAX register. This function uses the following calling sequence:

```
cs.IsEmpty( CSetValue );
```

---

[14] cs.setunion was used rather than cs.union because *union* is an HLA reserved word.

The single parameter may be a constant or a character set variable, altho█
it doesn't make much sense to pass a character set constant to this procedur█
(because you would know at compile time whether this set is empty).

The cs.member function tests to see if a character value is a member of █
set. This function returns true in the EAX register if the character is a mem█
of the set. Note that you can use the bt instruction to test this same conditi█
However, the cs.member function is probably a little more convenient to us█
the character argument is not a constant. The calling sequence for cs.membe█

---

```
cs.member( CharValue, CsetValue );
```

---

The first parameter is an 8-bit register, character variable, or a consta█
The second parameter is either a character set constant or a character set █
variable. It would be unusual for both parameters to be constants.

The cs.subset, cs.psubset (proper subset), cs.superset, and cs.psuperse█
(proper superset) functions let you check to see if one character set is a subse█
superset of another. The calling sequence for these four routines is nearl█
identical; it is one of the following:

---

```
cs.subset( CsetValue1, CsetValue2 );
cs.psubset( CsetValue1, CsetValue2 );
cs.superset( CsetValue1, CsetValue2 );
cs.psuperset( CsetValue1, CsetValue2 );
```

---

These routines compare the first parameter against the second parame█
and return true or false in the EAX register depending upon the result. O█
set is a subset of another if all the members of the first character set are pres█
in the second character set. It is a proper subset if the second (right) charac█
set also contains characters not found in the first (left) character set. Likewi█
one character set is a superset of another if it contains all the characters i█
the second set (and possibly more). A proper superset contains additiona█
characters beyond those found in the second set. The parameters can be
either character set variables or character set constants; however, it would
unusual for both parameters to be character set constants (because you c█
determine this at compile time, there would be no need to call a runtime
function to compute this).

The cs.eq and cs.ne functions check to see if two sets are equal or not
equal. These functions return true or false in EAX depending upon the s█
comparison. The calling sequence is identical to the sub/superset functio█
above:

---

```
cs.eq( CsetValue1, CsetValue2 );
cs.ne( CsetValue1, CsetValue2 );
```

---

Note that there are no functions that test for less than, less than or equal, greater than, or greater than or equal. The subset and proper subset functions are the equivalent of less than or equal and less than (respectively); likewise, the superset and proper superset functions are equivalent to greater than or equal and greater than (respectively).

The cs.extract routine removes an arbitrary character from a character set and returns that character in the EAX register.[15] The calling sequence is the following:

```
cs.extract( CsetVar );
```

The single parameter must be a character set variable. Note that this function will modify the character set variable by removing some character from the character set. This function returns $FFFF_FFFF (−1) in EAX if the character set was empty prior to the call.

In addition to the routines found in the cset.hhf (character set) library module, the string and standard output modules also provide functions that allow or expect character set parameters. For example, if you supply a character set value as a parameter to stdout.put, the stdout.put routine will print the characters currently in the set. See the HLA Standard Library documentation for more details on character set–handling procedures.

## 4.16  Using Character Sets in Your HLA Programs

Character sets are valuable for many different purposes in your programs. For example, one common use of character sets is to validate user input. This section will also present a couple of other applications for character sets to help you start thinking about how you could use them in your program.

Consider the following short code segment that gets a yes/no–type answer from the user:

```
static
    answer: char;
        .
        .
        .
    repeat
            .
            .
            .
        stdout.put( "Would you like to play again? " );
        stdin.FlushInput();
        stdin.get( answer );

    until( answer = 'n' );
```

---

[15] This routine returns the character in AL and zeros out the H.O. 3 bytes of EAX.

A major problem with this code sequence is that it will stop only if the user types a lowercase *n* character. If the user types anything other than *n* (including uppercase *N*), the program will treat this as an affirmative answer and transfer back to the beginning of the repeat..until loop. A better solution would be to validate the user input before the until clause above to ensure that the user has only typed *n*, *N*, *y*, or *Y*. The following code sequence will accomplish this:

```
repeat
        .
        .
        .
    repeat

        stdout.put( "Would you like to play again? " );
        stdin.FlushInput();
        stdin.get( answer );

    until( cs.member( answer, { 'n', 'N', 'Y', 'y' } ) );
    if( answer = 'N' ) then

        mov( 'n', answer );

    endif;

until( answer = 'n' );
```

## 4.17  Arrays

Along with strings, arrays are probably the most commonly used composite data. Yet most beginning programmers don't understand how arrays operate internally and their associated efficiency trade-offs. It's surprising how many novice (and even advanced!) programmers view arrays from a completely different perspective once they learn how to deal with arrays at the machine level.

Abstractly, an array is an aggregate data type whose members (elements) are all the same type. Selection of a member from the array is by an integer index.[16] Different indices select unique elements of the array. This text assumes that the integer indices are contiguous (though this is by no means required). That is, if the number *x* is a valid index into the array and *y* is also a valid index, with $x < y$, then all *i* such that $x < i < y$ are valid indices.

Whenever you apply the indexing operator to an array, the result is the specific array element chosen by that index. For example, A[i] chooses the *i*th element from array A. Note that there is no formal requirement that element *i* be anywhere near element *i+1* in memory. As long as A[i] always

---

[16] Or it could be some value whose underlying representation is integer, such as character, enumerated, and boolean types.

refers to the same memory location and A[i+1] always refers to its corresponding location (and the two are different), the definition of an array is satisfied.

In this text, we assume that array elements occupy contiguous locations in memory. An array with five elements will appear in memory as Figure 4-4 shows.

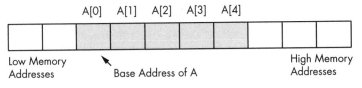

Figure 4-4: Array layout in memory

The *base address* of an array is the address of the first element on the array and always appears in the lowest memory location. The second array element directly follows the first in memory, the third element follows the second, and so on. Note that there is no requirement that the indices start at 0. They may start with any number as long as they are contiguous. However, for the purposes of discussion, this book will start all indexes at 0.

To access an element of an array, you need a function that translates an array index to the address of the indexed element. For a single-dimensional array, this function is very simple. It is:

Element_Address = Base_Address + ((Index - Initial_Index) * Element_Size)

where Initial_Index is the value of the first index in the array (which you can ignore if 0) and the value Element_Size is the size, in bytes, of an individual array element.

## 4.18 Declaring Arrays in Your HLA Programs

Before you can access elements of an array, you need to set aside storage for that array. Fortunately, array declarations build on the declarations you've already seen. To allocate n elements in an array, you would use a declaration like the following in one of the variable declaration sections:

ArrayName: basetype[n];

ArrayName is the name of the array variable and basetype is the type of an element of that array. This sets aside storage for the array. To obtain the base address of the array, just use ArrayName.

The [n] suffix tells HLA to duplicate the object n times. Now let's look at some specific examples.

```
static

    CharArray: char[128];     // Character array with elements 0..127.
    ByteArray: byte[10];      // Array of bytes with elements 0..9.
    PtrArray:  dword[4];      // Array of double words with elements 0..3.
```

These examples all allocate storage for uninitialized arrays. You may a
specify that the elements of the arrays be initialized using declarations lik
the following in the static and readonly sections:

```
RealArray: real32[8] := [ 1.0, 1.0, 1.0, 1.0, 1.0, 1.0, 1.0, 1.0 ];
IntegerAry: int32[8] := [ 1, 1, 1, 1, 1, 1, 1, 1 ];
```

These definitions both create arrays with eight elements. The first definiti
initializes each 4-byte real value to 1.0, the second declaration initializes ea
int32 element to 1. Note that the number of constants within the square brack
must exactly match the size of the array.

This initialization mechanism is fine if you want each element of the ar
to have the same value. What if you want to initialize each element of the
array with a (possibly) different value? No sweat, just specify a different set
values in the list surrounded by the square brackets in the example above:

```
RealArray: real32[8] := [ 1.0, 2.0, 3.0, 4.0, 5.0, 6.0, 7.0, 8.0 ];
IntegerAry: int32[8] := [ 1, 2, 3, 4, 5, 6, 7, 8 ];
```

## 4.19  HLA Array Constants

The last few examples in the previous section demonstrate the use of HLA
array constants. An HLA array constant is nothing more than a list of value
surrounded by a pair of brackets. The following are all legal array constan

```
[ 1, 2, 3, 4 ]
[ 2.0, 3.14159, 1.0, 0.5 ]
[ 'a', 'b', 'c', 'd' ]
[ "Hello", "world", "of", "assembly" ]
```

(Note that this last array constant contains four double-word pointers
the four HLA strings appearing elsewhere in memory.)

As you saw in the previous section, you can use array constants in the
static and readonly sections to provide initial values for array variables. The
number of comma-separated items in an array constant must exactly match
the number of array elements in the variable declaration. Likewise, the typ
of each of the array constant's elements must match the array variable's
declared base type.

Using array constants to initialize small arrays is very convenient. Of cours
if your array has several thousand elements, entering them will be tedious.
Most arrays initialized this way have no more than a couple hundred entrie
and generally far less than 100. It is reasonable to use an array constant to

initialize such variables. However, at some point initializing arrays in this manner will become far too tedious and error prone. You probably would not want to manually initialize an array with 1,000 different elements using an array constant. However, if you want to initialize all the elements of an array with the same value, HLA does provide a special array constant syntax for doing so. Consider the following declaration:

```
BigArray: uns32[ 1000 ] := 1000 dup [ 1 ];
```

This declaration creates a 1,000-element integer array initializing each element to one. The `1000 dup [ 1 ]` expression tells HLA to create an array constant by duplicating the single value `[ 1 ]` one thousand times. You can even use the `dup` operator to duplicate a series of values (rather than a single value), as the following example indicates:

```
SixteenInts: int32[16] := 4 dup [1,2,3,4];
```

This example initializes SixteenInts with four copies of the sequence 1,2,3,4, yielding a total of 16 different integers (i.e., 1, 2, 3, 4, 1, 2, 3, 4, 1, 2, 3, 4, 1, 2, 3, 4).

You will see some more possibilities with the `dup` operator when looking at multidimensional arrays in Section 4.22.

## 4.20 Accessing Elements of a Single-Dimensional Array

To access an element of a zero-based array, you can use the simplified formula

```
Element_Address = Base_Address + index * Element_Size
```

For the `Base_Address` entry you can use the name of the array (because HLA associates the address of the first element of an array with the name of that array). The `Element_Size` entry is the number of bytes for each array element. If the object is an array of bytes, the `Element_Size` field is 1 (resulting in a very simple computation). If each element of the array is a word (or other 2-byte type), then `Element_Size` is 2, and so on. To access an element of the SixteenInts array in the previous section, you'd use the following formula (the size is 4 because each element is an *int32* object):

```
Element_Address = SixteenInts + index*4
```

The 80x86 code equivalent to the statement eax := *SixteenInts[index]* is

```
        mov( index, ebx );
        shl( 2, ebx );          // Sneaky way to compute 4*ebx
        mov( SixteenInts[ ebx ], eax );
```

There are two important things to notice here. First of all, this code us
the shl instruction rather than the intmul instruction to compute 4*index. T
main reason for choosing shl is that it was more efficient. It turns out that s
is a *lot* faster than intmul on many processors.

The second thing to note about this instruction sequence is that it do
not explicitly compute the sum of the base address plus the index times 4.
Instead, it relies on the indexed addressing mode to implicitly compute th
sum. The instruction mov( SixteenInts[ ebx ], eax ); loads EAX from locati
SixteenInts + ebx, which is the base address plus index*4 (because EBX conta
index*4). Sure, you could have used

```
lea( eax, SixteenInts );
mov( index, ebx );
shl( 2, ebx );              // Sneaky way to compute 4*ebx
add( eax, ebx );            // Compute base address plus index*
mov( [ebx], eax );
```

in place of the previous sequence, but why use five instructions where thre
will do the same job? This is a good example of why you should know your
addressing modes inside and out. Choosing the proper addressing mode c:
reduce the size of your program, thereby speeding it up.

Of course, as long as we're discussing efficiency improvements, it's
worth pointing out that the 80x86 scaled indexed addressing modes let yc
automatically multiply an index by 1, 2, 4, or 8. Because this current examp
multiplies the index by 4, we can simplify the code even more by using the
scaled indexed addressing mode:

```
mov( index, ebx );
mov( SixteenInts[ ebx*4 ], eax );
```

Note, however, that if you need to multiply by some constant other tha
1, 2, 4 or 8, then you cannot use the scaled indexed addressing modes. Similar:
if you need to multiply by some element size that is not a power of 2, you w
not be able to use the shl instruction to multiply the index by the element
size; instead, you will have to use intmul or some other instruction sequenc
to do the multiplication.

The indexed addressing mode on the 80x86 is a natural for accessing
elements of a single-dimensional array. Indeed, its syntax even suggests an
array access. The important thing to keep in mind is that you must remember
multiply the index by the size of an element. Failure to do so will produce
incorrect results.

## 4.21   Sorting an Array of Values

Almost every textbook on this planet gives an example of a sort when
introducing arrays. Because you've probably seen how to do a sort in high-
level languages already, it's probably instructive to take a quick look at a so

in HLA. The example code in this section will use a variant of the bubble sort, which is great for short lists of data and lists that are nearly sorted but horrible for just about everything else.[17]

```
const
    NumElements := 16;

static
    DataToSort: uns32[ NumElements ] :=
                    [
                        1, 2, 16, 14,
                        3, 9, 4,  10,
                        5, 7, 15, 12,
                        8, 6, 11, 13
                    ];

    NoSwap: boolean;

        .
        .
        .

    // Bubble sort for the DataToSort array:

    repeat

        mov( true, NoSwap );
        for( mov( 0, ebx ); ebx <= NumElements-2; inc( ebx )) do

            mov( DataToSort[ ebx*4], eax );
            if( eax > DataToSort[ ebx*4 + 4] ) then

                mov( DataToSort[ ebx*4 + 4 ], ecx );
                mov( ecx, DataToSort[ ebx*4 ] );
                mov( eax, DataToSort[ ebx*4 + 4 ] ); // Note: eax contains
                mov( false, NoSwap );                //   DataToSort[ ebx*4 ]

            endif;

        endfor;

    until( NoSwap );
```

The bubble sort works by comparing adjacent elements in an array. The interesting thing to note in this code fragment is how it compares adjacent elements. You will note that the if statement compares EAX (which contains DataToSort[ebx*4]) against DataToSort[ebx*4 + 4]. Because each element of this array is 4 bytes (uns32), the index [ebx*4 + 4] references the next element beyond [ebx*4].

---

[17] Fear not, you'll see some better sorting algorithms in Chapter 5.

As is typical for a bubble sort, this algorithm terminates if the innerm
loop completes without swapping any data. If the data is already presorte
then the bubble sort is very efficient, making only one pass over the dat
Unfortunately, if the data is not sorted (worst case, if the data is sorted i
reverse order), then this algorithm is extremely inefficient. Indeed, althou
it is possible to modify the code above so that, on the average, it runs abo
twice as fast, such optimizations are wasted on such a poor algorithm. Howev
the bubble sort is very easy to implement and understand (which is why
introductory texts continue to use it in examples).

## 4.22  Multidimensional Arrays

The 80x86 hardware can easily handle single-dimensional arrays. Unfortunat
there is no magic addressing mode that lets you easily access elements of mul
mensional arrays. That's going to take some work and several instructions.

Before discussing how to declare or access multidimensional arrays, it
would be a good idea to figure out how to implement them in memory. T
first problem is to figure out how to store a multidimensional object into
one-dimensional memory space.

Consider for a moment a Pascal array of the form A:array[0..3,0..3] c
char;. This array contains 16 bytes organized as four rows of four characte
Somehow you've got to draw a correspondence with each of the 16 bytes i
this array and 16 contiguous bytes in main memory. Figure 4-5 shows one w
to do this.

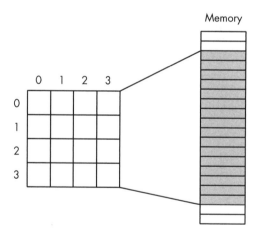

Figure 4-5: Mapping a 4×4 array to sequential
memory locations

The actual mapping is not important as long as two things occur: (1) Eac
element maps to a unique memory location (that is, no two entries in the
array occupy the same memory locations), and (2) the mapping is consiste
That is, a given element in the array always maps to the same memory locatio
So what you really need is a function with two input parameters (row and
column) that produces an offset into a linear array of 16 memory location

Now any function that satisfies the above constraints will work fine. Indeed, you could randomly choose a mapping as long as it was consistent. However, what you really want is a mapping that is efficient to compute at runtime and works for any size array (not just 4×4 or even limited to two dimensions). While a large number of possible functions fit this bill, there are two functions in particular that most programmers and high-level languages use: *row-major ordering* and *column-major ordering*.

## 4.22.1   Row-Major Ordering

Row-major ordering assigns successive elements, moving across the rows and then down the columns, to successive memory locations. This mapping is demonstrated in Figure 4-6.

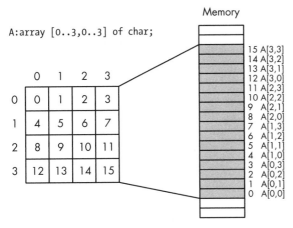

Figure 4-6: Row-major array element ordering

Row-major ordering is the method most high-level programming languages employ. It is very easy to implement and use in machine language. You start with the first row (row 0) and then concatenate the second row to its end. You then concatenate the third row to the end of the list, then the fourth row, and so on (see Figure 4-7).

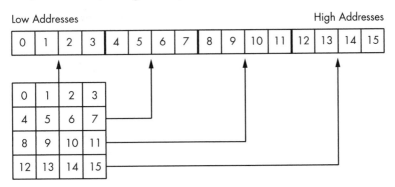

Figure 4-7: Another view of row-major ordering for a 4x4 array

The actual function that converts a list of index values into an offset slight modification of the formula for computing the address of an element of a single-dimensional array. The formula to compute the offset for a two dimensional row-major ordered array is:

$$Element\_Address = Base\_Address + (colindex * row\_size + rowindex) * Element\_S$$

As usual, *Base_Address* is the address of the first element of the array (A[0][0] in this case), and *Element_Size* is the size of an individual element the array, in bytes. *colindex* is the leftmost index, and *rowindex* is the rightm index into the array. *row_size* is the number of elements in one row of t array (four, in this case, because each row has four elements). Assumin *Element_Size* is 1, this formula computes the following offsets from the ba address:

| Column Index | Row Index | Offset into Array |
|---|---|---|
| 0 | 0 | 0 |
| 0 | 1 | 1 |
| 0 | 2 | 2 |
| 0 | 3 | 3 |
| 1 | 0 | 4 |
| 1 | 1 | 5 |
| 1 | 2 | 6 |
| 1 | 3 | 7 |
| 2 | 0 | 8 |
| 2 | 1 | 9 |
| 2 | 2 | 10 |
| 2 | 3 | 11 |
| 3 | 0 | 12 |
| 3 | 1 | 13 |
| 3 | 2 | 14 |
| 3 | 3 | 15 |

For a three-dimensional array, the formula to compute the offset into memory is the following:

$$Address = Base + ((depthindex * col\_size + colindex) * row\_size + rowindex) * Element\_Size$$

*col_size* is the number of items in a column, and *row_size* is the numb of items in a row. In C/C++, if you've declared the array as *type* A[i] [j] [k then *row_size* is equal to k and *col_size* is equal to j.

For a four-dimensional array, declared in C/C++ as *type* A[i] [j] [k] [m];, the formula for computing the address of an array element is:

$$Address = Base + (((LeftIndex * depth\_size + depthindex) * col\_size + colindex) * row\_size + rowindex) * Element\_S$$

*depth_size* is equal to j, *col_size* is equal to k, and *row_size* is equal to m. *LeftIndex* represents the value of the leftmost index.

By now you're probably beginning to see a pattern. There is a generic formula that will compute the offset into memory for an array with *any* number of dimensions; however, you'll rarely use more than four.

Another convenient way to think of row-major arrays is as arrays of arrays. Consider the following single-dimensional Pascal array definition:

---
A: array [0..3] of *sometype*;

---

Assume that *sometype* is the type *sometype* = array [0..3] of char;.

A is a single-dimensional array. Its individual elements happen to be arrays, but you can safely ignore that for the time being. The formula to compute the address of an element of a single-dimensional array is:

---
*Element_Address* = *Base* + *Index* * *Element_Size*

---

In this case *Element_Size* happens to be 4 because each element of A is an array of four characters. So what does this formula compute? It computes the base address of each row in this 4×4 array of characters (see Figure 4-8).

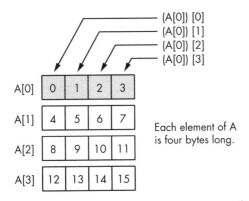

Figure 4-8: Viewing a 4x4 array as an array of arrays

Of course, once you compute the base address of a row, you can reapply the single-dimensional formula to get the address of a particular element. While this doesn't affect the computation, it's probably a little easier to deal with several single-dimensional computations rather than a complex multidimensional array computation.

Consider a Pascal array defined as A:array [0..3] [0..3] [0..3] [0..3] [0..3] of char;. You can view this five-dimensional array as a single-dimensional array of arrays. The following HLA code provides such a definition:

---
type
        OneD: char[4];
        TwoD: OneD[4];

```
            ThreeD: TwoD[4];
            FourD: ThreeD [4];
var
            A : FourD [4];
```

The size of OneD is 4 bytes. Because TwoD contains four OneD arrays, its size
16 bytes. Likewise, ThreeD is four TwoDs, so it is 64 bytes long. Finally, FourD is fo
ThreeDs, so it is 256 bytes long. To compute the address of A [b, c, d, e, f]
you could use the following steps:

1.  Compute the address of A [b] as *Base + b * size*. Here size is 256 bytes
    Use this result as the new base address in the next computation.

2.  Compute the address of A [b, c] by the formula *Base + c * size*, where
    *Base* is the value obtained in the previous step and *size* is 64. Use the
    result as the new base in the next computation.

3.  Compute the base address of A [b, c, d] by *Base + d * size*, with *Base*
    coming from the previous computation and *size* is 16. Use the result a
    the new base in the next computation.

4.  Compute the address of A [b, c, d, e] with the formula *Base + e * siz*
    with *Base* from the previous step with a size of 4. Use this value as the ba
    for the next computation.

5.  Finally, compute the address of A [b, c, d, e, f] using the formula *Base*
    *f * size*, where *Base* comes from the previous computation and *size* is
    (obviously you can simply ignore this final multiplication). The result
    you obtain at this point is the address of the desired element.

One of the main reasons you won't find higher-dimensional arrays in
assembly language is that assembly language emphasizes the inefficiencies
associated with such access. It's easy to enter something like A [b, c, d, e,
into a Pascal program, not realizing what the compiler is doing with the code.
Assembly language programmers are not so cavalier—they see the mess yo
wind up with when you use higher-dimensional arrays. Indeed, good assembly
language programmers try to avoid two-dimensional arrays and often reso
to tricks in order to access data in such an array when its use becomes absolute
mandatory.

## 4.22.2  Column-Major Ordering

Column-major ordering is the other function high-level languages frequen
used to compute the address of an array element. FORTRAN and various
dialects of BASIC (e.g., older versions of Microsoft BASIC) use this metho

In row-major ordering the rightmost index increases the fastest as you
move through consecutive memory locations. In column-major ordering th
leftmost index increases the fastest. Pictorially, a column-major ordered arr
is organized as shown in Figure 4-9.

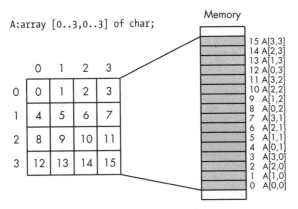

```
A:array [0..3,0..3] of char;
```

Figure 4-9: Column-major array element ordering

The formula for computing the address of an array element when using column-major ordering is very similar to that for row-major ordering. You simply reverse the indexes and sizes in the computation:

---

For a two-dimension column-major array:
Element_Address = Base_Address + (rowindex * col_size + colindex) *
                  Element_Size

For a three-dimension column-major array:
Address = Base + ((rowindex * col_size+colindex) * depth_size + depthindex) *
          Element_Size

For a four-dimension column-major array:
Address =
     Base + (((rowindex * col_size + colindex)*depth_size + depthindex) *
          Left_size + Leftindex) * Element_Size

---

# 4.23  Allocating Storage for Multidimensional Arrays

If you have an *m* × *n* array, it will have *m* * *n* elements and require *m* * *n* * Element_Size bytes of storage. To allocate storage for an array you must reserve this memory. As usual, there are several different ways of accomplishing this task. Fortunately, HLA's array-declaration syntax is very similar to high-level language array-declaration syntax, so C/C++, Java, BASIC, and Pascal programmers will feel right at home. To declare a multidimensional array in HLA, you use a declaration like the following:

---

ArrayName: elementType [ comma_separated_list_of_dimension_bounds ];

---

For example, here is a declaration for a 4×4 array of characters:

---

GameGrid: char[ 4, 4 ];

---

Here is another example that shows how to declare a three-dimension
array of strings:

```
NameItems: string[ 2, 3, 3 ];
```

Remember, string objects are really pointers, so this array declaration
reserves storage for 18 double-word pointers (2 * 3 * 3 = 18).

As was the case with single-dimensional arrays, you may initialize ever
element of the array to a specific value by following the declaration with t
assignment operator and an array constant. Array constants ignore dimensio
information; all that matters is that the number of elements in the array const
corresponds to the number of elements in the actual array. The following
example shows the GameGrid declaration with an initializer:

```
GameGrid: char[ 4, 4 ] :=
    [
        'a', 'b', 'c', 'd',
        'e', 'f', 'g', 'h',
        'i', 'j', 'k', 'l',
        'm', 'n', 'o', 'p'
    ];
```

Note that HLA ignores the indentation and extra whitespace characte
(e.g., newlines) appearing in this declaration. It was laid out to enhance
readability (which is always a good idea). HLA does not interpret the four
separate lines as representing rows of data in the array. Humans do, whi
is why it's good to write the data in this manner. All that matters is that the
are 16 (4 * 4) characters in the array constant. You'll probably agree that t
is much easier to read than

```
GameGrid: char[ 4,4 ] :=
    [ 'a', 'b', 'c', 'd', 'e', 'f', 'g', 'h', 'i', 'j', 'k', 'l', 'm',
      'n', 'o', 'p' ];
```

Of course, if you have a large array, an array with really large rows, or
array with many dimensions, there is little hope for winding up with somethin
readable. That's when comments that carefully explain everything come i
handy.

As for single-dimensional arrays, you can use the dup operator to initiali
each element of a large array with the same value. The following example
initializes a 256×64 array of bytes so that each byte contains the value $FF:

```
StateValue: byte[ 256, 64 ] := 256*64 dup [$ff];
```

Note the use of a constant expression to compute the number of array
elements rather than simply using the constant 16,384 (256 * 64). The use

of the constant expression more clearly suggests that this code is initializing each element of a 256×64 element array than does the simple literal constant 16,384.

Another HLA trick you can use to improve the readability of your programs is to use *nested array constants*. The following is an example of an HLA nested array constant:

```
[ [0, 1, 2], [3, 4], [10, 11, 12, 13] ]
```

Whenever HLA encounters an array constant nested inside another array constant, it simply removes the brackets surrounding the nested array constant and treats the whole constant as a single-array constant. For example, HLA converts this nested array constant to the following:

```
[ 0, 1, 2, 3, 4, 10, 11, 12, 13 ]
```

You can take advantage of this fact to help make your programs a little more readable. For multidimensional array constants you can enclose each row of the constant in square brackets to denote that the data in each row is grouped and separate from the other rows. Consider the following declaration for the GameGrid array that is identical (as far as HLA is concerned) to the earlier declaration for GameGrid:

```
GameGrid: char[ 4, 4 ] :=
    [
        [ 'a', 'b', 'c', 'd' ],
        [ 'e', 'f', 'g', 'h' ],
        [ 'i', 'j', 'k', 'l' ],
        [ 'm', 'n', 'o', 'p' ]
    ];
```

This declaration makes it clearer that the array constant is a 4×4 array rather than just a 16-element one-dimensional array whose elements wouldn't fit all on one line of source code. Little aesthetic improvements like this are what separate mediocre programmers from good programmers.

# 4.24 Accessing Multidimensional Array Elements in Assembly Language

Well, you've seen the formulas for computing the address of a multidimensional array element. Now it's time to see how to access elements of those arrays using assembly language.

The mov, shl, and intmul instructions make short work of the various equations that compute offsets into multidimensional arrays. Let's consider a two-dimensional array first.

```
static
     i:            int32;
     j:            int32;
     TwoD:         int32[ 4, 8 ];

                      .
                      .
                      .

// To perform the operation TwoD[i,j] := 5; you'd use code like the followi
// Note that the array index computation is (i*8 + j)*4.

          mov( i, ebx );
          shl( 3, ebx );       // Multiply by 8 (shl by 3 is a multiply by 8).
          add( j, ebx );
          mov( 5, TwoD[ ebx*4 ] );
```

Note that this code does *not* require the use of a two-register addressin mode on the 80x86. Although an addressing mode like TwoD[ebx][esi] lool like it should be a natural for accessing two-dimensional arrays, that isn't t purpose of this addressing mode.

Now consider a second example that uses a three-dimensional array:

```
static
     i:            int32;
     j:            int32;
     k:            int32;
     ThreeD:       int32[ 3, 4, 5 ];
                      .
                      .
                      .

// To perform the operation ThreeD[i,j,k] := esi; you'd use the following c
// that computes ((i*4 + j)*5 + k )*4 as the address of ThreeD[i,j,k].

          mov( i, ebx );
          shl( 2, ebx );                    // Four elements per column.
          add( j, ebx );
          intmul( 5, ebx );                 // Five elements per row.
          add( k, ebx );
          mov( esi, ThreeD[ ebx*4 ] );
```

Note that this code uses the intmul instruction to multiply the value in EBX by 5. Remember, the shl instruction can only multiply a register by a power of 2. While there are ways to multiply the value in a register by a consta other than a power of 2, the intmul instruction is more convenient.[18]

---

[18] A full discussion of multiplication by constants other than a power of 2 appears in Chapter

## 4.25 Records

Another major composite data structure is the Pascal record or C/C++/C# structure.[19] The Pascal terminology is probably better, because it tends to avoid confusion with the more general term *data structure*. Because HLA uses the term *record*, we'll adopt that term here.

Whereas an array is homogeneous, whose elements are all the same type, the elements in a record can have different types. Arrays let you select a particular element via an integer index. With records, you must select an element (known as a *field*) by name.

The whole purpose of a record is to let you encapsulate different, though logically related, data into a single package. The Pascal record declaration for a student is a typical example:

```
student =
    record
        Name:     string[64];
        Major:    integer;
        SSN:      string[11];
        Midterm1: integer;
        Midterm2: integer;
        Final:    integer;
        Homework: integer;
        Projects: integer;
    end;
```

Most Pascal compilers allocate each field in a record to contiguous memory locations. This means that Pascal will reserve the first 65 bytes for the name,[20] the next 2 bytes hold the major code, the next 12 bytes hold the Social Security number, and so on.

In HLA, you can also create record types using the record/endrecord declaration. You would encode the above record in HLA as follows:

```
type
    student:    record
        Name:     char[65];
        Major:    int16;
        SSN:      char[12];
        Midterm1: int16;
        Midterm2: int16;
        Final:    int16;
        Homework: int16;
        Projects: int16;
    endrecord;
```

---

[19] It also goes by some other names in other languages, but most people recognize at least one of these names.

[20] Strings require an extra byte, in addition to all the characters in the string, to encode the length.

As you can see, the HLA declaration is very similar to the Pascal declaration. Note that, to be true to the Pascal declaration, this example uses character arrays rather than strings for the Name and SSN (US Social Security number) fields. In a real HLA record declaration you'd probably use a string type for at least the name (keeping in mind that a string variable is only a 4-byte pointer).

The field names within the record must be unique. That is, the same name may not appear two or more times in the same record. However, all field names are local to that record. Therefore, you may reuse those field names elsewhere in the program or in different records.

The record/endrecord declaration may appear in a variable declaration section (e.g., static or var) or in a type declaration section. In the previous example the Student declaration appears in the type section, so this does not actually allocate any storage for a Student variable. Instead, you have to explicitly declare a variable of type Student. The following example demonstrates how to do this:

```
var
    John: Student;
```

This allocates 81 bytes of storage laid out in memory as shown in Figure 4-10.

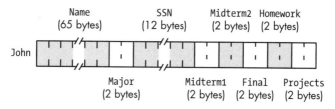

Figure 4-10: Student data structure storage in memory

If the label John corresponds to the *base address* of this record, then the Name field is at offset John+0, the Major field is at offset John+65, the SSN field is at offset John+67, and so on.

To access an element of a structure, you need to know the offset from the beginning of the structure to the desired field. For example, the Major field in the variable John is at offset 65 from the base address of John. Therefore you could store the value in AX into this field using the instruction

```
mov( ax, (type word John[65]) );
```

Unfortunately, memorizing all the offsets to fields in a record defeats the whole purpose of using them in the first place. After all, if you have to deal with these numeric offsets, why not just use an array of bytes instead of a record?

Fortunately, HLA lets you refer to field names in a record using the same mechanism C/C++/C# and Pascal use: the dot operator. To store AX into the Major field, you could use mov( ax, John.Major ); instead of the previous instruction. This is much more readable and certainly easier to use.

Note that the use of the dot operator does *not* introduce a new addressing mode. The instruction mov( ax, John.Major ); still uses the displacement-only addressing mode. HLA simply adds the base address of John with the offset to the Major field (65) to get the actual displacement to encode into the instruction.

Like any type declaration, HLA requires all record type declarations to appear in the program before you use them. However, you don't have to define all records in the type section to create record variables. You can use the record/endrecord declaration directly in a variable declaration section. This is convenient if you have only one instance of a given record object in your program. The following example demonstrates this:

```
storage
    OriginPoint:   record
        x: uns8;
        y: uns8;
        z: uns8;
    endrecord;
```

## 4.26 Record Constants

HLA lets you define record constants. In fact, HLA supports both manifest (symbolic) record constants and literal record constants. Record constants are useful as initializers for static record variables. They are also quite useful as compile-time data structures when using the HLA compile-time language (see the HLA reference manual for more details on the HLA compile-time language). This section discusses how to create record constants.

A literal record constant takes the following form:

RecordTypeName:[ List_of_comma_separated_constants ]

The RecordTypeName is the name of a record data type you've defined in an HLA type section prior to using the constant.

The constant list appearing between the brackets is the data for each of the fields in the specified record. The first item in the list corresponds to the first field of the record, the second item in the list corresponds to the second field, and so on. The data types of each of the constants appearing in this list must match their respective field types. The following example demonstrates how to use a literal record constant to initialize a record variable:

```
type
    point:      record
        x:int32;
        y:int32;
        z:int32;
    endrecord;

static
    Vector: point := point:[ 1, -2, 3 ];
```

This declaration initializes Vector.x with 1, Vector.y with −2, and Vector.z with 3.

You can also create manifest record constants by declaring record object*
the const or val sections of your program. You access fields of these symbc
record constants just as you would access the field of a record variable, us
the dot operator. Because the object is a constant, you can specify the fielc
a record constant anywhere a constant of that field's type is legal. You car
also employ symbolic record constants as variable initializers. The followi*
example demonstrates this:

```
type
        point:      record
                x:int32;
                y:int32;
                z:int32;
        endrecord;

const
        PointInSpace: point := point:[ 1, 2, 3 ];

static
        Vector: point := PointInSpace;
        XCoord: int32 := PointInSpace.x;
            .
            .
            .
        stdout.put( "Y Coordinate is ", PointInSpace.y, nl );
            .
            .
            .
```

## 4.27  Arrays of Records

It is a perfectly reasonable operation to create an array of records. To do *
you simply create a record type and then use the standard array declaratic
syntax. The following example demonstrates how you could do this:

```
type
        recElement:
            record
                << Fields for this record >>
            endrecord;
            .
            .
            .
static
        recArray: recElement[4];
```

To access an element of this array you use the standard array indexing
techniques. Because *recArray* is a single-dimensional array, you'd compute

the address of an element of this array using the formula *baseAddress* + *index*\*@size( *recElement* ). For example, to access an element of *recArray* you'd use code like the following:

```
// Access element i of recArray:

    intmul( @size( recElement ), i, ebx );   // ebx := i*@size( recElement )
    mov( recArray.someField[ebx], eax );
```

Note that the index specification follows the entire variable name; remember, this is assembly, not a high-level language (in a high-level language you'd probably use *recArray*[i].*someField*).

Naturally, you can create multidimensional arrays of records as well. You would use the row-major or column-major order functions to compute the address of an element within such records. The only thing that really changes (from the discussion of arrays) is that the size of each element is the size of the record object.

```
static
    rec2D: recElement[ 4, 6 ];
          .
          .
          .
    // Access element [i,j] of rec2D and load someField into eax:

    intmul( 6, i, ebx );
    add( j, ebx );
    intmul( @size( recElement ), ebx );
    mov( rec2D.someField[ ebx ], eax );
```

# 4.28  Arrays/Records as Record Fields

Records may contain other records or arrays as fields. Consider the following definition:

```
type
    Pixel:
        record
            Pt:         point;
            color:      dword;
        endrecord;
```

The definition above defines a single point with a 32-bit color component. When initializing an object of type Pixel, the first initializer corresponds to the Pt field, *not the x-coordinate field*. The following definition is incorrect:

```
static
    ThisPt: Pixel := Pixel:[ 5, 10 ];    // Syntactically incorrect!
```

The value of the first field (5) is not an object of type point. Therefore the assembler generates an error when encountering this statement. HLA will allow you to initialize the fields of Pixel using declarations like the following

```
static
    ThisPt: Pixel := Pixel:[ point:[ 1, 2, 3 ], 10 ];
    ThatPt: Pixel := Pixel:[ point:[ 0, 0, 0 ], 5 ];
```

Accessing Pixel fields is very easy. As in a high-level language, you use single period to reference the Pt field and a second period to access the x, and z fields of point:

```
        stdout.put( "ThisPt.Pt.x = ", ThisPt.Pt.x, nl );
        stdout.put( "ThisPt.Pt.y = ", ThisPt.Pt.y, nl );
        stdout.put( "ThisPt.Pt.z = ", ThisPt.Pt.z, nl );
            .
            .
            .
    mov( eax, ThisPt.Color );
```

You can also declare arrays as record fields. The following record create a data type capable of representing an object with eight points (for example cube):

```
type
    Object8:
        record
            Pts:        point[8];
            Color:      dword;
        endrecord;
```

This record allocates storage for eight different points. Accessing an element of the Pts array requires that you know the size of an object of typ point (remember, you must multiply the index into the array by the size of one element, 12 in this particular case). Suppose, for example, that you ha a variable Cube of type Object8. You could access elements of the Pts array as follows:

```
// Cube.Pts[i].x := 0;

        mov( i, ebx );
        intmul( 12, ebx );
        mov( 0, Cube.Pts.x[ebx] );
```

The one unfortunate aspect of all this is that you must know the size o each element of the Pts array. Fortunately, you can rewrite the code above using @size as follows:

```
// Cube.Pts[i].x := 0;

        mov( i, ebx );
```

```
        intmul( @size( point ), ebx );
        mov( 0, Cube.Pts.x[ebx] );
```

Note in this example that the index specification ([ebx]) follows the whole object name even though the array is Pts, not x. Remember, the [ebx] specification is an indexed addressing mode, not an array index. Indexes always follow the entire name, so you do not attach them to the array component as you would in a high-level language like C/C++ or Pascal. This produces the correct result because addition is commutative, and the dot operator (as well as the index operator) corresponds to addition. In particular, the expression Cube.Pts.x[ebx] tells HLA to compute the sum of Cube (the base address of the object) plus the offset to the Pts field, plus the offset to the x field, plus the value of EBX. Technically, we're really computing offset(Cube) + offset(Pts) + EBX + offset(x), but we can rearrange this because addition is commutative.

You can also define two-dimensional arrays within a record. Accessing elements of such arrays is no different than accessing any other two-dimensional array other than the fact that you must specify the array's field name as the base address for the array. For example:

```
type
     RecW2DArray:
          record
               intField: int32;
               aField:   int32[4,5];
                    .
                    .
                    .
          endrecord;

static
     recVar: RecW2DArray;
          .
          .
          .

     // Access element [i,j] of the aField field using row-major ordering:

     mov( i, ebx );
     intmul( 5, ebx );
     add( j, ebx );
     mov( recVar.aField[ ebx*4 ], eax );
          .
          .
          .
```

The code above uses the standard row-major calculation to index into a 4×5 array of double words. The only difference between this example and a standalone array access is the fact that the base address is recVar.aField.

There are two common ways to nest record definitions. As this section notes, you can create a record type in a type section and then use that type name as the data type of some field within a record (e.g., the Pt:point field in the Pixel data type above). It is also possible to declare a record directly within another record without creating a separate data type for that record the following example demonstrates this:

```
type
    NestedRecs:
        record
            iField: int32;
            sField: string;
            rField:
                record
                    i:int32;
                    u:uns32;
                endrecord;
            cField:char;
        endrecord;
```

Generally, it's a better idea to create a separate type rather than embed records directly in other records, but nesting them is perfectly legal.

If you have an array of records and one of the fields of that record type an array, you must compute the indexes into the arrays independently of on another and then use the sum of these indexes as the ultimate index. The following example demonstrates how to do this:

```
type
    recType:
        record
            arrayField: dword[4,5];
            << Other fields >>
        endrecord;

static
    aryOfRecs: recType[3,3];
        .
        .
        .

    // Access aryOfRecs[i,j].arrayField[k,l]:

    intmul( 5, i, ebx );            // Computes index into aryOfRecs
    add( j, ebx );                  // as (i*5 +j)*@size( recType ).
    intmul( @size( recType ), ebx );

    intmul( 3, k, eax );            // Computes index into aryOfRecs
    add( l, eax );                  // as (k*3 + j) (*4 handled later).

    mov( aryOfRecs.arrayField[ ebx + eax*4 ], eax );
```

Note the use of the base plus scaled indexed addressing mode to simplify this operation.

## 4.29 Aligning Fields Within a Record

To achieve maximum performance in your programs, or to ensure that HLA's records properly map to records or structures in some high-level language, you will often need to be able to control the alignment of fields within a record. For example, you might want to ensure that a double-word field's offset is an even multiple of 4. You use the align directive to do this. The following example shows how to align some fields on important boundaries:

```
type
    PaddedRecord:
        record
            c:  char;
            align(4);
            d:  dword;
            b:  boolean;
            align(2);
            w:  word;
        endrecord;
```

Whenever HLA encounters the align directive within a record declaration, it automatically adjusts the following field's offset so that it is an even multiple of the value the align directive specifies. It accomplishes this by increasing the offset of that field, if necessary. In the example above, the fields would have the following offsets: c:0, d:4, b:8, w:10. Note that HLA inserts 3 bytes of padding between c and d, and it inserts 1 byte of padding between b and w. It goes without saying that you should never assume that this padding is present. If you want to use those extra bytes, then you must declare fields for them.

Note that specifying alignment within a record declaration does not guarantee that the field will be aligned on that boundary in memory; it only ensures that the field's offset is a multiple of the value you specify. If a variable of type PaddedRecord starts at an odd address in memory, then the d field will also start at an odd address (because any odd address plus 4 is an odd address). If you want to ensure that the fields are aligned on appropriate boundaries in memory, you must also use the align directive before variable declarations of that record type. For example:

```
static
    .
    .
    .
    align(4);
    PRvar: PaddedRecord;
```

The value of the align operand should be an even value that is divisible by the largest align expression within the record type (4 is the largest value in this case, and it's already divisible by 2).

If you want to ensure that the record's size is a multiple of some value, then simply stick an align directive as the last item in the record declaration. HLA will emit an appropriate number of bytes of padding at the end of the record to fill it in to the appropriate size. The following example demonstrate how to ensure that the record's size is a multiple of 4 bytes:

```
type
     PaddedRec:
          record
               << Some field declarations >>

               align(4);
          endrecord;
```

HLA provides some additional alignment directives for records that let you easily control the alignment of all fields within a record and the starting offset of the fields in a record. If you're interested in more information, please consult the HLA reference manual.

## 4.30  Pointers to Records

During execution, your program may refer to record objects indirectly using a pointer. When you use a pointer to access fields of a structure, you must load one of the 80x86's 32-bit registers with the address of the desired record. Suppose you have the following variable declarations (assuming the Object structure from an earlier section):

```
static
     Cube:          Object8;
     CubePtr:       pointer to Object8 := &Cube;
```

CubePtr contains the address of (that is, it is a pointer to) the Cube object. To access the Color field of the Cube object, you could use an instruction like mov( Cube.Color, eax );. When accessing a field via a pointer, you first need to load the address of the object into a 32-bit register such as EBX. The instruction mov( CubePtr, ebx ); will do the trick. After doing so, you can access fields of the Cube object using the [ebx+offset] addressing mode. The only problem is "How do you specify which field to access?" Consider briefly the following *incorrect* code:

```
     mov( CubePtr, ebx );
     mov( [ebx].Color, eax );      // This does not work!
```

Because field names are local to a structure and it's possible to reuse a field name in two or more structures, how does HLA determine which offset Color represents? When accessing structure members directly (e.g., mov( Cube.Color, eax );), there is no ambiguity because Cube has a specific type that the assembler can check. [ebx], on the other hand, can point at *anything*. In particular, it can point at any structure that contains a Color field. So the assembler cannot, on its own, decide which offset to use for the Color symbol.

HLA resolves this ambiguity by requiring that you explicitly supply a type. To do this, you must coerce [ebx] to type Cube. Once you do this, you can use the normal dot operator notation to access the Color field:

```
mov( CubePtr, ebx );
mov( (type Cube [ebx]).Color, eax );
```

If you have a pointer to a record and one of that record's fields is an array, the easiest way to access elements of that field is by using the base-plus-indexed addressing mode. To do so, you just load the pointer's value into one register and compute the index into the array in a second register. Then you combine these two registers in the address expression. In the example above, the Pts field is an array of eight point objects. To access field x of the ith element of the Cube.Pts field, you'd use code like the following:

```
mov( CubePtr, ebx );
intmul( @size( point ), i, esi );   // Compute index into point array.
mov( (type Object8 [ebx]).Pts.x[ esi*4 ], eax );
```

If you use a pointer to a particular record type frequently in your program, typing a coercion operator like (type Object8 [ebx]) can get old very quickly. One way to reduce the typing needed to coerce EBX is to use a text constant. Consider the following statement:

```
const
    O8ptr: text := "(type Object8 [ebx])";
```

With this statement at the beginning of your program, you can use O8ptr in place of the type coercion operator, and HLA will automatically substitute the appropriate text. With a text constant like the above, the former example becomes a little more readable and writable:

```
mov( CubePtr, ebx );
intmul( @size( point ), i, esi );   // Compute index into point array.
mov( O8Ptr.Pts.x[ esi*4 ], eax );
```

## 4.31 Unions

A record definition assigns different offsets to each field in the record according to the size of those fields. This behavior is quite similar to the allocation of memory offsets in a var or static section. HLA provides a second type of structure declaration, the union, that does not assign different addresses to

each object; instead, each field in a union declaration has the same offset—
The following example demonstrates the syntax for a union declaration:

```
type
      unionType:
            union
                  << Fields (syntactically identical to record declarations) >>
            endunion;
```

You access the fields of a union exactly the same way you access the field
of a record: using dot notation and field names. The following is a concret
example of a union type declaration and a variable of the union type:

```
type
      numeric:
            union
                  i: int32;
                  u: uns32;
                  r: real64;
            endunion;
                  .
                  .
                  .
static
      number: numeric;
            .
            .
            .
      mov( 55, number.u );
            .
            .
            .
      mov( -5, number.i );
            .
            .
            .
      stdout.put( "Real value = ", number.r, nl );
```

The important thing to note about union objects is that all the fields of
union have the same offset in the structure. In the example above, the number.u,
number.i, and number.r fields all have the same offset: 0. Therefore, the fields
of a union overlap in memory; this is very similar to the way the 80x86 8-, 16-
and 32-bit registers overlap one another. Usually, you may access only one
field of a union at a time; that is, you do not manipulate separate fields of a
particular union variable concurrently because writing to one field overwrite
the other fields. In the example above, any modification of number.u would
also change number.i and number.r.

Programmers typically use unions for two different reasons: to conserve
memory or to create aliases. Memory conservation is the intended use of thi
data structure facility. To see how this works, let's compare the numeric unior
above with a corresponding record type.

```
type
    numericRec:
        record
                i: int32;
                u: uns32;
                r: real64;
        endrecord;
```

If you declare a variable, say n, of type numericRec, you access the fields as
n.i, n.u, and n.r exactly as though you had declared the variable to be type
numeric. The difference between the two is that numericRec variables allocate
separate storage for each field of the record, whereas numeric (union) objects
allocate the same storage for all fields. Therefore, @size(numericRec) is 16
because the record contains two double-word fields and a quad word (real64)
field. @size(numeric), however, is 8. This is because all the fields of a union occupy
the same memory locations, and the size of a union object is the size of the
largest field of that object (see Figure 4-11).

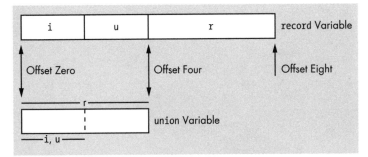

*Figure 4-11: Layout of a union versus a record variable*

In addition to conserving memory, programmers often use unions to
create aliases in their code. As you may recall, an alias is a different name for
the same memory object. Aliases are often a source of confusion in a program,
so you should use them sparingly; sometimes, however, using an alias can be
quite convenient. For example, in some section of your program you might
need to constantly use type coercion to refer to an object using a different
type. Although you can use an HLA text constant to simplify this process,
another way to do this is to use a union variable with the fields representing
the different types you want to use for the object. As an example, consider the
following code:

```
type
    CharOrUns:
        union
                c:char;
                u:uns32;
        endrecord;

static
    v:CharOrUns;
```

With a declaration like the above, you can manipulate an uns32 object
accessing v.u. If, at some point, you need to treat the L.O. byte of this uns3
variable as a character, you can do so by simply accessing the v.c variable, :
example,

```
mov( eax, v.u );
stdout.put( "v, as a character, is '", v.c, "'" nl );
```

You can use unions exactly the same way you use records in an HLA
program. In particular, union declarations may appear as fields in records,
record declarations may appear as fields in unions, array declarations may
appear within unions, you can create arrays of unions, and so on.

## 4.32  Anonymous Unions

Within a record declaration you can place a union declaration without specifyin
fieldname for the union object. The following example demonstrates the syn
for this:

```
type
    HasAnonUnion:
        record
            r:real64;
            union
                u:uns32;
                i:int32;
            endunion;
            s:string;
        endrecord;

static
    v: HasAnonUnion;
```

Whenever an anonymous union appears within a record you can acces
the fields of the union as though they were direct fields of the record. In the
example above, for example, you would access v's u and i fields using the
syntax v.u and v.i, respectively. The u and i fields have the same offset in t
record (8, because they follow a real64 object). The fields of v have the followi
offsets from v's base address:

| | |
|---|---|
| v.r | 0 |
| v.u | 8 |
| v.i | 8 |
| v.s | 12 |

@size(v) is 16 because the u and i fields consume only 4 bytes.
HLA also allows anonymous records within unions. Please see the HL
documentation for more details, though the syntax and usage are identica
to anonymous unions within records.

## 4.33  Variant Types

One big use of unions in programs is to create *variant* types. A variant variable can change its type dynamically while the program is running. A variant object can be an integer at one point in the program, switch to a string at a different part of the program, and then change to a real value at a later time. Many very-high-level language (VHLL) systems use a dynamic type system (that is, variant objects) to reduce the overall complexity of the program; indeed, proponents of many VHLLs insist that the use of a dynamic typing system is one of the reasons you can write complex programs with so few lines of code using those languages. Of course, if you can create variant objects in a VHLL, you can certainly do it in assembly language. In this section we'll look at how we can use the union structure to create variant types.

At any one given instant during program execution, a variant object has a specific type, but under program control the variable can switch to a different type. Therefore, when the program processes a variant object, it must use an if statement or switch statement (or something similar) to execute different instructions based on the object's current type. Very-high-level languages do this transparently. In assembly language you will have to provide the code to test the type yourself. To achieve this, the variant type needs some additional information beyond the object's value. Specifically, the variant object needs a field that specifies the current type of the object. This field (often known as the tag field) is an enumerated type or integer that specifies the object's type at any given instant. The following code demonstrates how to create a variant type:

```
type
    VariantType:
        record
            tag:uns32;    // 0-uns32, 1-int32, 2-real64
            union
                u:uns32;
                i:int32;
                r:real64;
            endunion;
        endrecord;

static
    v:VariantType;
```

The program would test the v.tag field to determine the current type of the v object. Based on this test, the program would manipulate the v.i, v.u, or v.r field.

Of course, when operating on variant objects, the program's code must constantly be testing the tag field and executing a separate sequence of instructions for uns32, int32, or real64 values. If you use the variant fields often, it makes a lot of sense to write procedures to handle these operations for you (e.g., *vadd*, *vsub*, *vmul*, and *vdiv*).

## 4.34  Namespaces

One really nice feature of records and unions is that the field names are lo
to a given record or union declaration. That is, you can reuse field names in
different records or unions. This is an important feature of HLA because
helps avoid *namespace pollution.* Namespace pollution occurs when you u
up all the "good" names within your program and you have to start creati
nondescriptive names for objects because you've already used the most
appropriate name for something else. We use the term *namespace* to descr
how HLA associates names with a particular object. The field names of a
record have a namespace that is limited to objects of that record type. HL
provides a generalization of this namespace mechanism that lets you crea
arbitrary namespaces. These namespace objects let you shield the names o
constants, types, variables, and other objects so their names do not interfe
with other declarations in your program.

An HLA namespace section encapsulates a set of generic declarations ir
much the same way that a record encapsulates a set of variable declarations
namespace declaration takes the following form:

```
namespace name;

    << declarations >>

end name;
```

The *name* identifier provides the name for the namespace. The identifier
after the end clause must exactly match the identifier after namespace. Note
that a namespace declaration section is a section unto itself. It does not have
appear in a type or var section. A namespace may appear anywhere one of th
HLA declaration sections is legal. A program may contain any number of
namespace declarations; in fact, the namespace identifiers don't even have t
be unique, as you will soon see.

The declarations that appear between the namespace and end clauses ar
all the standard HLA declaration sections except that you cannot nest namespa
declarations. You may, however, put const, val, type, static, readonly, and
storage sections within a namespace.[21] The following code provides an exam|
of a typical namespace declaration in an HLA program:

```
namespace myNames;

    type
        integer: int32;

    static
        i:integer;
        j:uns32;
```

---

[21] Procedure declarations, the subject of Chapter 5, are also legal within a namespace
declaration section.

```
const
     pi:real64 := 3.14159;


end myNames;
```

To access the fields of a namespace you use the same dot notation that records and unions use. For example, to access the fields of myNames outside of the namespace, you'd use the following identifiers:

| | |
|---|---|
| myNames.integer | A type declaration equivalent to int32 |
| myNames.i | An integer variable (int32) |
| myNames.j | An uns32 variable |
| myNames.pi | A real64 constant |

This example also demonstrates an important point about namespace declarations: Within a namespace you may reference other identifiers in that same namespace declaration without using the dot notation. For example, the i field above uses type integer from the myNames namespace without the mynames. prefix.

What is not obvious from the example above is that namespace declarations create a clean symbol table whenever you open up a namespace. The only external symbols that HLA recognizes in a namespace declaration are the predefined type identifiers (e.g., int32, uns32, and char). HLA does not recognize any symbols you've declared outside the namespace while it is processing your namespace declaration. This creates a problem if you want to use symbols from outside the namespace when declaring other symbols inside the namespace. For example, suppose the type integer had been defined outside myNames as follows:

```
type
     integer: int32;

namespace myNames;


     static
          i:integer;
          j:uns32;

     const
          pi:real64 := 3.14159;

end myNames;
```

If you were to attempt to compile this code, HLA would complain that the symbol integer is undefined. Clearly integer is defined in this program, but HLA hides all external symbols when creating a namespace so that you can reuse (and redefine) those symbols within the namespace. Of course, this doesn't help much if you actually want to use a name that you've defined outside myNames within that namespace. HLA provides a solution to this problem: the @global: operator. If, within a namespace declaration section, y prefix a name with @global:, then HLA will use the global definition of th name rather than the local definition (if a local definition even exists). To correct the problem in the previous example, you'd use the following cod

```
type
     integer: int32;

namespace myNames;


     static
          i:@global:integer;
          j:uns32;

     const
          pi:real64 := 3.14159;

end myNames;
```

With the @global: prefix, the i variable will be type int32 even if a different declaration of integer appears within the myNames namespace.

You cannot nest namespace declarations. Logically, there doesn't seem t be any need for this, hence its omission from the HLA language.

You can have multiple namespace declarations in the same program that use the same namespace identifier. For example:

```
namespace ns;

     << Declaration group #1 >>

end ns;
         .
         .
         .
namespace ns;

     << Declaration group #2 >>

end ns;
```

When HLA encounters a second namespace declaration for a given identifie it simply appends the declarations in the second group to the end of the symbol list it created for the first group. Therefore, after processing the tw namespace declarations, the ns namespace would contain the set of all symbo you've declared in both namespace blocks.

Perhaps the most common use of namespaces is in library modules. If you create a set of library routines to use in various projects or distribute to others, you have to be careful about the names you choose for your functions and other objects. If you use common names like get and put, the users of your module will complain when your names collide with theirs. An easy solution is to put all your code in a namespace block. Then the only name you have to worry about is the namespace identifier itself. This is the only name that will collide with other users' identifiers. This can happen, but it's much less likely to happen than if you don't use a namespace and your library module introduces dozens, if not hundreds, of new names into the global namespace.[22] The HLA Standard Library provides many good examples of namespaces in use. The HLA Standard Library defines several namespaces like stdout, stdin, str, cs, and chars. You refer to functions in these namespaces using names like stdout.put, stdin.get, cs.intersection, str.eq, and chars.toUpper. The use of namespaces in the HLA Standard Library prevents conflicts with similar names in your own programs.

## 4.35 Dynamic Arrays in Assembly Language

One problem with arrays as this chapter describes them is that their size is static. That is, the number of elements in all of the examples was chosen when writing the program; it was not selected while the program runs (that is, dynamically). Alas, sometimes you simply don't know how big an array needs to be when you're writing the program; you can only determine the size of the array while the program is running. This section describes how to allocate storage for arrays dynamically so you can set their size at runtime.

Allocating storage for a single-dimensional array, and accessing elements of that array, is a nearly trivial task at runtime. All you need to do is call the HLA Standard Library mem.alloc routine, specifying the size of the array in bytes. mem.alloc will return a pointer to the base address of the new array in the EAX register. Typically, you would save this address in a pointer variable and use that value as the base address of the array in all future array accesses.

To access an element of a single-dimensional dynamic array, you would generally load the base address into a register and compute the index in a second register. Then you could use the base-indexed addressing mode to access elements of that array. This is not a whole lot more work than accessing elements of a statically allocated array. The following code fragment demonstrates how to allocate and access elements of a single-dimensional dynamic array.

---

[22] The global namespace is the global section of your program.

```
static
        ArySize:                        uns32;
        BaseAdrs:                       pointer to uns32;
                .
                .
                .

        stdout.put( "How many elements do you want in your array? " );
        stdin.getu32();
        mov( eax, ArySize );  // Save away the upper bounds on this array.
        shl( 2, eax );        // Multiply eax by 4 to compute the number of bytes
        mem.alloc( eax );     // Allocate storage for the array.
        mov( eax, BaseAdrs ); // Save away the base address of the new array.
                .
                .
                .


        // Zero out each element of the array:

        mov( BaseAdrs, ebx );
        mov( 0, eax );
        for( mov(0, esi); esi < ArySize; inc( esi )) do

            mov( eax, [ebx + esi*4 ]);

        endfor;
```

Dynamically allocating storage for a multidimensional array is fairly straightforward. The number of elements in a multidimensional array is t▮ product of all the dimension values; for example, a 4×5 array has 20 elements. if you get the bounds for each dimension from the user, all you need to d▮ compute the product of all of these bound values and multiply the result ▮ the size of a single element. This computes the total number of bytes in th▮ array, the value that mem.alloc expects.

Accessing elements of multidimensional arrays is a little more problem atic. The problem is that you need to keep the dimension information (th▮ is, the bounds on each dimension) around because these values are neede when computing the row-major (or column-major) index into the array.[23] The conventional solution is to store these bounds into a static array (gen▮ ally you know the *arity*, or number of dimensions, at compile time, so it i possible to statically allocate storage for this array of dimension bounds) This array of dynamic array bounds is known as a *dope vector*. The following code fragment shows how to allocate storage for a two-dimensional dynam▮ array using a simple dope vector.

---

[23] Technically, you don't need the value of the leftmost dimension bound to compute an ind▮ into the array; however, if you want to check the index bounds using the bound instruction (o▮ some other technique), you will need this value around at runtime as well.

```
var
    ArrayPtr:   pointer to uns32;
    ArrayDims:  uns32[2];  // The dope vector
        .
        .
        .

    // Get the array bounds from the user:

    stdout.put( "Enter the bounds for dimension #1: " );
    stdin.get( ArrayDims[0] );

    stdout.put( "Enter the bounds for dimension #2: " );
    stdin.get( ArrayDims[1*4] );

    // Allocate storage for the array:

    mov( ArrayDims[0], eax );
    intmul( ArrayDims[1*4], eax );
    shl( 2, eax );        // Multiply by 4 because each element is 4 bytes.
    mem.alloc( eax );     // Allocate storage for the array and
    mov( eax, ArrayPtr ); // save away the pointer to the array.


    // Initialize the array:

    mov( 0, edx );
    mov( ArrayPtr, edi );
    for( mov( 0, ebx ); ebx < ArrayDims[0]; inc( ebx )) do

        for( mov( 0, ecx ); ecx < ArrayDims[1*4]; inc( ecx )) do

            // Compute the index into the array
            // as esi := ( ebx * ArrayDims[1*4] + ecx ) * 4
            // (Note that the final multiplication by 4 is
            //   handled by the scaled indexed addressing mode below.)

            mov( ebx, esi );
            intmul( ArrayDims[1*4], esi );
            add( ecx, esi );

            // Initialize the current array element with edx.

            mov( edx, [edi+esi*4] );
            inc( edx );

        endfor;

    endfor;
```

## 4.36  For More Information

In the electronic edition of this book, which you'll find at *http://webster.cs.ucr.e*
or *http://www.artofasm.com/*, you will find additional information about da
types. The HLA Standard Library documentation describes the HLA arra
package that provides support for dynamically allocated (and statically
allocated) arrays, indexing into arrays, and many other array options. You
should consult the HLA stdlib documentation for more details about this
array package. For additional information about data structure representati
in memory, you should consider reading my book *Write Great Code, Volume*
(No Starch Press, 2004). For an in-depth discussion of data types, you shou
consult a textbook on data structures and algorithms.

# 5

# PROCEDURES AND UNITS

 In a procedural programming language, the basic unit of code is the *procedure*. A procedure is a set of instructions that compute some value or take some action (such as printing or reading a character value). This chapter discusses how HLA implements procedures. It begins by discussing HLA's high-level syntax for procedure declarations and invocations, but it also describes the low-level implementation of procedures at the machine level. At this point, you should be getting comfortable with assembly language programming, so it's time to start presenting "pure" assembly language rather than continuing to rely on HLA's high-level syntax as a crutch.

## 5.1 Procedures

Most procedural programming languages implement procedures using the call/return mechanism. That is, some code calls a procedure, the procedure does its thing, and then the procedure returns to the caller. The call and return instructions provide the 80x86's *procedure invocation mechanism*. The calling code calls a procedure with the call instruction and the procedure returns to the caller with the ret instruction. For example, the following 80x86 instruction calls the HLA Standard Library stdout.newln routine:[1]

```
call stdout.newln;
```

The stdout.newln procedure prints a newline sequence to the console device and returns control to the instruction immediately following the ca stdout.newln; instruction.

Alas, the HLA Standard Library does not supply all the routines you w ever need. Most of the time you'll have to write your own procedures. T do this, you will use HLA's procedure-declaration facilities. A basic HLA procedure declaration takes the following form:

```
procedure ProcName;
    << Local declarations >>
begin ProcName;
    << Procedure statements >>
end ProcName;
```

Procedure declarations appear in the declaration section of your progra That is, anywhere you can put a static, const, type, or other declaration sectic you may place a procedure declaration. In the syntax example above, ProcNa represents the name of the procedure you wish to define. This can be any valid (and unique) HLA identifier. Whatever identifier follows the procedu: reserved word must also follow the begin and end reserved words in the p cedure. As you've probably noticed, a procedure declaration looks a whole like an HLA program. In fact, the only difference (so far) is the use of the procedure reserved word rather than the program reserved word.

Here is a concrete example of an HLA procedure declaration. This procedure stores zeros into the 256 double words that EBX points at upon entry into the procedure:

```
procedure zeroBytes;
begin zeroBytes;

    mov( 0, eax );
    mov( 256, ecx );
    repeat
        mov( eax, [ebx] );
        add( 4, ebx );
        dec( ecx );

    until( @z );  // That is, until ecx=0.

end zeroBytes;
```

---

[1] Normally you would call newln using the high-level newln(); syntax, but the call instruction works as well.

You can use the 80x86 call instruction to call this procedure. When, during program execution, the code falls into the end zeroBytes; statement, the procedure returns to whoever called it and begins executing the first instruction beyond the call instruction. The program in Listing 5-1 provides an example of a call to the zeroBytes routine.

```
program zeroBytesDemo;
#include( "stdlib.hhf" )


    procedure zeroBytes;
    begin zeroBytes;

        mov( 0, eax );
        mov( 256, ecx );
        repeat

            mov( eax, [ebx] );  // Zero out current dword.
            add( 4, ebx );      // Point ebx at next dword.
            dec( ecx );         // Count off 256 dwords.

        until( ecx = 0 );       // Repeat for 256 dwords.

    end zeroBytes;

static
    dwArray: dword[256];

begin zeroBytesDemo;

    lea( ebx, dwArray );
    call zeroBytes;

end zeroBytesDemo;
```

Listing 5-1: Example of a simple procedure

As you may have noticed when calling HLA Standard Library procedures, you don't have to use the call instruction to call HLA procedures. There is nothing special about the HLA Standard Library procedures versus your own procedures. Although the formal 80x86 mechanism for calling procedures is to use the call instruction, HLA provides a high-level extension that lets you call a procedure by simply specifying the procedure's name followed by an empty set of parentheses.[2] For example, either of the following statements will call the HLA Standard Library stdout.newln procedure:

```
call stdout.newln;
stdout.newln();
```

_____

[2] This assumes that the procedure does not have any parameters.

Likewise, either of the following statements will call the zeroBytes proced
in Listing 5-1:

```
call zeroBytes;
zeroBytes();
```

The choice of calling mechanism is strictly up to you. Most people,
however, find the high-level syntax easier to read.

## 5.2  Saving the State of the Machine

Take a look at the program in Listing 5-2. This section of code attempts to
print 20 lines of 40 spaces and an asterisk. Unfortunately, there is a subtle
bug that creates an infinite loop. The main program uses the repeat..unti
loop to call PrintSpaces 20 times. PrintSpaces uses ECX to count off the 40 spa
it prints. PrintSpaces returns with ECX containing 0. The main program th
prints an asterisk and a newline, decrements ECX, and then repeats becar
ECX isn't 0 (it will always contain $FFFF_FFFF at this point).

The problem here is that the PrintSpaces subroutine doesn't preserve t
ECX register. Preserving a register means you save it upon entry into the
subroutine and restore it before leaving. Had the PrintSpaces subroutine
preserved the contents of the ECX register, the program in Listing 5-2 wor
have functioned properly.

```
program nonWorkingProgram;
#include( "stdlib.hhf" );


    procedure PrintSpaces;
    begin PrintSpaces;

        mov( 40, ecx );
        repeat

            mov( ' ', al );
            stdout.putc( al );  // Print 1 of 40 spaces.
            dec( ecx );         // Count off 40 spaces.

        until( ecx = 0 );

    end PrintSpaces;

begin nonWorkingProgram;

    mov( 20, ecx );
    repeat

        PrintSpaces();
        stdout.put( '*', nl );
        dec( ecx );
```

```
            until( ecx = 0 );

end nonWorkingProgram;
```

*Listing 5-2: Program with an unintended infinite loop*

You can use the 80x86's push and pop instructions to preserve register values while you need to use them for something else. Consider the following code for PrintSpaces:

```
procedure PrintSpaces;
begin PrintSpaces;

    push( eax );
    push( ecx );
    mov( 40, ecx );
    repeat

        mov( ' ', al );
        stdout.putc( al );   // Print 1 of 40 spaces.
        dec( ecx );          // Count off 40 spaces.

    until( ecx = 0 );
    pop( ecx );
    pop( eax );

end PrintSpaces;
```

Note that PrintSpaces saves and restores EAX and ECX (because this procedure modifies these registers). Also, note that this code pops the registers off the stack in the reverse order that it pushed them. The last-in, first-out operation of the stack imposes this ordering.

Either the caller (the code containing the call instruction) or the callee (the subroutine) can take responsibility for preserving the registers. In the example above, the callee preserved the registers. The example in Listing 5-3 shows what this code might look like if the caller preserves the registers:

```
program callerPreservation;
#include( "stdlib.hhf" );


    procedure PrintSpaces;
    begin PrintSpaces;

        mov( 40, ecx );
        repeat

            mov( ' ', al );
            stdout.putc( al );   // Print 1 of 40 spaces.
            dec( ecx );          // Count off 40 spaces.

        until( ecx = 0 );

    end PrintSpaces;
```

```
begin callerPreservation;

    mov( 20, ecx );
    repeat

        push( eax );
        push( ecx );
        PrintSpaces();
        pop( ecx );
        pop( eax );
        stdout.put( '*', nl );
        dec( ecx );

    until( ecx = 0 );

end callerPreservation;
```

*Listing 5-3: Demonstration of caller register preservation*

There are two advantages to callee preservation: space and maintainabili∎ If the callee (the procedure) preserves all affected registers, then there is only one copy of the push and pop instructions, those the procedure contai∎ If the caller saves the values in the registers, the program needs a set of pu∎ and pop instructions around every call. Not only does this make your progra∎ longer, it also makes them harder to maintain. Remembering which registe∎ to push and pop on each procedure call is not easily done.

On the other hand, a subroutine may unnecessarily preserve some registe∎ if it preserves all the registers it modifies. In the examples above, the code∎ needn't save EAX. Although PrintSpaces changes AL, this won't affect the program's operation. If the caller is preserving the registers, it doesn't hav∎ to save registers it doesn't care about (see the program in Listing 5-4).

```
program callerPreservation2;
#include( "stdlib.hhf" );


    procedure PrintSpaces;
    begin PrintSpaces;

        mov( 40, ecx );
        repeat

            mov( ' ', al );
            stdout.putc( al );    // Print 1 of 40 spaces.
            dec( ecx );           // Count off 40 spaces.

        until( ecx = 0 );

    end PrintSpaces;

begin callerPreservation2;
```

```
    mov( 10, ecx );
    repeat

        push( ecx );
        PrintSpaces();
        pop( ecx );
        stdout.put( '*', nl );
        dec( ecx );

    until( ecx = 0 );


    mov( 5, ebx );
    while( ebx > 0 ) do

        PrintSpaces();

        stdout.put( ebx, nl );
        dec( ebx );

    endwhile;


    mov( 110, ecx );
    for( mov( 0, eax );  eax < 7; inc( eax )) do

        PrintSpaces();

        stdout.put( eax, " ", ecx, nl );
        dec( ecx );

    endfor;

end callerPreservation2;
```

*Listing 5-4: Demonstrating that caller preservation need not save all registers*

This example in Listing 5-4 provides three different cases. The first loop
(repeat..until) preserves only the ECX register. Modifying the AL register
won't affect the operation of this loop. Immediately after the first loop, this
code calls PrintSpaces again in the while loop. However, this code doesn't save
EAX or ECX because it doesn't care if PrintSpaces changes them.

One big problem with having the caller preserve registers is that your
program may change over time. You may modify the calling code or the
procedure to use additional registers. Such changes, of course, may change
the set of registers that you must preserve. Worse still, if the modification is
in the subroutine itself, you will need to locate *every* call to the routine and
verify that the subroutine does not change any registers the calling code uses.

Preserving registers isn't all there is to preserving the environment. You
can also push and pop variables and other values that a subroutine might
change. Because the 80x86 allows you to push and pop memory locations,
you can easily preserve these values as well.

## 5.3  Prematurely Returning from a Procedure

The HLA exit and exitif statements let you return from a procedure witho having to fall into the corresponding end statement in the procedure. The statements behave a whole lot like the break and breakif statements for loo except that they transfer control to the bottom of the procedure rather th out of the current loop. These statements are quite useful in many cases.

The syntax for these two statements is the following:

```
exit procedurename;
exitif( boolean_expression ) procedurename;
```

The *procedurename* operand is the name of the procedure you wish to e> If you specify the name of your main program, the exit and exitif stateme will terminate program execution (even if you're currently inside a procedu rather than the body of the main program).

The exit statement immediately transfers control out of the specified procedure or program. The conditional exitif statement first tests the boole expression and exits if the result is true. It is semantically equivalent to the following:

```
        if( boolean_expression ) then

            exit procedurename;

        endif;
```

Although the exit and exitif statements are invaluable in many cases, you should avoid using them without careful consideration. If a simple if statement will let you skip the rest of the code in your procedure, then by means use the if statement. Procedures that contain a lot of exit and exiti statements will be harder to read, understand, and maintain than procedur without these statements (after all, the exit and exitif statements are really nothing more than goto statements, and you've probably heard already abo the problems with gotos). exit and exitif are convenient when you have to return from a procedure inside a sequence of nested control structures, and slapping an if..endif around the remaining code in the procedure is impractical.

## 5.4  Local Variables

HLA procedures, like procedures and functions in most high-level languages, l you declare *local variables*. Local variables are generally accessible only withi the procedure; they are not accessible by the code that calls the procedure Local variable declarations are identical to variable declarations in your ma program except, of course, you declare the variables in the procedure's dec laration section rather than the main program's declaration section. Actually you may declare anything in the procedure's declaration section that is leg;

in the main program's declaration section, including constants, types, and even other procedures.[3] In this section, however, we'll concentrate on local variables.

Local variables have two important attributes that differentiate them from the variables in your main program (that is, *global* variables): *lexical scope* and *lifetime*. Lexical scope, or just *scope*, determines where an identifier is usable in your program. Lifetime determines when a variable has memory associated with it and is capable of storing data. Because these two concepts differentiate local and global variables, it is wise to spend some time discussing them.

Perhaps the best place to start when discussing the scope and lifetimes of local variables is with the scope and lifetimes of global variables—those variables you declare in your main program. Until now, the only rule you've had to follow concerning the declaration of your variables has been "you must declare all variables that you use in your programs." The position of the HLA declaration section with respect to the program statements automatically enforces the other major rule, which is "you must declare all variables before their first use." With the introduction of procedures, it is now possible to violate this rule because (1) procedures may access global variables, and (2) procedure declarations may appear anywhere in a declaration section, even before some variable declarations. The program in Listing 5-5 demonstrates this source code organization.

```
program demoGlobalScope;
#include( "stdlib.hhf" );

static
    AccessibleInProc: char;


    procedure aProc;
    begin aProc;

        mov( 'a', AccessibleInProc );

    end aProc;


static
    InaccessibleInProc: char;


begin demoGlobalScope;


    mov( 'b', InaccessibleInProc );
    aProc();
    stdout.put
```

---

[3] Strictly speaking, this is not true. You may not declare external objects within a procedure. External objects are the subject of Section 5.24.

```
        (
            "AccessibleInProc   = '",  AccessibleInProc,    "'" nl
            "InaccessibleInProc = '",  InaccessibleInProc,  "'" nl
        );


end demoGlobalScope;
```

*Listing 5-5: Demonstration of global scope*

This example demonstrates that a procedure can access global variable in the main program as long as you declare those global variables before the procedure. In this example, the aProc procedure cannot access the InaccessibleInProc variable because its declaration appears after the procedure declaration. However, aProc may reference AccessibleInProc because its declaration appears before the aProc procedure.

A procedure can access any static, storage, or readonly object exactly the same way the main program accesses such variables—by referencing the name. Although a procedure may access global var objects, a different syntax is necessary, and you need to learn a little more before you will understand the purpose of the additional syntax (for more details, please consult the HLA reference manual).

Accessing global objects is convenient and easy. Unfortunately, as you' probably learned when studying high-level language programming, accessing global objects makes your programs harder to read, understand, and maintain. Like most introductory programming texts, this book discourages the use of global variables within procedures. Accessing global variables within a procedure is sometimes the best solution to a given problem. However, such (legitimate) access typically occurs only in advanced programs involving multiple threads of execution or in other complex systems. Because it is unlikely you would be writing such code at this point, it is equally unlikely that you will absolutely need to access global variables in your procedures, so you should carefully consider your options before doing so.[4]

Declaring local variables in your procedures is very easy; you use the same declaration sections as the main program: static, readonly, storage, and var. The same rules and syntax for the declaration sections and the access of variables you declare in these sections apply in your procedure. The example code in Listing 5-6 demonstrates the declaration of a local variable.

```
program demoLocalVars;
#include( "stdlib.hhf" );

    // Simple procedure that displays 0..9 using
    // a local variable as a loop control variable.
```

---

[4] Note that this argument against accessing global variables does not apply to other global symbols. It is perfectly reasonable to access global constants, types, procedures, and other objects in your programs.

```
procedure CntTo10;
var
    i: int32;

begin CntTo10;

    for( mov( 0, i ); i < 10; inc( i )) do

        stdout.put( "i=" , i, nl );

    endfor;

end CntTo10;


begin demoLocalVars;

    CntTo10();

end demoLocalVars;
```

*Listing 5-6: Example of a local variable in a procedure*

Local variables in a procedure are accessible only within that procedure.[5] Therefore, the variable i in procedure CntTo10 in Listing 5-6 is not accessible in the main program.

For local variables, HLA relaxes the rule that identifiers must be unique in a program. In an HLA program, all identifiers must be unique within a given *scope.* Therefore, all global names must be unique with respect to one another. Similarly, all local variables within a given procedure must have unique names *but only with respect to other local symbols in that same procedure.* In particular, a local name may be the same as a global name. When this occurs, HLA creates two separate variables. Within the scope of the procedure, any reference to the common name accesses the local variable; outside that procedure, any reference to the common name references the global identifier. Although the quality of the resultant code is questionable, it is perfectly legal to have a global identifier named MyVar with the same local name in two or more different procedures. The procedures each have their own local variant of the object, which is independent of MyVar in the main program. Listing 5-7 provides an example of an HLA program that demonstrates this feature.

```
program demoLocalVars2;
#include( "stdlib.hhf" );

static
    i:  uns32 := 10;
    j:  uns32 := 20;
```

---

[5] Strictly speaking, this is not true. However, accessing nonlocal var objects is beyond the scope of this text. See the HLA documentation for more details.

```
// The following procedure declares i and j
// as local variables, so it does not have access
// to the global variables by the same name.

procedure First;
var
    i:int32;
    j:uns32;

begin First;

    mov( 10, j );
    for( mov( 0, i ); i < 10; inc( i )) do

        stdout.put( "i=", i," j=", j, nl );
        dec( j );

    endfor;

end First;


// This procedure declares only an i variable.
// It cannot access the value of the global i
// variable but it can access the value of the
// global j object because it does not provide
// a local variant of j.

procedure Second;
var
    i:uns32;

begin Second;

    mov( 10, j );
    for( mov( 0, i ); i < 10; inc( i )) do

        stdout.put( "i=", i," j=", j, nl );
        dec( j );

    endfor;

end Second;


begin demoLocalVars2;

    First();
    Second();

    // Because the calls to First and Second have not
    // modified variable i, the following statement
    // should print "i=10". However, because the Second
    // procedure manipulated global variable j, this
    // code will print "j=0" rather than "j=20".
```

```
        stdout.put( "i=", i, " j=", j, nl );

end demoLocalVars2;
```

Listing 5-7: Local variables need not have globally unique names.

There are good and bad points to be made about reusing global names within a procedure. On the one hand, there is the potential for confusion. If you use a name like ProfitsThisYear as a global symbol and you reuse that name within a procedure, someone reading the procedure might think that the procedure refers to the global symbol rather than the local symbol. On the other hand, simple names like i, j, and k are nearly meaningless (almost everyone expects the program to use them as loop-control variables or for other local uses), so reusing these names as local objects is probably a good idea. From a software engineering perspective, it is probably a good idea to keep all variables names that have a very specific meaning (like ProfitsThisYear) unique throughout your program. General names that have a nebulous meaning (like index and counter and names like i, j, or k) will probably be okay to reuse as global variables.

There is one last point to make about the scope of identifiers in an HLA program: variables in separate procedures are separate, even if they have the same name. The First and Second procedures in Listing 5-7, for example, share the same name (i) for a local variable. However, the i in First is a completely different variable from the i in Second.

The second major attribute that differentiates local variables from global variables is *lifetime*. The lifetime of a variable spans from the point when the program first allocates storage for a variable to the point when the program deallocates the storage for that variable. Note that lifetime is a dynamic attribute (controlled at runtime), whereas scope is a static attribute (controlled at compile time). In particular, a variable can actually have several lifetimes if the program repeatedly allocates and then deallocates the storage for that variable.

Global variables always have a single lifetime that spans from the moment when the main program first begins execution to the point when the main program terminates. Likewise, all static objects have a single lifetime that spans the execution of the program (remember, static objects are those you declare in the static, readonly, or storage sections). This is true even within procedures. So there is no difference between the lifetime of a local static object and the lifetime of a global static object. Variables you declare in the var section, however, are a different matter. HLA's var objects use *automatic storage allocation*. Automatic storage allocation means that the procedure automatically allocates storage for a local variable upon entry into a procedure. Similarly, the program deallocates storage for automatic objects when the procedure returns to its caller. Therefore, the lifetime of an automatic object is from the point of the execution of the first statement in a procedure to the point when it returns to its caller.

Perhaps the most important thing to note about automatic variables is that you cannot expect them to maintain their values between calls to the procedure. Once the procedure returns to its caller, the storage for the automatic variable is lost and, therefore, the value is lost as well. Thus, *you must always assume that a local var object is uninitialized upon entry into a proced* even if you know you've called the procedure before and the previous procedure invocation initialized that variable. Whatever value the last cal. stored into the variable was lost when the procedure returned to its call If you need to maintain the value of a variable between calls to a procedu you should use one of the static variable declaration types.

Given that automatic variables cannot maintain their values across p cedure calls, you might wonder why you would want to use them at all. Hc ever, there are several benefits to automatic variables that static variables not have. The biggest disadvantage to static variables is that they consume memory even when the (only) procedure that references them is not runni Automatic variables, on the other hand, consume storage only while the associated procedure is executing. Upon return, the procedure returns a automatic storage it allocated back to the system for reuse by other proc dures. You'll see some additional advantages to automatic variables later i this chapter.

## 5.5 Other Local and Global Symbol Types

As the previous section notes, HLA procedures let you declare constants. values, types, and almost everything else legal in the main program's decla tion section. The same rules for scope apply to these identifiers. Therefore you can reuse constant names, procedure names, type names, and the like local declarations.

Referencing global constants, values, and types does not present the same software engineering problems that occur when you reference globa variables. The problem with referencing global variables is that a procedu can change the value of a global variable in a nonobvious way. This makes programs more difficult to read, understand, and maintain because you can't often tell that a procedure is modifying memory by looking only at th call to that procedure. Constants, values, types, and other nonvariable objects don't suffer from this problem because you cannot change them at runtim Therefore, the pressure to avoid global objects at nearly all costs doesn't apply nonvariable objects.

Having said that it's okay to access global constants, types, and so on, i also worth pointing out that you should declare these objects locally withi a procedure if the only place your program references such objects is withi that procedure. Doing so will make your programs a little easier to read because the person reading your code won't have to search all over the plac for the symbol's definition.

## 5.6 Parameters

Although many procedures are totally self-contained, most procedures require some input data and return some data to the caller. Parameters are values that you pass to and from a procedure. In straight assembly language passing parameters can be a real chore. Fortunately, HLA provides a high-level-language-like syntax for procedure declarations and for procedure calls involving parameters. This section presents HLA's high-level parameter syntax. Later sections in this chapter deal with the low-level mechanisms for passing parameters in pure assembly code.

The first thing to consider when discussing parameters is *how* we pass them to a procedure. If you are familiar with Pascal or C/C++, you've probably seen two ways to pass parameters: pass by value and pass by reference. HLA certainly supports these two parameter-passing mechanisms. However, HLA also supports pass by value/result, pass by result, pass by name, and pass by lazy evaluation. Of course, HLA is assembly language, so it is possible to pass parameters in HLA using any scheme you can dream up (at least, any scheme that is possible at all on the CPU). However, HLA provides special high-level syntax for pass by value, reference, value/result, result, name, and lazy evaluation.

Because pass by value/result, result, name, and lazy evaluation are somewhat advanced, this book will not deal with those parameter-passing mechanisms. If you're interested in learning more about these parameter-passing schemes, see the HLA reference manual or check out the electronic versions of this text at *http://webster.cs.ucr.edu/* or *http://www.artofasm.com/*.

Another concern you will face when dealing with parameters is *where* you pass them. There are many different places to pass parameters; in this section we'll pass procedure parameters on the stack. You don't really need to concern yourself with the details because HLA abstracts them away for you; however, do keep in mind that procedure calls and procedure parameters make use of the stack. Therefore, whatever you push on the stack immediately before a procedure call is not going to be on the top of the stack upon entry into the procedure.

### 5.6.1 Pass by Value

A parameter passed by value is just that—the caller passes a value to the procedure. Pass-by-value parameters are input-only parameters. That is, you can pass them to a procedure, but the procedure cannot return values through them. Given the HLA procedure call

```
CallProc(I);
```

if you pass I by value, then CallProc does not change the value of I, regardless of what happens to the parameter inside CallProc.

Because you must pass a copy of the data to the procedure, you should use this method only for passing small objects like bytes, words, and double words. Passing large arrays and records by value is very inefficient (because you must create and pass a copy of the object to the procedure).

HLA, like Pascal and C/C++, passes parameters by value unless you specify otherwise. The following is what a typical function looks like with a single pass-by-value parameter.

```
procedure PrintNSpaces( N:uns32 );
begin PrintNSpaces;

    push( ecx );
    mov( N, ecx );
    repeat

        stdout.put( ' ' );    // Print 1 of N spaces.
        dec( ecx );           // Count off N spaces.

    until( ecx = 0 );
    pop( ecx );

end PrintNSpaces;
```

The parameter N in PrintNSpaces is known as a *formal parameter*. Anywhe
the name N appears in the body of the procedure, the program references t
value passed through N by the caller.

The calling sequence for PrintNSpaces can be any of the following:

```
PrintNSpaces( constant );
PrintNSpaces( reg32 );
PrintNSpaces( uns32_variable );
```

Here are some concrete examples of calls to PrintNSpaces:

```
PrintNSpaces( 40 );
PrintNSpaces( eax );
PrintNSpaces( SpacesToPrint );
```

The parameter in the calls to PrintNSpaces is known as an *actual parame*
In the examples above, 40, eax, and SpacesToPrint are the actual parameters

Note that pass-by-value parameters behave exactly like local variables y
declare in the var section with the single exception that the procedure's
caller initializes these local variables before it passes control to the procedur

HLA uses positional parameter notation just as most high-level languag
do. Therefore, if you need to pass more than one parameter, HLA will
associate the actual parameters with the formal parameters by their position
in the parameter list. The following PrintNChars procedure demonstrates a
simple procedure that has two parameters:

```
procedure PrintNChars( N:uns32; c:char );
begin PrintNChars;

    push( ecx );
    mov( N, ecx );
    repeat
```

```
        stdout.put( c );    // Print 1 of N characters.
        dec( ecx );         // Count off N characters.

    until( ecx = 0 );
    pop( ecx );

end PrintNChars;
```

The following is an invocation of the `PrintNChars` procedure that will print 20 asterisk characters:

```
PrintNChars( 20, '*' );
```

Note that HLA uses semicolons to separate the formal parameters in the procedure declaration, and it uses commas to separate the actual parameters in the procedure invocation (Pascal programmers should be comfortable with this notation). Also note that each HLA formal parameter declaration takes the following form:

```
parameter_identifier : type_identifier
```

In particular, note that the parameter type has to be an identifier. None of the following are legal parameter declarations because the data type is not a single identifier:

```
PtrVar: pointer to uns32
ArrayVar: uns32[10]
recordVar: record i:int32; u:uns32; endrecord
DynArray: array.dArray( uns32, 2 )
```

However, don't get the impression that you cannot pass pointer, array, record, or dynamic array variables as parameters. The trick is to declare a data type for each of these types in the type section. Then you can use a single identifier as the type in the parameter declaration. The following code fragment demonstrates how to do this with the four data types above:

```
type
    uPtr:       pointer to uns32;
    uArray10:   uns32[10];
    recType:    record i:int32; u:uns32; endrecord
    dType:      array.dArray( uns32, 2 );

    procedure FancyParms
    (
        PtrVar:     uPtr;
        ArrayVar: uArray10;
        recordVar:recType;
        DynArray: dType
    );
```

```
begin FancyParms;
        .
        .
        .
end FancyParms;
```

By default, HLA assumes that you intend to pass a parameter by value
HLA also lets you explicitly state that a parameter is a value parameter by
prefacing the formal parameter declaration with the val keyword. The
following is a version of the PrintNSpaces procedure that explicitly states
that N is a pass-by-value parameter:

```
procedure PrintNSpaces( val N:uns32 );
begin PrintNSpaces;

    push( ecx );
    mov( N, ecx );
    repeat

        stdout.put( ' ' );   // Print 1 of N spaces.
        dec( ecx );          // Count off N spaces.

    until( ecx = 0 );
    pop( ecx );

end PrintNSpaces;
```

Explicitly stating that a parameter is a pass-by-value parameter is a good
idea if you have multiple parameters in the same procedure declaration that
use different passing mechanisms.

When you pass a parameter by value and call the procedure using the
HLA high-level language syntax, HLA will automatically generate code that
will make a copy of the actual parameter's value and copy this data into the
local storage for that parameter (that is, the formal parameter). For small
objects, pass by value is probably the most efficient way to pass a parameter.
For large objects, however, HLA must generate code that copies each and
every byte of the actual parameter into the formal parameter. For large
arrays and records, this can be a very expensive operation.[6] Unless you have
specific semantic concerns that require you to pass a large array or record b
value, you should use pass by reference or some other parameter-passing
mechanism for arrays and records.

When passing parameters to a procedure, HLA checks the type of each
actual parameter and compares this type to the corresponding formal param
eter. If the types do not agree, HLA then checks to see if either the actual o
the formal parameter is a byte, word, or double-word object and the other
parameter is 1, 2, or 4 bytes in length (respectively). If the actual paramete
does not satisfy either of these conditions, HLA reports a parameter-type

---

[6] Note to C/C++ programmers: HLA does not automatically pass arrays by reference. If you
specify an array type as a formal parameter, HLA will emit code that makes a copy of each and
every byte of that array when you call the associated procedure.

mismatch error. If, for some reason, you need to pass a parameter to a procedure using a different type than the procedure calls for, you can always use the HLA type-coercion operator to override the type of the actual parameter.

## 5.6.2 Pass by Reference

To pass a parameter by reference, you must pass the address of a variable rather than its value. In other words, you must pass a pointer to the data. The procedure must dereference this pointer to access the data. Passing parameters by reference is useful when you must modify the actual parameter or when you pass large data structures between procedures.

To declare a pass-by-reference parameter, you must preface the formal parameter declaration with the var keyword. The following code fragment demonstrates this:

```
procedure UsePassByReference( var PBRvar: int32 );
begin UsePassByReference;
    .
    .
    .
end UsePassByReference;
```

Calling a procedure with a pass-by-reference parameter uses the same syntax as pass by value except that the parameter has to be a memory location; it cannot be a constant or a register. Furthermore, the type of the memory location must exactly match the type of the formal parameter. The following are legal calls to the procedure above (assuming i32 is an int32 variable):

```
UsePassByReference( i32 );
UsePassByReference( (type int32 [ebx] ) );
```

The following are all illegal UsePassbyReference invocations (assuming charVar is of type char):

```
UsePassByReference( 40 );        // Constants are illegal.
UsePassByReference( EAX );       // Bare registers are illegal.
UsePassByReference( charVar );   // Actual parameter type must match
                                 // the formal parameter type.
```

Unlike the high-level languages Pascal and C++, HLA does not completely hide the fact that you are passing a pointer rather than a value. In a procedure invocation, HLA will automatically compute the address of a variable and pass that address to the procedure. Within the procedure itself, however, you cannot treat the variable like a value parameter (as you could in most high-level languages). Instead, you treat the parameter as a double-word variable containing a pointer to the specified data. You must explicitly dereference this pointer when accessing the parameter's value. The example appearing in Listing 5-8 provides a simple demonstration of this.

```
program PassByRefDemo;
#include( "stdlib.hhf" );

var
    i:  int32;
    j:  int32;

    procedure pbr( var a:int32; var b:int32 );
    const
        aa: text := "(type int32 [ebx])";
        bb: text := "(type int32 [ebx])";

    begin pbr;

        push( eax );
        push( ebx );            // Need to use ebx to dereference a and b.

        // a = -1;

        mov( a, ebx );          // Get ptr to the "a" variable.
        mov( -1, aa );          // Store -1 into the "a" parameter.

        // b = -2;

        mov( b, ebx );          // Get ptr to the "b" variable.
        mov( -2, bb );          // Store -2 into the "b" parameter.

        // Print the sum of a+b.
        // Note that ebx currently contains a pointer to "b".

        mov( bb, eax );
        mov( a, ebx );          // Get ptr to "a" variable.
        add( aa, eax );
        stdout.put( "a+b=", (type int32 eax), nl );

    end pbr;

begin PassByRefDemo;

    // Give i and j some initial values so
    // we can see that pass by reference will
    // overwrite these values.

    mov( 50, i );
    mov( 25, j );

    // Call pbr passing i and j by reference

    pbr( i, j );

    // Display the results returned by pbr.
```

```
        stdout.put
        (
            "i=  ", i, nl,
            "j=  ", j, nl
        );

end PassByRefDemo;
```

*Listing 5-8: Accessing pass-by-reference parameters*

Passing parameters by reference can produce some peculiar results in some rare circumstances. Consider the pbr procedure in Listing 5-8. Were you to modify the call in the main program to be pbr(i,i) rather than pbr(i,j);, the program would produce the following nonintuitive output:

```
a+b=-4
i=  -2;
j=  25;
```

The reason this code displays a+b=-4 rather than the expected a+b=-3 is because the pbr(i,i); call passes the same actual parameter for a and b. As a result, the a and b reference parameters both contain a pointer to the same memory location—that of the variable i. In this case, a and b are *aliases* of one another. Therefore, when the code stores −2 at the location pointed at by b, it overwrites the −1 stored earlier at the location pointed at by a. When the program fetches the value pointed at by a and b to compute their sum, both a and b point at the same value, which is −2. Summing −2 + −2 produces the −4 result that the program displays. This nonintuitive behavior is possible anytime you encounter aliases in a program. Passing the same variable as two different reference parameters probably isn't very common. But you could also create an alias if a procedure references a global variable and you pass that same global variable by reference to the procedure (this is a good example of yet one more reason why you should avoid referencing global variables in a procedure).

Pass by reference is usually less efficient than pass by value. You must dereference all pass-by-reference parameters on each access; this is slower than simply using a value because it typically requires at least two instructions. However, when passing a large data structure, pass by reference is faster because you do not have to copy the large data structure before calling the procedure. Of course, you'd probably need to access elements of that large data structure (for example, an array) using a pointer, so very little efficiency is lost when you pass large arrays by reference.

## 5.7  Functions and Function Results

Functions are procedures that return some result to the caller. In assembly language, there are very few syntactical differences between a procedure and a function, which is why HLA doesn't provide a specific declaration for a function. Nevertheless, although there is very little *syntactical* difference between assembly procedures and functions, there are some *semantic* diffe ences. That is, although you can declare them the same way in HLA, you them differently.

Procedures are a sequence of machine instructions that fulfill some ta The end result of the execution of a procedure is the accomplishment of that activity. Functions, on the other hand, execute a sequence of machin instructions specifically to compute some value to return to the caller. O course, a function can perform some activity as well and procedures can undoubtedly compute some values, but the main difference is that the purpc of a function is to return some computed result; procedures don't have th requirement.

A good example of a procedure is the stdout.puti32 procedure. This procedure requires a single int32 parameter. The purpose of this procedu is to print the decimal conversion of this integer value to the standard outp device. Note that stdout.puti32 doesn't return any kind of value that is usak by the calling program.

A good example of a function is the cs.member function. This function expects two parameters: The first is a character value and the second is a character set value. This function returns true (1) in EAX if the character a member of the specified character set. It returns false if the character para eter is not a member of the character set.

Logically, the fact that cs.member returns a usable value to the calling code (in EAX) while stdout.puti32 does not is a good example of the mai difference between a function and a procedure. So, in general, a procedu becomes a function by virtue of the fact that you explicitly decide to retu a value somewhere upon procedure return. No special syntax is needed to declare and use a function. You still write the code as a procedure.

### 5.7.1   Returning Function Results

The 80x86's registers are the most common place to return function results. The cs.member routine in the HLA Standard Library is a good exampl of a function that returns a value in one of the CPU's registers. It returns true (1) or false (0) in the EAX register. By convention, programmers try return 8-, 16-, and 32-bit (nonreal) results in the AL, AX, and EAX registe respectively.[7] This is where most high-level languages return these types of results.

Of course, there is nothing particularly sacred about the AL/AX/EAX register. You could return function results in any register if it is more conve nient to do so. However, if you don't have a good reason for not using AL, AX/EAX, then you should follow the convention. Doing so will help other understand your code better because they will generally assume that your functions return small results in the AL/AX/EAX register set.

If you need to return a function result that is larger than 32 bits, you obviously must return it somewhere other than in EAX (which can hold on 32-bit values). For values slightly larger than 32 bits (e.g., 64 bits or maybe eve

---

[7] In Chapter 6 you'll see where most programmers return real results.

as many as 128 bits), you can split the result into pieces and return those parts in two or more registers. It is common to see programs returning 64-bit values in the EDX:EAX register pair (for example, the HLA Standard Library `stdin.geti64` function returns a 64-bit integer in the EDX:EAX register pair).

If you need to return a large object as a function result, say an array of 1,000 elements, you obviously are not going to be able to return the function result in the registers. There are two common ways to deal with large function return results: Either pass the return value as a reference parameter or allocate storage on the heap (using `mem.alloc`) for the object and return a pointer to it in a 32-bit register. Of course, if you return a pointer to storage you've allocated on the heap, the calling program must free this storage when it has finished with it.

## 5.7.2  Instruction Composition in HLA

Several HLA Standard Library functions allow you to call them as operands of other instructions. For example, consider the following code fragment:

```
if( cs.member( al, {'a'..'z'}) ) then
   .
   .
   .
endif;
```

As your high-level language experience (and HLA experience) should suggest, this code calls the `cs.member` function to check to see if the character in AL is a lowercase alphabetic character. If the `cs.member` function returns true, then this code fragment executes the then section of the if statement; however, if `cs.member` returns false, this code fragment skips the if..then body. There is nothing spectacular here except for the fact that HLA doesn't support function calls as boolean expressions in the if statement (look back at Chapter 1 to see the complete set of allowable expressions). How then, does this program compile and run, producing the intuitive results?

The next section describes how you can tell HLA that you want to use a function call in a boolean expression. However, to understand how this works, you need to first learn about *instruction composition* in HLA.

Instruction composition lets you use one instruction as the operand of another. For example, consider the mov instruction. It has two operands: a source operand and a destination operand. Instruction composition lets you substitute a valid 80x86 machine instruction for either (or both) operands. The following is a simple example:

```
mov( mov( 0, eax ), ebx );
```

Of course, the immediate question is, "What does this mean?" To understand what is going on, you must first realize that most instructions "return" a value to the compiler while they are being compiled. For most instructions, the value they "return" is their destination operand. Therefore, mov( 0, eax );

returns the string eax to the compiler during compilation because EAX i
the destination operand. Most of the time, specifically when an instructic
appears on a line by itself, the compiler ignores the returned string resul
However, HLA uses this string result whenever you supply an instruction
in place of some operand; specifically, HLA uses that string as the operand
place of the instruction. Therefore, the mov instruction above is equivalent
the following two-instruction sequence:

```
mov( 0, eax );      // HLA compiles interior instructions first.
mov( eax, ebx );    // HLA substituted "eax" for "mov( 0, eax )"
```

When processing composed instructions (that is, instruction sequence
that have other instructions as operands), HLA always works in a "left-to-rig
then depth-first (inside-out)" manner. To make sense of this, consider the
following instructions:

```
add( sub( mov( i, eax ), mov( j, ebx )), mov( k, ecx ));
```

To interpret what is happening here, begin with the source operand. I
consists of the following:

```
sub( mov( i, eax ), mov( j, ebx ))
```

The source operand for this instruction is mov( i, eax ) and this instru
tion does not have any composition, so HLA emits this instruction and return
its destination operand (eax) for use as the source to the sub instruction. Th
effectively gives us the following:

```
sub( eax, mov( j, ebx ))
```

Now HLA compiles the instruction that appears as the destination ope
and (mov( j, ebx )) and returns its destination operand (ebx) to substitute fc
this mov in the sub instruction. This yields the following:

```
sub( eax, ebx )
```

This is a complete instruction, without composition, that HLA can
compile. So it compiles this instruction and returns its destination operanc
(ebx) as the string result to substitute for the sub in the original add instructior
So the original add instruction now becomes

```
add( ebx, mov( k, ecx ));
```

HLA next compiles the mov instruction appearing in the destination
operand. It returns its destination operand as a string that HLA substitutes
for the mov, finally yielding the simple instruction

```
add( ebx, ecx );
```

The compilation of the original add instruction, therefore, yields the following instruction sequence:

```
mov( i, eax );
mov( j, ebx );
sub( eax, ebx );
mov( k, ecx );
add( ebx, ecx );
```

Whew! It's rather difficult to look at the original instruction and easily see that this sequence is the result. As you can see in this example, *overzealous use of instruction composition can produce nearly unreadable programs.* You should be very careful about using instruction composition in your programs. With only a few exceptions, writing a composed instruction sequence makes your program harder to read.

Note that the excessive use of instruction composition may make errors in your program difficult to decipher. Consider the following HLA statement:

```
add( mov( eax, i ), mov( ebx, j ) );
```

This instruction composition yields the following 80x86 instruction sequence:

```
mov( eax, i );
mov( ebx, j );
add( i, j );
```

Of course, the compiler will complain that you're attempting to add one memory location to another. However, the instruction composition effectively masks this fact and makes it difficult to comprehend the cause of the error message. Moral of the story: Avoid using instruction composition unless it really makes your program easier to read. The few examples in this section demonstrate how *not* to use instruction composition.

There are two main areas where using instruction composition can help make your programs more readable. The first is in HLA's high-level language control structures. The other is in procedure parameters. Although instruction composition is useful in these two cases (and probably a few others as well), this doesn't give you a license to use extremely convoluted instructions like the add instruction in the previous example. Instead, most of the time you will use a single instruction or a function call in place of a single operand in a high-level language boolean expression or in a procedure/function parameter.

While we're on the subject, exactly what does a procedure call return as the string that HLA substitutes for the call in an instruction composition? For that matter, what do statements like if..endif return? How about instructions that don't have a destination operand? Well, function return results are the subject of the next section, so you'll read about that in a few moments. As for all the other statements and instructions, you should check out the HLA reference manual. It lists each instruction and its returns value. The returns value is the string that HLA will substitute for the instruction when it appears as the operand to another instruction. Note that many HLA statements and instr**u**tions return the empty string as their returns value (by default, so do proc**e**dure calls). If an instruction returns the empty string as its composition value, then HLA will report an error if you attempt to use it as the operand **of** another instruction. For example, the if..then..endif statement returns th**e** empty string as its returns value, so you may not bury an if..then..endif inside another instruction.

## 5.7.3   The HLA @returns Option in Procedures

HLA procedure declarations allow a special option that specifies the string **to** use when a procedure invocation appears as the operand of another instru**c**tion: the @returns option. The syntax for a procedure declaration with the @returns option is as follows:

```
procedure ProcName ( optional_parameters );  @returns( string_constant );
    << Local declarations >>
begin ProcName;
    << Procedure statements >>
end ProcName;
```

If the @returns option is not present, HLA assigns the empty string to th**e** @returns value for the procedure. This effectively makes it illegal to use tha**t** procedure invocation as the operand to another instruction.

The @returns option requires a single-string expression surrounded by parentheses. HLA will substitute this string constant for the procedure call **if** it ever appears as the operand of another instruction. Typically this strin**g** constant is a register name; however, any text that would be legal as an instruction operand is okay here. For example, you could specify memory addresses or constants. For purposes of clarity, you should always specify th**e** location of a function's return value in the @returns parameter.

As an example, consider the following boolean function that returns tru**e** or false in the EAX register if the single-character parameter is an alphabeti**c** character:[8]

```
procedure IsAlphabeticChar( c:char ); @returns( "EAX" );
begin IsAlphabeticChar;

    // Note that cs.member returns true/false in eax.

    cs.member( c, {'a'..'z', 'A'..'Z'} );

end IsAlphabeticChar;
```

---

[8] Before you run off and actually use this function in your own programs, note that the HLA Standard Library provides the char.isAlpha function that provides this test. See the HLA documentation for more details.

Once you tack the @returns option on the end of this procedure declaration, you can legally use a call to IsAlphabeticChar as an operand to other HLA statements and instructions:

```
mov( IsAlphabeticChar( al ), ebx );
    .
    .
    .
if( IsAlphabeticChar( ch ) ) then
    .
    .
    .
endif;
```

The last example above demonstrates that, via the @returns option, you can embed calls to your own functions in the boolean expression field of various HLA statements. Note that the code above is equivalent to:

```
IsAlphabeticChar( ch );
if( eax ) then
    .
    .
    .
endif;
```

Not all HLA high-level language statements expand composed instructions before the statement. For example, consider the following while statement:

```
while( IsAlphabeticChar( ch ) ) do
    .
    .
    .
endwhile;
```

This code does not expand to the following:

```
IsAlphabeticChar( ch );
while( eax ) do
    .
    .
    .
endwhile;
```

Instead, the call to IsAlphabeticChar expands inside the while's boolean expression so that the program calls this function on each iteration of the loop.

You should exercise caution when entering the @returns parameter. H**
does not check the syntax of the string parameter when it is compiling the
procedure declaration (other than to verify that it is a string constant).
Instead, HLA checks the syntax when it replaces the function call with the
@returns string. So if you had specified eaz instead of eax as the @returns
parameter for IsAlphabeticChar in the previous examples, HLA would not
have reported an error until you actually used IsAlphabeticChar as an operan**
Then of course, HLA would complain about the illegal operand, and it's n**
at all clear what the problem is by looking at the IsAlphabeticChar invocation. So take special care not to introduce typographical errors into the
@returns string; figuring out such errors later can be very difficult.

# 5.8 Recursion

*Recursion* occurs when a procedure calls itself. The following, for example,**
a recursive procedure:

```
procedure Recursive;
begin Recursive;

    Recursive();

end Recursive;
```

Of course, the CPU will never return from this procedure. Upon entry
into Recursive, this procedure will immediately call itself again, and contro**
will never pass to the end of the procedure. In this particular case, runawa**
recursion results in an infinite loop.[9]

Like a looping structure, recursion requires a termination condition i**
order to stop infinite recursion. Recursive could be rewritten with a termination condition as follows:

```
procedure Recursive;
begin Recursive;

    dec( eax );
    if( @nz ) then

        Recursive();

    endif;

end Recursive;
```

---

[9] Well, not really infinite. The stack will overflow and Windows, Mac OS X, FreeBSD, or Linu**
will raise an exception at that point.

This modification to the routine causes `Recursive` to call itself the number of times appearing in the EAX register. On each call, `Recursive` decrements the EAX register by 1 and then calls itself again. Eventually, `Recursive` decrements EAX to 0 and returns from each call until it returns to the original caller.

So far, however, there hasn't been a real need for recursion. After all, you could efficiently code this procedure as follows:

```
procedure Recursive;
begin Recursive;

    repeat
        dec( eax );
    until( @z );

end Recursive;
```

Both examples would repeat the body of the procedure the number of times passed in the EAX register.[10] As it turns out, there are only a few recursive algorithms that you cannot implement in an iterative fashion. However, many recursively implemented algorithms are more efficient than their iterative counterparts, and most of the time the recursive form of the algorithm is much easier to understand.

The quicksort algorithm is probably the most famous algorithm that usually appears in recursive form. An HLA implementation of this algorithm appears in Listing 5-9.

```
program QSDemo;
#include( "stdlib.hhf" );

type
    ArrayType: uns32[ 10 ];

static
    theArray:   ArrayType := [1,10,2,9,3,8,4,7,5,6];


    procedure quicksort( var a:ArrayType; Low:int32; High:int32 );
    const
        i:      text := "(type int32 edi)";
        j:      text := "(type int32 esi)";
        Middle: text := "(type uns32 edx)";
        ary:    text := "[ebx]";

    begin quicksort;
```

---

[10] The latter version will do it considerably faster because it doesn't have the overhead of the call/ret instructions.

```
push( eax );
push( ebx );
push( ecx );
push( edx );
push( esi );
push( edi );

mov( a, ebx );        // Load BASE address of "a" into ebx.

mov( Low, edi);       // i := Low;
mov( High, esi );     // j := High;

// Compute a pivotal element by selecting the
// physical middle element of the array.

mov( i, eax );
add( j, eax );
shr( 1, eax );
mov( ary[eax*4], Middle );  // Put middle value in edx.

// Repeat until the edi and esi indexes cross one
// another (edi works from the start towards the end
// of the array, esi works from the end towards the
// start of the array).

repeat

    // Scan from the start of the array forward
    // looking for the first element greater or equal
    // to the middle element).

    while( Middle > ary[i*4] ) do

        inc( i );

    endwhile;

    // Scan from the end of the array backwards looking
    // for the first element that is less than or equal
    // to the middle element.

    while( Middle < ary[j*4] ) do

        dec( j );

    endwhile;

    // If we've stopped before the two pointers have
    // passed over one another, then we've got two
    // elements that are out of order with respect
    // to the middle element, so swap these two elements.

    if( i <= j ) then
```

```
                    mov( ary[i*4], eax );
                    mov( ary[j*4], ecx );
                    mov( eax, ary[j*4] );
                    mov( ecx, ary[i*4] );
                    inc( i );
                    dec( j );

            endif;

        until( i > j );

        // We have just placed all elements in the array in
        // their correct positions with respect to the middle
        // element of the array. So all elements at indexes
        // greater than the middle element are also numerically
        // greater than this element. Likewise, elements at
        // indexes less than the middle (pivotal) element are
        // now less than that element. Unfortunately, the
        // two halves of the array on either side of the pivotal
        // element are not yet sorted. Call quicksort recursively
        // to sort these two halves if they have more than one
        // element in them (if they have zero or one elements, then
        // they are already sorted).

        if( Low < j ) then

            quicksort( a, Low, j );

        endif;
        if( i < High ) then

quicksort( a, i, High );

        endif;

        pop( edi );
        pop( esi );
        pop( edx );
        pop( ecx );
        pop( ebx );
        pop( eax );

    end quicksort;

begin QSDemo;

    stdout.put( "Data before sorting: " nl );
    for( mov( 0, ebx ); ebx < 10; inc( ebx )) do

        stdout.put( theArray[ebx*4]:5 );

    endfor;
    stdout.newln();
```

```
        quicksort( theArray, 0, 9 );

        stdout.put( "Data after sorting: " nl );
        for( mov( 0, ebx ); ebx < 10; inc( ebx )) do

            stdout.put( theArray[ebx*4]:5 );

        endfor;
        stdout.newln();

end QSDemo;
```

*Listing 5-9: Recursive quicksort program*

Note that this quicksort procedure uses registers for all nonparameter local variables. Also note how quicksort uses text constant definitions to provide more readable names for the registers. This technique can often make an algorithm easier to read; however, one must take care when using this trick not to forget that those registers are being used.

# 5.9   Forward Procedures

As a general rule, HLA requires that you declare all symbols before their first use in a program.[11] Therefore, you must define all procedures before their first call. There are two reasons this isn't always practical: mutual recursion (two procedures call each other) and source code organization (you prefer to place a procedure in your code after the point where you've first called it). Fortunately, HLA lets you use a *forward procedure definition* to declare a procedure *prototype*. Forward declarations let you define a procedure before you actually supply the code for that procedure.

A forward procedure declaration is a familiar procedure declaration that uses the reserved word forward in place of the procedure's declaration section and body. The following is a forward declaration for the quicksort procedure appearing in the last section:

```
procedure quicksort( var a:ArrayType; Low:int32; High:int32 ); forward;
```

A forward declaration in an HLA program is a promise to the compiler that the actual procedure declaration will appear, exactly as stated in the forward declaration, at a later point in the source code.[12] The forward declaration must have the same parameters, they must be passed the same way, and they must all have the same types as the formal parameters in the procedure.

Routines that are mutually recursive (that is, procedure A calls procedure and procedure B calls procedure A) require at least one forward declaration because you may declare only one of procedure A or B before the other. In practice, however, mutual recursion (direct or indirect) doesn't occur very frequently, so you'll rarely forward declarations for this purpose.

---

[11] There are a few minor exceptions to this rule, but it is certainly true for procedure calls.

[12] Actually, *exactly* is too strong a word. You will see some exceptions in a moment.

In the absence of mutual recursion, it is always possible to organize your source code so that each procedure declaration appears before its first invocation. What's possible and what's desired are two different things, however. You might want to group a related set of procedures at the beginning of your source code and a different set of procedures toward the end of your source code. This logical grouping, by function rather than by invocation, may make your programs much easier to read and understand. However, this organization may also yield code that attempts to call a procedure before its declaration. No sweat; just use a forward procedure definition to resolve the problem.

One major difference between the forward definition and the actual procedure declaration has to do with the procedure options. Some options, like @returns, may appear only in the forward declaration (if a forward declaration is present). Other options may appear only in the actual procedure declaration (we haven't covered any of the other procedure options, so don't worry about them just yet). If your procedure requires an @returns option, the @returns option must appear before the forward reserved word. For example:

```
procedure IsItReady( valueToTest: dword ); @returns( "eax" ); forward;
```

The @returns option must not also appear in the actual procedure declaration later in your source file.

## 5.10  HLA v2.0 Procedure Declarations

HLA v2.0 and later support an alternate procedure declaration syntax that is similar to constant, type, and variable declarations. Though this book tends to prefer the original procedure declaration syntax (which HLA v2.0 and later still support), you will see examples of the new syntax in code that exists out in the real world; therefore, this section provides a brief discussion of the new procedure declaration syntax.

The new HLA v2.0 procedure declaration syntax uses the proc keyword to begin a procedure declaration section (similar to var or static beginning a variable declaration section). Within a proc section, procedure declarations take one of these forms:

```
procname:procedure( parameters );
begin procname;
    << body >>
end procname;
procname:procedure( parameters ) {options};
begin procname;
    << body >>
end procname;
procname:procedure( parameters ); external;
procname:procedure( parameters ) { options }; external;
```

Please see the HLA v2.0 (or later) reference manual for more details concerning this alternate procedure declaration syntax. Just be aware of it existence in case you come across it while reading example HLA code you' gotten from some other source.

## 5.11    Low-Level Procedures and the call Instruction

The 80x86 call instruction does two things. First, it pushes the address of t instruction immediately following the call onto the stack; then it transfers control to the address of the specified procedure. The value that call push onto the stack is known as the *return address*. When the procedure wants to return to the caller and continue execution with the first statement followi the call instruction, the procedure simply pops the return address off the stack and jumps (indirectly) to that address. Most procedures return to the caller by executing a ret (return) instruction. The ret instruction pops a return address off the stack and transfers control indirectly to the address pops off the stack.

By default, the HLA compiler automatically places a ret instruction (along with a few other instructions) at the end of each HLA procedure yc write. This is why you haven't had to explicitly use the ret instruction to this point. To disable the default code generation in an HLA procedure, specify the following options when declaring your procedures:

```
procedure ProcName; @noframe; @nodisplay;
begin ProcName;
    .
    .
    .
end ProcName;
```

The @noframe and @nodisplay clauses are examples of procedure *options.* HLA procedures support several such options, including @returns, @noframe, @nodisplay, and @noalignstack. You'll see the purpose of @noalignstack and a couple of other procedure options in Section 5.14. These procedure optio may appear in any order following the procedure name (and parameters, i any). Note that @noframe and @nodisplay (as well as @noalignstack) may appea only in an actual procedure declaration. You cannot specify these options i a forward declaration.

The @noframe option tells HLA that you don't want the compiler to automatically generate entry and exit code for the procedure. This tells HL/ not to automatically generate the ret instruction (along with several other instructions).

The @nodisplay option tells HLA that it should not allocate storage in procedure's local variable area for a *display*. The display is a mechanism you use to access nonlocal var objects in a procedure. Therefore, a display is necessary only if you nest procedures in your programs. This book will not consider the display or nested procedures; for more details on the display and nested procedures see the appropriate chapter in the electronic edition appearing at *http://www.artofasm.com/* or *http://webster.cs.ucr.edu/*, or check out the HLA reference manual. Until then, you can safely specify the @nodisplay option on all your procedures. Indeed, for all of the procedures appearing in this chapter up to this point, specifying the @nodisplay option makes a lot of sense because none of those procedures actually use the display. Procedures that have the @nodisplay option are a tiny bit faster and a tiny bit shorter than those procedures that do not specify this option.

The following is an example of the minimal procedure:

```
procedure minimal; @nodisplay; @noframe; @noalignstack;
begin minimal;

    ret();

end minimal;
```

If you call this procedure with the call instruction, minimal will simply pop the return address off the stack and return back to the caller. You should note that a ret instruction is absolutely necessary when you specify the @noframe procedure option.[13] If you fail to put the ret instruction in the procedure, the program will not return to the caller upon encountering the end minimal; statement. Instead, the program will fall through to whatever code happens to follow the procedure in memory. The example program in Listing 5-10 demonstrates this problem.

```
program missingRET;
#include( "stdlib.hhf" );

    // This first procedure has the @noframe
    // option but does not have a ret instruction.

    procedure firstProc; @noframe; @nodisplay;
    begin firstProc;

        stdout.put( "Inside firstProc" nl );

    end firstProc;
```

---

[13] Strictly speaking, this isn't true. But some mechanism that pops the return address off the stack and jumps to the return address is necessary in the procedure's body.

```
        // Because the procedure above does not have a
        // ret instruction, it will "fall through" to
        // the following instruction. Note that there
        // is no call to this procedure anywhere in
        // this program.

        procedure secondProc; @noframe; @nodisplay;
        begin secondProc;

            stdout.put( "Inside secondProc" nl );
            ret();

end secondProc;


begin missingRET;

        // Call the procedure that doesn't have
        // a ret instruction.

        call firstProc;

end missingRET;
```

Listing 5-10: Effect of a missing ret instruction in a procedure

Although this behavior might be desirable in certain rare circumstance it usually represents a defect in most programs. Therefore, if you specify th@noframe option, always remember to explicitly return from the procedure using the ret instruction.

## 5.12  Procedures and the Stack

Because procedures use the stack to hold the return address, you must exer cise caution when pushing and popping data within a procedure. Consider the following simple (and defective) procedure:

```
procedure MessedUp; @noframe; @nodisplay;
begin MessedUp;

    push( eax );
    ret();

end MessedUp;
```

At the point the program encounters the ret instruction, the 80x86 stack takes the form shown in Figure 5-1.

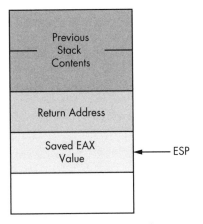

Figure 5-1: Stack contents before ret in MessedUp procedure

The ret instruction isn't aware that the value on the top of stack is not a valid address. It simply pops whatever value is on the top of the stack and jumps to that location. In this example, the top of stack contains the saved EAX value. Because it is very unlikely that EAX contains the proper return address (indeed, there is about a one in four billion chance it is correct), this program will probably crash or exhibit some other undefined behavior. Therefore, you must take care when pushing data onto the stack within a procedure that you properly pop that data prior to returning from the procedure.

**NOTE** *If you do not specify the @noframe option when writing a procedure, HLA automatically generates code at the beginning of the procedure that pushes some data onto the stack. Therefore, unless you understand exactly what is going on and you've taken care of this data HLA pushes on the stack, you should never execute the bare ret instruction inside a procedure that does not have the @noframe option. Doing so will attempt to return to the location specified by this data (which is not a return address) rather than properly returning to the caller. In procedures that do not have the @noframe option, use the exit or exitif statement to return from the procedure.*

Popping extra data off the stack prior to executing the ret statement can also create havoc in your programs. Consider the following defective procedure:

```
procedure messedUpToo; @noframe; @nodisplay;
begin messedUpToo;

    pop( eax );
    ret();

end messedUpToo;
```

Upon reaching the ret instruction in this procedure, the 80x86 stack look something like that shown in Figure 5-2.

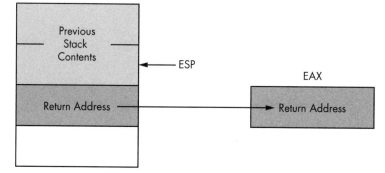

Figure 5-2: Stack contents before ret in messedUpToo

Once again, the ret instruction blindly pops whatever data happens to b on the top of the stack and attempts to return to that address. Unlike the previous example, where it was very unlikely that the top of stack contained valid return address (because it contained the value in EAX), there is a sma possibility that the top of stack in this example actually *does* contain a return address. However, this will not be the proper return address for the messedUpTo procedure; instead, it will be the return address for the procedure that calle messedUpToo. To understand the effect of this code, consider the program in Listing 5-11.

```
program extraPop;
#include( "stdlib.hhf" );


    // Note that the following procedure pops
    // excess data off the stack (in this case,
    // it pops messedUpToo's return address).

    procedure messedUpToo; @noframe; @nodisplay;
    begin messedUpToo;

        stdout.put( "Entered messedUpToo" nl );
        pop( eax );
        ret();

    end messedUpToo;



    procedure callsMU2; @noframe; @nodisplay;
    begin callsMU2;

        stdout.put( "calling messedUpToo" nl );
        messedUpToo();
```

```
    // Because messedUpToo pops extra data
    // off the stack, the following code
    // never executes (because the data popped
    // off the stack is the return address that
    // points at the following code).

    stdout.put( "Returned from messedUpToo" nl );
    ret();

end callsMU2;


begin extraPop;

    stdout.put( "Calling callsMU2" nl );
    callsMU2();
    stdout.put( "Returned from callsMU2" nl );

end extraPop;
```

*Listing 5-11: Effect of popping too much data off the stack*

Because a valid return address is sitting on the top of the stack, you might think that this program will actually work (properly). However, note that when returning from the messedUpToo procedure, this code returns directly to the main program rather than to the proper return address in the callsMU2 procedure. Therefore, all code in the callsMU2 procedure that follows the call to messedUpToo does not execute. When reading the source code, it may be very difficult to figure out why those statements are not executing because they immediately follow the call to the messedUpToo procedure. It isn't clear, unless you look very closely, that the program is popping an extra return address off the stack and therefore doesn't return to callsMU2 but rather returns directly to whoever calls callsMU2. Of course, in this example it's fairly easy to see what is going on (because this example is a demonstration of this problem). In real programs, however, determining that a procedure has accidentally popped too much data off the stack can be much more difficult. Therefore, you should always be careful about pushing and popping data in a procedure. You should always verify that there is a one-to-one relationship between the pushes in your procedures and the corresponding pops.

# 5.13  Activation Records

Whenever you call a procedure, there is certain information the program associates with that procedure call. The return address is a good example of some information the program maintains for a specific procedure call. Parameters and automatic local variables (that is, those you declare in the var section) are additional examples of information the program maintains for each procedure call. *Activation record* is the term we'll use to describe the information the program associates with a specific call to a procedure.[14]

---

[14] *Stack frame* is another term many people use to describe the activation record.

Activation record is an appropriate name for this data structure. The program creates an activation record when calling (activating) a procedure and the data in the structure is organized in a manner identical to records. Perhaps the only thing unusual about an activation record (when comparing it to a standard record) is that the base address of the record is in the middle of the data structure, so you must access fields of the record at positive and negative offsets.

Construction of an activation record begins in the code that calls a procedure. The caller pushes the parameter data (if any) onto the stack. Then the execution of the call instruction pushes the return address onto the stack. At this point, construction of the activation record continues within the procedure itself. The procedure pushes registers and other important state information and then makes room in the activation record for local variables. The procedure must also update the EBP register so that it points at the base address of the activation record.

To see what a typical activation record looks like, consider the following HLA procedure declaration:

```
procedure ARDemo( i:uns32; j:int32; k:dword ); @nodisplay;
var
        a:int32;
        r:real32;
        c:char;
        b:boolean;
        w:word;
begin ARDemo;
        .
        .
        .
end ARDemo;
```

Whenever an HLA program calls this ARDemo procedure, it begins by pushing the data for the parameters onto the stack. The calling code will push the parameters onto the stack in the order they appear in the parameter list, from left to right. Therefore, the calling code first pushes the value for the i parameter, then it pushes the value for the j parameter, and it finally pushes the data for the k parameter. After pushing the parameters, the program calls the ARDemo procedure. Immediately upon entry into the ARDemo procedure, the stack contains these four items arranged as shown in Figure 5-3.

The first few instructions in ARDemo (note that it does not have the @noframe option) will push the current value of EBP onto the stack and then copy the value of ESP into EBP. Next, the code drops the stack pointer down in memory to make room for the local variables. This produces the stack organization shown in Figure 5-4.

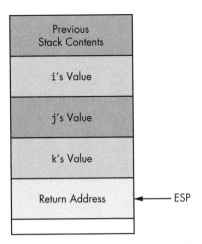

Figure 5-3: Stack organization immediately upon entry into ARDemo

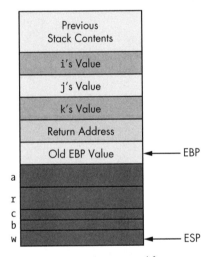

Figure 5-4: Activation record for ARDemo

To access objects in the activation record you must use offsets from the EBP register to the desired object. The two items of immediate interest to you are the parameters and the local variables. You can access the parameters at positive offsets from the EBP register; you can access the local variables at negative offsets from the EBP register, as Figure 5-5 shows.

Intel specifically reserves the EBP (Extended Base Pointer) register for use as a pointer to the base of the activation record. This is why you should never use the EBP register for general calculations. If you arbitrarily change the value in the EBP register, you will lose access to the current procedure's parameters and local variables.

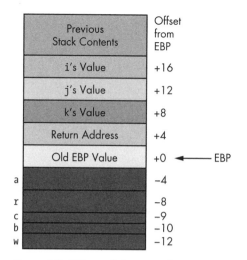

| Previous Stack Contents | Offset from EBP |
|---|---|
| i's Value | +16 |
| j's Value | +12 |
| k's Value | +8 |
| Return Address | +4 |
| Old EBP Value | +0 ◄——— EBP |
| a | −4 |
| r | −8 |
| c | −9 |
| b | −10 |
| w | −12 |

Figure 5-5: Offsets of objects in the ARDemo activation record

## 5.14  The Standard Entry Sequence

The caller of a procedure is responsible for pushing the parameters onto the stack. Of course, the call instruction pushes the return address onto the stack. It is the procedure's responsibility to construct the rest of the activation record. You can accomplish this by using the following "standard entry sequence" code:

```
push( ebp );        // Save a copy of the old ebp value.
mov( esp, ebp );    // Get pointer to base of activation record into ebp.
sub( NumVars, esp ); // Allocate storage for local variables.
```

If the procedure doesn't have any local variables, the third instruction above, sub( NumVars, esp );, isn't necessary. NumVars represents the number of bytes of local variables needed by the procedure. This is a constant that should be a multiple of 4 (so the ESP register remains aligned on a double-word boundary). If the number of bytes of local variables in the procedure is not a multiple of 4, you should round the value up to the next higher multiple of 4 before subtracting this constant from ESP. Doing so will slightly increase the amount of storage the procedure uses for local variables but will not otherwise affect the operation of the procedure.

**WARNING**  *If the* NumVars *constant is not a multiple of 4, subtracting this value from ESP (which, presumably, contains a double-word-aligned pointer) will virtually guarantee that all future stack accesses are misaligned because the program almost always pushes and pops double-word values. This will have a very negative performance impact on the program. Worse still, many OS API calls will fail if the stack is not double-word aligned upon entry into the operating system. Therefore, you must always ensure that your local variable allocation value is a multiple of 4.*

Because of the problems with a misaligned stack, by default HLA will also emit a fourth instruction as part of the standard entry sequence. The HLA compiler actually emits the following standard entry sequence for the ARDemo procedure defined earlier:

```
push( ebp );
mov( esp, ebp );
sub( 12, esp );            // Make room for ARDemo's local variables.
and( $FFFF_FFFC, esp );    // Force dword stack alignment.
```

The and instruction at the end of this sequence forces the stack to be aligned on a 4-byte boundary (it reduces the value in the stack pointer by 1, 2, or 3 if the value in ESP is not a multiple of 4). Although the ARDemo entry code correctly subtracts 12 from ESP for the local variables (12 is both a multiple of 4 and the number of bytes of local variables), this leaves ESP double-word aligned only if it was double-word aligned immediately upon entry into the procedure. Had the caller messed with the stack and left ESP containing a value that was not a multiple of 4, subtracting 12 from ESP would leave ESP containing an unaligned value. The and instruction in the sequence above, however, guarantees that ESP is dword aligned regardless of ESP's value upon entry into the procedure. The few bytes and CPU cycles needed to execute this instruction would pay off handsomely if ESP was not double-word aligned.

Although it is always safe to execute the and instruction in the standard entry sequence, it might not be necessary. If you always ensure that ESP contains a double-word-aligned value, the and instruction in the standard entry sequence above is unnecessary. Therefore, if you've specified the @noframe procedure option, you don't have to include that instruction as part of the entry sequence.

If you haven't specified the @noframe option (that is, you're letting HLA emit the instructions to construct the standard entry sequence for you), you can still tell HLA not to emit the extra and instruction if you're sure the stack will be double-word aligned whenever someone calls the procedure. To do this, use the @noalignstack procedure option. For example:

```
procedure NASDemo( i:uns32; j:int32; k:dword ); @noalignstack;
var
      LocalVar:int32;
begin NASDemo;
    .
    .
    .
end NASDemo;
```

HLA emits the following entry sequence for the procedure above:

```
push( ebp );
mov( esp, ebp );
sub( 4, esp );
```

## 5.15   The Standard Exit Sequence

Before a procedure returns to its caller, it needs to clean up the activation record. Although it is possible to share the cleanup duties between the procedure and the procedure's caller, Intel has included some features in the instruction set that allows the procedure to efficiently handle all the cleanup chores itself. Standard HLA procedures and procedure calls, therefore, assume that it is the procedure's responsibility to clean up the activation record (including the parameters) when the procedure returns to its caller.

If a procedure does not have any parameters, the exit sequence is very simple. It requires only three instructions:

```
mov( ebp, esp );    // Deallocate locals and clean up stack.
pop( ebp );         // Restore pointer to caller's activation record.
ret();              // Return to the caller.
```

If the procedure has some parameters, then a slight modification to the standard exit sequence is necessary in order to remove the parameter data from the stack. Procedures with parameters use the following standard exit sequence:

```
mov( ebp, esp );       // Deallocate locals and clean up stack.
pop( ebp );            // Restore pointer to caller's activation record.
ret( ParmBytes );      // Return to the caller and pop the parameters.
```

The ParmBytes operand of the ret instruction is a constant that specifies the number of bytes of parameter data to remove from the stack after the return instruction pops the return address. For example, the ARDemo example code in the previous sections has three double-word parameters. Therefore, the standard exit sequence would take the following form:

```
mov( ebp, esp );
pop( ebp );
ret( 12 );
```

If you've declared your parameters using HLA syntax (that is, a parameter list follows the procedure declaration), then HLA automatically creates a local constant in the procedure, _parms_, that is equal to the number of bytes of parameters in that procedure. Therefore, rather than counting the number of parameter bytes yourself, you can use the following standard exit sequence for any procedure that has parameters:

```
mov( ebp, esp );
pop( ebp );
ret( _parms_ );
```

Note that if you do not specify a byte constant operand to the ret instruction, the 80x86 will not pop the parameters off the stack upon return. Those parameters will still be sitting on the stack when you execute the first instruction following the call to the procedure. Similarly, if you specify a value that is too small, some of the parameters will be left on the stack upon return from the procedure. If the ret operand you specify is too large, the ret instruction will actually pop some of the caller's data off the stack, usually with disastrous consequences.

If you wish to return early from a procedure that doesn't have the @noframe option, and you don't particularly want to use the exit or exitif statement, you must execute the standard exit sequence to return to the caller. A simple ret instruction is insufficient because local variables and the old EBP value are probably sitting on the top of the stack.

# 5.16   Low-Level Implementation of Automatic (Local) Variables

Your program accesses local variables in a procedure using negative offsets from the activation record base address (EBP). Consider the following HLA procedure (which admittedly doesn't do much other than demonstrate the use of local variables):

```
procedure LocalVars; @nodisplay;
var
        a:int32;
        b:int32;
begin LocalVars;

    mov( 0, a );
    mov( a, eax );
    mov( eax, b );

end LocalVars;
```

The activation record for LocalVars appears in Figure 5-6.

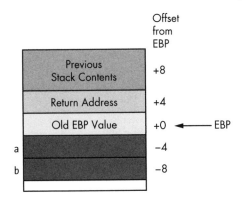

Figure 5-6: Activation record for the LocalVars procedure

The HLA compiler emits code that is roughly equivalent to the following[15] for the body of this procedure:

```
mov( 0, (type dword [ebp-4]));
mov( [ebp-4], eax );
mov( eax, [ebp-8] );
```

You could actually type these statements into the procedure yourself and they would work. Of course, using memory references like [ebp-4] and [ebp-8] rather than a or b makes your programs very difficult to read and understand. Therefore, you should always declare and use HLA symbolic names rather than offsets from EBP.

The standard entry sequence for this LocalVars procedure will be:[16]

```
push( ebp );
mov( esp, ebp );
sub( 8, esp );
```

This code subtracts 8 from the stack pointer because there are 8 bytes of local variables (two double-word objects) in this procedure. Unfortunately, as the number of local variables increases, especially if those variables have different types, computing the number of bytes of local variables becomes rather tedious. Fortunately, for those who wish to write the standard entry sequence themselves, HLA automatically computes this value for you and creates a constant, _vars_, that specifies the number of bytes of local variables.[1] Therefore, if you intend to write the standard entry sequence yourself, you should use the _vars_ constant in the sub instruction when allocating storage for the local variables:

```
push( ebp );
mov( esp, ebp );
sub( _vars_, esp );
```

Now that you've seen how assembly language allocates and deallocates storage for local variables, it's easy to understand why automatic (var) variables do not maintain their values between two calls to the same procedure. Because the memory associated with these automatic variables is on the stack, when a procedure returns to its caller the caller can push other data onto the stack, obliterating the values previously held on the stack. Furthermore, intervening calls to other procedures (with their own local variables) may wipe out the values on the stack. Also, upon reentry into a procedure, the procedure's local variables may correspond to different physical memory locations; hence the values of the local variables would not be in their proper locations.

---

[15] This ignores the code associated with the standard entry and exit sequences.

[16] This code assumes that ESP is dword aligned upon entry so the and( $FFFF_FFFC, esp ); instruction is unnecessary.

[17] HLA even rounds this constant up to the next even multiple of 4 so you don't have to worry about stack alignment.

One big advantage to automatic storage is that it efficiently shares a fixed pool of memory among several procedures. For example, if you call three procedures in a row, like so:

```
ProcA();
ProcB();
ProcC();
```

the first procedure (ProcA in the code above) allocates its local variables on the stack. Upon return, ProcA deallocates that stack storage. Upon entry into ProcB, the program allocates storage for ProcB's local variables *using the same memory locations just freed by ProcA*. Likewise, when ProcB returns and the program calls ProcC, ProcC uses the same stack space for its local variables that ProcB recently freed up. This memory reuse makes efficient use of the system resources and is probably the greatest advantage to using automatic (var) variables.

# 5.17 Low-Level Parameter Implementation

Earlier, when discussing HLA's high-level parameter passing mechanism, there were several questions concerning parameters. Some important questions are:

- Where is the data coming from?
- What mechanism do you use to pass and return data?
- How much data are you passing?

In this section we will take another look at the two most common parameter-passing mechanisms: pass by value and pass by reference. We will discuss three popular places to pass parameters by reference or by value: in the registers, on the stack, and in the code stream. The amount of parameter data has a direct bearing on where and how to pass it. The following sections take up these issues.

## 5.17.1 Passing Parameters in Registers

Having touched on *how* to pass parameters to a procedure in Section 5.6, the next thing to discuss is *where* to pass parameters. Where you pass parameters depends on the size and number of those parameters. If you are passing a small number of bytes to a procedure, then the registers are an excellent place to pass parameters to a procedure. If you are passing a single parameter to a procedure, you should use the following registers for the accompanying data types.

| Data Size | Pass in this Register |
|---|---|
| Byte: | al |
| Word: | ax |
| Double Word: | eax |
| Quad Word: | edx:eax |

This is not a hard-and-fast rule. If you find it more convenient to pass 16-bit values in the SI or BX register, then do so. However, most programmers use the registers above to pass parameters.

If you are passing several parameters to a procedure in the 80x86's registers, you should probably use up the registers in the following order:

| First | Last |
|---|---|
| eax, edx, ecx, esi, edi, ebx | |

In general, you should avoid using the EBP register. If you need more than six double words, perhaps you should pass your values elsewhere. This choice of priorities is not completely arbitrary. Many high-level languages will attempt to pass parameters in the EAX, EDX, and ECX registers (generally in that order). Furthermore, the Intel ABI (application binary interface) allows high-level language procedures to use EAX, EDX, and ECX without preserving their values. Hence, these three registers are a great place to pass parameters because a lot of code assumes their values are modified across procedure calls.

As an example, consider the following strfill( s,c ); procedure that copies the character c (passed by value in AL) to each character position in s (passed by reference in EDI) up to a zero-terminating byte:

```
// strfill-  Overwrites the data in a string with a character.
//
//      EDI-  Pointer to zero-terminated string (e.g., an HLA string)
//      AL-  Character to store into the string

procedure strfill; @nodisplay;
begin strfill;

    push( edi );  // Preserve this because it will be modified.
    while( (type char [edi] ) <> #0 ) do

        mov( al, [edi] );
        inc( edi );

    endwhile;
    pop( edi );

end strfill;
```

To call the strfill procedure you would load the address of the string data into EDI and the character value into AL prior to the call. The following code fragment demonstrates a typical call to strfill.

```
mov( s, edi );  // Get ptr to string data into edi (assumes s:string).
mov( ' ', al );
strfill();
```

Don't forget that HLA string variables are pointers. This example assumes that s is an HLA string variable and therefore contains a pointer to a zero-terminated string. Thus, the mov( s, edi ); instruction loads the address of the zero-terminated string into the EDI register (hence this code passes the address of the string data to strfill, that is, it passes the string by reference).

One way to pass parameters in the registers is to simply load them with the appropriate values prior to a call and then reference those registers within the procedure. This is the traditional mechanism for passing parameters in registers in an assembly language program. HLA, being somewhat more high-level than traditional assembly language, provides a formal parameter declaration syntax that lets you tell HLA you're passing certain parameters in the general-purpose registers. This declaration syntax is the following:

```
parmName: parmType in reg
```

Where *parmName* is the parameter's name, *parmType* is the type of the object, and *reg* is one of the 80x86's general-purpose 8-, 16-, or 32-bit registers. The size of the parameter's type must be equal to the size of the register or HLA will report an error. Here is a concrete example:

```
procedure HasRegParms( count: uns32 in ecx; charVal:char in al );
```

One nice feature to this syntax is that you can call a procedure that has register parameters exactly like any other procedure in HLA using the high-level syntax. For example:

```
HasRegParms( ecx, bl );
```

If you specify the same register as an actual parameter that you've declared for the formal parameter, HLA does not emit any extra code; it assumes that the parameter's value is already in the appropriate register. For example, in the call above, the first actual parameter is the value in ECX; because the procedure's declaration specifies that first parameter is in ECX, HLA will not emit any code. On the other hand, the second actual parameter is in BL, but the procedure will expect this parameter value in AL. Therefore, HLA will emit a mov( bl, al ); instruction prior to calling the procedure so that the value is in the proper register upon entry to the procedure.

You can also pass parameters by reference in a register. Consider the following declaration:

```
procedure HasRefRegParm( var myPtr:uns32 in edi );
```

A call to this procedure always requires some memory operand as the actual parameter. HLA will emit the code to load the address of that memory object into the parameter's register (EDI in this case). Note that when passing reference parameters, the register must be a 32-bit general-purpose register because addresses are 32 bits long. Here's an example of a call to HasRefRegParm:

```
HasRefRegParm( x );
```

HLA will emit either a mov( &x, edi); or lea( edi, x); instruction to load the address of x into the EDI registers prior to the call instruction.[18]

If you pass an anonymous memory object (for example, [edi] or [ecx]) as a parameter to HasRefRegParm, HLA will not emit any code if the memory reference uses the same register that you declare for the parameter (i.e., [edi]). It will use a simple mov instruction to copy the actual address into EDI if you specify an indirect addressing mode using a register other than EDI (e.g., [ecx]). It will use a lea instruction to compute the effective address of the anonymous memory operand if you use a more complex addressing mode like [edi+ecx*4+2].

Within the procedure's code, HLA creates text equates for those register parameters that map their names to the appropriate register. In the HasRegParm example, any time you reference the count parameter, HLA substitutes ecx for count. Likewise, HLA substitutes al for charVal throughout the procedure's body. Because these names are aliases for the registers, you should take care to always remember that you cannot use ECX and AL independently of these parameters. It would be a good idea to place a comment next to each use of these parameters to remind the reader that count is equivalent to ECX and charVal is equivalent to AL.

## 5.17.2   Passing Parameters in the Code Stream

Another place where you can pass parameters is in the code stream immediately after the call instruction. Consider the following print routine that prints a literal string constant to the standard output device:

```
call print;
byte "This parameter is in the code stream.",0;
```

Normally, a subroutine returns control to the first instruction immediately following the call instruction. Were that to happen here, the 80x86 would attempt to interpret the ASCII codes for "This . . . ." as an instruction. This would produce undesirable results. Fortunately, you can skip over this string when returning from the subroutine.

So how do you gain access to these parameters? Easy. The return address on the stack points at them. Consider the implementation of print appearing in Listing 5-12.

---

[18] The choice of instructions is dictated by whether x is a static variable (mov for static objects, lea for other objects).

```
program printDemo;
#include( "stdlib.hhf" );

    // print-
    //
    // This procedure writes the literal string
    // immediately following the call to the
    // standard output device. The literal string
    // must be a sequence of characters ending with
    // a zero byte (i.e., a C string, not an HLA
    // string).

    procedure print; @noframe; @nodisplay;
    const

        // RtnAdrs is the offset of this procedure's
        // return address in the activation record.

        RtnAdrs:text := "(type dword [ebp+4])";

    begin print;

        // Build the activation record (note the
        // @noframe option above).

        push( ebp );
        mov( esp, ebp );

        // Preserve the registers this function uses.

        push( eax );
        push( ebx );

        // Copy the return address into the ebx
        // register. Because the return address points
        // at the start of the string to print, this
        // instruction loads ebx with the address of
        // the string to print.

        mov( RtnAdrs, ebx );

        // Until we encounter a zero byte, print the
        // characters in the string.

        forever

            mov( [ebx], al );    // Get the next character.
            breakif( !al );      // Quit if it's zero.
            stdout.putc( al );   // Print it.
            inc( ebx );          // Move on to the next char.

        endfor;
```

```
// Skip past the zero byte and store the resulting
// address over the top of the return address so
// we'll return to the location that is one byte
// beyond the zero-terminating byte of the string.

inc( ebx );
mov( ebx, RtnAdrs );

// Restore eax and ebx.

pop( ebx );
pop( eax );

// Clean up the activation record and return.

pop( ebp );
ret();

end print;


begin printDemo;

// Simple test of the print procedure

call print;
byte "Hello World!", 13, 10, 0 ;

end printDemo;
```

*Listing 5-12: Print procedure implementation (using code stream parameters)*

Besides showing how to pass parameters in the code stream, the print routine also exhibits another concept: *variable-length parameters*. The string following the call can be any practical length. The zero terminating byte marks the end of the parameter list. There are two easy ways to handle variable-length parameters: Either use some special terminating value (like 0) or pass a special length value that tells the subroutine how many parameters you are passing. Both methods have their advantages and disadvantages. Using a special value to terminate a parameter list requires that you choose a value that never appears in the list. For example, print uses 0 as the terminating value, so it cannot print the NUL character (whose ASCII code is 0). Sometimes this isn't a limitation. Specifying a special-length parameter is another mechanism you can use to pass a variable-length parameter list. While this doesn't require any special codes or limit the range of possible values that can be passed to a subroutine, setting up the length parameter and maintaining the resulting code can be a real nightmare.[19]

Despite the convenience afforded by passing parameters in the code stream, there are some disadvantages to passing parameters there. First, if you fail to provide the exact number of parameters the procedure requires,

---

[19] This is especially true if the parameter list changes frequently.

the subroutine will get confused. Consider the print example. It prints a string of characters up to a zero-terminating byte and then returns control to the first instruction following the zero-terminating byte. If you leave off the zero-terminating byte, the print routine happily prints the following opcode bytes as ASCII characters until it finds a zero byte. Because zero bytes often appear in the middle of an instruction, the print routine might return control into the middle of some other instruction. This will probably crash the machine. Inserting an extra 0, which occurs more often than you might think, is another problem programmers have with the print routine. In such a case, the print routine would return upon encountering the first zero byte and attempt to execute the following ASCII characters as machine code. Once again, this usually crashes the machine. These are the some of the reasons why the HLA stdout.put code does *not* pass its parameters in the code stream. Problems notwithstanding, however, the code stream is an efficient place to pass parameters whose values do not change.

### 5.17.3 *Passing Parameters on the Stack*

Most high-level languages use the stack to pass parameters because this method is fairly efficient. By default, HLA also passes parameters on the stack. Although passing parameters on the stack is slightly less efficient than passing those parameters in registers, the register set is very limited and you can pass only a few value or reference parameters through registers. The stack, on the other hand, allows you to pass a large amount of parameter data without any difficulty. This is the principal reason that most programs pass their parameters on the stack.

HLA typically passes parameters you specify using the high-level procedure call syntax on the stack. For example, suppose you define strfill from earlier as follows:

```
procedure strfill( s:string; chr:char );
```

Calls of the form strfill( s, ' ' ); will pass the value of s (which is an address) and a space character on the 80x86 stack. When you specify a call to strfill in this manner, HLA automatically pushes the parameters for you, so you don't have to push them onto the stack yourself. Of course, if you choose to do so, HLA will let you manually push the parameters onto the stack prior to the call.

To manually pass parameters on the stack, push them immediately before calling the subroutine. The subroutine then reads this data from the stack memory and operates on it appropriately. Consider the following HLA procedure call:

```
CallProc(i,j,k);
```

HLA pushes parameters onto the stack in the order that they appear in the parameter list.[20] Therefore, the 80x86 code that HLA emits for this subroutine call (assuming you're passing the parameters by value) is:

```
push( i );
push( j );
push( k );
call CallProc;
```

Upon entry into CallProc, the 80x86's stack looks like that shown in Figure 5-7.

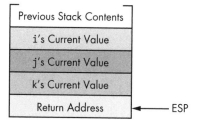

Figure 5-7: Stack layout upon entry into CallProc

You could gain access to the parameters passed on the stack by removing the data from the stack, as the following code fragment demonstrates:

```
// Note: To extract parameters off the stack by popping, it is very important
// to specify both the @nodisplay and @noframe procedure options.

static
        RtnAdrs: dword;
        p1Parm: dword;
        p2Parm: dword;
        p3Parm: dword;

procedure CallProc( p1:dword; p2:dword; p3:dword ); @nodisplay; @noframe;
begin CallProc;

        pop( RtnAdrs );
        pop( p3Parm );
        pop( p2Parm );
        pop( p1Parm );
        push( RtnAdrs );

                .
                .
                .
        ret();

end CallProc;
```

---

[20] This assumes, of course, that you don't instruct HLA otherwise. It is possible to tell HLA to reverse the order of the parameters on the stack. See the electronic edition for more details.

As you can see from this code, it first pops the return address off the stack and into the RtnAdrs variable; then it pops (in reverse order) the values of the p1, p2, and p3 parameters; finally, it pushes the return address back onto the stack (so the ret instruction will operate properly). Within the CallProc procedure, you may access the p1Parm, p2Parm, and p3Parm variables to use the p1, p2, and p3 parameter values.

There is, however, a better way to access procedure parameters. If your procedure includes the standard entry and exit sequences, then you may directly access the parameter values in the activation record by indexing off the EBP register. Consider the layout of the activation record for CallProc that uses the following declaration:

```
procedure CallProc( p1:dword; p2:dword; p3:dword ); @nodisplay; @noframe;
begin CallProc;

    push( ebp );      // This is the standard entry sequence.
    mov( esp, ebp ); // Get base address of A.R. into ebp.
        .
        .
        .
```

Take a look at the stack immediately after the execution of mov( esp, ebp ); in CallProc. Assuming you've pushed three double-word parameters onto the stack, it should look something like that shown in Figure 5-8.

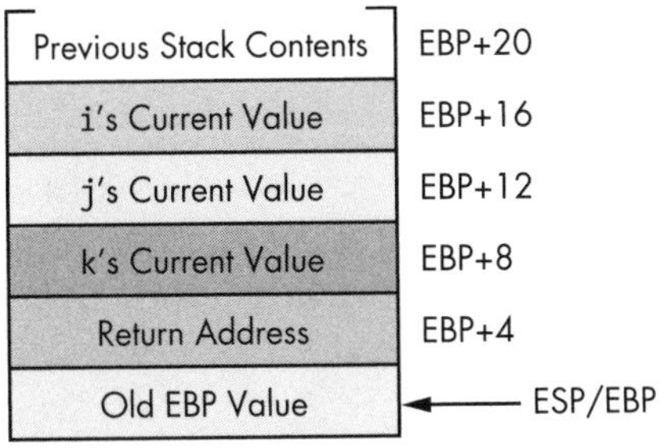

Figure 5-8: Activation record for CallProc
after standard entry sequence execution

Now you can access the parameters by indexing off the EBP register:

```
        mov( [ebp+16], eax );   // Accesses the first parameter.
        mov( [ebp+12], ebx );   // Accesses the second parameter.
        mov( [ebp+8], ecx );    // Accesses the third parameter.
```

Of course, as with local variables, you'd never really access the parameters in this way. You can use the formal parameter names (p1, p2, and p3), and HLA will substitute a suitable [ebp+displacement] memory address. Even though you shouldn't actually access parameters using address expressions like [ebp+12], it's important to understand their relationship to the parameters in your procedures.

Other items that often appear in the activation record are register valu[e]
that your procedure preserves. The most rational place to preserve registe[r]
in a procedure is in the code immediately following the standard entry
sequence. In a standard HLA procedure (one where you do not specify th[e]
@noframe option), this simply means that the code that preserves the registe[r]
should appear first in the procedure's body. Likewise, the code to restore
those register values should appear immediately before the end clause for th[e]
procedure.[21]

## 5.17.3.1 Accessing Value Parameters on the Stack

Accessing parameters passed by value is no different from accessing a local
var object. As long as you've declared the parameter in a formal parameter
list and the procedure executes the standard entry sequence upon entry in[to]
the program, all you need do is specify the parameter's name to reference th[e]
value of that parameter. Listing 5-13 provides an example program whose
procedure accesses a parameter the main program passes to it by value.

```
program AccessingValueParameters;
#include( "stdlib.hhf" )

    procedure ValueParm( theParameter: uns32 ); @nodisplay;
    begin ValueParm;

        mov( theParameter, eax );
        add( 2, eax );
        stdout.put
        (
            "theParameter + 2 = ",
            (type uns32 eax),
            nl
        );

    end ValueParm;


begin AccessingValueParameters;

    ValueParm( 10 );
    ValueParm( 135 );

end AccessingValueParameters;
```

*Listing 5-13: Demonstration of value parameters*

---

[21] Note that if you use the exit statement to exit a procedure, you must duplicate the code to[o]
pop the register values and place this code immediately before the exit clause. This is a goo[d]
example of a maintenance nightmare and is also a good reason why you should have only one ex[it]
point in your program.

Although you could access the value of theParameter using the anonymous address [EBP+8] within your code, there is absolutely no good reason for doing so. If you declare the parameter list using the HLA high-level language syntax, you can access the value parameter by specifying its name within the procedure.

### 5.17.3.2    Passing Value Parameters on the Stack

As Listing 5-13 demonstrates, passing a value parameter to a procedure is very easy. Just specify the value in the actual parameter list as you would for a high-level language call. Actually, the situation is a little more complicated than this. Passing value parameters is easy if you're passing constant, register, or variable values. It gets a little more complex if you need to pass the result of some expression. This section deals with the different ways you can pass a parameter by value to a procedure.

Of course, you do not have to use the HLA high-level syntax to pass value parameters to a procedure. You can push these values on the stack yourself. Because many times it is more convenient or more efficient to manually pass the parameters, describing how to do this is a good place to start.

As noted earlier in this chapter, when passing parameters on the stack you push the objects in the order they appear in the formal parameter list (from left to right). When passing parameters by value, you should push the values of the actual parameters onto the stack. The program in Listing 5-14 demonstrates how to do this.

```
program ManuallyPassingValueParameters;
#include( "stdlib.hhf" )

    procedure ThreeValueParms( p1:uns32; p2:uns32; p3:uns32 ); @nodisplay;
    begin ThreeValueParms;

        mov( p1, eax );
        add( p2, eax );
        add( p3, eax );
        stdout.put
        (
            "p1 + p2 + p3 = ",
            (type uns32 eax),
            nl
        );

    end ThreeValueParms;



static
    SecondParmValue:uns32 := 25;
```

```
begin ManuallyPassingValueParameters;

    pushd( 10 );                // Value associated with p1
    pushd( SecondParmValue);    // Value associated with p2
    pushd( 15 );                // Value associated with p3
    call ThreeValueParms;

end ManuallyPassingValueParameters;
```

Listing 5-14: Manually passing parameters on the stack

Note that if you manually push the parameters onto the stack as this example does, you must use the call instruction to call the procedure. If you attempt to use a procedure invocation of the form ThreeValueParms();, then HLA will complain about a mismatched parameter list. HLA won't realize that you've manually pushed the parameters (as far as HLA is concerned, those pushes appear to preserve some other data).

Generally, there is little reason to manually push a parameter onto the stack if the actual parameter is a constant, a register value, or a variable. HLA's high-level syntax handles most such parameters for you. There are several instances, however, where HLA's high-level syntax won't work. The first such example is passing the result of an arithmetic expression as a value parameter. Because runtime arithmetic expressions don't exist in HLA, you will have to manually compute the result of the expression and pass that value yourself. There are two possible ways to do this: calculate the result of the expression and manually push that result onto the stack, or compute the result of the expression into a register and pass the register as a parameter to the procedure. The program in Listing 5-15 demonstrates these two mechanisms.

```
program PassingExpressions;
#include( "stdlib.hhf" )

    procedure ExprParm( exprValue:uns32 ); @nodisplay;
    begin ExprParm;

        stdout.put( "exprValue = ", exprValue, nl );

    end ExprParm;


static
    Operand1: uns32 := 5;
    Operand2: uns32 := 20;
```

```
begin PassingExpressions;

    // ExprParm( Operand1 + Operand2 );
    //
    // Method one: Compute the sum and manually
    // push the sum onto the stack.

    mov( Operand1, eax );
    add( Operand2, eax );
    push( eax );
    call ExprParm;

    // Method two: Compute the sum in a register and
    // pass the register using the HLA high-level
    // language syntax.

    mov( Operand1, eax );
    add( Operand2, eax );
    ExprParm( eax );

end PassingExpressions;
```

*Listing 5-15: Passing the result of some arithmetic expression as a parameter*

The examples up to this point in this section have made an important assumption: that the parameter you are passing is a double-word value. The calling sequence changes somewhat if you're passing parameters that are not 4-byte objects. Because HLA can generate relatively inefficient code when passing objects that are not 4 bytes long, manually passing such objects is a good idea if you want to have the fastest possible code.

HLA requires that all value parameters be a multiple of 4 bytes long.[22] If you pass an object that is less than 4 bytes long, HLA requires that you *pad* the parameter data with extra bytes so that you always pass an object that is at least 4 bytes in length. For parameters that are larger than 4 bytes, you must ensure that you pass a multiple of 4 bytes as the parameter value, adding extra bytes at the high-order end of the object to pad it, as necessary.

Consider the following procedure prototype:

```
procedure OneByteParm( b:byte );
```

The activation record for this procedure appears in Figure 5-9.

---

[22] This applies only if you use the HLA high-level-language syntax to declare and access parameters in your procedures. Of course, if you manually push the parameters yourself and you access the parameters inside the procedure using an addressing mode like [ebp+8], then you can pass any size object you choose. Of course, keep in mind that most operating systems expect the stack to be dword aligned, so parameters you push should be a multiple of 4 bytes long.

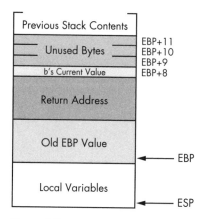

Figure 5-9: OneByteParm activation record

As you can see, there are 4 bytes on the stack associated with the b parameter, but only 1 of the 4 bytes contains valid data (the L.O. byte). The remaining 3 bytes are just padding, and the procedure should ignore these bytes. In particular, you should never assume that these extra bytes contain 0s or some other consistent value. Depending on the type of parameter you pass, HLA's automatic code generation may or may not push 0 bytes as the extra data on the stack.

When passing a byte parameter to a procedure, HLA will automatically emit code that pushes 4 bytes onto the stack. Because HLA's parameter-passing mechanism guarantees not to disturb any register or other values, HLA sometimes generates more code than is actually needed to pass a byte parameter. For example, if you decide to pass the AL register as the byte parameter, HLA will emit code that pushes the EAX register onto the stack. This single push instruction is a very efficient way to pass AL as a 4-byte parameter object. On the other hand, if you decide to pass the AH register as the byte parameter, pushing EAX won't work because this would leave the value in AH at offset EBP+9 in the activation record shown in Figure 5-9. Unfortunately, the procedure expects this value at offset EBP+8, so simply pushing EAX won't do the job. If you pass AH, BH, CH, or DH as a byte parameter, HLA emits code like the following:

```
sub( 4, esp );    // Make room for the parameter on the stack.
mov( ah, [esp] ); // Store ah into the L.O. byte of the parameter.
```

As you can clearly see, passing one of the H registers as a byte parameter is less efficient than passing one of the L registers. So you should attempt to use the L registers whenever possible if passing an 8-bit register as a parameter.[23] Note, by the way, that there is very little you can do about the efficiency issue even if you manually pass the parameters.

---

[23] Or better yet, pass the parameter directly in the register if you are writing the procedure yourself.

If the byte parameter you decide to pass is a variable rather than a register, HLA generates decidedly worse code. For example, suppose you call OneByteParm as follows:

```
OneByteParm( uns8Var );
```

For this call, HLA will emit code similar to the following to push this single-byte parameter:

```
push( eax );
push( eax );
mov( uns8Var, al );
mov( al, [esp+4] );
pop( eax );
```

As you can plainly see, this is a lot of code to pass a single byte onto the stack! HLA emits this much code because (1) it guarantees not to disturb any registers, and (2) it doesn't know whether uns8Var is the last variable in allocated memory. You can generate much better code if you don't have to enforce either of these two constraints.

If you have a spare 32-bit register lying around (especially one of EAX, EBX, ECX, or EDX), then you can pass a byte parameter onto the stack using only two instructions. Move (or move with zero/sign extension) the byte value into the register and then push the register onto the stack. For the current call to OneByteParm, the calling sequence would look like the following if EAX is available:

```
mov( uns8Var, al );
push( eax );
call OneByteParm;
```

If only ESI or EDI is available, you could use code like this:

```
movzx( uns8Var, esi );
push( esi );
call OneByteParm;
```

Another trick you can use to pass the parameter with only a single push instruction is to coerce the byte variable to a double-word object. For example:

```
push( (type dword uns8Var));
call OneByteParm;
```

This last example is very efficient. Note that it pushes the first 3 bytes of whatever value happens to follow uns8Var in memory as the padding bytes. HLA doesn't use this technique because there is a (very tiny) chance that using this scheme will cause the program to fail. If it turns out that the uns8Var object is the last byte of a given page in memory and the next page of memory is unreadable, the push instruction will cause a memory access exception. To be on the safe side, the HLA compiler does not use this scheme. However, you always ensure that the actual parameter you pass in this fashion is not t last variable you declare in a static section, then you can get away with co that uses this technique. Because it is nearly impossible for the byte object appear at the last accessible address on the stack, it is probably safe to use th technique with var objects.

When passing word parameters on the stack, you must also ensure that y include padding bytes so that each parameter consumes a multiple of 4 byte You can use the same techniques we use to pass bytes, except, of course, there are two valid bytes of data to pass instead of one. For example, you could use either of the following two schemes to pass a word object w to a OneWordParm procedure:

```
mov( w, ax );
push( eax );
call OneWordParm;
```

```
push( (type dword w) );
call OneWordParm;
```

When passing large objects by value on the stack (e.g., records and arrays you do not have to ensure that each element or field of the object consume a multiple of 4 bytes; all you need to do is ensure that the entire data structu consumes a multiple of 4 bytes on the stack. For example, if you have an array of ten 3-byte elements, the entire array will need 2 bytes of padding (10 * 3 is 30 bytes, which is not divisible by 4, but 10 * 3 + 2 is 32, which is divisible by 4). HLA does a fairly good job of passing large data objects by value to a procedure. For larger objects, you should use the HLA high-level language procedure invocation syntax unless you have some special require ments. Of course, if you want efficient operation, you should try to avoid passing large data structures by value.

By default, HLA guarantees that it won't disturb the values of any registe when it emits code to pass parameters to a procedure. Sometimes this guarante isn't necessary. For example, if you are returning a function result in EAX and you are not passing a parameter to a procedure in EAX, there really is no reason to preserve EAX upon entry into the procedure. Rather than generating some crazy code like the following to pass a byte parameter,

```
push( eax );
push( eax );
mov( uns8Var, al );
mov( al, [esp+4] );
pop( eax );
```

HLA could generate much better code if it knows that it can use EAX (or some other register) as follows.

```
        mov( uns8Var, al );
        push( eax );
```

You can use the @use procedure option to tell HLA that it can modify a register's value if doing so would improve the code it generates when passing parameters. The syntax for this option is:

```
@use reg32;
```

The *reg32* operand can be EAX, EBX, ECX, EDX, ESI, or EDI. You'll obtain the best results if this register is one of EAX, EBX, ECX, or EDX. You should note that you cannot specify EBP or ESP here (because the procedure already uses those registers).

The @use procedure option tells HLA that it's okay to modify the value of the register you specify as an operand. Therefore, if HLA can generate better code by not preserving that register's value, it will do so. For example, when the @use eax; option is provided for the OneByteParm procedure given earlier, HLA will only emit the two instructions immediately above rather than the five-instruction sequence that preserves EAX.

You must exercise care when specifying the @use procedure option. In particular, you should not be passing any parameters in the same register you specify in the @use option (because HLA may inadvertently scramble the parameter's value if you do this). Likewise, you must ensure that it's really okay for the procedure to change the register's value. As noted above, the best choice for an @use register is EAX when the procedure is returning a function result in EAX (because, clearly, the caller will not expect the procedure to preserve EAX).

If your procedure has a forward or external declaration (see Section 5.24), the @use option must appear only in the forward or external definition, not in the actual procedure declaration. If no such procedure prototype appears, then you must attach the @use option to the procedure declaration. Here's an example:

```
procedure OneByteParm( b:byte ); @nodisplay; @use EAX;
begin OneByteParm;

    << Do something with b. >>

end OneByteParm;
    .
    .
    .
static
    byteVar:byte;
        .
        .
        .
    OneByteParm( byteVar );
```

This call to OneByteParm emits the following instructions:

```
mov( uns8Var, al );
push( eax );
call OneByteParm;
```

### 5.17.3.3 Accessing Reference Parameters on the Stack

Because HLA passes the address for reference parameters, accessing the
reference parameters within a procedure is slightly more difficult than
accessing value parameters because you have to dereference the pointers
the reference parameters. Unfortunately, HLA's high-level syntax for pro
cedure declarations and invocations does not (and cannot) abstract this
detail away for you. You will have to manually dereference these pointers
yourself. This section reviews how you do this.

In Listing 5-16 the RefParm procedure has a single pass-by-reference
parameter. A pass-by-reference parameter is always a pointer to an object o
the type specified by the parameter's declaration. Therefore, theParameter i
actually an object of type pointer to uns32 rather than an uns32 value. In orde
to access the value associated with theParameter, this code has to load that
double-word address into a 32-bit register and access the data indirectly. Th
mov( theParameter, eax ); instruction in Listing 5-16 fetches this pointer into
the EAX register, and then procedure RefParm uses the [eax] addressing mod
to access the actual value of theParameter.

```
program AccessingReferenceParameters;
#include( "stdlib.hhf" )

    procedure RefParm( var theParameter: uns32 ); @nodisplay;
    begin RefParm;

        // Add 2 directly to the parameter passed by
        // reference to this procedure.

        mov( theParameter, eax );
        add( 2, (type uns32 [eax]) );

        // Fetch the value of the reference parameter
        // and print its value.

        mov( [eax], eax );
        stdout.put
        (
            "theParameter now equals ",
            (type uns32 eax),
            nl
        );

    end RefParm;
```

```
static
    p1: uns32 := 10;
    p2: uns32 := 15;

begin AccessingReferenceParameters;

    RefParm( p1 );
    RefParm( p2 );

    stdout.put( "On return, p1=", p1, " and p2=", p2, nl );

end AccessingReferenceParameters;
```

*Listing 5-16: Accessing a reference parameter*

Because this procedure accesses the data of the actual parameter, adding 2 to this data affects the values of the variables passed to the RefParm procedure from the main program. Of course, this should come as no surprise because these are the standard semantics for pass-by-reference parameters.

As you can see, accessing (small) pass-by-reference parameters is a little less efficient than accessing value parameters because you need an extra instruction to load the address into a 32-bit pointer register (not to mention you have to reserve a 32-bit register for this purpose). If you access reference parameters frequently, these extra instructions can really begin to add up, reducing the efficiency of your program. Furthermore, it's easy to forget to dereference a reference parameter and use the address of the value in your calculations (this is especially true when passing double-word parameters, like the uns32 parameter in the example above, to your procedures). Therefore, unless you really need to affect the value of the actual parameter, you should use pass by value to pass small objects to a procedure.

Passing large objects, like arrays and records, is where using reference parameters becomes efficient. When passing these objects by value, the calling code has to make a copy of the actual parameter; if the actual parameter is a large object, the copy process can be very inefficient. Because computing the address of a large object is just as efficient as computing the address of a small scalar object, there is no efficiency loss when passing large objects by reference. Within the procedure, you must still dereference the pointer to access the object, but the efficiency loss due to indirection is minimal when you contrast this with the cost of copying that large object. The program in Listing 5-17 demonstrates how to use pass by reference to initialize an array of records.

```
program accessingRefArrayParameters;
#include( "stdlib.hhf" )

const
    NumElements := 64;

type
    Pt: record
```

```
                    x:uns8;
                    y:uns8;

            endrecord;

        Pts: Pt[NumElements];


        procedure RefArrayParm( var ptArray: Pts ); @nodisplay;
        begin RefArrayParm;

            push( eax );
            push( ecx );
            push( edx );

            mov( ptArray, edx );     // Get address of parameter into edx.

            for( mov( 0, ecx ); ecx < NumElements; inc( ecx )) do

                // For each element of the array, set the x field
                // to (ecx div 8) and set the y field to (ecx mod 8).

                mov( cl, al );
                shr( 3, al );     // ecx div 8.
                mov( al, (type Pt [edx+ecx*2]).x );

                mov( cl, al );
                and( %111, al );  // ecx mod 8.
                mov( al, (type Pt [edx+ecx*2]).y );

            endfor;
            pop( edx );
            pop( ecx );
            pop( eax );

        end RefArrayParm;


static
    MyPts: Pts;

begin accessingRefArrayParameters;

    // Initialize the elements of the array.

    RefArrayParm( MyPts );


    // Display the elements of the array.

    for( mov( 0, ebx ); ebx < NumElements; inc( ebx )) do
```

```
        stdout.put
        (
            "RefArrayParm[",
            (type uns32 ebx):2,
            "].x=",
            MyPts.x[ ebx*2 ],

            "    RefArrayParm[",
            (type uns32 ebx):2,
            "].y=",
            MyPts.y[ ebx*2 ],
            nl
        );

    endfor;

end accessingRefArrayParameters;
```

*Listing 5-17: Passing an array of records by referencing*

As you can see from this example, passing large objects by reference is relatively efficient. Other than tying up the EDX register throughout the RefArrayParm procedure, plus a single instruction to load EDX with the address of the reference parameter, the RefArrayParm procedure doesn't require many more instructions than the same procedure where you would pass the parameter by value.

### 5.17.3.4    Passing Reference Parameters on the Stack

HLA's high-level syntax often makes passing reference parameters a breeze. All you need to do is specify the name of the actual parameter you wish to pass in the procedure's parameter list. HLA will automatically emit some code that will compute the address of the specified actual parameter and push this address onto the stack. However, like the code HLA emits for value parameters, the code HLA generates to pass the address of the actual parameter on the stack may not be the most efficient possible. Therefore, if you want to write fast code, you may want to manually write the code to pass reference parameters to a procedure. This section discusses how to do exactly that.

Whenever you pass a static object as a reference parameter, HLA generates very efficient code to pass the address of that parameter to the procedure. As an example, consider the following code fragment:

```
    procedure HasRefParm( var d:dword );
        .
        .
        .
    static
        FourBytes:dword;
```

```
var
    v: dword[2];
            .
            .
            .

HasRefParm( FourBytes );
            .
            .
            .
```

For the call to the HasRefParm procedure, HLA emits the following instruction sequence:

```
pushd( &FourBytes );
call HasRefParm;
```

You really aren't going to be able to do substantially better than this if you are passing your reference parameters on the stack. So if you're passing static objects as reference parameters, HLA generates fairly good code, and you should stick with the high-level syntax for the procedure call.

Unfortunately, when passing automatic (var) objects or indexed variable as reference parameters, HLA needs to compute the address of the object a runtime. This may require the use of the lea instruction. Unfortunately, the lea instruction requires a 32-bit register, and HLA promises not to disturb the values in any registers when it automatically generates code for you.[24] Therefore, HLA needs to preserve the value in whatever register it uses when it computes an address via lea to pass a parameter by reference. The following example shows you the code that HLA actually emits:

```
// Call to the HasRefParm procedure:

        HasRefParm( v[ebx*4] );

// HLA actually emits the following code for the above call:

        push( eax );
        push( eax );
        lea( eax, v[ebx*4] );
        mov( eax, [esp+4] );
        pop( eax );
        call HasRefParm;
```

As you can see, this is quite a bit of code, especially if you have a 32-bit register available and you don't need to preserve that register's value. The following is a better code sequence given the availability of EAX.

---

[24] This isn't entirely true. You'll see the exception in Chapter 12. Also, using the @use procedure option tells HLA that it's okay to modify the value in one of the registers.

```
          lea( eax, v[ebx*4] );
          push( eax );
          call HasRefParm;
```

Remember, when passing an actual parameter by reference, you must compute the address of that object and push the address onto the stack. For simple static objects you can use the address-of operator (&) to easily compute the address of the object and push it onto the stack; however, for indexed and automatic objects, you will probably need to use the lea instruction to compute the address of the object. Here are some examples that demonstrate this using the HasRefParm procedure from the previous examples:

```
static
      i:    int32;
      Ary:  int32[16];
      iptr: pointer to int32 := &i;

var
      v:    int32;
      AV:   int32[10];
      vptr: pointer to int32;
        .
        .
        .
      lea( eax, v );
      mov( eax, vptr );
        .
        .
        .
// HasRefParm( i );

      push( &i );                    // Simple static object, so just use &.
      call HasRefParm;

// HasRefParm( Ary[ebx] );        // Pass element of Ary by reference.

      lea( eax, Ary[ ebx*4 ]);   // Must use lea for indexed addresses.
      push( eax );
      call HasRefParm;

// HasRefParm( *iptr );   -- Pass object pointed at by iptr

      push( iptr );                  // Pass address (iptr's value) on stack.
      call HasRefParm;

// HasRefParm( v );

      lea( eax, v );                 // Must use lea to compute the address
      push( eax );                   // of automatic vars passed on stack.
      call HasRefParm;
```

```
// HasRefParm( AV[ esi ] );  -- Pass element of AV by reference.

    lea( eax, AV[ esi*4] );    // Must use lea to compute address of the
    push( eax );               // desired element.
    call HasRefParm;

// HasRefParm( *vptr );  -- Pass address held by vptr...

    push( vptr );              // Just pass vptr's value as the specified
    call HasRefParm;           // address.
```

If you have an extra register to spare, you can tell HLA to use that registe when computing the address-of reference parameters (without emitting th code to preserve that register's value). The @use option will tell HLA that it okay to use the specified register without preserving its value. As noted in th section on value parameters, the syntax for this procedure option is:

```
@use reg32;
```

where *reg32* may be any of EAX, EBX, ECX, EDX, ESI, or EDI. Because refe ence parameters always pass a 32-bit value, all of these registers are equivalen as far as HLA is concerned (unlike value parameters that may prefer the EAX, EBX, ECX, or EDX register). Your best choice would be EAX if the procedure is not passing a parameter in the EAX register and the procedu is returning a function result in EAX; otherwise, any currently unused regist will work fine.

With the @use eax; option, HLA emits the shorter code given in the previous examples. It does not emit all the extra instructions needed to preserve EAX's value. This makes your code much more efficient, especiall when passing several parameters by reference or when calling procedures with reference parameters several times.

### 5.17.3.5   Passing Formal Parameters as Actual Parameters

The examples in the previous two sections show how to pass static and auto matic variables as parameters to a procedure, either by value or by referenc There is one situation that these examples don't handle properly: the case when you are passing a formal parameter in one procedure as an actual parameter to another procedure. The following simple example demon strates the different cases that can occur for pass-by-value and pass-by-referenc parameters:

```
    procedure p1( val v:dword;  var r:dword );
    begin p1;
        .
        .
        .
    end p1;
```

```
procedure p2( val v2:dword; var r2:dword );
begin p2;

    p1( v2, r2 );    // (1) First call to p1
    p1( r2, v2 );    // (2) Second call to p1

end p2;
```

In the statement labeled (1) above, procedure p2 calls procedure p1 and passes its two formal parameters as parameters to p1. Note that this code passes the first parameter of both procedures by value, and it passes the second parameter of both procedures by reference. Therefore, in statement (1), the program passes the v2 parameter into p2 by value and passes it on to p1 by value; likewise, the program passes r2 in by reference and it passes the value onto p1 by reference.

Because p2's caller passes v2 in by value and p2 passes this parameter to p1 by value, all the code needs to do is make a copy of v2's value and pass this on to p1. The code to do this is nothing more than a single push instruction. For example:

```
push( v2 );
<< Code to handle r2 >>
call p1;
```

As you can see, this code is identical to passing an automatic variable by value. Indeed, it turns out that the code you need to write to pass a value parameter to another procedure is identical to the code you would write to pass a local automatic variable to that other procedure.

Passing r2 in statement (1) above requires a little more thought. You do not take the address of r2 using the lea instruction as you would a value parameter or an automatic variable. When passing r2 on through to p1, the author of this code probably expects the r formal parameter to contain the address of the variable whose address p2's caller passed into p2. In plain English, this means that p2 must pass the address of r2's actual parameter on through to p1. Because the r2 parameter is a double-word value containing the address of the corresponding actual parameter, this means that the code must pass the double-word value of r2 on to p1. The complete code for statement (1) above looks like the following:

```
push( v2 );    // Pass the value passed in through v2 to p1.
push( r2 );    // Pass the address passed in through r2 to p1.
call p1;
```

The important thing to note in this example is that passing a formal reference parameter (r2) as an actual reference parameter (r) does not involve taking the address of the formal parameter (r2). p2's caller has already done this; p2 simply passes this address on through to p1.

In the second call to p1 in the example above (2), the code swaps the actual parameters so that the call to p1 passes r2 by value and v2 by reference. Specifically, p1 expects p2 to pass it the value of the double-word object associated with r2; likewise, it expects p2 to pass it the address of the value associated with v2.

To pass the value of the object associated with r2, your code must dereference the pointer associated with r2 and directly pass the value. Here is the code HLA automatically generates to pass r2 as the first parameter to p1 in statement (2):

```
sub( 4, esp );      // Make room on stack for parameter.
push( eax );        // Preserve eax's value.
mov( r2, eax );     // Get address-of object passed in to p2.
mov( [eax], eax );  // Dereference to get the value of this object.
mov( eax, [esp+4]); // Put value-of parameter into its location on stack.
pop( eax );         // Restore original eax value.
```

As usual, HLA generates a little more code than may be necessary because it won't destroy the value in the EAX register (you may use the @use procedure option to tell HLA that it's okay to use EAX's value, thereby reducing the code it generates). You can write more efficient code if a register is available to use in this sequence. If EAX is unused, you could trim this down to the following:

```
mov( r2, eax );     // Get the pointer to the actual object.
pushd( [eax] );     // Push the value of the object onto the stack.
```

Because you can treat value parameters exactly like local (automatic) variables, you use the same code to pass v2 by reference to p1 as you would to pass a local variable in p2 to p1. Specifically, you use the lea instruction to compute the address of the value in the v2. The code HLA automatically emits for statement (2) above preserves all registers and takes the following form (same as passing an automatic variable by reference):

```
push( eax );        // Make room for the parameter.
push( eax );        // Preserve eax's value.
lea( eax, v2 );     // Compute address of v2's value.
mov( eax, [esp+4]); // Store away address as parameter value.
pop( eax );         // Restore eax's value.
```

Of course, if you have a register available, you can improve on this code. Here's the complete code that corresponds to statement (2) above:

```
mov( r2, eax );     // Get the pointer to the actual object.
pushd( [eax] );     // Push the value of the object onto the stack.
lea( eax, v2 );     // Push the address of v2 onto the stack.
push( eax );
call p1;
```

### 5.17.3.6 HLA Hybrid Parameter-Passing Facilities

Like control structures, HLA provides a high-level language syntax for procedure calls that is convenient to use and easy to read. However, this high-level language syntax is sometimes inefficient and may not provide the capabilities you need (for example, you cannot specify an arithmetic expression as a value parameter as you can in high-level languages). HLA lets you overcome these limitations by writing low-level ("pure") assembly language code. Unfortunately, low-level code is harder to read and maintain than procedure calls that use high-level syntax. Furthermore, it's quite possible that HLA generates perfectly fine code for certain parameters, while only one or two parameters present a problem. Fortunately, HLA provides a hybrid syntax for procedure calls that allows you to use both high-level and low-level syntax as appropriate for a given actual parameter. This lets you use high-level syntax where appropriate and then drop down into pure assembly language to pass those special parameters that HLA's high-level language syntax cannot handle efficiently (if at all).

Within an actual parameter list (using the high-level language syntax), if HLA encounters #{ followed by a sequence of statements and a closing }#, HLA will substitute the instructions between the braces in place of the code it would normally generate for that parameter. For example, consider the following code fragment:

```
procedure HybridCall( i:uns32; j:uns32 );
begin HybridCall;
    .
    .
    .
end HybridCall;
    .
    .
    .

    // Equivalent to HybridCall( 5, i+j );

    HybridCall
    (
        5,
        #{
            mov( i, eax );
            add( j, eax );
            push( eax );
        }#
    );
```

The call to HybridCall immediately above is equivalent to the following "pure" assembly language code.

```
pushd( 5 );
mov( i, eax );
add( j, eax );
push( eax );
call HybridCall;
```

As a second example, consider the example from the previous section:

```
procedure p2( val v2:dword; var r2:dword );
begin p2;

    p1( v2, r2 );    // (1) First call to p1
    p1( r2, v2 );    // (2) Second call to p1

end p2;
```

HLA generates exceedingly mediocre code for the second call to p1 in this example. If efficiency is important in the context of this procedure call and you have a free register available, you might want to rewrite this code a follows:[25]

```
procedure p2( val v2:dword; var r2:dword );
begin p2;

    p1( v2, r2 );    // (1) First call to p1
    p1              // (2) Second call to p1
    (                //     This code assumes eax is free.
        #{
            mov( r2, eax );
            pushd( [eax] );
        }#,

        #{
            lea( eax, v2 );
            push( eax );
        }#
    );

end p2;
```

Note that specifying the @use reg; option tells HLA that the register is always available for use wherever you call a procedure. If there is one case where the procedure's invocation must preserve the specified register, then you cannot use the @use option to generate better code. However, you may use the hybrid parameter-passing mechanism on a case-by-base basis to improve the performance of those particular calls.

---

[25] Of course, you could also use the @use eax; procedure option to achieve the same effect in this example.

### 5.17.3.7 Mixing Register and Stack-Based Parameters

You can mix register parameters and standard (stack-based) parameters in the same high-level procedure declaration. For example:

```
procedure HasBothRegAndStack( var dest:dword in edi; count:un32 );
```

When constructing the activation record, HLA ignores the parameters you pass in registers and processes only those parameters you pass on the stack. Therefore, a call to the HasBothRegAndStack procedure will push only a single parameter onto the stack (count). It will pass the dest parameter in the EDI register. When this procedure returns to its caller, it will remove only 4 bytes of parameter data from the stack.

Note that when you pass a parameter in a register, you should avoid specifying that same register in the @use procedure option. In the example above, HLA might not generate any code whatsoever at all for the dest parameter (because the value is already in EDI). Had you specified @use edi; and HLA decided it was okay to disturb EDI's value, this would destroy the parameter value in EDI; that won't actually happen in this particular example (because HLA never uses a register to pass a double-word value parameter like count), but keep this issue in mind.

## 5.18 Procedure Pointers

The 80x86 call instruction allows three basic forms: direct calls (via a procedure name), indirect calls through a 32-bit general-purpose register, and indirect calls through a double-word pointer variable. The call instruction supports the following (low-level) syntax:

```
call Procname;      // Direct call to procedure Procname (or Stmt label).
call( Reg32 );      // Indirect call to procedure whose address appears
                    // in the Reg32 general-purpose 32-bit register.
call( dwordVar );   // Indirect call to the procedure whose address
                    // appears in the dwordVar double word variable.
```

The first form we've been using throughout this chapter, so there is little need to discuss it here. The second form, the register indirect call, calls the procedure whose address is held in the specified 32-bit register. The address of a procedure is the byte address of the first instruction to execute within that procedure. Remember, on a Von Neumann architecture machine (like the 80x86), the system stores machine instructions in memory along with other data. The CPU fetches the instruction opcode values from memory prior to executing them. When you execute the register indirect call instruction, the 80x86 first pushes the return address onto the stack and then begins fetching the next opcode byte (instruction) from the address specified by the register's value.

The third form of the call instruction above fetches the address of some procedure's first instruction from a double-word variable in memory. Although this instruction suggests that the call uses the displacement-only addressing mode, you should realize that any legal memory addressing mode is legal here; for example, call( procPtrTable[ebx*4] ); is perfectly legitimate; this statement fetches the double word from the array of double words (procPtrTable) and calls the procedure whose address is the value contained within that double word.

HLA treats procedure names like static objects. Therefore, you can compute the address of a procedure by using the address-of (&) operator along with the procedure's name or by using the lea instruction. For example, &Procname is the address of the very first instruction of the Procname procedure. So all three of the following code sequences wind up calling the Procname procedure:

```
call Procname;
    .
    .
    .
mov( &Procname, eax );
call( eax );
    .
    .
    .
lea( eax, Procname );
call( eax );
```

Because the address of a procedure fits in a 32-bit object, you can store such an address into a double-word variable; in fact, you can initialize a double-word variable with the address of a procedure using code like the following:

```
procedure p;
begin p;
end p;
    .
    .
    .
static
    ptrToP: dword := &p;
    .
    .
    .
call( ptrToP );  // Calls the p procedure if ptrToP has not changed.
```

Because the use of procedure pointers occurs frequently in assembly language programs, HLA provides a special syntax for declaring procedure pointer variables and for calling procedures indirectly through such pointer variables. To declare a procedure pointer in an HLA program, you can use a variable declaration like the following:

```
static
    procPtr: procedure;
```

Note that this syntax uses the keyword procedure as a data type. It follows the variable name and a colon in one of the variable declaration sections (static, readonly, storage, or var). This sets aside exactly 4 bytes of storage for the *procPtr* variable. To call the procedure whose address is held by *procPtr*, you can use either of the following two forms:

```
call( procPtr );      // Low-level syntax
procPtr();            // High-level language syntax
```

Note that the high-level syntax for an indirect procedure call is identical to the high-level syntax for a direct procedure call. HLA can figure out whether to use a direct call or an indirect call by the type of the identifier. If you've specified a variable name, HLA assumes it needs to use an indirect call; if you specify a procedure name, HLA uses a direct call.

Like all pointer objects, you should not attempt to indirectly call a procedure through a pointer variable unless you've initialized that variable with an appropriate address. There are two ways to initialize a procedure pointer variable: static and readonly objects allow an initializer, or you can compute the address of a routine (as a 32-bit value) and store that 32-bit address directly into the procedure pointer at runtime. The following code fragment demonstrates both ways you can initialize a procedure pointer:

```
static
    ProcPointer: procedure := &p;    // Initialize ProcPointer with
                                     // the address of p.
    .
    .
    .
    ProcPointer();                   // First invocation calls p.

    mov( &q, ProcPointer );          // Reload ProcPointer with the address of q.
    .
    .
    .
    ProcPointer();                   // This invocation calls the q procedure.
```

Procedure pointer variable declarations also allow the declaration of parameters. To declare a procedure pointer with parameters, you must use a declaration like the following:

```
static
    p:procedure( i:int32; c:char );
```

This declaration states that p is a 32-bit pointer that contains the address of a procedure requiring two parameters. If desired, you could also initialize this variable p with the address of some procedure by using a static initializer. For example:

```
static
    p:procedure( i:int32; c:char ) := &SomeProcedure;
```

Note that *SomeProcedure* must be a procedure whose parameter list exactly matches p's parameter list (i.e., two value parameters, the first is an int32 parameter and the second is a char parameter). To indirectly call this procedure, you could use either of the following sequences:

```
push( Value_for_i );
push( Value_for_c );
call( p );
```

or

```
p( Value_for_i, Value_for_c );
```

The high-level language syntax has the same features and restrictions as the high-level syntax for a direct procedure call. The only difference is the actual call instruction HLA emits at the end of the calling sequence.

Although all the examples in this section use static variable declarations, don't get the idea that you can declare simple procedure pointers only in the static or other variable declaration sections. You can also declare procedure pointer types in the type section, and you can declare procedure pointers as fields of a record or a union. Assuming you create a type name for a procedure pointer in the type section, you can even create arrays of procedure pointers. The following code fragments demonstrate some of the possibilities:

```
type
        pptr:       procedure;
        prec:       record
                        p:pptr;
                        << Other fields >>
                    endrecord;
static
        p1:pptr;
        p2:pptr[2]
        p3:prec;
        .
        .
        .
        p1();
        p2[ebx*4]();
        p3.p();
```

One very important thing to keep in mind when using procedure pointers is that HLA does not (and cannot) enforce strict type checking on the pointer values you assign to a procedure pointer variable. In particular, if the parameter lists do not agree between the declarations of the pointer variable and the procedure whose address you assign to the pointer variable, the program will probably crash when you attempt to call the mismatched procedure indirectly through the pointer using the high-level syntax. Like the low-level "pure" procedure calls, it is your responsibility to ensure that the proper number and types of parameters are on the stack prior to the call.

## 5.19 Procedural Parameters

One place where procedure pointers are quite invaluable is in parameter lists. Selecting one of several procedures to call by passing the address of some procedure is a common operation. Therefore, HLA lets you declare procedure pointers as parameters.

There is nothing special about a procedure parameter declaration. It looks exactly like a procedure variable declaration except it appears within a parameter list rather than within a variable declaration section. The following are some typical procedure prototypes that demonstrate how to declare such parameters:

```
procedure p1( procparm: procedure ); forward;
procedure p2( procparm: procedure( i:int32 ) ); forward;
procedure p3( val procparm: procedure ); forward;
```

The last example above is identical to the first. It does point out, though, that you generally pass procedural parameters by value. This may seem counterintuitive because procedure pointers are addresses and you will need to pass an address as the actual parameter; however, a pass-by-reference procedure parameter means something else entirely. Consider the following (legal!) declaration:

```
procedure p4( var procPtr:procedure ); forward;
```

This declaration tells HLA that you are passing a procedure *variable* by reference to p4. The address HLA expects must be the address of a procedure pointer variable, not a procedure.

When passing a procedure pointer by value, you may specify either a procedure variable (whose value HLA passes to the actual procedure) or a procedure pointer constant. A procedure pointer constant consists of the address-of operator (&) immediately followed by a procedure name. Passing procedure constants is probably the most convenient way to pass procedural parameters. For example, the following calls to the Plot routine might plot out the function passed as a parameter from −2 to +2.

```
Plot( &sineFunc );
Plot( &cosFunc );
Plot( &tanFunc );
```

Note that you cannot pass a procedure as a parameter by simply specifying the procedure's name. That is, Plot( sineFunc ); will not work. Simply specifying the procedure name doesn't work because HLA will attempt to directly call the procedure whose name you specify (remember, a procedure name inside a parameter list invokes instruction composition). If you did not specify a parameter list—or at least an empty pair of parentheses—after the parameter/procedure's name, HLA would generate a syntax error message. Moral of the story: Don't forget to preface procedure parameter constant names with the address-of operator (&).

## 5.20 Untyped Reference Parameters

Sometimes you will want to write a procedure to which you pass a generic memory object by reference without regard to the type of that memory object. A classic example is a procedure that zeros out some data structure. Such a procedure might have the following prototype:

```
procedure ZeroMem( var mem:byte; count:uns32 );
```

This procedure would zero out count bytes starting at the address the first parameter specifies. The problem with this procedure prototype is that HLA will complain if you attempt to pass anything other than a byte object as the first parameter. Of course, you can overcome this problem using type coercion like the following, but if you call this procedure several times with a lot of different data types, then the following coercion operator is rather tedious to use:

```
ZeroMem( (type byte MyDataObject), @size( MyDataObject ));
```

Of course, you can always use hybrid parameter passing or manually push the parameters yourself, but these solutions are even more tedious than using the type coercion operation. Fortunately, HLA provides a convenient solution: untyped reference parameters.

Untyped reference parameters are exactly that—pass-by-reference parameters for which HLA doesn't bother to compare the type of the actual parameter against the type of the formal parameter. With an untyped reference parameter, the call to ZeroMem above would take the following form:

```
ZeroMem( MyDataObject, @size( MyDataObject ));
```

MyDataObject could be any type, and multiple calls to ZeroMem could pass different typed objects without any objections from HLA.

To declare an untyped reference parameter, you specify the parameter using the normal syntax except that you use the reserved word var in place of the parameter's type. This var keyword tells HLA that any variable object is legal for that parameter. Note that you must pass untyped reference parameters by reference, so the var keyword must precede the parameter's declaration as well. Here's the correct declaration for the ZeroMem procedure using an untyped reference parameter:

```
procedure ZeroMem( var mem:var; count:uns32 );
```

With this declaration, HLA will compute the address of whatever memory object you pass as an actual parameter to ZeroMem and pass this on the stack.

# 5.21   Managing Large Programs

Most assembly language source files are not standalone programs. In general, you will call various standard library or other routines that are not defined in your main program. For example, you've probably noticed by now that the 80x86 doesn't provide any machine instructions like read, write, or put for doing I/O operations. Of course, you can write your own procedures to accomplish this. Unfortunately, writing such routines is a complex task, and beginning assembly language programmers are not ready for such tasks. That's where the HLA Standard Library comes in. This is a package of procedures you can call to perform simple I/O operations like stdout.put.

The HLA Standard Library contains hundreds of thousands of lines of source code. Imagine how difficult programming would be if you had to merge these hundreds of thousands of lines of code into your simple programs! Imagine how slow compiling your programs would be if you had to compile those hundreds of thousands of lines with each program you write. Fortunately, you don't have to do this.

For small programs, working with a single source file is fine. For large programs, this gets very cumbersome (consider the example above of having to include the entire HLA Standard Library into each of your programs). Furthermore, once you've debugged and tested a large section of your code, continuing to assemble that same code when you make a small change to some other part of your program is a waste of time. The HLA Standard Library, for example, takes several minutes to assemble, even on a fast machine. Imagine having to wait 20 or 30 minutes on a fast PC to assemble a program to which you've made a one-line change!

As for high-level languages, the solution is *separate compilation*. First, you break up your large source files into manageable chunks. Then you compile the separate files into object code modules. Finally, you link the object modules together to form a complete program. If you need to make a small change to one of the modules, you only need to reassemble that one module; you do not need to reassemble the entire program.

The HLA Standard Library works in precisely this way. The Standard Library is already compiled and ready to use. You simply call routines in the Standard Library and link your code with the Standard Library using a *linker* program. This saves considerable time when developing a program that uses the Standard Library code. Of course, you can easily create your own object modules and link them together with your code. You could even add new routines to the Standard Library so they will be available for use in future programs you write.

"Programming in the large" is the term software engineers have coined to describe the processes, methodologies, and tools for handling the development of large software projects. While everyone has their own idea of what "large" is, separate compilation is one of the more popular techniques that support "programming in the large." The following sections describe the tools HLA provides for separate compilation and how to effectively employ these tools in your programs.

## 5.22 The #include Directive

The #include directive, when encountered in a source file, switches program input from the current file to the file specified in the parameter list of the #include directive. This allows you to construct text files containing common constants, types, source code, and other HLA items and include such files into the assembly of several separate programs. The syntax for the #include directive is:

---

#include( "Filename" )

---

*Filename* must be a valid filename. HLA merges the specified file into the compilation at the point of the #include directive. Note that you can nest #include statements inside files you include. That is, a file being included into another file during assembly may itself include a third file. In fact, the *stdlib.hhf* header file you see in most example programs is really nothing more than a bunch of #include statements (see Listing 5-18 for the original *stdlib.hhf* source code; note that this file is considerably different today, but the concept is still the same).

---

```
#include( "hla.hhf" )
#include( "x86.hhf" )
#include( "misctypes.hhf" )
#include( "hll.hhf" )

#include( "excepts.hhf" )
#include( "memory.hhf" )

#include( "args.hhf" )
#include( "conv.hhf" )
#include( "strings.hhf" )
#include( "cset.hhf" )
#include( "patterns.hhf" )
#include( "tables.hhf" )
#include( "arrays.hhf" )
#include( "chars.hhf" )

#include( "math.hhf" )
#include( "rand.hhf" )

#include( "stdio.hhf" )
#include( "stdin.hhf" )
#include( "stdout.hhf" )
```

---

*Listing 5-18: The original* stdlib.hhf *header file*

By including *stdlib.hhf* in your source code, you automatically include all the HLA library modules. It's often more efficient (in terms of compile time and size of code generated) to provide only those #include statements for the modules you actually need in your program. However, including *stdlib.hhf* is extremely convenient and takes up less space in this text, which is why most programs appearing in this text use *stdlib.hhf*.

Note that the #include directive does not need to end with a semicolon. If you put a semicolon after the #include, that semicolon becomes part of the source file and is the first character following the included source during compilation. HLA generally allows spare semicolons in various parts of the program, so you will sometimes see an #include statement ending with a semicolon. In general, though, you should not get in the habit of putting semicolons after #include statements because there is the slight possibility this could create a syntax error in certain circumstances.

Using the #include directive by itself does not provide separate compilation. You *could* use the #include directive to break up a large source file into separate modules and join these modules together when you compile your file. The following example would include the *printf.hla* and *putc.hla* files during the compilation of your program:

```
#include( "printf.hla" )
#include( "putc.hla" )
```

Now your program *will* benefit from the modularity gained by this approach. Alas, you will not save any development time. The #include directive inserts the source file at the point of the #include during compilation, exactly as though you had typed that code yourself. HLA still has to compile the code, and that takes time. Were you to include all the files for the Standard Library routines in this manner, your compilations would take *forever*.

In general, you should *not* use the #include directive to include source code as shown above.[26] Instead, you should use the #include directive to insert a common set of constants, types, external procedure declarations, and other such items into a program. Typically an assembly language include file does *not* contain any machine code (outside of a macro; see Chapter 9 for details). The purpose of using #include files in this manner will become clearer after you see how the external declarations work.

## 5.23 Ignoring Duplicate #include Operations

As you begin to develop sophisticated modules and libraries, you eventually discover a big problem: Some header files will need to include other header files (e.g., the *stdlib.hhf* header file includes all the other Standard Library header files). Well, this isn't actually a big problem, but a problem will occur when one header file includes another, and that second header file includes another, and that third header file includes another, and . . . that last header file includes the first header file. Now *this* is a big problem.

There are two problems with a header file indirectly including itself. First, this creates an infinite loop in the compiler. The compiler will happily go on about its business including all these files over and over again until it runs out of memory or some other error occurs. Clearly this is not a good thing. The second problem that occurs (usually before the first problem) is that the second time HLA includes a header file, it starts complaining bitterly

---

[26] There is nothing wrong with this, other than the fact that it does not take advantage of separate compilation.

about duplicate symbol definitions. After all, the first time it reads the header file it processes all the declarations in that file; the second time around it views all those symbols as duplicate symbols.

HLA provides a special include directive that eliminates this problem: #includeonce. You use this directive exactly like you use the #include directive. For example:

```
#includeonce( "myHeaderFile.hhf" )
```

If *myHeaderFile.hhf* directly or indirectly includes itself (with a #includeonce directive), then HLA will ignore the new request to include the file. Note, however, that if you use the #include directive, rather than #includeonce, HLA will include the file a second time. This was done in case you really do need to include a header file twice.

The bottom line is this: You should always use the #includeonce directive to include header files you've created. In fact, you should get in the habit of always using #includeonce, even for header files created by others (the HLA Standard Library already has provisions to prevent recursive includes, so you don't have to worry about using #includeonce with the Standard Library header files).

There is another technique you can use to prevent recursive includes—using conditional compilation. Chapter 9, the chapter on macros and the HLA Compile-Time Language, discusses this option.

## 5.24   Units and the external Directive

Technically, the #include directive provides you with all the facilities you need to create modular programs. You can create several modules, each containing some specific routine, and include those modules, as necessary, in your assembly language programs using #include. However, HLA provides a better way: external and public symbols.

One major problem with the #include mechanism is that once you've debugged a routine, including it into a compilation still wastes time because HLA must recompile bug-free code every time you assemble the main program. A much better solution would be to preassemble the debugged modules and link the object code modules together. This is what the external directive allows you to do.

To use the external facilities, you must create at least two source files. One file contains a set of variables and procedures used by the second. The second file uses those variables and procedures without knowing how they're implemented. The only problem is that if you create two separate HLA programs, the linker will get confused when you try to combine them. This is because both HLA programs have their own main program. Which main program does the OS run when it loads the program into memory?

To resolve this problem, HLA uses a different type of compilation module, the unit, to compile programs without a main program. The syntax for an HLA unit is actually simpler than that for an HLA program; it takes the following form:

```
unit unitname;

    << declarations >>

end unitname;
```

With one exception (the var section), anything that can go in the declaration section of an HLA program can go into the declaration section of an HLA unit. Notice that a unit does not have a begin clause and there are no program statements in the unit;[27] a unit contains only declarations.

In addition to the fact that a unit does not contain a main program section, there is one other difference between units and programs. Units cannot have a var section. This is because the var section declares automatic variables that are local to the main program's source code. Because there is no "main program" associated with a unit, var sections are illegal.[28]

To demonstrate, consider the two modules in Listings 5-19 and 5-20.

```
unit Number1;

static
    Var1:   uns32;
    Var2:   uns32;

    procedure Add1and2;
    begin Add1and2;

        push( eax );
        mov( Var2, eax );
        add( eax, Var1 );

    end Add1and2;

end Number1;
```

Listing 5-19: Example of a simple HLA unit

```
program main;
#include( "stdlib.hhf" );

begin main;
```

---

[27] Of course, units may contain procedures and those procedures may have statements, but the unit itself does not have any executable instructions associated with it.

[28] Procedures in the unit may have their own var sections, but the procedure's declaration section is separate from the unit's declaration section.

```
    mov( 2, Var2 );
    mov( 3, Var1 );
    Add1and2();
    stdout.put( "Var1=", Var1, nl );

end main;
```

*Listing 5-20: Main program that references external objects*

The main program references Var1, Var2, and Add1and2, yet these symbols are external to this program (they appear in unit Number1). If you attempt to compile the main program as it stands, HLA will complain that these three symbols are undefined.

Therefore, you must declare them external with the external option. An external procedure declaration looks just like a forward declaration except you use the reserved word external rather than forward. To declare external static variables, simply follow those variables' declarations with the reserved word external. The program in Listing 5-21 is a modification to the program in Listing 5-20 that includes the external declarations.

```
program main;
#include( "stdlib.hhf" );

    procedure Add1and2; external;

static
    Var1: uns32; external;
    Var2: uns32; external;

begin main;

    mov( 2, Var2 );
    mov( 3, Var1 );
    Add1and2();
    stdout.put( "Var1=", Var1, nl );

end main;
```

*Listing 5-21: Modified main program with external declarations*

If you attempt to compile this second version of main using the typical HLA compilation command HLA main2.hla, you will be somewhat disappointed. This program will actually compile without error. However, when HLA attempts to link this code it will report that the symbols Var1, Var2, and Add1and2 are undefined. This happens because you haven't compiled and linked in the associated unit with this main program. Before you try that and discover that it still doesn't work, you should know that all symbols in a unit, by default, are *private* to that unit. This means that those symbols are inaccessible in code outside that unit unless you explicitly declare those symbols as *public* symbols. To declare symbols as public, you simply put external declarations for those symbols in the unit before the actual symbol declarations. If an external declaration appears in the same source file as the actual declaration of a symbol, HLA assumes that the name is needed externally and makes that symbol a public (rather than private) symbol. The unit in Listing 5-22 is a correction to the Number1 unit that properly declares the external objects.

```
unit Number1;

static
    Var1:    uns32; external;
    Var2:    uns32; external;

    procedure Add1and2; external;

static
    Var1:    uns32;
    Var2:    uns32;


    procedure Add1and2;
    begin Add1and2;

        push( eax );
        mov( Var2, eax );
        add( eax, Var1 );

    end Add1and2;

end Number1;
```

Listing 5-22: Correct Number1 unit with external declarations

It may seem redundant declaring these symbols twice as occurs in Listings 5-21 and 5-22, but you'll soon see that you don't normally write the code this way.

If you attempt to compile the main program or the Number1 unit using the typical HLA statement, that is,

```
HLA main2.hla
HLA unit2.hla
```

you'll quickly discover that the linker still returns errors. It returns an error on the compilation of *main2.hla* because you still haven't told HLA to link in the object code associated with *unit2.hla*. Likewise, the linker complains if you attempt to compile *unit2.hla* by itself because it can't find a main program. The simple solution is to compile both of these modules together with the following single command:

```
HLA main2.hla unit2.hla
```

This command will properly compile both modules and link together their object code.

Unfortunately, the command above defeats one of the major benefits of separate compilation. When you issue this command it will compile both `main2` and `unit2` prior to linking them together. Remember, a major reason for separate compilation is to reduce compilation time on large projects. While the above command is convenient, it doesn't achieve this goal.

To separately compile the two modules you must run HLA separately on them. Of course, you saw earlier that attempting to compile these modules separately produced linker errors. To get around this problem, you need to compile the modules without linking them. The -c (compile-only) HLA command-line option achieves this. To compile the two source files without running the linker, you would use the following commands:

```
HLA -c main2.hla
HLA -c unit2.hla
```

This produces two object code files, *main2.obj* and *unit2.obj*, that you can link together to produce a single executable. You could run the linker program directly, but an easier way is to use the HLA compiler to link the object modules together for you:

```
HLA main2.obj unit2.obj
```

Under Windows, this command produces an executable file named *main2.exe*,[29] under Linux, Mac OS X, and FreeBSD this command produces a file named *main2*. You could also type the following command to compile the main program and link it with a previously compiled *unit2* object module:

```
HLA main2.hla unit2.obj
```

In general, HLA looks at the suffixes of the filenames following the HLA commands. If the filename doesn't have a suffix, HLA assumes it to be *.HLA*. If the filename has a suffix, then HLA will do the following with the file:

- If the suffix is *.HLA*, HLA will compile the file with the HLA compiler.
- If the suffix is *.ASM*, HLA will assemble the file with MASM (or some other default assembler such as FASM, NASM, or TASM under Windows) or Gas (Linux/Mac OS X/FreeBSD).
- If the suffix is *.OBJ* or *.LIB* (Windows), or *.o* or *.a* (Linux/Mac OS X/ FreeBSD), then HLA will link that module with the rest of the compilation

---

[29] If you want to explicitly specify the name of the output file, HLA provides a command-line option to achieve this. You can get a menu of all legal command-line options by entering the command HLA -?.

## 5.24.1   Behavior of the external Directive

Whenever you declare a symbol using the external directive, keep in mind several limitations of external objects:

- Only one external declaration of an object may appear in a given source file. That is, you cannot define the same symbol twice as an external object.
- Only procedure, static, readonly, and storage variable objects can be external. var, type, const, and parameter objects cannot be external.
- external objects must appear at the global declaration level. You cannot declare external objects within a procedure or other nested structure.[30]
- external objects publish their name globally. Therefore, you must carefully choose the names of your external objects so they do not conflict with other symbols.

This last point is especially important to keep in mind. HLA links your modules using a linker. At each step in this process, your choice of external names could create problems for you.

Consider the following HLA external/public declaration:

```
static
        extObj:         uns32; external;
        extObj:         uns32;
        localObject:    uns32;
```

When you compile a program containing these declarations, HLA automatically generates a "munged" name for the localObject variable that probably won't ever have any conflicts with system-global external symbols.[31] Whenever you declare an external symbol, however, HLA uses the object's name as the default external name. This can create some problems if you inadvertently use some global name as your variable name.

To get around the problem of conflicting external names, HLA supports an additional syntax for the external option that lets you explicitly specify the external name. The following example demonstrates this extended syntax:

```
static
    c: char; external( "var_c" );
    c: char;
```

If you follow the external keyword with a string constant enclosed by parentheses, HLA will continue to use the declared name (c in this example) as the identifier within your HLA source code. Externally (i.e., in the assembly

---

[30] There are a few exceptions, but you cannot declare external procedures or variables except at the global level.

[31] Typically, HLA creates a name like *001A_localObject* out of *localObject*. This is a legal MASM identifier, but it is not likely it will conflict with any other global symbols when HLA compiles the program with MASM.

code) HLA will substitute the name `var_c` whenever you reference c. This feature helps you avoid problems with the misuse of assembler reserved words, or other global symbols, in your HLA programs.

You should also note that this feature of the external option lets you create *aliases*. For example, you may want to refer to an object by the name `StudentCount` in one module while referring to the object as `PersonCount` in another module (you might do this because you have a general library module that deals with counting people and you want to use the object in a program that deals only with students). Using a declaration like the following lets you do this:

```
static
    StudentCount: uns32; external( "PersonCount" );
```

Of course, you've already seen some of the problems you might encounter when you start creating aliases. So you should use this capability sparingly in your programs. Perhaps a more reasonable use of this feature is to simplify certain OS APIs. For example, the Win32 API uses some really long names for certain procedure calls. You can use the external directive to provide a more meaningful name than the standard one the operating system specifies.

### 5.24.2   Header Files in HLA

HLA's technique of using the same external declaration to define public as well as external symbols may seem somewhat counterintuitive. Why not use public reserved word for public symbols and the external keyword for external definitions? Well, as counterintuitive as HLA's external declarations may seem, they are founded on decades of solid experience with the C/C++ programming language that uses a similar approach to public and external symbols.[32] Combined with a *header file*, HLA's external declarations make large-program maintenance a breeze.

An important benefit of the external directive (versus separate public and external directives) is that it lets you minimize duplication of effort in your source files. Suppose, for example, you want to create a module with a bunch of support routines and variables for use in several different programs (e.g., the HLA Standard Library). In addition to sharing some routines and some variables, suppose you want to share constants, types, and other items as well.

The #include file mechanism provides a perfect way to handle this. You simply create a #include file containing the constants, macros, and external definitions and include this file in the module that implements your routines and in the modules that use those routines (see Figure 5-10).

---

[32] Actually, C/C++ is a little different. All global symbols in a module are assumed to be public unless explicitly declared private. HLA's approach (forcing the declaration of public items via external) is a little safer.

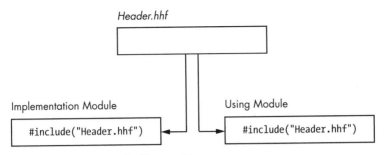

Figure 5-10: Using header files in HLA programs

A typical header file contains only const, val, type, static, readonly, storage, and procedure prototypes (plus a few others we haven't look at yet, like macros). Objects in the static, readonly, and storage sections, as well as all procedure declarations, are always external objects. In particular, you should not put any var objects in a header file, nor should you put any nonexternal variables or procedure bodies in a header file. If you do, HLA will make duplicate copies of these objects in the different source files that include the header file. Not only will this make your programs larger, but it will cause them to fail under certain circumstances. For example, you generally put a variable in a header file so you can share the value of that variable among several different modules. However, if you fail to declare that symbol as external in the header file and just put a standard variable declaration there, each module that includes the source file will get its own separate variable—the modules will not share a common variable.

If you create a standard header file, containing const, val, and type declarations and external objects, you should always be sure to include that file in the declaration section of all modules that need the definitions in the header file. Generally, HLA programs include all their header files in the first few statements after the program or unit header.

This text adopts the HLA Standard Library convention of using an *.hhf* suffix for HLA header files (*hhf* stands for *HLA header file*).

## 5.25 Namespace Pollution

One problem with creating libraries with a lot of different modules is namespace pollution. A typical library module will have a #include file associated with it that provides external definitions for all the routines, constants, variables, and other symbols provided in the library. Whenever you want to use some routines or other objects from the library, you would typically #include the library's header file in your project. As your libraries get larger and you add declarations in the header file, it becomes likely that the names you've chosen for your library's identifiers will conflict with names you want to use in your current project. This is known as *namespace pollution*: library header files pollute the namespace with names you typically don't need in order to gain easy access to the few routines in the library you actually use. Most of the time those names don't harm anything—unless you want to use those names for your own purposes.

HLA requires that you declare all external symbols at the global (progra unit) level. You cannot, therefore, include a header file with external declara tions within a procedure. Thus, there will be no naming conflicts between external library symbols and symbols you declare locally within a procedure the conflicts will occur only between the external symbols and your global symbols. While this is a good argument for avoiding global symbols as much as possible in your program, the fact remains that most symbols in an assembl language program will have global scope. So another solution is necessary.

HLA's solution is to put most of the library names in a namespace decla ration section. A namespace declaration encapsulates all declarations and exposes only a single name (the namespace identifier) at the global level. You access the names within the namespace by using the familiar dot notation (see the discussion of namespaces in Section 4.34). This reduces the effect of namespace pollution from many dozens or hundreds of names down to a single name.

Of course, one disadvantage of using a namespace declaration is that you have to type a longer name in order to reference a particular identifier in that namespace (that is, you have to type the namespace identifier, a period, and then the specific identifier you wish to use). For a few identifiers you use frequently, you might elect to leave those identifiers outside of any namespace declaration. For example, the HLA Standard Library does not define the symbol nl within a namespace. However, you want to minimize such declara-tions in your libraries to avoid conflicts with names in your own programs. Often, you can choose a namespace identifier to complement your routine names. For example, the HLA Standard Library's string copy routine was named after the equivalent C Standard Library function, strcpy. HLA's version is str.cpy. The actual function name is cpy; it happens to be a member of the str namespace, hence the full name str.cpy, which is very similar to the compa rable C function. The HLA Standard Library contains several examples of this convention. The arg.c and arg.v functions are another pair of such iden tifiers (corresponding to the C identifiers argc and argv).

Using a namespace in a header file is no different than using a namespace in a program or unit, though you do not normally put actual procedure bodies in a namespace. Here's an example of a typical header file containing a namespace declaration:

```
// myHeader.hhf -
//
// Routines supported in the myLibrary.lib file

namespace myLib;

    procedure func1; external;
    procedure func2; external;
    procedure func3; external;

end myLib;
```

Typically, you would compile each of the functions (func1..func3) as separate units (so each has its own object file and linking in one function doesn't link them all). Here's a sample unit declaration for one of these functions:

```
unit func1Unit;
#includeonce( "myHeader.hhf" )

procedure myLib.func1;
begin func1;

    << Code for func1 >>

end func1;

end func1Unit;
```

You should notice two important things about this unit. First, you do not put the actual func1 procedure code within a namespace declaration block. By using the identifier myLib.func1 as the procedure's name, HLA automatically realizes that this procedure declaration belongs in a namespace. The second thing to note is that you do not preface func1 with myLib. after the begin and end clauses in the procedure. HLA automatically associates the begin and end identifiers with the procedure declaration, so it knows that these identifiers are part of the myLib namespace and it doesn't make you type the whole name again.

Important note: When you declare external names within a namespace, as was done in func1Unit previously, HLA uses only the function name (func1 in this example) as the external name. This creates a namespace pollution problem in the external namespace. For example, if you have two different namespaces, myLib and yourLib, and they both define a func1 procedure, the linker will complain about a duplicate definition for func1 if you attempt to use functions from both these library modules. There is an easy workaround to this problem: Use the extended form of the external directive to explicitly supply an external name for all external identifiers appearing in a namespace declaration. For example, you could solve this problem with the following simple modification to the *myHeader.hhf* file above:

```
// myHeader.hhf -
//
// Routines supported in the myLibrary.lib file

namespace myLib;

    procedure func1; external( "myLib_func1" );
    procedure func2; external( "myLib_func2" );
    procedure func3; external( "myLib_func3" );

end myLib;
```

This example demonstrates an excellent convention you should adopt. When exporting names from a namespace, always supply an explicit extern name and construct that name by concatenating the namespace identifier with an underscore and the object's internal name.

The use of namespace declarations does not completely eliminate the problems of namespace pollution (after all, the namespace identifier is still global object, as anyone who has included *stdlib.hhf* and attempted to define a cs variable can attest), but namespace declarations come pretty close to eliminating this problem. Therefore, you should use namespace everywhere practical when creating your own libraries.

## 5.26  For More Information

The electronic edition of this book found at *http://www.artofasm.com/* or *http://webster.cs.ucr.edu/* contains a whole "volume" on advanced and intermediate procedures. The information in this chapter was taken from the introductory and intermediate chapters in the electronic edition. While the information appearing in this chapter covers 99 percent of the material assembly programmers typically use, there is additional information on procedures and parameters that you may find interesting. In particular, the electronic edition covers additional parameter-passing mechanisms (pass by value/result, pass by result, pass by name, and pass by lazy evaluation) and goes into greater detail about the places you can pass parameters. The electronic version of this text also covers iterators, thunks, and other advanced procedure types. You should also check out the HLA documentation for more details on HLA's procedure facilities. Finally, a good compiler construction textbook will cover additional details about runtime support for procedures.

This chapter discussed only 32-bit near procedures (appropriate for operating systems like Windows, Mac OS X, FreeBSD, and Linux). For information about procedures in 16-bit code (including near and far procedures) check out the 16-bit edition of this book, also found at *http://webster.cs.ucr.edu/* or *http://www.artofasm.com/*.

HLA supports the ability to nest procedures; that is, you can declare a procedure in the declaration section of some other procedure and use *display* and *static links* to access automatic variables in the enclosing procedures. HLA also supports advanced parameter-pointer facilities. This text does not discuss these features because they're somewhat advanced and very few assembly language programmers take advantage of these facilities in their programs. However, these features are very handy in certain situations. Once you're comfortable with procedures and assembly language programming in general, you should read about HLA's facilities for nested procedures in the HLA documentation and in the chapters on intermediate and advanced procedure in the electronic version of this book found at *http://webster.cs.ucr.edu/* or *http://www.artofasm.com/*.

Finally, the examples given for the code that HLA generates when passing parameters using the high-level syntax are incomplete. Over time, HLA has improved the quality of the code it generates when passing parameters on the stack. If you would like to see the type of code HLA generates for a particular parameter call sequence, you should supply the -sourcemode, -h, and -s command-line parameters to HLA and view the corresponding assembly language file that HLA emits (which will be a pseudo-HLA source file showing you the low-level code that HLA produces).

# 6

# ARITHMETIC

This chapter discusses arithmetic computation in assembly language. By the end of this chapter you should be able to translate arithmetic expressions and assignment statements from high-level languages like Pascal and C/C++ into 80x86 assembly language.

## 6.1  80x86 Integer Arithmetic Instructions

Before describing how to encode arithmetic expressions in assembly language, it would be a good idea to first discuss the remaining arithmetic instructions in the 80x86 instruction set. Previous chapters have covered most of the arithmetic and logical instructions, so this section covers the few remaining instructions you'll need.

## 6.1.1    The mul and imul Instructions

The multiplication instructions provide you with another taste of irregularity in the 80x86's instruction set. Instructions like add, sub, and many others in the 80x86 instruction set support two operands, just like the mov instruction. Unfortunately, there weren't enough bits in the 80x86's opcode byte to support all instructions, so the 80x86 treats the mul (unsigned multiply) and imul (signed integer multiply) instructions as single-operand instructions, just like the inc, dec, and neg instructions.

Of course, multiplication *is* a two-operand function. To work around this fact, the 80x86 always assumes the accumulator (AL, AX, or EAX) is the destination operand. This irregularity makes using multiplication on the 80x86 a little more difficult than other instructions because one operand has to be in the accumulator. Intel adopted this unorthogonal approach because it felt that programmers would use multiplication far less often than instructions like add and sub.

Another problem with the mul and imul instructions is that you cannot multiply the accumulator by a constant using these instructions. Intel quickly discovered the need to support multiplication by a constant and added the intmul instruction to overcome this problem. Nevertheless, you must be aware that the basic mul and imul instructions do not support the full range of operands as intmul.

There are two forms of the multiply instruction: unsigned multiplication (mul) and signed multiplication (imul). Unlike addition and subtraction, you need separate instructions for signed and unsigned operations.

The multiply instructions take the following forms:

Unsigned multiplication:

```
mul( reg8 );      // returns "ax"
mul( reg16 );     // returns "dx:ax"
mul( reg32 );     // returns "edx:eax"

mul( mem8 );      // returns "ax"
mul( mem16 );     // returns "dx:ax"
mul( mem32 );     // returns "edx:eax"
```

Signed (integer) multiplication:

```
imul( reg8 );     // returns "ax"
imul( reg16 );    // returns "dx:ax"
imul( reg32 );    // returns "edx:eax"

imul( mem8 );     // returns "ax"
imul( mem16 );    // returns "dx:ax"
imul( mem32 );    // returns "edx:eax"
```

The returns values above are the strings these instructions return for use with instruction composition in HLA. (i)mul, available on all 80x86 processors, multiplies 8-, 16-, or 32-bit operands.

When multiplying two *n*-bit values, the result may require as many as $2 * n$ bits. Therefore, if the operand is an 8-bit quantity, the result could require 16 bits. Likewise, a 16-bit operand produces a 32-bit result and a 32-bit operand requires 64 bits to hold the result.

The (i)mul instruction, with an 8-bit operand, multiplies AL by the operand and leaves the 16-bit product in AX. So

---
```
mul( operand8 );
```
---

or

---
```
imul( operand8 );
```
---

computes

---
```
ax := al * operand8
```
---

* represents an unsigned multiplication for mul and a signed multiplication for imul.

If you specify a 16-bit operand, then mul and imul compute

---
```
dx:ax := ax * operand16
```
---

* has the same meanings as above, and dx:ax means that DX contains the H.O. word of the 32-bit result and AX contains the L.O. word of the 32-bit result. If you're wondering why Intel didn't put the 32-bit result in EAX, just note that Intel introduced the mul and imul instructions in the earliest 80x86 processors, before the advent of 32-bit registers in the 80386 CPU.

If you specify a 32-bit operand, then mul and imul compute the following:

---
```
edx:eax := eax * operand32
```
---

* has the same meanings as above, and edx:eax means that EDX contains the H.O. double word of the 64-bit result and EAX contains the L.O. double word of the 64-bit result.

If an 8×8-, 16×16-, or 32×32-bit product requires more than 8, 16, or 32 bits (respectively), the mul and imul instructions set the carry and overflow flags. mul and imul scramble the sign and zero flags.

**NOTE** *Especially note that the sign and zero flags do not contain meaningful values after the execution of these two instructions.*

To help reduce some of the syntax irregularities with the use of the mul and imul instructions, HLA provides an extended syntax that allows the following two-operand forms:

Unsigned multiplication:

```
mul( reg8, al );
mul( reg16, ax );
mul( reg32, eax );
```

```
mul( mem8, al );
mul( mem16, ax );
mul( mem32, eax );

mul( constant8, al );
mul( constant16, ax );
mul( constant32, eax );
```

Signed (integer) multiplication:

```
imul( reg8, al );
imul( reg16, ax );
imul( reg32, eax );

imul( mem8, al );
imul( mem16, ax );
imul( mem32, eax );

imul( constant8, al );
imul( constant16, ax );
imul( constant32, eax );
```

The two-operand forms let you specify the (L.O.) destination register a the second operand. By specifying the destination register you can make you programs easier to read. Note that just because HLA allows two operands here, you can't specify an arbitrary register. The destination operand must always be AL, AX, or EAX, depending on the source operand.

HLA provides a form that lets you specify a constant. The 80x86 doesn actually support a mul or imul instruction that has a constant operand. HLA will take the constant you specify and create a variable in a read-only segmer in memory and initialize that variable with this value. Then HLA converts th instruction to the (i)mul( memory ); instruction. Note that when you speci a constant as the source operand, the instruction requires two operands (because HLA uses the second operand to determine whether the multiplic tion is 8, 16, or 32 bits).

You'll use the mul and imul instructions quite a lot when you learn abou extended-precision arithmetic in Chapter 8. Unless you're doing multiprec sion work, however, you'll probably just want to use the intmul instruction i place of the mul or imul because it is more general. However, intmul is not a complete replacement for these two instructions. Besides the number of operands, there are several differences between the intmul and the mul/imul instructions. The following rules apply specifically to the intmul instruction:

- There isn't an 8×8-bit intmul instruction available.
- The intmul instruction does not produce a $2 \times n$-bit result. That is, a 16×16-bit multiply produces a 16-bit result. Likewise, a 32×32-bit multipl produces a 32-bit result. These instructions set the carry and overflow flags if the result does not fit into the destination register.

## 6.1.2 The div and idiv Instructions

The 80x86 divide instructions perform a 64/32-bit division, a 32/16-bit division, or a 16/8-bit division. These instructions take the following forms:

```
div( reg8 );                    // returns "al"
div( reg16 );                   // returns "ax"
div( reg32 );                   // returns "eax"

div( reg8, ax );                // returns "al"
div( reg16, dx:ax );            // returns "ax"
div( reg32, edx:eax );          // returns "eax"

div( mem8 );                    // returns "al"
div( mem16 );                   // returns "ax"
div( mem32 );                   // returns "eax"

div( mem8, ax );                // returns "al"
div( mem16, dx:ax );            // returns "ax"
div( mem32, edx:eax );          // returns "eax"

div( constant8, ax );           // returns "al"
div( constant16, dx:ax );       // returns "ax"
div( constant32, edx:eax );     // returns "eax"

idiv( reg8 );                   // returns "al"
idiv( reg16 );                  // returns "ax"
idiv( reg32 );                  // returns "eax"

idiv( reg8, ax );               // returns "al"
idiv( reg16, dx:ax );           // returns "ax"
idiv( reg32, edx:eax );         // returns "eax"

idiv( mem8 );                   // returns "al"
idiv( mem16 );                  // returns "ax"
idiv( mem32 );                  // returns "eax"

idiv( mem8, ax );               // returns "al"
idiv( mem16, dx:ax );           // returns "ax"
idiv( mem32, edx:eax );         // returns "eax"

idiv( constant8, ax );          // returns "al"
idiv( constant16, dx:ax );      // returns "ax"
idiv( constant32, edx:eax );    // returns "eax"
```

The div instruction is an unsigned division operation. If the operand is an 8-bit operand, div divides the AX register by the operand leaving the quotient in AL and the remainder (modulo) in AH. If the operand is a 16-bit quantity, then the div instruction divides the 32-bit quantity in dx:ax by the operand, leaving the quotient in AX and the remainder in DX. With 32-bit operands div divides the 64-bit value in edx:eax by the operand, leaving the quotient in EAX and the remainder in EDX.

Like mul and imul, HLA provides special syntax to allow the use of consta operands even though the low-level machine instructions don't actually supp them. See the previous list of div instructions for these extensions.

The idiv instruction computes a signed quotient and remainder. Th syntax for the idiv instruction is identical to div (except for the use of the i mnemonic), though creating signed operands for idiv may require a differe sequence of instructions prior to executing idiv than for div.

You cannot, on the 80x86, simply divide one unsigned 8-bit value by another. If the denominator is an 8-bit value, the numerator must be a 16- value. If you need to divide one unsigned 8-bit value by another, you must zero extend the numerator to 16 bits. You can accomplish this by loading t numerator into the AL register and then moving 0 into the AH register. Th you can divide AX by the denominator operand to produce the correct resu *Failing to zero extend AL before executing div may cause the 80x86 to produce incorr results!* When you need to divide two 16-bit unsigned values, you must zero extend the AX register (which contains the numerator) into the DX registe To do this, just load 0 into the DX register. If you need to divide one 32-bi value by another, you must zero extend the EAX register into EDX (by loa ing a 0 into EDX) before the division.

When dealing with signed integer values, you will need to sign extend A into AX, AX into DX, or EAX into EDX before executing idiv. To do so, u the cbw, cwd, cdq, or movsx instruction. If the H.O. byte, word, or double wor does not already contain significant bits, then you must sign extend the val in the accumulator (AL/AX/EAX) before doing the idiv operation. Failu to do so may produce incorrect results.

There is one other issue with the 80x86's divide instructions: You can g a fatal error when using this instruction. First, of course, you can attempt t divide a value by 0. Another problem is that the quotient may be too large to fit into the EAX, AX, or AL register. For example, the 16/8-bit division $8000/2 produces the quotient $4000 with a remainder of 0. $4000 will not 1 into 8 bits. If this happens, or you attempt to divide by 0, the 80x86 will ge erate an ex.DivisionError exception or integer overflow error (ex.IntoInstr). This usually means your program will display the appropriate dialog and abort. If this happens to you, chances are you didn't sign or zero extend you numerator before executing the division operation. Because this error ma cause your program to crash, you should be very careful about the values yc select when using division. Of course, you can use the try..endtry block wit ex.DivisionError and ex.IntoInstr to trap this problem in your program.

The 80x86 leaves the carry, overflow, sign, and zero flags undefined aft a division operation. Therefore, you cannot test for problems after a divisio operation by checking the flag bits.

The 80x86 does not provide a separate instruction to compute the remainder of one number divided by another. The div and idiv instructior automatically compute the remainder at the same time they compute the quotient. HLA, however, provides mnemonics (instructions) for the mod an imod instructions. These special HLA instructions compile into the exact san code as their div and idiv counterparts. The only difference is the returns value for the instruction (because these instructions return the remainder i a different location than the quotient). The mod and imod instructions that HLA supports are as follows:

```
mod( reg8 );                        // returns "ah"
mod( reg16 );                       // returns "dx"
mod( reg32 );                       // returns "edx"

mod( reg8, ax );                    // returns "ah"
mod( reg16, dx:ax );                // returns "dx"
mod( reg32, edx:eax );              // returns "edx"

mod( mem8 );                        // returns "ah"
mod( mem16 );                       // returns "dx"
mod( mem32 );                       // returns "edx"

mod( mem8, ax );                    // returns "ah"
mod( mem16, dx:ax );                // returns "dx"
mod( mem32, edx:eax );              // returns "edx"

mod( constant8, ax );               // returns "ah"
mod( constant16, dx:ax );           // returns "dx"
mod( constant32, edx:eax );         // returns "edx"

imod( reg8 );                       // returns "ah"
imod( reg16 );                      // returns "dx"
imod( reg32 );                      // returns "edx"

imod( reg8, ax );                   // returns "ah"
imod( reg16, dx:ax );               // returns "dx"
imod( reg32, edx:eax );             // returns "edx"

imod( mem8 );                       // returns "ah"
imod( mem16 );                      // returns "dx"
imod( mem32 );                      // returns "edx"

imod( mem8, ax );                   // returns "ah"
imod( mem16, dx:ax );               // returns "dx"
imod( mem32, edx:eax );             // returns "edx"

imod( constant8, ax );              // returns "ah"
imod( constant16, dx:ax );          // returns "dx"
imod( constant32, edx:eax );        // returns "edx"
```

### 6.1.3 The cmp Instruction

The cmp (compare) instruction is identical to the sub instruction with one crucial semantic difference—it does not retain the difference it computes; it just sets the condition code bits in the flags register. The syntax for the cmp instruction is similar to that of sub (though the operands are reversed so it reads better); the generic form is:

```
cmp( LeftOperand, RightOperand );
```

This instruction computes *LeftOperand* - *RightOperand* (note the reversal from sub). The specific forms are:

```
cmp( reg, reg );      // Registers must be the same size.
cmp( reg, mem );      // Sizes must match.
cmp( reg, constant );
cmp( mem, constant );
```

The cmp instruction updates the 80x86's flags according to the result of the subtraction operation (*LeftOperand* - *RightOperand*). The 80x86 sets the flags in an appropriate fashion so that we can read this instruction as "compare *LeftOperand* to *RightOperand*." You can test the result of the comparison by checking the appropriate flags in the flags register using the conditional set instructions (see Section 6.1.4) or the conditional jump instructions (see Chapter 7).

Probably the first place to start when exploring the cmp instruction is to look at exactly how the cmp instruction affects the flags. Consider the following cmp instruction:

```
cmp( ax, bx );
```

This instruction performs the computation AX − BX and sets the flags depending upon the result of the computation. The flags are set as follows (also see Table 6-1):

**Z**  The zero flag is set if and only if AX = BX. This is the only time AX − BX produces a zero result. Hence, you can use the zero flag to test for equality or inequality.

**S**  The sign flag is set to 1 if the result is negative. At first glance, you might think that this flag would be set if AX is less than BX, but this isn't always the case. If AX = $7FFF and BX = −1 ($FFFF), then subtracting AX from BX produces $8000, which is negative (and so the sign flag will be set). So, for signed comparisons anyway, the sign flag doesn't contain the proper status. For unsigned operands, consider AX = $FFFF and BX = 1. AX is greater than BX but their difference is $FFFE, which is still negative. As it turns out, the sign flag and the overflow flag, taken together, can be used for comparing two signed values.

**O**  The overflow flag is set after a cmp operation if the difference of AX and BX produced an overflow or underflow. As mentioned above, the sign flag and the overflow flag are both used when performing signed comparisons.

**C**  The carry flag is set after a cmp operation if subtracting BX from AX requires a borrow. This occurs only when AX is less than BX where AX and BX are both unsigned values.

Given that the cmp instruction sets the flags in this fashion, you can test the comparison of the two operands with the following flags:

---

cmp( Left, Right );

---

**Table 6-1:** Condition Code Settings After cmp

| Unsigned Operands | Signed Operands |
|---|---|
| Z: Equality/inequality | Z: Equality/inequality |
| C: Left < Right (C = 1)<br>Left >= Right (C = 0) | C: No meaning |
| S: No meaning | S: See discussion in this section |
| O: No meaning | O: See discussion in this section |

For signed comparisons, the S (sign) and O (overflow) flags, taken together, have the following meaning:

- If [(S = 0) and (O = 1)] or [(S = 1) and (O = 0)] then Left < Right for a signed comparison.
- If [(S = 0) and (O = 0)] or [(S = 1) and (O = 1)] then Left >= Right for a signed comparison.

Note that (S xor O) is 1 if the left operand is less than the right operand. Conversely, (S xor O) is 0 if the left operand is greater or equal to the right operand.

To understand why these flags are set in this manner, consider the following examples:

```
Left            minus   Right           S   O
------                  ------          -   -

$FFFF (-1)       -      $FFFE (-2)       0   0
$8000            -      $0001            0   1
$FFFE (-2)       -      $FFFF (-1)       1   0
$7FFF (32767)    -      $FFFF (-1)       1   1
```

Remember, the cmp operation is really a subtraction; therefore, the first example above computes (−1) − (−2), which is (+1). The result is positive and an overflow did not occur, so both the S and O flags are 0. Because (S xor O) is 0, Left is greater than or equal to Right.

In the second example, the cmp instruction would compute (−32,768) − (+1), which is (−32,769). Because a 16-bit signed integer cannot represent this value, the value wraps around to $7FFF (+32,767) and sets the overflow flag. The result is positive (at least as a 16-bit value), so the CPU clears the sign flag. (S xor O) is 1 here, so Left is less than Right.

In the third example above, cmp computes (−2) − (−1), which produces (−1). No overflow occurred, so the O flag is 0, the result is negative, so the sign flag is 1. Because (S xor O) is 1, Left is less than Right.

In the fourth (and final) example, cmp computes $(+32,767) - (-1)$. Th
produces $(+32,768)$, setting the overflow flag. Furthermore, the value wra
around to $8000 $(-32,768)$, so the sign flag is set as well. Because (S xor O) is
Left is greater than or equal to Right.

You may test the flags after a cmp instruction using HLA high-level contr
statements and the boolean flag expressions (e.g., @c, @nc, @z, @nz, @o, @no, @s
@ns, and so on). Table 6-2 lists the boolean expressions HLA supports that
you check various conditions after a compare instruction.

**Table 6-2:** HLA Condition Code Boolean Expressions

| HLA Syntax | Condition | Comment |
|---|---|---|
| @c | Carry set | Carry flag is set if the first operand is less than the second operand (unsigned). Same condition as @b and @nae. |
| @nc | Carry clear (no carry) | Carry flag is clear if the first operand is greater than or equal to the second (using an unsigned comparison). Same condition as @nb and @ae. |
| @z | Zero flag set | Zero flag is set if the first operand equals the second operand. Same condition as @e. |
| @nz | Zero flag clear (no zero) | Zero flag is clear if the first operand is not equal to the second. Same condition as @ne. |
| @o | Overflow flag set | This flag is set if there was a signed arithmetic overflow as a result of the comparison operation. |
| @no | Overflow flag clear (no overflow) | The overflow flag is clear if there was no signed arithmetic overflow during the compare operation. |
| @s | Sign flag set | The sign flag is set if the result of the compare (subtraction) produces a negative result. |
| @ns | Sign flag clear (no sign) | The sign flag is clear if the compare operation produces a nonnegative (zero or positive) result. |
| @a | Above (unsigned greater than) | The @a condition checks the carry and zero flags to see if @c = 0 and @z = 0. This condition exists if the first (unsigned) operand is greater than the second (unsigned) operand. This is the same condition as @nbe. |
| @na | Not above | The @na condition checks to see if the carry flag is set (@c) or the zero flag is set (@z). This is equivalent to an unsigned "not greater than" condition. Note that this condition is the same as @be. |
| @ae | Above or equal (unsigned greater than or equal) | The @ae condition is true if the first operand is greater than or equal to the second using an unsigned comparison. This is equivalent to the @nb and @nc conditions. |
| @nae | Not above or equal | The @nae condition is true if the first operand is not greater than or equal to the second using an unsigned comparison. This is equivalent to the @b and @c conditions. |
| @b | Below (unsigned less than) | The @b condition is true if the first operand is less than the second using an unsigned comparison. This is equivalent to the @nae and @c conditions. |
| @nb | Not below | This condition is true if the first operand is not less than the second using an unsigned comparison. This condition is equivalent to the @nc and @ae conditions. |

| A Syntax | Condition | Comment |
|---|---|---|
| e | Below or equal (unsigned less than or equal) | The @be condition is true when the first operand is less than or equal to the second using an unsigned comparison. This condition is equivalent to @na. |
| e | Not below or equal | The @be condition is true when the first operand is not less than or equal to the second using an unsigned comparison. This condition is equivalent to @a. |
| | Greater (signed greater than) | The @g condition is true if the first operand is greater than the second using a signed comparison. This is equivalent to the @nle condition. |
| 3 | Not greater | The @ng condition is true if the first operand is not greater than the second using a signed comparison. This is equivalent to the @le condition. |
| e | Greater or equal (signed greater than or equal) | The @ge condition is true if the first operand is greater than or equal to the second using a signed comparison. This is equivalent to the @nl condition. |
| ge | Not greater or equal | The @nge condition is true if the first operand is not greater than or equal to the second using a signed comparison. This is equivalent to the @l condition. |
| | Less than (signed less than) | The @l condition is true if the first operand is less than the second using a signed comparison. This is equivalent to the @nge condition. |
| l | Not less than | The @ng condition is true if the first operand is not less than the second using a signed comparison. This is equivalent to the @ge condition. |
| e | Less than or equal (signed) | The @le condition is true if the first operand is less than or equal to the second using a signed comparison. This is equivalent to the @ng condition. |
| le | Not less than or equal | The @nle condition is true if the first operand is not less than or equal to the second using a signed comparison. This is equivalent to the @g condition. |
| | Equal (signed or unsigned) | This condition is true if the first operand equals the second. The @e condition is equivalent to the @z condition. |
| e | Not equal (signed or unsigned) | @ne is true if the first operand does not equal the second. This condition is equivalent to @nz. |

You may use the boolean conditions appearing in Table 6-2 within an if statement, while statement, or any other HLA high-level control statement that allows boolean expressions. Immediately after the execution of a cmp instruction, you would typically use one of these conditions in an if statement. For example:

```
cmp( eax, ebx );
if( @e ) then

    << Do something if eax = ebx. >>

endif;
```

Note that the example above is equivalent to the following:

```
if( eax = ebx ) then

    << Do something if eax = ebx. >>

endif;
```

## 6.1.4   The setcc Instructions

The *set on condition* (or setcc) instructions set a single-byte operand (register memory) to 0 or 1 depending on the values in the flags register. The general formats for the setcc instructions are:

```
setcc( reg8 );
setcc( mem8 );
```

setcc represents a mnemonic appearing in Tables 6-3, 6-4, and 6-5. These instructions store a 0 into the corresponding operand if the condition is false and they store a 1 into the 8-bit operand if the condition is true.

**Table 6-3:** setcc Instructions That Test Flags

| Instruction | Description | Condition | Comments |
|---|---|---|---|
| setc | Set if carry | Carry = 1 | Same as setb, setnae |
| setnc | Set if no carry | Carry = 0 | Same as setnb, setae |
| setz | Set if zero | Zero = 1 | Same as sete |
| setnz | Set if not zero | Zero = 0 | Same as setne |
| sets | Set if sign | Sign = 1 | |
| setns | Set if no sign | Sign = 0 | |
| seto | Set if overflow | Overflow = 1 | |
| setno | Set if no overflow | Overflow = 0 | |
| setp | Set if parity | Parity = 1 | Same as setpe |
| setpe | Set if parity even | Parity = 1 | Same as setp |
| setnp | Set if no parity | Parity = 0 | Same as setpo |
| setpo | Set if parity odd | Parity = 0 | Same as setnp |

The setcc instructions above simply test the flags without any other meaning attached to the operation. You could, for example, use setc to check the carry flag after a shift, rotate, bit test, or arithmetic operation. You might notice the setp, setpe, and setnp instructions above. They check the parity flag. These instructions appear here for completeness, but this text will not spend too much time discussing the parity flag (its use is somewhat obsolete).

The cmp instruction works synergistically with the setcc instructions. Immediately after a cmp operation the processor flags provide information concerning the relative values of those operands. They allow you to see if one operand is less than, equal to, or greater than the other.

Two additional groups of setcc instructions are very useful after a cmp operation. The first group deals with the result of an unsigned comparison; the second group deals with the result of a signed comparison.

**Table 6-4:** setcc Instructions for Unsigned Comparisons

| Instruction | Description | Condition | Comments |
| --- | --- | --- | --- |
| seta | Set if above (>) | Carry = 0, Zero = 0 | Same as setnbe |
| setnbe | Set if not below or equal (not <=) | Carry = 0, Zero = 0 | Same as seta |
| setae | Set if above or equal (>=) | Carry = 0 | Same as setnc, setnb |
| setnb | Set if not below (not <) | Carry = 0 | Same as setnc, setae |
| setb | Set if below (<) | Carry = 1 | Same as setc, setna |
| setnae | Set if not above or equal (not >=) | Carry = 1 | Same as setc, setb |
| setbe | Set if below or equal (<=) | Carry = 1 or Zero = 1 | Same as setna |
| setna | Set if not above (not >) | Carry = 1 or Zero = 1 | Same as setbe |
| sete | Set if equal (=) | Zero = 1 | Same as setz |
| setne | Set if not equal (!) | Zero = 0 | Same as setnz |

Table 6-5 lists the corresponding signed comparisons.

**Table 6-5:** setcc Instructions for Signed Comparisons

| Instruction | Description | Condition | Comments |
| --- | --- | --- | --- |
| setg | Set if greater (>) | Sign = Overflow and Zero = 0 | Same as setnle |
| setnle | Set if not less than or equal (not <=) | Sign = Overflow or Zero = 0 | Same as setg |
| setge | Set if greater than or equal (>=) | Sign = Overflow | Same as setnl |
| setnl | Set if not less than (not <) | Sign = Overflow | Same as setge |
| setl | Set if less than (<) | Sign ! Overflow | Same as setnge |
| setnge | Set if not greater or equal (not >=) | Sign ! Overflow | Same as setl |
| setl | Set if less than or equal (<=) | Sign ! Overflow or Zero = 1 | Same as setng |
| setng | Set if not greater than (not >) | Sign ! Overflow or Zero = 1 | Same as setle |
| sete | Set if equal (=) | Zero = 1 | Same as setz |
| setne | Set if not equal (!) | Zero = 0 | Same as setnz |

Note the correspondence between the setcc instructions and the HLA flag conditions that may appear in boolean instructions.

The setcc instructions are particularly valuable because they can conve the result of a comparison to a boolean value (false/true or 0/1). This is esp cially important when translating statements from a high-level language lik Pascal or C/C++ into assembly language. The following example shows ho to use these instructions in this manner:

```
// bool := a <= b

        mov( a, eax );
        cmp( eax, b );
        setle( bool );              // bool is a boolean or byte variable.
```

Because the setcc instructions always produce 0 or 1, you can use the results with the and and or instructions to compute complex boolean values

```
// bool := ((a <= b) and (d = e))

        mov( a, eax );
        cmp( eax, b );
        setle( bl );
        mov( d, eax );
        cmp( eax, e );
        sete( bh );
        and( bl, bh );
        mov( bh, bool );
```

## 6.1.5 The test Instruction

The 80x86 test instruction is to the and instruction what the cmp instruction to sub. That is, the test instruction computes the logical and of its two operand and sets the condition code flags based on the result; it does not, however, store the result of the logical and back into the destination operand. The synta for the test instruction is similar to and:

```
test( operand1, operand2 );
```

The test instruction sets the zero flag if the result of the logical and ope ation is 0. It sets the sign flag if the H.O. bit of the result contains a 1. The tes instruction always clears the carry and overflow flags.

The primary use of the test instruction is to check to see if an individua bit contains a 0 or a 1. Consider the instruction test( 1, al);. This instructio logically ands AL with the value 1; if bit 0 of AL contains 0, the result will be (setting the zero flag) because all the other bits in the constant 1 are 0. Con versely, if bit 1 of AL contains 1, then the result is not 0, so test clears the zer flag. Therefore, you can test the zero flag after this test instruction to see if bi 0 contains a 0 or a 1 (e.g., using a setz or setnz instruction).

The test instruction can also check to see if all the bits in a specified set of bits contain 0. The instruction test( $F, al); sets the zero flag if and only if the L.O. 4 bits of AL all contain 0.

One very important use of the test instruction is to check whether a register contains 0. The instruction test( *reg, reg* ); where both operands are the same register will logically and that register with itself. If the register contains 0, then the result is 0 and the CPU will set the zero flag. However, if the register contains a nonzero value, logically anding that value with itself produces that same nonzero value, so the CPU clears the zero flag. Therefore, you can check the zero flag immediately after the execution of this instruction (e.g., using the setz or setnz instructions or the @z and @nz boolean conditions) to see if the register contains 0. Here are some examples:

```
test( eax, eax );
setz( bl );        // bl is set to 1 if eax contains 0.
    .
    .
    .
test( bx, bx );
if( @nz ) then

    << Do something if bx <> 0. >>

endif;
```

# 6.2  Arithmetic Expressions

Probably the biggest shock to beginners facing assembly language for the very first time is the lack of familiar arithmetic expressions. Arithmetic expressions, in most high-level languages, look similar to their algebraic equivalents. For example:

```
x := y * z;
```

In assembly language, you'll need several statements to accomplish this same task:

```
mov( y, eax );
intmul( z, eax );
mov( eax, x );
```

Obviously the HLL version is much easier to type, read, and understand. This point, more than any other, is responsible for scaring people away from assembly language. Although there is a lot of typing involved, converting an arithmetic expression into assembly language isn't difficult at all. By attacking the problem in steps, the same way you would solve the problem by hand, you can easily break down any arithmetic expression into an equivalent sequence of assembly language statements. By learning how to convert such expression to assembly language in three steps, you'll discover there is little difficulty this task.

## 6.2.1 Simple Assignments

The easiest expressions to convert to assembly language are simple assign ments. Simple assignments copy a single value into a variable and take one two forms:

```
variable := constant
```

or

```
var1 := var2
```

Converting the first form to assembly language is simple—just use the assembly language statement:

```
mov( constant, variable );
```

This mov instruction copies the constant into the variable.

The second assignment above is slightly more complicated because the 80x86 doesn't provide a memory-to-memory mov instruction. Therefore, to copy one memory variable into another, you must move the data through a register. By convention (and for slight efficiency reasons), most programme tend to favor AL/AX/EAX for this purpose. For example:

```
var1 := var2;
```

becomes

```
mov( var2, eax );
mov( eax, var1 );
```

This is assuming, of course, that *var1* and *var2* are 32-bit variables. Use A if they are 8-bit variables; use AX if they are 16-bit variables.

Of course, if you're already using AL, AX, or EAX for something else, on of the other registers will suffice. Regardless, you will generally use a registe to transfer one memory location to another.

## 6.2.2 Simple Expressions

The next level of complexity is a simple expression. A simple expression take the following form:

```
var1 := term1 op term2;
```

*var1* is a variable, *term1* and *term2* are variables or constants, and *op* is some arithmetic operator (addition, subtraction, multiplication, and so on). Most expressions take this form. It should come as no surprise, then, that the 80x86 architecture was optimized for just this type of expression.

A typical conversion for this type of expression takes the following form:

```
mov( term1, eax );
op( term2, eax );
mov( eax, var1 )
```

*op* is the mnemonic that corresponds to the specified operation (e.g., + is add, - is sub, etc.).

Note that the simple expression *var1 := const1 op const2;* is easily handled with a compile-time expression and a single mov instruction. For example, to compute *var1 := 5+3;*, just use the single instruction mov( 5+3, var1 );.

There are a few inconsistencies you need to be aware of. When dealing with the (i)mul, (i)div, and (i)mod instructions on the 80x86, you must use the AL/AX/EAX and DX/EDX registers. You cannot use arbitrary registers as you can with other operations. Also, don't forget the sign extension instructions if you're performing a division operation and you're dividing one 16/32-bit number by another. Finally, don't forget that some instructions may cause overflow. You may want to check for an overflow (or underflow) condition after an arithmetic operation.

Here are some examples of common simple expressions:

```
x := y + z;

        mov( y, eax );
        add( z, eax );
        mov( eax, x );

x := y - z;

        mov( y, eax );
        sub( z, eax );
        mov( eax, x );

x := y * z; {unsigned}

        mov( y, eax );
        mul( z, eax );      // Don't forget this wipes out edx.
        mov( eax, x );

x := y * z; {signed}

        mov( y, eax );
        intmul( z, eax );   // Does not affect edx!
        mov( eax, x );
```

```
x := y div z; {unsigned div}

            mov( y, eax );
            mov( 0, edx );          // Zero extend eax into edx.
            div( z, edx:eax );
            mov( eax, x );

x := y idiv z; {signed div}

            mov( y, eax );
            cdq();                  // Sign extend eax into edx.
            idiv( z, edx:eax );
            mov( eax, z );

x := y mod z; {unsigned remainder}

            mov( y, eax );
            mov( 0, edx );          // Zero extend eax into edx.
            mod( z, edx:eax );
            mov( edx, x );          // Note that remainder is in edx.

x := y imod z; {signed remainder}

            mov( y, eax );
            cdq();                  // Sign extend eax into edx.
            imod( z, edx:eax );
            mov( edx, x );          // Remainder is in edx.
```

Certain unary operations also qualify as simple expressions, producing additional inconsistencies in the general rule. A good example of a unary operation is negation. In a high-level language, negation takes one of two possible forms:

```
    var := -var
```

or

```
    var1 := -var2
```

Note that *var := -constant* is really a simple assignment, not a simple expression. You can specify a negative constant as an operand to the mov instruction:

```
    mov( -14, var );
```

To handle *var1 = -var1;*, use this single assembly language statement:

```
    // var1 = -var1;

    neg( var1 );
```

If two different variables are involved, then use the following.

```
// var1 = -var2;

mov( var2, eax );
neg( eax );
mov( eax, var1 );
```

## 6.2.3  Complex Expressions

A complex expression is any arithmetic expression involving more than two terms and one operator. Such expressions are commonly found in programs written in a high-level language. Complex expressions may include parentheses to override operator precedence, function calls, array accesses, and so on. While the conversion of many complex expressions to assembly language is fairly straightforward, other conversions require some effort. This section outlines the rules you use to convert such expressions.

A complex expression that is easy to convert to assembly language is one that involves three terms and two operators. For example:

```
w := w - y - z;
```

Clearly the straightforward assembly language conversion of this statement will require two sub instructions. However, even with an expression as simple as this one, the conversion is not trivial. There are actually *two ways* to convert this from the statement above into assembly language:

```
mov( w, eax );
sub( y, eax );
sub( z, eax );
mov( eax, w );
```

and

```
mov( y, eax );
sub( z, eax );
sub( eax, w );
```

The second conversion, because it is shorter, looks better. However, it produces an incorrect result (assuming Pascal-like semantics for the original statement). *Associativity* is the problem. The second sequence above computes w := w - (y - z), which is not the same as w := (w - y) - z. How we place the parentheses around the subexpressions can affect the result. Note that if you are interested in a shorter form, you can use the following sequence:

```
mov( y, eax );
add( z, eax );
sub( eax, w );
```

This computes w := w - (y + z). This is equivalent to w := (w - y) - z.

*Precedence* is another issue. Consider this Pascal expression:

```
x := w * y + z;
```

Once again there are two ways we can evaluate this expression:

```
x := (w * y) + z;
```

or

```
x := w * (y + z);
```

By now, you're probably thinking that this text is crazy. Everyone knows the correct way to evaluate these expressions is by the second form. However you're wrong to think that way. The APL programming language, for example evaluates expressions solely from right to left and does not give one operator precedence over another. Which way is "correct" depends entirely on how you define precedence in your arithmetic system.

Most high-level languages use a fixed set of precedence rules to describe the order of evaluation in an expression involving two or more different operators. Such programming languages usually compute multiplication and division before addition and subtraction. Those that support exponentiation (for example, FORTRAN and BASIC) usually compute that before multiplication and division. These rules are intuitive because almost everyone learns them before high school. Consider the expression

```
x op1 y op2 z
```

If *op1* takes precedence over *op2*, then this evaluates to (x *op1* y) *op2* z; otherwise, if *op2* takes precedence over *op1*, then this evaluates to x *op1* (y *op2* z). Depending upon the operators and operands involved, these two computations could produce different results. When converting an expression of this form into assembly language, you must be sure to compute the subexpression with the highest precedence first. The following example demonstrates this technique:

```
// w := x + y * z;

        mov( x, ebx );
        mov( y, eax );      // Must compute y * z first because "*"
        intmul( z, eax );   // has higher precedence than "+".
        add( ebx, eax );
        mov( eax, w );
```

If two operators appearing within an expression have the same precedence, then you determine the order of evaluation using *associativity* rules. Most operators are *left associative*, meaning that they evaluate from left to right. Addition, subtraction, multiplication, and division are all left associative.

A *right-associative* operator evaluates from right to left. The exponentiation operator in FORTRAN and BASIC is a good example of a right-associative operator:

---

2^2^3 is equal to 2^(2^3) *not* (2^2)^3

---

The precedence and associativity rules determine the order of evaluation. Indirectly, these rules tell you where to place parentheses in an expression to determine the order of evaluation. Of course, you can always use parentheses to override the default precedence and associativity. However, the ultimate point is that your assembly code must complete certain operations before others to correctly compute the value of a given expression. The following examples demonstrate this principle:

---

```
// w := x - y - z

        mov( x, eax );      // All the same operator, so we need
        sub( y, eax );      // to evaluate from left to right
        sub( z, eax );      // because they all have the same
        mov( eax, w );      // precedence and are left associative.

// w := x + y * z

        mov( y, eax );      // Must compute y * z first because
        intmul( z, eax );   // multiplication has a higher
        add( x, eax );      // precedence than addition.
        mov( eax, w );


// w := x / y - z

        mov( x, eax );      // Here we need to compute division
        cdq();              // first because it has the highest
        idiv( y, edx:eax ); // precedence.
        sub( z, eax );
        mov( eax, w );

// w := x * y * z

        mov( y, eax );      // Addition and multiplication are
        intmul( z, eax );   // commutative; therefore the order
        intmul( x, eax );   // of evaluation does not matter.
        mov( eax, w );
```

---

There is one exception to the associativity rule. If an expression involves multiplication and division, it is generally better to perform the multiplication first. For example, given an expression of the form

---

w := x / y * z      // Note: This is (x * z) / y, not x / (y * z).

---

it is usually better to compute x * z and then divide the result by y rather tha[n] divide x by y and multiply the quotient by z. There are two reasons why this approach is better. First, remember that the imul instruction always produce[s] a 64-bit result (assuming 32-bit operands). By doing the multiplication first you automatically *sign extend* the product into the EDX register so you do n[ot] have to sign extend EAX prior to the division. A second reason for doing th[e] multiplication first is to increase the accuracy of the computation. Remembe[r] (integer) division often produces an inexact result. For example, if you co[m] pute 5/2 you will get the value 2, not 2.5. Computing (5 / 2) * 3 produces 6. However, if you compute (5 * 3) / 2 you get the value 7, which is a little clos[e] to the real quotient (7.5). Therefore, if you encounter an expression of th[e] form

```
w := x / y * z;
```

you can usually convert it to the following assembly code:

```
mov( x, eax );
imul( z, eax );          // Note the use of imul, not intmul!
idiv( y, edx:eax );
mov( eax, w );
```

Of course, if the algorithm you're encoding depends on the truncation effect of the division operation, you cannot use this trick to improve the algorithm. Moral of the story: Always make sure you fully understand any expression you are converting to assembly language. Obviously, if the semantic[s] dictate that you must perform the division first, then do so.

Consider the following Pascal statement:

```
w := x - y * x;
```

This is similar to a previous example except it uses subtraction rather than addition. Because subtraction is not commutative, you cannot comput[e] y * x and then subtract x from this result. This tends to complicate the conversion a tiny amount. Rather than use a straightforward multiplication-and-addition sequence, you'll have to load x into a register, multiply y and x leaving their product in a different register, and then subtract this produc[t] from x. For example:

```
mov( x, ebx );
mov( y, eax );
intmul( x, eax );
sub( eax, ebx );
mov( ebx, w );
```

This is a trivial example that demonstrates the need for *temporary variables* in an expression. This code uses the EBX register to temporarily hold a copy of x until it computes the product of y and x. As your expressions increase in complexity, the need for temporaries grows. Consider the following Pascal statement:

```
w := (a + b) * (y + z);
```

Following the normal rules of algebraic evaluation, you compute the subexpressions inside the parentheses (that is, the two subexpressions with the highest precedence) first and set their values aside. When you've computed the values for both subexpressions, you can compute their sum. One way to deal with a complex expression like this one is to reduce it to a sequence of simple expressions whose results wind up in temporary variables. For example, you can convert the single expression above into the following sequence:

```
temp1 := a + b;
temp2 := y + z;
w := temp1 * temp2;
```

Because converting simple expressions to assembly language is quite easy, it's now a snap to compute the former complex expression in assembly. The code is:

```
mov( a, eax );
add( b, eax );
mov( eax, temp1 );
mov( y, eax );
add( z, eax );
mov( eax, temp2 );
mov( temp1, eax );
intmul( temp2, eax );
mov( eax, w );
```

Of course, this code is grossly inefficient, and it requires that you declare a couple of temporary variables in your data segment. However, it is very easy to optimize this code by keeping temporary variables, as much as possible, in 80x86 registers. By using 80x86 registers to hold the temporary results, this code becomes:

```
mov( a, eax );
add( b, eax );
mov( y, ebx );
add( z, ebx );
intmul( ebx, eax );
mov( eax, w );
```

Here's yet another example:

```
x := (y + z) * (a - b) / 10;
```

This can be converted to a set of four simple expressions:

```
temp1 := (y + z)
temp2 := (a - b)
temp1 := temp1 * temp2
X := temp1 / 10
```

You can convert these four simple expressions into the following assembly language statements:

```
mov( y, eax );         // Compute eax = y + z
add( z, eax );
mov( a, ebx );         // Compute ebx = a - b
sub( b, ebx );
imul( ebx, eax );      // This also sign extends eax into edx.
idiv( 10, edx:eax );
mov( eax, x );
```

The most important thing to keep in mind is that you should attempt to keep temporary values in registers. Remember, accessing an 80x86 register is much more efficient than accessing a memory location. Use memory locations to hold temporaries only if you've run out of registers.

Ultimately, converting a complex expression to assembly language is little different than solving the expression by hand. Instead of actually computing the result at each stage of the computation, you simply write the assembly code that computes the result. Because you were probably taught to compute only one operation at a time, this means that manual computation works on "simple expressions" that exist in a complex expression. Of course, converting those simple expressions to assembly is fairly simple. Therefore, anyone who can solve a complex expression by hand can convert it to assembly language following the rules for simple expressions.

### 6.2.4 Commutative Operators

If *op* represents some operator, that operator is *commutative* if the following relationship is always true:

```
(A op B) = (B op A)
```

As you saw in the previous section, commutative operators are nice because the order of their operands is immaterial, and this lets you rearrange a computation, often making that computation easier or more efficient. Often, rearranging a computation allows you to use fewer temporary variables. Whenever you encounter a commutative operator in an expression, you should always check to see if there is a better sequence you can use to improve the size or speed of your code. Tables 6-6 and 6-7, respectively, list the commutative and noncommutative operators you typically find in high-level languages.

**Table 6-6:** Some Common Commutative Binary Operators

| Pascal | C/C++ | Description |
| --- | --- | --- |
| + | + | Addition |
| * | * | Multiplication |
| and | && or & | Logical or bitwise and |
| or | \|\| or \| | Logical or bitwise or |
| xor | ^ | (Logical or) bitwise exclusive-or |
| = | == | Equality |
| <> | != | Inequality |

**Table 6-7:** Some Common Noncommutative Binary Operators

| Pascal | C/C++ | Description |
| --- | --- | --- |
| - | - | Subtraction |
| / or div | / | Division |
| mod | % | Modulo or remainder |
| < | < | Less than |
| <= | <= | Less than or equal |
| > | > | Greater than |
| >= | >= | Greater than or equal |

# 6.3 Logical (Boolean) Expressions

Consider the following expression from a Pascal program:

```
b := ((x = y) and (a <= c)) or ((z - a) <> 5);
```

b is a boolean variable and the remaining variables are all integers.

How do we represent boolean variables in assembly language? Although it takes only a single bit to represent a boolean value, most assembly language programmers allocate a whole byte or word for this purpose (thus, HLA also allocates a whole byte for a boolean variable). With a byte, there are 256 possible values we can use to represent the two values *true* and *false*. So which two values (or which two sets of values) do we use to represent these boolean values? Because of the machine's architecture, it's much easier to test for conditions like zero or not zero and positive or negative rather than to test for one of two particular boolean values. Most programmers (and, indeed, some programming languages like C) choose 0 to represent false and anything else to represent true. Some people prefer to represent true and false with 1 and 0 (respectively) and not allow any other values. Others select all

1 bits ($FFFF_FFFF, $FFFF, or $FF) for true and 0 for false. You could also use a positive value for true and a negative value for false. All these mechanisms have their advantages and drawbacks.

Using only 0 and 1 to represent false and true offers two very big advantages: (1) The setcc instructions produce these results, so this scheme is compatible with those instructions; (2) the 80x86 logical instructions (and, or, xor, and, to a lesser extent, not) operate on these values exactly as you would expect. That is, if you have two boolean variables A and B, then the following instructions perform the basic logical operations on these two variables:

```
// c = a AND b;

    mov( a, al );
    and( b, al );
    mov( al, c );

// c = a OR b;

    mov( a, al );
    or( b, al );
    mov( al, c );

// c = a XOR b;

    mov( a, al );
    xor( b, al );
    mov( al, c );

// b = NOT a;

    mov( a, al );      // Note that the NOT instruction does not
    not( al );         // properly compute al = NOT al by itself.
    and( 1, al );      // I.e., (NOT 0) does not equal one. The AND
    mov( al, b );      // instruction corrects this problem.

    mov( a, al );      // Another way to do b = NOT a;
    xor( 1, al );      // Inverts bit 0.
    mov( al, b );
```

Note, as pointed out above, that the not instruction will not properly compute logical negation. The bitwise not of 0 is $FF and the bitwise not of 1 is $FE. Neither result is 0 or 1. However, by anding the result with 1 you get the proper result. Note that you can implement the not operation more efficiently using the xor( 1, ax ); instruction because it affects only the L.O. bit.

As it turns out, using 0 for false and anything else for true has a lot of subtle advantages. Specifically, the test for true or false is often implicit in the execution of any logical instruction. However, this mechanism suffers from a very big disadvantage: You cannot use the 80x86 and, or, xor, and not instructions to implement the boolean operations of the same name. Consider the two values $55 and $AA. They're both nonzero so they both represent the value true. However, if you logically and $55 and $AA together using the 80x86 and instruction, the result is 0. True and true should produce true, not false. Although you can account for situations like this, it usually requires a few extra instructions and is somewhat less efficient when computing boolean operations.

A system that uses nonzero values to represent true and 0 to represent false is an *arithmetic logical system*. A system that uses the two distinct values like 0 and 1 to represent false and true is called a *boolean logical system*, or simply a boolean system. You can use either system, as convenient. Consider again the boolean expression

```
b := ((x = y) and (a <= d)) or ((z - a) <> 5);
```

The simple expressions resulting from this expression might be:

```
mov( x, eax );
cmp( y, eax );
sete( al );        // al := x = y;

mov( a, ebx );
cmp( ebx, d );
setle( bl );       // bl := a <= d;
and( al, bl );     // bl := (x = y) and (a <= d);

mov( z, eax );
sub( a, eax );
cmp( eax, 5 );
setne( al );
or( bl, al );      // al := ((x = y) and (a <= d)) or ((z - a) <> 5);
mov( al, b );
```

When working with boolean expressions don't forget that you might be able to optimize your code by simplifying those boolean expressions. You can use algebraic transformations to help reduce the complexity of an expression. In the chapter on control structures, you'll also see how to use control flow to calculate a boolean result. This is generally quite a bit more efficient than using *complete boolean evaluation* as the examples in this section teach.

## 6.4  Machine and Arithmetic Idioms

An idiom is an idiosyncrasy. Several arithmetic operations and 80x86 instructions have idiosyncrasies that you can take advantage of when writing assembly language code. Some people refer to the use of machine and arithmetic idioms as "tricky programming" that you should always avoid in well-written programs. While it is wise to avoid tricks just for the sake of tricks, many machine and arithmetic idioms are well known and commonly found in assembly language programs. Some of them are little more than tricks, but a good number of them are simply "tricks of the trade." This text cannot even begin to present all of the idioms in common use today; they are too numerous and the list is constantly changing. Nevertheless, there are some very important idioms that you will see all the time, so it makes sense to discuss those.

### 6.4.1 Multiplying without mul, imul, or intmul

When multiplying by a constant, you can sometimes write faster code by using shifts, additions, and subtractions in place of multiplication instructions.

Remember, a shl instruction computes the same result as multiplying the specified operand by 2. Shifting to the left two bit positions multiplies the operand by 4. Shifting to the left three bit positions multiplies the operand by 8. In general, shifting an operand to the left $n$ bits multiplies it by $2^n$. You can multiply any value by some constant using a series of shifts and additions or shifts and subtractions. For example, to multiply the AX register by 10, you need only multiply it by 8 and then add in two times the original value. That is, 10 * ax = 8 * ax + 2 * ax. The code to accomplish this is:

```
shl( 1, ax );        // Multiply ax by two.
mov( ax, bx);        // Save 2*ax for later.
shl( 2, ax );        // Multiply ax by eight (*4 really,
                     // but ax contains *2).
add( bx, ax );       // Add in ax*2 to ax*8 to get ax*10.
```

Many x86 processors can multiply the AX register (or just about any register, for that matter) by various constant values much faster by using shl than by using the mul instruction. This may seem hard to believe because it takes only one instruction to compute this product:

```
intmul( 10, ax );
```

However, if you look at the instruction timings, the shift and add example above requires fewer clock cycles on many processors in the 80x86 family than the mul instruction. Of course, the code is somewhat larger (by a few bytes), but the performance improvement is usually worth it.

You can also use subtraction with shifts to perform a multiplication operation. Consider the following multiplication by 7:

```
mov( eax, ebx );     // Save eax * 1
shl( 3, eax );       // eax = eax * 8
sub( ebx, eax );     // eax * 8 - eax * 1 is eax * 7
```

A common error beginning assembly language programmers make is subtracting or adding 1 or 2 rather than eax * 1 or eax * 2. The following does not compute eax * 7:

```
shl( 3, eax );
sub( 1, eax );
```

It computes (8 * eax) - 1, something entirely different (unless, of course, EAX = 1). Beware of this pitfall when using shifts, additions, and subtractions to perform multiplication operations.

You can also use the lea instruction to compute certain products. The trick is to use the scaled index addressing modes. The following examples demonstrate some simple cases:

```
lea( eax, [ecx][ecx] );       // eax := ecx * 2
lea( eax, [eax][eax*2] );     // eax := eax * 3
lea( eax, [eax*4] );          // eax := eax * 4
lea( eax, [ebx][ebx*4] );     // eax := ebx * 5
lea( eax, [eax*8] );          // eax := eax * 8
lea( eax, [edx][edx*8] );     // eax := edx * 9
```

## 6.4.2   Division Without div or idiv

Just as the shl instruction is useful for simulating a multiplication by a power of 2, the shr and sar instructions can simulate a division by a power of 2. Unfortunately, you cannot easily use shifts, additions, and subtractions to perform a division by an arbitrary constant. Therefore, keep in mind that this trick is useful only when dividing by powers of 2. Also, don't forget that the sar instruction rounds towards negative infinity rather than toward 0; this is not the way the idiv instruction operates (it rounds toward 0).

Another way to perform division is to use the multiply instructions. You can divide by some value by multiplying by its reciprocal. Because the multiply instruction is faster than the divide instruction, multiplying by a reciprocal is usually faster than division.

Now you're probably wondering, "How does one multiply by a reciprocal when the values we're dealing with are all integers?" The answer, of course, is that we must cheat to do this. If you want to multiply by 1/10, there is no way you can load the value 1/10 into an 80x86 integer register prior to performing the multiplication. However, we could multiply 1/10 by 10, perform the multiplication, and then divide the result by 10 to get the final result. Of course, this wouldn't buy you anything; in fact, it would make things worse because you're now doing a multiplication by 10 as well as a division by 10. However, suppose you multiply 1/10 by 65,536 (6,553), perform the multiplication, and then divide by 65,536. This would still perform the correct operation, and, as it turns out, if you set up the problem correctly, you can get the division operation for free. Consider the following code that divides AX by 10:

```
mov( 6554, dx );        // 6,554 = round( 65,536/10 )
mul( dx, ax );
```

This code leaves AX/10 in the DX register.

To understand how this works, consider what happens when you multiply AX by 65,536 ($1_0000). This simply moves AX into DX and sets AX to 0 (a multiply by $1_0000 is equivalent to a shift left by 16 bits). Multiplying by 6,554 (65,536 divided by 10) puts AX divided by 10 into the DX register. Because mul is faster than div, this technique runs a little faster than using a division.

Multiplying by a reciprocal works well when you need to divide by a constant. You could even use it to divide by a variable, but the overhead to compute the reciprocal pays off only if you perform the division many, many times (by the same value).

### 6.4.3 Implementing Modulo-N Counters with and

If you want to implement a counter variable that counts up to $2^n - 1$ and then resets to 0, simply use the following code:

```
inc( CounterVar );
and( nBits, CounterVar );
```

where nBits is a binary value containing $n$ bits containing ones right justified in the number. For example, to create a counter that cycles between 0 and 1 $(2^4 - 1)$, you could use the following:

```
inc( CounterVar );
and( %00001111, CounterVar );
```

# 6.5 Floating-Point Arithmetic

When the 8086 CPU first appeared in the late 1970s, semiconductor technology was not to the point where Intel could put floating-point instructions directly on the 8086 CPU. Therefore, Intel devised a scheme whereby it could use a second chip to perform the floating-point calculations—the floating-point unit (or FPU).[1] By the release of the Intel Pentium chip, semiconductor technology had advanced to the point that the FPU was fully integrated onto the 80x86 CPU. Therefore, almost all modern 80x86 CPU devices fully support floating-point arithmetic directly on the CPU.

### 6.5.1 FPU Registers

The 80x86 FPUs add 13 registers to the 80x86: eight floating-point data registers, a control register, a status register, a tag register, an instruction pointer, and a data pointer. The data registers are similar to the 80x86's general-purpose register set insofar as all floating-point calculations take place in these registers. The control register contains bits that let you decide how the FPU handles certain degenerate cases like rounding of inaccurate computations; it also contains bits that control precision and so on. The status register is similar to the 80x86's flags register; it contains the condition code bits and several other floating-point flags that describe the state of the FPU. The tag register contains several groups of bits that determine the state of the value in each of the eight floating-point data registers. The instruction and data pointer registers

---

[1] Intel has also referred to this device as the Numeric Data Processor (NDP), Numeric Processor Extension (NPX), and math coprocessor.

contain certain state information about the last floating-point instruction executed. We will not consider the last three registers here; see the Intel documentation for more details.

### 6.5.1.1 FPU Data Registers

The FPUs provide eight 80-bit data registers organized as a stack. This is a significant departure from the organization of the general-purpose registers on the 80x86 CPU. HLA refers to these registers as ST0, ST1, . . . ST7.

The biggest difference between the FPU register set and the 80x86 register set is the stack organization. On the 80x86 CPU, the AX register is always the AX register, no matter what happens. On the FPU, however, the register set is an eight-element stack of 80-bit floating-point values (see Figure 6-1).

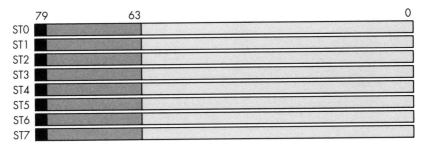

*Figure 6-1: FPU floating-point register stack*

ST0 refers to the item on the top of the stack, ST1 refers to the next item on the stack, and so on. Many floating-point instructions push and pop items on the stack; therefore, ST1 will refer to the previous contents of ST0 after you push something onto the stack. It will take some thought and practice to get used to the fact that the register numbers change, but this is an easy problem to overcome.

### 6.5.1.2 The FPU Control Register

When Intel designed the 80x87 (and, essentially, the IEEE floating-point standard), there were no standards in floating-point hardware. Different (mainframe and mini) computer manufacturers all had different and incompatible floating-point formats. Unfortunately, several applications had been written taking into account the idiosyncrasies of these different floating-point formats. Intel wanted to design an FPU that could work with the majority of the software out there (keep in mind that the IBM-PC was three to four years away when Intel began designing the 8087, so Intel couldn't rely on that "mountain" of software available for the PC to make its chip popular). Unfortunately, many of the features found in these older floating-point formats were mutually incompatible. For example, in some floating-point systems rounding would occur when there was insufficient precision; in others, truncation would occur. Some applications would work with one floating-point system but not with the other. Intel wanted as many applications as possible to work with as few changes as possible on its 80x87 FPUs, so it added a special register, the FPU *control register*, that lets the user choose one of several possible operating modes for the FPU.

The 80x87 control register contains 16 bits organized as shown in Figure 6-2.

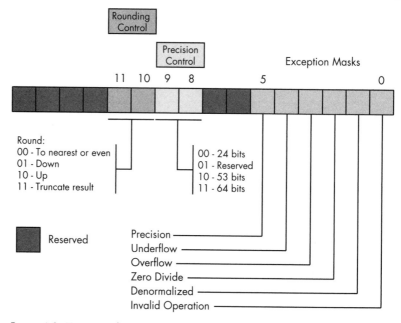

Figure 6-2: FPU control register

Bits 10 and 11 of the FPU control register provide rounding control according to the values appearing in Table 6-8.

**Table 6-8:** Rounding Control

| Bits 10 & 11 | Function |
|---|---|
| 00 | To nearest or even |
| 01 | Round down |
| 10 | Round up |
| 11 | Truncate |

The 00 setting is the default. The FPU rounds up values above one-half of the least significant bit. It rounds down values below one-half of the least significant bit. If the value below the least significant bit is exactly one-half of the least significant bit, then the FPU rounds the value toward the value whose least significant bit is 0. For long strings of computations, this provides a reasonable, automatic way to maintain maximum precision.

The round-up and round-down options are present for those computations where it is important to keep track of the accuracy during a computation. By setting the rounding control to round down and performing the operation, then repeating the operation with the rounding control set to round up, you can determine the minimum and maximum ranges between which the true result will fall.

The truncate option forces all computations to truncate any excess bits during the computation. You will rarely use this option if accuracy is important to you. However, if you are porting older software to the FPU, you might use this option to help when porting the software. One place where this option is extremely useful is when converting a floating-point value to an integer. Because most software expects floating-point-to-integer conversions to truncate the result, you will need to use the truncation/rounding mode to achieve this.

Bits 8 and 9 of the control register specify the precision during computation. This capability is provided to allow compatibility with older software as required by the IEEE 754 standard. The precision control bits use the values in Table 6-9.

**Table 6-9:** Mantissa Precision Control Bits

| Bits 8 & 9 | Precision Control |
|------------|-------------------|
| 00 | 24 bits |
| 01 | Reserved |
| 10 | 53 bits |
| 11 | 64 bits |

Some CPUs may operate faster with floating-point values whose precision is 53 bits (i.e., 64-bit floating-point format) rather than 64 bits (i.e., 80-bit floating-point format). Please see the documentation for your specific processor for details. Generally, the CPU defaults these bits to %11 to select the 64-bit mantissa precision.

Bits 0..5 are the *exception masks*. These are similar to the interrupt enable bit in the 80x86's flags register. If these bits contain a 1, the corresponding condition is ignored by the FPU. However, if any bit contains 0, and the corresponding condition occurs, then the FPU immediately generates an interrupt so the program can handle the degenerate condition (typically, this would wind up raising an HLA exception; see the *excepts.hhf* header file for the exception values).

Bit 0 corresponds to an invalid operation error. This generally occurs as the result of a programming error. Situations that raise the invalid operation exception (ex.fInvalidOperation) include pushing more than eight items onto the stack or attempting to pop an item off an empty stack, taking the square root of a negative number, or loading a nonempty register.

Bit 1 masks the *denormalized* interrupt that occurs whenever you try to manipulate denormalized values. Denormalized exceptions occur when you load arbitrary extended-precision values into the FPU or work with very small numbers just beyond the range of the FPU's capabilities. Normally, you would probably *not* enable this exception. If you enable this exception and the FPU generates this interrupt, the HLA runtime system raises the ex.fDenormal exception.

Bit 2 masks the *zero divide* exception. If this bit contains 0, the FPU will generate an interrupt if you attempt to divide a nonzero value by 0. If you do not enable the zero division exception, the FPU will produce NaN (not a number) whenever you perform a zero division. It's probably a good idea to enable this exception by programming a 0 into this bit. Note that if your program generates this interrupt, the HLA runtime system will raise the ex.fDivByZero exception.

Bit 3 masks the *overflow* exception. The FPU will raise the overflow exception if a calculation overflows or if you attempt to store a value that is too large to fit into the destination operand (for example, storing a large extended-precision value into a single-precision variable). If you enable this exception and the FPU generates this interrupt, the HLA runtime system raises the ex.fOverflow exception.

Bit 4, if set, masks the *underflow* exception. Underflow occurs when the result is too *small* to fit in the destination operand. Like overflow, this exception can occur whenever you store a small extended-precision value into a smaller variable (single or double precision) or when the result of a computation is too small for extended precision. If you enable this exception and the FPU generates this interrupt, the HLA runtime system raises the ex.fUnderflow exception.

Bit 5 controls whether the *precision* exception can occur. A precision exception occurs whenever the FPU produces an imprecise result, generally the result of an internal rounding operation. Although many operations will produce an exact result, many more will not. For example, dividing 1 by 10 will produce an inexact result. Therefore, this bit is usually 1 because inexact results are very common. If you enable this exception and the FPU generates this interrupt, the HLA runtime system raises the ex.InexactResult exception.

Bits 6..7 and 12..15 in the control register are currently undefined and reserved for future use (bits 7 and 12 were valid on older FPUs but are no longer used).

The FPU provides two instructions, fldcw (load control word) and fstcw (store control word), that let you load and store the contents of the control register. The single operand to these instructions must be a 16-bit memory location. The fldcw instruction loads the control register from the specified memory location. fstcw stores the control register into the specified memory location. The syntax for these instructions is:

```
fldcw( mem16 );
fstcw( mem16 );
```

Here's some example code that sets the rounding control to "truncate result" and sets the rounding precision to 24 bits:

```
static
    fcw16: word;
        .
        .
        .
```

```
fstcw( fcw16 );
mov( fcw16, ax );
and( $f0ff, ax );      // Clears bits 8-11.
or( $0c00, ax );       // Rounding control=%11, Precision = %00.
mov( ax, fcw16 );
fldcw( fcw16 );
```

### 6.5.1.3    The FPU Status Register

The FPU status register provides the status of the FPU at the instant you read it. The fstsw instruction stores the 16-bit floating-point status register into a word variable. The status register is a 16-bit register; its layout appears in Figure 6-3.

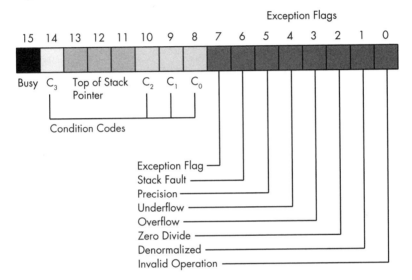

*Figure 6-3: The FPU status register*

Bits 0 through 5 are the exception flags. These bits appear in the same order as the exception masks in the control register. If the corresponding condition exists, then the bit is set. These bits are independent of the exception masks in the control register. The FPU sets and clears these bits regardless of the corresponding mask setting.

Bit 6 indicates a *stack fault*. A stack fault occurs whenever there is a stack overflow or underflow. When this bit is set, the $C_1$ condition code bit determines whether there was a stack overflow ($C_1 = 1$) or stack underflow ($C_1 = 0$) condition.

Bit 7 of the status register is set if *any* error condition bit is set. It is the logical or of bits 0 through 5. A program can test this bit to quickly determine if an error condition exists.

Bits 8, 9, 10, and 14 are the coprocessor condition code bits. Various instructions set the condition code bits, as shown in Tables 6-10 and 6-11, respectively.

**Table 6-10:** FPU Condition Code Bits (X = "Don't care")

| Instruction | Condition Code Bits | | | | Condition |
|---|---|---|---|---|---|
| | $C_3$ | $C_2$ | $C_1$ | $C_0$ | |
| fcom<br>fcomp<br>fcompp<br>ficom<br>ficomp | 0<br>0<br>1<br>1 | 0<br>0<br>0<br>1 | X<br>X<br>X<br>X | 0<br>1<br>0<br>1 | ST > source<br>ST < source<br>ST = source<br>ST or source undefined |
| ftst | 0<br>0<br>1<br>1 | 0<br>0<br>0<br>1 | X<br>X<br>X<br>X | 0<br>1<br>0<br>1 | ST is positive<br>ST is negative<br>ST is 0 (+ or −)<br>ST is uncomparable |
| fxam | 0<br>0<br>0<br>0<br>1<br>1<br>1<br>1<br>0<br>0<br>0<br>0<br>1 | 0<br>0<br>1<br>1<br>0<br>0<br>1<br>1<br>0<br>0<br>1<br>1<br>X | 0<br>1<br>0<br>1<br>0<br>1<br>0<br>1<br>0<br>1<br>0<br>1<br>X | 0<br>0<br>0<br>0<br>0<br>0<br>0<br>0<br>1<br>1<br>1<br>1<br>1 | + Unnormalized<br>− Unnormalized<br>+ Normalized<br>− Normalized<br>+ 0<br>− 0<br>+ Denormalized<br>− Denormalized<br>+ NaN<br>− NaN<br>+ Infinity<br>− Infinity<br>Empty register |
| fucom<br>fucomp<br>fucompp | 0<br>0<br>1<br>1 | 0<br>0<br>0<br>1 | X<br>X<br>X<br>X | 0<br>1<br>0<br>1 | ST > source<br>ST < source<br>ST = source<br>Unordered |

**Table 6-11:** Condition Code Interpretations (X = "Don't care")

| Instruction | Condition Code Bits | | | | Condition |
|---|---|---|---|---|---|
| | $C_3$ | $C_2$ | $C_1$ | $C_0$ | |
| fcom<br>fcomp<br>fcompp<br>ficom<br>ficomp | 0<br>0<br>1<br>1 | 0<br>0<br>0<br>1 | X<br>X<br>X<br>X | 0<br>1<br>0<br>1 | ST > source<br>ST < source<br>ST = source<br>ST or source undefined |
| ftst | 0<br>0<br>1<br>1 | 0<br>0<br>0<br>1 | X<br>X<br>X<br>X | 0<br>1<br>0<br>1 | ST is positive<br>ST is negative<br>ST is 0 (+ or −)<br>ST is uncomparable |

**Table 6-11:** Condition Code Interpretations (X = "Don't care") (continued)

| Instruction | Condition Code Bits | | | | Condition |
|---|---|---|---|---|---|
| | $C_3$ | $C_2$ | $C_1$ | $C_0$ | |
| fxam | 0 | 0 | 0 | 1 | + Unnormalized |
| | 0 | 0 | 1 | 0 | − Unnormalized |
| | 0 | 1 | 0 | 0 | + Normalized |
| | 0 | 1 | 1 | 0 | − Normalized |
| | 1 | 0 | 0 | 0 | + 0 |
| | 1 | 0 | 1 | 0 | − 0 |
| | 1 | 1 | 0 | 0 | + Denormalized |
| | 1 | 1 | 1 | 0 | − Denormalized |
| | 0 | 0 | 0 | 1 | + NaN |
| | 0 | 0 | 1 | 1 | − NaN |
| | 0 | 1 | 0 | 1 | + Infinity |
| | 0 | 1 | 1 | 1 | − Infinity |
| | 1 | X | X | 1 | Empty register |
| fucom | 0 | 0 | X | 0 | ST > source |
| fucomp | 0 | 0 | X | 1 | ST < source |
| fucompp | 1 | 0 | X | 0 | ST = source |
| | 1 | 1 | X | 1 | Unordered |

Bits 11–13 of the FPU status register provide the register number of the top of stack. During computations, the FPU adds (modulo-8) the *logical* register numbers supplied by the programmer to these three bits to determine the *physical* register number at runtime.

Bit 15 of the status register is the *busy* bit. It is set whenever the FPU is busy. This bit is a historical artifact from the days when the FPU was a separate chip; most programs will have little reason to access this bit.

## 6.5.2 FPU Data Types

The FPU supports seven different data types: three integer types, a packed decimal type, and three floating-point types. The integer type supports 64-bit integers, although it is often faster to do the 64-bit arithmetic using the integer unit of the CPU (see Chapter 8). Certainly it is faster to do 16-bit and 32-bit integer arithmetic using the standard integer registers. The packed decimal type provides a 17-digit signed decimal (BCD) integer. The primary purpose of the BCD format is to convert between strings and floating-point values. The remaining three data types are the 32-bit, 64-bit, and 80-bit floating-point data types. The 80x87 data types appear in Figures 6-4, 6-5, and 6-6.

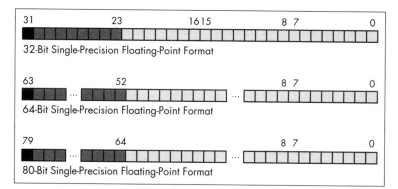

Figure 6-4: FPU floating-point formats

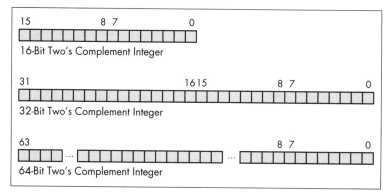

Figure 6-5: FPU integer formats

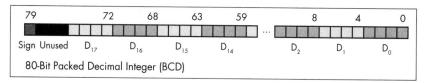

Figure 6-6: FPU packed decimal format

The FPU generally stores values in a *normalized* format. When a floating-point number is normalized, the H.O. bit of the mantissa is always 1. In the 32- and 64-bit floating-point formats, the FPU does not actually store this bit; the FPU always assumes that it is 1. Therefore, 32- and 64-bit floating-point numbers are always normalized. In the extended-precision 80-bit floating-point format, the FPU does *not* assume that the H.O. bit of the mantissa is 1; the H.O. bit of the mantissa appears as part of the string of bits.

Normalized values provide the greatest precision for a given number of bits. However, there are a large number of nonnormalized values that we *cannot* represent with the 80-bit format. These values are very close to 0 and represent the set of values whose mantissa H.O. bit is not 0. The FPUs support a special 80-bit form known as *denormalized* values. Denormalized values allow the FPU to encode very small values it cannot encode using normalized values, but denormalized values offer fewer bits of precision than normalized values. Therefore, using denormalized values in a computation may introduce some slight inaccuracy into a computation. Of course, this is always better than underflowing the denormalized value to 0 (which could make the computation even less accurate), but you must keep in mind that if you work with very small values you may lose some accuracy in your computations. Note that the FPU status register contains a bit you can use to detect when the FPU uses a denormalized value in a computation.

### 6.5.3 The FPU Instruction Set

The FPU adds many instructions to the 80x86 instruction set. We can classify these instructions as data movement instructions, conversions, arithmetic instructions, comparisons, constant instructions, transcendental instructions, and miscellaneous instructions. The following sections describe each of the instructions in these categories.

### 6.5.4 FPU Data Movement Instructions

The data movement instructions transfer data between the internal FPU registers and memory. The instructions in this category are fld, fst, fstp, and fxch. The fld instruction always pushes its operand onto the floating-point stack. The fstp instruction always pops the top of stack after storing the top of stack (TOS). The remaining instructions do not affect the number of items on the stack.

#### 6.5.4.1 The fld Instruction

The fld instruction loads a 32-bit, 64-bit, or 80-bit floating-point value onto the stack. This instruction converts 32- and 64-bit operands to an 80-bit extended-precision value before pushing the value onto the floating-point stack.

The fld instruction first decrements the TOS pointer (bits 11–13 of the status register) and then stores the 80-bit value in the physical register specified by the new TOS pointer. If the source operand of the FLD instruction is a floating-point data register, sti, then the actual register the FPU uses for the load operation is the register number *before* decrementing the TOS pointer. Therefore, fld( st0 ); duplicates the value on the top of the stack.

The fld instruction sets the stack fault bit if stack overflow occurs. It sets the denormalized exception bit if you load an 80-bit denormalized value. It sets the invalid operation bit if you attempt to load an empty floating-point register onto the top of stack (or perform some other invalid operation).

Here are some examples:

```
fld( st1 );
fld( real32_variable );
fld( real64_variable );
fld( real80_variable );
fld( (type real64 [ebx]) );
fld( real_constant );
```

Note that there is no way to directly load a 32-bit integer register onto the floating-point stack, even if that register contains a real32 value. To accomplish this, you must first store the integer register into a memory location; then you can push that memory location onto the FPU stack using the fld instruction. For example:

```
mov( eax, tempReal32 );   // Save real32 value in eax to memory.
fld( tempReal32 );        // Push that real value onto the FPU stack.
```

Note that loading a constant via fld is actually an HLA extension. The FPU doesn't support this instruction type. HLA creates a real80 object in the constants segment and uses the address of this memory object as the true operand for fld.

### 6.5.4.2 The fst and fstp Instructions

The fst and fstp instructions copy the value on the top of the floating-point stack to another floating-point register or to a 32-, 64-, or 80-bit memory variable. When copying data to a 32- or 64-bit memory variable, the FPU rounds the 80-bit extended-precision value on the top of stack to the smaller format as specified by the rounding control bits in the FPU control register.

The fstp instruction pops the value off the top of the stack when moving it to the destination location. It does this by incrementing the TOS pointer in the status register after accessing the data in ST0. If the destination operand is a floating-point register, the FPU stores the value at the specified register number *before* popping the data off the top of the stack.

Executing an fstp( st0 ); instruction effectively pops the data off the top of stack with no data transfer. Here are some examples:

```
fst( real32_variable );
fst( real64_variable );
fst( realArray[ ebx*8 ] );
fst( st2 );
fstp( st1 );
```

The last example above effectively pops ST1 while leaving ST0 on the top of stack.

The fst and fstp instructions will set the stack exception bit if a stack underflow occurs (attempting to store a value from an empty register stack). They will set the precision bit if there is a loss of precision during the store operation (this will occur, for example, when storing an 80-bit extended-precision value into a 32- or 64-bit memory variable and some bits are lost during conversion). They will set the underflow exception bit when storing an 80-bit value into a 32- or 64-bit memory variable, but the value is too small to fit into the destination operand. Likewise, these instructions will set the overflow exception bit if the value on the top of stack is too big to fit into a 32- or 64-bit memory variable. The fst and fstp instructions set the denormalized flag when you try to store a denormalized value into an 80-bit register or variable.[2] They set the invalid operation flag if an invalid operation (such as storing into an empty register) occurs. Finally, these instructions set the $C_1$ condition bit if rounding occurs during the store operation (this occurs only when storing into a 32- or 64-bit memory variable and you have to round the mantissa to fit into the destination).

**NOTE** *Because of an idiosyncrasy in the FPU instruction set related to the encoding of the instructions, you cannot use the fst instruction to store data into a real80 memory variable. You may, however, store 80-bit data using the fstp instruction.*

### 6.5.4.3 The fxch Instruction

The fxch instruction exchanges the value on the top of stack with one of the other FPU registers. This instruction takes two forms: one with a single FPU register as an operand and the second without any operands. The first form exchanges the top of stack with the specified register. The second form of fxch swaps the top of stack with ST1.

Many FPU instructions, for example, fsqrt, operate only on the top of the register stack. If you want to perform such an operation on a value that is not on the top of stack, you can use the fxch instruction to swap that register with TOS, perform the desired operation, and then use the fxch to swap the TOS with the original register. The following example takes the square root of ST2:

```
fxch( st2 );
fsqrt();
fxch( st2 );
```

The fxch instruction sets the stack exception bit if the stack is empty. It sets the invalid operation bit if you specify an empty register as the operand. This instruction always clears the $C_1$ condition code bit.

## 6.5.5 Conversions

The FPU performs all arithmetic operations on 80-bit real quantities. In a sense, the fld and fst/fstp instructions are conversion instructions because they automatically convert between the internal 80-bit real format and the 32- and 64-bit memory formats. Nonetheless, we'll simply classify them as data movement operations, rather than conversions, because they are moving real values to and from memory. The FPU provides six other instructions that convert to or from integer or binary-coded decimal (BCD) format when moving data. These instructions are fild, fist, fistp, fisttp, fbld, and fbstp.

---

[2] Storing a denormalized value into a 32- or 64-bit memory variable will always set the underflow exception bit.

### 6.5.5.1 The fild Instruction

The fild (integer load) instruction converts a 16-, 32-, or 64-bit two's compl ment integer to the 80-bit extended-precision format and pushes the result onto the stack. This instruction always expects a single operand. This operand must be the address of a word, double-word, or quad-word integer variable. You cannot specify one of the 80x86's 16- or 32-bit general-purpose register If you want to push the value of an 80x86 general-purpose register onto the FPU stack, you must first store it into a memory variable and then use fild to push that memory variable.

The fild instruction sets the stack exception bit and $C_1$ (accordingly) if stack overflow occurs while pushing the converted value. Look at these examples:

```
fild( word_variable );
fild( dword_val[ ecx*4 ] );
fild( qword_variable );
fild( (type int64 [ebx]) );
```

### 6.5.5.2 The fist, fistp, and fisttp Instructions

The fist, fistp, and fisttp instructions convert the 80-bit extended-precision variable on the top of stack to a 16-, 32-, or 64-bit integer and store the resul away into the memory variable specified by the single operand. The fist an fistp instructions convert the value on TOS to an integer according to the rounding setting in the FPU control register (bits 10 and 11). The fisttp instruction always does the conversion using the truncation mode. As for the fild instruction, the fist, fistp, and fisttp instructions will not let you specif one of the 80x86's general-purpose 16- or 32-bit registers as the destination operand.

The fist instruction converts the value on the top of stack to an integer and then stores the result; it does not otherwise affect the floating-point registe stack. The fistp and fisttp instructions pop the value off the floating-point register stack after storing the converted value.

These instructions set the stack exception bit if the floating-point registe stack is empty (this will also clear $C_1$). They set the precision (imprecise operation) and $C_1$ bits if rounding occurs (that is, if there is any fractional component to the value in ST0). These instructions set the underflow excep tion bit if the result is too small (that is, less than 1 but greater than 0 or less than 0 but greater than −1). Here are some examples:

```
fist( word_var[ ebx*2 ] );
fist( qword_var );
fisttp( dword_var );
fistp( dword_var );
```

Don't forget that the fist and fistp instructions use the rounding contro settings to determine how they will convert the floating-point data to an inte ger during the store operation. Be default, the rounding control is usually se to "round" mode; yet most programmers expect fist/fistp to truncate the decimal portion during conversion. If you want fist/fistp to truncate floating-point values when converting them to an integer, you will need to set the rounding control bits appropriately in the floating-point control register (or use the fisttp instruction to truncate the result regardless of the rounding control bits). Here's an example:

```
static
      fcw16:        word;
      fcw16_2:      word;
      IntResult:    int32;
         .
         .
         .
      fstcw( fcw16 );
      mov( fcw16, ax );
      or( $0c00, ax );       // Rounding control=%11 (truncate).
      mov( ax, fcw16_2 );    // Store into memory and reload the ctrl word.
      fldcw( fcw16_2 );

      fistp( IntResult );    // Truncate ST0 and store as int32 object.

      fldcw( fcw16 );        // Restore original rounding control.
```

### 6.5.5.3  The fbld and fbstp Instructions

The fbld and fbstp instructions load and store 80-bit BCD values. The fbld instruction converts a BCD value to its 80-bit extended-precision equivalent and pushes the result onto the stack. The fbstp instruction pops the extended-precision real value on TOS, converts it to an 80-bit BCD value (rounding according to the bits in the floating-point control register), and stores the converted result at the address specified by the destination memory operand. Note that there is no fbst instruction.

The fbld instruction sets the stack exception bit and $C_1$ if stack overflow occurs. It sets the invalid operation bit if you attempt to load an invalid BCD value. The fbstp instruction sets the stack exception bit and clears $C_1$ if stack underflow occurs (the stack is empty). It sets the underflow flag under the same conditions as fist and fistp. Look at these examples:

```
// Assuming fewer than 8 items on the stack, the following
// code sequence is equivalent to an fbst instruction:

      fld( st0 );
      fbstp( tbyte_var );

// The following example easily converts an 80-bit BCD value to
// a 64-bit integer:

      fbld( tbyte_var );
      fist( qword_var );
```

These two instructions are especially useful for converting between string and floating-point formats. See the floating-point-to-string and string-to-floating-point conversion routines in the HLA Standard Library for more details.

### 6.5.6  Arithmetic Instructions

The arithmetic instructions make up a small but important subset of the FPU's instruction set. These instructions fall into two general categories: those that operate on real values and those that operate on a real and an integer value.

#### 6.5.6.1  The fadd and faddp Instructions

These two instructions take the following forms:

```
fadd()
faddp()
fadd( st0, sti );
fadd( sti, st0 );
faddp( st0, sti );
fadd( mem_32_64 );
fadd( real_constant );
```

The fadd instruction, with no operands, adds the value in ST0 to the value in ST1 and stores the result into ST1. The faddp instruction (with no operands) pops the two values on the top of stack, adds them, and pushes their sum back onto the stack.

The next two forms of the fadd instruction, those with two FPU register operands, behave like the 80x86's add instruction. They add the value in the source register operand to the value in the destination register operand. Note that one of the register operands must be ST0.

The faddp instruction with two operands adds ST0 (which must always be the source operand) to the destination operand and then pops ST0. The destination operand must be one of the other FPU registers.

The last form above, fadd with a memory operand, adds a 32- or 64-bit floating-point variable to the value in ST0. This instruction will convert the 32- or 64-bit operands to an 80-bit extended-precision value before performing the addition. Note that this instruction does *not* allow an 80-bit memory operand.

These instructions can raise the stack, precision, underflow, overflow, denormalized, and illegal operation exceptions, as appropriate. If a stack fault exception occurs, $C_1$ denotes stack overflow or underflow.

Like fld( real_constant), the fadd( real_constant ) instruction is an HLA extension. Note that it creates a 64-bit variable holding the constant value and emits the fadd( mem64 ) instruction, specifying the read-only object it creates in the constants segment.

## 6.5.6.2 The fsub, fsubp, fsubr, and fsurpb Instructions

These four instructions take the following forms:

```
fsub()
fsubp()
fsubr()
fsubrp()

fsub( st0, sti )
fsub( sti, st0 );
fsubp( st0, sti );
fsub( mem_32_64 );
fsub( real_constant );

fsubr( st0, sti )
fsubr( sti, st0 );
fsubrp( st0, sti );
fsubr( mem_32_64 );
fsubr( real_constant );
```

With no operands, the fsub instruction subtracts ST0 from ST1 and leaves the result in ST1. With no operands the fsubp instruction pops ST0 and ST1 from the register stack, computes st1 - st0 and then pushes the difference back onto the stack. The fsubr and fsubrp instructions (reverse subtraction) operate in an almost identical fashion except they compute st0 - st1.

With two register operands (*source, destination*) the fsub instruction computes *destination := destination - source*. One of the two registers must be ST0. With two registers as operands, the fsubp also computes *destination := destination - source*, and then it pops ST0 off the stack after computing the difference. For the fsubp instruction, the source operand must be ST0.

With two register operands, the fsubr and fsubrp instructions work in a similar fashion to fsub and fsubp, except they compute *destination := source - destination*.

The fsub( *mem* ) and fsubr( *mem* ) instructions accept a 32- or 64-bit memory operand. They convert the memory operand to an 80-bit extended-precision value and subtract this from ST0 (fsub) or subtract ST0 from this value (fsubr) and store the result back into ST0.

These instructions can raise the stack, precision, underflow, overflow, denormalized, and illegal operation exceptions, as appropriate. If a stack fault exception occurs, $C_1$ denotes stack overflow or underflow.

**NOTE**    *The instructions that have real constants as operands aren't true FPU instructions. These are extensions provided by HLA. HLA generates a constant segment memory object initialized with the constant's value.*

### 6.5.6.3 The fmul and fmulp Instructions

The `fmul` and `fmulp` instructions multiply two floating-point values. These instructions allow the following forms:

```
fmul()
fmulp()

fmul( sti, sto );
fmul( sto, sti );
fmul( mem_32_64 );
fmul( real_constant );

fmulp( sto, sti );
```

With no operands, `fmul` will compute sto * st1 and store the product in ST1. The `fmulp` instruction, with no operands, will pop ST0 and ST1, multiply these values, and push their product back onto the stack. The `fmul` instruction with two register operands compute *destination := destination * source*. One of the registers (source or destination) must be ST0.

The `fmulp( sto, sti )` instruction computes sti := sti * sto and then pop ST0. This instruction uses the value for STi before popping ST0. The `fmul( mem )` instruction requires a 32- or 64-bit memory operand. It converts the specified memory variable to an 80-bit extended-precision value and then multiplies ST0 by this value.

These instructions can raise the stack, precision, underflow, overflow, denormalized, and illegal operation exceptions, as appropriate. If rounding occurs during the computation, these instructions set the $C_1$ condition code bit. If a stack fault exception occurs, $C_1$ denotes stack overflow or underflow.

**NOTE** *The instruction that has a real constant as its operand isn't a true FPU instruction. is an extension provided by HLA (see the note at the end of Section 6.5.6.2 for detail.*

### 6.5.6.4 The fdiv, fdivp, fdivr, and fdivrp Instructions

These four instructions allow the following forms:

```
fdiv()
fdivp()
fdivr()
fdivrp()

fdiv( sti, sto );
fdiv( sto, sti );
fdivp( sto, sti );

fdivr( sti, sto );
fdivr( sto, sti );
fdivrp( sto, sti );
```

```
fdiv( mem_32_64 );
fdivr( mem_32_64 );
fdiv( real_constant );
fdivr( real_constant );
```

With no operands, the fdivp instruction pops ST0 and ST1, computes st1/st0, and pushes the result back onto the stack. The fdiv instruction with no operands computes st1 := st1/st0. The fdivr and fdivrp instructions work in a similar fashion to fdiv and fdivp except that they compute st0/st1 rather than st1/st0.

With two register operands, these instructions compute the following quotients:

```
fdiv( sti, st0 );        // st0 := st0/sti
fdiv( st0, sti );        // sti := sti/st0
fdivp( st0, sti );       // sti := sti/st0 then pop st0
fdivr( st0, sti );       // st0 := st0/sti
fdivrp( st0, sti );      // sti := st0/sti then pop st0
```

The fdivp and fdivrp instructions also pop ST0 after performing the division operation. The value for $i$ in these two instructions is computed before popping ST0.

These instructions can raise the stack, precision, underflow, overflow, denormalized, zero divide, and illegal operation exceptions, as appropriate. If rounding occurs during the computation, these instructions set the $C_1$ condition code bit. If a stack fault exception occurs, $C_1$ denotes stack overflow or underflow.

Note that the instructions that have real constants as operands aren't true FPU instructions. These are extensions provided by HLA.

### 6.5.6.5 The fsqrt Instruction

The fsqrt routine does not allow any operands. It computes the square root of the value on top of stack (TOS) and replaces ST0 with this result. The value on TOS must be 0 or positive; otherwise fsqrt will generate an invalid operation exception.

This instruction can raise the stack, precision, denormalized, and invalid operation exceptions, as appropriate. If rounding occurs during the computation, fsqrt sets the $C_1$ condition code bit. If a stack fault exception occurs, $C_1$ denotes stack overflow or underflow.

Here's an example:

```
// Compute z := sqrt(x**2 + y**2);

    fld( x );           // Load x.
    fld( st0 );         // Duplicate x on TOS.
    fmulp();            // Compute x**2.
```

```
fld( y );              // Load y.
fld( st0 );            // Duplicate y.
fmul();                // Compute y**2.

faddp();               // Compute x**2 + y**2.
fsqrt();               // Compute sqrt( x**2 + y**2 ).
fstp( z );             // Store result away into z.
```

### 6.5.6.6  The fprem and fprem1 Instructions

The fprem and fprem1 instructions compute a *partial remainder*. Intel designed
the fprem instruction before the IEEE finalized its floating-point standard.
In the final draft of the IEEE floating-point standard, the definition of
fprem was a little different than Intel's original design. Unfortunately, Intel
needed to maintain compatibility with the existing software that used the
fprem instruction, so it designed a new version to handle the IEEE partial
remainder operation, fprem1. You should always use fprem1 in new software;
therefore we will discuss only fprem1 here, although you use fprem in an
identical fashion.

fprem1 computes the *partial* remainder of st0/st1. If the difference between
the exponents of ST0 and ST1 is less than 64, fprem1 can compute the exact
remainder in one operation. Otherwise you will have to execute the fprem1
two or more times to get the correct remainder value. The $C_2$ condition code
bit determines when the computation is complete. Note that fprem1 does not
pop the two operands off the stack; it leaves the partial remainder in ST0 and
the original divisor in ST1 in case you need to compute another partial product to complete the result.

The fprem1 instruction sets the stack exception flag if there aren't two values
on the top of stack. It sets the underflow and denormal exception bits if the
result is too small. It sets the invalid operation bit if the values on TOS are
inappropriate for this operation. It sets the $C_2$ condition code bit if the partial
remainder operation is not complete. Finally, it loads $C_3$, $C_1$, and $C_0$ with bits 0,
1, and 2 of the quotient, respectively.

An example follows:

```
// Compute z := x mod y

        fld( y );
        fld( x );
        repeat

            fprem1();
            fstsw( ax );    // Get condition code bits into ax.
            and( 1, ah );   // See if C2 is set.

        until( @z );        // Repeat until C2 is clear.
        fstp( z );          // Store away the remainder.
        fstp( st0 );        // Pop old y value.
```

### 6.5.6.7 The frndint Instruction

The frndint instruction rounds the value on the top of stack (TOS) to the nearest integer using the rounding algorithm specified in the control register.

This instruction sets the stack exception flag if there is no value on the TOS (it will also clear $C_1$ in this case). It sets the precision and denormal exception bits if there was a loss of precision. It sets the invalid operation flag if the value on the TOS is not a valid number. Note that the result on TOS is still a floating-point value; it simply does not have a fractional component.

### 6.5.6.8 The fabs Instruction

fabs computes the absolute value of ST0 by clearing the mantissa sign bit of ST0. It sets the stack exception bit and invalid operation bits if the stack is empty.

Here's an example:

```
// Compute x := sqrt(abs(x));

        fld( x );
        fabs();
        fsqrt();
        fstp( x );
```

### 6.5.6.9 The fchs Instruction

fchs changes the sign of ST0's value by inverting the mantissa sign bit (that is, this is the floating-point negation instruction). It sets the stack exception bit and invalid operation bits if the stack is empty.

Look at this example:

```
// Compute x := -x if x is positive, x := x if x is negative.
// That is, force x to be a negative value.

        fld( x );
        fabs();
        fchs();
        fstp( x );
```

## 6.5.7 Comparison Instructions

The FPU provides several instructions for comparing real values. The fcom, fcomp, and fcompp instructions compare the two values on the top of stack and set the condition codes appropriately. The ftst instruction compares the value on the top of stack with 0.

Generally, most programs test the condition code bits immediately after a comparison. Unfortunately, there are no FPU instructions that test the FPU condition codes. Instead, you use the fstsw instruction to copy the floating-point status register into the AX register; then you can use the sahf instruction to copy the AH register into the 80x86's condition code bits. After doing this,

you can test the standard 80x86 flags to check for some condition. This tec‑
nique copies $C_0$ into the carry flag, $C_2$ into the parity flag, and $C_3$ into the ze‑
flag. The sahf instruction does not copy $C_1$ into any of the 80x86's flag bits

Because the sahf instruction does not copy any FPU status bits into the
sign or overflow flags, you cannot use signed comparison instructions. Instea‑
use unsigned operations (e.g., seta, setb) when testing the results of a floatin‑
point comparison. *Yes, these instructions normally test unsigned values, and
floating-point numbers are signed values.* However, use the unsigned operatior
anyway; the fstsw and sahf instructions set the 80x86 flags register as thoug
you had compared unsigned values with the cmp instruction.

The Pentium II and (upward) compatible processors provide an extra s‑
of floating-point comparison instructions that directly affect the 80x86 con‑
tion code flags. These instructions circumvent having to use fstsw and sahf
to copy the FPU status into the 80x86 condition codes. These instructions
include fcomi and fcomip. You use them just like the fcom and fcomp instruc‑
tions, except, of course, you do not have to manually copy the status bits to
the FLAGS register.

### 6.5.7.1 The fcom, fcomp, and fcompp Instructions

The fcom, fcomp, and fcompp instructions compare ST0 to the specified operan‑
and set the corresponding FPU condition code bits based on the result of th‑
comparison. The legal forms for these instructions are:

```
fcom()
fcomp()
fcompp()

fcom( sti )
fcomp( sti )

fcom( mem_32_64 )
fcomp( mem_32_64 )
fcom( real_constant )
fcomp( real_constant )
```

With no operands, fcom, fcomp, and fcompp compare ST0 against ST1 an‑
set the FPU flags accordingly. In addition, fcomp pops ST0 off the stack and
fcompp pops both ST0 and ST1 off the stack.

With a single-register operand, fcom and fcomp compare ST0 against the
specified register. fcomp also pops ST0 after the comparison.

With a 32- or 64-bit memory operand, the fcom and fcomp instructions
convert the memory variable to an 80-bit extended-precision value and the‑
compare ST0 against this value, setting the condition code bits accordingly
fcomp also pops ST0 after the comparison.

These instructions set $C_2$ (which winds up in the parity flag) if the two
operands are not comparable (e.g., NaN). If it is possible for an illegal floatin‑
point value to wind up in a comparison, you should check the parity flag fo‑
an error before checking the desired condition (e.g., using HLA's @p and @n‑
conditions, or by using the setp/setnp instructions).

These instructions set the stack fault bit if there aren't two items on the top of the register stack. They set the denormalized exception bit if either or both operands are denormalized. They set the invalid operation flag if either or both operands are quiet NaNs. These instructions always clear the $C_1$ condition code.

Note that the instructions that have real constants as operands aren't true FPU instructions. These are extensions provided by HLA. When HLA encounters such an instruction, it creates a real64 read-only variable in the constants segment and initializes this variable with the specified constant. Then HLA translates the instruction to one that specifies a real64 memory operand.

**NOTE** *Because of the precision differences (64 bits versus 80 bits), if you use a constant operand in a floating-point instruction you may not get results that are as precise as you would expect.*

Let's look at an example of a floating-point comparison:

```
fcompp();
fstsw( ax );
sahf();
setb( al );    // al = true if st1 < st0.
        .
        .
        .
```

Note that you cannot compare floating-point values in an HLA runtime boolean expression (e.g., within an if statement). You may, however, test the conditions in such statements after a floating-point comparison like the sequence above. For example:

```
fcompp();
fstsw( ax );
sahf();
if( @b ) then

        << Code that executes if st1 < st0 >>

endif;
```

### 6.5.7.2 The fcomi and fcomip Instructions

The fcomi and fcomip instructions compare ST0 to the specified operand and set the corresponding EFLAG condition code bits based on the result of the comparison. You use these instructions in a similar manner to fcom and fcomp except you can test the CPU's flag bits directly after the execution of these instructions without first moving the FPU status bits into the EFLAGS register. The legal forms for these instructions are as follows:

```
fcomi()
fcomip()
```

```
fcomi( sti )
fcomip( sti )

fcomi( mem_32_64 )
fcomip( mem_32_64 )
fcomi( real_constant )
fcomip( real_constant )
```

### 6.5.7.3 The ftst Instruction

The ftst instruction compares the value in ST0 against 0.0. It behaves just lik the fcom instruction would if ST1 contained 0.0. Note that this instruction does not differentiate −0.0 from +0.0. If the value in ST0 is either of these values, ftst will set $C_3$ to denote equality. This instruction does *not* pop ST( off the stack.

Here's an example:

```
ftst();
fstsw( ax );
sahf();
sete( al );                          // Set al to 1 if TOS = 0.0
```

## 6.5.8 Constant Instructions

The FPU provides several instructions that let you load commonly used cor stants onto the FPU's register stack. These instructions set the stack fault, invalid operation, and $C_1$ flags if a stack overflow occurs; they do not otherwise affect the FPU flags. The specific instructions in this category include th following:

```
fldz()          // Pushes +0.0.
fld1()          // Pushes +1.0.
fldpi()         // Pushes pi.
fldl2t()        // Pushes log2(10).
fldl2e()        // Pushes log2(e).
fldlg2()        // Pushes log10(2).
fldln2()        // Pushes ln(2).
```

## 6.5.9 Transcendental Instructions

The FPU provides eight transcendental (logarithmic and trigonometric) instructions to compute sine, cosine, partial tangent, partial arctangent, $2x -$ $y * \log_2(x)$, and $y * \log_2(x + 1)$. Using various algebraic identities, it is easy t compute most of the other common transcendental functions using these instructions.

### 6.5.9.1 The f2xm1 Instruction

f2xm1 computes $2^{ST0} - 1$. The value in ST0 must be in the range −1.0..ST0..+1.0 If ST0 is out of range, f2xm1 generates an undefined result but raises no excep tions. The computed value replaces the value in ST0.

Here's an example computing $10^x$ using the identity $10^x = 2^{x*\log2(10)}$. This is only useful for a small range of $x$ that doesn't put ST0 outside of the previously mentioned valid range.

```
fld( x );
fldl2t();
fmul();
f2xm1();
fld1();
fadd();
```

Note that f2xm1 computes $2x - 1$, which is why the code above adds 1.0 to the result at the end of the computation.

### 6.5.9.2 The fsin, fcos, and fsincos Instructions

These instructions pop the value off the top of the register stack and compute the sine, cosine, or both and push the result(s) back onto the stack. The fsincos instruction pushes the sine followed by the cosine of the original operand; hence it leaves cos(ST0) in ST0 and sin(ST0) in ST1.

These instructions assume ST0 specifies an angle in radians and this angle must be in the range $-2^{63} <$ ST0 $< +2^{63}$. If the original operand is out of range, these instructions set the $C_2$ flag and leave ST0 unchanged. You can use the fprem1 instruction, with a divisor of $2\pi$, to reduce the operand to a reasonable range.

These instructions set the stack fault/$C_1$, precision, underflow, denormalized, and invalid operation flags according to the result of the computation.

### 6.5.9.3 The fptan Instruction

fptan computes the tangent of ST0 and pushes this value, and then it pushes 1.0 onto the stack. Like the fsin and fcos instructions, the value of ST0 must be in radians and in the range $-2^{63} <$ ST0 $< +2^{63}$. If the value is outside this range, fptan sets $C_2$ to indicate that the conversion did not take place. As with the fsin, fcos, and fsincos instructions, you can use the fprem1 instruction to reduce this operand to a reasonable range using a divisor of $2\pi$.

If the argument is invalid (i.e., zero or $\pi$ radians, which causes a division by 0), the result is undefined and this instruction raises no exceptions. fptan will set the stack fault, precision, underflow, denormal, invalid operation, $C_2$, and $C_1$ bits as required by the operation.

### 6.5.9.4 The fpatan Instruction

This instruction expects two values on the top of stack. It pops them and computes ST0 = $\tan^{-1}$(ST1/ST0).

The resulting value is the arctangent of the ratio on the stack expressed in radians. If you have a value you wish to compute the tangent of, use fld1 to create the appropriate ratio and then execute the fpatan instruction.

This instruction affects the stack fault/$C_1$, precision, underflow, denormal, and invalid operation bits if a problem occurs during the computation. It sets the $C_1$ condition code bit if it has to round the result.

### 6.5.9.5  The fyl2x Instruction

This instruction expects two operands on the FPU stack: y is found in ST1 and x is found in ST0. This function computes ST0 = ST1 * $\log_2$(ST0).

This instruction has no operands (to the instruction itself). The instruction uses the following syntax:

```
fyl2x();
```

Note that this instruction computes the base-2 logarithm. Of course, it a trivial matter to compute the log of any other base by multiplying by the appropriate constant.

### 6.5.9.6  The fyl2xp1 Instruction

This instruction expects two operands on the FPU stack: y is found in ST1 and x is found in ST0. This function computes ST0 = ST1 * $\log_2$(ST0 + 1.0).

The syntax for this instruction is:

```
fyl2xp1();
```

Otherwise, the instruction is identical to fyl2x.

## 6.5.10  Miscellaneous Instructions

The FPU includes several additional instructions that control the FPU, synchronize operations, and let you test or set various status bits. These instructions include finit/fninit, fldcw, fstcw, fclex/fnclex, and fstsw.

### 6.5.10.1  The finit and fninit Instructions

The finit instruction initializes the FPU for proper operation. Your application should execute this instruction before executing any other FPU instruction. This instruction initializes the control register to $37F, the status register to 0 and the tag word to $FFFF. The other registers are unaffected.

Here are some examples:

```
finit();
fninit();
```

The difference between finit and fninit is that finit first checks for any pending floating-point exceptions before initializing the FPU; fninit does not.

### 6.5.10.2  The fldcw and fstcw Instructions

The fldcw and fstcw instructions require a single 16-bit memory operand:

```
fldcw( mem16 );
fstcw( mem16 );
```

These two instructions load the control register from a memory location (`fldcw`) or store the control word to a 16-bit memory location (`fstcw`).

When using the `fldcw` instruction to turn on one of the exceptions, if the corresponding exception flag is set when you enable that exception, the FPU will generate an immediate interrupt before the CPU executes the next instruction. Therefore, you should use the `fclex` instruction to clear any pending interrupts before changing the FPU exception enable bits.

### 6.5.10.3  The fclex and fnclex Instructions

The `fclex` and `fnclex` instructions clear all exception bits, the stack fault bit, and the busy flag in the FPU status register.

Here are some examples:

```
fclex();
fnclex();
```

The difference between these instructions is the same as between `finit` and `fninit`.

### 6.5.10.4  The fstsw and fnstsw Instructions

These instructions store the FPU status register into a 16-bit memory location or the AX register.

```
fstsw( ax );
fnstsw( ax );
fstsw( mem16 );
fnstsw( mem16 );
```

These instructions are unusual in the sense that they can copy an FPU value into one of the 80x86 general-purpose registers (specifically, AX). Of course, the whole purpose behind allowing the transfer of the status register into AX is to allow the CPU to easily test the condition code register with the `sahf` instruction. The difference between `fstsw` and `fnstsw` is the same as for `fclex` and `fnclex`.

## 6.5.11  Integer Operations

The FPU provides special instructions that combine integer-to-extended-precision conversion with various arithmetic and comparison operations. These instructions are the following:

```
fiadd( int_16_32 );
fisub( int_16_32 );
fisubr( int_16_32 );
fimul( int_16_32 );
fidiv( int_16_32 );
fidivr( int_16_32 );
```

```
ficom( int_16_32 );
ficomp( int_16_32 );
```

These instructions convert their 16- or 32-bit integer operands to an 80-[...]
extended-precision floating-point value and then use this value as the sour[...]
operand for the specified operation. These instructions use ST0 as the des[...]
nation operand.

## 6.6 Converting Floating-Point Expressions to Assembly Language

Because the FPU register organization is different than the 80x86 integer r[...]
ister set, translating arithmetic expressions involving floating-point operan[...]
is a little different than the techniques for translating integer expressions.
Therefore, it makes sense to spend some time discussing how to manually
translate floating-point expressions into assembly language.

In one respect, it's actually easier to translate floating-point expression[...]
into assembly language. The stack architecture of the Intel FPU eases the
translation of arithmetic expressions into assembly language. If you've eve[...]
used a Hewlett-Packard calculator, you'll be right at home on the FPU becaus[...]
like the HP calculator, the FPU uses *postfix notation* (also called *Reverse Poli[...]
notation*, or *RPN*), for arithmetic operations. Once you get used to using po[...]
fix notation, it's actually a bit more convenient for translating expression[...]
because you don't have to worry about allocating temporary variables—the[...]
always wind up on the FPU stack.

Postfix notation, as opposed to standard *infix notation*, places the operands before the operator. The following examples give some simple exampl[...]
of infix notation and the corresponding postfix notation:

| infix notation | postfix notation |
|----------------|------------------|
| 5 + 6          | 5  6  +          |
| 7 - 2          | 7  2  -          |
| x * y          | x  y  *          |
| a / b          | a  b  /          |

A postfix expression like 5 6 + says, "push 5 onto the stack, push 6 ont[...]
the stack, and then pop the value off the top of stack (6) and add it to the ne[...]
top of stack." Sound familiar? This is exactly what the fld and fadd instructio[...]
do. In fact, you can calculate this using the following code:

```
fld( 5.0 );
fld( 6.0 );
fadd();                        // 11.0 is now on the top of the FPU stack.
```

As you can see, postfix is a convenient notation because it's very easy to
translate this code into FPU instructions.

One advantage to postfix notation is that it doesn't require any parentheses. The following examples demonstrate some slightly more complex infix-to-postfix conversions:

| infix notation | postfix notation |
| --- | --- |
| (x + y) * 2 | x  y + 2 * |
| x * 2 - (a + b) | x 2 * a b + - |
| (a + b) * (c + d) | a b + c d + * |

The postfix expression x y + 2 * says, "Push x, then push y; next, add those values on the stack (producing x + y on the stack). Next, push 2 and then multiply the two values (2 and x + y) on the stack to produce two times the quantity x + y." Once again, we can translate these postfix expressions directly into assembly language. The following code demonstrates the conversion for each of the above expressions:

```
//        x y + 2 *

        fld( x );
        fld( y );
        fadd();
        fld( 2.0 );
        fmul();

//        x 2 * a b + -

        fld( x );
        fld( 2.0 );
        fmul();
        fld( a );
        fld( b );
        fadd();
        fsub();

//        a b + c d + *

        fld( a );
        fld( b );
        fadd();
        fld( c );
        fld( d );
        fadd();
        fmul();
```

### 6.6.1  Converting Arithmetic Expressions to Postfix Notation

Because the process of translating arithmetic expressions into assembly language involves postfix notation (RPN), converting arithmetic expressions into postfix notation seems like a good place to begin our discussion of floating-point expression conversion. This section will concentrate on postfix conversion.

For simple expressions, those involving two operands and a single expression, the translation is trivial. Simply move the operator from the infix position to the postfix position (that is, move the operator from between the operands to after the second operand). For example, 5 + 6 becomes 5 6 Other than separating your operands so you don't confuse them (i.e., is it and 6 or 56?), converting simple infix expressions into postfix notation is straightforward.

For complex expressions, the idea is to convert the simple subexpressio into postfix notation and then treat each converted subexpression as a sing operand in the remaining expression. The following discussion surrounds completed conversions with square brackets so it is easy to see which text needs to be treated as a single operand in the conversion.

As for integer expression conversion, the best place to start is in the innermost parenthetical subexpression and then work your way outward co sidering precedence, associativity, and other parenthetical subexpressions. a concrete working example, consider the following expression:

```
x = ((y - z) * a) - ( a + b * c ) / 3.14159
```

A possible first translation is to convert the subexpression (y - z) into postfix notation:

```
x = ([y z -] * a) - ( a + b * c ) / 3.14159
```

Square brackets surround the converted postfix code just to separate from the infix code. These exist only to make the partial translations mor readable. Remember, for the purposes of conversion we will treat the tex inside the square brackets as a single operand. Therefore, you would trea [y z -] as though it were a single variable name or constant.

The next step is to translate the subexpression ([y z -] * a ) into postfi form. This yields the following:

```
x = [y z - a *] - ( a + b * c ) / 3.14159
```

Next, we work on the parenthetical expression ( a + b * c ). Because multiplication has higher precedence than addition, we convert b * c first:

```
x = [y z - a *] - ( a + [b c *]) / 3.14159
```

After converting b * c we finish the parenthetical expression:

```
x = [y z - a *] - [a b c * +] / 3.14159
```

This leaves only two infix operators: subtraction and division. Because division has the higher precedence, we'll convert that first:

```
x = [y z - a *] - [a b c * + 3.14159 /]
```

Finally, we convert the entire expression into postfix notation by dealing with the last infix operation, subtraction:

```
x = [y z - a *] [a b c * + 3.14159 /] -
```

Removing the square brackets to give us true postfix notation yields the following postfix expression:

```
x = y z - a * a b c * + 3.14159 / -
```

The following steps demonstrate another infix-to-postfix conversion for the expression:

```
a = (x * y - z + t) / 2.0
```

1. Work inside the parentheses. Because multiplication has the highest precedence, convert that first:

   ```
   a = ( [x y *] - z + t) / 2.0
   ```

2. Still working inside the parentheses, we note that addition and subtraction have the same precedence, so we rely on associativity to determine what to do next. These operators are left associative, so we must translate the expressions in a left-to-right order. This means translate the subtraction operator first:

   ```
   a = ( [x y * z -] + t) / 2.0
   ```

3. Now translate the addition operator inside the parentheses. Because this finishes the parenthetical operators, we can drop the parentheses:

   ```
   a = [x y * z - t +] / 2.0
   ```

4. Translate the final infix operator (division). This yields the following:

   ```
   a = [x y * z - t + 2.0 / ]
   ```

5. Drop the square brackets and we're done:

   ```
   a = x y * z - t + 2.0 /
   ```

### 6.6.2   Converting Postfix Notation to Assembly Language

Once you've translated an arithmetic expression into postfix notation, finishing the conversion to assembly language is easy. All you have to do is issue an fld instruction whenever you encounter an operand and issue an appropriate

arithmetic instruction when you encounter an operator. This section uses th
completed examples from the previous section to demonstrate how little the
is to this process.

```
x = y z - a * a b c * + 3.14159 / -
```

1.  Convert y to fld(y).
2.  Convert z to fld(z).
3.  Convert - to fsub().
4.  Convert a to fld(a).
5.  Convert * to fmul().
6.  Continuing in a left-to-right fashion, generate the following code for th
    expression:

```
fld( y );
fld( z );
fsub();
fld( a );
fmul();
fld( a );
fld( b );
fld( c );
fmul();
fadd();
fldpi();        // Loads pi (3.14159)
fdiv();
fsub();

fstp( x );      // Store result away into x.
```

Here's the translation for the second example in the previous section:

```
a = x y * z - t + 2.0 /
fld( x );
fld( y );
fmul();
fld( z );
fsub();
fld( t );
fadd();
fld( 2.0 );
fdiv();

fstp( a );      // Store result away into a.
```

As you can see, the translation is fairly simple once you've converted the infix notation to postfix notation. Also note that, unlike integer expression conversion, you don't need any explicit temporaries. It turns out that the FPU stack provides the temporaries for you.[3] For these reasons, conversion of floating-point expressions into assembly language is actually easier than converting integer expressions.

## 6.7  HLA Standard Library Support for Floating-Point Arithmetic

Chapter 2 briefly mentioned the stdin.getf function. What it left out of that discussion is where stdin.getf returns the floating-point value is reads from the standard input. Now that you've seen the floating-point extensions to the 80x86, it's possible to finish the discussion of that standard library function. The stdin.getf function reads a string of characters from the standard input, converts those characters to an 80-bit floating-point number, and leaves the result sitting on the FPU stack (in ST0).

The HLA Standard Library also provides the math.hhf module that includes several mathematical functions that the FPU doesn't directly support as well as support for various functions (like sine and cosine) that the FPU partially supports. Some of the functions that the math.hhf module provides are acos, acot, acsc, asec, asin, cot, csc, sec, $2^x$, $10^x$, $y^x$, $e^x$, log, and ln. Please consult the HLA standard library documentation for more information about these functions and other mathematical functions the HLA standard library supports.

## 6.8  For More Information

The Intel/AMD processor manuals fully describe the operation of each of the integer and floating-point arithmetic instructions, including a detailed description of how these instructions affect the condition code bits and other flags in the EFLAGS and FPU status registers. To write the best possible assembly language code, you need to be intimately familiar with how the arithmetic instructions affect the execution environment, so spending time with the Intel/AMD manuals is a good idea.

The HLA Standard Library provides a large number of floating-point functions for which there are no individual machine instructions. The HLA Standard Library also provides functions like math.sin and math.cos that overcome limitations of the native machine instructions. See the HLA Standard Library reference manual for more details. Also, the HLA Standard Library is available in source code form, so you can look at the implementation of these mathematical functions for more examples of floating-point coding.

---

[3] This assumes, of course, that your calculations aren't so complex that you exceed the eight-element limitation of the FPU stack.

Chapter 8 discusses multiprecision integer arithmetic. See that chapter for details on handling integer operands that are greater than 32 bits in si

The 80x86 SSE instruction set found on later members of the CPU provides support for floating-point arithmetic using the SSE register set. Consu *http://webster.cs.ucr.edu/* or the Intel/AMD documentation for details concern ing the SSE floating-point instruction set.

# 7

## LOW-LEVEL CONTROL STRUCTURES

 This chapter discusses "pure" assembly language control statements. You'll need to master these low-level control structures before you can claim to be an assembly language programmer. By the time you finish this chapter, you should be able to stop using HLA's high-level control statements and synthesize them using low-level 80x86 machine instructions.

The last section of this chapter discusses *hybrid* control structures that combine the features of HLA's high-level control statements with the 80x86 control instructions. These combine the power and efficiency of the low-level control statements with the readability of high-level control statements. Advanced assembly programmers may want to use these hybrid statements to improve their programs' readability without sacrificing efficiency.

## 7.1 Low-Level Control Structures

Until now, most of the control structures you've seen and have used in your programs are similar to the control structures found in high-level languages like Pascal, C++, and Ada. While these control structures make learning assembly language easy, they are not true assembly language statements. Instead, the HLA compiler translates these control structures into a sequence of "pure" machine instructions that achieve the same result as the high-level control structures. This text uses the high-level control structures to allow you to learn assembly language without having to learn everything all at once. Now, however, it's time to put aside these high-level control structures and learn how to write your programs in *real* assembly language, using low-level control structures.

## 7.2 Statement Labels

Assembly language low-level control structures make extensive use of *labels* within your source code. A low-level control structure usually transfers control between two points in your program. You typically specify the destination of such a transfer using a statement label. A statement label consists of a valid (unique) HLA identifier and a colon. For example:

---

```
aLabel:
```

---

Of course, as for procedure, variable, and constant identifiers, you should attempt to choose descriptive and meaningful names for your labels. The example identifier above, aLabel, is hardly descriptive or meaningful.

Statement labels have one important attribute that differentiates them from most other identifiers in HLA: You don't have to declare a label before you use it. This is important, because low-level control structures must often transfer control to some point later in the code; therefore the label may not be defined by the time you reference it.

You can do three things with labels: transfer control to a label via a jump (goto) instruction, call a label via the call instruction, and take the address of a label. There is very little else you can directly do with a label (of course, there is very little else you would want to do with a label, so this is hardly a restriction). The program in Listing 7-1 demonstrates two ways to take the address of a label in your program and print out the address (using the lea instruction and using the & address-of operator):

---

```
program labelDemo;
#include( "stdlib.hhf" );

begin labelDemo;

    lbl1:

        lea( ebx, lbl1 );
        mov( &lbl2, eax );
        stdout.put( "&lbl1=$", ebx, " &lbl2=", eax, nl );
```

```
        lbl2:

end labelDemo;
```

*Listing 7-1: Displaying the address of statement labels in a program*

HLA also allows you to initialize double-word variables with the addresses of statement labels. However, there are some restrictions on labels that appear in the initialization portions of variable declarations. The most important restriction is that you must define the statement label at the same lexical level as the variable declaration. That is, if you reference a statement label in the initializer of a variable declaration appearing in the main program, the statement label must also be in the main program. Conversely, if you take the address of a statement label in a local variable declaration, that symbol must appear in the same procedure as the local variable. Listing 7-2 demonstrates the use of statement labels in variable initialization:

```
program labelArrays;
#include( "stdlib.hhf" );

static
    labels:dword[2] := [ &lbl1, &lbl2 ];

    procedure hasLabels;
    static
        stmtLbls: dword[2] := [ &label1, &label2 ];

    begin hasLabels;

        label1:

            stdout.put
            (
                "stmtLbls[0]= $", stmtLbls[0], nl,
                "stmtLbls[1]= $", stmtLbls[4], nl
            );

        label2:

    end hasLabels;

begin labelArrays;

    hasLabels();
    lbl1:

        stdout.put( "labels[0]= $", labels[0], " labels[1]=", labels[4], nl );

    lbl2:

end labelArrays;
```

*Listing 7-2: Initializing dword variables with the address of statement labels*

Once in a while, you'll need to refer to a label that is not within the current procedure. The need for this is sufficiently rare that this text will not describe all the details. See the HLA documentation for more details should you ever need to do this.

## 7.3 Unconditional Transfer of Control (jmp)

The jmp (jump) instruction unconditionally transfers control to another point in the program. There are three forms of this instruction: a direct jump and two indirect jumps. These instructions take the following forms:

```
jmp label;
jmp( reg32 );
jmp( mem32 );
```

The first instruction is a direct jump above. For direct jumps you normally specify the target address using a statement label. The label appears either on the same line as an executable machine instruction or by itself on a line preceding an executable machine instruction. The direct jump is completely equivalent to a goto statement in a high-level language.[1]

Here's an example:

```
        << statements >>
        jmp laterInPgm;
              .
              .
              .
laterInPgm:
        << statements >>
```

The second form of the jmp instruction given earlier—jmp( reg32 );—is *register indirect* jump instruction. This instruction transfers control to the instruction whose address appears in the specified 32-bit general-purpose register. To use this form of the jmp instruction, you must load a 32-bit register with the address of some machine instruction prior to the execution of the jmp. You could use this instruction to implement a *state machine* by loading a register with the address of some label at various points throughout your program and then use a single indirect jump at a common point to transfer control to one of those labels. The short sample program in Listing 7-3 demonstrates how you could use the jmp in this manner.

```
program regIndJmp;
#include( "stdlib.hhf" );

static
    i:int32;
```

---

[1] Unlike high-level languages, where your instructors usually forbid you to use goto statements, you will find that the use of the jmp instruction in assembly language is essential.

```
begin regIndJmp;

    // Read an integer from the user and set ebx to
    // denote the success or failure of the input.

    try

        stdout.put( "Enter an integer value between 1 and 10: " );
        stdin.get( i );
        mov( i, eax );
        if( eax in 1..10 ) then

            mov( &GoodInput, ebx );

        else

            mov( &valRange, ebx );

        endif;

      exception( ex.ConversionError )

        mov( &convError, ebx );

      exception( ex.ValueOutOfRange )

        mov( &valRange, ebx );

    endtry;

    // Okay, transfer control to the appropriate
    // section of the program that deals with
    // the input.

    jmp( ebx );

    valRange:
        stdout.put( "You entered a value outside the range 1..10" nl );
        jmp Done;

    convError:
        stdout.put( "Your input contained illegal characters" nl );
        jmp Done;

    GoodInput:
        stdout.put( "You entered the value ", i, nl );

    Done:


end regIndJmp;
```

*Listing 7-3: Using register-indirect jmp instructions*

The third form of the jmp instruction given earlier is a memory-indirect jmp. This form of the jmp instruction fetches the double-word value from the memory location and jumps to that address. This is similar to the register-indirect jmp except the address appears in a memory location rather than in register. Listing 7-4 demonstrates a rather trivial use of this form of the jmp instruction.

```
program memIndJmp;
#include( "stdlib.hhf" );

static
    LabelPtr:dword := &stmtLabel;

begin memIndJmp;

    stdout.put( "Before the JMP instruction" nl );
    jmp( LabelPtr );

        stdout.put( "This should not execute" nl );

    stmtLabel:

        stdout.put( "After the LabelPtr label in the program" nl );

end memIndJmp;
```

Listing 7-4: Using memory-indirect jmp instructions

**WARNING**     *Unlike the HLA high-level control structures, the low-level jmp instructions can cause you a lot of trouble. In particular, if you do not initialize a register with the address of a valid instruction and you jump indirectly through that register, the results are undefined (though this will usually cause a general protection fault). Similarly, if you do not initialize a double-word variable with the address of a legal instruction, jumping indirectly through that memory location will probably crash your program.*

## 7.4 The Conditional Jump Instructions

Although the jmp instruction provides transfer of control, it is inconvenient to use when making decisions such as those you'll need to implement statement like if and while. The 80x86's conditional jump instructions handle this task

The conditional jumps test one or more CPU flags to see if they match some particular pattern. If the flag settings match the condition, the conditional jump instruction transfers control to the target location. If the match fails, the CPU ignores the conditional jump and execution continues with the instruction following the conditional jump. Some conditional jump instructions simply test the setting of the sign, carry, overflow, and zero flags. For example, after the execution of a shl instruction, you could test the carry flag to determine if the shl shifted a 1 out of the H.O. bit of its operand. Likewise you could test the zero flag after a test instruction to check if the result was 0. Most of the time, however, you will probably execute a conditional jump after a cmp instruction. The cmp instruction sets the flags so that you can test for less than, greater than, equality, and so on.

The conditional jmp instructions take the following form:

```
jcc label;
```

The cc in jcc indicates that you must substitute some character sequence that specifies the type of condition to test. These are the same characters the setcc instruction uses. For example, js stands for *jump* if the sign flag is set. A typical js instruction is:

```
js ValueIsNegative;
```

In this example, the js instruction transfers control to the ValueIsNegative label if the sign flag is currently set; control falls through to the next instruction following the js instruction if the sign flag is clear.

Unlike the unconditional jmp instruction, the conditional jump instructions do not provide an indirect form. They only allow a branch to a statement label in your program.

**NOTE** *Intel's documentation defines various synonyms or instruction aliases for many conditional jump instructions.*

Tables 7-1, 7-2, and 7-3 list all the aliases for a particular instruction. These tables also list the opposite branches. You'll soon see the purpose of the opposite branches.

**Table 7-1:** jcc Instructions That Test Flags

| Instruction | Description | Condition | Aliases | Opposite |
|---|---|---|---|---|
| jc | Jump if carry | Carry = 1 | jb, jnae | jnc |
| jnc | Jump if no carry | Carry = 0 | jnb, jae | jc |
| jz | Jump if zero | Zero = 1 | je | jnz |
| jnz | Jump if not zero | Zero = 0 | jne | jz |
| js | Jump if sign | Sign = 1 | | jns |
| jns | Jump if no sign | Sign = 0 | | js |
| jo | Jump if overflow | Overflow = 1 | | jno |
| jno | Jump if no overflow | Overflow = 0 | | jo |
| jp | Jump if parity | Parity = 1 | jpe | jnp |
| jpe | Jump if parity even | Parity = 1 | jp | jpo |
| jnp | Jump if no parity | Parity = 0 | jpo | jp |
| jpo | Jump if parity odd | Parity = 0 | jnp | jpe |

**Table 7-2:** jcc Instructions for Unsigned Comparisons

| Instruction | Description | Condition | Aliases | Opposite |
|---|---|---|---|---|
| ja | Jump if above (>) | Carry = 0, Zero = 0 | jnbe | jna |
| jnbe | Jump if not below or equal (not <=) | Carry = 0, Zero = 0 | ja | jbe |
| jae | Jump if above or equal (>=) | Carry = 0 | jnc, jnb | jnae |
| jnb | Jump if not below (not <) | Carry = 0 | jnc, jae | jb |
| jb | Jump if below (<) | Carry = 1 | jc, jnae | jnb |
| jnae | Jump if not above or equal (not >=) | Carry = 1 | jc, jb | jae |
| jbe | Jump if below or equal (<=) | Carry = 1 or Zero = 1 | jna | jnbe |
| jna | Jump if not above (not >) | Carry = 1 or Zero = 1 | jbe | ja |
| je | Jump if equal (=) | Zero = 1 | jz | jne |
| jne | Jump if not equal (¦) | Zero = 0 | jnz | je |

**Table 7-3:** jcc Instructions for Signed Comparisons

| Instruction | Description | Condition | Aliases | Opposite |
|---|---|---|---|---|
| jg | Jump if greater (>) | Sign = Overflow or Zero = 0 | jnle | jng |
| jnle | Jump if not less than or equal (not <=) | Sign = Overflow or Zero = 0 | jg | jle |
| jge | Jump if greater than or equal (>=) | Sign = Overflow | jnl | jge |
| jnl | Jump if not less than (not <) | Sign = Overflow | jge | jl |
| jl | Jump if less than (<) | Sign <> Overflow | jnge | jnl |
| jnge | Jump if not greater or equal (not >=) | Sign <> Overflow | jl | jge |
| jle | Jump if less than or equal (<=) | Sign <> Overflow or Zero = 1 | jng | jnle |
| jng | Jump if not greater than (not >) | Sign <> Overflow or Zero = 1 | jle | jg |
| je | Jump if equal (=) | Zero = 1 | jz | jne |
| jne | Jump if not equal (¦) | Zero = 0 | jnz | je |

One brief comment about the Opposite column is in order. In many instances you will need to be able to generate the opposite of a specific branch instruction (examples appear later in this section). With only two exceptions a very simple rule completely describes how to generate an opposite branch

- If the second letter of the jcc instruction is not an n, insert an n after the j. For example, je becomes jne and jl becomes jnl.

- If the second letter of the jcc instruction is an n, then remove that n from the instruction. For example, jng becomes jg and jne becomes je.

The two exceptions to this rule are jpe (jump if parity is even) and jpo (jump if parity is odd). These exceptions cause few problems because (1) you'll hardly ever need to test the parity flag, and (2) you can use the aliases jp and jnp as synonyms for jpe and jpo. The "N/No N" rule applies to jp and jnp.

Though you *know* that jge is the opposite of jl, get in the habit of using jnl rather than jge as the opposite jump instruction for jl. It's too easy in an important situation to start thinking "greater is the opposite of less" and substitute jg instead. You can avoid this confusion by always using the "N/No N" rule.

The 80x86 conditional jump instructions give you the ability to split program flow into one of two paths depending on some condition. Suppose you want to increment the AX register if BX is equal to CX. You can accomplish this with the following code:

```
            cmp( bx, cx );
            jne SkipStmts;
            inc( ax );
SkipStmts:
```

The trick is to use the *opposite* branch to skip over the instructions you want to execute if the condition is true. Always use the "opposite branch (N/No N)" rule given earlier to select the opposite branch.

You can also use the conditional jump instructions to synthesize loops. For example, the following code sequence reads a sequence of characters from the user and stores each character in successive elements of an array until the user presses the ENTER key (carriage return):

```
            mov( 0, edi );
RdLnLoop:
            stdin.getc();               // Read a character into the al register.
            mov( al, Input[ edi ] );    // Store away the character.
            inc( edi );                 // Move on to the next character.
            cmp( al, stdio.cr );        // See if the user pressed Enter.
            jne RdLnLoop;
```

Like the setcc instructions, the conditional jump instructions come in two basic categories: those that test specific processor flags (e.g., jz, jc, jno) and those that test some condition (less than, greater than, etc.). When testing a condition, the conditional jump instructions almost always follow a cmp instruction. The cmp instruction sets the flags so that you can use a ja, jae, jb, jbe, je, or jne instruction to test for unsigned less than, less than or equal, equal, unequal, greater than, or greater than or equal. Simultaneously, the cmp instruction sets the flags so that you can also do a signed comparison using the jl, jle, je, jne, jg, and jge instructions.

The conditional jump instructions only test the 80x86 flags; they do not affect any of them.

## 7.5 "Medium-Level" Control Structures: jt and jf

HLA provides two special conditional jump instructions: jt (jump if true) and jf (jump if false). These instructions take the following syntax:

```
jt( boolean_expression ) target_label;
jf( boolean_expression ) target_label;
```

The *boolean_expression* is the standard HLA boolean expression allowed by if..endif and other HLA high-level language statements. These instruction evaluate the boolean expression and jump to the specified label if the expre sion evaluates true (jt) or false (jf).

These are not real 80x86 instructions. HLA compiles them into a sequenc of one or more 80x86 machine instructions that achieve the same result. In general, you should not use these two instructions in your main code; they offer few benefits over using an if..endif statement and they are no more readable than the pure assembly language sequences they compile into. HL provides these "medium-level" instructions so that you may create your own high-level control structures using macros (see Chapter 9 and the HLA refe ence manual for more details).

# 7.6 Implementing Common Control Structures in Assembly Language

Because a primary goal of this chapter is to teach you how to use the low-leve machine instructions to implement decisions, loops, and other control cor structs, it would be wise to show you how to implement these high-level statements using pure assembly language. The following sections provide this information.

# 7.7 Introduction to Decisions

In its most basic form, a *decision* is some sort of branch within the code that switches between two possible execution paths based on some condition. Normally (though not always), conditional instruction sequences are imple mented with the conditional jump instructions. Conditional instructions correspond to the if..then..endif statement in HLA:

```
if( expression ) then
    << statements >>
endif;
```

Assembly language, as usual, offers much more flexibility when dealing with conditional statements. Consider the following C/C++ statement:

```
if( (( x < y ) && ( z > t )) || ( a != b ) )
    stmt1;
```

A "brute force" approach to converting this statement into assembly language might produce the following:

```
mov( x, eax );
cmp( eax, y );
setl( bl );        // Store x<y in bl.
mov( z, eax );
cmp( eax, t );
```

```
        setg( bh );       // Store z>t in bh.
        and( bh, bl );     // Put (x<y) && (z>t) into bl.
        mov( a, eax );
        cmp( eax, b );
        setne( bh );       // Store a != b into bh.
        or( bh, bl );      // Put (x<y) && (z>t) || (a!=b) into bl
        je SkipStmt1;      // Branch if result is false.

    << Code for Stmt1 goes here. >>

SkipStmt1:
```

As you can see, it takes a considerable number of conditional statements just to process the expression in the example above. This roughly corresponds to the (equivalent) C/C++ statements:

```
        bl = x < y;
        bh = z > t;
        bl = bl && bh;
        bh = a != b;
        bl = bl || bh;
        if( bl )
            << Stmt1 >>;
```

Now compare this with the following "improved" code:

```
        mov( a, eax );
        cmp( eax, b );
        jne DoStmt;
        mov( x, eax );
        cmp( eax, y );
        jnl SkipStmt;
        mov( z, eax );
        cmp( eax, t );
        jng SkipStmt;
DoStmt:
        << Place code for Stmt1 here. >>
SkipStmt:
```

Two things should be apparent from the code sequences above: First, a single conditional statement in C/C++ (or some other HLL) may require several conditional jumps in assembly language; second, organization of complex expressions in a conditional sequence can affect the efficiency of the code. Therefore, you should exercise care when dealing with conditional sequences in assembly language.

Conditional statements may be broken down into three basic categories: if statements, switch/case statements, and indirect jumps. The following sections describe these program structures, how to use them, and how to write them in assembly language.

## 7.7.1 if..then..else Sequences

The most common conditional statements are the if..then..endif and if..then..else..endif statements. These two statements take the form shown in Figure 7-1.

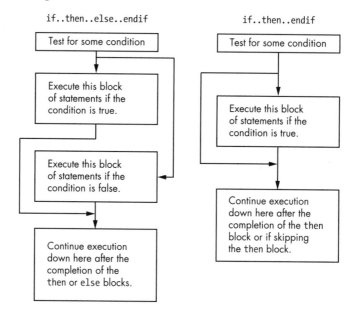

Figure 7-1: *if..then..else..endif and if..then..endif statement flow*

The if..then..endif statement is just a special case of the if..then.. else..endif statement (with an empty else block). Therefore, we'll consider only the more general if..then..else..endif form. The basic implementation of an if..then..else..endif statement in 80x86 assembly language looks something like this:

```
<< Sequence of statements to test some condition >>
        jcc ElseCode;
<< Sequence of statements corresponding to the THEN block >>

        jmp EndOfIf;

ElseCode:
<< Sequence of statements corresponding to the ELSE block >>

EndOfIf:
```

Note that *jcc* represents some conditional jump instruction. For example, to convert the C/C++ statement

```
if( a == b )
        c = d;
else
        b = b + 1;
```

to assembly language, you could use the following 80x86 code:

```
        mov( a, eax );
        cmp( eax, b );
        jne ElsePart;
        mov( d, c );
        jmp EndOfIf;

ElseBlk:
        inc( b );

EndOfIf:
```

For simple expressions like ( a == b ) generating the proper code for an if..then..else..endif statement is almost trivial. Should the expression become more complex, the code complexity increases as well. Consider the following C/C++ if statement presented earlier:

```
if( (( x > y ) && ( z < t )) || ( a != b ) )
    c = d;
```

When processing complex if statements such as this one, you'll find the conversion task easier if you break the if statement into a sequence of three different if statements as follows:

```
if( a != b ) c = d;
else if( x > y)
    if( z < t )
        c = d;
```

This conversion comes from the following C/C++ equivalents:

```
if( expr1 && expr2 ) stmt;
```

is equivalent to

```
if( expr1 ) if( expr2 ) stmt;
```

and

```
if( expr1 || expr2 ) stmt;
```

is equivalent to

```
if( expr1 ) stmt;
else if( expr2 ) stmt;
```

In assembly language, the former if statement becomes

```
// if( (( x > y ) && ( z < t )) || ( a != b ) )
//       c = d;

        mov( a, eax );
        cmp( eax, b );
        jne DoIF;
        mov( x, eax );
        cmp( eax, y );
        jng EndOfIF;
        mov( z, eax );
        cmp( eax, t );
        jnl EndOfIf;
DoIf:
        mov( d, eax );
        mov( eax, c );
EndOfIf:
```

As you can see, testing a condition can easily become more complex than the statements appearing in the else and then blocks. Although it seems somewhat paradoxical that it may take more effort to test a condition than to act on the results of that condition, it happens all the time. Therefore, you should be prepared to accept this.

Probably the biggest problem with complex conditional statements in assembly language is trying to figure out what you've done after you've written the code. A big advantage high-level languages offer over assembly language is that expressions are much easier to read and comprehend. The high-level version is (more) self-documenting, whereas assembly language tends to hide the true nature of the code. Therefore, well-written comments are an essential ingredient to assembly language implementations of if..then..else..endif statements. An elegant implementation of the example above is as follows:

```
// if ((x > y) && (z < t)) or (a != b)   c = d;
// Implemented as:
// if (a != b) then goto DoIf;

        mov( a, eax );
        cmp( eax, b );
        jne DoIf;

// if not (x > t) then goto EndOfIf;

        mov( x, eax );
        cmp( eax, y );
        jng EndOfIf;

// if not (z < t) then goto EndOfIf;
```

```
            mov( z, eax );
            cmp( eax, t );
            jnl EndOfIf;

// then block:

DoIf:
            mov( d, eax );
            mov( eax, c );

// End of if statement

EndOfIf:
```

Admittedly, this appears to be going overboard for such a simple example. The following would probably suffice:

```
// if ( (( x > y ) && ( z < t )) || ( a != b ) )  c = d;
// Test the boolean expression:

            mov( a, eax );
            cmp( eax, b );
            jne DoIf;
            mov( x, eax );
            cmp( eax, y );
            jng EndOfIf;
            mov( z, eax );
            cmp( eax, t );
            jnl EndOfIf;

// then block:

DoIf:
            mov( d, eax );
            mov( eax, c );

// End of if statement

EndOfIf:
```

However, as your if statements become complex, the density (and quality) of your comments become more and more important.

### 7.7.2  Translating HLA if Statements into Pure Assembly Language

Translating HLA if statements into pure assembly language is very easy. The boolean expressions that the HLA if statement supports were specifically chosen to expand into a few simple machine instructions. The following paragraphs discuss the conversion of each supported boolean expression into pure machine code.

### if( *flag_specification* ) then *stmts* endif;

This form is, perhaps, the easiest HLA if statement to convert. To execute the code immediately following the then keyword if a particular flag is set (or clear), all you need do is skip over the code if the flag is clear (set). This requires only a single conditional jump instruction for implementation, as the following examples demonstrate:

```
// if( @c ) then inc( eax );  endif;

        jnc SkipTheInc;

            inc( eax );

        SkipTheInc:

// if( @ns ) then neg( eax ); endif;

        js SkipTheNeg;

            neg( eax );

        SkipTheNeg:
```

### if( *register* ) then *stmts* endif;

This form uses the test instruction to check the specified register for 0. If the register contains 0 (false), then the program jumps around the statements after the then clause with a jz instruction. Converting this statement to assembly language requires a test instruction and a jz instruction, as the following examples demonstrate:

```
// if( eax ) then mov( false, eax );  endif;

        test( eax, eax );
        jz DontSetFalse;

            mov( false, eax );

        DontSetFalse:

// if( al ) then mov( bl, cl );  endif;

        test( al, al );
        jz noMove;

            mov( bl, cl );

        noMove:
```

### if( !*register* ) then *stmts* endif;

This form of the if statement uses the test instruction to check the specified register to see if it is 0. If the register is not 0 (true), then the program jumps around the statements after the then clause with a jnz instruction. Converting this statement to assembly language requires a test instruction and a jnz instruction in a manner identical to the previous examples.

### if( *boolean_variable* ) then *stmts* endif;

This form of the if statement compares the boolean variable against 0 (false) and branches around the statements if the variable contains false. HLA implements this statement by using the cmp instruction to compare the boolean variable to 0, and then it uses a jz (je) instruction to jump around the statements if the variable is false. The following example demonstrates the conversion:

```
// if( bool ) then mov( 0, al );  endif;

        cmp( bool, false );
        je SkipZeroAL;

            mov( 0, al );

        SkipZeroAL:
```

### if( !*boolean_variable* ) then *stmts* endif;

This form of the if statement compares the boolean variable against 0 (false) and branches around the statements if the variable contains true (the opposite condition of the previous example). HLA implements this statement by using the cmp instruction to compare the boolean variable to 0 and then it uses a jnz (jne) instruction to jump around the statements if the variable contains true. The following example demonstrates the conversion:

```
// if( !bool ) then mov( 0, al );  endif;

        cmp( bool, false );
        jne SkipZeroAL;

            mov( 0, al );

        SkipZeroAL:
```

### if( *mem_reg relop mem_reg_const* ) then *stmts* endif;

HLA translates this form of the if statement into a cmp instruction and a conditional jump that skips over the statements on the opposite condition specified by the relop operator. Table 7-4 lists the correspondence between operators and conditional jump instructions.

**Table 7-4:** `if` Statement Conditional Jump Instructions

| Relational operation | Conditional jump instruction if both operands are unsigned | Conditional jump instruction if either operand is signed |
|---|---|---|
| = or == | jne | jne |
| <> or != | je | je |
| < | jnb | jnl |
| <= | jnbe | jnle |
| > | jna | jng |
| >= | jnae | jnge |

Here are a few examples of `if` statements translated into pure assembly language that use expressions involving relational operators:

```
// if( al == ch ) then inc( cl ); endif;

        cmp( al, ch );
        jne SkipIncCL;

            inc( cl );

        SkipIncCL:

// if( ch >= 'a' ) then and( $5f, ch ); endif;

        cmp( ch, 'a' );
        jnae NotLowerCase

            and( $5f, ch );

        NotLowerCase:

// if( (type int32 eax ) < -5 ) then mov( -5, eax );  endif;

        cmp( eax, -5 );
        jnl DontClipEAX;

            mov( -5, eax );

        DontClipEAX:

// if( si <> di ) then inc( si );  endif;

        cmp( si, di );
        je DontIncSI;

            inc( si );

        DontIncSI:
```

## if( *reg/mem* in *LowConst..HiConst* ) then *stmts* endif;

HLA translates this if statement into a pair of cmp instructions and a pair of conditional jump instructions. It compares the register or memory location against the lower-valued constant and jumps if less than (signed) or below (unsigned) past the statements after the then clause. If the register or memory location's value is greater than or equal to *LowConst*, the code falls through to the second cmp and conditional jump pair that compares the register or memory location against the higher constant. If the value is greater than (above) this constant, a conditional jump instruction skips the statements in the then clause.

Here's an example:

```
// if( eax in 1000..125_000 ) then sub( 1000, eax );  endif;

        cmp( eax, 1000 );
        jb DontSub1000;
        cmp( eax, 125_000 );
        ja DontSub1000;

            sub( 1000, eax );

        DontSub1000:

// if( i32 in -5..5 ) then add( 5, i32 ); endif;

        cmp( i32, -5 );
        jl NoAdd5;
        cmp( i32, 5 );
        jg NoAdd5;

            add(5, i32 );

        NoAdd5:
```

## if( *reg/mem* not in *LowConst..HiConst* ) then *stmts* endif;

This form of the HLA if statement tests a register or memory location to see if its value is outside a specified range. The implementation is very similar to the previous code except you branch to the then clause if the value is less than the *LowConst* value or greater than the *HiConst* value, and you branch over the code in the then clause if the value is within the range specified by the two constants. The following examples demonstrate how to do this conversion:

```
// if( eax not in 1000..125_000 ) then add( 1000, eax );  endif;

        cmp( eax, 1000 );
        jb Add1000;
        cmp( eax, 125_000 );
        jbe SkipAdd1000;
```

```
                    Add1000:
                    add( 1000, eax );

            SkipAdd1000:

// if( i32 not in -5..5 ) then mov( 0, i32 );  endif;

                    cmp( i32, -5 );
                    jl Zeroi32;
                    cmp( i32, 5 );
                    jle SkipZero;

                        Zeroi32:
                        mov( 0, i32 );

                SkipZero:
```

## 7.7.3  Implementing Complex if Statements Using Complete Boolean Evaluation

Many boolean expressions involve conjunction (and) or disjunction (or) operations. This section describes how to convert boolean expressions into assembly language. There are two different ways to convert complex boolean expressions involving conjunction and disjunction into assembly language: using complete boolean evaluation or using short-circuit boolean evaluation. This section discusses complete boolean evaluation. The next section discusses short-circuit boolean evaluation.

Conversion via complete boolean evaluation is almost identical to converting arithmetic expressions into assembly language. Indeed, the previous chapter on arithmetic covers this conversion process. About the only thing worth noting about that process is that you do not need to store the result in some variable; once the evaluation of the expression is complete, you check to see if you have a false (0) or true (1, or nonzero) result to take whatever action the boolean expression dictates. As you can see in the examples in the preceding sections, you can often use the fact that the last logical instruction (and/or) sets the zero flag if the result is false and clears the zero flag if the result is true. This lets you avoid explicitly testing for the result. Consider the following if statement and its conversion to assembly language using complete boolean evaluation:

```
//      if( (( x < y ) && ( z > t )) || ( a != b ) )
//          << Stmt1 >>;

        mov( x, eax );
        cmp( eax, y );
        setl( bl );       // Store x<y in bl.
        mov( z, eax );
        cmp( eax, t );
        setg( bh );       // Store z>t in bh.
        and( bh, bl );    // Put (x<y) && (z>t) into bl.
```

```
        mov( a, eax );
        cmp( eax, b );
        setne( bh );    // Store a != b into bh.
        or( bh, bl );   // Put (x<y) && (z>t) || (a != b) into bl.
        je SkipStmt1;   // Branch if result is false.

    << Code for Stmt1 goes here. >>

SkipStmt1:
```

This code computes a boolean result in the BL register and then, at the end of the computation, tests this value to see if it contains true or false. If the result is false, this sequence skips over the code associated with Stmt1. The important thing to note in this example is that the program will execute each and every instruction that computes this boolean result (up to the je instruction).

### 7.7.4   Short-Circuit Boolean Evaluation

If you are willing to expend a little more effort, you can usually convert a boolean expression to a much shorter and faster sequence of assembly language instructions using *short-circuit boolean evaluation*. Short-circuit boolean evaluation attempts to determine whether an expression is true or false by executing only some of the instructions that would compute the complete expression. For this reason, plus the fact that short-circuit boolean evaluation doesn't require the use of any temporary registers, HLA uses short-circuit evaluation when translating complex boolean expressions into assembly language.

Consider the expression a && b. Once we determine that a is false, there is no need to evaluate b because there is no way the expression can be true. If a and b represent subexpressions rather than simple variables, the savings possible with short-circuit boolean evaluation are apparent. As a concrete example, consider the subexpression ((x<y) && (z>t)) from the previous section. Once you determine that x is not less than y, there is no need to check to see if z is greater than t because the expression will be false regardless of z and t's values. The following code fragment shows how you can implement short-circuit boolean evaluation for this expression:

```
// if( (x<y) && (z>t) ) then ...

        mov( x, eax );
        cmp( eax, y );
        jnl TestFails;
        mov( z, eax );
        cmp( eax, t );
        jng TestFails;

            << Code for THEN clause of IF statement >>

        TestFails:
```

Notice how the code skips any further testing once it determines that x is not less than y. Of course, if x is less than y, then the program has to test z to see if it is greater than t; if not, the program skips over the then clause. Only if the program satisfies both conditions does the code fall through to the then clause.

For the logical or operation the technique is similar. If the first subexpression evaluates to true, then there is no need to test the second operand. Whatever the second operand's value is at that point, the full expression still evaluates to true. The following example demonstrates the use of short-circuit evaluation with disjunction (or):

```
// if( ch < 'A' || ch > 'Z' )
//     then stdout.put( "Not an uppercase char" );
// endif;

        cmp( ch, 'A' );
        jb ItsNotUC
        cmp( ch, 'Z' );
        jna ItWasUC;

            ItsNotUC:
            stdout.put( "Not an uppercase char" );

        ItWasUC:
```

Because the conjunction and disjunction operators are commutative, you can evaluate the left or right operand first if it is more convenient to do so.[2] As one last example in this section, consider the full boolean expression from the previous section:

```
// if( (( x < y ) && ( z > t )) || ( a != b ) ) << Stmt1 >>;

        mov( a, eax );
        cmp( eax, b );
        jne DoStmt1;
        mov( x, eax );
        cmp( eax, y );
        jnl SkipStmt1;
        mov( z, eax );
        cmp( eax, t );
jng SkipStmt1;

            DoStmt1:
            << Code for Stmt1 goes here. >>

        SkipStmt1:
```

---

[2] However, be aware of the fact that some expressions depend on the leftmost subexpression evaluating one way in order for the rightmost subexpression to be valid; for example, a common test in C/C++ is if( x != NULL && x->y )...

Notice how the code in this example chose to evaluate a != b first and the remaining subexpression last. This is a common technique assembly language programmers use to write better code.

## 7.7.5  Short-Circuit vs. Complete Boolean Evaluation

When using complete boolean evaluation, every statement in the sequence for that expression will execute; short-circuit boolean evaluation, on the other hand, may not require the execution of every statement associated with the boolean expression. As you've seen in the previous two sections, code based on short-circuit evaluation is usually shorter and faster. So it would seem that short-circuit evaluation is the technique of choice when converting complex boolean expressions to assembly language.

Sometimes, unfortunately, short-circuit boolean evaluation may not produce the correct result. In the presence of *side effects* in an expression, short-circuit boolean evaluation will produce a different result than complete boolean evaluation. Consider the following C/C++ example:

```
if( ( x == y ) && ( ++z != 0 )) << Stmt >>;
```

Using complete boolean evaluation, you might generate the following code:

```
        mov( x, eax );      // See if x == y.
        cmp( eax, y );
        sete( bl );
        inc( z );           // ++z
        cmp( z, 0 );        // See if incremented z is 0.
        setne( bh );
        and( bh, bl );      // Test x == y && ++z != 0.
        jz SkipStmt;

        << Code for Stmt goes here. >>

SkipStmt:
```

Using short-circuit boolean evaluation, you might generate the following code:

```
        mov( x, eax );      // See if x == y.
        cmp( eax, y );
        jne SkipStmt;
        inc( z );           // ++z
        cmp( z, 0 );        // See if incremented z is 0.
        je SkipStmt;

        << Code for Stmt goes here. >>

SkipStmt:
```

Notice a very subtle but important difference between these two conver sions: If x is equal to y, then the first version above *still increments* z and compare it to 0 before it executes the code associated with Stmt; the short-circuit version, on the other hand, skips the code that increments z if it turns out that is equal to y. Therefore, the behavior of these two code fragments is differen if x is equal to y. Neither implementation is particularly wrong; depending or the circumstances you may or may not want the code to increment [z if x is equal to y. However, it is important that you realize that these two schemes produce different results, so you can choose an appropriate implementatior if the effect of this code on z matters to your program.

Many programs take advantage of short-circuit boolean evaluation and rely on the fact that the program may not evaluate certain components of the expression. The following C/C++ code fragment demonstrates what is proba bly the most common example that requires short-circuit boolean evaluatior

```
if( Ptr != NULL && *Ptr == 'a' ) << Stmt >>;
```

If it turns out that Ptr is NULL, then the expression is false and there is nc need to evaluate the remainder of the expression (and, therefore, code thar uses short-circuit boolean evaluation will not evaluate the remainder of this expression). This statement relies on the semantics of short-circuit boolean evaluation for correct operation. Were C/C++ to use complete boolean eval uation, and the variable Ptr contained NULL, then the second half of the expression would attempt to dereference a NULL pointer (which tends to crash most programs). Consider the translation of this statement using complete and short-circuit boolean evaluation:

```
// Complete boolean evaluation:

        mov( Ptr, eax );
        test( eax, eax );    // Check to see if eax is 0 (NULL is 0).
        setne( bl );
        mov( [eax], al );    // Get *Ptr into al.
        cmp( al, 'a' );
        sete( bh );
        and( bh, bl );
        jz SkipStmt;

        << Code for Stmt goes here. >>

SkipStmt:
```

Notice in this example that if Ptr contains NULL (0), then this program will attempt to access the data at location 0 in memory via the mov( [eax], al ); instruction. Under most operating systems this will cause a memory access fault (general protection fault).

Now consider the short-circuit boolean conversion:

```
// Short-circuit boolean evaluation

        mov( Ptr, eax );    // See if Ptr contains NULL (0) and
        test( eax, eax );   // immediately skip past Stmt if this
        jz SkipStmt;        // is the case.

        mov( [eax], al );   // If we get to this point, Ptr contains
        cmp( al, 'a' );     // a non-NULL value, so see if it points
        jne SkipStmt;       // at the character 'a'.

        << Code for Stmt goes here. >>

SkipStmt:
```

As you can see in this example, the problem with dereferencing the NULL pointer doesn't exist. If Ptr contains NULL, this code skips over the statements that attempt to access the memory address Ptr contains.

## 7.7.6 Efficient Implementation of if Statements in Assembly Language

Encoding if statements efficiently in assembly language takes a bit more thought than simply choosing short-circuit evaluation over complete boolean evaluation. To write code that executes as quickly as possible in assembly language, you must carefully analyze the situation and generate the code appropriately. The following paragraphs provide some suggestions you can apply to your programs to improve their performance.

### 7.7.6.1 Know Your Data!

A mistake programmers often make is the assumption that data is random. In reality, data is rarely random, and if you know the types of values that your program commonly uses, you can use this knowledge to write better code. To see how, consider the following C/C++ statement:

```
if(( a == b ) && ( c < d )) ++i;
```

Because C/C++ uses short-circuit evaluation, this code will test to see if a is equal to b. If so, then it will test to see if c is less than d. If you expect a to be equal to b most of the time but don't expect c to be less than d most of the time, this statement will execute slower than it should. Consider the following HLA implementation of this code:

```
        mov( a, eax );
        cmp( eax, b );
        jne DontIncI;
```

```
        mov( c, eax );
        cmp( eax, d );
        jnl DontIncI;

            inc( i );

    DontIncI:
```

As you can see in this code, if a is equal to b most of the time and c is not less than d most of the time, you will have to execute all six instructions nearly every time in order to determine that the expression is false. Now consider the following implementation of the above C/C++ statement that takes advantage of this knowledge and the fact that the && operator is commutative:

```
        mov( c, eax );
        cmp( eax, d );
        jnl DontIncI;

        mov( a, eax );
        cmp( eax, b );
        jne DontIncI;

            inc( i );

    DontIncI:
```

In this example the code first checks to see if c is less than d. If most of the time c is less than d, then this code determines that it has to skip to the label DontIncI after executing only three instructions in the typical case (compared with six instructions in the previous example). This fact is much more obvious in assembly language than in a high-level language; this is one of the main reasons why assembly programs are often faster than their high-level language counterparts: optimizations are more obvious in assembly language than in a high-level language. Of course, the key here is to understand the behavior of your data so you can make intelligent decisions such as the one above.

### 7.7.6.2 Rearranging Expressions

Even if your data is random (or you can't determine how the input values will affect your decisions), there may still be some benefit to rearranging the terms in your expressions. Some calculations take far longer to compute than others. For example, the div instruction is much slower than a simple cmp instruction. Therefore, if you have a statement like the following, you may want to rearrange the expression so that the cmp comes first:

```
if( (x % 10 = 0 ) && (x != y ) ++x;
```

Converted to assembly code, this if statement becomes:

```
mov( x, eax );          // Compute X % 10.
cdq();                  // Must sign extend eax -> edx:eax.
imod( 10, edx:eax );    // Remember, remainder goes into edx.
test( edx, edx );       // See if edx is 0.
jnz SkipIf;

mov( x, eax );
cmp( eax, y );
je SkipIf;

    inc( x );

SkipIf:
```

The `imod` instruction is very expensive (often 50–100 times slower than most of the other instructions in this example). Unless it is 50–100 times more likely that the remainder is 0 rather than x is equal to y, it would be better to do the comparison first and the remainder calculation afterward:

```
mov( x, eax );
cmp( eax, y );
je SkipIf;

mov( x, eax );          // Compute X % 10.
cdq();                  // Must sign extend eax -> edx:eax.
imod( 10, edx:eax );    // Remember, remainder goes into edx.
test( edx, edx );       // See if edx is 0.
jnz SkipIf;

    inc( x );

SkipIf:
```

Of course, in order to rearrange the expression in this manner, the code must not assume the use of short-circuit evaluation semantics (because the && and || operators are not commutative if the code must compute one subexpression before another).

### 7.7.6.3 Destructuring Your Code

Although there are many good things to be said about structured programming techniques, there are some drawbacks to writing structured code. Specifically, structured code is sometimes less efficient than unstructured code. Most of the time this is tolerable because unstructured code is difficult to read and maintain; it is often acceptable to sacrifice some performance in exchange for maintainable code. In certain instances, however, you may need all the performance you can get. In those rare instances you might choose to compromise the readability of your code in order to gain some additional performance.

One classic way to do this is to use code movement to move code your program rarely uses out of the way of code that executes most of the time. For example, consider the following pseudo C/C++ statement:

```
if( See_If_an_Error_Has_Occurred )
{
    << Statements to execute if no error >>
}
else
{
    << Error handling statements >>
}
```

In normal code, one does not expect errors to be frequent. Therefore you would normally expect the then section of the above if to execute far more often than the else clause. The code above could translate into the following assembly code:

```
cmp( See_If_an_Error_Has_Occurred, true );
je HandleTheError;

    << Statements to execute if no error >>
    jmp EndOfIF;

HandleTheError:
    << Error handling statements >>
EndOfIf:
```

Notice that if the expression is false, this code falls through to the normal statements and then jumps over the error-handling statements. Instructions that transfer control from one point in your program to another (for example, jmp instructions) tend to be slow. It is much faster to execute a sequential set of instructions rather than jump all over the place in your program. Unfortunately, the code above doesn't allow this. One way to rectify this problem is to move the else clause of the code somewhere else in your program. That is, you could rewrite the code as follows:

```
cmp( See_If_an_Error_Has_Occurred, true );
je HandleTheError;

    << Statements to execute if no error >>

EndOfIf:
```

At some other point in your program (typically after a jmp instruction) you would insert the following code:

```
HandleTheError:
    << Error handling statements >>
    jmp EndOfIf;
```

Note that the program isn't any shorter. The jmp you removed from the original sequence winds up at the end of the else clause. However, because the else clause rarely executes, moving the jmp instruction from the then clause (which executes frequently) to the else clause is a big performance win because the then clause executes using only straight-line code. This technique is surprisingly effective in many time-critical code segments.

There is a difference between writing *destructured* code and writing *unstructured* code. Unstructured code is written in an unstructured way to begin with. It is generally hard to read, difficult to maintain, and often contains defects. Destructured code, on the other hand, starts out as structured code, and you make a conscious decision to eliminate the structure in order to gain a small performance boost. Generally, you've already tested the code in its structured form before destructuring it. Therefore, destructured code is often easier to work with than unstructured code.

### 7.7.6.4 Calculation Rather Than Branching

On many processors in the 80x86 family, branches (jumps) are very expensive compared to many other instructions. For this reason it is sometimes better to execute more instructions in a sequence than fewer instructions that involve branching. For example, consider the simple assignment eax = abs( eax );. Unfortunately, there is no 80x86 instruction that computes the absolute value of an integer. The obvious way to handle this is with an instruction sequence like the following:

```
        test( eax, eax );
        jns ItsPositive;

            neg( eax );

ItsPositive:
```

However, as you can plainly see in this example, it uses a conditional jump to skip over the neg instruction (that creates a positive value in EAX if EAX was negative). Now consider the following sequence that will also do the job:

```
// Set edx to $FFFF_FFFF if eax is negative, $0000_0000 if eax is
// 0 or positive:

        cdq();

// If eax was negative, the following code inverts all the bits in eax;
// otherwise it has no effect on eax.

        xor( edx, eax );

// If eax was negative, the following code adds 1 to eax; otherwise
// it doesn't modify eax's value.
```

```
        and( 1, edx );      // edx = 0 or 1 (1 if eax was negative).
        add( edx, eax );
```

This code will invert all the bits in EAX and then add 1 to EAX if EAX wa
negative prior to the sequence; that is, it negates the value in EAX. If EAX
was 0 or positive, then this code does not change the value in EAX.

Note that this sequence takes four instructions rather than the three th
previous example requires. However, because there are no transfer-of-contro
instructions in this sequence, it may execute faster on many CPUs in the
80x86 family.

### 7.7.7   switch/case Statements

The HLA switch statement takes the following form:

```
switch( reg32 )
    case( const1 )
        << Stmts1: code to execute if reg32 equals const1 >>

    case( const2 )
        << Stmts2: code to execute if reg32 equals const2 >>
        .
        .
        .
    case( constn )
        << Stmtsn: code to execute if reg32 equals constn >>

    default      // Note that the default section is optional.
        << Stmts_default: code to execute if reg32
           does not equal any of the case values >>

endswitch;
```

When this statement executes, it checks the value of the register agains
the constants const1..constn. If a match is found, then the corresponding
statements execute. HLA places a few restrictions on the switch statement.
First, the HLA switch statement allows only a 32-bit register as the switch
expression. Second, all the constants in the case clauses must be unique. The
reason for these restrictions will become clear in a moment.

Most introductory programming texts introduce the switch/case statement
by explaining it as a sequence of if..then..elseif..else..endif statements.
They might claim that the following two pieces of HLA code are equivalent

```
switch( eax )
    case(0) stdout.put("i=0");
    case(1) stdout.put("i=1");
    case(2) stdout.put("i=2");
endswitch;
```

```
if( eax = 0 ) then
    stdout.put("i=0")
elseif( eax = 1 ) then
    stdout.put("i=1")
elseif( eax = 2 ) then
    stdout.put("i=2");
endif;
```

While semantically these two code segments may be the same, their implementation is usually different. Whereas the if..then..elseif..else..endif chain does a comparison for each conditional statement in the sequence, the switch statement normally uses an indirect jump to transfer control to any one of several statements with a single computation. Consider the two examples presented above; they could be written in assembly language with the following code:

```
// if..then..else..endif form:

        mov( i, eax );
        test( eax, eax );   // Check for 0.
        jnz Not0;
            stdout.put( "i=0" );
            jmp EndCase;

        Not0:
        cmp( eax, 1 );
        jne Not1;
            stdou.put( "i=1" );
            jmp EndCase;

        Not1:
        cmp( eax, 2 );
        jne EndCase;
            stdout.put( "i=2" );
    EndCase:


// Indirect Jump Version

readonly
    JmpTbl:dword[3] := [ &Stmt0, &Stmt1, &Stmt2 ];
        .
        .
        .
    mov( i, eax );
    jmp( JmpTbl[ eax*4 ] );

        Stmt0:
            stdout.put( "i=0" );
            jmp EndCase;
```

```
          Stmt1:
                stdout.put( "I=1" );
                jmp EndCase;

          Stmt2:
                stdout.put( "I=2" );

     EndCase:
```

The implementation of the if..then..elseif..else..endif version is fairly
obvious and needs little in the way of explanation. The indirect jump version,
however, is probably quite mysterious to you, so let's consider how this particular implementation of the switch statement works.

Remember that there are three common forms of the jmp instruction. The
standard unconditional jmp instruction, like the jmp EndCase; instruction in the
previous examples, transfers control directly to the statement label specified
as the jmp operand. The second form of the jmp instruction—jmp( reg32 );—
transfers control to the memory location specified by the address found in a
32-bit register. The third form of the jmp instruction, the one the previous
example uses, transfers control to the instruction specified by the contents
of a double-word memory location. As this example clearly illustrates, that
memory location can use any addressing mode. You are not limited to the
displacement-only addressing mode. Now let's consider exactly how this second implementation of the switch statement works.

To begin with, a switch statement requires that you create an array of
pointers with each element containing the address of a statement label in
your code (those labels must be attached to the sequence of instructions to
execute for each case in the switch statement). In the example above, the
JmpTbl array serves this purpose. Note that this code initializes JmpTbl with the
address of the statement labels Stmt0, Stmt1, and Stmt2. The program places
this array in the readonly section because the program should never change
these values during execution.

**WARNING**    *Whenever you initialize an array with a set of addresses of statement labels as in this
example, the declaration section in which you declare the array (e.g., readonly in this
case) must be in the same procedure that contains the statement labels.[3]*

During the execution of this code sequence, the program loads the EAX
register with i's value. Then the program uses this value as an index into the
JmpTbl array and transfers control to the 4-byte address found at the specified
location. For example, if EAX contains 0, the jmp( JmpTbl[eax*4] ); instruction
will fetch the double word at address JmpTbl+0 ( eax*4=0 ). Because the first
double word in the table contains the address of Stmt0, the jmp instruction
transfers control to the first instruction following the Stmt0 label. Likewise, if i
(and therefore, EAX) contains 1, then the indirect jmp instruction fetches the
double word at offset 4 from the table and transfers control to the first instruction following the Stmt1 label (because the address of Stmt1 appears at offset

---

[3] If the switch statement appears in your main program, you must declare the array in the
declaration section of your main program.

4 in the table). Finally, if i/EAX contains 2, then this code fragment transfers control to the statements following the Stmt2 label because it appears at offset 8 in the JmpTbl table.

You should note that as you add more (consecutive) cases, the jump table implementation becomes more efficient (in terms of both space and speed) than the if/elseif form. Except for simple cases, the switch statement is almost always faster and usually by a large margin. As long as the case values are consecutive, the switch statement version is usually smaller as well.

What happens if you need to include nonconsecutive case labels or you cannot be sure that the switch value doesn't go out of range? With the HLA switch statement, such an occurrence will transfer control to the first statement after the endswitch clause (or to a default case, if one is present in the switch). However, this doesn't happen in the example above. If variable i does not contain 0, 1, or 2, executing the code above produces undefined results. For example, if i contains 5 when you execute the code in the previous example, the indirect jmp instruction will fetch the dword at offset 20 (5 * 4) in JmpTbl and transfer control to that address. Unfortunately, JmpTbl doesn't have six entries; so the program will wind up fetching the value of the third double word following JmpTbl and use that as the target address. This will often crash your program or transfer control to an unexpected location.

The solution is to place a few instructions before the indirect jmp to verify that the switch selection value is within some reasonable range. In the previous example, we'd probably want to verify that i's value is in the range 0..2 before executing the jmp instruction. If i's value is outside this range, the program should simply jump to the endcase label (this corresponds to dropping down to the first statement after the endswitch clause). The following code provides this modification:

```
readonly
    JmpTbl:dword[3] := [ &Stmt0, &Stmt1, &Stmt2 ];
      .
      .
      .
    mov( i, eax );
    cmp( eax, 2 );          // Verify that i is in the range
    ja EndCase;             // 0..2 before the indirect jmp.
    jmp( JmpTbl[ eax*4 ] );


        Stmt0:
            stdout.put( "i=0" );
            jmp EndCase;

        Stmt1:
            stdout.put( "i=1" );
            jmp EndCase;
```

```
    Stmt2:
        stdout.put( "i=2" );

EndCase:
```

Although the example above handles the problem of selection values being outside the range 0..2, it still suffers from a couple of severe restrictions

- The cases must start with the value 0. That is, the minimum case constant has to be 0 in this example.
- The case values must be contiguous.

Solving the first problem is easy, and you deal with it in two steps. First you must compare the case selection value against a lower and upper bound before determining if the case value is legal. For example:

```
// SWITCH statement specifying cases 5, 6, and 7:
// WARNING: This code does *NOT* work. Keep reading to find out why.

    mov( i, eax );
    cmp( eax, 5 );
    jb EndCase
    cmp( eax, 7 );                  // Verify that i is in the range
    ja EndCase;                     // 5..7 before the indirect jmp.
    jmp( JmpTbl[ eax*4 ] );


        Stmt5:
            stdout.put( "i=5" );
            jmp EndCase;

        Stmt6:
            stdout.put( "i=6" );
            jmp EndCase;

        Stmt7:
            stdout.put( "i=7" );

EndCase:
```

As you can see, this code adds a pair of extra instructions, cmp and jb, to test the selection value to ensure it is in the range 5..7. If not, control drops down to the EndCase label; otherwise control transfers via the indirect jmp instruction. Unfortunately, as the comments point out, this code is broken. Consider what happens if variable i contains the value 5: the code will verify that 5 is in the range 5..7 and then it will fetch the dword at offset 20 (5*@size(dword)) and jump to that address. As before, however, this loads 4 bytes outside the bounds of the table and does not transfer control to a defined location. One solution is to subtract the smallest case selection value from EAX before executing the jmp instruction, as shown in the following example.

```
// SWITCH statement specifying cases 5, 6, and 7:
// WARNING: There is a better way to do this. Keep reading.

readonly
    JmpTbl:dword[3] := [ &Stmt5, &Stmt6, &Stmt7 ];
            .
            .
            .
    mov( i, eax );
    cmp( eax, 5 );
    jb EndCase
    cmp( eax, 7 );              // Verify that i is in the range
    ja EndCase;                 // 5..7 before the indirect jmp.
    sub( 5, eax );              // 5->0, 6->1, 7->2.
    jmp( JmpTbl[ eax*4 ] );


        Stmt5:
            stdout.put( "i=5" );
            jmp EndCase;

        Stmt6:
            stdout.put( "i=6" );
            jmp EndCase;

        Stmt7:
            stdout.put( "i=7" );

    EndCase:
```

By subtracting 5 from the value in EAX, this code forces EAX to take on
the value 0, 1, or 2 prior to the jmp instruction. Therefore, case-selection value 5
jumps to Stmt5, case-selection value 6 transfers control to Stmt6, and case-selection
value 7 jumps to Stmt7.

There is a sneaky way to improve the code above. You can eliminate the
sub instruction by merging this subtraction into the jmp instruction's address
expression. Consider the following code that does this:

```
// SWITCH statement specifying cases 5, 6, and 7:

readonly
    JmpTbl:dword[3] := [ &Stmt5, &Stmt6, &Stmt7 ];
            .
            .
            .
    mov( i, eax );
    cmp( eax, 5 );
    jb EndCase
    cmp( eax, 7 );                  // Verify that i is in the range
    ja EndCase;                     // 5..7 before the indirect jmp.
    jmp( JmpTbl[ eax*4 - 5*@size(dword)] );
```

```
        Stmt5:
                stdout.put( "i=5" );
                jmp EndCase;

        Stmt6:
                stdout.put( "i=6" );
                jmp EndCase;

        Stmt7:
                stdout.put( "i=7" );

EndCase:
```

The HLA switch statement provides a default clause that executes if the case-selection value doesn't match any of the case values. For example:

```
switch( ebx )

        case( 5 )  stdout.put( "ebx=5" );
        case( 6 )  stdout.put( "ebx=6" );
        case( 7 )  stdout.put( "ebx=7" );
        default
                stdout.put( "ebx does not equal 5, 6, or 7" );

endswitch;
```

Implementing the equivalent of the default clause in pure assembly language is very easy. Just use a different target label in the jb and ja instruction at the beginning of the code. The following example implements an HLA switch statement similar to the one immediately above:

```
// SWITCH statement specifying cases 5, 6, and 7 with a DEFAULT clause:

readonly
        JmpTbl:dword[3] := [ &Stmt5, &Stmt6, &Stmt7 ];
                .
                .
                .
        mov( i, eax );
        cmp( eax, 5 );
        jb DefaultCase;
        cmp( eax, 7 );                  // Verify that i is in the range
        ja DefaultCase;                 // 5..7 before the indirect jmp.
        jmp( JmpTbl[ eax*4 - 5*@size(dword)] );


        Stmt5:
                stdout.put( "i=5" );
                jmp EndCase;
```

```
Stmt6:
     stdout.put( "i=6" );
     jmp EndCase;

Stmt7:
     stdout.put( "i=7" );
     jmp EndCase;

DefaultCase:
     stdout.put( "i does not equal 5, 6, or 7" );
EndCase:
```

The second restriction noted earlier, that the case values need to be contiguous, is easy to handle by inserting extra entries into the jump table. Consider the following HLA switch statement:

```
switch( ebx )

     case( 1 ) stdout.put( "ebx = 1" );
     case( 2 ) stdout.put( "ebx = 2" );
     case( 4 ) stdout.put( "ebx = 4" );
     case( 8 ) stdout.put( "ebx = 8" );
     default
          stdout.put( "ebx is not 1, 2, 4, or 8" );

endswitch;
```

The minimum switch value is 1 and the maximum value is 8. Therefore, the code before the indirect jmp instruction needs to compare the value in EBX against 1 and 8. If the value is between 1 and 8, it's still possible that EBX might not contain a legal case-selection value. However, because the jmp instruction indexes into a table of double words using the case-selection table, the table must have eight double-word entries. To handle the values between 1 and 8 that are not case-selection values, simply put the statement label of the default clause (or the label specifying the first instruction after the endswitch if there is no default clause) in each of the jump table entries that don't have a corresponding case clause. The following code demonstrates this technique:

```
readonly
    JmpTbl2: dword :=
                [
                    &Case1, &Case2, &dfltCase, &Case4,
                    &dfltCase, &dfltCase, &dfltCase, &Case8
                ];
        .
        .
        .
```

```
        cmp( ebx, 1 );
        jb dfltCase;
        cmp( ebx, 8 );
        ja dfltCase;
        jmp( JmpTbl2[ ebx*4 - 1*@size(dword) ] );

            Case1:
                stdout.put( "ebx = 1" );
                jmp EndOfSwitch;

            Case2:
                stdout.put( "ebx = 2" );
                jmp EndOfSwitch;

            Case4:
                stdout.put( "ebx = 4" );
                jmp EndOfSwitch;

            Case8:
                stdout.put( "ebx = 8" );
                jmp EndOfSwitch;

            dfltCase:
                stdout.put( "ebx is not 1, 2, 4, or 8" );

        EndOfSwitch:
```

There is a problem with this implementation of the switch statement. If the case values contain nonconsecutive entries that are widely spaced, the jump table could become exceedingly large. The following switch statement would generate an extremely large code file:

```
switch( ebx )

    case( 1      ) << Stmt1 >>;
    case( 100    ) << Stmt2 >>;
    case( 1_000  ) << Stmt3 >>;
    case( 10_000 ) << Stmt4 >>;
    default << Stmt5 >>;

endswitch;
```

In this situation, your program will be much smaller if you implement the switch statement with a sequence of if statements rather than using an indirect jump statement. However, keep one thing in mind—the size of the jump table does not normally affect the execution speed of the program. If the jump table contains two entries or two thousand, the switch statement will execute the multiway branch in a constant amount of time. The if statement implementation requires a linearly increasing amount of time for each case label appearing in the case statement.

Probably the biggest advantage to using assembly language over an HLL like Pascal or C/C++ is that you get to choose the actual implementation of statements like switch. In some instances you can implement a switch statement as a sequence of if..then..elseif statements, or you can implement it as a jump table, or you can use a hybrid of the two:

```
switch( eax )

        case( 0   ) << Stmt0 >>;
        case( 1   ) << Stmt1 >>;
        case( 2   ) << Stmt2 >>;
        case( 100 ) << Stmt3 >>;
        default << Stmt4 >>;

endswitch;
```

This could become

```
        cmp( eax, 100 );
        je DoStmt3;
        cmp( eax, 2 );
        ja TheDefaultCase;
        jmp( JmpTbl[ eax*4 ]);
        . . .
```

Of course, HLA supports the following code high-level control structures:

```
    if( ebx = 100 ) then
        << Stmt3 >>;
    else
        switch( eax )
            case(0) << Stmt0 >>;
            case(1) << Stmt1 >>;
            case(2) << Stmt2 >>;
            Otherwise << Stmt4 >>;
        endswitch;
    endif;
```

But this tends to destroy the readability of the program. On the other hand, the extra code to test for 100 in the assembly language code doesn't adversely affect the readability of the program (perhaps because it's so hard to read already). Therefore, most people will add the extra code to make their program more efficient.

The C/C++ switch statement is very similar to the HLA switch statement. There is only one major semantic difference: The programmer must explicitly place a break statement in each case clause to transfer control to the first statement beyond the switch. This break corresponds to the jmp instruction at the end of each case sequence in the assembly code above. If the corresponding

break is not present, C/C++ transfers control into the code of the following
case. This is equivalent to leaving off the jmp at the end of the case's sequence

```
switch (i)
{
    case 0: << Stmt1 >>;
    case 1: << Stmt2 >>;
    case 2: << Stmt3 >>;
        break;
    case 3: << Stmt4 >>;
        break;
    default: << Stmt5 >>;
}
```

This translates into the following 80x86 code:

```
readonly
    JmpTbl: dword[4] := [ &case0, &case1, &case2, &case3 ];
        .
        .
        .
    mov( i, ebx );
    cmp( ebx, 3 );
    ja DefaultCase;
    jmp( JmpTbl[ ebx*4 ]);

        case0:
            Stmt1;

        case1:
            Stmt2;

        case2:
            Stmt3;
            jmp EndCase;     // Emitted for the break stmt.

        case3:
            Stmt4;
            jmp EndCase;     // Emitted for the break stmt.

        DefaultCase:
            Stmt5;

    EndCase:
```

## 7.8 State Machines and Indirect Jumps

Another control structure commonly found in assembly language programs
is the *state machine*. A state machine uses a *state variable* to control program
flow. The FORTRAN programming language provides this capability with
the assigned goto statement. Certain variants of C (for example, GNU's GCC
from the Free Software Foundation) provide similar features. In assembly
language, the indirect jump can implement state machines.

So what is a state machine? In very basic terms, it is a piece of code that keeps track of its execution history by entering and leaving certain "states." For the purposes of this chapter, we'll just assume that a state machine is a piece of code that (somehow) remembers the history of its execution (its *state*) and executes sections of code based on that history.

In a very real sense, all programs are state machines. The CPU registers and values in memory constitute the state of that machine. However, we'll use a much more constrained view. Indeed, for most purposes only a single variable (or the value in the EIP register) will denote the current state.

Now let's consider a concrete example. Suppose you have a procedure that you want to perform one operation the first time you call it, a different operation the second time you call it, yet something else the third time you call it, and then something new again on the fourth call. After the fourth call it repeats these four different operations in order. For example, suppose you want the procedure to add EAX and EBX the first time, subtract them on the second call, multiply them on the third, and divide them on the fourth. You could implement this procedure as follows:

```
procedure StateMachine;
static
    State:byte := 0;
begin StateMachine;

    cmp( State, 0 );
    jne TryState1;

        // State 0: Add ebx to eax and switch to State 1:

        add( ebx, eax );
        inc( State );
        exit StateMachine;

    TryState1:
    cmp( State, 1 );
    jne TryState2;

        // State 1: Subtract ebx from eax and switch to State 2:

        sub( ebx, eax );
        inc( State );       // State 1 becomes State 2.
        exit StateMachine;

    TryState2:
    cmp( State, 2 );
    jne MustBeState3;

        // If this is State 2, multiply ebx by eax and switch to State 3:

        intmul( ebx, eax );
        inc( State );       // State 2 becomes State 3.
        exit StateMachine;
```

```
    // If it isn't one of the above states, we must be in State 3,
    // so divide eax by ebx and switch back to State 0.

    MustBeState3:
    push( edx );          // Preserve this 'cause it gets whacked by div.
    xor( edx, edx );      // Zero extend eax into edx.
    div( ebx, edx:eax);
    pop( edx );           // Restore edx's value preserved above.
    mov( 0, State );      // Reset the state back to 0.

end StateMachine;
```

Technically, this procedure is not the state machine. Instead, it is the va~~ri~~able State and the cmp/jne instructions that constitute the state machine.

There is nothing particularly special about this code. It's little more tha~~n~~ a switch statement implemented via the if..then..elseif construct. The onl~~y~~ thing unique about this procedure is that it remembers how many times it ha~~s~~ been called[4] and behaves differently depending upon the number of calls. While this is a *correct* implementation of the desired state machine, it is not particularly efficient. The astute reader, of course, would recognize that th~~e~~ code could be made a little faster using an actual switch statement rather tha~~n~~ the if..then..elseif implementation. However, there is an even better solutio~~n~~.

A common implementation of a state machine in assembly language is ~~to~~ use an indirect jump. Rather than having a state variable that contains a valu~~e~~ like 0, 1, 2, or 3, we could load the state variable with the *address* of the cod~~e~~ to execute upon entry into the procedure. By simply jumping to that addres~~s~~ the state machine could save the tests needed to select the proper code fra~~g~~ment. Consider the following implementation using the indirect jump:

```
procedure StateMachine;
static
     State:dword := &State0;
begin StateMachine;

    jmp( State );

        // State 0: Add ebx to eax and switch to State 1:

    State0:
        add( ebx, eax );
        mov( &State1, State );
        exit StateMachine;

    State1:

        // State 1: Subtract ebx from eax and switch to State 2:
```

---

[4] Actually, it remembers how many times, modulo 4, that it has been called.

```
            sub( ebx, eax );
            mov( &State2, State );    // State 1 becomes State 2.
            exit StateMachine;

        State2:

            // If this is State 2, multiply ebx by eax and switch to State 3:

            intmul( ebx, eax );
            mov( &State3, State );    // State 2 becomes State 3.
            exit StateMachine;

        // State 3: Divide eax by ebx and switch back to State 0.

        State3:
            push( edx );              // Preserve this 'cause it gets whacked by div.
            xor( edx, edx );          // Zero extend eax into edx.
            div( ebx, edx:eax);
            pop( edx );               // Restore edx's value preserved above.
            mov( &State0, State );    // Reset the state back to 0.

    end StateMachine;
```

---

The jmp instruction at the beginning of the StateMachine procedure transfers control to the location pointed at by the State variable. The first time you call StateMachine it points at the State0 label. Thereafter, each subsection of code sets the State variable to point at the appropriate successor code.

## 7.9 Spaghetti Code

One major problem with assembly language is that it takes several statements to realize a simple idea encapsulated by a single high-level language statement. All too often an assembly language programmer will notice that she or he can save a few bytes or cycles by jumping into the middle of some program structure. After a few such observations (and corresponding modifications) the code contains a whole sequence of jumps in and out of portions of the code. If you were to draw a line from each jump to its destination, the resulting listing would end up looking like someone dumped a bowl of spaghetti on your code, hence the term *spaghetti code*.

Spaghetti code suffers from one major drawback—it's difficult (at best) to read such a program and figure out what it does. Most programs start out in a "structured" form only to become spaghetti code when sacrificed at the altar of efficiency. Alas, spaghetti code is rarely efficient. Because it's difficult to figure out exactly what's going on, it's very difficult to determine if you can use a better algorithm to improve the system. Hence, spaghetti code may wind up less efficient than structured code.

While it's true that producing some spaghetti code in your programs m improve its efficiency, doing so should always be a last resort after you've trie everything else and you still haven't achieved what you need. Always start o writing your programs with straightforward if and switch statements. Start combining sections of code (via jmp instructions) once everything is workir and well understood. Of course, you should never obliterate the structure your code unless the gains are worth it.

A famous saying in structured programming circles is, "After gotos, poir ers are the next most dangerous element in a programming language." A similar saying is "Pointers are to data structures what gotos are to control stru tures." In other words, avoid excessive use of pointers. If pointers and gotos are bad, then the indirect jump must be the worst construct of all because involves both gotos and pointers! Seriously, though, the indirect jump instru tion should be avoided for casual use. Its use tends to make a program hard to read. After all, an indirect jump can (theoretically) transfer control to ar point within a program. Imagine how hard it would be to follow the flow through a program if you have no idea what a pointer contains and you con across an indirect jump using that pointer. Therefore, you should always exe cise care when using jump indirect instructions.

## 7.10  Loops

Loops represent the final basic control structure (sequences, decisions, an loops) that make up a typical program. Like so many other structures in asser bly language, you'll find yourself using loops in places you've never dreamed using loops. Most high-level languages have implied loop structures hidder away. For example, consider the BASIC statement if A$ = B$ then 100. This statement compares two strings and jumps to statement 100 if they are equa In assembly language, you would need to write a loop to compare each cha acter in A$ to the corresponding character in B$ and then jump to statemen 100 if and only if all the characters matched. In BASIC, there is no loop to b seen in the program. Assembly language requires a loop to compare the inc vidual characters in the string.[5] This is but a small example that shows how loops seem to pop up everywhere.

Program loops consist of three components: an optional initialization component, an optional loop termination test, and the body of the loop. Th order in which you assemble these components can dramatically affect the loop's operation. Three permutations of these components appear frequentl in programs. Because of their frequency, these loop structures are given speci names in high-level languages: while loops, repeat..until loops (do..while in C/C++), and infinite loops (e.g., forever..endfor in HLA).

---

[5] Of course, the HLA Standard Library provides the str.eq routine that compares the strings fo you, effectively hiding the loop even in an assembly language program.

## 7.10.1 while Loops

The most general loop is the while loop. In HLA's high-level syntax it takes the following form:

```
while( expression ) do statements endwhile;
```

There are two important points to note about the while loop. First, the test for termination appears at the beginning of the loop. Second, as a direct consequence of the position of the termination test, the body of the loop may never execute if the boolean expression is always false.

Consider the following HLA while loop:

```
mov( 0, i );
while( i < 100 ) do

    inc( i );

endwhile;
```

The mov( 0, i ); instruction is the initialization code for this loop. i is a loop-control variable, because it controls the execution of the body of the loop. i < 100 is the loop termination condition. That is, the loop will not terminate as long as i is less than 100. The single instruction inc( i ); is the loop body that executes on each loop iteration.

Note that an HLA while loop can be easily synthesized using if and jmp statements. For example, you may replace the previous HLA while loop with the following HLA code:

```
mov( 0, i );
WhileLp:
if( i < 100 ) then

    inc( i );
    jmp WhileLp;

endif;
```

More generally, you can construct any while loop as follows:

```
<< Optional initialization code >>

UniqueLabel:
if( not_termination_condition ) then

    << Loop body >>
    jmp UniqueLabel;

endif;
```

Therefore, you can use the techniques from earlier in this chapter to conve if statements to assembly language and add a single jmp instruction to produ a while loop. The example we've been looking at in this section translates the following pure 80x86 assembly code:[6]

```
mov( 0, i );
WhileLp:
      cmp( i, 100 );
      jnl WhileDone;
      inc( i );
      jmp WhileLp;

WhileDone:
```

## 7.10.2  repeat..until Loops

The repeat..until (do..while) loop tests for the termination condition at th end of the loop rather than at the beginning. In HLA high-level syntax, the repeat..until loop takes the following form:

```
<< Optional initialization code >>
repeat

      << Loop body >>

until( termination_condition );
```

This sequence executes the initialization code, then executes the loop body, and finally tests some condition to see if the loop should repeat. If th boolean expression evaluates to false, the loop repeats; otherwise the loop te minates. The two things you should note about the repeat..until loop are th the termination test appears at the end of the loop and, as a direct consequenc of this, the loop body always executes at least once.

Like the while loop, the repeat..until loop can be synthesized with an i statement and a jmp. You could use the following:

```
<< Initialization code >>
SomeUniqueLabel:

      << Loop body >>

if( not_the_termination_condition ) then jmp SomeUniqueLabel; endif;
```

---

[6] Note that HLA will actually convert most while statements to different 80x86 code than this section presents. The reason for the difference appears in Section 7.11, when we explore how write more efficient loop code.

Based on the material presented in the previous sections, you can easily synthesize repeat..until loops in assembly language. The following is a simple example:

```
repeat

        stdout.put( "Enter a number greater than 100: " );
        stdin.get( i );

    until( i > 100 );

// This translates to the following if/jmp code:

    RepeatLabel:

        stdout.put( "Enter a number greater than 100: " );
        stdin.get( i );

    if( i <= 100 ) then jmp RepeatLabel; endif;

// It also translates into the following "pure" assembly code:

    RepeatLabel:

        stdout.put( "Enter a number greater than 100: " );
        stdin.get( i );

    cmp( i, 100 );
    jng RepeatLabel;
```

### 7.10.3 forever..endfor Loops

If while loops test for termination at the beginning of the loop and repeat..until loops check for termination at the end of the loop, the only place left to test for termination is in the middle of the loop. The HLA high-level forever..endfor loop, combined with the break and breakif statements, provides this capability. The forever..endfor loop takes the following form:

```
forever

    << Loop body >>

endfor;
```

Note that there is no explicit termination condition. Unless otherwise provided for, the forever..endfor construct forms an infinite loop. A breaki statement usually handles loop termination. Consider the following HLA code that employs a forever..endfor construct:

```
forever

    stdin.get( character );
    breakif( character = '.' );
    stdout.put( character );

endfor;
```

Converting a forever loop to pure assembly language is easy. All you nee is a label and a jmp instruction. The breakif statement in this example is rea nothing more than an if and a jmp instruction. The pure assembly languag version of the code above looks something like the following:

```
foreverLabel:

    stdin.get( character );
    cmp( character, '.' );
    je ForIsDone;
    stdout.put( character );
    jmp foreverLabel;

ForIsDone:
```

## 7.10.4  for Loops

The for loop is a special form of the while loop that repeats the loop body specific number of times. In HLA, the for loop takes the following form:

```
for( Initialization_Stmt; Termination_Expression; inc_Stmt ) do

    << statements >>

endfor;
```

This is completely equivalent to the following:

```
Initialization_Stmt;
while( Termination_Expression ) do

    << statements >>

    inc_Stmt;

endwhile;
```

Traditionally, programs use the for loop to process arrays and other objects accessed in sequential order. One normally initializes a loop-control variable with the initialization statement and then uses the loop-control variable as an index into the array (or other data type). For example:

```
for( mov( 0, esi ); esi < 7; inc( esi )) do

    stdout.put( "Array Element = ", SomeArray[ esi*4 ], nl );

endfor;
```

To convert this to pure assembly language, begin by translating the for loop into an equivalent while loop:

```
        mov( 0, esi );
        while( esi < 7 ) do

            stdout.put( "Array Element = ", SomeArray[ esi*4 ], nl );

            inc( esi );
        endwhile;
```

Now, using the techniques from the section on while loops, translate the code into pure assembly language:

```
        mov( 0, esi );
        WhileLp:
        cmp( esi, 7 );
        jnl EndWhileLp;

            stdout.put( "Array Element = ", SomeArray[ esi*4 ], nl );

            inc( esi );
            jmp WhileLp;

        EndWhileLp:
```

### 7.10.5  The break and continue Statements

The HLA break and continue statements both translate into a single jmp instruction. The break instruction exits the loop that immediately contains the break statement; the continue statement restarts the loop that immediately contains the continue statement.

Converting a break statement to pure assembly language is very easy. Just emit a jmp instruction that transfers control to the first statement following the endxxxx (or until) clause of the loop to exit. You can do this by placing a label after the associated endxxxx clause and jumping to that label. The following code fragments demonstrate this technique for the various loops.

```
// Breaking out of a FOREVER loop:

forever
    << stmts >>
            // break;
            jmp BreakFromForever;
    << stmts >>
endfor;
BreakFromForever:

// Breaking out of a FOR loop;
for( initStmt; expr; incStmt ) do
    << stmts >>
            // break;
            jmp BrkFromFor;
    << stmts >>
endfor;
BrkFromFor:

// Breaking out of a WHILE loop:

while( expr ) do
    << stmts >>
            // break;
            jmp BrkFromWhile;
    << stmts >>
endwhile;
BrkFromWhile:

// Breaking out of a REPEAT..UNTIL loop:

repeat
    << stmts >>
            // 20break;
            jmp BrkFromRpt;
    << stmts >>
until( expr );
BrkFromRpt:
```

The continue statement is slightly more complex than the break statement. The implementation is still a single jmp instruction; however, the target label doesn't wind up going in the same spot for each of the differen loops. Figures 7-2, 7-3, 7-4, and 7-5 show where the continue statement transfer control for each of the HLA loops.

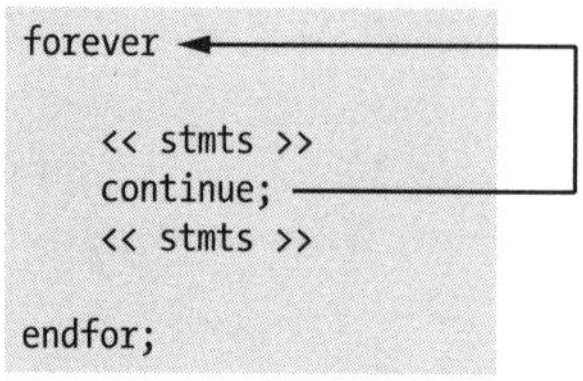

Figure 7-2: continue destination
for the forever loop

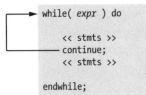

```
while( expr ) do

    << stmts >>
    continue;
    << stmts >>

endwhile;
```

Figure 7-3: continue destination and the while loop

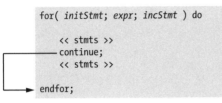

```
for( initStmt; expr; incStmt ) do

    << stmts >>
    continue;
    << stmts >>

endfor;
```

Note: continue forces the execution of the incStmt clause and then transfers control to the test for loop termination.

Figure 7-4: continue destination and the for loop

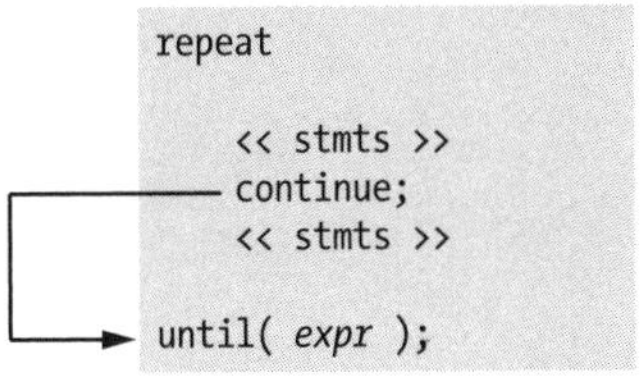

```
repeat

    << stmts >>
    continue;
    << stmts >>

until( expr );
```

Figure 7-5: continue destination and the repeat..until loop

The following code fragments demonstrate how to convert the continue statement into an appropriate jmp instruction for each of these loop types.

### forever..continue..endfor

```
// Conversion of forever loop with continue
// to pure assembly:
forever
    << stmts >>
    continue;
    << stmts >>
endfor;

// Converted code:

foreverLbl:
    << stmts >>
        // continue;
        jmp foreverLbl;
    << stmts >>
    jmp foreverLbl;
```

### while..continue..endwhile

```
// Conversion of while loop with continue
// into pure assembly:
```

```
while( expr ) do
    << stmts >>
    continue;
    << stmts >>
endwhile;

// Converted code:

whlLabel:
<< Code to evaluate expr >>
jcc EndOfWhile;        // Skip loop on expr failure.
    << stmts >>
        // continue;
        jmp whlLabel; // Jump to start of loop on continue.
    << stmts >>
    jmp whlLabel;      // Repeat the code.
EndOfwhile:
```

## for..continue..endfor

```
// Conversion for a for loop with continue
// into pure assembly:

for( initStmt; expr; incStmt ) do
    << stmts >>
    continue;
    << stmts >>
endfor;

// Converted code:

initStmt
ForLpLbl:
<< Code to evaluate expr >>
jcc EndOfFor;          // Branch if expression fails.
    << stmts >>
        // continue;
        jmp ContFor;  // Branch to incStmt on continue.
    << stmts >>

    ContFor:
    incStmt
    jmp ForLpLbl;
EndOfFor:
```

## repeat..continue..until

```
repeat
    << stmts >>
    continue;
    << stmts >>
until( expr );
```

```
// Converted code:

RptLpLbl:
     << stmts >>
          // continue;
          jmp ContRpt;   // Continue branches to loop termination test.
          << stmts >>
     ContRpt:
     << Code to test expr >>
     jcc RptLpLbl;        // Jumps if expression evaluates false.
```

## 7.10.6   Register Usage and Loops

Given that the 80x86 accesses registers more efficiently than memory locations, registers are the ideal spot to place loop-control variables (especially for
small loops). However, there are some problems associated with using registers within a loop. The primary problem with using registers as loop-control
variables is that registers are a limited resource. The following will not work
properly because it attempts to reuse a register (CX) that is already in use:

```
          mov( 8, cx );
          loop1:
               mov( 4, cx );
               loop2:
                    << stmts >>
                    dec( cx );
                    jnz loop2;
               dec( cx );
          jnz loop1;
```

The intent here, of course, was to create a set of nested loops, that is, one
loop inside another. The inner loop (loop2) should repeat four times for each
of the eight executions of the outer loop (loop1). Unfortunately, both loops
use the same register as a loop-control variable. Therefore, this will form an
infinite loop because CX will contain 0 at the end of the first loop. Because
CX is always 0 upon encountering the second dec instruction, control will
always transfer to the loop1 label (because decrementing 0 produces a nonzero result). The solution here is to save and restore the CX register or to use
a different register in place of CX for the outer loop:

```
          mov( 8, cx );
          loop1:
               push( cx );
               mov( 4, cx );
               loop2:
                    << stmts >>
                    dec( cx );
                    jnz loop2;

               pop( cx );
```

```
        dec( cx );
        jnz loop1;
```

or

```
    mov( 8, dx );
    loop1:
        mov( 4, cx );
        loop2:
            << stmts >>
            dec( cx );
            jnz loop2;

        dec( dx );
        jnz loop1;
```

Register corruption is one of the primary sources of bugs in loops in assembly language programs, so always keep an eye out for this problem.

# 7.11 Performance Improvements

The 80x86 microprocessors execute sequences of instructions at blinding speed. Therefore, you'll rarely encounter a slow program that doesn't contain any loops. Because loops are the primary source of performance problems within a program, they are the place to look when attempting to speed up your software. While a treatise on how to write efficient programs is beyond the scope of this chapter, there are some things you should be aware of when designing loops in your programs. They're all aimed at removing unnecessary instructions from your loops in order to reduce the time it takes to execute single iteration of the loop.

## 7.11.1 *Moving the Termination Condition to the End of a Loop*

Consider the following flow graphs for the three types of loops presented earlier

```
repeat..until loop:
    Initialization code
        Loop body
    Test for termination
    Code following the loop

while loop:
    Initialization code
    Loop termination test
        Loop body
        Jump back to test
    Code following the loop
```

```
forever..endfor loop:
    Initialization code
        Loop body part one
        Loop termination test
        Loop body part two
        Jump back to Loop body part one
    Code following the loop
```

As you can see, the repeat..until loop is the simplest of the bunch. This is reflected in the assembly language implementation of these loops. Consider the following repeat..until and while loops that are semantically identical:

```
// Example involving a WHILE loop:

    mov( edi, esi );
    sub( 20, esi );
    while( esi <= edi ) do

        << stmts >>
        inc( esi );

    endwhile;

// Conversion of the code above into pure assembly language:

    mov( edi, esi );
    sub( 20, esi );
    whlLbl:
    cmp( esi, edi );
    jnle EndOfWhile;

        << stmts >>
        inc( esi );
        << stmts >>
        jmp whlLbl;

    EndOfWhile:


// Example involving a REPEAT..UNTIL loop:

    mov( edi, esi );
    sub( 20, esi );
    repeat

        << stmts >>
        inc( esi );

    until( esi > edi );
```

```
// Conversion of the REPEAT..UNTIL loop into pure assembly:

    rptLabel:
        << stmts >>
        inc( esi );
        cmp( esi, edi );
        jng rptLabel;
```

As you can see by carefully studying the conversion to pure assembly la
guage, testing for the termination condition at the end of the loop allowed
to remove a jmp instruction from the loop. This can be significant if this loc
is nested inside other loops. In the preceding example there wasn't a proble
with executing the body at least once. Given the definition of the loop, you
can easily see that the loop will be executed exactly 20 times. This suggests
that the conversion to a repeat..until loop is trivial and always possible. Unfo
tunately, it's not always quite this easy. Consider the following HLA code:

```
    while( esi <= edi ) do
        << stmts >>
        inc( esi );
    endwhile;
```

In this particular example, we haven't the slightest idea what ESI contai
upon entry into the loop. Therefore, we cannot assume that the loop body
will execute at least once. So we must test for loop termination before exec
ing the body of the loop. The test can be placed at the end of the loop with
the inclusion of a single jmp instruction:

```
    jmp WhlTest;
    TopOfLoop:
        << stmts >>
        inc( esi );
    WhlTest:
        cmp( esi, edi );
        jle TopOfLoop;
```

Although the code is as long as the original while loop, the jmp instructio
executes only once rather than on each repetition of the loop. Note that th
slight gain in efficiency is obtained via a slight loss in readability. The secon
code sequence above is closer to spaghetti code than the original impleme
tation. Such is often the price of a small performance gain. Therefore, you
should carefully analyze your code to ensure that the performance boost is
worth the loss of clarity. More often than not, assembly language programme
sacrifice clarity for dubious gains in performance, producing impossible-to
understand programs.

Note, by the way, that HLA translates its high-level while statement into
sequence of instructions that test the loop termination condition at the botto
of the loop using exactly the technique this section describes.

## 7.11.2  Executing the Loop Backwards

Because of the nature of the flags on the 80x86, loops that repeat from some number down to (or up to) 0 are more efficient than loops that execute from 0 to some other value. Compare the following HLA for loop and the code it generates:

```
for( mov( 1, j ); j <= 8; inc( j ) ) do
    << stmts >>
endfor;

// Conversion to pure assembly (as well as using a REPEAT..UNTIL form):

mov( 1, j );
ForLp:
    << stmts >>
    inc( j );
    cmp( j, 8 );
    jnge ForLp;
```

Now consider another loop that also has eight iterations but runs its loop-control variable from 8 down to 1 rather than 1 up to 8:

```
mov( 8, j );
LoopLbl:
    << stmts >>
    dec( j );
    jnz LoopLbl;
```

Note that by running the loop from 8 down to 1 we saved a comparison on each repetition of the loop.

Unfortunately, you cannot force all loops to run backward. However, with a little effort and some coercion you should be able to write many for loops so that they operate backward. Saving the execution time of the cmp instruction on each iteration of the loop may result in faster code.

The example above worked out well because the loop ran from 8 down to 1. The loop terminated when the loop-control variable became 0. What happens if you need to execute the loop when the loop-control variable goes to 0? For example, suppose that the loop above needed to range from 7 down to 0. As long as the upper bound is positive, you can substitute the jns instruction in place of the jnz instruction in the earlier code:

```
mov( 7, j );
LoopLbl:
    << stmts >>
    dec( j );
    jns LoopLbl;
```

This loop will repeat eight times, with j taking on the values 7..0. When it decrements 0 to −1, it sets the sign flag and the loop terminates.

Keep in mind that some values may look positive but are actually negative. If the loop-control variable is a byte, then values in the range 128..255 are negative in the two's complement system. Therefore, initializing the loop-control variable with any 8-bit value in the range 129..255 (or, of course, 0) terminates the loop after a single execution. This can get you into trouble if you're not careful.

## 7.11.3  Loop-Invariant Computations

A *loop-invariant computation* is some calculation that appears within a loop that always yields the same result. You needn't do such computations inside the loop. You can compute them outside the loop and reference the value of the computations inside the loop. The following HLA code demonstrates an invariant computation:

```
for( mov( 0, eax ); eax < n; inc( eax )) do

    mov( eax, edx );
    add( j, edx );
    sub( 2, edx );
    add( edx, k );

endfor;
```

Because j never changes throughout the execution of this loop, the sub-expression j-2 can be computed outside the loop:

```
mov( j, ecx );
sub( 2, ecx );
for( mov( 0, eax ); eax < n; inc( eax )) do

    mov( eax, edx );
    add( ecx, edx );
    add( edx, k );

endfor;
```

Although we've eliminated a single instruction by computing the sub-expression j-2 outside the loop, there is still an invariant component to this calculation. Note that this invariant component executes *n* times in the loop; this means that we can translate the previous code to the following:

```
mov( j, ecx );
sub( 2, ecx );
intmul( n, ecx );   // Compute n*(j-2) and add this into k outside
add( ecx, k );      // the loop.
for( mov( 0, eax ); eax < n; inc( eax )) do
```

```
    add( eax, k );

endfor;
```

As you can see, we've shrunk the loop body from four instructions down to one. Of course, if you're really interested in improving the efficiency of this particular loop, you can compute the result without using a loop at all (there is a formula that corresponds to the iterative calculation above). Still, this simple example demonstrates elimination of loop-invariant calculations from a loop.

## 7.11.4  Unraveling Loops

For small loops, that is, those whose body is only a few statements, the overhead required to process a loop may constitute a significant percentage of the total processing time. For example, look at the following Pascal code and its associated 80x86 assembly language code:

```
for i := 3 downto 0 do A[i] := 0;

mov( 3, i );
LoopLbl:
    mov( i, ebx );
    mov( 0, A[ ebx*4 ] );
    dec( i );
    jns LoopLbl;
```

Four instructions execute on each repetition of the loop. Only one instruction is doing the desired operation (moving a 0 into an element of A). The remaining three instructions control the loop. Therefore, it takes 16 instructions to do the operation logically required by 4.

While there are many improvements we could make to this loop based on the information presented thus far, consider carefully exactly what it is that this loop is doing—it's storing four 0s into A[0] through A[3]. A more efficient approach is to use four mov instructions to accomplish the same task. For example, if A is an array of double words, then the following code initializes A much faster than the code above:

```
mov( 0, A[0] );
mov( 0, A[4] );
mov( 0, A[8] );
mov( 0, A[12] );
```

Although this is a simple example, it shows the benefit of *loop unraveling* (also known as *loop unrolling*). If this simple loop appeared buried inside a set of nested loops, the 4:1 instruction reduction could possibly double the performance of that section of your program.

Of course, you cannot unravel all loops. Loops that execute a variable number of times are difficult to unravel because there is rarely a way to deter mine (at assembly time) the number of loop iterations. Therefore, unraveling a loop is a process best applied to loops that execute a known number of times (and the number of times is known at assembly time).

Even if you repeat a loop some fixed number of iterations, it may not be a good candidate for loop unraveling. Loop unraveling produces impressive per formance improvements when the number of instructions controlling the loop (and handling other overhead operations) represents a significant percentage of the total number of instructions in the loop. Had the previous loop contained 36 instructions in the body (exclusive of the 4 overhead instructions), then the performance improvement would be, at best, only 10 percent (compared with the 300–400 percent it now enjoys). Therefore, the costs of unraveling a loop, that is, all the extra code that must be inserted into your program, quickly reach a point of diminishing returns as the body of the loop grows larger or as the number of iterations increases. Furthermore, entering that code into your program can become quite a chore. Therefore, loop unravel ing is a technique best applied to small loops.

Note that the superscalar 80x86 chips (Pentium and later) have *branch- prediction hardware* and use other techniques to improve performance. Loop unrolling on such systems may actually *slow down* the code because these pro cessors are optimized to execute short loops.

### 7.11.5  Induction Variables

Consider the following loop:

```
for i := 0 to 255 do csetVar[i] := {};
```

Here the program is initializing each element of an array of character sets to the empty set. The straightforward code to achieve this is the following:

```
mov( 0, i );
FLp:

    // Compute the index into the array (note that each element
    // of a CSET array contains 16 bytes).

    mov( i, ebx );
    shl( 4, ebx );

    // Set this element to the empty set (all 0 bits).

    mov( 0, csetVar[ ebx ] );
    mov( 0, csetVar[ ebx+4 ] );
    mov( 0, csetVar[ ebx+8 ] );
    mov( 0, csetVar[ ebx+12 ] );
```

```
        inc( i );
        cmp( i, 256 );
        jb FLp;
```

Although unraveling this code will still produce a performance improvement, it will take 1,024 instructions to accomplish this task, too many for all but the most time-critical applications. However, you can reduce the execution time of the body of the loop using *induction variables*. An induction variable is one whose value depends entirely on the value of some other variable. In the example above, the index into the array csetVar tracks the loop-control variable (it's always equal to the value of the loop-control variable times 16). Because i doesn't appear anywhere else in the loop, there is no sense in performing the computations on i. Why not operate directly on the array index value? The following code demonstrates this technique:

```
mov( 0, ebx );
FLp:
        mov( 0, csetVar[ ebx ]);
        mov( 0, csetVar[ ebx+4 ] );
        mov( 0, csetVar[ ebx+8 ] );
        mov( 0, csetVar[ ebx+12 ] );

        add( 16, ebx );
        cmp( ebx, 256*16 );
        jb FLp;
```

The induction that takes place in this example occurs when the code increments the loop-control variable (moved into EBX for efficiency reasons) by 16 on each iteration of the loop rather than by 1. Multiplying the loop-control variable by 16 (and also the final loop-termination constant value) allows the code to eliminate multiplying the loop-control variable by 16 on each iteration of the loop (that is, this allows us to remove the shl instruction from the previous code). Further, because this code no longer refers to the original loop-control variable (i), the code can maintain the loop-control variable strictly in the EBX register.

## 7.12  Hybrid Control Structures in HLA

The HLA high-level language control structures have a few drawbacks: (1) they're not true assembly language instructions, (2) complex boolean expressions support only short-circuit evaluation, and (3) they often introduce inefficient coding practices into a language that most people use only when they need to write high-performance code. On the other hand, while the 80x86 low-level control structures let you write efficient code, the resulting code is very difficult to read and maintain. HLA provides a set of hybrid control structures that allow you to use pure assembly language statements to evaluate boolean expressions while using the high-level control structures to delineate the statements controlled by the boolean expressions. The result is code that is much more readable than pure assembly language without being a whole lot less efficient.

HLA provides hybrid forms of the if..elseif..else..endif, while..endwhile, repeat..until, breakif, exitif, and continueif statements (that is, those that involve a boolean expression). For example, a hybrid if statement takes the following form:

```
if( #{ instructions }# ) then statements endif;
```

Note the use of #{ and }# operators to surround a sequence of instructions within this statement. This is what differentiates the hybrid control structures from the standard high-level language control structures. The remaining hybrid control structures take the following forms:

```
while( #{ statements }# ) statements endwhile;
repeat statements until( #{ statements }# );
breakif( #{ statements }# );
exitif( #{ statements }# );
continueif( #{ statements }# );
```

The statements within the curly braces replace the normal boolean expression in an HLA high-level control structure. These particular statements are special insofar as HLA defines two pseudo-labels, true and false, within their context. HLA associates the label true with the code that would normally execute if a boolean expression were present and that expression's result was true. Similarly, HLA associates the label false with the code that would execute if a boolean expression in one of these statements evaluated false. As a simple example, consider the following two (equivalent) if statements:

```
if( eax < ebx ) then inc( eax ); endif;

if
( #{
    cmp( eax, ebx );
    jnb false;
}# ) then
    inc( eax );

endif;
```

The jnb that transfers control to the false label in this latter example will skip over the inc instruction if EAX is not less than EBX. Note that if EAX is less than EBX, then control falls through to the inc instruction. This is roughly equivalent to the following pure assembly code:

```
cmp( eax, ebx );
jnb falseLabel;
    inc( eax );
falseLabel:
```

As a slightly more complex example, consider the statement

```
if( eax >= j && eax <= k ) then sub( j, eax ); endif;
```

The following hybrid if statement accomplishes the above:

```
if
( #{
    cmp( eax, j );
    jnae false;
    cmp( eax, k );
    jnae false;
}# ) then
    sub( j, eax );

endif;
```

As one final example of the hybrid if statement, consider the following:

```
// if( ((eax > ebx) && (eax < ecx)) || (eax = edx)) then
//     mov( ebx, eax );
// endif;

if
( #{
    cmp( eax, edx );
    je true;
    cmp( eax, ebx );
    jng false;
    cmp( eax, ecx );
    jnb false;
}# ) then
    mov( ebx, eax );

endif;
```

Because these examples are rather trivial, they don't really demonstrate how much more readable the code can be when using hybrid statements rather than pure assembly code. However, one thing you should notice is that using hybrid statements eliminates the need to insert labels throughout your code. This can make your programs easier to read and understand.

For the if statement, the true label corresponds to the then clause of the statement; the false label corresponds to the elseif, else, or endif clause (whichever follows the then clause). For the while loop, the true label corresponds to the body of the loop, whereas the false label is attached to the first statement following the corresponding endwhile. For the repeat..until statement, the true label is attached to the code following the until clause, whereas the false label is attached to the first statement of the body of the loop. The breakif, exitif, and continueif statements associate the false label with the statement immediately following one of these statements; they associate the true label with the code normally associated with a break, exit, or continue statement.

## 7.13 For More Information

HLA contains a few additional high-level control structures beyond those th[...] chapter describes. Examples include the try..endtry block and the foreach statement. A discussion of these statements does not appear in this chapter because these are advanced control structures and their implementation is too complex to describe this early in the text. For more information on the implementation, see the electronic edition at *http://www.artofasm.com/* (or *http://webster.cs.ucr.edu/*) or the HLA reference manual.

# 8

# ADVANCED ARITHMETIC

 This chapter deals with those arithmetic operations for which assembly language is especially well suited. It covers four main topics: extended-precision arithmetic, arithmetic on operands whose sizes are different, decimal arithmetic, and computation via table lookup.

By far, the most extensive subject this chapter covers is multiprecision arithmetic. By the conclusion of this chapter you will know how to apply arithmetic and logical operations to integer operands of any size. If you need to work with integer values outside the range ±2 billion (or with unsigned values beyond 4 billion), no sweat; this chapter shows you how to get the job done.

Different-size operands also present some special problems. For example, you may want to add a 64-bit unsigned integer to a 128-bit signed integer value. This chapter discusses how to convert these two operands to a compatible format.

This chapter also discusses decimal arithmetic using the 80x86 BCD (binary-coded decimal) instructions and the FPU (floating-point unit). This lets you use decimal arithmetic in those few applications that absolutely require base-10 operations.

Finally, this chapter concludes by discussing how to speed up complex computations using table lookups.

# 8.1 Multiprecision Operations

One big advantage of assembly language over high-level languages is that assembly language does not limit the size of integer operations. For example, the standard C programming language defines three different integer sizes: short int, int, and long int.[1] On the PC, these are often 16- and 32-bit integers. Although the 80x86 machine instructions limit you to processing 8-, 16-, or 32-bit integers with a single instruction, you can always use multiple instructions to process integers of any size. If you want to add 256-bit integer values together, no problem; it's relatively easy to accomplish this in assembly language. The following sections describe how to extend various arithmetic and logical operations from 16 or 32 bits to as many bits as you please.

### 8.1.1 HLA Standard Library Support for Extended-Precision Operations

Although it is important for you to understand how to do extended-precision arithmetic yourself, you should note that the HLA Standard Library provides a full set of 64-bit and 128-bit arithmetic and logical functions that you can use. These routines are general purpose and very convenient to use. This section briefly describes the HLA Standard Library support for extended-precision arithmetic.

As noted in earlier chapters, the HLA compiler supports several different 64-bit and 128-bit data types. These extended data types are:

- uns64: 64-bit unsigned integers
- int64: 64-bit signed integers
- qword: 64-bit untyped values
- uns128: 128-bit unsigned integers
- int128: 128-bit signed integers
- lword: 128-bit untyped values

HLA also provides a tbyte type, but we will not consider that here (see Section 8.2).

HLA fully supports 64-bit and 128-bit literal constants and constant arithmetic. This allows you to initialize 64- and 128-bit static objects using standard decimal, hexadecimal, or binary notation. For example:

```
static
    u128    :uns128 := 123456789012345678901233567890;
    i64     :int64  := -12345678901234567890;
    lw      :lword  := $1234_5678_90ab_cdef_0000_ffff;
```

---

[1] Newer C standards also provide for a long long int, which is usually a 64-bit integer.

In order to easily manipulate 64-bit and 128-bit values, the HLA Standard Library's math.hhf module provides a set of functions that handle most of the standard arithmetic and logical operations. You use these functions in a manner similar to the 32-bit arithmetic and logical instructions. For example, consider the math.addq (qword) and math.addl (lword) functions:

```
math.addq( left64, right64, dest64 );
math.addl( left128, right128, dest128 );
```

These functions compute the following:

```
dest64 := left64 + right64;       // dest64, left64, and right64
                                  // must be 8-byte operands
dest128 := left128 + right128;  // dest128, left128, and right128
                                  // must be 16-byte operands
```

These functions set the 80x86 flags the same way you'd expect after the execution of an add instruction. Specifically, these functions set the zero flag if the (full) result is 0, they set the carry flag if there is a carry from the H.O. bit, they set the overflow flag if there is a signed overflow, and they set the sign flag if the H.O. bit of the result contains 1.

Most of the remaining arithmetic and logical routines use the same calling sequence as math.addq and math.addl. Briefly, here are those functions:

```
math.andq( left64, right64, dest64 );
math.andl( left128, right128, dest128 );
math.divq( left64, right64, dest64 );
math.divl( left128, right128, dest128 );
math.idivq( left64, right64, dest64 );
math.idivl( left128, right128, dest128 );
math.modq( left64, right64, dest64 );
math.modl( left128, right128, dest128 );
math.imodq( left64, right64, dest64 );
math.imodl( left128, right128, dest128 );
math.mulq( left64, right64, dest64 );
math.mull( left128, right128, dest128 );
math.imulq( left64, right64, dest64 );
math.imull( left128, right128, dest128 );
math.orq( left64, right64, dest64 );
math.orl( left128, right128, dest128 );
math.subq( left64, right64, dest64 );
math.subl( left128, right128, dest128 );
math.xorq( left64, right64, dest64 );
math.xorl( left128, right128, dest128 );
```

These functions set the flags the same way as the corresponding 32-bit machine instructions and, in the case of the division and remainder (modulo) functions, raise the same exceptions. Note that the multiplication functions do not produce an extended-precision result. The destination value is the same size as the source operands. These functions set the overflow and carry

flags if the result does not fit into the destination operand. All of these fun-
tions compute the following:

```
dest64 := left64 op right64;
dest128 := left128 op right128;
```

where *op* represents the specific operation.

In addition to these functions, the HLA Standard Library's math modul
also provides a few additional functions whose syntax is slightly different fro
math.addq and math.addl. These functions include math.negq, math.negl, math.not
math.notl, math.shlq, math.shll, math.shrq, and math.shrl. Note that there are n
rotates or arithmetic shift-right functions. However, you'll soon see that thes
operations are easy to synthesize using standard instructions. Here are the
prototypes for these additional functions:

```
math.negq( source:qword; var dest:qword );
math.negl( source:lword; var dest:lword );
math.notq( source:qword; var dest:qword );
math.notl( source:lword; var dest:lword );
math.shlq( count:uns32; source:qword; var dest:qword );
math.shll( count:uns32; source:lword; var dest:lword );
math.shrq( count:uns32; source:qword; var dest:qword );
math.shrl( count:uns32; source:lword; var dest:lword );
```

Again, all these functions set the flags exactly the same way the correspon-
ing machine instructions would set the flags were they to support 64-bit or
128-bit operands.

The HLA Standard Library also provides a full complement of I/O and
conversion routines for 64-bit and 128-bit values. For example, you can use
stdout.put to display 64- and 128-bit values, you may use stdin.get to read thes
values, and there is a set of routines in the HLA conversions module that co:
vert between these values and their string equivalents. In general, anything
you can do with a 32-bit value can be done with a 64-bit or 128-bit value as
well. See the HLA Standard Library documentation for more details.

### 8.1.2 Multiprecision Addition Operations

The 80x86 add instruction adds two 8-, 16-, or 32- bit numbers. After the exec
tion of the add instruction, the 80x86 carry flag is set if there is an overflow ou
of the H.O. bit of the sum. You can use this information to do multiprecision
addition operations. Consider the way you manually perform a multidigit
(multiprecision) addition operation:

```
Step 1: Add the least significant digits together:

        289                    289
       +456    produces       +456
       ----                   ----
                              5 with carry 1.
```

Step 2: Add the next significant digits plus the carry:

```
       1 (previous carry)
      289                             289
     +456          produces          +456
     ----                            ----
        5                            45 with carry 1.
```

Step 3: Add the most significant digits plus the carry:

```
                                       1 (previous carry)
      289                             289
     +456          produces          +456
     ----                            ----
       45                             745
```

The 80x86 handles extended-precision arithmetic in an identical fashion, except instead of adding the numbers a digit at a time, it adds them together a byte, word, or double word at a time. Consider the three double-word (96-bit) addition operation in Figure 8-1.

Step 1: Add the least significant words together.

Step 2: Add the middle words together.

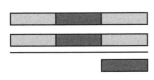
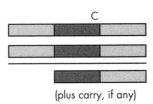

(plus carry, if any)

Step 3: Add the most significant words together.

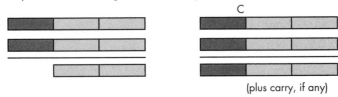

(plus carry, if any)

Figure 8-1: Adding two 96-bit objects together

As you can see from this figure, the idea is to break up a larger operation into a sequence of smaller operations. Since the x86 processor family is capable of adding together, at most, 32 bits at a time, the operation must proceed in blocks of 32 bits or less. So the first step is to add the two L.O. double words together just as you would add the two L.O. digits of a decimal number together in the manual algorithm. There is nothing special about this operation; you can use the add instruction to achieve this.

The second step involves adding together the second pair of double words in the two 96-bit values. Note that in step 2, the calculation must also add in the carry out of the previous addition (if any). If there is a carry out of the L.O. addition, the add instruction sets the carry flag to 1; conversely, if there is no carry out of the L.O. addition, the earlier add instruction clears the carry flag. Therefore, in this second addition, we really need to compute the sum of the two double words plus the carry out of the first instruction. Fortunately, the x86 CPUs provide an instruction that does exactly this: the adc (add with carry) instruction. The adc instruction uses the same syntax as the add instruction and performs almost the same operation:

```
adc( source, dest );   // dest := dest + source + C
```

As you can see, the only difference between the add and adc instructions is that the adc instruction adds in the value of the carry flag along with the source and destination operands. It also sets the flags the same way the add instruction does (including setting the carry flag if there is an unsigned overflow). This is exactly what we need to add together the middle two double words of our 96-bit sum.

In step 3 of Figure 8-1, the algorithm adds together the H.O. double words of the 96-bit value. This addition operation must also incorporate the carry out of the sum of the middle two double words; hence the adc instruction is needed here as well. To sum it up, the add instruction adds the L.O. double words together. The adc (add with carry) instruction adds all other double-word pairs together. At the end of the extended-precision addition sequence, the carry flag indicates unsigned overflow (if set), a set overflow flag indicates signed overflow, and the sign flag indicates the sign of the result. The zero flag doesn't have any real meaning at the end of the extended-precision addition (it simply means that the sum of the two H.O. double words is 0 and does not indicate that the whole result is 0). If you want to see how to check for an extended-precision zero result, see the source code for the HLA Standard Library math.addq or math.addl function.

For example, suppose that you have two 64-bit values you wish to add together, defined as follows:

```
static
    X: qword;
    Y: qword;
```

Suppose also that you want to store the sum in a third variable, Z, which is also a qword. The following 80x86 code will accomplish this task:

```
mov( (type dword X), eax );      // Add together the L.O. 32 bits
add( (type dword Y), eax );      // of the numbers and store the
mov( eax, (type dword Z) );      // result into the L.O. dword of Z.
```

```
mov( (type dword X[4]), eax );      // Add together (with carry) the
adc( (type dword Y[4]), eax );      // H.O. 32 bits and store the result
mov( eax, (type dword Z[4]) );      // into the H.O. dword of Z.
```

Remember, these variables are qword objects. Therefore the compiler will not accept an instruction of the form mov( X, eax ); because this instruction would attempt to load a 64-bit value into a 32-bit register. This code uses the coercion operator to coerce symbols X, Y, and Z to 32 bits. The first three instructions add the L.O. double words of X and Y together and store the result at the L.O. double word of Z. The last three instructions add the H.O. double words of X and Y together, along with the carry from the L.O. word, and store the result in the H.O. double word of Z. Remember, address expressions of the form X[4] access the H.O. double word of a 64-bit entity. This is because the x86 memory space addresses bytes, and it takes 4 consecutive bytes to form a double word.

You can extend this to any number of bits by using the adc instruction to add in the higher-order values. For example, to add together two 128-bit values, you could use code like the following:

```
type
    tBig: dword[4];        // Storage for four dwords is 128 bits.

static
    BigVal1: tBig;
    BigVal2: tBig;
    BigVal3: tBig;
        .
        .
        .
    mov( BigVal1[0], eax );    // Note there is no need for (type dword BigValx)
    add( BigVal2[0], eax );    // because the base type of BitValx is dword.
    mov( eax, BigVal3[0] );

    mov( BigVal1[4], eax );
    adc( BigVal2[4], eax );
    mov( eax, BigVal3[4] );

    mov( BigVal1[8], eax );
    adc( BigVal2[8], eax );
    mov( eax, BigVal3[8] );

    mov( BigVal1[12], eax );
    adc( BigVal2[12], eax );
    mov( eax, BigVal3[12] );
```

## 8.1.3  Multiprecision Subtraction Operations

The 80x86 performs multibyte subtraction, just as it does addition, the same way you would manually, except it subtracts whole bytes, words, or double words at a time rather than decimal digits. The mechanism is similar to that for the add operation. You use the sub instruction on the L.O. byte/word/double word and the sbb (subtract with borrow) instruction on the high-order value.

The following example demonstrates a 64-bit subtraction using the 32-bit registers on the 80x86:

```
static
    Left:       qword;
    Right:      qword;
    Diff:       qword;
       .
       .
       .

    mov( (type dword Left), eax );
    sub( (type dword Right), eax );
    mov( eax, (type dword Diff) );

    mov( (type dword Left[4]), eax );
    sbb( (type dword Right[4]), eax );
    mov( (type dword Diff[4]), eax );
```

The following example demonstrates a 128-bit subtraction:

```
type
    tBig: dword[4];  // Storage for four dwords is 128 bits.

static
    BigVal1: tBig;
    BigVal2: tBig;
    BigVal3: tBig;
       .
       .
       .

    // Compute BigVal3 := BigVal1 - BigVal2

    mov( BigVal1[0], eax ); // Note there is no need for (type dword BigValx)
    sub( BigVal2[0], eax ); // because the base type of BitValx is dword.
    mov( eax, BigVal3[0] );

    mov( BigVal1[4], eax );
    sbb( BigVal2[4], eax );
    mov( eax, BigVal3[4] );

    mov( BigVal1[8], eax );
    sbb( BigVal2[8], eax );
    mov( eax, BigVal3[8] );

    mov( BigVal1[12], eax );
    sbb( BigVal2[12], eax );
    mov( eax, BigVal3[12] );
```

## 8.1.4 Extended-Precision Comparisons

Unfortunately, there isn't a "compare with borrow" instruction that you can use to perform extended-precision comparisons. Since the cmp and sub instructions perform the same operation, at least as far as the flags are concerned, you'd probably guess that you could use the sbb instruction to synthesize an extended-precision comparison; however, that approach won't always work. Fortunately, there is a better solution.

Consider the two unsigned values $2157 and $1293. The L.O. bytes of these two values do not affect the outcome of the comparison. Simply comparing the H.O. bytes, $21 with $12, tells us that the first value is greater than the second. In fact, the only time you ever need to look at both bytes of these values is if the H.O. bytes are equal. In all other cases comparing the H.O. bytes tells you everything you need to know about the values. Of course, this is true for any number of bytes, not just 2. The following code compares two signed 64-bit integers by comparing their H.O. double words first and comparing their L.O. double words only if the H.O. double words are equal:

```
// This sequence transfers control to location "IsGreater" if
// QwordValue > QwordValue2. It transfers control to "IsLess" if
// QwordValue < QwordValue2. It falls through to the instruction
// following this sequence if QwordValue = QwordValue2. To test for
// inequality, change the "IsGreater" and "IsLess" operands to "NotEqual"
// in this code.

        mov( (type dword QWordValue[4]), eax );  // Get H.O. dword.
        cmp( eax, (type dword QWordValue2[4]));
        jg IsGreater;
        jl IsLess;

        mov( (type dword QWordValue[0]), eax );  // If H.O. dwords were equal,
        cmp( eax, (type dword QWordValue2[0]));  // then we must compare the
        jg IsGreater;                            // L.O. dwords.
        jl IsLess;

// Fall through to this point if the two values were equal.
```

To compare unsigned values, simply use the ja and jb instructions in place of jg and jl.

You can easily synthesize any possible comparison from the preceding sequence. The following examples show how to do this. These examples demonstrate signed comparisons; just substitute ja, jae, jb, and jbe for jg, jge, jl, and jle (respectively) if you want unsigned comparisons. Each of the following examples assumes these declarations:

```
static
    QW1: qword;
    QW2: qword;
```

```
const
    QW1d: text := "(type dword QW1)";
    QW2d: text := "(type dword QW2)";
```

The following code implements a 64-bit test to see if QW1 < QW2 (signed)
Control transfers to IsLess label if QW1 < QW2. Control falls through to the nex
statement if this is not true.

```
    mov( QW1d[4], eax );    // Get H.O. dword.
    cmp( eax, QW2d[4] );
    jg NotLess;
    jl IsLess;

    mov( QW1d[0], eax );    // Fall through to here if the H.O. dwords are equal.
    cmp( eax, QW2d[0] );
    jl IsLess;
NotLess:
```

Here is a 64-bit test to see if QW1 <= QW2 (signed). This code jumps to
IsLessEq if the condition is true.

```
    mov( QW1d[4], eax );    // Get H.O. dword.
    cmp( eax, QW2d[4] );
    jg NotLessEQ;
    jl IsLessEQ;

    mov( QW1d[0], eax );    // Fall through to here if the H.O. dwords are equal.
    cmp( eax, QW2d[0] );
    jle IsLessEQ;
NotLessEQ:
```

This is a 64-bit test to see if QW1 > QW2 (signed). It jumps to IsGtr if this con
dition is true.

```
    mov( QW1d[4], eax );    // Get H.O. dword.
    cmp( eax, QW2d[4] );
    jg IsGtr;
    jl NotGtr;

    mov( QW1d[0], eax );    // Fall through to here if the H.O. dwords are equal.
    cmp( eax, QW2d[0] );
    jg IsGtr;
NotGtr:
```

The following is a 64-bit test to see if QW1 >= QW2 (signed). This code jump
to label IsGtrEQ if this is the case.

```
    mov( QW1d[4], eax );    // Get H.O. dword.
    cmp( eax, QW2d[4] );
    jg IsGtrEQ;
    jl NotGtrEQ;
```

```
        mov( QW1d[0], eax );    // Fall through to here if the H.O. dwords are equal.
        cmp( eax, QW2d[0] );
        jge IsGtrEQ;
NotGtrEQ:
```

Here is a 64-bit test to see if QW1 = QW2 (signed or unsigned). This code branches to the label IsEqual if QW1 = QW2. It falls through to the next instruction if they are not equal.

```
        mov( QW1d[4], eax );    // Get H.O. dword.
        cmp( eax, QW2d[4] );
        jne NotEqual;

        mov( QW1d[0], eax );    // Fall through to here if the H.O. dwords are equal.
        cmp( eax, QW2d[0] );
        je IsEqual;
NotEqual:
```

The following is a 64-bit test to see if QW1 <> QW2 (signed or unsigned). This code branches to the label NotEqual if QW1 <> QW2. It falls through to the next instruction if they are equal.

```
        mov( QW1d[4], eax );    // Get H.O. dword.
        cmp( eax, QW2d[4] );
        jne IsNotEqual;

        mov( QW1d[0], eax );    // Fall through to here if the H.O. dwords are equal.
        cmp( eax, QW2d[0] );
        jne IsNotEqual;

// Fall through to this point if they are equal.
```

You cannot directly use the HLA high-level control structures if you need to perform an extended-precision comparison. However, you may use the HLA hybrid control structures and bury the appropriate comparison in the boolean expression. Doing so may produce easier to read code. For example, the following if..then..else..endif statement checks to see if QW1 > QW2 using a 64-bit extended-precision unsigned comparison:

```
if
( #{
        mov( QW1d[4], eax );
        cmp( eax, QW2d[4] );
        jg true;

        mov( QW1d[0], eax );
        cmp( eax, QW2d[0] );
        jng false;
}# ) then

    << Code to execute if QW1 > QW2 >>
```

```
else

    << Code to execute if QW1 <= QW2 >>

endif;
```

If you need to compare objects that are larger than 64 bits, it is very ea
to generalize the code given above for 64-bit operands. Always start the con
parison with the H.O. double words of the objects and work your way down
the L.O. double words of the objects as long as the corresponding doubl
words are equal. The following example compares two 128-bit values to see
the first is less than or equal (unsigned) to the second:

```
static
    Big1: uns128;
    Big2: uns128;
       .
       .
       .
    if
    ( #{
        mov( Big1[12], eax );
        cmp( eax, Big2[12] );
        jb true;
        ja false;
        mov( Big1[8], eax );
        cmp( eax, Big2[8] );
        jb true;
        ja false;
        mov( Big1[4], eax );
        cmp( eax, Big2[4] );
        jb true;
        ja false;
        mov( Big1[0], eax );
        cmp( eax, Big2[0] );
        jnbe false;
    }# ) then

        << Code to execute if Big1 <= Big2 >>

    else

        << Code to execute if Big1 > Big2 >>

    endif;
```

## 8.1.5  Extended-Precision Multiplication

Although an 8×8-bit, 16×16-bit, or 32×32-bit multiplication is usually sufficient,
there are times when you may want to multiply larger values. You will use the x8
single operand mul and imul instructions for extended-precision multiplicatio
operations.

Not surprisingly (in view of how we achieved extended-precision addition using adc and sbb), you use the same techniques to perform extended-precision multiplication on the 80x86 that you employ when manually multiplying two values. Consider a simplified form of the way you perform multidigit multiplication by hand:

---

1) Multiply the first two
   digits together (5*3):

```
123
 45
---
 15
```

2) Multiply 5*2:

```
123
 45
---
 15
 10
```

3) Multiply 5*1:

```
123
 45
---
 15
 10
  5
```

4) Multiply 4*3:

```
123
 45
---
 15
 10
  5
 12
```

5) Multiply 4*2:

```
123
 45
---
 15
 10
  5
 12
  8
```

6) Multiply 4*1:

```
123
 45
---
 15
 10
  5
 12
  8
  4
```

7) Add all the partial products together:

```
  123
   45
  ---
   15
   10
    5
   12
    8
    4
------
 5535
```

---

The 80x86 does extended-precision multiplication in the same manner except that it works with bytes, words, and double words rather than digits. Figure 8-2 shows how this works.

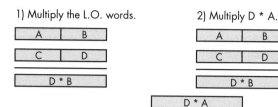

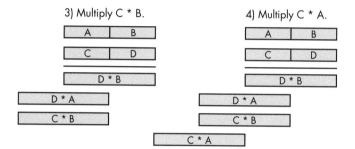

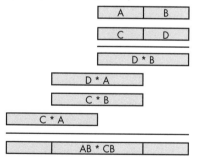

Figure 8-2: Extended-precision multiplication

Probably the most important thing to remember when performing an extended-precision multiplication is that you must also perform a multiple-precision addition at the same time. Adding up all the partial products require several additions that will produce the result. Listing 8-1 demonstrates the proper way to multiply two 64-bit values on a 32-bit processor.

```
program testMUL64;
#include( "stdlib.hhf" )


procedure MUL64( Multiplier:qword; Multiplicand:qword; var Product:lword );
const
    mp: text := "(type dword Multiplier)";
    mc: text := "(type dword Multiplicand)";
    prd:text := "(type dword [edi])";

begin MUL64;

    mov( Product, edi );

    // Multiply the L.O. dword of Multiplier times Multiplicand.

    mov( mp, eax );
    mul( mc, eax );        // Multiply L.O. dwords.
    mov( eax, prd );       // Save L.O. dword of product.
    mov( edx, ecx );       // Save H.O. dword of partial product result.


    mov( mp, eax );
    mul( mc[4], eax );     // Multiply mp(L.O.) * mc(H.O.)
    add( ecx, eax );       // Add to the partial product.
    adc( 0, edx );         // Don't forget the carry!
    mov( eax, ebx );       // Save partial product for now.
    mov( edx, ecx );


    // Multiply the H.O. word of Multiplier with Multiplicand.

    mov( mp[4], eax );     // Get H.O. dword of Multiplier.
    mul( mc, eax );        // Multiply by L.O. word of Multiplicand.
    add( ebx, eax );       // Add to the partial product.
    mov( eax, prd[4] );    // Save the partial product.
    adc( edx, ecx );       // Add in the carry!


    mov( mp[4], eax );     // Multiply the two H.O. dwords together.
    mul( mc[4], eax );
    add( ecx, eax );       // Add in partial product.
    adc( 0, edx );         // Don't forget the carry!
    mov( eax, prd[8] );    // Save the partial product.
    mov( edx, prd[12] );

end MUL64;

static
    op1: qword;
    op2: qword;
    rslt: lword;
```

```
begin testMUL64;

    // Initialize the qword values (note that static objects
    // are initialized with 0 bits).

    mov( 1234, (type dword op1 ));
    mov( 5678, (type dword op2 ));
    MUL64( op1, op2, rslt );

    // The following only prints the L.O. qword, but
    // we know the H.O. qword is 0 so this is okay.

    stdout.put( "rslt=" );
    stdout.putu64( (type qword rslt));

end testMUL64;
```

*Listing 8-1: Extended-precision multiplication*

One thing you must keep in mind concerning this code is that it works only for unsigned operands. To multiply two signed values you must note the signs of the operands before the multiplication, take the absolute value of the two operands, do an unsigned multiplication, and then adjust the sign of the resulting product based on the signs of the original operands. Multiplication of signed operands is left as an exercise to the reader (or you could just check out the source code in the HLA Standard Library).

The example in Listing 8-1 was fairly straightforward because it was possible to keep the partial products in various registers. If you need to multiply large values together, you will need to maintain the partial products in temporary (memory) variables. Other than that, the algorithm that Listing 8-1 uses generalizes to any number of double words.

### 8.1.6  Extended-Precision Division

You cannot synthesize a general $n$-bit/$m$-bit division operation using the div and idiv instructions. Extended-precision division requires a sequence of shift and subtract instructions and is extremely messy. However, a less-general operation, dividing an $n$-bit quantity by a 32-bit quantity, is easily synthesized using the div instruction. This section presents both methods for extended-precision division.

Before we describe how to perform a multiprecision division operation, you should note that some operations require an extended-precision division even though they may look calculable with a single div or idiv instruction. Dividing a 64-bit quantity by a 32-bit quantity is easy, as long as the resulting quotient fits into 32 bits. The div and idiv instructions will handle this directly. However, if the quotient does not fit into 32 bits, then you have to handle this problem as an extended-precision division. The trick here is to divide the (zero- or sign-extended) H.O. double word of the dividend by the divisor and then repeat the process with the remainder and the L.O. dword of the dividend. The following sequence demonstrates this.

```
static
    dividend: dword[2] := [$1234, 4];   // = $4_0000_1234.
    divisor:  dword := 2;               // dividend/divisor = $2_0000_091A
    quotient: dword[2];
    remainder:dword;
    .
    .
    .
    mov( divisor, ebx );
    mov( dividend[4], eax );
    xor( edx, edx );                    // Zero extend for unsigned division.
    div( ebx, edx:eax );
    mov( eax, quotient[4] );            // Save H.O. dword of the quotient (2).
    mov( dividend[0], eax );            // Note that this code does *NOT* zero extend
    div( ebx, edx:eax );                // eax into edx before this div instr.
    mov( eax, quotient[0] );            // Save L.O. dword of the quotient ($91a).
    mov( edx, remainder );              // Save away the remainder.
```

Since it is perfectly legal to divide a value by 1, it is possible that the resulting quotient could require as many bits as the dividend. That is why the quotient variable in this example is the same size (64 bits) as the dividend variable (note the use of an array of two double words rather than a qword type; this spares the code from having to coerce the operands to double words). Regardless of the size of the dividend and divisor operands, the remainder is always no larger than the size of the division operation (32 bits in this case). Hence the remainder variable in this example is just a double word.

Before analyzing this code to see how it works, let's take a brief look at why a single 64/32 division will not work for this particular example even though the div instruction does indeed calculate the result for a 64/32 division. The naive approach, assuming that the x86 were capable of this operation, would look something like the following:

```
// This code does *NOT* work!

    mov( dividend[0], eax );    // Get dividend into edx:eax
    mov( dividend[4], edx );
    div( divisor, edx:eax );    // Divide edx:eax by divisor.
```

Although this code is syntactically correct and will compile, if you attempt to run this code it will raise an ex.DivideError[2] exception. The reason is that the quotient must fit into 32 bits. Because the quotient turns out to be $2_0000_091A, it will not fit into the EAX register, hence the resulting exception.

Now let's take another look at the former code that correctly computes the 64/32 quotient. This code begins by computing the 32/32 quotient of dividend[4]/divisor. The quotient from this division (2) becomes the H.O. double word of the final quotient. The remainder from this division (0) becomes the extension in EDX for the second half of the division operation. The second half of the code divides edx:dividend[0] by divisor to produce the

---

[2] Windows may translate this to an ex.IntoInstr exception.

L.O. double word of the quotient and the remainder from the division. Note th
the code does not zero extend EAX into EDX prior to the second div instructio
EDX already contains valid bits, and this code must not disturb them.

The 64/32 division operation above is actually just a special case of the
general division operation that lets you divide an arbitrary size value by a 32-t
divisor. To achieve this, you begin by moving the H.O. double word of the d
idend into EAX and zero extending this into EDX. Next, you divide this valu
by the divisor. Then, without modifying EDX along the way, you store away th
partial quotients, load EAX with the next-lower double word in the dividen
and divide it by the divisor. You repeat this operation until you've processe
all the double words in the dividend. At that time the EDX register will cor
tain the remainder. The program in Listing 8-2 demonstrates how to divide
128-bit quantity by a 32-bit divisor, producing a 128-bit quotient and a 32-b
remainder.

```
program testDiv128;
#include( "stdlib.hhf" )

procedure div128
(
        Dividend:    lword;
        Divisor:     dword;
    var QuotAdrs:    lword;
    var Remainder:   dword
); @nodisplay;

const
    Quotient: text := "(type dword [edi])";

begin div128;

    push( eax );
    push( edx );
    push( edi );

    mov( QuotAdrs, edi );        // Pointer to quotient storage.

    mov( (type dword Dividend[12]), eax ); // Begin division with the H.O. dword
    xor( edx, edx );             // Zero extend into edx.
    div( Divisor, edx:eax );     // Divide H.O. dword.
    mov( eax, Quotient[12] );    // Store away H.O. dword of quotient.

    mov( (type dword Dividend[8]), eax ); // Get dword #2 from the dividend.
    div( Divisor, edx:eax );     // Continue the division.
    mov( eax, Quotient[8] );     // Store away dword #2 of the quotient.

    mov( (type dword Dividend[4]), eax ); // Get dword #1 from the dividend.
    div( Divisor, edx:eax );     // Continue the division.
    mov( eax, Quotient[4] );     // Store away dword #1 of the quotient.
```

```
        mov( (type dword Dividend[0]), eax );     // Get the L.O. dword of the
                                                  // dividend.
        div( Divisor, edx:eax );    // Finish the division.
        mov( eax, Quotient[0] );    // Store away the L.O. dword of the quotient.

        mov( Remainder, edi );      // Get the pointer to the remainder's value.
        mov( edx, [edi] );          // Store away the remainder value.

        pop( edi );
        pop( edx );
        pop( eax );

end div128;

static
    op1:    lword    := $8888_8888_6666_6666_4444_4444_2222_2221;
    op2:    dword    := 2;
    quo:    lword;
    rmndr:  dword;


begin testDiv128;

    div128( op1, op2, quo, rmndr );

    stdout.put
    (
        nl
        nl
        "After the division: " nl
        nl
        "Quotient = $",
        quo[12], "_",
        quo[8], "_",
        quo[4], "_",
        quo[0], nl

        "Remainder = ", (type uns32 rmndr )
    );

end testDiv128;
```

*Listing 8-2: Unsigned 128/32-bit extended-precision division*

You can extend this code to any number of bits by simply adding additional mov/div/mov instructions to the sequence. Like the extended-precision multiplication the previous section presents, this extended-precision division algorithm works only for unsigned operands. If you need to divide two signed quantities, you must note their signs, take their absolute values, do the unsigned division, and then set the sign of the result based on the signs of the operands.

If you need to use a divisor larger than 32 bits, you're going to have to implement the division using a shift-and-subtract strategy. Unfortunately, such algorithms are very slow. In this section we'll develop two division algorithms that operate on an arbitrary number of bits. The first is slow but easier to understand; the second is quite a bit faster (in the average case).

As for multiplication, the best way to understand how the computer pe forms division is to study how you were taught to do long division by hand. Consider the operation 3,456/12 and the steps you would take to manually perform this operation, as shown in Figure 8-3.

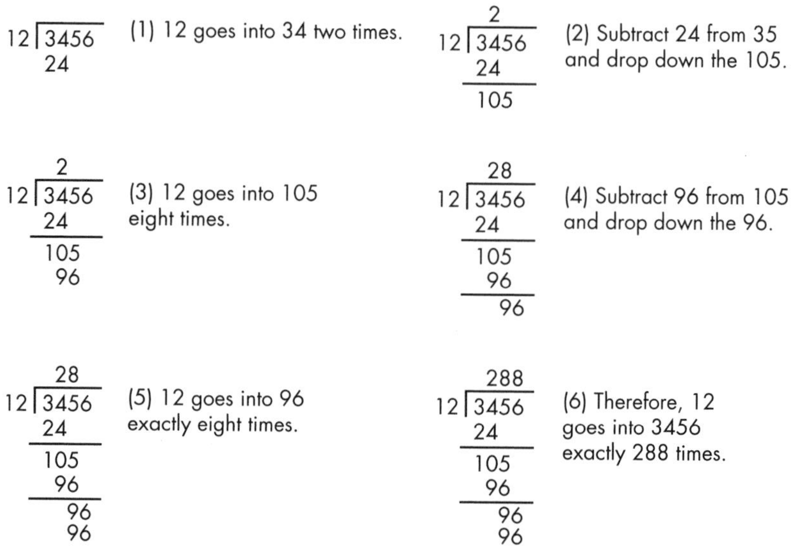

```
         2
12 ⟌ 3456        (1) 12 goes into 34 two times.
     24
```

```
           2
12 ⟌ 3456          (2) Subtract 24 from 35
     24            and drop down the 105.
    ─────
     105
```

```
          2
12 ⟌ 3456          (3) 12 goes into 105
     24            eight times.
    ─────
     105
      96
```

```
          28
12 ⟌ 3456          (4) Subtract 96 from 105
     24            and drop down the 96.
    ─────
     105
      96
     ─────
      96
```

```
          28
12 ⟌ 3456          (5) 12 goes into 96
     24            exactly eight times.
    ─────
     105
      96
     ─────
      96
      96
```

```
         288
12 ⟌ 3456          (6) Therefore, 12
     24            goes into 3456
    ─────          exactly 288 times.
     105
      96
     ─────
      96
      96
```

Figure 8-3: Manual digit-by-digit division operation

This algorithm is actually easier in binary because at each step you do no have to guess how many times 12 goes into the remainder, nor do you have t multiply 12 by your guess to obtain the amount to subtract. At each step in th binary algorithm the divisor goes into the remainder exactly zero or one times. As an example, consider the division of 27 (11011) by 3 (11) that is shown i Figure 8-4.

There is a novel way to implement this binary division algorithm that computes the quotient and the remainder at the same time. The algorithm i the following:

```
Quotient := Dividend;
Remainder := 0;
for i := 1 to NumberBits do

    Remainder:Quotient := Remainder:Quotient SHL 1;
    if Remainder >= Divisor then

        Remainder := Remainder - Divisor;
        Quotient := Quotient + 1;

    endif
endfor
```

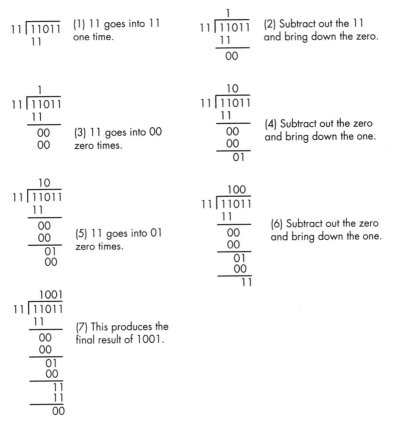

*Figure 8-4: Longhand division in binary*

NumberBits is the number of bits in the Remainder, Quotient, Divisor, and Dividend variables. Note that the Quotient := Quotient + 1; statement sets the L.O. bit of Quotient to 1 because this algorithm previously shifts Quotient 1 bit to the left. The program in Listing 8-3 implements this algorithm.

```
program testDiv128b;
#include( "stdlib.hhf" )



// div128-
//
// This procedure does a general 128/128 division operation using the
// following algorithm (all variables are assumed to be 128-bit objects):
//
// Quotient := Dividend;
// Remainder := 0;
// for i := 1 to NumberBits do
//
```

```
//   Remainder:Quotient := Remainder:Quotient SHL 1;
//   if Remainder >= Divisor then
//
//       Remainder := Remainder - Divisor;
//       Quotient := Quotient + 1;
//
//   endif
// endfor
//

procedure div128
(
        Dividend:    lword;
        Divisor:     lword;
    var QuotAdrs:    lword;
    var RmndrAdrs:   lword
);  @nodisplay;

const
    Quotient: text := "Dividend";    // Use the Dividend as the Quotient.

var
    Remainder: lword;

begin div128;

    push( eax );
    push( ecx );
    push( edi );

    mov( 0, eax );                        // Set the remainder to 0.
    mov( eax, (type dword Remainder[0]) );
    mov( eax, (type dword Remainder[4]) );
    mov( eax, (type dword Remainder[8]) );
    mov( eax, (type dword Remainder[12]));

    mov( 128, ecx );                      // Count off 128 bits in ecx.
    repeat

        // Compute Remainder:Quotient := Remainder:Quotient SHL 1:

        shl( 1, (type dword Dividend[0]) );   // See Section 8.1.12 to see
        rcl( 1, (type dword Dividend[4]) );   // how this code shifts 256
        rcl( 1, (type dword Dividend[8]) );   // bits to the left by 1 bit.
        rcl( 1, (type dword Dividend[12]));
        rcl( 1, (type dword Remainder[0]) );
        rcl( 1, (type dword Remainder[4]) );
        rcl( 1, (type dword Remainder[8]) );
        rcl( 1, (type dword Remainder[12]));

        // Do a 128-bit comparison to see if the remainder
        // is greater than or equal to the divisor.
```

```
          if
          ( #{
              mov( (type dword Remainder[12]), eax );
              cmp( eax, (type dword Divisor[12]) );
              ja true;
              jb false;

              mov( (type dword Remainder[8]), eax );
              cmp( eax, (type dword Divisor[8]) );
              ja true;
              jb false;

              mov( (type dword Remainder[4]), eax );
              cmp( eax, (type dword Divisor[4]) );
              ja true;
              jb false;

              mov( (type dword Remainder[0]), eax );
              cmp( eax, (type dword Divisor[0]) );
              jb false;
          }# ) then

              // Remainder := Remainder - Divisor

              mov( (type dword Divisor[0]), eax );
              sub( eax, (type dword Remainder[0]) );

              mov( (type dword Divisor[4]), eax );
              sbb( eax, (type dword Remainder[4]) );

              mov( (type dword Divisor[8]), eax );
              sbb( eax, (type dword Remainder[8]) );

              mov( (type dword Divisor[12]), eax );
              sbb( eax, (type dword Remainder[12]) );

              // Quotient := Quotient + 1;

              add( 1, (type dword Quotient[0]) );
              adc( 0, (type dword Quotient[4]) );
              adc( 0, (type dword Quotient[8]) );
              adc( 0, (type dword Quotient[12]) );

          endif;
          dec( ecx );

until( @z );


// Okay, copy the quotient (left in the Dividend variable)
// and the remainder to their return locations.
```

```
        mov( QuotAdrs, edi );
        mov( (type dword Quotient[0]), eax );
        mov( eax, [edi] );
        mov( (type dword Quotient[4]), eax );
        mov( eax, [edi+4] );
        mov( (type dword Quotient[8]), eax );
        mov( eax, [edi+8] );
        mov( (type dword Quotient[12]), eax );
        mov( eax, [edi+12] );

        mov( RmndrAdrs, edi );
        mov( (type dword Remainder[0]), eax );
        mov( eax, [edi] );
        mov( (type dword Remainder[4]), eax );
        mov( eax, [edi+4] );
        mov( (type dword Remainder[8]), eax );
        mov( eax, [edi+8] );
        mov( (type dword Remainder[12]), eax );
        mov( eax, [edi+12] );


        pop( edi );
        pop( ecx );
        pop( eax );

end div128;



// Some simple code to test out the division operation:

static
    op1:    lword    := $8888_8888_6666_6666_4444_4444_2222_2221;
    op2:    lword    := 2;
    quo:    lword;
    rmndr:  lword;


begin testDiv128b;

    div128( op1, op2, quo, rmndr );

    stdout.put
    (
        nl
        nl
        "After the division: " nl
        nl
        "Quotient = $",
        (type dword quo[12]), "_",
        (type dword quo[8]), "_",
        (type dword quo[4]), "_",
        (type dword quo[0]), nl
```

```
            "Remainder = ", (type uns32 rmndr )
    );

end testDiv128b;
```

*Listing 8-3: Extended-precision division*

This code looks simple but there are a few problems with it: It does not check for division by 0 (it will produce the value $FFFF_FFFF_FFFF_FFFF if you attempt to divide by 0), it handles only unsigned values, and it is very slow. Handling division by 0 is very simple; just check the divisor against 0 prior to running this code and return an appropriate error code if the divisor is 0 (or raise the ex.DivisionError exception). Dealing with signed values is the same as the earlier division algorithm: Note the signs, take the operands' absolute values, do the unsigned division, and then fix the sign afterward. The performance of this algorithm, however, leaves a lot to be desired. It's around an order of magnitude or two worse than the div/idiv instructions on the 80x86, and they are among the slowest instructions on the CPU.

There is a technique you can use to boost the performance of this division by a fair amount: Check to see if the divisor variable uses only 32 bits. Often, even though the divisor is a 128-bit variable, the value itself fits just fine into 32 bits (that is, the H.O. double words of Divisor are 0). In this special case, which occurs frequently, you can use the div instruction, which is much faster. The algorithm is a bit more complex because you have to first compare the H.O. double words for 0, but on the average it runs much faster while remaining capable of dividing any two pairs of values.

### 8.1.7   Extended-Precision neg Operations

Although there are several ways to negate an extended-precision value, the shortest way for smaller values (96 bits or less) is to use a combination of neg and sbb instructions. This technique uses the fact that neg subtracts its operand from 0. In particular, it sets the flags the same way the sub instruction would if you subtracted the destination value from 0. This code takes the following form (assuming you want to negate the 64-bit value in EDX:EAX):

```
neg( edx );
neg( eax );
sbb( 0, edx );
```

The sbb instruction decrements EDX if there is a borrow out of the L.O. word of the negation operation (which always occurs unless EAX is 0).

Extending this operation to additional bytes, words, or double words is easy; all you have to do is start with the H.O. memory location of the object you want to negate and work toward the L.O. byte. The following code computes a 128-bit negation.

```
static
    Value: dword[4];
        .
        .
        .
    neg( Value[12] );      // Negate the H.O. double word.
    neg( Value[8] );       // Neg previous dword in memory.
    sbb( 0, Value[12] );   // Adjust H.O. dword.

    neg( Value[4] );       // Negate the second dword in the object.
    sbb( 0, Value[8] );    // Adjust third dword in object.
    sbb( 0, Value[12] );   // Adjust the H.O. dword.

    neg( Value );          // Negate the L.O. dword.
    sbb( 0, Value[4] );    // Adjust second dword in object.
    sbb( 0, Value[8] );    // Adjust third dword in object.
    sbb( 0, Value[12] );   // Adjust the H.O. dword.
```

Unfortunately, this code tends to get really large and slow because you need to propagate the carry through all the H.O. words after each negation operation. A simpler way to negate larger values is to simply subtract that value from 0:

```
static
    Value: dword[5];    // 160-bit value.
        .
        .
        .
    mov( 0, eax );
    sub( Value, eax );
    mov( eax, Value );

    mov( 0, eax );
    sbb( Value[4], eax );
    mov( eax, Value[4] );

    mov( 0, eax );
    sbb( Value[8], eax );
    mov( eax, Value[8] );

    mov( 0, eax );
    sbb( Value[12], eax );
    mov( eax, Value[12] );

    mov( 0, eax );
    sbb( Value[16], eax );
    mov( eax, Value[16] );
```

## 8.1.8　Extended-Precision and Operations

Performing an *n*-byte and operation is very easy: Simply and the corresponding bytes between the two operands, saving the result. For example, to perform the and operation where all operands are 64 bits long, you could use the following code:

```
mov( (type dword source1), eax );
and( (type dword source2), eax );
mov( eax, (type dword dest) );

mov( (type dword source1[4]), eax );
and( (type dword source2[4]), eax );
mov( eax, (type dword dest[4]) );
```

This technique easily extends to any number of words; all you need to do is logically and the corresponding bytes, words, or double words together in the operands. Note that this sequence sets the flags according to the value of the last and operation. If you and the H.O. double words last, this sets all but the zero flag correctly. If you need to test the zero flag after this sequence, you will need to logically or the two resulting double words together (or otherwise compare them both against 0).

## 8.1.9　Extended-Precision or Operations

Multibyte logical or operations are performed in the same way as multibyte and operations. You simply or the corresponding bytes in the two operands together. For example, to logically or two 96-bit values, use the following code:

```
mov( (type dword source1), eax );
or( (type dword source2), eax );
mov( eax, (type dword dest) );

mov( (type dword source1[4]), eax );
or( (type dword source2[4]), eax );
mov( eax, (type dword dest[4]) );

mov( (type dword source1[8]), eax );
or( (type dword source2[8]), eax );
mov( eax, (type dword dest[8]) );
```

As for the previous example, this does not set the zero flag properly for the entire operation. If you need to test the zero flag after a multiprecision or, you must logically or all the resulting double words together.

## 8.1.10 Extended-Precision xor Operations

Extended-precision xor operations are performed in a manner identical to and/or—simply xor the corresponding bytes in the two operands to obtain th extended-precision result. The following code sequence operates on two 64-b operands, computes their exclusive-or, and stores the result into a 64-bit variab

```
mov( (type dword source1), eax );
xor( (type dword source2), eax );
mov( eax, (type dword dest) );

mov( (type dword source1[4]), eax );
xor( (type dword source2[4]), eax );
mov( eax, (type dword dest[4]) );
```

The comment about the zero flag in the previous two sections applies here.

## 8.1.11 Extended-Precision not Operations

The not instruction inverts all the bits in the specified operand. An extende precision not is performed by simply executing the not instruction on all th affected operands. For example, to perform a 64-bit not operation on the value in (edx:eax), all you need to do is execute the following instructions:

```
not( eax );
not( edx );
```

Keep in mind that if you execute the not instruction twice, you wind up with the original value. Also note that exclusive-oring a value with all 1s ($F $FFFF, or $FFFF_FFFF) performs the same operation as the not instruction

## 8.1.12 Extended-Precision Shift Operations

Extended-precision shift operations require a shift and a rotate instruction. Consider what must happen to implement a 64-bit shl using 32-bit operatior (see Figure 8-5):

1. A 0 must be shifted into bit 0.
2. Bits 0 through 30 are shifted into the next-higher bit.
3. Bit 31 is shifted into bit 32.
4. Bits 32 through 62 must be shifted into the next-higher bit.
5. Bit 63 is shifted into the carry flag.

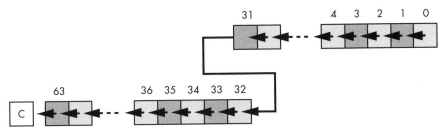

*Figure 8-5: 64-bit shift-left operation*

The two instructions you can use to implement this 64-bit shift are shl and rcl. For example, to shift the 64-bit quantity in (EDX:EAX) one position to the left, you'd use the following instructions:

```
shl( 1, eax );
rcl( 1, eax );
```

Note that using this technique you can shift an extended-precision value only 1 bit at a time. You cannot shift an extended-precision operand several bits using the CL register. Nor can you specify a constant value greater than 1 using this technique.

To understand how this instruction sequence works, consider the operation of the individual instructions. The shl instruction shifts a 0 into bit 0 of the 64-bit operand and shifts bit 31 into the carry flag. The rcl instruction then shifts the carry flag into bit 32 and then shifts bit 63 into the carry flag. The result is exactly what we want.

To perform a shift left on an operand larger than 64 bits, you simply use additional rcl instructions. An extended-precision shift-left operation always starts with the least-significant double word, and each succeeding rcl instruction operates on the next-most-significant double word. For example, to perform a 96-bit shift-left operation on a memory location, you could use the following instructions:

```
shl( 1, (type dword Operand[0]) );
rcl( 1, (type dword Operand[4]) );
rcl( 1, (type dword Operand[8]) );
```

If you need to shift your data by 2 or more bits, you can either repeat the above sequence the desired number of times (for a constant number of shifts) or you can place the instructions in a loop to repeat them some number of times. For example, the following code shifts the 96-bit value *Operand* to the left the number of bits specified in ECX:

```
ShiftLoop:
    shl( 1, (type dword Operand[0]) );
    rcl( 1, (type dword Operand[4]) );
    rcl( 1, (type dword Operand[8]) );
    dec( ecx );
    jnz ShiftLoop;
```

You implement shr and sar in a similar way, except you must start at the H.O. word of the operand and work your way down to the L.O. word:

```
// Extended-precision SAR:

    sar( 1, (type dword Operand[8]) );
    rcr( 1, (type dword Operand[4]) );
    rcr( 1, (type dword Operand[0]) );

// Double-precision SHR:

    shr( 1, (type dword Operand[8]) );
    rcr( 1, (type dword Operand[4]) );
    rcr( 1, (type dword Operand[0]) );
```

There is one major difference between the extended-precision shifts described here and their 8/16/32-bit counterparts—the extended-precision shifts set the flags differently than the single-precision operations. This is because the rotate instructions affect the flags differently than the shift instructions. Fortunately, the carry flag is the one you'll test most often after a shift operation, and the extended-precision shift operations (i.e., rotate instructions) properly set this flag.

The shld and shrd instructions let you efficiently implement multiprecision shifts of several bits. These instructions have the following syntax:

```
    shld( constant, Operand1, Operand2 );
    shld( cl, Operand1, Operand2 );
    shrd( constant, Operand1, Operand2 );
    shrd( cl, Operand1, Operand2 );
```

The shld instruction works as shown in Figure 8-6.

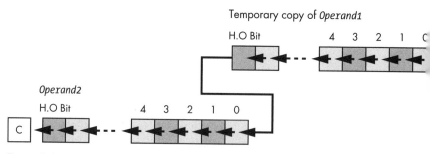

Figure 8-6: shld operation

Operand1 must be a 16- or 32-bit register. Operand2 can be a register or a memory location. Both operands must be the same size. The immediate operand can be a value in the range 0 through $n-1$, where $n$ is the number of bits in the two operands; this operand specifies the number of bits to shift.

The shld instruction shifts bits in Operand2 to the left. The H.O. bits shift into the carry flag, and the H.O. bits of Operand1 shift into the L.O. bits of Operand2. Note that this instruction does not modify the value of Operand1; it uses a temporary copy of *Operand1* during the shift. The immediate operand specifies the number of bits to shift. If the count is $n$, then shld shifts bit $n-1$ into the carry flag. It also shifts the H.O. $n$ bits of *Operand1* into the L.O. $n$ bits of *Operand2*. The shld instruction sets the flag bits as follows:

1. If the shift count is 0, the shld instruction doesn't affect any flags.
2. The carry flag contains the last bit shifted out of the H.O. bit of the *Operand2*.
3. If the shift count is 1, the overflow flag will contain 1 if the sign bit of *Operand2* changes during the shift. If the count is not 1, the overflow flag is undefined.
4. The zero flag will be 1 if the shift produces a 0 result.
5. The sign flag will contain the H.O. bit of the result.

The shrd instruction is similar to shld except, of course, it shifts its bits right rather than left. To get a clear picture of the shrd instruction, consider Figure 8-7.

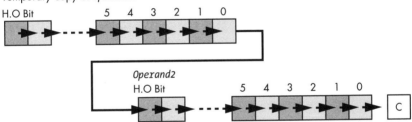

Figure 8-7: shrd operation

The shrd instruction sets the flag bits as follows:

1. If the shift count is 0, the shrd instruction doesn't affect any flags.
2. The carry flag contains the last bit shifted out of the L.O. bit of the *Operand2*.
3. If the shift count is 1, the overflow flag will contain 1 if the H.O. bit of *Operand2* changes. If the count is not 1, the overflow flag is undefined.
4. The zero flag will be 1 if the shift produces a 0 result.
5. The sign flag will contain the H.O. bit of the result.

Consider the following code sequence:

```
static
    ShiftMe: dword[3] := [ $1234, $5678, $9012 ];
        .
        .
        .
```

```
mov( ShiftMe[4], eax )
shld( 6, eax, ShiftMe[8] );
mov( ShiftMe[0], eax );
shld( 6, eax, ShiftMe[4] );
shl( 6, ShiftMe[0] );
```

The first shld instruction above shifts the bits from ShiftMe[4] into ShiftMe[
without affecting the value in ShiftMe[4]. The second shld instruction shifts
the bits from ShiftMe into ShiftMe[4]. Finally, the shl instruction shifts the L.(
double word the appropriate amount. There are two important things to no
about this code. First, unlike the other extended-precision shift-left operation
this sequence works from the H.O. double word down to the L.O. double
word. Second, the carry flag does not contain the carry from the H.O. shift
operation. If you need to preserve the carry flag at that point, you will need
push the flags after the first shld instruction and pop the flags after the shl
instruction.

You can do an extended-precision shift-right operation using the shrd
instruction. It works almost the same way as the code sequence above, except
you work from the L.O. double word to the H.O. double word. The solutio
is left as an exercise for the reader.

### 8.1.13  Extended-Precision Rotate Operations

The rcl and rcr operations extend in a manner almost identical to shl and
shr. For example, to perform 96-bit rcl and rcr operations, use the following
instructions:

```
rcl( 1, (type dword Operand[0]) );
rcl( 1, (type dword Operand[4]) );
rcl( 1, (type dword Operand[8]) );

rcr( 1, (type dword Operand[8]) );
rcr( 1, (type dword Operand[4]) );
rcr( 1, (type dword Operand[0]) );
```

The only difference between this code and the code for the extended-
precision shift operations is that the first instruction is a rcl or rcr rather tha
a shl or shr instruction.

Performing an extended-precision rol or ror operation isn't quite as
simple. You can use the bt, shld, and shrd instructions to implement an
extended-precision rol or ror instruction. The following code shows how to
use the shld instruction to do an extended-precision rol:

```
// Compute rol( 4, edx:eax );

        mov( edx, ebx );
        shld, 4, eax, edx );
        shld( 4, ebx, eax );
        bt( 0, eax );           // Set carry flag, if desired.
```

An extended-precision ror instruction is similar; just keep in mind that you work on the L.O. end of the object first and the H.O. end last.

## 8.1.14 Extended-Precision I/O

Once you can do extended-precision arithmetic, the next problem is how to get those extended-precision values into your program and how to display their values to the user. HLA's Standard Library provides routines for unsigned decimal, signed decimal, and hexadecimal I/O for values that are 8, 16, 32, 64, or 128 bits in length. So as long as you're working with values whose size is less than or equal to 128 bits in length, you can use the Standard Library code. If you need to input or output values that are greater than 128 bits in length, you will need to write your own procedures to handle the operation. This section discusses the strategies you will need to write such routines.

The examples in this section work specifically with 128-bit values. The algorithms are perfectly general and extend to any number of bits (indeed, the 128-bit algorithms in this section are really nothing more than the algorithms the HLA Standard Library uses for 128-bit values). Of course, if you need a set of 128-bit unsigned I/O routines, you can use the Standard Library code as is. If you need to handle larger values, simple modifications to the following code are all that should be necessary.

The sections that follow use a common set of 128-bit data types in order to avoid having to coerce lword/uns128/int128 values in each instruction. Here are these types:

```
type
    h128        :dword[4];
    u128        :dword[4];
    i128        :dword[4];
```

### 8.1.14.1 Extended-Precision Hexadecimal Output

Extended-precision hexadecimal output is very easy. All you have to do is output each double-word component of the extended-precision value from the H.O. double word to the L.O. double word using a call to the stdout.puth32 routine. The following procedure does exactly this to output an lword value:

```
procedure puth128( b128: h128 ); @nodisplay;
begin puth128;

    stdout.puth32( b128[12] );
    stdout.puth32( b128[8] );
    stdout.puth32( b128[4] );
    stdout.puth32( b128[0] );

end puth128;
```

Of course, the HLA Standard Library supplies a stdout.puth128 procedure that directly writes lword values, so you can call stdout.puth128 multiple times when outputting larger values (e.g., a 256-bit value). As it turns out, the implementation of the HLA stdlib.puth128 routine is very similar to puth128, above.

### 8.1.14.2 Extended-Precision Unsigned Decimal Output

Decimal output is a little more complicated than hexadecimal output because the H.O. bits of a binary number affect the L.O. digits of the decimal representation (this was not true for hexadecimal values, which is why hexadecimal output is so easy). Therefore, we will have to create the decimal representation for a binary number by extracting one decimal digit at a time from the number.

The most common solution for unsigned decimal output is to successively divide the value by 10 until the result becomes 0. The remainder after the first division is a value in the range 0..9, and this value corresponds to the L.O. digit of the decimal number. Successive divisions by 10 (and their corresponding remainder) extract successive digits from the number.

Iterative solutions to this problem generally allocate storage for a string of characters large enough to hold the entire number. Then the code extracts the decimal digits in a loop and places them in the string one by one. At the end of the conversion process, the routine prints the characters in the string in reverse order (remember, the divide algorithm extracts the L.O. digits first and the H.O. digits last, the opposite of the way you need to print them).

In this section, we employ a recursive solution because it is a little more elegant. The recursive solution begins by dividing the value by 10 and saving the remainder in a local variable. If the quotient is not 0, the routine recursively calls itself to print any leading digits first. On return from the recursive call (which prints all the leading digits), the recursive algorithm prints the digit associated with the remainder to complete the operation. Here's how the operation works when printing the decimal value 789:

1. Divide 789 by 10. Quotient is 78, and remainder is 9.

2. Save the remainder (9) in a local variable and recursively call the routine with the quotient.

3. [Recursive entry 1] Divide 78 by 10. Quotient is 7, and remainder is 8.

4. Save the remainder (8) in a local variable and recursively call the routine with the quotient.

5. [Recursive entry 2] Divide 7 by 10. Quotient is 0, and remainder is 7.

6. Save the remainder (7) in a local variable. Because the quotient is 0, don't call the routine recursively.

7. Output the remainder value saved in the local variable (7). Return to the caller (recursive entry 1).

8. [Return to recursive entry 1] Output the remainder value saved in the local variable in recursive entry 1 (8). Return to the caller (original invocation of the procedure).

9. [Original invocation] Output the remainder value saved in the local variable in the original call (9). Return to the original caller of the output routine.

The only operation that requires extended-precision calculation through this entire algorithm is the "divide by 10" statement. Everything else is simple and straightforward. We are in luck with this algorithm, because we are dividing an extended-precision value by a value that easily fits into a double word, and we can use the fast (and easy) extended-precision division algorithm that uses the div instruction. The program in Listing 8-4 implements a 128-bit decimal output routine utilizing this technique.

```
program out128;

#include( "stdlib.hhf" );

// 128-bit unsigned integer data type:

type
    u128: dword[4];



// DivideBy10-
//
//   Divides "divisor" by 10 using fast
//   extended-precision division algorithm
//   that employs the div instruction.
//
//   Returns quotient in "quotient".
//   Returns remainder in eax.
//   Trashes ebx, edx, and edi.

procedure DivideBy10( dividend:u128; var quotient:u128 ); @nodisplay;
begin DivideBy10;

    mov( quotient, edi );
    xor( edx, edx );
    mov( dividend[12], eax );
    mov( 10, ebx );
    div( ebx, edx:eax );
    mov( eax, [edi+12] );

    mov( dividend[8], eax );
    div( ebx, edx:eax );
    mov( eax, [edi+8] );
```

```
        mov( dividend[4], eax );
        div( ebx, edx:eax );
        mov( eax, [edi+4] );

        mov( dividend[0], eax );
        div( ebx, edx:eax );
        mov( eax, [edi+0] );
        mov( edx, eax );

    end DivideBy10;



    // Recursive version of putu128.
    // A separate "shell" procedure calls this so that
    // this code does not have to preserve all the registers
    // it uses (and DivideBy10 uses) on each recursive call.

    procedure recursivePutu128( b128:u128 ); @nodisplay;
    var
        remainder: byte;

    begin recursivePutu128;

        // Divide by 10 and get the remainder (the char to print).

        DivideBy10( b128, b128 );
        mov( al, remainder );       // Save away the remainder (0..9).

        // If the quotient (left in b128) is not 0, recursively
        // call this routine to print the H.O. digits.

        mov( b128[0], eax );    // If we logically OR all the dwords
        or( b128[4], eax );     // together, the result is 0 if and
        or( b128[8], eax );     // only if the entire number is 0.
        or( b128[12], eax );
        if( @nz ) then

            recursivePutu128( b128 );

        endif;

        // Okay, now print the current digit.

        mov( remainder, al );
        or( '0', al );          // Converts 0..9 -> '0'..'9'.
        stdout.putc( al );

    end recursivePutu128;
```

```
// Nonrecursive shell to the above routine so we don't bother
// saving all the registers on each recursive call.

procedure putu128( b128:u128 ); @nodisplay;
begin putu128;

    push( eax );
    push( ebx );
    push( edx );
    push( edi );

    recursivePutu128( b128 );

    pop( edi );
    pop( edx );
    pop( ebx );
    pop( eax );

end putu128;




// Code to test the routines above:

static
    b0: u128 := [0, 0, 0, 0];              // decimal = 0
    b1: u128 := [1234567890, 0, 0, 0];     // decimal = 1234567890
    b2: u128 := [$8000_0000, 0, 0, 0];     // decimal = 2147483648
    b3: u128 := [0, 1, 0, 0 ];             // decimal = 4294967296

    // Largest uns128 value
    // (decimal=340,282,366,920,938,463,463,374,607,431,768,211,455):

    b4: u128 := [$FFFF_FFFF, $FFFF_FFFF, $FFFF_FFFF, $FFFF_FFFF ];

begin out128;

    stdout.put( "b0 = " );
    putu128( b0 );
    stdout.newln();

    stdout.put( "b1 = " );
    putu128( b1 );
    stdout.newln();

    stdout.put( "b2 = " );
    putu128( b2 );
    stdout.newln();

    stdout.put( "b3 = " );
    putu128( b3 );
    stdout.newln();
```

```
    stdout.put( "b4 = " );
    putu128( b4 );
    stdout.newln();

end out128;
```

*Listing 8-4: 128-bit extended-precision decimal output routine*

### 8.1.14.3   Extended-Precision Signed Decimal Output

Once you have an extended-precision unsigned decimal output routine, writing an extended-precision signed decimal output routine is very easy. Th basic algorithm takes the following form:

1. Check the sign of the number.
2. If it is positive, call the unsigned output routine to print it. If the numbe is negative, print a minus sign. Then negate the number and call the unsigned output routine to print it.

To check the sign of an extended-precision integer, of course, you simpl test the H.O. bit of the number. To negate a large value, the best solution is probably to subtract that value from 0. Here's a quick version of puti128 tha uses the putu128 routine from the previous section:

```
procedure puti128( i128: u128 ); @nodisplay;
begin puti128;

    if( (type int32 i128[12]) < 0 ) then

        stdout.put( '-' );

        // Extended-precision Negation:

        push( eax );
        mov( 0, eax );
        sub( i128[0], eax );
        mov( eax, i128[0] );

        mov( 0, eax );
        sbb( i128[4], eax );
        mov( eax, i128[4] );

        mov( 0, eax );
        sbb( i128[8], eax );
        mov( eax, i128[8] );

        mov( 0, eax );
        sbb( i128[12], eax );
```

```
        mov( eax, i128[12] );
        pop( eax );

    endif;
    putu128( i128 );

end puti128;
```

### 8.1.14.4    Extended-Precision Formatted Output

The code in the previous two sections prints signed and unsigned integers using the minimum number of necessary print positions. To create nicely formatted tables of values you will need the equivalent of a puti128Size or putu128Size routine. Once you have the "unformatted" versions of these routines, implementing the formatted versions is very easy.

The first step is to write i128Size and u128Size routines that compute the minimum number of digits needed to display the value. The algorithm to accomplish this is very similar to the numeric output routines. In fact, the only difference is that you initialize a counter to 0 upon entry into the routine (for example, the nonrecursive shell routine), and you increment this counter rather than outputting a digit on each recursive call. (Don't forget to increment the counter inside i128Size if the number is negative; you must allow for the output of the minus sign.) After the calculation is complete, these routines should return the size of the operand in the EAX register.

Once you have the i128Size and u128Size routines, writing the formatted output routines is easy. Upon initial entry into puti128Size or putu128Size, these routines call the corresponding size routine to determine the number of print positions for the number to display. If the value that the size routine returns is greater than the absolute value of the minimum size parameter (passed into puti128Size or putu128Size), all you need to do is call the put routine to print the value; no other formatting is necessary. If the absolute value of the parameter size is greater than the value i128Size or u128Size returns, then the program must compute the difference between these two values and print that many spaces (or other filler characters) before printing the number (if the parameter size value is positive) or after printing the number (if the parameter size value is negative). The actual implementation of these two routines is left as an exercise to the reader (or just check out the source code in the HLA Standard Library for the stdout.putiSize128 and stdout.putuSize128 routines).

The HLA Standard Library implements the i128Size and u128Size by doing a set of successive extended-precision comparisons to determine the number of digits in the values. Interested readers may want to look at the source code for these routines as well as the source code for the stdout.puti128 and stdout.putu128 procedures (this source code appears on Webster at *http://webster.cs.ucr.edu/* or *http://www.artofasm.com/*).

### 8.1.14.5 Extended-Precision Input Routines

There are a couple of fundamental differences between the extended-precision output routines and the extended-precision input routines. First of all, numeric output generally occurs without possibility of error;[3] numeric input, on the other hand, must handle the very real possibility of an input error such as illegal characters and numeric overflow. Also, HLA's Standard Library and runtime system encourage a slightly different approach to input conversion. This section discusses those issues that differentiate input conversion from output conversion.

Perhaps the biggest difference between input and output conversion is the fact that output conversion is not bracketed. That is, when converting a numeric value to a string of characters for output, the output routine does not concern itself with characters preceding the output string, nor is it concerned with the characters following the numeric value in the output stream. Numeric output routines convert their data to a string and print that string without considering the context (that is, the characters before and after the string representation of the numeric value). Numeric input routines cannot be so cavalier; the contextual information surrounding the numeric string is very important.

A typical numeric input operation consists of reading a string of characters from the user and then translating this string of characters into an internal numeric representation. For example, a statement like stdin.get(i32); typically reads a line of text from the user and converts a sequence of digits appearing at the beginning of that line of text into a 32-bit signed integer (assuming i32 is an int32 object). Note, however, that the stdin.get routine skips over certain characters in the string that may appear before the actual numeric characters. For example, stdin.get automatically skips any leading spaces in the string. Likewise, the input string may contain additional data beyond the end of the numeric input (for example, it is possible to read two integer values from the same input line), and therefore the input conversion routine must somehow determine where the numeric data ends in the input stream. Fortunately, HLA provides a simple mechanism that lets you easily determine the start and end of the input data: the Delimiters character set.

The Delimiters character set is a variable, internal to the HLA Standard Library, that contains the set of legal characters that may precede or follow a legal numeric value. By default, this character set includes the end-of-string marker (a 0 byte), a tab character, a line-feed character, a carriage-return character, a space, a comma, a colon, and a semicolon. Therefore, HLA's numeric input routines will automatically ignore any characters in this set that occur on input before a numeric string. Likewise, characters from this set may legally follow a numeric string on input (conversely, if any non-delimiter character follows the numeric string, HLA will raise an ex.ConversionError exception).

---

[3] Technically speaking, this isn't entirely true. It is possible for a device error (e.g., disk full) to occur. The likelihood of this is so low that we can effectively ignore this possibility.

The Delimiters character set is a private variable inside the HLA Standard Library. Although you do not have direct access to this object, the HLA Standard Library does provide two accessor functions, conv.setDelimiters and conv.getDelimiters, that let you access and modify the value of this character set. These two functions have the following prototypes (found in the *conv.hhf* header file):

```
procedure conv.setDelimiters( Delims:cset );
procedure conv.getDelimiters( var Delims:cset );
```

The conv.setDelimiters procedure will copy the value of the Delims parameter into the internal Delimiters character set. Therefore, you can use this procedure to change the character set if you want to use a different set of delimiters for numeric input. The conv.getDelimiters call returns a copy of the internal Delimiters character set in the variable you pass as a parameter to the conv.getDelimiters procedure. We will use the value returned by conv.getDelimiters to determine the end of numeric input when writing our own extended-precision numeric input routines.

When reading a numeric value from the user, the first step is to get a copy of the Delimiters character set. The second step is to read and discard input characters from the user as long as those characters are members of the Delimiters character set. Once a character is found that is not in the Delimiters set, the input routine must check this character and verify that it is a legal numeric character. If not, the program should raise an ex.IllegalChar exception if the character's value is outside the range $00..$7F, or it should raise the ex.ConversionError exception if the character is not a legal numeric character. Once the routine encounters a numeric character, it should continue reading characters as long as they are valid numeric characters; while reading the characters, the conversion routine should be translating them to the internal representation of the numeric data. If, during conversion, an overflow occurs, the procedure should raise the ex.ValueOutOfRange exception.

Conversion to numeric representation should end when the procedure encounters the first delimiter character at the end of the string of digits. However, it is very important that the procedure does not consume the delimiter character that ends the string. That is, the following is incorrect:

```
static
    Delimiters: cset;
        .
        .
        .
    conv.getDelimiters( Delimiters );

    // Skip over leading delimiters in the string:

    while( stdin.getc() in Delimiters ) do  /* getc did the work */ endwhile;
    while( al in '0'..'9') do
```

```
    // Convert character in al to numeric representation and
    // accumulate result...

    stdin.getc();

endwhile;
if( al not in Delimiters ) then

    raise( ex.ConversionError );

endif;
```

The first while loop reads a sequence of delimiter characters. When this first while loop ends, the character in AL is not a delimiter character. The second while loop processes a sequence of decimal digits. First, it checks the character read in the previous while loop to see if it is a decimal digit; if so, it processes that digit and reads the next character. This process continues until the call to stdin.getc (at the bottom of the loop) reads a nondigit character. After the second while loop, the program checks the last character read to ensure that it is a legal delimiter character for a numeric input value.

The problem with this algorithm is that it consumes the delimiter character after the numeric string. For example, the colon symbol is a legal delimiter in the default Delimiters character set. If the user types the input **123:456** and executes the code above, this code will properly convert 123 to the numeric value 123. However, the very next character read from the input stream will be the character 4, not the colon character (:). While this may be acceptable in certain circumstances, most programmers expect numeric input routines to consume only leading delimiter characters and the numeric digit characters. They do not expect the input routine to consume any trailing delimiter characters (for example, many programs will read the next character and expect a colon as input if presented with the string **123:456**). Because stdin.getc consumes an input character, and there is no way to put the character back onto the input stream, some other way of reading input characters from the user that doesn't consume those characters is needed.[4]

The HLA Standard Library comes to the rescue by providing the stdin.peekc function. Like stdin.getc, the stdin.peekc routine reads the next input character from HLA's internal buffer. There are two major differences between stdin.peekc and stdin.getc. First, stdin.peekc will not force the input of a new line of text from the user if the current input line is empty (or you've already read all the text from the input line). Instead, stdin.peekc simply returns 0 in the AL register to indicate that there are no more characters on the input line. Because #0 (the NUL character) is (by default) a legal delimiter character for numeric values, and the end of line is certainly a legal way to terminate numeric input, this works out rather well. The second difference between stdin.getc and stdin.peekc is that stdin.peekc does not consume the character

---

[4] The HLA Standard Library routines actually buffer up input lines in a string and process characters out of the string. This makes it easy to "peek" ahead one character when looking for delimiter to end the input value. Your code can also do this; however, the code in this chapter uses a different approach.

read from the input buffer. If you call stdin.peekc several times in a row, it will always return the same character; likewise, if you call stdin.getc immediately after stdin.peekc, the call to stdin.getc will generally return the same character as returned by stdin.peekc (the only exception being the end-of-line condition). So, although we cannot put characters back onto the input stream after we've read them with stdin.getc, we can peek ahead at the next character on the input stream and base our logic on that character's value. A corrected version of the previous algorithm might be the following:

```
static
    Delimiters: cset;
        .
        .
        .
        conv.getDelimiters( Delimiters );

    // Skip over leading delimiters in the string:

    while( stdin.peekc() in Delimiters ) do

        // If at the end of the input buffer, we must explicitly read a
        // new line of text from the user. stdin.peekc does not do this
        // for us.

        if( al = #0 ) then

            stdin.ReadLn();

        else

            stdin.getc();  // Remove delimiter from the input stream.

        endif;

    endwhile;
    while( stdin.peekc in '0'..'9') do

        stdin.getc();     // Remove the input character from the input stream.

        // Convert character in al to numeric representation and
        // accumulate result...

    endwhile;
    if( al not in Delimiters ) then

        raise( ex.ConversionError );

    endif;
```

Note that the call to stdin.peekc in the second while does not consume the delimiter character when the expression evaluates false. Hence, the delimiter character will be the next character read after this algorithm finishes.

The only remaining comment to make about numeric input is to point out that the HLA Standard Library input routines allow arbitrary underscore to appear within a numeric string. The input routines ignore these underscore characters. This allows the user to input strings like FFFF_F012 and 1_023_596, which are a little more readable than FFFFF012 and 1023596. Allowing underscores (or any other symbol you choose) within a numeric input routine is quite simple; just modify the second while loop above as follows:

```
while( stdin.peekc in {'0'..'9', '_'}) do

    stdin.getc();  // Read the character from the input stream.

    // Ignore underscores while processing numeric input.

    if( al <> '_' ) then

        // Convert character in al to numeric representation and
        // accumulate result...

    endif;

endwhile;
```

### 8.1.14.6  Extended-Precision Hexadecimal Input

As was the case for numeric output, hexadecimal input is the easiest numeric input routine to write. The basic algorithm for hexadecimal-string-to-numeric conversion is the following:

1.  Initialize the extended-precision value to 0.
2.  For each input character that is a valid hexadecimal digit, do the following:
    a.  Convert the hexadecimal character to a value in the range 0..15 ($0..$F).
    b.  If the H.O. 4 bits of the extended-precision value are nonzero, raise an exception.
    c.  Multiply the current extended-precision value by 16 (i.e., shift left 4 bits).
    d.  Add the converted hexadecimal digit value to the accumulator.
    e.  Check the last input character to ensure it is a valid delimiter. Raise an exception if it is not.

The program in Listing 8-5 implements this extended-precision hexadecimal input routine for 128-bit values.

```
program Xin128;

#include( "stdlib.hhf" );

// 128-bit unsigned integer data type:

type
    b128: dword[4];




procedure getb128( var inValue:b128 ); @nodisplay;
const
    HexChars   := {'0'..'9', 'a'..'f', 'A'..'F', '_'};
var
    Delimiters: cset;
    LocalValue: b128;

begin getb128;

    push( eax );
    push( ebx );

    // Get a copy of the HLA standard numeric input delimiters:

    conv.getDelimiters( Delimiters );

    // Initialize the numeric input value to 0:

    xor( eax, eax );
    mov( eax, LocalValue[0] );
    mov( eax, LocalValue[4] );
    mov( eax, LocalValue[8] );
    mov( eax, LocalValue[12] );

    // By default, #0 is a member of the HLA Delimiters
    // character set. However, someone may have called
    // conv.setDelimiters and removed this character
    // from the internal Delimiters character set. This
    // algorithm depends upon #0 being in the Delimiters
    // character set, so let's add that character in
    // at this point just to be sure.

    cs.unionChar( #0, Delimiters );


    // If we're at the end of the current input
    // line (or the program has yet to read any input),
    // for the input of an actual character.
```

```
            if( stdin.peekc() = #0 ) then

                stdin.readLn();

        endif;




        // Skip the delimiters found on input. This code is
        // somewhat convoluted because stdin.peekc does not
        // force the input of a new line of text if the current
        // input buffer is empty. We have to force that input
        // ourselves in the event the input buffer is empty.

        while( stdin.peekc() in Delimiters ) do

                // If we're at the end of the line, read a new line
                // of text from the user; otherwise, remove the
                // delimiter character from the input stream.

                if( al = #0 ) then

                    stdin.readLn(); // Force a new input line.

                else

                    stdin.getc();    // Remove the delimiter from the input buffer.

                endif;

        endwhile;

        // Read the hexadecimal input characters and convert
        // them to the internal representation:

        while( stdin.peekc() in HexChars ) do

                // Actually read the character to remove it from the
                // input buffer.

                stdin.getc();

                // Ignore underscores, process everything else.

                if( al <> '_' ) then

                    if( al in '0'..'9' ) then

                        and( $f, al );  // '0'..'9' -> 0..9

                    else

                        and( $f, al );  // 'a'/'A'..'f'/'F' -> 1..6
                        add( 9, al );   // 1..6 -> 10..15
```

```
            endif;

            // Conversion algorithm is the following:
            //
            // (1) LocalValue := LocalValue * 16.
            // (2) LocalValue := LocalValue + al
            //
            // Note that "* 16" is easily accomplished by
            // shifting LocalValue to the left 4 bits.
            //
            // Overflow occurs if the H.O. 4 bits of LocalValue
            // contain a nonzero value prior to this operation.

            // First, check for overflow:

            test( $F0, (type byte LocalValue[15]));
            if( @nz ) then

                raise( ex.ValueOutOfRange );

            endif;

            // Now multiply LocalValue by 16 and add in
            // the current hexadecimal digit (in eax).

            mov( LocalValue[8], ebx );
            shld( 4, ebx, LocalValue[12] );
            mov( LocalValue[4], ebx );
            shld( 4, ebx, LocalValue[8] );
            mov( LocalValue[0], ebx );
            shld( 4, ebx, LocalValue[4] );
            shl( 4, ebx );
            add( eax, ebx );
            mov( ebx, LocalValue[0] );

        endif;

    endwhile;

// Okay, we've encountered a non-hexadecimal character.
// Let's make sure it's a valid delimiter character.
// Raise the ex.ConversionError exception if it's invalid.

if( al not in Delimiters ) then

    raise( ex.ConversionError );

endif;

// Okay, this conversion has been a success. Let's store
// away the converted value into the output parameter.
```

```
        mov( inValue, ebx );
        mov( LocalValue[0], eax );
        mov( eax, [ebx] );

        mov( LocalValue[4], eax );
        mov( eax, [ebx+4] );

        mov( LocalValue[8], eax );
        mov( eax, [ebx+8] );

        mov( LocalValue[12], eax );
        mov( eax, [ebx+12] );

        pop( ebx );
        pop( eax );

end getb128;



// Code to test the routines above:

static
    b1:b128;

begin Xin128;

    stdout.put( "Input a 128-bit hexadecimal value: " );
    getb128( b1 );
    stdout.put
    (
        "The value is: $",
        b1[12], '_',
        b1[8],  '_',
        b1[4],  '_',
        b1[0],
        nl
    );

end Xin128;
```

*Listing 8-5: Extended-precision hexadecimal input*

Extending this code to handle objects that are greater than 128 bits long is very easy. There are only three changes necessary: You must zero out the whole object at the beginning of the getb128 routine; when checking for overflow (the test( $F, (type byte LocalValue[15]) ); instruction), you must test the H.O. 4 bits of the new object you're processing; and you must modify the code that multiplies LocalValue by 16 (via shld) so that it multiplies your object by 16 (i.e., shifts it to the left 4 bits).

## 8.1.14.7 Extended-Precision Unsigned Decimal Input

The algorithm for extended-precision unsigned decimal input is nearly identical to that for hexadecimal input. In fact, the only difference (beyond only accepting decimal digits) is that you multiply the extended-precision value by 10 rather than 16 for each input character (in general, the algorithm is the same for any base; just multiply the accumulating value by the input base). The code in Listing 8-6 demonstrates how to write a 128-bit unsigned decimal input routine.

```
program Uin128;

#include( "stdlib.hhf" );

// 128-bit unsigned integer data type:

type
    u128: dword[4];



procedure getu128( var inValue:u128 ); @nodisplay;
var
    Delimiters: cset;
    LocalValue: u128;
    PartialSum: u128;

begin getu128;

    push( eax );
    push( ebx );
    push( ecx );
    push( edx );

    // Get a copy of the HLA standard numeric input delimiters:

    conv.getDelimiters( Delimiters );

    // Initialize the numeric input value to 0:

    xor( eax, eax );
    mov( eax, LocalValue[0] );
    mov( eax, LocalValue[4] );
    mov( eax, LocalValue[8] );
    mov( eax, LocalValue[12] );

    // By default, #0 is a member of the HLA Delimiters
    // character set. However, someone may have called
    // conv.setDelimiters and removed this character
    // from the internal Delimiters character set. This
    // algorithm depends upon #0 being in the Delimiters
    // character set, so let's add that character in
    // at this point just to be sure.
```

```
                cs.unionChar( #0, Delimiters );


                // If we're at the end of the current input
                // line (or the program has yet to read any input),
                // wait for the input of an actual character.

                if( stdin.peekc() = #0 ) then

                    stdin.readLn();

                endif;



                // Skip the delimiters found on input. This code is
                // somewhat convoluted because stdin.peekc does not
                // force the input of a new line of text if the current
                // input buffer is empty. We have to force that input
                // ourselves in the event the input buffer is empty.

                while( stdin.peekc() in Delimiters ) do

                    // If we're at the end of the line, read a new line
                    // of text from the user; otherwise, remove the
                    // delimiter character from the input stream.

                    if( al = #0 ) then

                        stdin.readLn(); // Force a new input line.

                    else

                        stdin.getc();    // Remove the delimiter from the input buffer.

                    endif;

                endwhile;

                // Read the decimal input characters and convert
                // them to the internal representation:

                while( stdin.peekc() in '0'..'9' ) do

                    // Actually read the character to remove it from the
                    // input buffer.

                    stdin.getc();

                    // Ignore underscores, process everything else.
```

```
if( al <> '_' ) then

    and( $f, al );                // '0'..'9' -> 0..9
    mov( eax, PartialSum[0] );    // Save to add in later.

    // Conversion algorithm is the following:
    //
    // (1) LocalValue := LocalValue * 10.
    // (2) LocalValue := LocalValue + al
    //
    // First, multiply LocalValue by 10:

    mov( 10, eax );
    mul( LocalValue[0], eax );
    mov( eax, LocalValue[0] );
    mov( edx, PartialSum[4] );

    mov( 10, eax );
    mul( LocalValue[4], eax );
    mov( eax, LocalValue[4] );
    mov( edx, PartialSum[8] );

    mov( 10, eax );
    mul( LocalValue[8], eax );
    mov( eax, LocalValue[8] );
    mov( edx, PartialSum[12] );

    mov( 10, eax );
    mul( LocalValue[12], eax );
    mov( eax, LocalValue[12] );

    // Check for overflow. This occurs if edx
    // contains a nonzero value.

    if( edx /* <> 0 */ ) then

        raise( ex.ValueOutOfRange );

    endif;

    // Add in the partial sums (including the
    // most recently converted character).

    mov( PartialSum[0], eax );
    add( eax, LocalValue[0] );

    mov( PartialSum[4], eax );
    adc( eax, LocalValue[4] );

    mov( PartialSum[8], eax );
    adc( eax, LocalValue[8] );
```

```
                    mov( PartialSum[12], eax );
                    adc( eax, LocalValue[12] );

                    // Another check for overflow. If there
                    // was a carry out of the extended-precision
                    // addition above, we've got overflow.

                    if( @c ) then

                        raise( ex.ValueOutOfRange );

                    endif;

                endif;

            endwhile;

            // Okay, we've encountered a non-decimal character.
            // Let's make sure it's a valid delimiter character.
            // Raise the ex.ConversionError exception if it's invalid.

            if( al not in Delimiters ) then

                raise( ex.ConversionError );

            endif;

            // Okay, this conversion has been a success. Let's store
            // away the converted value into the output parameter.

            mov( inValue, ebx );
            mov( LocalValue[0], eax );
            mov( eax, [ebx] );

            mov( LocalValue[4], eax );
            mov( eax, [ebx+4] );

            mov( LocalValue[8], eax );
            mov( eax, [ebx+8] );

            mov( LocalValue[12], eax );
            mov( eax, [ebx+12] );

            pop( edx );
            pop( ecx );
            pop( ebx );
            pop( eax );

end getu128;
```

```
// Code to test the routines above:

static
    b1:u128;

begin Uin128;

    stdout.put( "Input a 128-bit decimal value: " );
    getu128( b1 );
    stdout.put
    (
        "The value is: $",
        b1[12], '_',
        b1[8],  '_',
        b1[4],  '_',
        b1[0],
        nl
    );

end Uin128;
```

*Listing 8-6: Extended-precision unsigned decimal input*

As for hexadecimal input, extending this decimal input to some number of bits beyond 128 is fairly easy. All you need do is modify the code that zeros out the LocalValue variable and the code that multiplies LocalValue by 10 (overflow checking is done in this same code, so there are only two spots in this code that require modification).

### 8.1.14.8 Extended-Precision Signed Decimal Input

Once you have an unsigned decimal input routine, writing a signed decimal input routine is easy. The following algorithm describes how to accomplish this:

1. Consume any delimiter characters at the beginning of the input stream.
2. If the next input character is a minus sign, consume this character and set a flag noting that the number is negative.
3. Call the unsigned decimal input routine to convert the rest of the string to an integer.
4. Check the return result to make sure its H.O. bit is clear. Raise the ex.ValueOutOfRange exception if the H.O. bit of the result is set.
5. If the code encountered a minus sign in step 2, negate the result.

The actual code is left as a programming exercise for the reader (or see the conversion routines in the HLA Standard Library for concrete examples).

## 8.2 Operating on Different-Size Operands

Occasionally you may need to do some computation on a pair of operands that are not the same size. For example, you may need to add a word and a double word together or subtract a byte value from a word value. The solution is simple: just extend the smaller operand to the size of the larger operand and then do the operation on two similarly sized operands. For signed operands you would sign extend the smaller operand to the same size as the larger operand; for unsigned values, you zero extend the smaller operand. This works for any operation, although the following examples demonstrate this for the addition operation.

To extend the smaller operand to the size of the larger operand, use a sign extension or zero extension operation (depending upon whether you're adding signed or unsigned values). Once you've extended the smaller value to the size of the larger, the addition can proceed. Consider the following code that adds a byte value to a word value:

```
static
    var1: byte;
    var2: word;
       .
       .
       .
// Unsigned addition:

    movzx( var1, ax );
    add( var2, ax );

// Signed addition:

    movsx( var1, ax );
    add( var2, ax );
```

In both cases, the byte variable was loaded into the AL register, extended to 16 bits, and then added to the word operand. This code works out really well if you can choose the order of the operations (for example, adding the 8-bit value to the 16-bit value). Sometimes, you cannot specify the order of the operations. Perhaps the 16-bit value is already in the AX register and you want to add an 8-bit value to it. For unsigned addition, you could use the following code:

```
mov( var2, ax );      // Load 16-bit value into ax.
   .                  // Do some other operations leaving
   .                  // a 16-bit quantity in ax.
add( var1, al );      // Add in the 8-bit value.
adc( 0, ah );         // Add carry into the H.O. word.
```

The first add instruction in this example adds the byte at var1 to the L.O. byte of the value in the accumulator. The adc instruction above adds the carry from the addition of the L.O. bytes into the H.O. byte of the accumulator. You must take care to ensure that this adc instruction is present. If you leave it out, you may not get the correct result.

Adding an 8-bit signed operand to a 16-bit signed value is a little more difficult. Unfortunately, you cannot add an immediate value (as above) to the H.O. word of AX. This is because the H.O. extension byte can be either $00 or $FF. If a register is available, the best thing to do is the following:

```
mov( ax, bx );          // bx is the available register.
movsx( var1, ax );
add( bx, ax );
```

If an extra register is not available, you might try the following code:

```
push( ax );             // Save word value.
movsx( var1, ax );      // Sign extend 8-bit operand to 16 bits.
add( [esp], ax );       // Add in previous word value.
add( 2, esp );          // Pop junk from stack.
```

Another alternative is to store the 16-bit value in the accumulator into a memory location and then proceed as before:

```
mov( ax, temp );
movsx( var1, ax );
add( temp, ax );
```

All the examples above added a byte value to a word value. By zero or sign extending the smaller operand to the size of the larger operand, you can easily add any two different-size variables together.

As a last example, consider adding an 8-bit signed value to a quadword (64-bit) value:

```
static
    QVal:qword;
    BVal:int8;
    .
    .
    .
    movsx( BVal, eax );
    cdq();
    add( (type dword QVal), eax );
    adc( (type dword QVal[4]), edx );
```

## 8.3 Decimal Arithmetic

The 80x86 CPUs use the binary numbering system for their native internal representation. The binary numbering system is, by far, the most common numbering system in use in computer systems today. In the early days, however, there were computer systems that were based on the decimal (base 10) numbering system instead of the binary numbering system. Consequently, their arithmetic system was decimal based rather than binary. Such computer systems were very popular in systems targeted for business/commercial systems.[5] Although systems designers have discovered that binary arithmetic is almost always better than decimal arithmetic for general calculations, the myth still persists that decimal arithmetic is better for money calculations than binary arithmetic. Therefore, many software systems still specify the use of decimal arithmetic in their calculations (not to mention that there is lots of legacy code out there whose algorithms are stable only if they use decimal arithmetic). Therefore, despite the fact that decimal arithmetic is generally inferior to binary arithmetic, the need for decimal arithmetic persists.

Of course, the 80x86 is not a decimal computer; therefore, we have to play tricks in order to represent decimal numbers using the native binary format. The most common technique, even employed by most so-called decimal computers, is to use the binary-coded decimal, or BCD, representation. The BCD representation uses 4 bits to represent the 10 possible decimal digits (see Table 8-1). The binary value of those 4 bits is equal to the corresponding decimal value in the range 0..9. Of course, with 4 bits we can actually represent 16 different values; the BCD format ignores the remaining six bit combinations.

Because each BCD digit requires 4 bits, we can represent a 2-digit BCD value with a single byte. This means that we can represent the decimal value in the range 0..99 using a single byte (versus 0..255 if we treat the value as an unsigned binary number). Clearly it takes more memory to represent the same value in BCD than it does to represent the same value in binary. For example, with a 32-bit value you can represent BCD values in the range 0..99,999,999 (eight significant digits). However, you can represent values in the range 0..4,294,967,295 (more than nine significant digits) by using binary representation.

Not only does the BCD format waste memory on a binary computer (because it uses more bits to represent a given integer value), decimal arithmetic is also slower. For these reasons, you should avoid the use of decimal arithmetic unless it is absolutely mandated for a given application.

Binary-coded decimal representation does offer one big advantage over binary representation: It is fairly simple to convert between the string representation of a decimal number and the BCD representation. This feature is particularly beneficial when working with fractional values because fixed and floating-point binary representations cannot exactly represent many

---

[5] In fact, until the release of the IBM 360 in the mid-1960s, most scientific computer systems were binary based, whereas most commercial/business systems were decimal based. IBM pushed its system\360 as a single-purpose solution for both business and scientific applications. Indeed, the model designation (360) was derived from the 360 degrees on a compass so as to suggest that the system\360 was suitable for computations "at all points of the compass" (i.e., business and scientific).

commonly used values between 0 and 1 (e.g., 1/10). Therefore, BCD operations can be efficient when reading from a BCD device, doing a simple arithmetic operation (for example, a single addition), and then writing the BCD value to some other device.

**Table 8-1:** Binary-Coded Decimal (BCD) Representation

| BCD Representation | Decimal Equivalent |
| --- | --- |
| 0000 | 0 |
| 0001 | 1 |
| 0010 | 2 |
| 0011 | 3 |
| 0100 | 4 |
| 0101 | 5 |
| 0110 | 6 |
| 0111 | 7 |
| 1000 | 8 |
| 1001 | 9 |
| 1010 | Illegal |
| 1011 | Illegal |
| 1100 | Illegal |
| 1101 | Illegal |
| 1110 | Illegal |
| 1111 | Illegal |

## 8.3.1 Literal BCD Constants

HLA does not provide, nor do you need, a special literal BCD constant. Because BCD is just a special form of hexadecimal notation that does not allow the values $A..$F, you can easily create BCD constants using HLA's hexadecimal notation. Of course, you must take care not to include the symbols A..F in a BCD constant because they are illegal BCD values. As an example, consider the following mov instruction that copies the BCD value 99 into the AL register:

```
mov( $99, al );
```

The important thing to keep in mind is that you must not use HLA literal decimal constants for BCD values. That is, mov( 95, al ); does not load the BCD representation for 95 into the AL register. Instead, it loads $5F into AL, and that's an illegal BCD value. Any computations you attempt with illegal BCD values will produce garbage results. Always remember that, even though it seems counterintuitive, you use hexadecimal literal constants to represent literal BCD values.

## 8.3.2  The 80x86 daa and das Instructions

The integer unit on the 80x86 does not directly support BCD arithmetic. Instead, the 80x86 requires that you perform the computation using binary arithmetic and use some auxiliary instructions to convert the binary result to BCD. To support packed BCD addition and subtraction with two digits per byte, the 80x86 provides two instructions: decimal adjust after addition (daa) and decimal adjust after subtraction (das). You would execute these two instructions immediately after an add/adc or sub/sbb instruction to correct the binary result in the AL register.

To add a pair of two-digit (i.e., single-byte) BCD values together, you would use the following sequence:

```
mov( bcd_1, al );    // Assume that bcd_1 and bcd_2 both contain
add( bcd_2, al );    // valid BCD values.
daa();
```

The first two instructions above add the 2-byte values together using standard binary arithmetic. This may not produce a correct BCD result. For example, if bcd_1 contains $9 and bcd_2 contains $1, then the first two instructions above will produce the binary sum $A instead of the correct BCD result $10. The daa instruction corrects this invalid result. It checks to see if there was a carry out of the low-order BCD digit and adjusts the value (by adding 6 to it) if there was an overflow. After adjusting for overflow out of the L.O. digit, the daa instruction repeats this process for the H.O. digit. daa sets the carry flag if there was a (decimal) carry out of the H.O. digit of the operation.

The daa instruction operates only on the AL register. It will not adjust (properly) for a decimal addition if you attempt to add a value to AX, EAX, or any other register. Specifically note that daa limits you to adding two decimal digits (a single byte) at a time. This means that for the purposes of computing decimal sums, you have to treat the 80x86 as though it were an 8-bit processor capable of adding only 8 bits at a time. If you wish to add more than two digits together, you must treat this as a multiprecision operation. For example, to add four decimal digits together (using daa), you must execute a sequence like the following:

```
// Assume "bcd_1:byte[2];", "bcd_2:byte[2];", and "bcd_3:byte[2];"

mov( bcd_1[0], al );
add( bcd_2[0], al );
daa();
mov( al, bcd_3[0] );
mov( bcd_1[1], al );
adc( bcd_2[1], al );
daa();
mov( al, bcd_3[1], al );

// Carry is set at this point if there was unsigned overflow.
```

Because a binary addition of two words (producing a word result) requires only three instructions, you can see that decimal arithmetic is expensive.[6]

The das (decimal adjust after subtraction) instruction adjusts the decimal result after a binary sub or sbb instruction. You use it the same way you use the daa instruction. Here are some examples:

```
// Two-digit (1-byte) decimal subtraction:

    mov( bcd_1, al );    // Assume that bcd_1 and bcd_2 both contain
    sub( bcd_2, al );    // valid BCD values.
    das();

// Four-digit (2-byte) decimal subtraction.
// Assume "bcd_1:byte[2];", "bcd_2:byte[2];", and "bcd_3:byte[2];"

    mov( bcd_1[0], al );
    sub( bcd_2[0], al );
    das();
    mov( al, bcd_3[0] );
    mov( bcd_1[1], al );
    sbb( bcd_2[1], al );
    das();
    mov( al, bcd_3[1], al );

// Carry is set at this point if there was unsigned overflow.
```

Unfortunately, the 80x86 provides support only for addition and subtraction of packed BCD values using the daa and das instructions. It does not support multiplication, division, or any other arithmetic operations. Because decimal arithmetic using these instructions is so limited, you'll rarely see any programs use these instructions.

### 8.3.3 The 80x86 aaa, aas, aam, and aad Instructions

In addition to the packed decimal instructions (daa and das), the 80x86 CPUs support four unpacked decimal adjustment instructions. Unpacked decimal numbers store only one digit per 8-bit byte. As you can imagine, this data representation scheme wastes a considerable amount of memory. However, the unpacked decimal adjustment instructions support the multiplication and division operations, so they are marginally more useful.

The instruction mnemonics aaa, aas, aam, and aad stand for "ASCII adjust for Addition, Subtraction, Multiplication, and Division" (respectively). Despite their names, these instructions do not process ASCII characters. Instead, they support an unpacked decimal value in AL whose L.O. 4 bits contain the decimal digit and the H.O. 4 bits contain 0. Note, though, that you can easily convert an ASCII decimal digit character to an unpacked decimal number by simply anding AL with the value $0F.

---

[6] You'll also soon see that it's rare to find decimal arithmetic done this way. So it hardly matters.

The aaa instruction adjusts the result of a binary addition of two unpacked decimal numbers. If the addition of those two values exceeds 10, then aaa will su tract 10 from AL and increment AH by 1 (as well as set the carry flag). aaa assume that the two values you add together are legal unpacked decimal values. Other than the fact that aaa works with only one decimal digit at a time (rather than two), you use it the same way you use the daa instruction. Of course, if you need t add together a string of decimal digits, using unpacked decimal arithmetic will require twice as many operations and, therefore, twice the execution time.

You use the aas instruction the same way you use the das instruction excep of course, it operates on unpacked decimal values rather than packed decimal values. As for aaa, aas will require twice the number of operations to add the sam number of decimal digits as the das instruction. If you're wondering why anyon would want to use the aaa or aas instruction, keep in mind that the unpacked fc mat supports multiplication and division, while the packed format does not. Since packing and unpacking the data is usually more expensive than working o the data a digit at a time, the aaa and aas instructions are more efficient if you have to work with unpacked data (because of the need for multiplication and division).

The aam instruction modifies the result in the AX register to produce correct unpacked decimal result after multiplying two unpacked decimal di its using the mul instruction. Because the largest product you may obtain i 81 (9 * 9 produces the largest possible product of two single-digit values), th result will fit in the AL register. aam unpacks the binary result by dividing it b 10, leaving the quotient (H.O. digit) in AH and the remainder (L.O. digit) i AL. Note that aam leaves the quotient and remainder in different registers tha a standard 8-bit div operation.

Technically, you do not have to use the aam instruction for BCD multipl cation operations. aam simply divides AL by 10 and leaves the quotient and remainder in AH and AL (respectively). If you have need of this particular operation, you may use the aam instruction for this purpose (indeed, that's about the only use for aam in most programs these days).

If you need to multiply more than two unpacked decimal digits together using mul and aam, you will need to devise a multiprecision multiplication that uses the manual algorithm from earlier in this chapter. Since that is a lot of work, this section will not present that algorithm. If you need a multiprecision decimal multiplication, see Section 8.3.4; it presents a better solution.

The aad instruction, as you might expect, adjusts a value for unpacked decimal division. The unusual thing about this instruction is that you must execute it before a div operation. It assumes that AL contains the least-significant digit of a two-digit value and AH contains the most-significant digit of a two-digit unpacked decimal value. It converts these two numbers t binary so that a standard div instruction will produce the correct unpacked decimal result. Like aam, this instruction is nearly useless for its intended pu pose because extended-precision operations (for example, division of more than one or two digits) are extremely inefficient. However, this instruction is actually quite useful in its own right. It computes AX = AH * 10 + AL (assuming that AH and AL contain single-digit decimal values). You can use this instruction to convert a two-character string containing the ASCII representation of a value in the range 0..99 to a binary value. For example:

```
mov( '9', al );
mov( '9', ah );    // "99" is in ah:al.
and( $0F0F, ax );  // Convert from ASCII to unpacked decimal.
aad();             // After this, ax contains 99.
```

The decimal and ASCII adjust instructions provide an extremely poor implementation of decimal arithmetic. To better support decimal arithmetic on 80x86 systems, Intel incorporated decimal operations into the FPU. The next section discusses how to use the FPU for this purpose. However, even with FPU support, decimal arithmetic is inefficient and less precise than binary arithmetic. Therefore, you should consider carefully if you really need to use decimal arithmetic before incorporating it into your programs.

### 8.3.4  Packed Decimal Arithmetic Using the FPU

To improve the performance of applications that rely on decimal arithmetic, Intel incorporated support for decimal arithmetic directly into the FPU. Unlike the packed and unpacked decimal formats of the previous sections, the FPU easily supports values with up to 18 decimal digits of precision, all at FPU speeds. Furthermore, all the arithmetic capabilities of the FPU (for example, transcendental operations) are available in addition to addition, subtraction, multiplication, and division. Assuming you can live with only 18 digits of precision and a few other restrictions, decimal arithmetic on the FPU is the right way to go if you must use decimal arithmetic in your programs.

The first fact you must note when using the FPU is that it doesn't really support decimal arithmetic. Instead, the FPU provides two instructions, fbld and fbstp, that convert between packed decimal and binary floating-point formats when moving data to and from the FPU. The fbld (float/BCD load) instruction loads an 80-bit packed BCD value unto the top of the FPU stack after converting that BCD value to the IEEE binary floating-point format. Likewise, the fbstp (float/BCD store and pop) instruction pops the floating-point value off the top of stack, converts it to a packed BCD value, and stores the BCD value into the destination memory location.

Once you load a packed BCD value into the FPU, it is no longer BCD. It's just a floating-point value. This presents the first restriction on the use of the FPU as a decimal integer processor: Calculations are done using binary arithmetic. If you have an algorithm that absolutely positively depends on the use of decimal arithmetic, it may fail if you use the FPU to implement it.[7]

---

[7] An example of such an algorithm might be a multiplication by 10 by shifting the number one digit to the left. However, such operations are not possible within the FPU itself, so algorithms that misbehave inside the FPU are actually quite rare.

The second limitation is that the FPU supports only one BCD data type: 10-byte 18-digit packed decimal value. It will not support smaller values, nor will it support larger values. Since 18 digits are usually sufficient and memory is cheap, this isn't a big restriction.

A third consideration is that the conversion between packed BCD and the floating-point format is not a cheap operation. The fbld and fbstp instructions can be quite slow (more than two orders of magnitude slower than fld and fstp, for example). Therefore, these instructions can be costly if you're doing simple additions or subtractions; the cost of conversion far outweighs the time spent adding the values a byte at a time using the daa and das instructions (multiplication and division, however, are going to be faster on the FPU).

You may be wondering why the FPU's packed decimal format supports only 18 digits. After all, with 10 bytes it should be possible to represent 20 BCD digits. As it turns out, the FPU's packed decimal format uses the first 9 bytes to hold the packed BCD value in a standard packed decimal format (the first byte contains the two L.O. digits and the ninth byte holds the two H.O. digits). The H.O. bit of the tenth byte holds the sign bit, and the FPU ignores the remaining bits in the tenth byte. If you're wondering why Intel didn't squeeze in one more digit (that is, use the L.O. 4 bits of the tenth byte to allow for 19 digits of precision), just keep in mind that doing so would create some possible BCD values that the FPU could not exactly represent in the native floating-point format. Hence, you have the limitation of 18 digits.

The FPU uses a one's complement notation for negative BCD values. That is, the sign bit contains a 1 if the number is negative or 0 and it contains a 0 if the number is positive or 0 (like the binary one's complement format, there are two distinct representations for 0).

HLA's tbyte type is the standard data type you would use to define packed BCD variables. The fbld and fbstp instructions require a tbyte operand (which you can initialize with a hexadecimal/BCD value).

Because the FPU converts packed decimal values to the internal floating-point format, you can mix packed decimal, floating point, and (binary) integer formats in the same calculation. The program in Listing 8-7 demonstrates how you might achieve this.

```
program MixedArithmetic;
#include( "stdlib.hhf" )

static
    tb: tbyte := $654321;

begin MixedArithmetic;

    fbld( tb );
    fmul( 2.0 );
    fiadd( 1 );
    fbstp( tb );
    stdout.put( "bcd value is " );
```

```
    stdout.puth80( tb );
    stdout.newln();

end MixedArithmetic;
```

*Listing 8-7: Mixed-mode FPU arithmetic*

The FPU treats packed decimal values as integer values. Therefore, if your calculations produce fractional results, the fbstp instruction will round the result according to the current FPU rounding mode. If you need to work with fractional values, you need to stick with floating-point results.

# 8.4  Tables

The term *table* has different meanings to different programmers. To most assembly language programmers, a table is nothing more than an array that is initialized with some data. The assembly language programmer often uses tables to compute complex or otherwise slow functions. Many very-high-level languages (for example, SNOBOL4 and Icon) directly support a table data type. Tables in these languages are essentially associative arrays whose elements you can access with a noninteger index (for example, floating point, string, or any other data type). HLA provides a table module that lets you index an array using a string. However, in this chapter we will adopt the assembly language programmer's view of tables.

A table is an array containing initialized values that do not change during the execution of the program. In assembly language, you can use tables for a variety of purposes: computing functions, controlling program flow, or simply looking things up. In general, tables provide a fast mechanism for performing some operation at the expense of some space in your program (the extra space holds the tabular data). In the following sections we'll explore some of the many possible uses of tables in an assembly language program.

Note that because tables typically contain initialized data that does not change during program execution, the readonly section is a good place to put your table objects.

## 8.4.1  Function Computation via Table Lookup

Tables can do all kinds of things in assembly language. In high-level languages like Pascal, it's easy to create a formula that computes some value. A simple-looking high-level-language arithmetic expression can be equivalent to a considerable amount of 80x86 assembly language code and, therefore, could be expensive to compute. Assembly language programmers often precompute many values and use a table lookup of those values to speed up their programs. This has the advantage of being easier, and it's often more efficient as well. Consider the following Pascal statement:

```
if (character >= 'a') and (character <= 'z') then character :=
chr(ord(character) - 32);
```

This Pascal if statement converts the character variable's value from lower case to uppercase if *character* is in the range a..z. The HLA code that does the same thing follows:

```
    mov( character, al );
    if( al in 'a'..'z' ) then

        and( $5f, al );      // Same as sub( 32, al ) in this code.

    endif;
    mov( al, character );
```

Note that HLA's high-level if statement translates into four machine instructions in this particular example. Hence, this code requires a total of seven machine instructions.

Had you buried this code in a nested loop, you'd be hard pressed to reduce the size of this code without using a table lookup. Using a table lookup, however, allows you to reduce this sequence of instructions to just four instructions:

```
    mov( character, al );
    lea( ebx, CnvrtLower );
    xlat
    mov( al, character );
```

You're probably wondering how this code works and asking, "What is the new instruction, xlat?" The xlat, or translate, instruction does the following:

```
mov( [ebx+al*1], al );
```

That is, it uses the current value of the AL register as an index into the array whose base address is found in EBX. It fetches the byte at that index in the array and copies that byte into the AL register. Intel calls this instruction *translate* because programmers typically use it to translate characters from one form to another using a lookup table. That's exactly how we are using it here.

In the previous example, CnvrtLower is a 256-byte table that contains the values 0..$60 at indices 0..$60, $41..$5A at indices $61..$7A, and $7B..$FF at indices $7Bh..0FF. Therefore, if AL contains a value in the range $0..$60, the xlat instruction returns the value $0..$60, effectively leaving AL unchanged. However, if AL contains a value in the range $61..$7A (the ASCII codes for a..z), then the xlat instruction replaces the value in AL with a value in the range $41..$5A. The values $41..$5A just happen to be the ASCII codes for A..Z. Therefore, if AL originally contains a lowercase character ($61..$7A), the xlat instruction replaces the value in AL with a corresponding value in the range $61..$7A, effectively converting the original lowercase character ($61..$7A) to an uppercase character ($41..$5A). The remaining entries in the table, like entries $0..$60, simply contain the index into the table of their particular element. Therefore, if AL originally contains a value in the range $7A..$FF, the xlat instruction will return the corresponding table entry that also contains $7A..$FF.

As the complexity of the function increases, the performance benefits of the table lookup method increase dramatically. While you would almost never use a lookup table to convert lowercase to uppercase, consider what happens if you want to swap cases, for example, via computation:

```
mov( character, al );
if( al in 'a'..'z' ) then

    and( $5f, al );

elseif( al in 'A'..'Z' ) then

    or( $20, al );

endif;
mov( al, character ):
```

The if and elseif statements generate 4 and 5 actual machine instructions, respectively, so this code is equivalent to 13 actual machine instructions.

The table lookup code to compute this same function is:

```
mov( character, al );
lea( ebx, SwapUL );
xlat();
mov( al, character );
```

As you can see, when using a table lookup to compute a function, only the table changes; the code remains the same.

Table lookups suffer from one major problem—functions computed via table lookup have a limited domain. The domain of a function is the set of possible input values (parameters) it will accept. For example, the upper-case/lowercase conversion functions above have the 256-character ASCII character set as their domain.

A function such as SIN or COS accepts the set of real numbers as possible input values. Clearly the domain for SIN and COS is much larger than for the upper/lowercase conversion function. If you are going to do computations via table lookup, you must limit the domain of a function to a small set. This is because each element in the domain of a function requires an entry in the lookup table. You won't find it very practical to implement a function via table lookup whose domain is the set of real numbers.

Most lookup tables are quite small, usually 10 to 256 entries. Rarely do lookup tables grow beyond 1,000 entries. Most programmers don't have the patience to create (and verify the correctness) of a 1,000-entry table.

Another limitation of functions based on lookup tables is that the elements in the domain of the function must be fairly contiguous. Table lookups take the input value for a function, use this input value as an index into the table, and return the value at that entry in the table. If you do not pass a function any values other than 0, 100, 1,000, and 10,000, it would seem an ideal candidate for implementation via table lookup; its domain consists of only four items. However, the table would actually require 10,001 different elements due to the range of the input values. Therefore, you cannot efficiently create such a function via a table lookup. Throughout this section on tables, we'll assume that the domain of the function is a fairly contiguous set of values.

The best functions you can implement via table lookups are those whose domain and range are always 0..255 (or some subset of this range). You can efficiently implement such functions on the 80x86 via the xlat instruction. The uppercase/lowercase conversion routines presented earlier are good examples of such a function. Any function in this class (those whose domain and range take on the values 0..255) can be computed using the same two instructions: lea( table, ebx ); and xlat();. The only thing that ever changes is the lookup table.

You cannot (conveniently) use the xlat instruction to compute a function value once the range or domain of the function takes on values outside 0..255. There are three situations to consider:

- The domain is outside 0..255 but the range is within 0..255.
- The domain is inside 0..255 but the range is outside 0..255.
- Both the domain and range of the function take on values outside 0..255.

We will consider each of these cases separately.

If the domain of a function is outside 0..255, but the range of the function falls within this set of values, our lookup table will require more than 256 entries but we can represent each entry with a single byte. Therefore, the lookup table can be an array of bytes. Other than those lookups that can use the xlat instruction, functions falling into this class are the most efficient. The following Pascal function invocation

```
B := Func(X);
```

where Func is

```
function Func(X:dword):byte;
```

is easily converted to the following HLA code:

```
mov( X, ebx );
mov( FuncTable[ ebx ], al );
mov( al, B );
```

This code loads the function parameter into ebx, uses this value (in the range 0..??) as an index into the FuncTable table, fetches the byte at that location, and stores the result into B. Obviously, the table must contain a valid entry for each possible value of X. For example, suppose you wanted to map a cursor position on the video screen in the range 0..1,999 (there are 2,000 character positions on an 80×25 video display) to its X or Y coordinate on the screen. You could easily compute the X coordinate via the function

```
X := Posn mod 80
```

and the Y coordinate with the formula

```
Y := Posn div 80
```

(where Posn is the cursor position on the screen). This can be easily computed using the 80x86 code:

```
        mov( Posn, ax );
        div( 80, ax );

// X is now in ah, Y is now in al
```

However, the div instruction on the 80x86 is very slow. If you need to do this computation for every character you write to the screen, you will seriously degrade the speed of your video display code. The following code, which realizes these two functions via table lookup, may improve the performance of your code considerably:

```
        movzx( Posn, ebx );        // Use a plain mov instr if Posn is
        mov( YCoord[ebx], al );    // uns32 rather than an uns16 value.
        mov( XCoord[ebx], ah );
```

If the domain of a function is within 0..255 but the range is outside this set, the lookup table will contain 256 or fewer entries, but each entry will require 2 or more bytes. If both the range and domains of the function are outside 0..255, each entry will require 2 or more bytes and the table will contain more than 256 entries.

Recall from the chapter on arrays that the formula for indexing into a single-dimensional array (of which a table is a special case) is:

```
        Address := Base + index * size
```

If elements in the range of the function require 2 bytes, then you must multiply the index by 2 before indexing into the table. Likewise, if each entry requires 3, 4, or more bytes, the index must be multiplied by the size of each table entry before being used as an index into the table. For example, suppose you have a function, F(x), defined by the following (pseudo) Pascal declaration:

```
function F(x:dword):word;
```

You can easily create this function using the following 80x86 code (and, of course, the appropriate table named F):

```
        mov( X, ebx );
        mov( F[ebx*2], ax );
```

Any function whose domain is small and mostly contiguous is a good candidate for computation via table lookup. In some cases, noncontiguous domains are acceptable as well, as long as the domain can be coerced into a appropriate set of values. Such operations are called *conditioning* and are th subject of the next section.

### 8.4.2 Domain Conditioning

Domain conditioning is taking a set of values in the domain of a function an massaging them so that they are more acceptable as inputs to that function Consider the following function:

$$\sin x = \sin x | (x \in [-2\pi, 2\pi])$$

This says that the (computer) function sin(x) is equivalent to the (math ematical) function sin *x* where

$$-2\pi \ldots x \ldots 2\pi$$

As we all know, sine is a circular function, which will accept any real val ued input. The formula used to compute sine, however, accepts only a sma set of these values.

This range limitation doesn't present any real problems; by simply compu ing sin(X mod (2\*pi)) we can compute the sine of any input value. Modifying an input value so that we can easily compute a function is called *conditionin the input*. In the example above we computed X mod 2\*pi and used the result a the input to the sin function. This truncates X to the domain sin needs with out affecting the result. We can apply input conditioning to table lookups a well. In fact, scaling the index to handle word entries is a form of input con ditioning. Consider the following Pascal function:

```
function val(x:word):word; begin
    case x of
        0: val := 1;
        1: val := 1;
        2: val := 4;
        3: val := 27;
        4: val := 256;
        otherwise val := 0;
    end;
end;
```

This function computes some value for x in the range 0..4 and it returns if x is outside this range. Since x can take on 65,536 different values (being 16-bit word), creating a table containing 65,536 words where only the first fiv entries are nonzero seems to be quite wasteful. However, we can still comput this function using a table lookup if we use input conditioning. The following assembly language code presents this principle:

```
mov( 0, ax );              // ax = 0, assume x > 4.
movzx( x, ebx );           // Note that H.O. bits of ebx must be 0!
if( bx <= 4 ) then

    mov( val[ ebx*2 ], ax );

endif;
```

This code checks to see if x is outside the range 0..4. If so, it manually sets AX to 0; otherwise it looks up the function value through the val table. With input conditioning, you can implement several functions that would otherwise be impractical to do via table lookup.

### 8.4.3 Generating Tables

One big problem with using table lookups is creating the table in the first place. This is particularly true if there is a large number of entries in the table. Figuring out the data to place in the table, then laboriously entering the data, and, finally, checking that data to make sure it is valid is a very time-consuming and boring process. For many tables, there is no way around this process. For other tables, there is a better way—using the computer to generate the table for you. An example is probably the best way to describe this. Consider the following modification to the sine function:

$$\sin(x) \times r = \left\langle \frac{(r \times (1000 \times \sin x))}{1000} \middle| [x \in 0, 359] \right\rangle$$

This states that $x$ is an integer in the range 0..359 and $r$ must be an integer. The computer can easily compute this with the following code:

```
movzx( x, ebx );
mov( Sines[ ebx*2], eax );   // Get sin(X) * 1000
imul( r, eax );              // Note that this extends eax into edx.
idiv( 1000, edx:eax );       // Compute (r*(sin(X)*1000)) / 1000
```

Note that integer multiplication and division are not associative. You cannot remove the multiplication by 1,000 and the division by 1,000 because they appear to cancel one another out. Furthermore, this code must compute this function in exactly this order. All that we need to complete this function is a table containing 360 different values corresponding to the sine of the angle (in degrees) times 1,000. Entering such a table into an assembly language program containing such values is extremely boring and you'd probably make several mistakes entering and verifying this data. However, you can have the program generate this table for you. Consider the HLA program in Listing 8-8.

```
program GenerateSines;
#include( "stdlib.hhf" );

var
    outFile: dword;
    angle:   int32;
    r:       int32;

readonly
    RoundMode: uns16 := $23f;



begin GenerateSines;

    // Open the file:

    mov( fileio.openNew( "sines.hla" ), outFile );

    // Emit the initial part of the declaration to the output file:

    fileio.put
    (
        outFile,
        stdio.tab,
        "sines: int32[360] := " nl,
        stdio.tab, stdio.tab, stdio.tab, "[" nl );

    // Enable rounding control (round to the nearest integer).

    fldcw( RoundMode );

    // Emit the sines table:

    for( mov( 0, angle); angle < 359; inc( angle )) do

        // Convert angle in degrees to an angle in radians using
        // radians := angle * 2.0 * pi / 360.0;

        fild( angle );
        fld( 2.0 );
        fmulp();
        fldpi();
        fmulp();
        fld( 360.0 );
        fdivp();

        // Okay, compute the sine of st0.
```

```
fsin();

// Multiply by 1000 and store the rounded result into
// the integer variable r.

fld( 1000.0 );
fmulp();
fistp( r );

// Write out the integers eight per line to the source file.
// Note: If (angle AND %111) is 0, then angle is evenly
// divisible by 8 and we should output a newline first.

test( %111, angle );
if( @z ) then

    fileio.put
    (
        outFile,
        nl,
        stdio.tab,
        stdio.tab,
        stdio.tab,
        stdio.tab,
        r:5,
        ','
    );

else

    fileio.put( outFile, r:5, ',' );

endif;

endfor;

// Output sine(359) as a special case (no comma following it).
// Note: This value was computed manually with a calculator.

fileio.put
(
    outFile,
    "  -17",
    nl,
    stdio.tab,
    stdio.tab,
    stdio.tab,
    "];",
    nl
);
fileio.close( outFile );

end GenerateSines;
```

*Listing 8-8: An HLA program that generates a table of sines*

The program above produces the following output (truncated for brevity

```
sines: int32[360] :=
    [

        0,   17,   35,   52,   70,   87,  105,  122,
      139,  156,  174,  191,  208,  225,  242,  259,
      276,  292,  309,  326,  342,  358,  375,  391,
      407,  423,  438,  454,  469,  485,  500,  515,
      530,  545,  559,  574,  588,  602,  616,  629,
      643,  656,  669,  682,  695,  707,  719,  731,
                                                  .
                                                  .
                                                  .

     -643, -629, -616, -602, -588, -574, -559, -545,
     -530, -515, -500, -485, -469, -454, -438, -423,
     -407, -391, -375, -358, -342, -326, -309, -292,
     -276, -259, -242, -225, -208, -191, -174, -156,
     -139, -122, -105,  -87,  -70,  -52,  -35,  -17
    ];
```

Obviously it's much easier to write the HLA program that generated the data than to enter (and verify) this data by hand. Of course, you don't even have to write the table-generation program in HLA. If you prefer, you might find it easier to write the program in Pascal/Delphi, C/C++, or some other high-level language. Because the program will only execute once, the performance of the table-generation program is not an issue. If it's easier to write the table-generation program in a high-level language, by all means do so. Note also that HLA has a built-in interpreter that allows you to easily create tables without having to use an external program. For more details, see Chapter 9.

Once you run your table-generation program, all that remains to be done is to cut and paste the table from the file (*sines.hla* in this example) into the program that will actually use the table.

### 8.4.4 Table Lookup Performance

In the early days of PCs, table lookups were a preferred way to do high-performance computations. However, as the speed of new CPUs vastly outpaces the speed of memory, the advantages of lookup tables have been waning. Today, it is not uncommon for a CPU to be 10 to 100 times faster than main memory. As a result, using a table lookup may not be faster than doing the same calculation with machine instructions. So it's worthwhile to briefly discuss when table lookups offer a big advantage.

Although the CPU is much faster than main memory, the on-chip CPU cache memory subsystems operate at near CPU speeds. Therefore, table lookups can be cost effective if your table resides in cache memory on the CPU. This means that the way to get good performance using table lookups is to use small tables (because there's only so much room on the cache) and use tables whose entries you reference frequently (so the tables stay in the cache). See

*Write Great Code, Volume 1* (No Starch Press) or the electronic version of *The Art of Assembly Language* at *http://webster.cs.ucr.edu/* or *http://www.artofasm.com/* for details concerning the operation of cache memory and how you can optimize your use of cache memory.

## 8.5 For More Information

The HLA Standard Library reference manual contains lots of information about the HLA Standard Library's extended-precision arithmetic capabilities. You'll also want to check out the source code for several of the HLA Standard Library routines to see how to do various extended-precision operations (that properly set the flags once the computation is complete). The HLA Standard Library source code also covers the extended-precision I/O operations that do not appear in this chapter.

Donald Knuth's *The Art of Computer Programming, Volume Two: Seminumerical Algorithms* contains a lot of useful information about decimal arithmetic and extended-precision arithmetic, though that text is generic and doesn't describe how to do this in x86 assembly language.

# 9

## MACROS AND THE HLA COMPILE-TIME LANGUAGE

 This chapter discusses the HLA compile-time language. This discussion includes what is perhaps the most important component of the HLA compile-time language, *macros*. Many people judge the power of an assembler by the power of its macro processing capabilities. If you happen to be one of these people, you'll probably agree that HLA is one of the more powerful assemblers on the planet after reading this chapter, because HLA has one of the most powerful macro processing facilities of any computer language processing system.

## 9.1 Introduction to the Compile-Time Language (CTL)

HLA is actually two languages rolled into a single program. The *runtime language* is the standard 80x86/HLA assembly language you've been reading about in all the previous chapters. This is called the runtime language because the programs you write execute when you run the executable file. HLA contains an interpreter for a second language, the HLA compile-time language (CTL), which executes programs while HLA is compiling a program.

The source code for the CTL program is embedded in an HLA assembly language source file; that is, HLA source files contain instructions for both the HLA CTL and the runtime program. HLA executes the CTL program during compilation. Once HLA completes compilation, the CTL program terminates; the CTL application is not a part of the runtime executable that HLA emits, although the CTL application can *write* part of the runtime program for you, and, in fact, this is the major purpose of the CTL (see Figure 9-1).

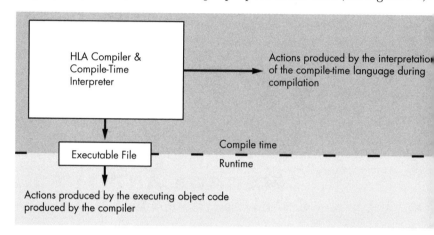

Figure 9-1: Compile-time versus runtime execution

It may seem confusing to have two separate languages built into the same compiler. Perhaps you're even questioning why anyone would need a compile-time language. To understand the benefits of a compile-time language, consider the following statement that you should be very comfortable with at this point:

```
stdout.put("i32=",i32," strVar=",strVar," charVar=",charVar,nl);
```

This statement is neither a statement in the HLA language nor a call to some HLA Standard Library procedure. Instead, stdout.put is actually a statement in a CTL application provided by the HLA Standard Library. The stdout.put "application" processes the parameter list and generates calls to various other Standard Library procedures; it chooses the procedure to call based on the type of the parameter it is currently processing. For example, the stdout.put "application" above will emit the following statements to the runtime executable:

```
stdout.puts( "i32=" );
stdout.puti32( i32 );
stdout.puts( " strVar=" );
stdout.puts( strVar );
stdout.puts( " charVar=" );
stdout.putc( charVar );
stdout.newln();
```

Clearly the stdout.put statement is much easier to read and write than the sequence of statements that stdout.put emits in response to its parameter list. This is one of the more powerful capabilities of the HLA programming language: the ability to modify the language to simplify common programming tasks. Printing different data objects in a sequential fashion is a common task; the stdout.put "application" greatly simplifies this process.

The HLA Standard Library is *loaded* with many HLA CTL examples. In addition to Standard Library usage, the HLA CTL is quite adept at handling "one-use" applications. A classic example is filling in the data for a lookup table. Chapter 8 noted that it is possible to construct lookup tables using the HLA CTL. Not only is this possible, but it is often far less work to use the HLA CTL to construct these tables.

Although the CTL itself is relatively inefficient and you would not normally use it to write end-user applications, it does maximize the use of your time. By learning how to use the HLA CTL and applying it properly, you can develop assembly language applications as rapidly as high-level language applications (even faster because HLA's CTL lets you create *very* high-level-language constructs).

## 9.2   The #print and #error Statements

You may recall that Chapter 1 began with the typical first program most people write when learning a new language, the "Hello, world!" program. It is only fitting for this chapter to present that same program when discussing the second language of this book. Listing 9-1 provides the basic "Hello, world!" program written in the HLA compile-time language.

```
program ctlHelloWorld;
begin ctlHelloWorld;

    #print( "Hello, World of HLA/CTL" )

end ctlHelloWorld;
```

*Listing 9-1: The CTL "Hello, world!" program*

The only CTL statement in this program is the #print statement. The remaining lines are needed just to keep the compiler happy (though we could have reduced the overhead to two lines by using a unit rather than a program declaration).

The #print statement displays the textual representation of its argument list during the compilation of an HLA program. Therefore, if you compile the program above with the command hla ctlHW.hla, the HLA compiler will immediately print the text:

```
Hello, World of HLA/CTL
```

Note that there is a big difference between the following two statemen
in an HLA source file:

```
#print( "Hello World" )
stdout.puts( "Hello World" nl );
```

The first statement prints Hello World (and a new line) during the com
lation process. This first statement does not have any effect on the executab
program. The second line doesn't affect the compilation process (other tha
the emission of code to the executable file). However, when you run the ex
cutable file, the second statement prints the string Hello World followed by
newline sequence.

The HLA/CTL #print statement uses the following basic syntax:

```
#print( list_of_comma_separated_constants )
```

Note that a semicolon does not terminate this statement. Semicolons
terminate runtime statements; they generally do not terminate compile-tim
statements (there is one big exception, as you will see a little later).

The #print statement must have at least one operand; if multiple operand
appear in the parameter list, you must separate each operand with a comm
(just like stdout.put). If a particular operand is not a string constant, HLA w
translate that constant to its corresponding string representation and print
that string. Here's an example:

```
#print( "A string Constant ", 45, ' ', 54.9, ' ', true )
```

You may specify named symbolic constants and constant expressions.
However, all #print operands must be constants (either literal constants o
constants you define in the const or val sections), and those constants must b
defined before you use them in the #print statement. For example:

```
const
    pi := 3.14159;
    charConst := 'c';

#print( "PI = ", pi, "  CharVal=", charConst )
```

The HLA #print statement is particularly invaluable for debugging CTI
programs. This statement is also useful for displaying the progress of the co
pilation and displaying assumptions and default actions that take place durin
compilation. Other than displaying the text associated with the #print param
ter list, the #print statement has no effect on the compilation of the program

The #error statement allows a single-string constant operand. Like #prin
this statement will display the string to the console during compilation. Ho
ever, the #error statement treats the string as an error message and displays
the string as part of an HLA error diagnostic. Further, the #error statement
increments the error count, and this will cause HLA to stop the compilatio
(without assembling or linking) after processing the current source file. Yo

would normally use the #error statement to display an error message during compilation if your CTL code discovers something that prevents it from creating valid code. For example:

```
#error( "Statement must have exactly one operand" )
```

Like the #print statement, the #error statement does not end with a semicolon. Although #error allows only a single-string operand, it's very easy to print other values by using the compile-time string concatenation operator and several of the HLA built-in compile-time functions. You'll learn about these a little later in this chapter.

## 9.3 Compile-Time Constants and Variables

Just as the runtime language does, the compile-time language supports constants and variables. You declare compile-time constants in the const section, just as you would with the runtime language. You declare compile-time variables in the val section. Objects you declare in the val section are constants to the runtime language, but remember that you can change the value of an object you declare in the val section throughout the source file. Hence the term "compile-time variable." See Chapter 4 for more details.

The CTL assignment statement (?) computes the value of the constant expression to the right of the assignment operator (:=) and stores the result into the val object name appearing immediately to the left of the assignment operator.[1] This example code may appear anywhere in your HLA source file, not just in the val section of the program.

```
?ConstToPrint := 25;
#print( "ConstToPrint = ", ConstToPrint )
?ConstToPrint := ConstToPrint + 5;
#print( "Now ConstToPrint = ", ConstToPrint )
```

## 9.4 Compile-Time Expressions and Operators

The HLA CTL supports constant expressions in the CTL assignment statement. Unlike the runtime language (where you have to translate algebraic notation into a sequence of machine instructions), the HLA CTL allows a full set of arithmetic operations using familiar expression syntax. This gives the HLA CTL considerable power, especially when combined with the built-in compile-time functions the next section discusses.

Tables 9-1 and 9-2 list operators that the HLA CTL supports in compile-time expressions.

---

[1] If the identifier to the left of the assignment operator is undefined, HLA will automatically declare this object at the current scope level.

**Table 9-1:** Compile-Time Operators

| Operator(s) | Operand Types* | Description |
|---|---|---|
| - (unary) | numeric | Negates the specific numeric value (int, uns, real). |
| | cset | Returns the complement of the specified character set. |
| ! (unary) | integer | Inverts all the bits in the operand (bitwise not). |
| | boolean | Boolean not of the operand. |
| * | numericL * numericR | Multiplies the two operands. |
| | csetL * csetR | Computes the intersection of the two sets. |
| div | integerL divintegerR | Computes the integer quotient of the two integer (int/uns/dword) operands. |
| mod | integerL modintegerR | Computes the remainder of the division of the two integer (int/uns/dword) operands. |
| / | numericL / numericR | Computes the real quotient of the two numeric operands. Returns a real result even if both operands are integers. |
| << | integerL << integerR | Shifts integerL operand to the left the number of bits specified by the integerR operand. |
| >> | integerL >> integerR | Shifts integerL operand to the right the number of bits specified by the integerR operand. |
| + | numericL + numericR | Adds the two numeric operands. |
| | csetL + csetR | Computes the union of the two sets. |
| | strL + strR | Concatenates the two strings. |
| - | numericL numericR | Computes the difference between numericL and numericR. |
| | csetL - csetR | Computes the set difference of csetL - csetR. |
| = or == | numericL = numericR | Returns true if the two operands have the same value. |
| | csetL = csetR | Returns true if the two sets are equal. |
| | strL = strR | Returns true if the two strings/chars are equal. |
| | typeL = typeR | Returns true if the two values are equal. They must be the same type. |
| <> or != | typeL <> typeR (sameas !=) | Returns false if the two (compatible) operands are not equal to one another (numeric, cset, or string). |
| < | numericL < numericR | Returns true if numericL is less than numericR. |
| | csetL < csetR | Returns true if csetL is a proper subset of csetR. |
| | strL < strR | Returns true if strL is less than strR. |
| | booleanL < booleanR | Returns true if the left operand is less than the right operand (note: false < true). |
| | enumL < enumR | Returns true if enumL appears in the same enumlist as enumR and enumL appears first. |

**Table 9-1:** Compile-Time Operators (continued)

| Operator(s) | Operand Types* | Description |
|---|---|---|
| <= | Same as < | Returns true if the left operand is less than or equal to the right operand. For character sets, this means that the left operand is a subset of the right operand. |
| > | Same as < | Returns true if the left operand is greater than the right operand. For character sets, this means that the left operand is a proper superset of the right operand. |
| >= | Same as <= | Returns true if the left operand is greater than or equal to the right operand. For character sets, this means that the left operand is a superset of the right operand. |
| & | integerL & integerR | Computes the bitwise and of the two operands. |
|  | booleanL & booleanR | Computes the logical and of the two operands. |
| \| | integerL \| integerR | Computes the bitwise or of the two operands. |
|  | booleanL \| booleanR | Computes the logical or of the two operands. |
| ^ | integerL ^ integerR | Computes the bitwise xor of the two operands. |
|  | booleanL ^ booleanR | Computes the logical xor of the two operands. Note that this is equivalent to booleanL <> booleanR. |
| in | charL in csetR | Returns true if charL is a member of csetR. |

* Type numeric is {int*XX*, uns*XX*, byte, word, dword, and real*XX*} values. Type cset is a character set operand. Type integer is {int*XX*, uns*XX*, byte, word, dword}. Type str is any string or character value. Type indicates an arbitrary HLA type. Other types specify an explicit HLA data type.

**Table 9-2:** Operator Precedence and Associativity

| Associativity | Precedence (Highest to Lowest) | Operator |
|---|---|---|
| Right to left | 6 | ! (unary) |
|  |  | - (unary) |
| Left to right | 5 | * |
|  |  | div |
|  |  | mod |
|  |  | / |
|  |  | >> |
|  |  | << |
| Left to right | 4 | + |
|  |  | - |

*(continued)*

**Table 9-2:** Operator Precedence and Associativity (continued)

| Associativity | Precedence (Highest to Lowest) | Operator |
|---|---|---|
| Left to right | 3 | = or == |
| | | <> or != |
| | | < |
| | | <= |
| | | > |
| | | >= |
| Left to right | 2 | & |
| | | \| |
| | | ^ |
| Nonassociative | 1 | in |

Of course, you can always override the default precedence and associativi of an operator by using parentheses in an expression.

## 9.5 Compile-Time Functions

HLA provides a wide range of compile-time functions you can use. These fun tions compute values during compilation the same way a high-level-language function computes values at runtime. The HLA compile-time language includes a wide variety of numeric, string, and symbol table functions that help you write sophisticated compile-time programs.

Most of the names of the built-in compile-time functions begin with the special symbol @ and have names like @sin or @length. The use of these speci identifiers prevents conflicts with common names you might want to use in your own programs (like length). The remaining compile-time functions (those that do not begin with @) are typically data conversion functions tha use type names like int8 and real64. You can even create your own compile-time functions using macros (which is discussed in Section 9.8).

HLA organizes the compile-time functions into various classes dependir on the type of operation. For example, there are functions that convert con stants from one form to another (such as string-to-integer conversion), ther are many useful string functions, and HLA provides a full set of compile-tim numeric functions.

The complete list of HLA compile-time functions is too lengthy to present here. Instead, a complete description of each of the compile-time objects and functions appears in the HLA reference manual (found at *http://webster.cs.ucr.edu/* or *http://www.artofasm.com/*); this section highlights a few o the functions in order to demonstrate their use. Later sections in this chapte as well as future chapters, make extensive use of the various compile-time functions.

Perhaps the most important concept to understand about the compile-time functions is that they are equivalent to constants in your assembly language code (i.e., the runtime program). For example, the compile-time function invocation @sin(3.1415265358979328) is roughly equivalent to specifying 0.0 at that point in your program.[2] A function invocation like @sin( x ) is legal only if x is a constant with a previous declaration at the point of the function call in the source file. In particular, x cannot be a runtime variable or other object whose value exists at runtime rather than compile time. Because HLA replaces compile-time function calls with their constant result, you may ask why you should even bother with compile-time functions. After all, it's probably more convenient to type *0.0* than it is to type *@sin(3.1415265358979328)* in your program. However, compile-time functions are handy for generating lookup tables and other mathematical results that may change whenever you change a const value in your program. Section 9.9 will explore this idea further.

### 9.5.1 Type-Conversion Compile-Time Functions

Probably the most commonly used compile-time functions are the type-conversion functions. These functions take a single parameter of one type and convert that information to some specified type. These functions use several of the HLA built-in data type names as the function names. Functions in this category are the following:

- boolean
- int8, int16, int32, int64, and int128
- uns8, uns16, uns32, uns64, and uns128
- byte, word, dword, qword, and lword (these are effectively equivalent to uns8, uns16, uns32, uns64, and uns128, respectively)
- real32, real64, and real80
- char
- string
- cset
- text

These functions accept a single constant expression parameter and, if at all reasonable, convert that expression's value to the type specified by the type name. For example, the following function call returns the value −128 because it converts the string constant to the corresponding integer value:

```
int8( "-128" )
```

Certain conversions don't make sense or have restrictions associated with them. For example, the boolean function will accept a string parameter, but that string must be "true" or "false" or the function will generate a compile-time error. Likewise, the numeric conversion functions (e.g., int8) allow a string oper-

---

[2] Actually, because @sin's parameter in this example is not exactly pi, you will get a small positive number instead of zero as the function result, but in theory you should get zero.

and, but the string operand must represent a legal numeric value. Some conversions (for example, int8 with a character set parameter) simply don' make sense and are always illegal.

One of the most useful functions in this category is the string function This function accepts nearly all the constant expression types, and it generat a string that represents the parameter's data. For example, the invocation string( 128 ) produces the string 128 as the return result. This function is handy when you have a value that you wish to use where HLA requires a strin For example, the #error compile-time statement allows only a single-string operand. You can use the string function and the string concatenation operator (+) to easily get around this limitation. For example:

```
#error( "theValue (" + string( theValue ) + ") is out of range" )
```

Note that these type functions actually perform a conversion. This mea that the bit pattern these functions return may be considerably different tha the bit pattern you pass as an argument. For example, consider the followin invocation of the real32 function:

```
real32( $3F80_0000 )
```

Now it turns out that $3F80_0000 is the hexadecimal equivalent of the real32 value 1.0. However, the preceding function invocation does not retur 1.0; instead it attempts to convert the integer value $3F80_0000 (1,065,353,21€ to a real32 value but fails because the value is too large to exactly represent using a real32 object. Contrast this with the following constant function:

```
char( 65 )
```

This CTL function invocation returns the character A (because 65 is th ASCII code for A). Notice how the char function simply uses the bit pattern c the integer argument you pass it as an ASCII code, whereas the real32 function attempts to translate the integer argument to a floating-point value. Althoug the semantics are quite different between these two functions, the bottom line is that they tend to do the intuitive operation, even at the expense of consistency.

Sometimes, however, you might not want these functions to do the "int itive" thing. For example, you might want the real32 function to simply trea the bit pattern you pass it as a real32 value. To handle this situation, HLA provides a second set of type functions, which are simply the type names wit an @ prefix that treat the argument as a bit pattern of the final type. So if yo really want to produce 1.0 from $3F80_0000, then you could use the followin function invocation:

```
@real32( $3F80_0000 )
```

Generally, type coercion of this form is somewhat advanced in the compile-time language, so you'll probably not use it very often. However, when it is needed, it's nice to have around.

### 9.5.2 Numeric Compile-Time Functions

The functions in this category perform standard mathematical operations at compile time. These functions are handy for generating lookup tables and "parameterizing" your source code by recalculating functions on constants defined at the beginning of your program. Functions in this category include the following:

| | |
|---|---|
| • @abs( *n* ) | Absolute value of numeric argument |
| • @ceil( *r* ), @floor( *r* ) | Extract integer component of floating-point value |
| • @sin( *r* ), @cos( *r* ), @tan( *r* ) | Standard trig functions |
| • @exp( *r* ), @log( *r* ), @log10( *r* ) | Standard log/exponent functions |
| • @min( *list* ), @max( *list* ) | Return min/max value from a list of values |
| • @random, @randomize | Return a pseudo-random int32 value |
| • @sqrt( *n* ) | Computes the square root of its numeric argument (real result) |

See the HLA reference manual at *http://webster.cs.ucr.edu/* or *http://www.artofasm.com/* for more details on these functions.

### 9.5.3 Character-Classification Compile-Time Functions

The functions in this group all return a boolean result. They test a character (or all the characters in a string) to see if it belongs to a certain class of characters. The functions in this category include the following:

- @isAlpha( *c* ), @isAlphanum( *c* )
- @isDigit( *c* ), @isxDigit( *c* )
- @isLower( *c* ), @isUpper( *c* )
- @isSpace( *c* )

In addition to these character-classification functions, the HLA language provides a set of pattern-matching functions that you can also use to classify character and string data. See the HLA reference manual at for the discussion of these routines.

### 9.5.4 Compile-Time String Functions

The functions in this category operate on string parameters. Most return a string result, although a few (for example, @length and @index) return integer results. These functions do not directly affect the values of their parameters;

instead, they return an appropriate result that you can assign back to the parameter if you wish to do so.

- @delete, @insert
- @index, @rindex
- @length
- @lowercase, @uppercase
- @strbrk, @strspan
- @strset
- @substr, @tokenize, @trim

For specific details concerning these functions, their parameters, and their types, see the HLA reference manual. Note that these are the compile time equivalents of many of the string functions found in the HLA Standard Library.

The @length function deserves a special discussion because it is probably the most popular function in this category. It returns an uns32 constant spec fying the number of characters found in its string parameter. The syntax is the following:

---

@length( *string_expression* )

---

where *string_expression* represents any compile-time string expression. As noted this function returns the length, in characters, of the specified expression.

### 9.5.5  Compile-Time Symbol Information

During compilation HLA maintains an internal database known as the *symbo table*. The symbol table contains lots of useful information concerning all the identifiers you've defined up to a given point in the program. In order to ger erate machine code output, HLA needs to query this database to determine how to treat certain symbols. In your compile-time programs, it is often nec essary to query the symbol table to determine how to handle an identifier or expression in your code. The HLA compile-time symbol-information functions handle this task.

Many of the compile-time symbol-information functions are well beyond the scope of this text. This chapter will present a few of the functions. For a complete list of the compile-time symbol-table functions, see the HLA refer ence manual. The functions we will consider in this chapter include the following:

- @size
- @defined
- @typeName
- @elements
- @elementSize

Without question, the @size function is probably the most important function in this group. Indeed, previous chapters have made use of this function already. The @size function requires a single HLA identifier or constant expression as a parameter. It returns the size, in bytes, of the data type of that object (or expression). If you supply an identifier, it can be a constant, type, or variable identifier. As you've seen in previous chapters, this function is invaluable for allocating storage via mem.alloc and allocating storage for arrays.

Another very useful function in this group is the @defined function. This function accepts a single HLA identifier as a parameter. For example:

---

```
@defined( MyIdentifier )
```

---

This function returns true if the identifier is defined at that point in the program; it returns false otherwise.

The @typeName function returns a string specifying the type name of the identifier or expression you supply as a parameter. For example, if i32 is an int32 object, then @typeName( i32 ) returns the string int32. This function is useful for testing the types of objects you are processing in your compile-time programs.

The @elements function requires an array identifier or expression. It returns the total number of array elements as the function result. Note that for multidimensional arrays this function returns the product of all the array dimensions.[3]

The @elementSize function returns the size, in bytes, of an element of an array whose name you pass as a parameter. This function is extremely valuable for computing indices into an array (that is, this function computes the element_size component of the array index calculation; see Chapter 4 for more details).

## 9.5.6 Miscellaneous Compile-Time Functions

The HLA compile-time language contains several additional functions that don't fall into one of the categories above. Some of the more useful miscellaneous functions include the following:

- @odd
- @lineNumber
- @text

The @odd function takes an ordinal value (i.e., nonreal numeric or character) as a parameter and returns true if the value is odd, false if it is even. The @lineNumber function requires no parameters; it returns the current line number in the source file. This function is quite useful for debugging compile-time (and runtime!) programs.

The @text function is probably the most useful function in this group. It requires a single-string parameter. It expands that string as text in place of the

---

[3] There is an @dim function that returns an array specifying the bounds on each dimension of a multidimensional array. See the documentation at *http://webster.cs.ucr.edu/* or *http://www.artofasm .com/* for more details if you're interested in this function.

@text function call. This function is quite useful in conjunction with the compile-time string-processing functions. You can build an instruction (or portion of an instruction) using the string-manipulation functions and then convert that string to program source code using the @text function. The following is a trivial example of this function in operation:

```
?id1:string := "eax";
?id2:string := "i32";
@text( "mov( " + id1 + ", " + id2 + ");" )
```

The preceding sequence compiles to

```
mov( eax, i32 );
```

## 9.5.7  Compile-Time Type Conversions of Text Objects

Once you create a text constant in your program, it's difficult to manipulate that object. The following example demonstrates a programmer's desire to change the definition of a text symbol within a program:

```
val
        t:text := "stdout.put";
            .
            .
            .
        ?t:text := "fileio.put";
```

The basic idea in this example is that the symbol t expands to stdout.put in the first half of the code, and it expands to fileio.put in the second half of the program. Unfortunately, this simple example will not work. The problem is that HLA will expand a text symbol in place almost anywhere it finds that symbol. This includes occurrences of t within a ? statement. Therefore, the previous code expands to the following (incorrect) text:

```
val
        t:text := "stdout.put";
            .
            .
            .
        ?stdout.put:text := "fileio.put";
```

HLA doesn't know how to deal with this ? statement, so it generates a syntax error.

At times you may not want HLA to expand a text object. Your code may want to process the string data held by the text object. HLA provides a couple of ways to deal with these two problems:

- @string( *identifier* )
- @toString:*identifier*

For @string( *identifier* ), HLA returns a string constant corresponding to the text data associated with the text object. In other words, this operator lets you treat a text object as though it were a string constant within an expression.

Unfortunately, the @string function converts a text object to a string constant, not a string identifier. Therefore, you cannot say something like

```
?@string(t) := "Hello"
```

This doesn't work because @string(t) replaces itself with the string constant associated with the text object t. Given the former assignment to t, this statement expands to

```
?"stdout.put" := "Hello";
```

This statement is still illegal.

The @toString:*identifier* operator comes to the rescue in this case. The @toString: operator requires a text object as the associated identifier. It converts this text object to a string object (still maintaining the same string data) and then returns the identifier. Because the identifier is now a string object, you can assign a value to it (and change its type to something else, for example, text, if that's what you need). To achieve the original goal, therefore, you'd use code like the following:

```
val
    t:text := "stdout.put";
        .
        .
        .
    ?@toString:t : text := "fileio.put";
```

# 9.6 Conditional Compilation (Compile-Time Decisions)

HLA's compile-time language provides an if statement, #if, that lets you make decisions at compile time. The #if statement has two main purposes: The traditional use of #if is to support *conditional compilation* (or *conditional assembly*), allowing you to include or exclude code during a compilation depending on the status of various symbols or constant values in your program. The second use of this statement is to support the standard if statement decision-making process in the HLA compile-time language. This section discusses these two uses for the HLA #if statement.

The simplest form of the HLA compile-time #if statement uses the following syntax:

```
#if( constant_boolean_expression )
    << text >>
#endif
```

Note that you do not place semicolons after the #endif clause. If you place a semicolon after the #endif, it becomes part of the source code, and this would be identical to inserting that semicolon immediately before the next item in the program.

At compile time, HLA evaluates the expression in the parentheses after the #if. This must be a constant expression, and its type must be boolean. If the expression evaluates true, HLA continues to process the text in the source file as though the #if statement was not present. However, if the expression evaluates false, HLA treats all the text between the #if and the corresponding #endif clause as though it were a comment (that is, it ignores the text), as shown in Figure 9-2.

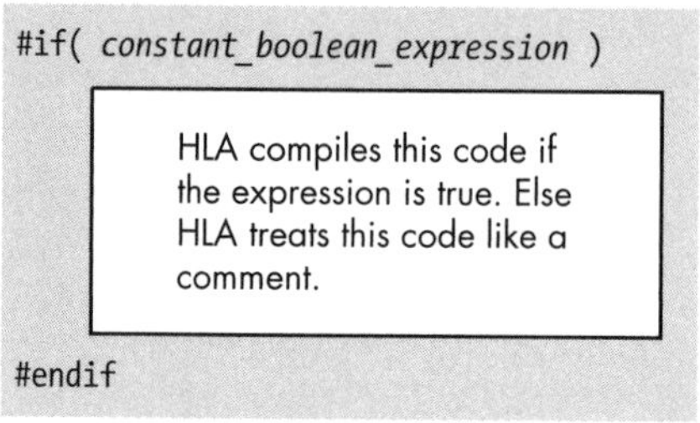

Figure 9-2: Operation of an HLA compile-time #if statement

Keep in mind that HLA's constant expressions support a full expression syntax like you'd find in a high-level language like C or Pascal. The #if expression syntax is not limited to the syntax allowed by expressions in the HLA if statement. Therefore, it is perfectly reasonable to write fancy expressions like the following:

```
#if( @length( someStrConst ) < 10*i & ( (MaxItems*2 + 2) < 100 | MinItems-5 < 10 ))
    << text >>
#endif
```

Also keep in mind that the identifiers in a compile-time expression must all be const or val identifiers or an HLA compile-time function call (with appropriate parameters). In particular, remember that HLA evaluates these expressions at compile time so they cannot contain runtime variables.[4] HLA's compile-time language uses complete boolean evaluation, so any side effects that occur in the expression may produce undesired results.

The HLA #if statement supports optional #elseif and #else clauses that behave in the intuitive fashion. The complete syntax for the #if statement looks like the following:

```
#if( constant_boolean_expression_1 )
    << text >>
#elseif( constant_boolean_expression_2 )
    << text >>
```

---

[4] Except, of course, as parameters to certain HLA compile-time functions like @size or @typeName.

```
#else
    << text >>
#endif
```

If the first boolean expression evaluates true, then HLA processes the text up to the #elseif clause. It then skips all text (that is, treats it like a comment) until it encounters the #endif clause. HLA continues processing the text after the #endif clause in the normal fashion.

If the first boolean expression above evaluates false, then HLA skips all the text until it encounters a #elseif, #else, or #endif clause. If it encounters a #elseif clause (as above), then HLA evaluates the boolean expression associated with that clause. If it evaluates true, HLA processes the text between the #elseif and the #else clauses (or to the #endif clause if the #else clause is not present). If, during the processing of this text, HLA encounters another #elseif or, as above, a #else clause, then HLA ignores all further text until it finds the corresponding #endif.

If both the first and second boolean expressions in the previous example evaluate false, HLA skips their associated text and begins processing the text in the #else clause. As you can see, the #if statement behaves in a relatively intuitive fashion once you understand how HLA "executes" the body of these statements; the #if statement processes the text or treats it as a comment, depending on the state of the boolean expression. Of course, you can create a nearly infinite variety of different #if statement sequences by including zero or more #elseif clauses and optionally supplying the #else clause. Because the construction is identical to the HLA if..then..elseif..else..endif statement, there is no need to elaborate further here.

A very traditional use of conditional compilation is to develop software that you can easily configure for several different environments. For example, the fcomip instruction makes floating-point comparisons very easy, but this instruction is available only on Pentium Pro and later processors. If you want to use this instruction on the processors that support it and fall back to the standard floating-point comparison on the older processors, you would normally have to write two versions of the program—one with the fcomip instruction and one with the traditional floating-point comparison sequence. Unfortunately, maintaining two different source files (one for newer processors and one for older processors) is very difficult. Most engineers prefer to use conditional compilation to embed the separate sequences in the same source file. The following example demonstrates how to do this:

```
const
    // Set true to use FCOMIxx instrs.
    PentProOrLater: boolean := false;
        .
        .
        .
    #if( PentProOrLater )

        fcomip();      // Compare st1 to st0 and set flags.
```

```
    #else
        fcomp();        // Compare st1 to st0.
        fstsw( ax );    // Move the FPU condition code bits
        sahf();         // into the flags register.

    #endif
```

As currently written, this code fragment will compile the three-instruction sequence in the #else clause and ignore the code between the #if and #else clauses (because the constant PentProOrLater is false). By changing the value of PentProOrLater to true, you can tell HLA to compile the single fcomip instruction rather than the three-instruction sequence. Of course, you can use the PentProOrLater constant in other #if statements throughout your program to control how HLA compiles your code.

Note that conditional compilation does not let you create a single *executable* that runs efficiently on all processors. When using this technique you will still have to create two executable programs (one for Pentium Pro and later processors, one for the earlier processors) by compiling your source file twice: During the first compilation you must set the PentProOrLater constant to false; during the second compilation you must set this constant to true. Although you must create two separate executables, you need only maintain a single source file.

If you are familiar with conditional compilation in other languages, such as the C/C++ language, you may be wondering if HLA supports a statement like C's #ifdef statement. The answer is no, it does not. However, you can use the HLA compile-time function @defined to easily test to see if a symbol has been defined earlier in the source file. Consider the following modification to the preceding code that uses this technique:

```
const
    // Note: Uncomment the following line if you are compiling this
    // code for a Pentium Pro or later CPU.

    // PentProOrLater :=0;  // Value and type are irrelevant.
        .
        .
        .
#if( @defined( PentProOrLater ) )

    fcomip();       // Compare st1 to st0 and set flags.

#else

    fcomp();        // Compare st1 to st0.
    fstsw( ax ); // Move the FPU condition code bits
    sahf();         // into the flags register.

#endif
```

Another common use of conditional compilation is to introduce debugging and testing code into your programs. A typical debugging technique that many HLA programmers use is to insert "print" statements at strategic points throughout their code; this enables them to trace through their code and display important values at various checkpoints. A big problem with this technique, however, is that they must remove the debugging code prior to completing the project. The software's customer (or a student's instructor) probably doesn't want to see debugging output in the middle of a report the program produces. Therefore, programmers who use this technique tend to insert code temporarily and then remove the code once they run the program and determine what is wrong. There are at least two problems with this technique:

- Programmers often forget to remove some debugging statements, and this creates defects in the final program.

- After removing a debugging statement, these programmers often discover that they need that same statement to debug some different problem at a later time. Hence they are constantly inserting and removing the same statements over and over again.

Conditional compilation can provide a solution to this problem. By defining a symbol (say, debug) to control debug output in your program, you can easily activate or deactivate *all* debugging output by simply modifying a single line of source code. The following code fragment demonstrates this:

```
const
    // Set to true to activate debug output.
    debug: boolean := false;
        .
        .
        .
#if( debug )

    stdout.put( "At line ", @lineNumber, " i=", i, nl );

#endif
```

As long as you surround all debugging output statements with an #if statement like the preceding, you don't have to worry about debug output accidentally appearing in your final application. By setting the debug symbol to false, you can automatically disable all such output. Likewise, you don't have to remove all your debugging statements from your programs once they've served their immediate purpose. By using conditional compilation, you can leave these statements in your code because they are so easy to deactivate. Later, if you decide you need to view this same debugging information during a compilation, you won't have to reenter the debugging statement; you simply reactivate it by setting the debug symbol to true.

Although program configuration and debugging control are two of the more common, traditional uses for conditional compilation, don't forget that the #if statement provides the basic conditional statement in the HLA compile-time language. You will use the #if statement in your compile-time program the same way you would use an if statement in HLA or some other language. Later sections in this text will present lots of examples of using the #if statement in this capacity.

## 9.7 Repetitive Compilation (Compile-Time Loops)

HLA's #while..#endwhile and #for..#endfor statements provide compile-time loop constructs. The #while statement tells HLA to process the same sequence of statements repetitively during compilation. This is very handy for constructing data tables as well as providing a traditional looping structure for compile-time programs. Although you will not employ the #while statement anywhere near as often as the #if statement, this compile-time control structure is very important when you write advanced HLA programs.

The #while statement uses the following syntax:

```
#while( constant_boolean_expression )
    << text >>
#endwhile
```

When HLA encounters the #while statement during compilation, it will evaluate the constant boolean expression. If the expression evaluates false, HLA will skip over the text between the #while and the #endwhile clauses (the behavior is similar to the #if statement if the expression evaluates false). If the expression evaluates true, then HLA will process the statements between the #while and #endwhile clauses and then "jump back" to the start of the #while statement in the source file and repeat this process, as shown in Figure 9-3.

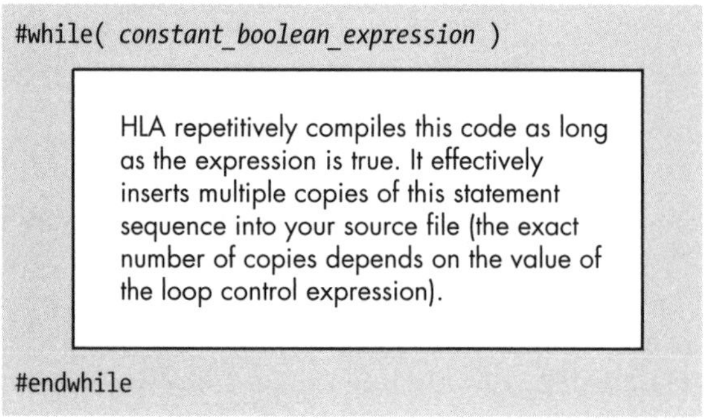

```
#while( constant_boolean_expression )

    HLA repetitively compiles this code as long
    as the expression is true. It effectively
    inserts multiple copies of this statement
    sequence into your source file (the exact
    number of copies depends on the value of
    the loop control expression).

#endwhile
```

Figure 9-3: HLA compile-time #while statement operation

To understand how this process works, consider the program in Listing 9-9.

```
program ctWhile;
#include( "stdlib.hhf" )
```

```
static
ary: uns32[5] := [ 2, 3, 5, 8, 13 ];

begin ctWhile;

    ?i := 0;
    #while( i < 5 )

        stdout.put( "array[ ", i, " ] = ", ary[i*4], nl );
        ?i := i + 1;

    #endwhile

end ctWhile;
```

*Listing 9-2: #while..#endwhile demonstration*

As you can probably surmise, the output from this program is the following:

```
array[ 0 ] = 2
array[ 1 ] = 3
array[ 2 ] = 4
array[ 3 ] = 5
array[ 4 ] = 13
```

What is not quite obvious is how this program generates this output. Remember, the #while..#endwhile construct is a compile-time language feature, not a runtime control construct. Therefore, the previous #while loop repeats five times during *compilation*. On each repetition of the loop, the HLA compiler processes the statements between the #while and #endwhile clauses. Therefore, the preceding program is really equivalent to the code that is shown in Listing 9-3.

```
program ctWhile;
#include( "stdlib.hhf" )

static
    ary: uns32[5] := [ 2, 3, 5, 8, 13 ];

begin ctWhile;

    stdout.put( "array[ ", 0, " ] = ", ary[0*4], nl );
    stdout.put( "array[ ", 1, " ] = ", ary[1*4], nl );
    stdout.put( "array[ ", 2, " ] = ", ary[2*4], nl );
    stdout.put( "array[ ", 3, " ] = ", ary[3*4], nl );
    stdout.put( "array[ ", 4, " ] = ", ary[4*4], nl );

end ctWhile;
```

*Listing 9-3: Program equivalent to the code in Listing 9-2*

As you can see in this example, the #while statement is very convenient for constructing repetitive-code sequences. This is especially invaluable for unrolling loops.

HLA provides three forms of the #for..#endfor loop. These three loops take the following general form:

```
#for( valObject := startExpr to endExpr )
        .
        .
        .
    #endfor

    #for( valObject := startExpr downto endExpr )
        .
        .
        .
    #endfor

    #for( valObject in composite_expr )
        .
        .
        .
    #endfor
```

*Listing 9-4: HLA #for loops*

As its name suggests, *valObject* must be an object you've defined in a va: declaration.

For the first two forms of the #for loop above, the *startExpr* and *endExpr* components can be any HLA constant expression that yields an integer value The first of these #for loops is semantically equivalent to the following #whil code:

```
?valObject := startExpr;
    #while( valObject <= endExpr )
            .
            .
            .
            ?valObject := valObject + 1;
    #endwhile
```

The second of these #for loops is semantically equivalent to the #while loop:

```
?valObject := startExpr;
    #while( valObject >= endExpr )
```

```
        .
        .
        .
    ?valObject := valObject - 1;
#endwhile
```

The third of these #for loops (the one using the in keyword) is especially useful for processing individual items from some composite data type. This loop repeats once for each element, field, character, and so on of the composite value you specify for *composite_expr*. This can be an array, string, record, or character set expression. For arrays, this #for loop repeats once for each element of the array and on each iteration of the loop; the loop control variable contains the current element's value. For example, the following compile-time loop displays the values 1, 10, 100, and 1,000:

```
#for( i in [1, 10, 100, 1000])
        #print( i )
#endfor
```

If the *composite_expr* constant is a string constant, the #for loop repeats once for each character in the string and sets the value of the loop control variable to the current character. If the *composite_expr* constant expression is a record constant, then the loop will repeat once for each field of the record, and for each iteration the loop control variable will take on the *type and value* of the current field. If the *composite_expr* expression is a character set, the loop will repeat once for each character in the set, and the loop control variable will be assigned that character.

The #for loop actually turns out to be more useful than the #while loop because the larger number of compile-time loops you encounter repeat a fixed number of times (for example, processing a fixed number of array elements, macro parameters, and so on).

## 9.8  Macros (Compile-Time Procedures)

Macros are objects that a language processor replaces with other text during compilation. Macros are great devices for replacing long, repetitive sequences of text with much shorter sequences of text. In additional to the traditional role that macros play (e.g., #define in C/C++), HLA's macros also serve as the equivalent of a compile-time language procedure or function. Therefore, macros are very important in HLA's compile-time language—just as important as functions and procedures are in other high-level languages.

Although macros are nothing new, HLA's implementation of macros far exceeds the macro-processing capabilities of most other programming languages (high level or low level). The following sections explore HLA's macro-processing facilities and the relationship between macros and other HLA CTL control constructs.

## 9.8.1  Standard Macros

HLA supports a straightforward macro facility that lets you define macros in a manner that is similar to declaring a procedure. A typical, simple macro declaration takes the following form:

```
#macro macroname;
    << Macro body >>
#endmacro
```

Although macro and procedure declarations are similar, there are several immediate differences between the two that are obvious from this example. First, of course, macro declarations use the reserved word #macro rather than procedure. Second, you do not begin the body of the macro with a begin macroname; clause. Finally, you will note that macros end with the #endmacro clause rather than end macroname;. The following code is a concrete example of a macro declaration:

```
#macro neg64;

    neg( edx );
    neg( eax );
    sbb( 0, edx );

#endmacro
```

Execution of this macro's code will compute the two's complement of the 64-bit value in EDX:EAX (see the description of extended-precision neg in Section 8.1.7).

To execute the code associated with neg64, you simply specify the macro's name at the point you want to execute these instructions. For example:

```
    mov( (type dword i64), eax );
    mov( (type dword i64[4]), edx );
    neg64;
```

Note that you do *not* follow the macro's name with a pair of empty parentheses as you would a procedure call (the reason for this will become clear a little later).

Other than the lack of parentheses following neg64's invocation,[5] this look just like a procedure call. You could implement this simple macro as a procedure using the following procedure declaration:

```
procedure neg64p;
begin neg64p;
```

---

[5] To differentiate between macros and procedures, this text will use the term *invocation* when describing the use of a macro and *call* when describing the use of a procedure.

```
    neg( edx );
    neg( eax );
    sbb( 0, edx );

end neg64p;
```

Note that the following two statements will both negate the value in EDX:EAX:

```
neg64;          neg64p();
```

The difference between these two (the macro invocation versus the procedure call) is the fact that macros expand their text inline, whereas a procedure call emits a call to the corresponding procedure elsewhere in the text. That is, HLA replaces the invocation neg64; directly with the following text:

```
    neg( edx );
    neg( eax );
    sbb( 0, edx );
```

On the other hand, HLA replaces the procedure call neg64p(); with the single call instruction:

```
call neg64p;
```

Presumably, you've defined the neg64p procedure earlier in the program.

You should make the choice of macro versus procedure call on the basis of efficiency. Macros are slightly faster than procedure calls because you don't execute the call and corresponding ret instructions. On the other hand, the use of macros can make your program larger because a macro invocation expands to the text of the macro's body on each invocation. Procedure calls jump to a single instance of the procedure's body. Therefore, if the macro body is large and you invoke the macro several times throughout your program, it will make your final executable much larger. Also, if the body of your macro executes more than a few simple instructions, the overhead of a call/ret sequence has little impact on the overall execution time of the code, so the execution time savings are nearly negligible. On the other hand, if the body of a procedure is very short (like the neg64 example above), you'll discover that the macro implementation is much faster and doesn't expand the size of your program by much. A good rule of thumb is:

**NOTE**    *Use macros for short, time-critical program units. Use procedures for longer blocks of code and when execution time is not as critical.*

Macros have many other disadvantages over procedures. Macros cannot have local (automatic) variables, macro parameters work differently than procedure parameters, macros don't support (runtime) recursion, and macros are a little more difficult to debug than procedures (just to name a few disadvantages). Therefore, you shouldn't really use macros as a substitute for procedures except in cases where performance is absolutely critical.

## 9.8.2  Macro Parameters

Like procedures, macros allow you to define parameters that let you supply different data on each macro invocation. This lets you write generic macros whose behavior can vary depending on the parameters you supply. By processing these macro parameters at compile time, you can write very sophisticated macros.

Macro parameter declaration syntax is very straightforward. You simply supply a list of parameter names within parentheses in a macro declaration:

```
#macro neg64( reg32HO, reg32LO );

    neg( reg32HO );
    neg( reg32LO );
    sbb( 0, reg32HO );

#endmacro;
```

Note that you do not associate a data type with a macro parameter as you do for procedural parameters. This is because HLA macros are generally text objects.

When you invoke a macro, you simply supply the actual parameters the same way you would for a procedure call:

```
    neg64( edx, eax );
```

Note that a macro invocation that requires parameters expects you to enclose the parameter list within parentheses.

### 9.8.2.1  Standard Macro Parameter Expansion

As the previous section explains, HLA automatically associates the type text with macro parameters. This means that during a macro expansion, HLA substitutes the text you supply as the actual parameter everywhere the formal parameter name appears. The semantics of "pass by textual substitution" are a little different than "pass by value" or "pass by reference," so it is worthwhile exploring those differences here.

Consider the following macro invocations, using the neg64 macro from the previous section:

```
    neg64( edx, eax );
    neg64( ebx, ecx );
```

These two invocations expand into the following code:

```
// neg64(edx, eax );

    neg( edx );
    neg( eax );
    sbb( 0, edx );

// neg64( ebx, ecx );

    neg( ebx );
    neg( ecx );
    sbb( 0, ebx );
```

Note that macro invocations do not make a local copy of the parameters (as "pass by value" does), nor do they pass the address of the actual parameter to the macro. Instead, a macro invocation of the form neg64( edx, eax ); is equivalent to the following:

```
  ?reg32HO: text := "edx";
  ?reg32LO: text := "eax";

  neg( reg32HO );
  neg( reg32LO );
  sbb( 0, reg32HO );
```

Of course, the text objects immediately expand their string values inline, producing the former expansion for neg64( edx, eax );.

Note that macro parameters are not limited to memory, register, or constant operands as are instruction or procedure operands. Any text is fine as long as its expansion is legal wherever you use the formal parameter. Similarly, formal parameters may appear anywhere in the macro body, not just where memory, register, or constant operands are legal. Consider the following macro declaration and sample invocations:

```
#macro chkError( instr, jump, target );

    instr;
    jump target;

#endmacro;

    chkError( cmp( eax, 0 ), jnl, RangeError );      // Example 1
        ...
    chkError( test( 1, bl ), jnz, ParityError );     // Example 2

// Example 1 expands to

    cmp( eax, 0 );
    jnl RangeError;
```

```
// Example 2 expands to

    test( 1, bl );
    jnz ParityError;
```

In general, HLA assumes that all text between commas constitutes a single macro parameter. If HLA encounters any opening bracketing symbols (left parentheses, left braces, or left brackets), then it will include all text up to the appropriate closing symbol, ignoring any commas that may appear within the bracketing symbols. This is why the chkError invocations above treat cmp( eax, 0 and test( 1, bl ) as single parameters rather than as a pair of parameters. Of course, HLA does not consider commas (and bracketing symbols) within a string constant as the end of an actual parameter. So the following macro and invocation are perfectly legal:

```
#macro print( strToPrint );

    stdout.out( strToPrint );

#endmacro;
      .
      .
      .
    print( "Hello, world!" );
```

HLA treats the string Hello, world! as a single parameter because the comma appears inside a literal string constant, just as your intuition suggests.

If you are unfamiliar with textual macro parameter expansion in other languages, you should be aware that there are some problems you can run into when HLA expands your actual macro parameters. Consider the following macro declaration and invocation:

```
#macro Echo2nTimes( n, theStr );
    #for( echoCnt := 1 to n*2 )
        #print( theStr )
    #endfor
#endmacro;
      .
      .
      .
Echo2nTimes( 3+1, "Hello" );
```

This example displays Hello five times during compilation rather than the eight times you might intuitively expect. This is because the #for statement above expands to

```
    #for( echoCnt := 1 to 3+1*2 )
```

The actual parameter for *n* is 3+1; because HLA expands this text directly in place of *n*, you get an erroneous text expansion. Of course, at compile time HLA computes 3+1*2 as the value 5 rather than as the value 8 (which you would get had HLA passed this parameter by value rather than by textual substitution).

The common solution to this problem when passing numeric parameters that may contain compile-time expressions is to surround the formal parameter in the macro with parentheses; for example, you would rewrite the macro above as follows:

```
#macro Echo2nTimes( n, theStr );

    #for( echoCnt := 1 to  (n)*2 )

        #print( theStr )

    #endfor

#endmacro;
```

The earlier invocation would expand to the following code:

```
#for( echoCnt := 1 to (3+1)*2 )
    #print( theStr )
#endfor
```

This version of the macro produces the intuitive result.

If the number of actual parameters does not match the number of formal parameters, HLA will generate a diagnostic message during compilation. As with procedures, the number of actual parameters must agree with the number of formal parameters. If you would like to have optional macro parameters, then keep reading.

### 9.8.2.2 Macros with a Variable Number of Parameters

You may have noticed by now that some HLA macros don't require a fixed number of parameters. For example, the stdout.put macro in the HLA Standard Library allows one or more actual parameters. HLA uses a special array syntax to tell the compiler that you wish to allow a variable number of parameters in a macro parameter list. If you follow the last macro parameter in the formal parameter list with [ ], then HLA will allow a variable number of actual parameters (zero or more) in place of that formal parameter. For example:

```
#macro varParms( varying[] );

    << Macro body >>
```

```
#endmacro;
        .
        .
        .
    varParms( 1 );
    varParms( 1, 2 );
    varParms( 1, 2, 3 );
    varParms();
```

Note the last invocation especially. If a macro has any formal parameter you must supply parentheses with the macro list after the macro invocation. This is true even if you supply zero actual parameters to a macro with a varying parameter list. Keep in mind this important difference between a macro with no parameters and a macro with a varying parameter list but no actual parameters.

When HLA encounters a formal macro parameter with the [ ] suffix (which must be the last parameter in the formal parameter list), HLA create a constant string array and initializes that array with the text associated with the remaining actual parameters in the macro invocation. You can determine the number of actual parameters assigned to this array using the @elements compile-time function. For example, @elements( varying ) will return some value, or greater, that specifies the total number of parameters associated with that parameter. The following declaration for varParms demonstrates how you might use this:

```
#macro varParms( varying[] );

    #for( vpCnt := 0 to @elements( varying ) - 1 )

        #print( varying[ vpCnt ] )

    #endfor

#endmacro;
        .
        .
        .
varParms( 1 );          // Prints "1" during compilation.
varParms( 1, 2 );       // Prints "1" and "2" on separate lines.
varParms( 1, 2, 3 );    // Prints "1", "2", and "3" on separate lines.
varParms();             // Doesn't print anything.
```

Because HLA doesn't allow arrays of text objects, the varying parameter must be an array of strings. This, unfortunately, means you must treat the varying parameters differently than you handle standard macro parameters. If you want some element of the varying string array to expand as text within the macro body, you can always use the @text function to achieve this. Conversely, if you want to use a nonvarying formal parameter as a string object, you can always use the @string( *name* ) function. The following example demonstrates this:

```
#macro ReqAndOpt( Required, optional[] );
    ?@text( optional[0] ) := @string( ReqAndOpt );
    #print( @text( optional[0] ))

    #endmacro;
    .
    .
    .
    ReqAndOpt( i, j );

// The macro invocation above expands to

    ?@text( "j" ) := @string( i );
    #print( "j" )

// The above further expands to

    j := "i";
    #print( j )

// The above simply prints "i" during compilation.
```

Of course, it would be a good idea, in a macro like the above, to verify that there are at least two parameters before attempting to reference element zero of the optional parameter. You can easily do this as follows:

```
#macro ReqAndOpt( Required, optional[] );

    #if( @elements( optional ) > 0 )

        ?@text( optional[0] ) := @string( ReqAndOpt );
        #print( @text( optional[0] ))

    #else

        #error( "ReqAndOpt must have at least two parameters" )

    #endif

#endmacro;
```

### 9.8.2.3   Required vs. Optional Macro Parameters

As the previous section notes, HLA requires exactly one actual parameter for each nonvarying formal macro parameter. If there is no varying macro parameter (and there can be at most one), then the number of actual parameters must exactly match the number of formal parameters. If a varying formal parameter is present, then there must be at least as many actual macro parameters as there are nonvarying (or required) formal macro parameters. If there is a single, varying actual parameter, then a macro invocation may have zero or more actual parameters.

There is one big difference between a macro invocation of a macro with no parameters and a macro invocation of a macro with a single, varying parameter that has no actual parameters: The macro with the varying parameter list must have an empty set of parentheses after it, while the macro invocation of the macro without any parameters does not allow this. You can use this fact to your advantage if you wish to write a macro that doesn't have any parameters but you want to follow the macro invocation with ( ) so that it matches the syntax of a procedure call with no parameters. Consider the following macro:

```
#macro neg64( JustForTheParens[] );

    #if( @elements( JustForTheParens ) = 0 )

        neg( edx );
        neg( eax );
        sbb( 0, edx );

    #else

        #error( "Unexpected operand(s)" )

    #endif

#endmacro;
```

The preceding macro requires invocations of the form neg64(); to use the same syntax you would use for a procedure call. This feature is useful if you want the syntax of your parameterless macro invocations to match the syntax of a parameterless procedure call. It's not a bad idea to do this, just in the off chance you need to convert the macro to a procedure at some point (or vice versa, for that matter).

### 9.8.3 Local Symbols in a Macro

Consider the following macro declaration:

```
macro JZC( target );

        jnz NotTarget;
        jc target;
```

```
    NotTarget:

endmacro;
```

The purpose of this macro is to simulate an instruction that jumps to the specified target location if the zero flag is set *and* the carry flag is set. Conversely, if either the zero flag is clear or the carry flag is clear, this macro transfers control to the instruction immediately following the macro invocation.

There is a serious problem with this macro. Consider what happens if you use this macro more than once in your program:

```
JZC( Dest1 );
   .
   .
   .
JZC( Dest2 );
   .
   .
   .
```

The preceding macro invocations expand to the following code:

```
   jnz NotTarget;
   jc Dest1;
NotTarget:
      .
      .
      .
   jnz NotTarget;
   jc Dest2;
NotTarget:
      .
      .
      .
```

The problem with the expansion of these two macro invocations is that they both emit the same label, NotTarget, during macro expansion. When HLA processes this code it will complain about a duplicate symbol definition. Therefore, you must take care when defining symbols inside a macro because multiple invocations of that macro may lead to multiple definitions of that symbol.

HLA's solution to this problem is to allow the use of *local symbols* within a macro. Local macro symbols are unique to a specific invocation of a macro. For example, had NotTarget been a local symbol in the preceding JZC macro invocations, the program would have compiled properly because HLA treats each occurrence of NotTarget as a unique symbol.

HLA does not automatically make internal macro symbol definitions local to that macro.[6] Instead, you must explicitly tell HLA which symbols must be local. You do this in a macro declaration using the following generic syntax:

```
#macro macroname( optional_parameters ):optional_list_of_local_names ;
    << Macro body >>
#endmacro;
```

The list of local names is a sequence of one or more HLA identifiers separated by commas. Whenever HLA encounters this name in a particular macro invocation, it automatically substitutes some unique name for that identifier. For each macro invocation, HLA substitutes a different name for the local symbol.

You can correct the problem with the JZC macro by using the following macro code:

```
#macro JZC( target ):NotTarget;

        jnz NotTarget;
        jc target;
    NotTarget:

#endmacro;
```

Now whenever HLA processes this macro it will automatically associate a unique symbol with each occurrence of NotTarget. This will prevent the duplicate-symbol error that occurs if you do not declare NotTarget as a local symbol.

HLA implements local symbols by substituting a symbol like _nnnn_ (where nnnn is a four-digit hexadecimal number) wherever the local symbol appears in a macro invocation. For example, a macro invocation of the form JZC( SomeLabel ); might expand to

```
        jnz _010A_;
        jc SomeLabel;
    _010A_:
```

For each local symbol appearing within a macro expansion, HLA will generate a unique temporary identifier by simply incrementing this numeric value for each new local symbol it needs. As long as you do not explicitly create labels of the form _nnnn_Text_ (where nnnn is a hexadecimal value), there will never be a conflict in your program. HLA explicitly reserves all symbols that begin and end with a single underscore for its own private use (and for use by the HLA Standard Library). As long as you honor this restriction, there should be no conflicts between HLA local symbol generation and labels in your own programs because all HLA-generated symbols begin and end with single underscore.

---

[6] Sometimes you actually want the symbols to be global.

HLA implements local symbols by effectively converting that local symbol to a text constant that expands to the unique symbol HLA generates for the local label. That is, HLA effectively treats local symbol declarations as indicated by the following example:

```
#macro JZC( target );
    ?NotTarget:text := "_010A_Text_";

        jnz NotTarget;
        jc target;

    NotTarget:

#endmacro;
```

Whenever HLA expands this macro it will substitute _010A_Text_ for each occurrence of NotTarget it encounters in the expansion. This analogy isn't perfect because the text symbol NotTarget in this example is still accessible after the macro expansion, whereas this is not the case when defining local symbols within a macro. But this does give you an idea of how HLA implements local symbols.

## 9.8.4 Macros as Compile-Time Procedures

Although programmers typically use macros to expand to some sequence of machine instructions, there is absolutely no requirement that a macro body contain any executable instructions. Indeed, many macros contain only compile-time language statements (for example, #if, #while, #for, ? assignments, and the like). By placing only compile-time language statements in the body of a macro, you can effectively write compile-time procedures and functions using macros.

The following unique macro is a good example of a compile-time function that returns a string result. Consider the definition of this macro:

```
#macro unique:theSym;
    @string(theSym)
#endmacro;
```

Whenever your code references this macro, HLA replaces the macro invocation with the text @string(theSym), which, of course, expands to some string like _021F_Text_. Therefore, you can think of this macro as a compile-time function that returns a string result.

Be careful that you don't take the function analogy too far. Remember, macros always expand to their body text at the point of invocation. Some expansions may not be legal at any arbitrary point in your programs. Fortunately, most compile-time statements are legal anywhere whitespace is legal in your programs. Therefore, macros behave as you would expect functions or procedures to behave during the execution of your compile-time programs.

Of course, the only difference between a procedure and a function is th
a function returns some explicit value, while procedures simply do some act
ity. There is no special syntax for specifying a compile-time function return
value. As the example above indicates, simply specifying the value you wish
return as a statement in the macro body suffices. A compile-time procedur
on the other hand, would not contain any non-compile-time language state
ments that expand into some sort of data during macro invocation.

## 9.8.5   Simulating Function Overloading with Macros

The C++ language supports a nifty feature known as *function overloading*. Fur
tion overloading lets you write several different functions or procedures th
all have the same name. The difference between these functions is the type
of their parameters or the number of parameters. A procedure declaration
is unique in C++ if it has a different number of parameters than other
functions with the same name or if the types of its parameters differ from
other functions with the same name. HLA does not directly support procedure overloading, but you can use macros to achieve the same result. This
section explains how to use HLA's macros and the compile-time language
to achieve function/procedure overloading.

One good use for procedure overloading is to reduce the number of
Standard Library routines you must remember how to use. For example, th
HLA Standard Library provides five different "puti" routines that output a
integer value: stdout.puti128, stdout.puti64, stdout.puti32, stdout.puti16, and
stdout.puti8. The different routines, as their names suggest, output integer
values according to the size of their integer parameter. In the C++ languag
(or another other language supporting procedure/function overloading)
the engineer designing the input routines would probably have chosen to
name them all stdout.puti and leave it up to the compiler to select the appr
priate one based on the operand size.[7] The macro in Listing 9-5 demonstrate
how to do this in HLA using the compile-time language to figure out the siz
of the parameter operand.

```
// Puti.hla
//
// This program demonstrates procedure overloading via macros.
//
// It defines a "puti" macro that calls stdout.puti8, stdout.puti16,
// stdout.puti32, or stdout.puti64, depending on the size of
// the operand.

program putiDemo;
#include( "stdlib.hhf" )
```

---

[7] By the way, the HLA Standard Library does this as well. Although it doesn't provide stdout.puti,
it does provide stdout.put, which will choose an appropriate output routine based upon the
parameter's type. This is a bit more flexible than a puti routine.

```
// puti-
//
// Automatically decides whether we have a 64-, 32-, 16-, or 8-bit
// operand and calls the appropriate stdout.putiX routine to
// output this value.

#macro puti( operand );

    // If we have an 8-byte operand, call puti64:

    #if( @size( operand ) = 8 )

        stdout.puti64( operand );


    // If we have a 5-byte operand, call puti32:

    #elseif( @size( operand ) = 4 )

        stdout.puti32( operand );


    // If we have a 2-byte operand, call puti16:

    #elseif( @size( operand ) = 2 )

        stdout.puti16( operand );


    // If we have a 1-byte operand, call puti8:

    #elseif( @size( operand ) = 1 )

        stdout.puti8( operand );


    // If it's not an 8-, 4-, 2-, or 1-byte operand,
    // then print an error message:

    #else

        #error( "Expected a 64-, 32-, 16-, or 8-bit operand" )

    #endif

#endmacro;


// Some sample variable declarations so we can test the macro above:
```

```
static
    i8:   int8    := -8;
    i16:  int16   := -16;
    i32:  int32   := -32;
    i64:  qword;


begin putiDemo;

    // Initialize i64 because we can't do this in the static section.

    mov( -64, (type dword i64 ));
    mov( $FFFF_FFFF, (type dword i64[4]));

    // Demo the puti macro:

    puti( i8  ); stdout.newln();
    puti( i16 ); stdout.newln();
    puti( i32 ); stdout.newln();
    puti( i64 ); stdout.newln();

end putiDemo;
```

*Listing 9-5: Simple procedure overloading based on operand size*

The example above simply tests the size of the operand to determine which output routine to use. You can use other HLA compile-time functions such as @typename, to do more sophisticated processing. Consider the program in Listing 9-6, which demonstrates a macro that overloads stdout.puti32, stdout.putu32, and stdout.putd depending on the type of the operand.

```
// put32.hla
//
// This program demonstrates procedure overloading via macros.
//
// It defines a put32 macro that calls stdout.puti32, stdout.putu32,
// or stdout.putdw depending on the type of the operand.


program put32Demo;
#include( "stdlib.hhf" )


// put32-
//
// Automatically decides whether we have an int32, uns32, or dword
// operand and calls the appropriate stdout.putX routine to
// output this value.

#macro put32( operand );
```

```
// If we have an int32 operand, call puti32:

    #if( @typename( operand ) = "int32" )

        stdout.puti32( operand );


    // If we have an uns32 operand, call putu32:

    #elseif( @typename( operand ) = "uns32" )

        stdout.putu32( operand );


    // If we have a dword operand, call puth32:

    #elseif( @typename( operand ) = "dword" )

        stdout.puth32( operand );

    // If it's not a 32-bit integer value, report an error:

    #else

        #error( "Expected an int32, uns32, or dword operand" )

    #endif

#endmacro;


// Some sample variable declarations so we can test the macro above:

static
    i32: int32    := -32;
    u32: uns32    := 32;
    d32: dword    := $32;

begin put32Demo;


    // Demo the put32 macro:

    put32( d32 );   stdout.newln();
    put32( u32 );   stdout.newln();
    put32( i32 );   stdout.newln();

end put32Demo;
```

*Listing 9-6: Procedure overloading based on operand type*

You can easily extend this macro to output 8- and 16-bit operands as well as 32-bit operands. That is left as an exercise for the reader.

The number of actual parameters is another way to resolve which overloaded procedure to call. If you specify a variable number of macro parameters (using the [ ] syntax; see the discussion in Section 9.8.2.2), you can use the @elements compile-time function to determine exactly how many parameters are present and call the appropriate routine. The sample in Listing 9-7 uses this trick to determine whether it should call stdout.puti32 or stdout.puti32Size.

```
// puti32.hla
//
// This program demonstrates procedure overloading via macros.
//
// It defines a puti32 macro that calls
// stdout.puti32 or stdout.puti32size
// depending on the number of parameters present.


program puti32Demo;
#include( "stdlib.hhf" )


// puti32-
//
// Automatically decides whether we have an int32, uns32, or dword
// operand and calls the appropriate stdout.putX routine to
// output this value.

#macro puti32( operand[] );

    // If we have a single operand, call stdout.puti32:

    #if( @elements( operand ) = 1 )

        stdout.puti32( @text(operand[0]) );


    // If we have two operands, call stdout.puti32size and
    // supply a default value of ' ' for the padding character:

    #elseif( @elements( operand ) = 2 )

        stdout.puti32Size
        (
            @text(operand[0]),
            @text(operand[1]),
            ' '
        );
```

```
    // If we have three parameters, then pass all three of them
    // along to puti32size:

#elseif( @elements( operand ) = 3 )

    stdout.puti32Size
    (
        @text(operand[0]),
        @text(operand[1]),
        @text(operand[2])
    );


    // If we don't have one, two, or three operands, report an error:

#else

    #error( "Expected one, two, or three operands" )

#endif

#endmacro;


// A sample variable declaration so we can test the macro above:

Static
    i32: int32 := -32;

begin puti32Demo;


        // Demo the put32 macro:

    puti32( i32 );   stdout.newln();
    puti32( i32, 5 );   stdout.newln();
    puti32( i32, 5, '*' );   stdout.newln();

end puti32Demo;
```

*Listing 9-7: Using the number of parameters to resolve overloaded procedures*

All the examples up to this point provide procedure overloading for Standard Library routines (specifically, the integer output routines). Of course, you are not limited to overloading procedures in the HLA Standard Library. You can create your own overloaded procedures as well. All you have to do is write a set of procedures, all with unique names, and then use a single macro to decide which routine to actually call based on the macro's parameters. Rather than call the individual routines, invoke the common macro and let it decide which procedure to actually call.

## 9.9 Writing Compile-Time "Programs"

The HLA compile-time language provides a powerful facility with which to write "programs" that execute while HLA is compiling your assembly language programs. Although it is possible to write some general-purpose programs using the HLA compile-time language, the real purpose of the HLA compile-time language is to allow you to write short programs *that write other programs*. In particular, the primary purpose of the HLA compile-time language is to automate the creation of large or complex assembly language sequences. The following subsections provide some simple examples of such compile-time programs.

### 9.9.1 Constructing Data Tables at Compile Time

Earlier, this book suggested that you could write programs to generate large complex lookup tables for your assembly language programs (see the discussion of tables in Section 8.4.3). Chapter 8 provides examples in HLA but suggests that writing a separate program is unnecessary. This is true; you can generate most lookup tables you'll need using nothing more than the HLA compile-time language facilities. Indeed, filling in table entries is one of the principle uses of the HLA compile-time language. In this section we will take a look at using the HLA compile-time language to construct data tables during compilation.

In Section 8.4.3, you saw an example of an HLA program that writes a text file containing a lookup table for the trigonometric sine function. The table contains 360 entries with the index into the table specifying an angle in degrees. Each int32 entry in the table contains the value $\sin(angle)*1{,}000$ where *angle* is equal to the index into the table. Section 8.4.3 suggests running this program and then including the text output from that program into the actual program that used the resulting table. You can avoid much of this work by using the compile-time language. The HLA program in Listing 9-8 includes a short compile-time code fragment that constructs this table of sines directly.

```
// demoSines.hla
//
// This program demonstrates how to create a lookup table
// of sine values using the HLA compile-time language.

program demoSines;
#include( "stdlib.hhf" )

const
    pi :real80 := 3.1415926535897;
```

```
readonly
    sines:  int32[ 360 ] :=
            [
                // The following compile-time program generates
                // 359 entries (out of 360). For each entry
                // it computes the sine of the index into the
                // table and multiplies this result by 1000
                // in order to get a reasonable integer value.

                ?angle := 0;
                #while( angle < 359 )

                    // Note: HLA's @sin function expects angles
                    // in radians. radians = degrees*pi/180.
                    // The int32 function truncates its result,
                    // so this function adds 1/2 as a weak attempt
                    // to round the value up.

                    int32( @sin( angle * pi / 180.0 ) * 1000 + 0.5 ),
                    ?angle := angle + 1;

                #endwhile

                // Here's the 360th entry in the table. This code
                // handles the last entry specially because a comma
                // does not follow this entry in the table.

                int32( @sin( 359 * pi / 180.0 ) * 1000 + 0.5 )
            ];
begin demoSines;

    // Simple demo program that displays all the values in the table:

    for( mov( 0, ebx); ebx<360; inc( ebx )) do

        mov( sines[ ebx*4 ], eax );
        stdout.put
        (
            "sin( ",
            (type uns32 ebx ),
            " )*1000 = ",
            (type int32 eax ),
            nl
        );

    endfor;


end demoSines;
```

Listing 9-8: Generating a sine lookup table with the compile-time language

Another common use for the compile-time language is to build ASCII character lookup tables for use by the xlat instruction at runtime. Common examples include lookup tables for alphabetic case manipulation. The program in Listing 9-9 demonstrates how to construct an uppercase conversion table and a lowercase conversion table.[8] Note the use of a macro as a compile-time procedure to reduce the complexity of the table-generating code:

```
// demoCase.hla
//
// This program demonstrates how to create a lookup table
// of alphabetic case conversion values using the HLA
// compile-time language.

program demoCase;
#include( "stdlib.hhf" )

const

        // emitCharRange
        //
        // This macro emits a set of character entries
        // for an array of characters. It emits a list
        // of values (with a comma suffix on each value)
        // from the starting value up to, but not including,
        // the ending value.

        #macro emitCharRange( start, last ): index;

            ?index:uns8 := start;
            #while( index < last )

                char( index ),
                ?index := index + 1;

            #endwhile

        #endmacro;

    readonly

    // toUC:
    // The entries in this table contain the value of the index
    // into the table except for indices #$61..#$7A (those entries
    // whose indices are the ASCII codes for the lowercase
    // characters). Those particular table entries contain the
    // codes for the corresponding uppercase alphabetic characters.
```

---

[8] Note that on modern processors, using a lookup table is probably not the most efficient way convert between alphabetic cases. However, this is just an example of filling in the table using the compile-time language. The principles are correct, even if the code is not exactly the best could be.

```
// If you use an ASCII character as an index into this table and
// fetch the specified byte at that location, you will effectively
// translate lowercase characters to uppercase characters and
// leave all other characters unaffected.

toUC: char[ 256 ] :=
        [
                // The following compile-time program generates
                // 255 entries (out of 256). For each entry
                // it computes toupper( index ) where index is
                // the character whose ASCII code is an index
                // into the table.

                emitCharRange( 0, uns8('a') )

                // Okay, we've generated all the entries up to
                // the start of the lowercase characters. Output
                // uppercase characters in place of the lowercase
                // characters here.

                emitCharRange( uns8('A'), uns8('Z') + 1 )

                // Okay, emit the nonalphabetic characters
                // through to byte code #$FE:

                emitCharRange( uns8('z') + 1, $FF )

                // Here's the last entry in the table. This code
                // handles the last entry specially because a comma
                // does not follow this entry in the table.

                #$FF

        ];


// The following table is very similar to the one above.
// You would use this one, however, to translate uppercase
// characters to lowercase while leaving everything else alone.
// See the comments in the previous table for more details.

TOlc: char[ 256 ] :=
        [
                emitCharRange( 0, uns8('A') )
                emitCharRange( uns8('a'), uns8('z') + 1 )
                emitCharRange( uns8('Z') + 1, $FF )

                #$FF
        ];
```

```
begin demoCase;
    for( mov( uns32( ' ' ), eax ); eax <= $FF; inc( eax )) do

        mov( toUC[ eax ], bl );
        mov( TOlc[ eax ], bh );
        stdout.put
        (
            "toupper( '",
            (type char al),
            "' ) = '",
            (type char bl),
            "'    tolower( '",
            (type char al),
            "' ) = '",
            (type char bh),
            "'",
            nl
        );

    endfor;

end demoCase;
```

*Listing 9-9: Generating case-conversion tables with the compile-time language*

One important thing to note about this example is the fact that a semicolon does not follow the emitCharRange macro invocations. Macro invocations do not require a closing semicolon. Often, it is legal to go ahead and add one to the end of the macro invocation because HLA is normally very forgiving about having extra semicolons inserted into the code. In this case, however, the extra semicolons are illegal because they would appear between adjacent entries in the TOlc and toUC tables. Keep in mind that macro invocations don't require a semicolon, especially when using macro invocations as compile-time procedures.

### 9.9.2  Unrolling Loops

In the chapter on low-level control structures, this text points out that you can unravel loops to improve the performance of certain assembly language programs. One problem with unraveling, or unrolling, loops is that you may need to do a lot of extra typing, especially if there are many loop iterations. Fortunately, HLA's compile-time language facilities, especially the #while and #for loops, come to the rescue. With a small amount of extra typing plus one copy of the loop body, you can unroll a loop as many times as you please.

If you simply want to repeat the same exact code sequence some number of times, unrolling the code is especially trivial. All you have to do is wrap an HLA #for..#endfor loop around the sequence and count off a val object the specified number of times. For example, if you wanted to print Hello World 10 times, you could encode this as follows.

```
#for( count := 1 to 10 )
    stdout.put( "Hello World", nl );
#endfor
```

Although the code above looks very similar to an HLA for loop you could write in your program, remember the fundamental difference: The preceding code simply consists of 10 straight stdout.put calls in the program. Were you to encode this using an HLA for loop, there would be only one call to stdout.put and lots of additional logic to loop back and execute that single call 10 times.

Unrolling loops becomes slightly more complicated if any instructions in that loop refer to the value of a loop control variable or another value, which changes with each iteration of the loop. A typical example is a loop that zeros the elements of an integer array:

```
mov( 0, eax );
for( mov( 0, ebx ); ebx < 20; inc( ebx )) do

    mov( eax, array[ ebx*4 ] );

endfor;
```

In this code fragment the loop uses the value of the loop control variable (in EBX) to index into *array*. Simply copying mov( eax, array[ ebx*4 ]); 20 times is not the proper way to unroll this loop. You must substitute an appropriate constant index in the range 0..76 (the corresponding loop indices, times 4) in place of ebx*4 in this example. Correctly unrolling this loop should produce the following code sequence:

```
            mov( eax, array[ 0*4 ] );
            mov( eax, array[ 1*4 ] );
            mov( eax, array[ 2*4 ] );
            mov( eax, array[ 3*4 ] );
            mov( eax, array[ 4*4 ] );
            mov( eax, array[ 5*4 ] );
            mov( eax, array[ 6*4 ] );
            mov( eax, array[ 7*4 ] );
            mov( eax, array[ 8*4 ] );
            mov( eax, array[ 9*4 ] );
            mov( eax, array[ 10*4 ] );
            mov( eax, array[ 11*4 ] );
            mov( eax, array[ 12*4 ] );
            mov( eax, array[ 13*4 ] );
            mov( eax, array[ 14*4 ] );
            mov( eax, array[ 15*4 ] );
            mov( eax, array[ 16*4 ] );
            mov( eax, array[ 17*4 ] );
            mov( eax, array[ 18*4 ] );
            mov( eax, array[ 19*4 ] );
```

You can easily do this using the following compile-time code sequence:

```
#for( iteration := 0 to 19 )
    mov( eax, array[ iteration*4 ] );
#endfor
```

If the statements in a loop make use of the loop control variable's value, it is only possible to unroll such loops if those values are known at compile time. You cannot unroll loops when user input (or other runtime information) controls the number of iterations.

## 9.10  Using Macros in Different Source Files

Unlike procedures, macros do not have a fixed piece of code at some address in memory. Therefore, you cannot create external macros and link them with other modules in your program. However, it is very easy to share macros with different source files: Just put the macros you wish to reuse in a header file and include that file using the #include directive. You can make the macro available to any source file you choose using this simple trick.

## 9.11  For More Information

Although this chapter has spent a considerable amount of time describing various features of HLA's macro support and compile-time language features, the truth is this chapter has barely described what's possible with HLA. Indeed, this chapter made the claim that HLA's macro facilities are far more powerful than those provided by other assemblers; however, this chapter doesn't do HLA's macros justice. If you've ever used a language with decent macro facilities, you're probably wondering, "What's the big deal?" Well, the really sophisticated stuff is beyond the scope of this chapter. If you're interested in learning more about HLA's powerful macro facilities, please consult the HLA reference manual and the electronic editions of *The Art of Assembly Language* at *http://webster.cs.ucr.edu/* or *http://www.artofasm.com/*. You'll discover that it's actually possible to create your own high-level languages using HLA's macro facilities. However, this chapter does not assume the reader has the prerequisite knowledge to do that type of programming (yet!), so this chapter defers that discussion to the material that you'll also find on the websites.

# 10

## BIT MANIPULATION

 Manipulating bits in memory is, perhaps, the feature for which assembly language is most famous. Indeed, one of the reasons peopleclaimthattheCprogramminglanguage is a medium-level language rather than a high-level language is because of the vast array of bit-manipulation operators that C provides. Even with this wide array of bit-manipulation operations, the C programming language doesn't provide as complete a set of bit-manipulation operations as assembly language.

This chapter discusses how to manipulate strings of bits in memory and registers using 80x86 assembly language. It begins with a review of the bit-manipulation instructions covered thus far, and it also introduces a few new instructions. This chapter reviews information on packing and unpacking bit strings in memory because this is the basis for many bit-manipulation operations. Finally, this chapter discusses several bit-centric algorithms and their implementation in assembly language.

## 10.1 What Is Bit Data, Anyway?

Before describing how to manipulate bits, it might not be a bad idea to defin exactly what this text means by *bit data*. Most readers probably assume that b manipulation programs twiddle individual bits in memory. While programs that do this are definitely bit-manipulation programs, we're not going to lim our definition to just those programs. For our purposes, *bit manipulation* refers to working with data types that consist of strings of bits that are nonco tiguous or are not a multiple of 8 bits long. Generally, such bit objects will no represent numeric integers, although we will not place this restriction on ou bit strings.

A *bit string* is some contiguous sequence of one or more bits. Note that bit string does not have to start or end at any special point. For example, a b string could start in bit 7 of one byte in memory and continue through to bit of the next byte in memory. Likewise, a bit string could begin in bit 30 of EAX, consume the upper 2 bits of EAX, and then continue from bit 0 through bit 1 of EBX. In memory, the bits must be physically contiguous (that is, the bit numbers are always increasing except when crossing a byte boundary, and a byte boundaries the memory address increases by 1 byte). In registers, if a b string crosses a register boundary, the application defines the continuation register, but the bit string always continues in bit 0 of that second register.

A *bit set* is a collection of bits, not necessarily contiguous, within some larger data structure. For example, bits 0..3, 7, 12, 24, and 31 from some doub word form a set of bits. Usually, we will limit bit sets to some reasonably size *container object* (the data structure that encapsulates the bit set), but the def nition doesn't specifically limit the size. Normally, we will deal with bit sets that are part of an object no more than about 32 or 64 bits in size, though th limit is completely artificial. Note that bit strings are special cases of bit sets

A *bit run* is a sequence of bits with all the same value. A *run of zeros* is a b string that contains all zeros, and a *run of ones* is a bit string containing all one The *first set bit* in a bit string is the bit position of the first bit containing a 1 i a bit string, that is, the first 1 bit following a possible run of zeros. A similar definition exists for the *first clear bit*. The *last set bit* is the last bit position in bit string that contains 1; the remainder of the string forms an uninterrupte run of zeros. A similar definition exists for the *last clear bit*.

A *bit offset* is the number of bits from some boundary position (usually a byte boundary) to the specified bit. As noted in Chapter 2, we number the bi starting from 0 at the boundary location.

A *mask* is a sequence of bits that we'll use to manipulate certain bits in another value. For example, the bit string %0000_1111_0000, when it's use with the and instruction, can mask away (clear) all the bits except bits 4 throug 7. Likewise, if you use the same value with the or instruction, it can force bits through 7 to ones in the destination operand. The term *mask* comes from th use of these bit strings with the and instruction; in those situations the 1 an 0 bits behave like masking tape when you're painting something; they pass through certain bits unchanged while masking out (clearing) the other bits

Armed with these definitions, we're ready to start manipulating some bit

## 10.2 Instructions That Manipulate Bits

Bit manipulation generally consists of six activities: setting bits, clearing bits, inverting bits, testing and comparing bits, extracting bits from a bit string, and inserting bits into a bit string. By now you should be familiar with most of the instructions we'll use to perform these operations; their introduction started way back in the earliest chapters of this text. Nevertheless, it's worthwhile to review the old instructions here as well as present the few bit-manipulation instructions we've yet to consider.

The most basic bit-manipulation instructions are the `and`, `or`, `xor`, `not`, `test`, and shift and rotate instructions. Indeed, on the earliest 80x86 processors, these were the only instructions available for bit manipulation. The following paragraphs review these instructions, concentrating on how you could use them to manipulate bits in memory or registers.

The `and` instruction provides the ability to strip away unwanted bits from some bit sequence, replacing the unwanted bits with zeros. This instruction is especially useful for isolating a bit string or a bit set that is merged with other, unrelated data (or, at least, data that is not part of the bit string or bit set). For example, suppose that a bit string consumes bit positions 12 through 24 of the EAX register; we can isolate this bit string by setting all other bits in EAX to 0 by using the following instruction:

```
and( %1_1111_1111_1111_0000_0000_0000, eax );
```

Most programs use the `and` instruction to clear bits that are not part of the desired bit string. In theory, you could use the `or` instruction to mask all unwanted bits to ones rather than zeros, but later comparisons and operations are often easier if the unneeded bit positions contain 0 (see Figure 10-1).

| | | | | | | | | | | | | | | | | | | | | | | | | | | | | | | | |
|---|---|---|---|---|---|---|---|---|---|---|---|---|---|---|---|---|---|---|---|---|---|---|---|---|---|---|---|---|---|---|---|
| X | X | X | X | X | X | X | S | S | S | S | S | S | S | S | S | S | S | S | S | X | X | X | X | X | X | X | X | X | X | X | X |
| 0 | 0 | 0 | 0 | 0 | 0 | 0 | 1 | 1 | 1 | 1 | 1 | 1 | 1 | 1 | 1 | 1 | 1 | 1 | 1 | 0 | 0 | 0 | 0 | 0 | 0 | 0 | 0 | 0 | 0 | 0 | 0 |
| 0 | 0 | 0 | 0 | 0 | 0 | 0 | S | S | S | S | S | S | S | S | S | S | S | S | S | 0 | 0 | 0 | 0 | 0 | 0 | 0 | 0 | 0 | 0 | 0 | 0 |

Using a bit mask to isolate bits 12..24 in EAX

Top: Original Value in EAX   Middle: Bit Mask   Bottom: Final Value in EAX

*Figure 10-1: Isolating a bit string using the and instruction*

Once you've cleared the unneeded bits in a set of bits, you can often operate on the bit set in place. For example, to see if the string of bits in positions 12 through 24 of EAX contains $12F3, you could use the following code:

```
and( %1_1111_1111_1111_0000_0000_0000, eax );
cmp( eax, %1_0010_1111_0011_0000_0000_0000 );
```

Here's another solution, using constant expressions, that's a little easier to digest:

```
and( %1_1111_1111_1111_0000_0000_0000, eax );
cmp( eax, $12F3 << 12 );  // "<<12" shifts $12F3 to the left 12 bits.
```

Most of the time, however, you'll want (or need) the bit string aligned with bit 0 in EAX prior to any operations you would want to perform. Of course, you can use the shr instruction to properly align the value after you've masked it, like this:

```
and( %1_1111_1111_1111_0000_0000_0000, eax );
shr( 12, eax );
cmp( eax, $12F3 );
<< Other operations that require the bit string at bit #0 >>
```

Now that the bit string is aligned to bit 0, the constants and other values you use in conjunction with this value are easier to deal with.

You can also use the or instruction to mask unwanted bits. However, the or instruction does not let you clear bits; it allows you to set bits to ones. In some instances setting all the bits around your bit set may be desirable; most software, however, is easier to write if you clear the surrounding bits rather than set them.

The or instruction is especially useful for inserting a bit set into some other bit string. To do this, there are several steps you must go through:

- Clear all the bits surrounding your bit set in the source operand.
- Clear all the bits in the destination operand where you wish to insert the bit set.
- or the bit set and destination operand together.

For example, suppose you have a value in bits 0..12 of EAX that you wish to insert into bits 12..24 of EBX without affecting any of the other bits in EBX. You would begin by stripping out bits 13 and above from EAX; then you would strip out bits 12..24 in EBX. Next, you would shift the bits in EAX so the bit string occupies bits 12..24 of EAX. Finally, you would or the value in EAX into EBX (see Figure 10-2), as shown here:

```
and( $1FFF, eax );       // Strip all but bits 0..12 from eax.
and( $FE00_0FFF, ebx );  // Clear bits 12..24 in ebx.
shl( 12, eax );          // Move bits 0..12 to 12..24 in eax.
or( eax, ebx );          // Merge the bits into ebx.
```

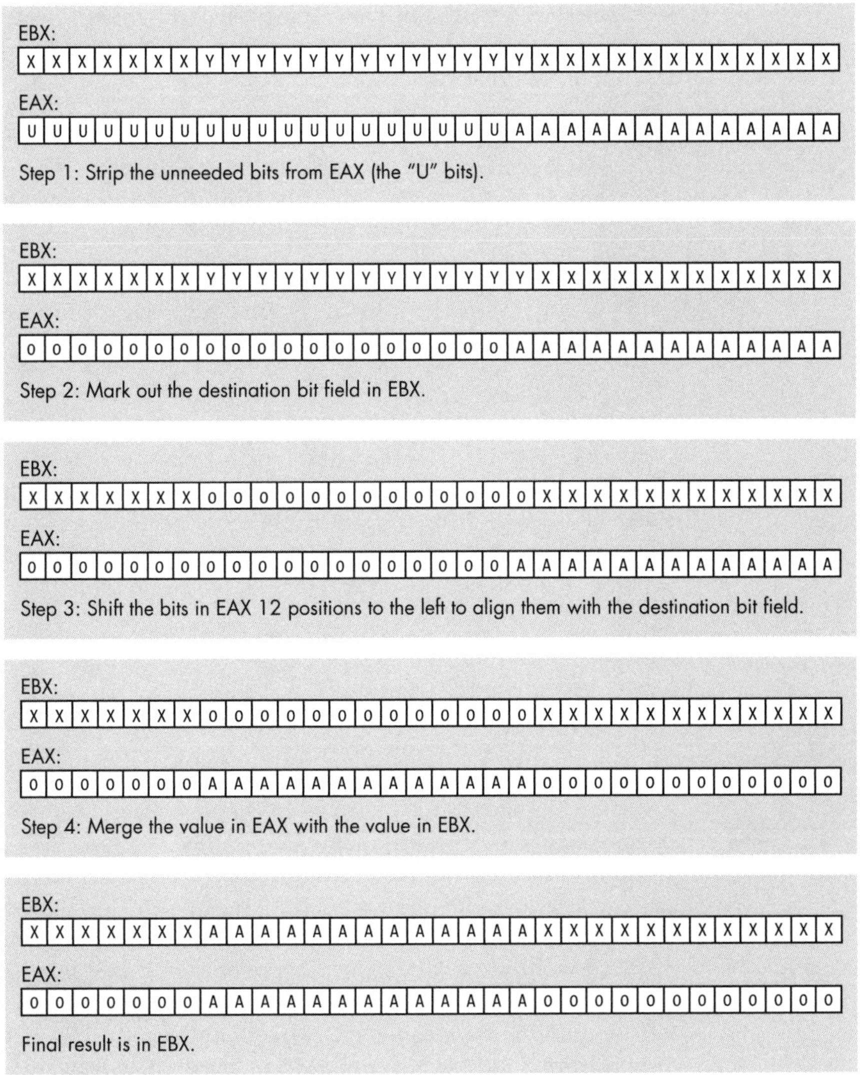

EBX:

| X | X | X | X | X | X | X | Y | Y | Y | Y | Y | Y | Y | Y | Y | Y | Y | Y | Y | X | X | X | X | X | X | X | X | X | X | X | X |

EAX:

| U | U | U | U | U | U | U | U | U | U | U | U | U | U | U | U | U | U | U | U | A | A | A | A | A | A | A | A | A | A | A | A |

Step 1: Strip the unneeded bits from EAX (the "U" bits).

EBX:

| X | X | X | X | X | X | X | Y | Y | Y | Y | Y | Y | Y | Y | Y | Y | Y | Y | Y | X | X | X | X | X | X | X | X | X | X | X | X |

EAX:

| 0 | 0 | 0 | 0 | 0 | 0 | 0 | 0 | 0 | 0 | 0 | 0 | 0 | 0 | 0 | 0 | 0 | 0 | 0 | 0 | A | A | A | A | A | A | A | A | A | A | A | A |

Step 2: Mark out the destination bit field in EBX.

EBX:

| X | X | X | X | X | X | X | X | 0 | 0 | 0 | 0 | 0 | 0 | 0 | 0 | 0 | 0 | 0 | 0 | 0 | X | X | X | X | X | X | X | X | X | X | X |

EAX:

| 0 | 0 | 0 | 0 | 0 | 0 | 0 | 0 | 0 | 0 | 0 | 0 | 0 | 0 | 0 | 0 | 0 | 0 | 0 | 0 | A | A | A | A | A | A | A | A | A | A | A | A |

Step 3: Shift the bits in EAX 12 positions to the left to align them with the destination bit field.

EBX:

| X | X | X | X | X | X | X | X | 0 | 0 | 0 | 0 | 0 | 0 | 0 | 0 | 0 | 0 | 0 | 0 | 0 | X | X | X | X | X | X | X | X | X | X | X |

EAX:

| 0 | 0 | 0 | 0 | 0 | 0 | 0 | A | A | A | A | A | A | A | A | A | A | A | A | A | 0 | 0 | 0 | 0 | 0 | 0 | 0 | 0 | 0 | 0 | 0 | 0 |

Step 4: Merge the value in EAX with the value in EBX.

EBX:

| X | X | X | X | X | X | X | X | A | A | A | A | A | A | A | A | A | A | A | A | A | X | X | X | X | X | X | X | X | X | X | X |

EAX:

| 0 | 0 | 0 | 0 | 0 | 0 | 0 | A | A | A | A | A | A | A | A | A | A | A | A | A | 0 | 0 | 0 | 0 | 0 | 0 | 0 | 0 | 0 | 0 | 0 | 0 |

Final result is in EBX.

*Figure 10-2: Inserting bits 0..12 of EAX into bits 12..24 of EBX*

In this figure the desired bits (AAAAAAAAAAAA) formed a bit string. However, this algorithm still works fine even if you're manipulating a noncontiguous set of bits. All you have to do is to create an appropriate bit mask you can use for anding that has ones in the appropriate places.

When working with bit masks, it is incredibly poor programming style to use literal numeric constants as in the past few examples. You should always create symbolic constants in the HLA const (or val) section for your bit masks.

Combined with some constant expressions, you can produce code that is muc
easier to read and maintain. The current example code is more properly
written as the following:

```
const
    StartPosn := 12;
    BitMask: dword := $1FFF << StartPosn; // Mask occupies bits 12..24.
        .
        .
        .
    shl( StartPosn, eax );   // Move into position.
    and( BitMask, eax );     // Strip all but bits 12..24 from eax.
    and( !BitMask, ebx );    // Clear bits 12..24 in ebx.
    or( eax, ebx );          // Merge the bits into ebx.
```

Notice the use of the compile time not operator (!) to invert the bit mas
in order to clear the bit positions in EBX where the code inserts the bits fro
EAX. This saves having to create another constant in the program that has t
be changed anytime you modify the BitMask constant. Having to maintain tw
separate symbols whose values are dependent on one another is not a good
thing in a program.

Of course, in addition to merging one bit set with another, the or instru
tion is also useful for forcing bits to 1 in a bit string. By setting various bits i
a source operand to 1, you can force the corresponding bits in the destinatio
operand to 1 by using the or instruction.

The xor instruction allows you to invert selected bits in a bit set. Althoug
inverting bits isn't as common as setting or clearing them, the xor instructio
often appears in bit-manipulation programs. Of course, if you want to inve
all the bits in some destination operand, the not instruction is probably mor
appropriate than the xor instruction; however, to invert selected bits while n
affecting others, the xor is the way to go.

One interesting fact about xor's operation is that it lets you manipulate
known data in just about any way imaginable. For example, if you know tha
a field contains %1010, you can force that field to 0 by xoring it with %101(
Similarly, you can force it to %1111 by xoring it with %0101. Although this
might seem like a waste, because you can easily force this 4-bit string to 0 or a
ones using and/or, the xor instruction has two advantages: (1) You are not lim
ited to forcing the field to all zeros or all ones; you can actually set these bi
to any of the 16 valid combinations via xor; and (2) if you need to manipulat
other bits in the destination operand at the same time, and/or may not be ab
to accommodate you. For example, suppose that you know that one field co
tains %1010 that you want to force to 0 and another field contains %1000 an
you wish to increment that field by 1 (i.e., set the field to %1001). You canno
accomplish both operations with a single and or or instruction, but you can d
this with a single xor instruction; just xor the first field with %1010 and th
second field with %0001. Remember, however, that this trick works only if yo
know the current value of a bit set within the destination operand. Of cours
while you're adjusting the values of bit fields containing known values, you
can invert bits in other fields simultaneously.

In addition to setting, clearing, and inverting bits in some destination operand, the and, or, and xor instructions also affect various condition codes in the flags register. These instructions affect the flags as follows:

- These instructions always clear the carry and overflow flags.
- These instructions set the sign flag if the result has a 1 in the H.O. bit; they clear it otherwise. That is, these instructions copy the H.O. bit of the result into the sign flag.
- These instructions set/clear the zero flag if the result is 0.
- These instructions set the parity flag if there is an even number of set bits in the L.O. byte of the destination operand; they clear the parity flag if there is an odd number of 1 bits in the L.O. byte of the destination operand.

The first thing to note is that these instructions always clear the carry and overflow flags. This means that you cannot expect the system to preserve the state of these two flags across the execution of these instructions. A very common mistake in many assembly language programs is the assumption that these instructions do not affect the carry flag. Many people will execute an instruction that sets/clears the carry flag, execute an and/or/xor instruction, and then attempt to test the state of the carry from the previous instruction. This simply will not work.

One of the more interesting aspects to these instructions is that they copy the H.O. bit of their result into the sign flag. This means that you can easily test the setting of the H.O. bit of the result by testing the sign flag (using sets/setns or js/jns instructions, or using the @s/@ns flags in a boolean expression). For this reason, many assembly language programmers will often place an important boolean variable in the H.O. bit of some operand so they can easily test the state of that bit using the sign flag after a logical operation.

We haven't talked much about the parity flag in this text. We're not going to get into a big discussion of this flag and what you use it for because the primary purpose for this flag has been taken over by hardware.[1] However, because this is a chapter on bit manipulation, and parity computation is a bit-manipulation operation, it seems only fitting to provide a brief discussion of the parity flag at this time.

Parity is a very simple error-detection scheme originally employed by telegraphs and other serial communication protocols. The idea was to count the number of set bits in a character and include an extra bit in the transmission to indicate whether that character contained an even or odd number of set bits. The receiving end of the transmission would also count the bits and verify that the extra "parity" bit indicated a successful transmission. We're not going to explore the information-theory aspects of this error-checking scheme at this point other than to point out that the purpose of the parity flag is to help compute the value of this extra bit.

---

[1] Serial communications chips and other communications hardware that use parity for error checking normally compute the parity in hardware; you don't have to use software for this purpose.

The 80x86 and, or, and xor instructions set the parity bit if the L.O. byte their operand contains an even number of set bits. An important fact bear repeating here: The parity flag reflects only the number of set bits in the L.( byte of the destination operand; it does not include the H.O. bytes in a wor double-word, or other-sized operand. The instruction set uses the L.O. byt only to compute the parity because communication programs that use pari are typically character-oriented transmission systems (there are better erro checking schemes if you transmit more than 8 bits at a time).

The zero flag setting is one of the more important results the and/or/x instructions produce. Indeed, programs reference this flag so often after th and instruction that Intel added a separate instruction, test, whose main pu pose is to logically and two results and set the flags without otherwise affectin either instruction operand.

There are three main uses of the zero flag after the execution of an and test instruction: (1) checking to see if a particular bit in an operand is set, (' checking to see if at least one of several bits in a bit set is 1, and (3) checkin to see if an operand is 0. Using (1) is actually a special case of (2) in which th bit set contains only a single bit. We'll explore each of these uses in the follc ing paragraphs.

A common use for the and instruction, and also the original reason for th inclusion of the test instruction in the 80x86 instruction set, is to test to see a particular bit is set in a given operand. To perform this type of test, you would normally and/test a constant value containing a single set bit with th operand you wish to test. This clears all the other bits in the second operan leaving a 0 in the bit position under test if the operand contains a 0 in that k position. anding with a 1 leaves a 1 in that position if it originally contained 1. Because all of the other bits in the result are 0, the entire result will be 0 that particular bit is 0; the entire result will be nonzero if that bit position cc tains a 1. The 80x86 reflects this status in the zero flag (Z = 1 indicates a 0 b Z = 0 indicates a 1 bit). The following instruction sequence demonstrates hc to test to see if bit 4 is set in EAX:

```
test( %1_0000, eax ); // Check bit #4 to see if it is 0/1.
if( @nz ) then

    << Do this if the bit is set. >>

else

    << Do this if the bit is clear. >>

endif;
```

You can also use the and/test instructions to see if any one of several bi is set. Simply supply a constant that has a 1 in all the positions you want to te (and zeros everywhere else). anding such a value with an unknown quantity will produce a nonzero value if one or more of the bits in the operand und test contain a 1. The following example tests to see if the value in EAX contains a 1 in bit positions 1, 2, 4, and 7:

```
test( %1001_0110, eax );
if( @nz ) then // At least one of the bits is set.

    << Do whatever needs to be done if one of the bits is set. >>

endif;
```

Note that you cannot use a single and or test instruction to see if all the corresponding bits in the bit set are equal to 1. To accomplish this, you must first mask out the bits that are not in the set and then compare the result against the mask itself. If the result is equal to the mask, then all the bits in the bit set contain ones. You must use the and instruction for this operation because the test instruction does not mask out any bits. The following example checks to see if all the bits in a bit set (bitMask) are equal to 1:

```
and( bitMask, eax );
cmp( eax, bitMask );
if( @e ) then

    // All the bit positions in eax corresponding to the set
    // bits in bitMask are equal to 1 if we get here.

    << Do whatever needs to be done if the bits match. >>

endif;
```

Of course, once we stick the cmp instruction in there, we don't really have to check to see if all the bits in the bit set contain ones. We can check for any combination of values by specifying the appropriate value as the operand to the cmp instruction.

Note that the test/and instructions will set the zero flag in the above code sequences only if all the bits in EAX (or other destination operand) have zeros in the positions where ones appear in the constant operand. This suggests another way to check for all ones in the bit set: Invert the value in EAX prior to using the and or test instruction. Then if the zero flag is set, you know that there were all ones in the (original) bit set. For example:

```
not( eax );
test( bitMask, eax );
if( @z ) then
    // At this point, eax contained all ones in the bit positions
    // occupied by ones in the bitMask constant.

    << Do whatever needs to be done at this point. >>

endif;
```

The previous paragraphs all suggest that the bitMask (the source operand) is a constant. This was for purposes of example only. In fact, you can use a variable or other register here, if you prefer. Simply load that variable or register with the appropriate bit mask before you execute the test, and, or or instructions in the examples above.

Another set of instructions we've already seen that we can use to manipulate bits are the bit test instructions. These instructions include bt (bit test), bts (bit test and set), btc (bit test and complement), and btr (bit test and reset). We've used these instructions to manipulate bits in HLA character-set variables; we can also use them to manipulate bits in general. The btx instructions allow the following syntactical forms:

```
btx( BitNumber, BitsToTest );
btx( reg16, reg16 );
btx( reg32, reg32 );
btx( constant, reg16 );
btx( constant, reg32 );
btx( reg16, mem16 );
btx( reg32, mem32 );
btx( constant, mem16 );
btx( constant, mem32 );
```

The btx instruction's first operand is a bit number that specifies which bit to check in the second operand. If the second operand is a register, then the first operand must contain a value between 0 and the size of the register (in bits) minus 1; because the 80x86's largest registers are 32 bits, this value has the maximum value 31 (for 32-bit registers). If the second operand is a memory location, then the bit count is not limited to values in the range 0..31. If the first operand is a constant, it can be any 8-bit value in the range 0..255. If the first operand is a register, it has no limitation.

The bt instruction copies the specified bit from the second operand into the carry flag. For example, the bt( 8, eax ); instruction copies bit 8 of the EAX register into the carry flag. You can test the carry flag after this instruction to determine whether bit 8 was set or clear in EAX.

The bts, btc, and btr instructions manipulate the bit they test while they are testing it. These instructions may be slow (depending on the processor you're using), and you should avoid them if performance is your primary concern and you're using an older CPU. If performance (versus convenience) is an issue, you should always try two different algorithms—one that uses these instructions, one that uses and/or instructions—and measure the performance difference; then choose the best of the two approaches.

The shift and rotate instructions are another group of instructions you can use to manipulate and test bits. These instructions move the H.O. (left shift/rotate) or L.O. (right shift/rotate) bits into the carry flag. Therefore, you can test the carry flag after you execute one of these instructions to determine the original setting of the operand's H.O. or L.O. bit. The shift and rotate instructions are invaluable for aligning bit strings and packing and unpacking data. Chapter 2 has several examples of this, and some earlier examples in this chapter also use the shift instructions for this purpose.

## 10.3 The Carry Flag as a Bit Accumulator

The btx, shift, and rotate instructions set or clear the carry flag depending on the operation and selected bit. Because these instructions place their "bit result" in the carry flag, it is often convenient to think of the carry flag as a 1-bit register or accumulator for bit operations. In this section we will explore some of the operations possible with this bit result in the carry flag.

Instructions that will be useful for manipulating bit results in the carry flag are those that use the carry flag as some sort of input value. The following is a sampling of such instructions:

- adc, sbb
- rcl, rcr
- cmc (We'll throw in clc and stc even though they don't use the carry as input.)
- jc, jnc
- setc, setnc

The adc and sbb instructions add or subtract their operands along with the carry flag. So if you've computed some bit result into the carry flag, you can figure that result into an addition or subtraction using these instructions.

To merge a bit result into the carry flag, you most often use the rotate through carry instructions (rcl and rcr). These instructions move the carry flag into the L.O. or H.O. bits of their destination operand. These instructions are very useful for packing a set of bit results into a byte, word, or double-word value.

The cmc (complement carry) instruction lets you easily invert the result of some bit operation. You can also use the clc and stc instructions to initialize the carry flag prior to some string of bit operations involving the carry flag.

Instructions that test the carry flag are going to be very popular after a calculation that leaves a bit result in the carry flag. The jc, jnc, setc, and setnc instructions are quite useful here. You can also use the HLA @c and @nc operands in a boolean expression to test the result in the carry flag.

If you have a sequence of bit calculations and you would like to test to see if the calculations produce a specific set of 1-bit results, the easiest way to do this is to clear a register or memory location and use the rcl or rcr instruction to shift each result into that location. Once the bit operations are complete, then you can compare the register or memory location holding the result against a constant value. If you want to test a sequence of results involving conjunction and disjunction (that is, strings of results involving ands and ors), then you could use the setc and setnc instruction to set a register to 0 or 1 and then use the and/or instructions to merge the results.

## 10.4 Packing and Unpacking Bit Strings

A common bit operation is inserting a bit string into an operand or extracting a bit string from an operand. Chapter 2 provided simple examples of packing and unpacking such data; now it is time to formally describe how to do this.

For our purposes we will assume that we're dealing with bit strings—th
is, a contiguous sequence of bits. In Section 10.11 we'll look at how to extra
and insert bit sets. Another simplification we'll make is that the bit string co
pletely fits within a byte, word, or double-word operand. Large bit strings th
cross object boundaries require additional processing; a discussion of bit strin
that cross double-word boundaries appears later in this section.

A bit string has two attributes that we must consider when packing and
unpacking that bit string: a starting bit position and a length. The starting k
position is the bit number of the L.O. bit of the string in the larger operan
The length is the number of bits in the operand. To insert (pack) data into
destination operand, you start with a bit string of the appropriate length th
is right justified (that is, starts in bit position 0) and is zero extended to 8, 1
or 32 bits. The task is to insert this data at the appropriate starting position
some other operand that is 8-, 16-, or 32-bits wide. There is no guarantee th
the destination bit positions contain any particular value.

The first two steps (which can occur in any order) are to clear out the c
responding bits in the destination operand and to shift (a copy of) the bi
string so that the L.O. bit begins at the appropriate bit position. The thir
step is to or the shifted result with the destination operand. This inserts the k
string into the destination operand (see Figure 10-3).

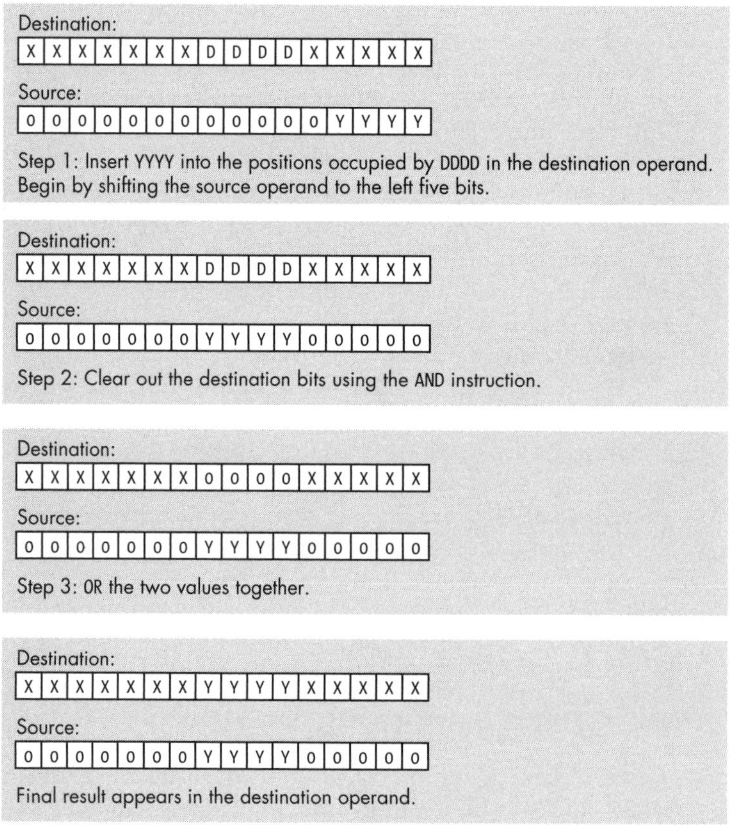

Destination:

| X | X | X | X | X | X | X | X | D | D | D | D | X | X | X | X | X |

Source:

| 0 | 0 | 0 | 0 | 0 | 0 | 0 | 0 | 0 | 0 | 0 | 0 | 0 | Y | Y | Y | Y |

Step 1: Insert YYYY into the positions occupied by DDDD in the destination operand.
Begin by shifting the source operand to the left five bits.

Destination:

| X | X | X | X | X | X | X | D | D | D | D | X | X | X | X | X |

Source:

| 0 | 0 | 0 | 0 | 0 | 0 | 0 | 0 | Y | Y | Y | Y | 0 | 0 | 0 | 0 | 0 |

Step 2: Clear out the destination bits using the AND instruction.

Destination:

| X | X | X | X | X | X | X | X | 0 | 0 | 0 | 0 | 0 | X | X | X | X | X |

Source:

| 0 | 0 | 0 | 0 | 0 | 0 | 0 | 0 | Y | Y | Y | Y | 0 | 0 | 0 | 0 | 0 |

Step 3: OR the two values together.

Destination:

| X | X | X | X | X | X | X | X | Y | Y | Y | Y | X | X | X | X | X |

Source:

| 0 | 0 | 0 | 0 | 0 | 0 | 0 | 0 | Y | Y | Y | Y | 0 | 0 | 0 | 0 | 0 |

Final result appears in the destination operand.

Figure 10-3: Inserting a bit string into a destination operand

It takes only three instructions to insert a bit string of known length into a destination operand. The following three instructions demonstrate how to handle the insertion operation in Figure 10-3. These instructions assume that the source operand is in BX and the destination operand is AX:

```
shl( 5, bx );
and( %111111000011111, ax );
or( bx, ax );
```

If the length and the starting position aren't known when you're writing the program (that is, you have to calculate them at runtime), then bit-string insertion is a little more difficult. However, with the use of a lookup table it's still an easy operation to accomplish. Let's assume that we have two 8-bit values: a starting bit position for the field we're inserting and a nonzero 8-bit length value. Also assume that the source operand is in EBX and the destination operand is in EAX. The code to insert one operand into another could take the following form:

```
readonly
    // The index into the following table specifies the length
    // of the bit string at each position:

    MaskByLen: dword[ 33 ] :=
        [
            0,  $1,  $3,  $7, $f, $1f, $3f, $7f,
            $ff, $1ff, $3ff, $7ff, $fff, $1fff, $3fff, $7fff, $ffff,
            $1_ffff, $3_ffff, $7_ffff, $f_ffff,
            $1f_ffff, $3f_ffff, $7f_ffff, $ff_ffff,
            $1ff_ffff, $3ff_ffff, $7ff_ffff, $fff_ffff,
            $1fff_ffff, $3fff_ffff, $7fff_ffff, $ffff_ffff
        ];
        .
        .
        .

    movzx( Length, edx );
    mov( MaskByLen[ edx*4 ], edx );
    mov( StartingPosition, cl );
    shl( cl, edx );
    not( edx );
    shl( cl, ebx );
    and( edx, eax );
    or( ebx, eax );
```

Each entry in the MaskByLen table contains the number of 1 bits specified by the index into the table. Using the *Length* value as an index into this table fetches a value that has as many 1 bits as the *Length* value. The code above fetches an appropriate mask, shifts it to the left so that the L.O. bit of this run of ones matches the starting position of the field into which we want to insert the data, and then inverts the mask and uses the inverted value to clear the appropriate bits in the destination operand.

Extracting a bit string from a larger operand is just as easy as inserting bit string into some larger operand. All you have to do is mask out the unwant bits and then shift the result until the L.O. bit of the bit string is in bit 0 of t destination operand. For example, to extract the 4-bit field starting at bit po tion 5 in EBX and leave the result in EAX, you could use the following co

```
mov( ebx, eax );              // Copy data to destination.
and( %1_1110_0000, eax );     // Strip unwanted bits.
shr( 5, eax );                // Right justify to bit position 0.
```

If you do not know the bit string's length and starting position when you're writing the program, you can still extract the desired bit string. The code is very similar to insertion (though a little simpler). Assuming you ha the *Length* and *StartingPosition* values we used when inserting a bit string, yo can extract the corresponding bit string using the following code (assumin source = EBX and dest = EAX):

```
movzx( Length, edx );
mov( MaskByLen[ edx*4 ], edx );
mov( StartingPosition, cl );
mov( ebx, eax );
shr( cl, eax );
and( edx, eax );
```

The examples up to this point all assume that the bit string appears co pletely within a double-word (or smaller) object. This will always be the case the bit string is less than or equal to 32 bits in length. However, if the lengt of the bit string plus its starting position (modulo 8) within an object is great than 32, then the bit string will cross a double-word boundary within the objec Extracting such bit strings requires up to three operations: one operation extract the start of the bit string (up to the first double-word boundary), an operation that copies whole double words (assuming the bit string is so lor that it consumes several double words), and a final operation that copies leftover bits in the last double word at the end of the bit string. The actua implementation of this operation is left as an exercise for the reader.

## 10.5 Coalescing Bit Sets and Distributing Bit Strings

Inserting and extracting bit sets is little different than inserting and extract b strings if the "shape" of the bit set you're inserting (or resulting bit set you'r extracting) is the same as the bit set in the main object. The shape of a bit s is the distribution of the bits in the set, ignoring the starting bit position of the set. So a bit set that includes bits 0, 4, 5, 6, and 7 has the same shape as bit set that includes bits 12, 16, 17, 18, and 19 because the distribution of th bits is the same. The code to insert or extract this bit set is nearly identical t that of the previous section; the only difference is the mask value you use. Fo example, to insert this bit set starting at bit 0 in EAX into the corresponding bit set starting at position 12 in EBX, you could use the following code:

```
and( !%1111_0001_0000_0000_0000, ebx );// Mask out destination bits.
shl( 12, eax );                        // Move source bits into position.
or( eax, ebx );                        // Merge the bit set into ebx.
```

However, suppose you have 5 bits in bit positions 0 through 4 in EAX and you want to merge them into bits 12, 16, 17, 18, and 19 in EBX. Somehow you have to distribute the bits in EAX prior to logically oring the values into EBX. Given the fact that this particular bit set has only two runs of 1 bits, the process is somewhat simplified. The following code achieves this in a somewhat sneaky fashion:

```
and( !%1111_0001_0000_0000_0000, ebx );
shl( 3, eax );   // Spread out the bits: 1-4 goes to 4-7 and 0 to 3.
btr( 3, eax );   // Bit 3->carry and then clear bit 3.
rcl( 12, eax );  // Shift in carry and put bits into final position.
or( eax, ebx );  // Merge the bit set into ebx.
```

This trick with the btr (bit test and reset) instruction worked well because we had only 1 bit out of place in the original source operand. Alas, had the bits all been in the wrong location relative to one another, this scheme might not have worked quite as well. We'll see a more general solution in just a moment.

Extracting this bit set and collecting ("coalescing") the bits into a bit string is not quite as easy. However, there are still some sneaky tricks we can pull. Consider the following code that extracts the bit set from EBX and places the result into bits 0..4 of EAX:

```
mov( ebx, eax );
and( %1111_0001_0000_0000_0000, eax );  // Strip unwanted bits.
shr( 5, eax );                          // Put bit 12 into bit 7, etc.
shr( 3, ah );                           // Move bits 11..14 to 8..11.
shr( 7, eax );                          // Move down to bit 0.
```

This code moves (original) bit 12 into bit position 7, the H.O. bit of AL. At the same time it moves bits 16..19 down to bits 11..14 (bits 3..6 of AH). Then the code shifts bits 3..6 in AH down to bit 0. This positions the H.O. bits of the bit set so that they are adjacent to the bit left in AL. Finally, the code shifts all the bits down to bit 0. Again, this is not a general solution, but it shows a clever way to attack this problem if you think about it carefully.

The problem with the coalescing and distribution algorithms above is that they are not general. They apply only to their specific bit sets. Usually specific solutions will provide the most efficient solution. A generalized solution (perhaps one that lets you specify a mask, and the code distributes or coalesces the bits accordingly) is going to be a bit more difficult. The following code demonstrates how to distribute the bits in a bit string according to the values in a bit mask:

```
// eax- Originally contains some value into which we
//        insert bits from ebx.
// ebx- L.O. bits contain the values to insert into eax.
// edx- Bitmap with ones indicating the bit positions in eax to insert.
// cl- Scratchpad register.

            mov( 32, cl );   // Count number of bits we rotate.
            jmp DistLoop;

CopyToEAX:rcr( 1, ebx );     // Don't use SHR here, must preserve Z-flag.
            rcr( 1, eax );
            jz  Done;
DistLoop: dec( cl );
            shr( 1, edx );
            jc CopyToEAX;
            ror( 1, eax );   // Keep current bit in eax.
            jnz DistLoop;

Done:       ror( cl, eax );  // Reposition remaining bits.
```

In the code above, if we load EDX with %1100_1001, then this code will copy bits 0..3 to bits 0, 3, 6, and 7 in EAX. Notice the short-circuit test that checks to see if we've exhausted the values in EDX (by checking for a 0 in EDX). Note that the rotate instructions do not affect the zero flag but the shift instructions do. Hence the shr instruction above will set the zero flag when there are no more bits to distribute (when EDX becomes 0).

The general algorithm for coalescing bits is a tad more efficient than distribution. Here's the code that will extract bits from EBX via the bit mask in EDX and leave the result in EAX:

```
// eax- Destination register.
// ebx- Source register.
// edx- Bitmap with ones representing bits to copy to eax.
// ebx and edx are not preserved.
        sub( eax, eax );  // Clear destination register.
        jmp ShiftLoop;

ShiftInEAX:
        rcl( 1, ebx );    // Up here we need to copy a bit from
        rcl( 1, eax );    // ebx to eax.
ShiftLoop:
        shl( 1, edx );    // Check mask to see if we need to copy a bit.
        jc ShiftInEAX;    // If carry set, go copy the bit.
        rcl( 1, ebx );    // Current bit is uninteresting, skip it.
        jnz ShiftLoop;    // Repeat as long as there are bits in edx.
```

This sequence takes advantage of a sneaky trait of the shift and rotate instructions: the shift instructions affect the zero flag, whereas the rotate instructions do not. Therefore, the shl( 1, edx ); instruction sets the zero flag when EDX becomes 0 (after the shift). If the carry flag was also set, the code will make one additional pass through the loop in order to shift a bit into EAX, but the next time the code shifts EDX 1 bit to the left, EDX is still 0 and so the carry will be clear. On this iteration, the code falls out of the loop.

Another way to coalesce bits is via table lookup. By grabbing a byte of data at a time (so your tables don't get too large), you can use that byte's value as an index into a lookup table that coalesces all the bits down to bit 0. Finally, you can merge the bits at the low end of each byte together. This might produce a more efficient coalescing algorithm in certain cases. The implementation is left to the reader.

## 10.6 Packed Arrays of Bit Strings

Although it is far more efficient to create arrays whose elements have an integral number of bytes, it is quite possible to create arrays of elements whose size is not a multiple of 8 bits. The drawback is that calculating the "address" of an array element and manipulating that array element involves a lot of extra work. In this section we'll take a look at a few examples of packing and unpacking array elements in an array whose elements are an arbitrary number of bits long.

Before proceeding, it's probably worthwhile to discuss why you would want to bother with arrays of bit objects. The answer is simple: space. If an object consumes only 3 bits, you can get 2.67 times as many elements into the same space if you pack the data rather than allocating a whole byte for each object. For very large arrays, this can be a substantial savings. Of course, the cost of this space savings is speed: You have to execute extra instructions to pack and unpack the data, thus slowing down access to the data.

The calculation for locating the bit offset of an array element in a large block of bits is almost identical to the standard array access; it is:

---

```
Element_Address_in_bits =
        Base_address_in_bits + index * element_size_in_bits
```

---

Once you calculate the element's address in bits, you need to convert it to a byte address (because we have to use byte addresses when accessing memory) and extract the specified element. Because the base address of an array element (almost) always starts on a byte boundary, we can use the following equations to simplify this task:

---

```
Byte_of_1st_bit =
    Base_Address + (index * element_size_in_bits )/8

Offset_to_1st_bit =
    (index * element_size_in_bits) % 8 (note "%" = MOD)
```

---

For example, suppose we have an array of 200 3-bit objects that we declar
as follows:

```
static
    AO3Bobjects: byte[ int32((200*3)/8 + 2) ];  // "+2" handles
                                                 // truncation.
```

The constant expression in the dimension above reserves space for enoug
bytes to hold 600 bits (200 elements, each 3 bits long). As the comment note
the expression adds 2 extra bytes at the end to ensure we don't lose any od
bits (that won't happen in this example because 600 is evenly divisible by 8
but in general you can't count on this; one extra byte usually won't hurt thing:
and also to allow us to access 1 byte beyond the end of the array (when storin
data to the array).

Now suppose you want to access the *i*th 3-bit element of this array. You
can extract these bits by using the following code:

```
// Extract the ith group of 3 bits in AO3Bobjects
// and leave this value in eax.

    sub( ecx, ecx );            // Put i/8 remainder here.
    mov( i, eax );              // Get the index into the array.
    lea( eax, [eax+eax*2] );    // eax := eax * 3 (3 bits/element).
    shrd( 3, eax, ecx );        // eax/8 -> eax and eax mod 8 -> ecx
                                // (H.O. bits).
    shr( 3, eax );              // Remember, shrd doesn't modify eax.
    rol( 3, ecx );              // Put remainder into L.O. 3
                                // bits of ecx.

// Okay, fetch the word containing the 3 bits we want to
// extract. We have to fetch a word because the last bit or two
// could wind up crossing the byte boundary (i.e., bit offset 6
// and 7 in the byte).

    mov( (type word AO3Bobjects[eax]), ax );
    shr( cl, ax );              // Move bits down to bit 0.
    and( %111, eax );           // Remove the other bits.
```

Inserting an element into the array is a bit more difficult. In addition t
computing the base address and bit offset of the array element, you also hav
to create a mask to clear out the bits in the destination where you're going t
insert the new data. The following code inserts the L.O. 3 bits of EAX into th
*i*th element of the AO3Bobjects array.

```
// Insert the L.O. 3 bits of ax into the ith element
// of AO3Bobjects:

readonly
    Masks:
        word[8] :=
        [
```

```
            !%0111,                !%0011_1000,
            !%0001_1100_0000,      !%1110,
            !%0111_0000,           !%0011_1000_0000,
            !%0001_1100,           !%1110_0000
        ];

                        .

                        .

                        .

        mov( i, ebx );              // Get the index into the array.
        mov( ebx, ecx );            // Use L.O. 3 bits as index
        and( %111, ecx );           // into Masks table.
        mov( Masks[ecx*2], dx );    // Get bit mask.

        // Convert index into the array into a bit index.
        // To do this, multiply the index by 3:

        lea( ebx, [ebx+ebx*2]);

        // Divide by 8 to get the byte index into ebx
        // and the bit index (the remainder) into ecx:

        shrd( 3,ebx, ecx );
        shr( 3, ebx );
        rol( 3, ecx );

        // Grab the bits and clear those we're inserting.

        and( (type word AO3Bobjects[ ebx ]), dx );

        // Put our 3 bits in their proper location.

        shl( cl, ax );

        // Merge bits into destination.

        or( ax, dx );

        // Store back into memory.

        mov( dx, (type word AO3Bobjects[ ebx ]) );
```

Notice the use of a lookup table to generate the masks needed to clear out the appropriate position in the array. Each element of this array contains all ones except for three zeros in the position we need to clear for a given bit offset (note the use of the ! operator to invert the constants in the table).

## 10.7  Searching for a Bit

A very common bit operation is to locate the end of some run of bits. A special case of this operation is to locate the first (or last) set or clear bit in a 16- or 32-bit value. In this section we'll explore ways to accomplish this.

Before describing how to search for the first or last bit of a given value, perhaps it's wise to discuss exactly what the terms *first* and *last* mean in this context. The term *first set bit* means the first bit in a value, scanning from bit toward the high-order bit, which contains a 1. A similar definition exists for the *first clear bit*. The *last set bit* is the first bit in a value, scanning from the high order bit toward bit 0, which contains a 1. A similar definition exists for the *last clear bit*.

One obvious way to scan for the first or last bit is to use a shift instruction in a loop and count the number of iterations before you shift out a 1 (or 0) into the carry flag. The number of iterations specifies the position. Here's some sample code that checks for the first set bit in EAX and returns that bit position in ECX:

```
         mov( -32, ecx );   // Count off the bit positions in ecx.
TstLp:   shr( 1, eax );     // Check to see if current bit
                            // position contains a 1.
         jc Done;           // Exit loop if it does.
         inc( ecx );        // Bump up our bit counter by 1.
         jnz TstLp;         // Exit if we execute this loop 32 times.

Done:    add( 32, cl );     // Adjust loop counter so it holds
                            // the bit position.

// At this point, ecx contains the bit position of the first set bit.
// ecx contains 32 if eax originally contained 0 (no set bits).
```

The only thing tricky about this code is the fact that it runs the loop counter from −32 up to 0 rather than 32 down to 0. This makes it slightly easier to calculate the bit position once the loop terminates.

The drawback to this particular loop is that it's expensive. This loop repeats as many as 32 times depending on the original value in EAX. If the values you're checking often have lots of zeros in the L.O. bits of EAX, this code runs rather slowly.

Searching for the first (or last) set bit is such a common operation that Intel added a couple of instructions on the 80386 specifically to accelerate this process. These instructions are bsf (bit scan forward) and bsr (bit scan reverse). Their syntax is as follows:

```
         bsr( source, destReg );
         bsf( source, destReg );
```

The source and destinations operands must be the same size, and they must both be 16- or 32-bit objects. The destination operand has to be a register. The source operand can be a register or a memory location.

The bsf instruction scans for the first set bit (starting from bit position 0 in the source operand. The bsr instruction scans for the last set bit in the source operand by scanning from the H.O. bit toward the L.O. bit. If these instructions find a bit that is set in the source operand, then they clear the zero flag and put the bit position into the destination register. If the source register contains 0 (that is, there are no set bits), then these instructions set the zero flag and leave an indeterminate value in the destination register. Note that you should test the zero flag immediately after the execution of these instructions to validate the destination register's value. Here's an example:

```
mov( SomeValue, ebx );   // Value whose bits we want to check.
bsf( ebx, eax );         // Put position of first set bit in eax.
jz NoBitsSet;            // Branch if SomeValue contains 0.
mov( eax, FirstBit );    // Save location of first set bit.
        .
        .
        .
```

You use the bsr instruction in an identical fashion except that it computes the bit position of the last set bit in an operand (that is, the first set bit it finds when scanning from the H.O. bit toward the L.O. bit).

The 80x86 CPUs do not provide instructions to locate the first bit containing a 0. However, you can easily scan for a 0 bit by first inverting the source operand (or a copy of the source operand if you must preserve the source operand's value) and then search for the first 1 bit; this corresponds to the first 0 bit in the original operand value.

The bsf and bsr instructions are very complex 80x86 instructions. Therefore, these instructions may be slower than other instructions. Indeed, in some circumstances it may be faster to locate the first set bit using discrete instructions. However, because the execution time of these instructions varies widely from CPU to CPU, you should test the performance of these instructions prior to using them in time-critical code.

Note that the bsf and bsr instructions do not affect the source operand. A common operation is to extract the first (or last) set bit you find in some operand. That is, you might want to clear the bit once you find it. If the source operand is a register (or you can easily move it into a register), then you can use the btr (or btc) instruction to clear the bit once you've found it. Here's some code that achieves this result:

```
bsf( eax, ecx );       // Locate first set bit in eax.
if( @nz ) then         // If we found a bit, clear it.

    btr( ecx, eax );   // Clear the bit we just found.

endif;
```

At the end of this sequence, the zero flag indicates whether we found a bit (note that btr does not affect the zero flag). Alternately, you could add an else section to the if statement above that handles the case when the source operand (EAX) contains 0 at the beginning of this instruction sequence.

Because the bsf and bsr instructions support only 16- and 32-bit operands, you will have to compute the first bit position of an 8-bit operand a little differently. There are a couple of reasonable approaches. First, of course, you can usually zero extend an 8-bit operand to 16 or 32 bits and then use the bsf or bsr instruction on this operand. Another alternative is to create a lookup table where each entry in the table contains the number of bits in the value you use as an index into the table; then you can use the xlat instruction to "compute" the first bit position in the value (note that you will have to handle the value 0 as a special case). Another solution is to use the shift algorithm appearing at the beginning of this section; for an 8-bit operand, this is not an entirely inefficient solution.

One interesting use of the bsf and bsr instructions is to fill in a character set with all the values from the lowest valued character in the set through the highest valued character. For example, suppose a character set contains the values {'A', 'M', 'a'..'n', 'z'}; if we filled in the gaps in this character set we would have the values {'A'..'z'}. To compute this new set we can use bsf to determine the ASCII code of the first character in the set and bsr to determine the ASCII code of the last character in the set. After doing this, we can feed those two ASCII codes to the HLA Standard Library cs.rangeChar function to compute the new set.

You can also use the bsf and bsr instructions to determine the size of a run of bits, assuming that you have a single run of bits in your operand. Simply locate the first and last bits in the run (as above) and then compute the difference (plus 1) of the two values. Of course, this scheme is valid only if there are no intervening zeros between the first and last set bits in the value.

## 10.8  Counting Bits

The last example in the previous section demonstrates a specific case of a very general problem: counting bits. Unfortunately, that example has a severe limitation: It only counts a single run of 1 bits appearing in the source operand. This section discusses a more general solution to this problem.

Hardly a week goes by that someone doesn't ask on one of the Internet newsgroups how to count the number of bits in a register operand. This is a common request, undoubtedly, because many assembly language course instructors assign this task as a project to their students as a way to teach them about the shift and rotate instructions. Undoubtedly, the solution these instructors expect is something like the following:

```
// BitCount1:
//
// Counts the bits in the eax register, returning the count in ebx.

          mov( 32, cl );    // Count the 32 bits in eax.
          sub( ebx, ebx );  // Accumulate the count here.
CntLoop:  shr( 1, eax );    // Shift next bit out of eax and into Carry.
          adc( 0, bl );     // Add the carry into the ebx register.
          dec( cl );        // Repeat 32 times.
          jnz CntLoop;
```

The "trick" worth noting here is that this code uses the adc instruction to add the value of the carry flag into the BL register. Because the count is going to be less than 32, the result will fit comfortably into BL.

Tricky code or not, this instruction sequence is not particularly fast. As you can tell with just a small amount of analysis, the loop above always executes 32 times, so this code sequence executes 130 instructions (4 instructions per iteration plus 2 extra instructions). You might ask if there is a more efficient solution; the answer is yes. The following code, taken from the AMD Athlon optimization guide, provides a faster solution (see the comments for a description of the algorithm):

```
// bitCount
//
// Counts the number of "1" bits in a dword value.
// This function returns the dword count value in eax.

procedure bitCount( BitsToCnt:dword ); @nodisplay;

const
    EveryOtherBit       := $5555_5555;
    EveryAlternatePair  := $3333_3333;
    EvenNibbles         := $0f0f_0f0f;

begin bitCount;

    push( edx );
    mov( BitsToCnt, eax );
    mov( eax, edx );

    // Compute sum of each pair of bits
    // in eax. The algorithm treats
    // each pair of bits in eax as a
    // 2-bit number and calculates the
    // number of bits as follows (description
    // is for bits 0 and 1, it generalizes
    // to each pair):
    //
    // edx =   Bit1 Bit0
    // eax = 0 Bit1
    //
    // edx-eax =   00 if both bits were 0.
    // 01 if Bit0=1 and Bit1=0.
    // 01 if Bit0=0 and Bit1=1.
    // 10 if Bit0=1 and Bit1=1.
    //
    // Note that the result is left in edx.

    shr( 1, eax );
    and( EveryOtherBit, eax );
    sub( eax, edx );

    // Now sum up the groups of 2 bits to
    // produces sums of 4 bits. This works
    // as follows:
    //
```

```
// edx = bits 2,3, 6,7, 10,11, 14,15, ..., 30,31
// in bit positions 0,1, 4,5, ..., 28,29 with
// zeros in the other positions.
//
// eax = bits 0,1, 4,5, 8,9, ... 28,29 with zeros
// in the other positions.
//
// edx+eax produces the sums of these pairs of bits.

// The sums consume bits 0,1,2, 4,5,6, 8,9,10, ... 28,29,30
// in eax with the remaining bits all containing 0.

mov( edx, eax );
shr( 2, edx );
and( EveryAlternatePair, eax );
and( EveryAlternatePair, edx );
add( edx, eax );

// Now compute the sums of the even and odd nibbles in the
// number. Because bits 3, 7, 11, etc. in eax all contain
// 0 from the above calculation, we don't need to AND
// anything first, just shift and add the two values.
// This computes the sum of the bits in the 4 bytes
// as four separate values in eax (al contains number of
// bits in original al, ah contains number of bits in
// original ah, etc.)

mov( eax, edx );
shr( 4, eax );
add( edx, eax );
and( EvenNibbles, eax );

// Now for the tricky part.
// We want to compute the sum of the 4 bytes
// and return the result in eax. The following
// multiplication achieves this. It works
// as follows:
// (1) the $01 component leaves bits 24..31
//      in bits 24..31.
//
// (2) the $100 component adds bits 17..23
//      into bits 24..31.
//
// (3) the $1_0000 component adds bits 8..15
//      into bits 24..31.
//
// (4) the $1000_0000 component adds bits 0..7
//      into bits 24..31.
//
// Bits 0..23 are filled with garbage, but bits
// 24..31 contain the actual sum of the bits
// in eax's original value. The shr instruction
// moves this value into bits 0..7 and zeros
// out the H.O. bits of eax.
```

```
            intmul( $0101_0101, eax );
            shr( 24, eax );

            pop( edx );

        end bitCount;
```

## 10.9 Reversing a Bit String

Another common programming project instructors assign, and a useful function in its own right, is a program that reverses the bits in an operand. That is,
it swaps the L.O. bit with the H.O. bit, bit 1 with the next-to-H.O. bit, and so
on. The typical solution an instructor probably expects for this assignment is
the following:

```
// Reverse the 32-bits in eax, leaving the result in ebx:

                mov( 32, cl );
RvsLoop:        shr( 1, eax );   // Move current bit in eax to
                                 // the carry flag.
                rcl( 1, ebx );   // Shift the bit back into
                                 // ebx, backwards.
                dec( cl );
                jnz RvsLoop;
```

As with the previous examples, this code suffers from the fact that it repeats
the loop 32 times, for a grand total of 129 instructions. By unrolling the loop
you can get it down to 64 instructions, but this is still somewhat expensive.

As usual, the best solution to an optimization problem is often a better
algorithm rather than attempting to tweak your code by trying to choose
faster instructions to speed up some code. However, a little intelligence goes
a long way when manipulating bits. In the last section, for example, we were
able to speed up counting the bits in a string by substituting a more complex
algorithm for the simplistic "shift and count" algorithm. In the example
above, we are once again faced with a very simple algorithm with a loop that
repeats for 1 bit in each number. The question is "Can we discover an algorithm that doesn't execute 129 instructions to reverse the bits in a 32-bit
register?" The answer is yes, and the trick is to do as much work as possible in
parallel.

Suppose that all we wanted to do was swap the even and odd bits in a 32-bit
value. We can easily swap the even and odd bits in EAX using the following code:

```
mov( eax, edx );            // Make a copy of the odd bits.
shr( 1, eax );              // Move even bits to the odd positions.
and( $5555_5555, edx );     // Isolate the odd bits.
and( $5555_5555, eax );     // Isolate the even bits.
shl( 1, edx );              // Move odd bits to even positions.
or( edx, eax );             // Merge the bits and complete the swap.
```

Of course, swapping the even and odd bits, while somewhat interesting, does not solve our larger problem of reversing all the bits in the number. But it does take us part of the way there. For example, if after executing the preceding code sequence you swap adjacent pairs of bits, you've managed to swap the bits in all the nibbles in the 32-bit value. Swapping adjacent pairs of bits is done in a manner very similar to the above; the code is:

```
mov( eax, edx );      // Make a copy of the odd-numbered bit pairs.
shr( 2, eax );        // Move the even bit pairs to the odd position.
and( $3333_3333, edx ); // Isolate the odd pairs.
and( $3333_3333, eax ); // Isolate the even pairs.
shl( 2, edx );        // Move the odd pairs to the even positions.
or( edx, eax );       // Merge the bits and complete the swap.
```

After completing the preceding sequence, you swap the adjacent nibbles in the 32-bit register. Again, the only difference is the bit mask and the length of the shifts. Here's the code:

```
mov( eax, edx );      // Make a copy of the odd-numbered nibbles.
shr( 4, eax );        // Move the even nibbles to the odd position.
and( $0f0f_0f0f, edx ); // Isolate the odd nibbles.
and( $0f0f_0f0f, eax ); // Isolate the even nibbles.
shl( 4, edx );        // Move the odd pairs to the even positions.
or( edx, eax );       // Merge the bits and complete the swap.
```

You can probably see the pattern developing and can figure out that in the next two steps you have to swap the bytes and then the words in this object. You can use code like the above, but there is a better way: Use the bswap instruction. The bswap (byte swap) instruction uses the following syntax:

```
bswap( reg32 );
```

This instruction swaps bytes 0 and 3, and it swaps bytes 1 and 2 in the specified 32-bit register. The principle use of this instruction is to convert data between the so-called little-endian and big-endian data formats.[2] Although you don't specifically use this instruction for this purpose here, the bswap instruction does swap the bytes and words in a 32-bit object exactly the way you want them when reversing bits. Rather than sticking in another 12 instructions to swap the bytes and then the words, you can simply use a bswap( eax ) instruction to complete the job after the instructions above. The final code sequence is:

```
mov( eax, edx );      // Make a copy of the odd bits in the data.
shr( 1, eax );        // Move the even bits to the odd positions.
and( $5555_5555, edx ); // Isolate the odd bits.
and( $5555_5555, eax ); // Isolate the even bits.
```

---

[2] In the little-endian system, which is the native 80x86 format, the L.O. byte of an object appears at the lowest address in memory. In the big-endian system, which various RISC processors use, the H.O. byte of an object appears at the lowest address in memory. The bswap instruction converts between these two data formats.

```
        shl( 1, edx );          // Move the odd bits to the even positions.
        or( edx, eax );         // Merge the bits and complete the swap.

        mov( eax, edx );        // Make a copy of the odd numbered bit pairs.
        shr( 2, eax );          // Move the even bit pairs to the odd position.
        and( $3333_3333, edx ); // Isolate the odd pairs.
        and( $3333_3333, eax ); // Isolate the even pairs.
        shl( 2, edx );          // Move the odd pairs to the even positions.
        or( edx, eax );         // Merge the bits and complete the swap.

        mov( eax, edx );        // Make a copy of the odd numbered nibbles.
        shr( 4, eax );          // Move the even nibbles to the odd position.
        and( $0f0f_0f0f, edx ); // Isolate the odd nibbles.
        and( $0f0f_0f0f, eax ); // Isolate the even nibbles.
        shl( 4, edx );          // Move the odd pairs to the even positions.
        or( edx, eax );         // Merge the bits and complete the swap.

        bswap( eax );           // Swap the bytes and words.
```

This algorithm requires only 19 instructions, and it executes much faster than the bit-shifting loop appearing earlier. Of course, this sequence does consume a little more memory. If you're trying to save memory rather than clock cycles, the loop is probably a better solution.

## 10.10  Merging Bit Strings

Another common bit string operation is producing a single bit string by merging, or interleaving, bits from two different sources. The following example code sequence creates a 32-bit string by merging alternate bits from two 16-bit strings:

```
// Merge two 16-bit strings into a single 32-bit string.
// ax - Source for even numbered bits.
// bx - Source for odd numbered bits.
// cl - Scratch register.
// edx- Destination register.

          mov( 16, cl );
MergeLp:  shrd( 1, eax, edx );   // Shift a bit from eax into edx.
          shrd( 1, ebx, edx );   // Shift a bit from ebx into edx.
          dec( cl );
          jne MergeLp;
```

This particular example merged two 16-bit values together, alternating their bits in the result value. For a faster implementation of this code, unrolling the loop is probably your best bet because this eliminates half the instructions.

With a few slight modifications, we could also have merged four 8-bit values together, or we could have generated the result using other bit sequences. For example, the following code copies bits 0..5 from EAX, then bits 0..4 from

EBX, then bits 6..11 from EAX, then bits 5..15 from EBX, and finally bits 12..
from EAX:

```
shrd( 6, eax, edx );
shrd( 5, ebx, edx );
shrd( 6, eax, edx );
shrd( 11, ebx, edx );
shrd( 4, eax, edx );
```

## 10.11  Extracting Bit Strings

Of course, we can easily accomplish the converse of merging two bit stream
that is, we can extract and distribute bits in a bit string among multiple des
nations. The following code takes the 32-bit value in EAX and distributes
alternate bits among the BX and DX registers:

```
          mov( 16, cl );   // Count the loop iterations.
ExtractLp: shr( 1, eax );  // Extract even bits to (e)bx.
          rcr( 1, ebx );
          shr( 1, eax );   // Extract odd bits to (e)dx.
          rcr( 1, edx );
          dec( cl );       // Repeat 16 times.
          jnz ExtractLp;
          shr( 16, ebx );  // Need to move the results from the H.O.
          shr( 16, edx );  // bytes of ebx/edx to the L.O. bytes.
```

This sequence executes 99 instructions. This isn't terrible, but we can
probably do a little better by using an algorithm that extracts bits in paralle
Employing the technique we used to reverse bits in a register, we can come ι
with the following algorithm that relocates all the even bits to the L.O. wor
of EAX and all the odd bits to the H.O. word of EAX.

```
// Swap bits at positions (1,2), (5,6), (9,10), (13,14), (17,18),
// (21,22), (25,26), and (29, 30).

    mov( eax, edx );
    and( $9999_9999, eax );  // Mask out the bits we'll keep for now.
    mov( edx, ecx );
    shr( 1, edx );           // Move 1st bits in tuple above to the
    and( $2222_2222, ecx );  // correct position and mask out the
    and( $2222_2222, edx );  // unneeded bits.
    shl( 1, ecx );           // Move 2nd bits in tuples above.
    or( edx, ecx );          // Merge all the bits back together.
    or( ecx, eax );

// Swap bit pairs at positions ((2,3), (4,5)),
// ((10,11), (12,13)), etc.

    mov( eax, edx );
    and( $c3c3_c3c3, eax );  // The bits we'll leave alone.
    mov( edx, ecx );
```

```
shr( 2, edx );
and( $0c0c_0c0c, ecx );
and( $0c0c_0c0c, edx );
shl( 2, ecx );
or( edx, ecx );
or( ecx, eax );

// Swap nibbles at nibble positions (1,2), (5,6), (9,10), etc.

mov( eax, edx );
and( $f00f_f00f, eax );
mov( edx, ecx );
shr(4, edx );
and( $0f0f_0f0f, ecx );
and( $0f0f_0f0f, ecx );
shl( 4, ecx );
or( edx, ecx );
or( ecx, eax );

// Swap bits at positions 1 and 2.

ror( 8, eax );
xchg( al, ah );
rol( 8, eax );
```

This sequence requires 30 instructions. At first blush it looks like a winner because the original loop executes 64 instructions. However, this code isn't quite as good as it looks. After all, if we're willing to write this much code, why not unroll the loop above 16 times? That sequence requires only 64 instructions. So the complexity of the previous algorithm may not gain much on instruction count. As to which sequence is faster, well, you'll have to time them to figure this out. However, the shrd instructions are not particularly fast on all processors and neither are the instructions in the other sequence. This example appears here not to show you a better algorithm but rather to demonstrate that writing really tricky code doesn't always provide a big performance boost.

Extracting other bit combinations is left as an exercise for the reader.

## 10.12  Searching for a Bit Pattern

Another bit-related operation you may need is the ability to search for a particular bit pattern in a string of bits. For example, you might want to locate the bit index of the first occurrence of %1011 starting at some particular position in a bit string. In this section we'll explore some simple algorithms to accomplish this task.

To search for a particular bit pattern we're going to need to know four things: (1) the pattern to search for (the *pattern*), (2) the length of the pattern we're searching for, (3) the bit string that we're going to search through (the *source*), and (4) the length of the bit string to search through. The basic idea behind the search is to create a mask based on the length of the pattern and mask a copy of the source with this value. Then we can directly compare

the pattern with the masked source for equality. If they are equal, you're fin
ished; if they're not equal, then increment a bit position counter, shift the
source one position to the right, and try again. You repeat this operation
length(*source*) - length(*pattern*) times. The algorithm fails if it does not
detect the bit pattern after this many attempts (because we will have exhausted
all the bits in the source operand that could match the pattern's length).
Here's a simple algorithm that searches for a 4-bit pattern throughout the
EBX register:

```
        mov( 28, cl );        // 28 attempts because 32-4 = 28
                              // (len(src) - len(pat)).
        mov( %1111, ch );     // Mask for the comparison.
        mov( pattern, al );   // Pattern to search for.
        and( ch, al );        // Mask unnecessary bits in al.
        mov( source, ebx );   // Get the source value.
ScanLp: mov( bl, dl );        // Copy the L.O. 4 bits of ebx
        and( ch, dl );        // Mask unwanted bits.
        cmp( dl, al );        // See if we match the pattern.
        jz Matched;
        dec( cl );            // Repeat the specified number of times.
        shl( 1, ebx );
        jnz ScanLp;

// Do whatever needs to be done if we failed to match the bit string.

        jmp Done;

Matched:

// If we get to this point, we matched the bit string. We can compute
// the position in the original source as 28-cl.

Done:
```

Bit-string scanning is a special case of string matching. String matching
a well-studied problem in computer science, and many of the algorithms you
can use for string matching are applicable to bit-string matching as well. Such
algorithms are beyond the scope of this chapter, but to give you a preview of
how this works, you compute some function (like xor or sub) between the pattern and the current source bits and use the result as an index into a lookup
table to determine how many bits you can skip. Such algorithms let you skip
several bits rather than shifting only once for each iteration of the scanning
loop (as is done by the previous algorithm).

## 10.13   The HLA Standard Library Bits Module

The HLA Standard Library provides the bits.hhf module that provides several
bit-related functions, including built-in functions for many of the algorithms
we've studied in this chapter. This section describes some of the functions
available in the HLA Standard Library.

```
procedure bits.cnt( b:dword ); @returns( "eax" );
```

This procedure returns the number of 1 bits present in the b parameter. It returns the count in the EAX register. To count the number of 0 bits in the parameter value, invert the value of the parameter before passing it to bits.cnt. If you want to count the number of bits in a 16-bit operand, simply zero extend it to 32 bits prior to calling this function. Here are a couple of examples:

```
// Compute the number of bits in a 16-bit register:

    pushw( 0 );
    push( ax );
    call bits.cnt;

// If you prefer to use a higher-level syntax, try the following:

    bits.cnt( #{ pushw(0); push(ax); }# );

// Compute the number of bits in a 16-bit memory location:

    pushw( 0 );
    push( mem16 );
    call bits.cnt;
```

If you want to compute the number of bits in an 8-bit operand, it's probably faster to write a simple loop that rotates all the bits in the source operand and adds the carry into the accumulating sum. Of course, if performance isn't an issue, you can zero extend the byte to 32 bits and call the bits.cnt procedure.

```
procedure bits.distribute( source:dword; mask:dword; dest:dword );
    @returns( "eax" );
```

This function takes the L.O. $n$ bits of source, where $n$ is the number of 1 bits in mask, and inserts these bits into dest at the bit positions specified by the 1 bits in mask (that is, the same as the distribute algorithm appearing earlier in this chapter). This function does not change the bits in dest that correspond to the zeros in the mask value. This function does not affect the value of the actual dest parameter; it returns the new value in the EAX register.

```
procedure bits.coalesce( source:dword; mask:dword );
    @returns( "eax" );
```

This function is the converse of bits.distribute. It extracts all the bits in source whose corresponding positions in mask contain a 1. This function coalesces (right justifies) these bits in the L.O. bit positions of the result and returns the result in EAX.

```
procedure bits.extract( var d:dword );
    @returns( "eax" ); // Really a macro.
```

This function extracts the first set bit in d searching from bit 0 and returns the index of this bit in the EAX register; the function also returns the zero flag clear in this case. This function also clears that bit in the operand. If d contains 0, then this function returns the zero flag set and EAX will contain −1.

Note that HLA actually implements this function as a macro, not a procedure. This means that you can pass any double-word operand as a parameter (a memory or a register operand). However, the results are undefined if you pass EAX as the parameter (because this function computes the bit number in EAX).

```
procedure bits.reverse32( d:dword ); @returns( "eax" );
procedure bits.reverse16( w:word ); @returns( "ax" );
procedure bits.reverse8( b:byte ); @returns( "al" );
```

These three routines return their parameter value with its bits reversed in the accumulator register (AL/AX/EAX). Call the routine appropriate for your data size.

```
procedure bits.merge32( even:dword; odd:dword ); @returns( "edx:eax" );
procedure bits.merge16( even:word; odd:word ); @returns( "eax" );
procedure bits.merge8( even:byte; odd:byte ); @returns( "ax" );
```

These routines merge two streams of bits to produce a value whose size is the combination of the two parameters. The bits from the even parameter occupy the even bit positions in the result; the bits from the odd parameter occupy the odd bit positions in the result. Notice that these functions return 16, 32, or 64 bits based on byte, word, and double-word parameter values.

```
procedure bits.nibbles32( d:dword ); @returns( "edx:eax" );
procedure bits.nibbles16( w:word ); @returns( "eax" );
procedure bits.nibbles8( b:byte ); @returns( "ax" );
```

These routines extract each nibble from the parameter and place those nibbles into individual bytes. The bits.nibbles8 function extracts the two nibbles from the b parameter and places the L.O. nibble in AL and the H.O. nibble in AH. The bits.nibbles16 function extracts the four nibbles in w and places them in each of the 4 bytes of EAX. You can use the bswap or rox instructions to gain access to the nibbles in the H.O. word of EAX. The bits.nibbles32 function extracts the eight nibbles in EAX and distributes them through the 8 bytes in EDX:EAX. Nibble 0 winds up in AL and nibble 7 winds up in the H.O. byte of EDX. Again, you can use bswap or the rotate instructions to access the upper bytes of EAX and EDX.

## 10.14 For More Information

The electronic edition of *The Art of Assembly Language* at *http://webster.cs.ucr.edu/* and *http://www.artofasm.com/* contains some additional information you may find useful when developing bit-manipulation algorithms. In particular, the chapter on digital design discusses boolean algebra, a subject that you will find essential when working with bits. The HLA Standard Library reference manual contains more information about the HLA Standard Library bit-manipulation routines. See that documentation on the website for more information about those functions. As noted in the section on bit counting, the AMD Athlon optimization guide contains some useful algorithms for bit-based computations. Finally, to learn more about bit searching algorithms, you should pick up a textbook on data structures and algorithms and study the section on string-matching algorithms.

# 11

# THE STRING INSTRUCTIONS

A *string* is a collection of values stored in contiguous memory locations. Strings are usually arrays of bytes, words, or (on 80386 andlaterprocessors)doublewords.The80x86 microprocessor family supports several instructions specifically designed to cope with strings. This chapter explores some of the uses of these string instructions.

The 80x86 CPUs can process three types of strings: byte strings, word strings, and double-word strings. They can move strings, compare strings, search for a specific value within a string, initialize a string to a fixed value, and do other primitive operations on strings. The 80x86's string instructions are also useful for manipulating arrays, tables, and records. You can easily assign or compare such data structures using the string instructions. Using string instructions may speed up your array-manipulation code considerably.

# 11.1  The 80x86 String Instructions

All members of the 80x86 family support five different string instructions: movs*x*, cmps*x*, scas*x*, lods*x*, and stos*x*.[1] (*x* = b, w, or d for byte, word, or double word, respectively; this text will generally drop the *x* suffix when talking about these string instructions in a general sense.) They are the string primitives c which you can build most other string operations. How you use these five instructions is the topic of the sections that follow.

```
For MOVS:
        movsb();
        movsw();
        movsd();

For CMPS:
        cmpsb();
        cmpsw();
        cmpsd();

For SCAS:
        scasb();
        scasw();
        scasd();

For STOS:
        stosb();
        stosw();
        stosd();

For LODS:
        lodsb();
        lodsw();
        lodsd();
```

## 11.1.1  How the String Instructions Operate

The string instructions operate on blocks (contiguous linear arrays) of memor For example, the movs instruction moves a sequence of bytes from one mem ory location to another. The cmps instruction compares two blocks of memor The scas instruction scans a block of memory for a particular value. These string instructions often require three operands: a destination block addres a source block address, and (optionally) an element count. For example, whe using the movs instruction to copy a string, you need a source address, a des nation address, and a count (the number of string elements to move).

---

[1] The 80x86 processor support two additional string instructions, ins and outs, which input strings of data from an input port or output strings of data to an output port. We will not consider these instructions because they are privileged instructions, and you cannot execute them in a standard 32-bit OS application.

Unlike other instructions, which operate on memory, the string instructions don't have any explicit operands. The operands for the string instructions are as follows:

- ESI (source index) register
- EDI (destination index) register
- ECX (count) register
- AL/AX/EAX register
- The direction flag in the FLAGS register

For example, one variant of the movs (move string) instruction copies ECX elements from the source address specified by ESI to the destination address specified by EDI. Likewise, the cmps instruction compares the string pointed at by ESI, of length ECX, to the string pointed at by EDI.

Not all string instructions have source and destination memory operands (only movs and cmps support them). For example, the scas instruction (scan a string) compares the value in the accumulator (AL, AX, or EAX) to values in memory.

### 11.1.2   The rep/repe/repz and repnz/repne Prefixes

The string instructions, by themselves, do not operate on strings of data. The movs instruction, for example, will only copy a single byte, word, or double word. When the movs instruction executes, it ignores the value in the ECX register. The repeat prefixes tell the 80x86 to do a multibyte string operation. The syntax for the repeat prefix is as follows:

```
For MOVS:
     rep.movsb();
     rep.movsw();
     rep.movsd();

For CMPS:
     repe.cmpsb();      // Note: repz is a synonym for repe.
     repe.cmpsw();
     repe.cmpsd();

     repne.cmpsb();     // Note: repnz is a synonym for repne.
     repne.cmpsw();
     repne.cmpsd();

For SCAS:
     repe.scasb();      // Note: repz is a synonym for repe.
     repe.scasw();
     repe.scasd();
```

```
    repne.scasb();    // Note: repnz is a synonym for repne.
    repne.scasw();
    repne.scasd();

For STOS:
    rep.stosb();
    rep.stosw();
    rep.stosd();
```

You don't normally use the repeat prefixes with the lods instruction.

When specifying the repeat prefix before a string instruction, the strin[g] instruction repeats its operation ECX times.[2] Without the repeat prefix, the instruction operates only on a single element (byte, word, or double wor[d]).

You can use repeat prefixes to process entire strings with a single instr[uc]tion. You can use the string instructions, without the repeat prefix, as strin[g] primitive operations to synthesize more powerful string operations.

### 11.1.3   The Direction Flag

In addition to the ESI, EDI, ECX, and AL/AX/EAX registers, one other re[g]ister controls the operation of the 80x86's string instructions—the EFLAG[S] register. Specifically, the *direction flag* in the flags register controls how the CPU processes strings.

If the direction flag is clear, the CPU increments ESI and EDI after op[er]ating on each string element. For example, executing movs will move the byt[e,] word, or double word at ESI to EDI and will then increment ESI and EDI b[y] 1, 2, or 4. When specifying the rep prefix before this instruction, the CPU increments ESI and EDI for each element in the string (the count in ECX specifies the number of elements). At completion, the ESI and EDI registe[rs] will be pointing at the first item beyond the strings.

If the direction flag is set, the 80x86 decrements ESI and EDI after it processes each string element (again, ECX specifies the number of string elements). After a repeated string operation, the ESI and EDI registers will b[e] pointing at the first byte, word, or double word before the strings if the direction flag was set.

You can change the direction flag's value using the cld (clear direction flag) and std (set direction flag) instructions. When using these instruction[s] inside a procedure, keep in mind that they modify the machine state. There[e]fore, you may need to save the direction flag during the execution of that procedure. The following example exhibits the kinds of problems you mig[ht] encounter.

---

[2] Except for the cmps instruction, which repeats *at most* the number of times specified in the EC[X] register.

```
procedure Str2; @nodisplay;
begin Str2;

        std();
    << Do some string operations. >>
            .
            .
            .

end Str2;
            .
            .
            .
        cld();
    << Do some operations. >>
        Str2();
    << Do some string operations requiring D=0. >>
```

This code will not work properly. The calling code assumes that the direction flag is clear after Str2 returns. However, this isn't true. Therefore, the string operations executed after the call to Str2 will not function properly.

There are a couple of ways to handle this problem. The first, and probably the most obvious, is always to insert the cld or std instructions immediately before executing a sequence of one or more string instructions. This ensures that the direction flag is always set properly for your code. The other alternative is to save and restore the direction flag using the pushfd and popfd instructions. Using these two techniques, the code above would look like the following examples.

Always issuing cld or std before a string instruction:

```
procedure Str2; @nodisplay;
begin Str2;

        std();
    << Do some string operations. >>
            .
            .
            .

end Str2;
            .
            .
            .
        cld();
    << Do some operations. >>
        Str2();
        cld();
    << Do some string operations requiring D=0. >>
```

Saving and restoring the flags register:

```
procedure Str2; @nodisplay;
begin Str2;

        pushfd();
        std();
    << Do some string operations. >>
            .

            .

            .
        popfd();
end Str2;
            .

            .

        cld();
    << Do some operations. >>
        Str2();
    << Do some string operations requiring D=0. >>
```

If you use the pushfd and popfd instructions to save and restore the flags register, keep in mind that you're saving and restoring all the flags. This make it somewhat difficult to return information in other flag bits. For example, it a bit of work to return an error condition in the carry flag if you use pushfd an popfd to preserve the direction flag in the procedure.

A third solution is to always ensure that the direction flag is clear excep for the execution of a particular sequence that requires it to be set. For example, many library calls and some operating systems always assume tha the direction flag is clear when you call them. Most standard C library function work this way, for example. You can follow this convention by always assumin that the direction flag is clear, and then make sure you clear it immediately after a sequence that requires the use of std.

### 11.1.4   The movs Instruction

The movs instruction uses the following syntax:

```
movsb()
movsw()
movsd()
rep.movsb()
rep.movsw()
rep.movsd()
```

The movsb (move string, bytes) instruction fetches the byte at address ESI, stores it at address EDI, and then increments or decrements the ESI and EDI registers by 1. If the rep prefix is present, the CPU checks ECX to see if it contains 0. If not, then it moves the byte from ESI to EDI and decrements the ECX register. This process repeats until ECX becomes 0. If ECX contains 0 upon initial execution, the movs instruction will not copy any data bytes.

The movsw (move string, words) instruction fetches the word at address ESI, stores it at address EDI, and then increments or decrements ESI and EDI by 2. If there is a rep prefix, then the CPU repeats this procedure ECX times.

The movsd instruction operates in a similar fashion on double words. It increments or decrements ESI and EDI by 4 after each data movement.

When you use the rep prefix, the movsb instruction moves the number of bytes you specify in the ECX register. The following code segment copies 384 bytes from CharArray1 to CharArray2:

```
CharArray1: byte[ 384 ];
CharArray2: byte[ 384 ];
    .
    .
    .
    cld();
    lea( esi, CharArray1 );
    lea( edi, CharArray2 );
    mov( 384, ecx );
    rep.movsb();
```

If you substitute movsw for movsb, then the preceding code will move 384 words (768 bytes) rather than 384 bytes:

```
WordArray1: word[ 384 ];
WordArray2: word[ 384 ];
    .
    .
    .
    cld();
    lea( esi, WordArray1 );
    lea( edi, WordArray2 );
    mov( 384, ecx );
    rep.movsw();
```

Remember, the ECX register contains the element count, not the byte count. When using the movsw instruction, the CPU moves the number of words specified in the ECX register. Similarly, movsd moves the number of double words you specify in the ECX register, not the number of bytes.

If you've set the direction flag before executing a movsb/movsw/movsd instruction, the CPU decrements the ESI and EDI registers after moving each string element. This means that the ESI and EDI registers must point at the last element of their respective strings before executing a movsb, movsw, or mov instruction. For example:

```
CharArray1: byte[ 384 ];
CharArray2: byte[ 384 ];
      .
      .
      .
    cld();
    lea( esi, CharArray1[383] );
    lea( edi, CharArray2[383] );
    mov( 384, ecx );
    rep.movsb();
```

Although there are times when processing a string from tail to head is useful (see the cmps description in Section 11.1.5), generally you'll process strings in the forward direction because that's more straightforward. The is one class of string operations where being able to process strings in both directions is absolutely mandatory: moving strings when the source and des nation blocks overlap. Consider what happens in the following code:

```
CharArray1: byte;
CharArray2: byte[ 384 ];
      .
      .
      .
    cld();
    lea( esi, CharArray1 );
    lea( edi, CharArray2 );
    mov( 384, ecx );
    rep.movsb();
```

This sequence of instructions treats CharArray1 and CharArray2 as a pair 384-byte strings. However, the last 383 bytes in the CharArray1 array overlap th first 383 bytes in the CharArray2 array. Let's trace the operation of this code byte by byte.

When the CPU executes the movsb instruction, it copies the byte at ESI (CharArray1) to the byte pointed at by EDI (CharArray2). Then it increments ESI and EDI, decrements ECX by 1, and repeats this process. Now the ESI r ister points at CharArray1+1 (which is the address of CharArray2), and the ED register points at CharArray2+1. The movsb instruction copies the byte pointed by ESI to the byte pointed at by EDI. However, this is the byte originally copie from location CharArray1. So the movsb instruction copies the value originally i location CharArray1 to both locations CharArray2 and CharArray2+1. Again, the CP increments ESI and EDI, decrements ECX, and repeats this operation. Now th movsb instruction copies the byte from location CharArray1+2 (CharArray2+1) to location CharArray2+2. But once again, this is the value that originally appeare in location CharArray1. Each repetition of the loop copies the next element in CharArray1[0] to the next available location in the CharArray2 array. Pictorially, it looks something like Figure 11-1.

The end result is that the movsb instruction replicates X throughout the string. The movsb instruction copies the source operand into the memory location, which will become the source operand for the very next move operation, which causes the replication.

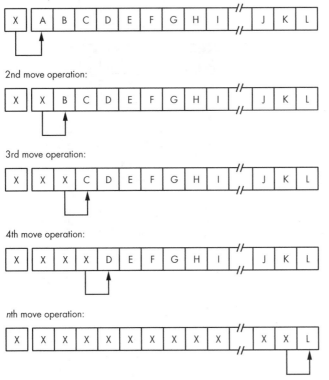

Figure 11-1: Copying data between two overlapping arrays (forward direction)

If you really want to move one array into another when they overlap like this, you should move each element of the source string to the destination string starting at the end of the two strings, as shown in Figure 11-2.

Setting the direction flag and pointing ESI and EDI at the end of the strings will allow you to (correctly) move one string to another when the two strings overlap and the source string begins at a lower address than the destination string. If the two strings overlap and the source string begins at a higher address than the destination string, then clear the direction flag and point ESI and EDI at the beginning of the two strings.

If the two strings do not overlap, then you can use either technique to move the strings around in memory. Generally, operating with the direction flag clear is the easiest, so that makes the most sense.

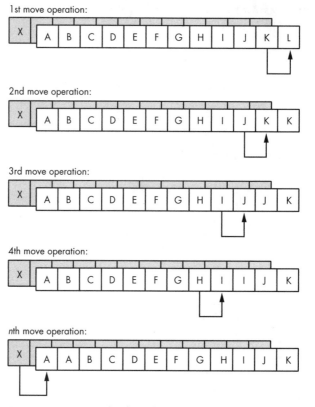

*Figure 11-2: Using a backward copy to copy data in overlapping arrays*

You shouldn't use the movsx instruction to fill an array with a single byte, word, or double-word value. Another string instruction, stos, is much better for this purpose. However, for arrays whose elements are 1, 2, or 4 bytes, you can use the movs instruction to initialize the entire array to the content of the first element.

The movs instruction is sometimes more efficient when copying double words than it is copying bytes or words. On some systems, it typically takes the same amount of time to copy a byte using movsb as it does to copy a double word using movsd. Therefore, if you are moving a large number of bytes from one array to another, the copy operation will be faster if you can use the movsd instruction rather than the movsb instruction. If the number of bytes you wish to move is an even multiple of 4, this is a trivial change; just divide the number of bytes to copy by 4, load this value into ECX, and then use the movsb instruction. If the number of bytes is not evenly divisible by 4, then you can use the movsd instruction to copy all but the last 1, 2, or 3 bytes of the array (that is, the remainder after you divide the byte count by 4). For example, if you want to efficiently move 4,099 bytes, you can do so with the following instruction sequence.

```
lea( esi, Source );
lea( edi, Destination );
mov( 1024, ecx );     // Copy 1024 dwords = 4096 bytes.
rep.movsd();
movsw();              // Copy bytes 4097 and 4098.
movsb();              // Copy the last byte.
```

Using this technique to copy data never requires more than three movsx instructions because you can copy 1, 2, or 3 bytes with no more than two movsb and movsw instructions. The scheme above is most efficient if the two arrays are aligned on double-word boundaries. If not, you might want to move the movsb or movsw instruction (or both) before the movsd so that the movsd instruction works with double-word-aligned data.

If you do not know the size of the block you are copying until the program executes, you can still use code like the following to improve the performance of a block move of bytes:

```
lea( esi, Source );
lea( edi, Dest );
mov( Length, ecx );
shr( 2, ecx );      // Divide by 4.
if( @nz ) then      // Only execute movsd if 4 or more bytes.

    rep.movsd();    // Copy the dwords.

endif;
mov( Length, ecx );
and( %11, ecx );    // Compute (Length mod 4).
if( @nz ) then      // Only execute movsb if #bytes/4 <> 0.

    rep.movsb();    // Copy the remaining 1, 2, or 3 bytes.

endif;
```

On many computer systems, the movsd instruction provides about the fastest way to copy bulk data from one location to another. While there are, arguably, faster ways to copy the data on certain CPUs, ultimately the memory bus performance is the limiting factor, and the CPUs are generally much faster than the memory bus. Therefore, unless you have a special system, writing fancy code to improve memory-to-memory transfers is probably a waste of time. Also note that Intel has improved the performance of the movsx instructions on later processors so that movsb operates almost as efficiently as movsw and movsd when copying the same number of bytes. Therefore, when working on a later 80x86 processor, it may be more efficient to simply use movsb to copy the specified number of bytes rather than go through all the complexity outlined above. The bottom line is this: If the speed of a block move matters to you, try it several different ways and pick the fastest (or the simplest, if they all run the same speed, which is likely).

## 11.1.5　The cmps Instruction

The cmps instruction compares two strings. The CPU compares the string referenced by EDI to the string pointed at by ESI. ECX contains the length of the two strings (when using the repe or repne prefix). Like the movs instruction, HLA allows several different forms of this instruction:

```
cmpsb();
cmpsw();
cmpsd();

repe.cmpsb();
repe.cmpsw();
repe.cmpsd();

repne.cmpsb();
repne.cmpsw();
repne.cmpsd();
```

As for the movs instruction, you specify the actual operand addresses in the ESI and EDI registers.

Without a repeat prefix, the cmps instruction subtracts the value at location EDI from the value at ESI and updates the flags. Other than updating the flags, the CPU doesn't use the difference produced by this subtraction. After comparing the two locations, cmps increments or decrements the ESI and EDI registers by 1, 2, or 4 (for cmpsb/cmpsw/cmpsd, respectively). cmps increments the ESI and EDI registers if the direction flag is clear and decrements them otherwise.

Of course, you will not tap the real power of the cmps instruction using to compare single bytes, words, or double words in memory. This instruction shines when you use it to compare whole strings. With cmps, you can compare consecutive elements in a string until you find a match or until consecutive elements do not match.

To compare two strings to see if they are equal or not equal, you must compare corresponding elements in a string until they don't match. Consider the following strings:

```
"String1"
"String1"
```

The only way to determine that these two strings are equal is to compare each character in the first string to the corresponding character in the second. After all, the second string could have been String2, which definitely is not equal to String1. Once you encounter a character in the destination string that does not equal the corresponding character in the source string, the comparison can stop. You needn't compare any other characters in the two strings.

The repe prefix accomplishes this operation. It will compare successive elements in a string as long as they are equal and ECX is greater than 0. We could compare the two strings above using the following 80x86 assembly language code:

```
cld();
mov( AdrsString1, esi );
mov( AdrsString2, edi );
mov( 7, ecx );
repe.cmpsb();
```

After the execution of the cmpsb instruction, you can test the flags using the standard (unsigned) conditional jump instructions. This lets you check for equality, inequality, less than, greater than, and so on.

Character strings are usually compared using *lexicographical ordering*. In lexicographical ordering, the least significant element of a string carries the most weight. This is in direct contrast to standard integer comparisons, where the most significant portion of the number carries the most weight. Furthermore, the length of a string affects the comparison only if the two strings are identical up to the length of the shorter string. For example, Zebra is less than Zebras because it is the shorter of the two strings; however, Zebra is greater than AAAAAAAAAAH! even though Zebra is shorter. Lexicographical comparisons compare corresponding elements until encountering a character that doesn't match or until encountering the end of the shorter string. If a pair of corresponding characters do not match, then this algorithm compares the two strings based on that single character. If the two strings match up to the length of the shorter string, we must compare their length. The two strings are equal if and only if their lengths are equal and each corresponding pair of characters in the two strings are identical. Lexicographical ordering is the standard alphabetical ordering you've grown up with.

For character strings, use the cmps instruction in the following manner:

- The direction flag must be cleared before comparing the strings.

- Use the cmpsb instruction to compare the strings on a byte-by-byte basis. Even if the strings contain an even number of characters, you cannot use the cmpsw or cmpsd instructions. They do not compare strings in lexicographical order.

- You must load the ECX register with the length of the smaller string.

- Use the repe prefix.

- The ESI and EDI registers must point at the very first character in the two strings you want to compare.

After the execution of the cmps instruction, if the two strings were equal, their lengths must be compared in order to finish the comparison. The following code compares a couple of character strings:

```
mov( AdrsStr1, esi );
mov( AdrsStr2, edi );
```

```
    mov( LengthSrc, ecx );
    if( ecx > LengthDest ) then    // Put the length of the
                                    // shorter string in ecx.
        mov( LengthDest, ecx );

    endif;
    repe.cmpsb();
    if( @z ) then                   // If equal to the length of the
                                    // shorter string, cmp lengths.
        mov( LengthSrc, ecx );
        cmp( ecx, LengthDest );

    endif;
```

If you're using bytes to hold the string lengths, you should adjust this code appropriately (that is, use a movzx instruction to load the lengths into ECX). HLA strings use a double word to hold the current length value, so this isn't an issue when using HLA strings.

You can also use the cmps instruction to compare multiword integer values (that is, extended-precision integer values). Because of the amount of setup required for a string comparison, this isn't practical for integer values less than six or eight double words in length, but for large integer values, it's an excellent way to compare such values. Unlike for character strings, we cannot compare integer strings using lexicographical ordering. When comparing strings, we compare the characters from the least significant byte to the most significant byte. When comparing integers, we must compare the values from the most significant byte (or word/double word) down to the least significant byte, word, or double word. So, to compare two 32-byte (256-bit) integer values, use the following code on the 80x86:

```
    std();
    lea( esi, SourceInteger[28] );
    lea( edi, DestInteger[28] );
    mov( 8, ecx );
    rep.cmpsd();
```

This code compares the integers from their most significant dword down to the least significant dword. The cmpsd instruction finishes when the two values are unequal or upon decrementing ECX to 0 (implying that the two values are equal). Once again, the flags provide the result of the comparison.

The repne prefix will instruct the cmps instruction to compare successive string elements as long as they do not match. The 80x86 flags are of little use after the execution of this instruction. Either the ECX register is 0 (in which case the two strings are totally different), or it contains the number of elements compared in the two strings until a match is found. While this form of the cmps instruction isn't particularly useful for comparing strings, it is useful for locating the first pair of matching items in a couple of byte, word, or double-word arrays. In general, though, you'll rarely use the repne prefix with cmps.

One last thing to keep in mind with using the cmps instruction: The value in the ECX register determines the number of elements to process, not the number of bytes. Therefore, when using cmpsw, ECX specifies the number of words to compare. Likewise, for cmpsd, ECX contains the number of double words to process.

## 11.1.6   The scas Instruction

The cmps instruction compares two strings against each other. You do not use it to search for a particular element within a string. For example, you could not use the cmps instruction to quickly scan for a 0 throughout some other string. You can use the scas (scan string) instruction for this task.

Unlike the movs and cmps instructions, the scas instruction requires only a destination string (pointed at by EDI) rather than both a source and destination string. The source operand is the value in the AL (scasb), AX (scasw), or EAX (scasd) register. The scas instruction compares the value in the accumulator (AL, AX, or EAX) against the value pointed at by EDI and then increments (or decrements) EDI by 1, 2, or 4. The CPU sets the flags according to the result of the comparison. While this might be useful on occasion, scas is a lot more useful when using the repe and repne prefixes.

With the repe prefix (repeat while equal), scas scans the string searching for an element that does not match the value in the accumulator. When using the repne prefix (repeat while not equal), scas scans the string, searching for the first string element that is equal to the value in the accumulator.

You're probably wondering, "Why do these prefixes do exactly the opposite of what they ought to do?" The preceding paragraphs haven't quite phrased the operation of the scas instruction properly. When using the repe prefix with scas, the 80x86 scans through the string while the value in the accumulator is equal to the string operand. This is equivalent to searching through the string for the first element that does not match the value in the accumulator. The scas instruction with repne scans through the string while the accumulator is not equal to the string operand. Of course, this form searches for the first value in the string that matches the value in the accumulator register. The scas instructions take the following forms:

```
scasb()
scasw()
scasd()

repe.scasb()
repe.scasw()
repe.scasd()

repne.scasb()
repne.scasw()
repne.scasd()
```

Like the cmps and movs instructions, the value in the ECX register specifies the number of elements, not bytes, to process when using a repeat prefix.

## 11.1.7  The stos Instruction

The stos instruction stores the value in the accumulator at the location spe[cified] by EDI. After storing the value, the CPU increments or decrements ED[I] depending on the state of the direction flag. Although the stos instruction has many uses, its primary use is to initialize arrays and strings to a constan[t] value. For example, if you have a 256-byte array you want to clear out with zeros, use the following code:

```
cld();
lea( edi, DestArray );
mov( 64, ecx );          // 64 double words = 256 bytes.
xor( eax, eax );         // Zero out eax.
rep.stosd();
```

This code writes 64 double words rather than 256 bytes because a singl[e] stosd operation is faster than four stosb operations.

The stos instructions take six forms. They are:

```
stosb();
stosw();
stosd();

rep.stosb();
rep.stosw();
rep.stosd();
```

The stosb instruction stores the value in the AL register into the spec[i]fied memory location(s), the stosw instruction stores the AX register into th[e] specified memory location(s), and the stosd instruction stores EAX into the specified location(s).

Keep in mind that the stos instruction is useful only for initializing a byt[e,] word, or double-word array to a constant value. If you need to initialize an arr[ay] with elements that have different values, you cannot use the stos instruction.

## 11.1.8  The lods Instruction

The lods instruction is unique among the string instructions. You will probab[ly] never use a repeat prefix with this instruction. The lods instruction copies th[e] byte, word, or double word pointed at by ESI into the AL, AX, or EAX registe[r,] after which it increments or decrements the ESI register by 1, 2, or 4. Repe[at]ing this instruction via the repeat prefix would serve almost no purpose whatsoever because the accumulator register will be overwritten each time the lods instruction repeats. At the end of the repeat operation, the accum[u]lator will contain the last value read from memory.

Instead, use the lods instruction to fetch bytes (lodsb), words (lodsw), o[r] double words (lodsd) from memory for further processing. By using the lo[ds] and stos instructions, you can synthesize powerful string operations.

Like the stos instruction, the lods instructions take six forms:

```
lodsb();
lodsw();
lodsd();

rep.lodsb();
rep.lodsw();
rep.lodsd();
```

As mentioned earlier, you'll rarely, if ever, use the rep prefixes with these instructions.[3] The 80x86 increments or decrements ESI by 1, 2, or 4 depending on the direction flag and whether you're using the lodsb, lodsw, or lodsd instruction.

## 11.1.9  Building Complex String Functions from lods and stos

The 80x86 supports only five different string instructions: movs, cmps, scas, lods, and stos.[4] These certainly aren't the only string operations you'll ever want to use. However, you can use the lods and stos instructions to easily generate any particular string operation you like. For example, suppose you wanted a string operation that converts all the uppercase characters in a string to lowercase. You could use the following code:

```
mov( StringAddress, esi );   // Load string address into esi.
mov( esi, edi );             // Also point edi here.
mov( (type str.strRec [esi]).length, ecx );

repeat

    lodsb();                 // Get the next character in the string.
    if( al in 'A'..'Z' ) then

        or( $20, al );       // Convert uppercase to lowercase.

    endif;
    stosb();                 // Store converted char into string.
    dec( ecx );

until( @z );                 // Zero flag is set when ecx is 0.
```

Because the lods and stos instructions use the accumulator as an intermediary location, you can use any accumulator operation to quickly manipulate string elements.

---

[3] They appear here simply because they are allowed. They're not very useful, but they are allowed. About the only use for this form of the instruction is to "touch" items in the cache so they are preloaded into the cache. However, there are better ways to accomplish this.

[4] Not counting ins and outs, which we're ignoring here.

## 11.2  Performance of the 80x86 String Instructions

In the early 80x86 processors, the string instructions provided the most efficient way to manipulate strings and blocks of data. However, these instructions are not part of Intel's RISC Core instruction set, and as such, they can be slower than doing the same operations using discrete instructions. Intel has optimized the movs instruction on later processors so that it operates about as rapidly as possible, but the other string instructions can be fairly slow. As always, it's a good idea to implement performance-critical algorithms using different algorithms (with and without the string instructions) and compare their performance to determine which solution to use.

Keep in mind that the string instructions run at different speeds relative to other instructions depending on which processor you're using. Therefore, it's a good idea to try your experiments on the processors where you expect your code to run. Note that on most processors, the movs instruction is faster than the corresponding discrete instructions. Intel has worked hard to keep movs optimized because so much performance-critical code uses it.

Although the string instructions can be slower than discrete instructions, there is no question that the string instructions are generally more compact than the discrete code that achieves the same result.

## 11.3  For More Information

The HLA Standard Library contains hundreds of string and pattern-matching functions you may find useful. All of this appears in source form at *http://www.artofasm.com/* or *http://webster.cs.ucr.edu/*; you should check out some of that source code if you want to see some examples of string instructions in action. Note also that some of the HLA Standard Library routines use discrete instructions to implement certain high-performance algorithms. You may want to look at that code as an example of such code. The 16-bit edition of this book (which appears on the website) discusses the implementation of several character-string functions using the 80x86 string instructions. Check out that edition for additional examples (those examples do not appear here because of the performance problems with the string instructions). Finally, for general information about string functions, check out the HLA Standard Library reference manual. It explains the operation of the string and pattern-matching functions found in the HLA Standard Library.

# 12

## CLASSES AND OBJECTS

Many modern high-level languages support the notion of classes and objects. C++ (an object-oriented version of C), Java, and Delphi(anobject-orientedversionofPascal)are good examples. Of course, these high-level language compilers translate their source code into low-level machine code, so it should be pretty obvious that some mechanism exists in machine code for implementing classes and objects.

Although it has always been possible to implement classes and objects in machine code, most assemblers provide poor support for writing object-oriented assembly language programs. HLA does not suffer from this drawback because it provides good support for writing object-oriented assembly language programs. This chapter discusses the general principles behind object-oriented programming (OOP) and how HLA supports OOP.

## 12.1  General Principles

Before discussing the mechanisms behind OOP, it is probably a good idea to take a step back and explore the benefits of using OOP (especially in assembly language programs). Most texts that describe the benefits of OOP will use buzzwords like *code reuse, abstract data types, improved development efficiency,* and so on. While all of these features are nice and are good attributes for a programming paradigm, a good software engineer would question the use of assembly language in an environment where "improved development efficiency" is an important goal. After all, you can probably obtain far better efficiency by using a high-level language (even in a non-OOP fashion) than you can by using objects in assembly language. If the purported features of OOP don't seem to apply to assembly language programming, then why bother using OOP in assembly? This section will explore some of those reasons.

The first thing you should realize is that the use of assembly language does not negate the aforementioned OOP benefits. OOP in assembly language does promote code reuse. It provides a good method for implementing abstract data types, and it can improve development efficiency *in assembly language.* In other words, if you're dead set on using assembly language, there are benefits to using OOP.

To understand one of the principle benefits of OOP, consider the concept of a global variable. Most programming texts strongly recommend against the use of global variables in a program (as does this text). Interprocedural communication through global variables is dangerous because it is difficult to keep track of all the possible places in a large program that modify a given global object. Worse, it is very easy when making enhancements to accidentally reuse a global object for something other than its intended purpose; this tends to introduce defects into the system.

Despite the well-understood problems with global variables, the semantics of global objects (extended lifetimes and accessibility from different procedures) are absolutely necessary in various situations. Objects solve this problem by letting the programmer determine the lifetime of an object[1] as well as allowing access to data fields from different procedures. Objects have several advantages over simple global variables insofar as objects can control access to their data fields (making it difficult for procedures to accidentally access the data), and you can also create multiple instances of an object, allowing separate sections of your program to use their own unique "global" object without interference from other sections.

Of course, objects have many other valuable attributes. One could write several volumes on the benefits of objects and OOP; this single chapter cannot do the subject justice. This chapter presents objects with an eye toward using them in HLA/assembly programs. However, if you are new to OOP or wish more information about the object-oriented paradigm, you should consult other texts on this subject.

---

[1] Lifetime means the time during which the system allocates memory for an object.

An important use for classes and objects is to create *abstract data types (ADTs)*. An abstract data type is a collection of data objects and the functions (which we'll call *methods*) that operate on the data. In a pure abstract data type, the ADT's methods are the only code that has access to the data fields of the ADT; external code may access the data only by using function calls to get or set data field values (these are the ADT's *accessor* methods). In real life, for efficiency reasons, most languages that support ADTs allow at least limited access to the data fields of an ADT by external code.

Assembly language is not a language most people associate with ADTs. Nevertheless, HLA provides several features to allow the creation of rudimentary ADTs. While some might argue that HLA's facilities are not as complete as those in a language such as C++ or Java, keep in mind that these differences exist because HLA is an assembly language.

True ADTs should support *information hiding*. This means that the ADT does not allow the user of an ADT access to internal data structures and routines that manipulate those structures. In essence, information hiding restricts ADT access to the ADT's accessor methods. Assembly language, of course, provides very few restrictions. If you are dead set on accessing an object directly, there is very little HLA can do to prevent you from doing this. However, HLA has some facilities that will provide a limited form of information hiding. Combining these with some care on your part, you will be able to enjoy many of the benefits of information hiding within your programs.

The primary facilities HLA provides to support information hiding are separate compilation, linkable modules, and the #include/#includeonce directives. For our purposes, an abstract data type definition will consist of two sections: an *interface* section and an *implementation* section.

The interface section contains the definitions that must be visible to the application program. In general, it should not contain any specific information that would allow the application program to violate the information-hiding principle, but this is often impossible given the nature of assembly language. Nevertheless, you should attempt to reveal only what is absolutely necessary within the interface section.

The implementation section contains the code, data structures, and so on to actually implement the ADT. While some of the methods and data types appearing in the implementation section may be public (by virtue of appearance within the interface section), many of the subroutines, data items, and so on will be private to the implementation code. The implementation section is where you hide all the details from the application program.

If you wish to modify the abstract data type at some point in the future, you will only have to change the interface and implementation sections. Unless you delete some previously visible object that the applications use, there will be no need to modify the applications at all.

Although you could place the interface and implementation sections directly in an application program, this would not promote information hiding or maintainability, especially if you have to include the code in several different applications. The best approach is to place the implementation section in an include file that any interested application reads using the HLA #include directive and to place the implementation section in a separate module that you link with your applications.

The include file would contain external directives, any necessary macros and other definitions you want made public. It generally would not contain 80x86 code except, perhaps, in some macros. When an application wants to make use of an ADT, it would include this file.

The separate assembly file containing the implementation section would contain all the procedures, functions, data objects, and so on to actually implement the ADT. Those names that you want to be public should appear in the interface include file and have the external attribute. You should also include the interface include file in the implementation file so you do not have to maintain two sets of external directives.

One problem with using procedures for data access methods is the fact that many accessor methods are especially trivial (e.g., just a mov instruction) and the overhead of the call and return instructions is expensive for such trivial operations. For example, suppose you have an ADT whose data object is a structure, but you do not want to make the field names visible to the application and you really do not want to allow the application to access the fields of the data structure directly (because the data structure may change in the future). The normal way to handle this is to supply a GetField method that returns the value of the desired field. However, as pointed out above, this can be very slow. An alternative for simple access methods is to use a macro to emit the code to access the desired field. Although code to directly access the data object appears in the application program (via macro expansion), a recompile will automatically update it if you ever change the macro in the interface section.

Although it is quite possible to create ADTs using nothing more than separate compilation and, perhaps, records, HLA does provide a better solution: the class. Read on to find out about HLA's support for classes and objects as well as how to use these to create ADTs.

## 12.2  Classes in HLA

Fundamentally, a *class* is a record declaration that allows the definition of non-data fields (e.g., procedures, constants, and macros). The inclusion of other objects in the class definition dramatically expands the capabilities of a class. For example, with a class it is now possible to easily define an ADT because classes may include data and methods (procedures) that operate on that data.

The principle way to create an abstract data type in HLA is to declare a class data type. Classes in HLA always appear in the type section and use the following syntax:

```
classname : class

        << Class declaration section >>

    endclass;
```

The class declaration section is very similar to the local declaration section for a procedure insofar as it allows const, val, var, storage, readonly, static, and proc variable declaration sections. Classes also let you define macros and specify procedure, iterator,[2] and *method* prototypes (method declarations are legal only in classes). Conspicuously absent from this list is the type declaration section. You cannot declare new types within a class.

A *method* is a special type of procedure that appears only within a class. A little later you will see the difference between procedures and methods; for now you can treat them as being the same. Other than a few subtle details regarding class initialization and the use of pointers to classes, their semantics are identical.[3] Generally, if you don't know whether to use a procedure or method in a class, the safest bet is to use a method.

You do not place procedure/iterator/method code within a class. Instead you simply supply *prototypes* for these routines. A routine prototype consists of the procedure, iterator, or method reserved word, the routine name, any parameters, and a couple of optional procedure attributes (@use, @returns, and external). The actual routine definition (the body of the routine and any local declarations it needs) appears outside the class.

The following example demonstrates a typical class declaration appearing in the type section:

```
TYPE
    TypicalClass:  class

        Const
            TCconst := 5;

        Val
            TCval := 6;

        var
            TCvar : uns32; // Private field used only by TCproc.
```

---

[2] This text does not discuss iterators. See the HLA reference manual for details on this type of function.

[3] Note, however, that the difference between procedures and methods makes all the difference in the world to the object-oriented programming paradigm, hence the inclusion of methods in HLA's class definitions.

```
static
    TCstatic : int32;

procedure TCproc( u:uns32 ); @returns( "eax" );
iterator TCiter( i:int32 ); external;

method TCmethod( c:char );

endclass;
```

As you can see, classes are very similar to records in HLA. Indeed, you can think of a record as being a class that allows only var declarations. HLA implements classes in a fashion quite similar to records insofar as it allocates sequentia data fields in sequential memory locations. In fact, with only one minor excep tion, there is almost no difference between a record declaration and a class declaration that has only a var declaration section. Later you'll see exactly how HLA implements classes, but for now you can assume that HLA implements them the same as it does records, and you won't be too far off the mark

You can access the TCvar and TCstatic fields (in the class above) just like a record's fields. You access the const and val fields in a similar manner. If a variable of type TypicalClass has the name obj, you can access the fields of ob as follows:

```
mov ( obj.TCconst, eax );
mov( obj.TCval, ebx );
add( obj.TCvar, eax );
add( obj.TCstatic, ebx );
obj.TCproc( 20 );  // Calls the TCproc procedure in TypicalClass.
etc.
```

If an application program includes the class declaration above, it can create variables using the TypicalClass type and perform operations using the mentioned methods. Unfortunately, the application program can also acces the fields of the ADT with impunity. For example, if a program created a var able MyClass of type TypicalClass, then it could easily execute instructions like mov( MyClass.TCvar, eax ); even though this field might be private to the impl mentation section. Unfortunately, if you are going to allow an application to declare a variable of type TypicalClass, the field names will have to be visible While there are some tricks we could play with HLA's class definitions to hel hide the private fields, the best solution is to thoroughly comment the private fields and then exercise some restraint when accessing the fields of that class Specifically, this means that ADTs you create using HLA's classes cannot be "pure" ADTs because HLA allows direct access to the data fields. However, with a little discipline, you can simulate a pure ADT by simply electing not to access such fields outside the class's methods, procedures, and iterators.

Prototypes appearing in a class are effectively forward declarations. Like normal forward declarations, all procedures, iterators, and methods you defin in a class must have an actual implementation later in the code. Alternately you may attach the external option to the end of a procedure, iterator, or method declaration within a class to inform HLA that the actual code appears in a separate module. As a general rule, class declarations appear in header files and represent the interface section of an ADT. The procedure, iterator, and method bodies appear in the implementation section, which is usually a separate source file that you compile separately and link with the modules that use the class.

The following is an example of a sample class procedure implementation:

```
procedure TypicalClass.TCproc( u:uns32 ); @nodisplay;
    << Local declarations for this procedure >>
begin TCproc;

    << Code to implement whatever this procedure does >>

end TCProc;
```

There are several differences between a standard procedure declaration and a class procedure declaration. First, and most obvious, the procedure name includes the class name (e.g., `TypicalClass.TCproc`). This differentiates this class procedure definition from a regular procedure that just happens to have the name `TCproc`. Note, however, that you do not have to repeat the class name before the procedure name in the `begin` and `end` clauses of the procedure (this is similar to procedures you define in HLA namespaces).

A second difference between class procedures and nonclass procedures is not obvious. Some procedure attributes (`@use`, `external`, `@returns`, `@cdecl`, `@pascal`, and `@stdcall`) are legal only in the prototype declaration appearing within the class, while other attributes (`@noframe`, `@nodisplay`, `@noalignstack`, and `@align`) are legal only within the procedure definition and not within the class. Fortunately, HLA provides helpful error messages if you stick the option in the wrong place, so you don't have to memorize this rule.

If a class routine's prototype does not have the `external` option, the compilation unit (that is, the program or unit) containing the class declaration must also contain the routine's definition or HLA will generate an error at the end of the compilation. For small, local classes (that is, when you're embedding the class declaration and routine definitions in the same compilation unit) the convention is to place the class's procedure, iterator, and method definitions in the source file shortly after the class declaration. For larger systems (that is, when separately compiling a class's routines), the convention is to place the class declaration in a header file by itself and place all the procedure, iterator, and method definitions in a separate HLA unit and compile them by themselves.

# 12.3 Objects

Remember, a class definition is just a type. Therefore, when you declare a class type you haven't created a variable whose fields you can manipulate. An *object* is an *instance* of a class; that is, an object is a variable whose type is some class. You declare objects (i.e., class variables) the same way you declare other variables: in a var, static, or storage section.[4] Here is a pair of sample object declarations:

```
var
    T1: TypicalClass;
    T2: TypicalClass;
```

For a given class object, HLA allocates storage for each variable appearing in the var section of the class declaration. If you have two objects, T1 and T2, of type TypicalClass, then T1.TCvar is unique, as is T2.TCvar. This is the intuitive result (similar to record declarations); most data fields you define in a class will appear in the var declaration section of the class.

Static data objects (for example, those you declare in the static or storage sections of a class declaration) are not unique among the objects of that class; that is, HLA allocates only a single static variable that all variables of that class share. For example, consider the following (partial) class declaration and object declarations:

```
type
    sc: class

            var
                i:int32;

            static
                s:int32;
                .
                .
                .
    endclass;
var
    s1: sc;
    s2: sc;
```

In this example, s1.i and s2.i are different variables. However, s1.s and s2.s are aliases of one another. Therefore, an instruction like mov(5, s1.s) also stores 5 into s2.s. Generally you use static class variables to maintain information about the whole class, while you use class var objects to maintain information about the specific object. Because keeping track of class information is relatively rare, you will probably declare most class data fields in a var section.

You can also create dynamic instances of a class and refer to those dynamic objects via pointers. In fact, this is probably the most common form of object

---

[4] Technically, you could also declare an object in a readonly section, but HLA does not allow you to define class constants, so there is little utility in declaring class objects in the readonly section.

storage and access. The following code shows how to create pointers to objects and how you can dynamically allocate storage for an object:

```
var
     pSC: pointer to sc;
          .
          .
          .
     mem.alloc( @size( sc ) );
     mov( eax, pSC );
          .
          .
          .
     mov( pSC, ebx );
     mov( (type sc [ebx]).i, eax );
```

Note the use of type coercion to cast the pointer in EBX as type sc.

## 12.4  Inheritance

Inheritance is one of the most fundamental ideas behind object-oriented programming. The basic idea is that a class inherits, or copies, all the fields from some class and then possibly expands the number of fields in the new data type. For example, suppose you created a data type point that describes a point in the planar (two-dimensional) space. The class for this point might look like the following:

```
type
     point: class

          var
               x:int32;
               y:int32;

          method distance;

     endclass;
```

Suppose you want to create a point in 3D space rather than 2D space. You can easily build such a data type as follows:

```
type
     point3D: class inherits( point )

          var
               z:int32;

     endclass;
```

The inherits option on the class declaration tells HLA to insert the fields of point at the beginning of the class. In this case, point3D inherits the fields of point. HLA always places the inherited fields at the beginning of a class object. The reason for this will become clear a little later. If you have an instance of point3D, which you call P3, then the following 80x86 instructions are all legal:

```
mov( P3.x, eax );
add( P3.y, eax );
mov( eax, P3.z );
P3.distance();
```

Note that the p3.distance method invocation in this example calls the point.distance method. You do not have to write a separate distance method for the point3D class unless you really want to do so (see the next section for details). Just like the x and y fields, point3D objects inherit point's methods.

## 12.5 Overriding

*Overriding* is the process of replacing an existing method in an inherited class with one more suitable for the new class. In the point and point3D examples appearing in the previous section, the distance method (presumably) computes the distance from the origin to the specified point. For a point on a two-dimensional plane, you can compute the distance using the following function:

$$d = \sqrt{x^2 + y^2}$$

However, the distance for a point in 3D space is given by this equation:

$$d = \sqrt{x^2 + y^2 + z^2}$$

Clearly, if you call the distance function for point for a point3D object, you will get an incorrect answer. In the previous section, however, you saw that the P3 object calls the distance function inherited from the point class. Therefore, this would produce an incorrect result.

In this situation the point3D data type must override the distance method with one that computes the correct value. You cannot simply redefine the point3D class by adding a distance method prototype:

```
type
     point3D:    class inherits( point )

          var
               z:int32;
          method distance; // This doesn't work!
     endclass;
```

The problem with the `distance` method declaration above is that `point3D` already has a `distance` method—the one that it inherits from the `point` class. HLA will complain because it doesn't like two methods with the same name in a single class.

To solve this problem, we need some mechanism by which we can override the declaration of `point.distance` and replace it with a declaration for `point3D.distance`. To do this, you use the `override` keyword before the method declaration:

```
type
    point3D: class inherits( point )

        var
            z:int32;

        override method distance; // This will work!

    endclass;
```

The `override` prefix tells HLA to ignore the fact that `point3D` inherits a method named `distance` from the `point` class. Now, any call to the `distance` method via a `point3D` object will call the `point3D.distance` method rather than `point.distance`. Of course, once you override a method using the `override` prefix, you must supply the method in the implementation section of your code. For example:

```
method point3D.distance; @nodisplay;

    << Local declarations for the distance function >>

begin distance;

    << Code to implement the distance function >>

end distance;
```

## 12.6   Virtual Methods vs. Static Procedures

A little earlier, this chapter suggested that you could treat class methods and class procedures the same. There are, in fact, some major differences between the two (after all, why have methods if they're the same as procedures?). As it turns out, the differences between methods and procedures are crucial if you want to develop object-oriented programs. Methods provide the second feature necessary to support true polymorphism: virtual procedure calls.[5] A virtual procedure call is just a fancy name for an indirect procedure call (using a

---

[5] *Polymorphism* literally means "many-faced." In the context of object-oriented programming, polymorphism means that the same method name, for example, distance, refers to one of several different methods.

pointer associated with the object). The key benefit of virtual procedures is that the system automatically calls the right method when using pointers to generic objects.

Consider the following declarations using the point class from the previous sections:

```
var
    P2: point;
    P:  pointer to point;
```

Given the declarations above, the following assembly statements are all legal:

```
    mov( P2.x, eax );
    mov( P2.y, ecx );
    P2.distance();          // Calls point3D.distance.

    lea( ebx, P2 );         // Store address of P2 into P.
    mov( ebx, P );
    P.distance();           // Calls point.distance.
```

Note that HLA lets you call a method via a pointer to an object rather than directly via an object variable. This is a crucial feature of objects in HLA and a key to implementing *virtual method calls*.

The magic behind polymorphism and inheritance is that object pointer are *generic*. In general, when your program references data indirectly through a pointer, the value of the pointer should be the address of some value of th underlying data type associated with that pointer. For example, if you have pointer to a 16-bit unsigned integer, you wouldn't normally use that pointe to access a 32-bit signed integer value. Similarly, if you have a pointer to som record, you would not normally cast that pointer to some other record type and access the fields of that other type.[6] With pointers to class objects, however, we can lift this restriction a little. Pointers to objects may legally contai the address of the object's type *or the address of any object that inherits the fields* that type. Consider the following declarations that use the point and point3D types from the previous examples:

```
var
    P2: point;
    P3: point3D;
    p:  pointer to point;
        .
        .
        .
```

_____

[6] Of course, assembly language programmers break rules like this all the time. For now, let's assume we're playing by the rules and access the data using only the data type associated wit the pointer.

```
lea( ebx, P2 );
mov( ebx, p );
p.distance();          // Calls the point.distance method.
   .
   .
   .
lea( ebx, P3 );
mov( ebx, p );         // Yes, this is semantically legal.
p.distance();          // Surprise, this calls point3D.distance.
```

Because p is a pointer to a point object, it might seem intuitive for p.distance to call the point.distance method. However, methods are *polymorphic.* If you have a pointer to an object and you call a method associated with that object, the system will call the actual (overridden) method associated with the object, not the method specifically associated with the pointer's class type.

Class procedures behave differently than methods with respect to overridden procedures. When you call a class procedure indirectly through an object pointer, the system will always call the procedure associated with the underlying class. So had distance been a procedure rather than a method in the previous examples, the p.distance(); invocation would always call point.distance, even if p were pointing at a point3D object. Section 12.9 explains why methods and procedures are different.

## 12.7  Writing Class Methods and Procedures

For each class procedure and method prototype appearing in a class definition, there must be a corresponding procedure or method appearing within the program (for the sake of brevity, this section will use the term *routine* to mean procedure or method from this point forward). If the prototype does not contain the external option, then the code must appear in the same compilation unit as the class declaration. If the external option does follow the prototype, then the code may appear in the same compilation unit or a different compilation unit (as long as you link the resulting object file with the code containing the class declaration). Like external (non-class) procedures, if you fail to provide the code, the linker will complain when you attempt to create an executable file. To reduce the size of the following examples, they will all define their routines in the same source file as the class declaration.

HLA class routines must always follow the class declaration in a compilation unit. If you are compiling your routines in a separate unit, the class declarations must still precede the implementation of the routines from the class (usually via an #include file). If you haven't defined the class by the time you define a routine like point.distance, HLA doesn't know that point is a class and, therefore, doesn't know how to handle the routine's definition.

Consider the following declarations for a point2D class:

```
type
    point2D: class
        const
            UnitDistance: real32 := 1.0;

        var
            x: real32;
            y: real32;

        static
            LastDistance: real32;

        method distance
        (
            fromX: real32;
            fromY: real32
        ); @returns( "st0" );
        procedure InitLastDistance;

    endclass;
```

The distance function for this class should compute the distance from the object's point to (fromX, fromY). The following formula describes this computation:

$$d = \sqrt{(x - fromX)^2 + (y - fromY)^2}$$

A first pass at writing the distance method might produce the following code

```
method point2D.distance( fromX:real32; fromY:real32 ); @nodisplay;
begin distance;

        fld( x );           // Note: this doesn't work!
        fld( fromX );       // Compute (x-fromX)
        fsubp();
        fld( st0 );         // Duplicate value on TOS.
        fmulp();            // Compute square of difference.

        fld( y );           // This doesn't work either.
        fld( fromY );       // Compute (y-fromY)
        fsubp();
        fld( st0 );         // Compute the square of the difference.
        fmulp();
        faddp();
        fsqrt();

end distance;
```

This code probably looks like it should work to someone who is familiar with an object-oriented programming language like C++ or Delphi. However, as the comments indicate, the instructions that push the x and y variables onto the FPU stack don't work; HLA doesn't automatically define the symbols associated with the data fields of a class within that class's routines.

To learn how to access the data fields of a class within that class's routines, we need to back up a moment and discuss some very important implementation details concerning HLA's classes. To do this, consider the following variable declarations:

```
var
    Origin:     point2D;
    PtInSpace:  point2D;
```

Remember, whenever you create two objects like Origin and PtInSpace, HLA reserves storage for the x and y data fields for both of these objects. However, there is only one copy of the point2D.distance method in memory. Therefore, were you to call Origin.distance and PtInSpace.distance, the system would call the same routine for both method invocations. Once inside that method, one has to wonder what an instruction like fld( x ); would do. How does it associate x with Origin.x or PtInSpace.x? Worse still, how would this code differentiate between the data field x and a global object x? In HLA, the answer is, it doesn't. You do not specify the data field names within a class routine by simply using their names as though they were common variables.

To differentiate Origin.x from PtInSpace.x within class routines, HLA automatically passes a pointer to an object's data fields whenever you call a class routine. Therefore, you can reference the data fields indirectly off this pointer. HLA passes this object pointer in the ESI register. This is one of the few places where HLA-generated code will modify one of the 80x86 registers behind your back: *Anytime you call a class routine, HLA automatically loads the ESI register with the object's address.* Obviously, you cannot count on ESI's value being preserved across class routine calls, nor can you pass parameters to the class routine in the ESI register (though it is perfectly reasonable to specify @use esi; to allow HLA to use the ESI register when setting up other parameters). For class methods (but not procedures), HLA will also load the EDI register with the address of the classes' *virtual method table*. While the virtual method table address isn't as interesting as the object address, keep in mind that *HLA-generated code will overwrite any value in the EDI register when you call a class method or an iterator.* Again, "EDI" is a good choice for the @use operand for methods because HLA will wipe out the value in EDI anyway.

Upon entry into a class routine, ESI contains a pointer to the (nonstatic) data fields associated with the class. Therefore, to access fields like x and y (in our point2D example), you could use an address expression like the following:

```
(type point2D [esi]).x
```

Because you use ESI as the base address of the object's data fields, it's a good idea not to disturb ESI's value within the class routines (or, at least, preserve ESI's value across the code where you must use ESI for some other purpose). Note that within a method you do not have to preserve EDI (unless, for some reason, you need access to the virtual method table, which is unlikely).

Accessing the fields of a data object within a class's routines is such a common operation that HLA provides a shorthand notation for casting ESI as a pointer to the class object: this. Within a class in HLA, the reserved word this automatically expands to a string of the form (type *classname* [esi]), substituting, of course, the appropriate class name for *classname*. Using the this keyword, we can (correctly) rewrite the previous distance method as follows:

```
method point2D.distance( fromX:real32; fromY:real32 ); @nodisplay;
begin distance;

            fld( this.x );
            fld( fromX );      // Compute (x-fromX).
            fsubp();
            fld( st0 );        // Duplicate value on TOS.
            fmulp();           // Compute square of difference.

            fld( this.y );
            fld( fromY );      // Compute (y-fromY).
            fsubp();
            fld( st0 );        // Compute the square of the difference.
            fmulp();
            faddp();
            fsqrt();

end distance;
```

Don't forget that calling a class routine wipes out the value in the ESI register. This isn't obvious from the syntax of the routine's invocation. It is especially easy to forget this when calling some class routine from inside some other class routine; remember that if you do this, the internal call wipes out the value in ESI and on return from that call ESI no longer points at the original object. Always push and pop ESI (or otherwise preserve ESI's value) in this situation. For example:

```
            .
            .
            .
            fld( this.x );         // esi points at current object.
            .
            .
            .
```

```
        push( esi );              // Preserve esi across this method call.
        SomeObject.SomeMethod();
        pop( esi );
        .
        .
        .
        lea( ebx, this.x );       // esi points at original object here.
```

The this keyword provides access to the class variables you declare in the var section of a class. You can also use this to call other class routines associated with the current object. For example:

```
this.distance( 5.0, 6.0 );
```

To access class constants and static data fields, you generally do not use the this pointer. HLA associates constant and static data fields with the whole class, not a specific object (just like static fields in a class). To access these class members, use the class name in place of the object name. For example, to access the UnitDistance constant in the point2d class you could use a statement like the following:

```
fld( point2D.UnitDistance );
```

As another example, if you wanted to update the LastDistance field in the point2D class each time you computed a distance, you could rewrite the point2D.distance method as follows:

```
method point2D.distance( fromX:real32; fromY:real32 ); @nodisplay;
begin distance;

        fld( this.x );
        fld( fromX );         // Compute (x-fromX).
        fsubp();
        fld( st0 );           // Duplicate value on TOS.
        fmulp();              // Compute square of difference.

        fld( this.y );
        fld( fromY );         // Compute (y-fromY).
        fsubp();
        fld( st0 );           // Compute the square of the difference.
        fmulp();
        faddp();
        fsqrt();

        fst( point2D.LastDistance ); // Update shared (STATIC) field.

end distance;
```

The next section will explain why you use the class name when referring to constants and static objects but you use this to access var objects.

Class procedures are also static objects, so it is possible to call a class procedure by specifying the class name rather than an object name in the procedure invocation; for example, both of the following are legal:

```
Origin.InitLastDistance();
point2D.InitLastDistance();
```

There is, however, a subtle difference between these two class procedure calls. The first call above loads ESI with the address of the origin object prior to actually calling the InitLastDistance procedure. The second call, however, is a direct call to the class procedure without referencing an object; therefore, HLA doesn't know what object address to load into the ESI register. In this case, HLA loads NULL (0) into ESI prior to calling the InitLastDistance procedure. Because you can call class procedures in this manner, it's always a good idea to check the value in ESI within your class procedures to verify that HLA contains a valid object address. Checking the value in ESI is a good way to determine which calling mechanism is in use. Section 12.9 discusses constructors and object initialization; then you will see a good use for static procedures and calling those procedures directly (rather than through the use of an object).

## 12.8 Object Implementation

In a high-level object-oriented language like C++ or Delphi, it is quite possible to master the use of objects without really understanding how the machine implements them. One of the reasons for learning assembly language programming is to fully comprehend low-level implementation details so you can make educated decisions concerning the use of programming constructs like objects. Further, because assembly language allows you to poke around with data structures at a very low level, knowing how HLA implements objects can help you create certain algorithms that would not be possible without a detailed knowledge of object implementation. Therefore, this section and its corresponding subsections explain the low-level implementation details you will need to know in order to write object-oriented HLA programs.

HLA implements objects in a manner quite similar to records. In particular, HLA allocates storage for all var objects in a class in a sequential fashion, just like records. Indeed, if a class consists of only var data fields, the memory representation of that class is nearly identical to that of a corresponding record declaration. Consider the student record declaration taken from Chapter 4 and the corresponding class (see Figures 12-1 and 12-2, respectively

```
type
     student: record
          Name:     char[65];
          Major:    int16;
          SSN:      char[12];
          Midterm1: int16;
          Midterm2: int16;
          Final:    int16;
          Homework: int16;
          Projects: int16;
     endrecord;
     student2: class
          var
               Name:     char[65];
               Major:    int16;
               SSN:      char[12];
               Midterm1: int16;
               Midterm2: int16;
               Final:    int16;
               Homework: int16;
               Projects: int16;
     endclass;
```

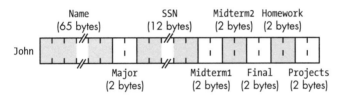

*Figure 12-1: student record implementation in memory*

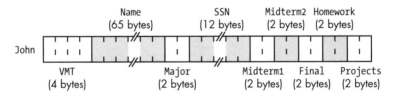

*Figure 12-2: student class implementation in memory*

If you look carefully at Figures 12-1 and 12-2, you'll discover that the only difference between the class and the record implementations is the inclusion of the VMT (virtual method table) pointer field at the beginning of the class object. This field, which is always present in a class, contains the address of the class's virtual method table that, in turn, contains the addresses of all the class's methods and iterators. The VMT field, by the way, is present even if a class doesn't contain any methods or iterators.

As pointed out in previous sections, HLA does not allocate storage for static objects within the object. Instead, HLA allocates a single instance of each static data field that all objects share. As an example, consider the following class and object declarations:

```
type
        tHasStatic: class

            var
                i:int32;
                j:int32;
                r:real32;

            static
                c:char[2];
                b:byte;

        endclass;

var
        hs1: tHasStatic;
        hs2: tHasStatic;
```

Figure 12-3 shows the storage allocation for these two objects in memory

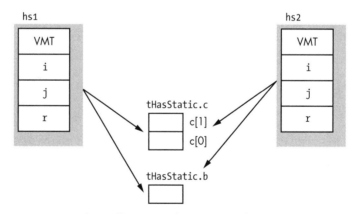

*Figure 12-3: Object allocation with static data fields*

Of course, const, val, and #macro objects do not have any runtime memory requirements associated with them, so HLA does not allocate any storage for these fields. Like the static data fields, you may access const, val, and #macro fields using the class name as well as an object name. Hence, even if tHasStatic has these types of fields, the memory organization for tHasStatic objects would still be the same as shown in Figure 12-3.

Other than the presence of the virtual method table (VMT) pointer, the presence of methods and procedures has no impact on the storage allocation of an object. Of course, the machine instructions associated with these routines do appear somewhere in memory. So in a sense the code for the routines is quite similar to static data fields insofar as all the objects share a single instance of the routine.

## 12.8.1   Virtual Method Tables

When HLA calls a class procedure, it directly calls that procedure using a call instruction, just like any normal procedure call. Methods are another story altogether. Each object in the system carries a pointer to a virtual method table, which is an array of pointers to all the methods and iterators appearing within the object's class (see Figure 12-4).

SomeObject

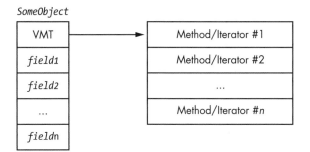

Figure 12-4: Virtual method table organization

Each iterator or method you declare in a class has a corresponding entry in the virtual method table. That double-word entry contains the address of the first instruction of that iterator or method. Calling a class method or iterator is a bit more work than calling a class procedure (it requires one additional instruction plus the use of the EDI register). Here is a typical calling sequence for a method:

```
mov( ObjectAdrs, ESI );    // All class routines do this.
mov( [esi], edi );         // Get the address of the VMT into edi
call( (type dword [edi+n])); // "n" is the offset of the method's
                           // entry in the VMT.
```

For a given class there is only one copy of the virtual method table in memory. This is a static object, so all objects of a given class type share the same virtual method table. This is reasonable because all objects of the same class type have exactly the same methods and iterators (see Figure 12-5).

Although HLA builds the VMT record structure as it encounters methods and iterators within a class, HLA does not automatically create the virtual method table for you. You must explicitly declare this table in your program. To do this, you include a statement like the following in a static or readonly declaration section of your program. For example:

```
readonly
    VMT( classname );
```

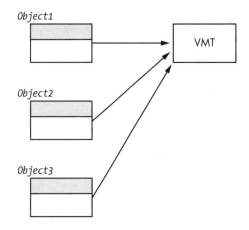

Note: Objects are all the same class type.

*Figure 12-5: All objects that are the same class type share the same VMT.*

Because the addresses in a virtual method table should never change during program execution, the readonly section is probably the best choice for declaring virtual method tables. It should go without saying that changing the pointers in a virtual method table is, in general, a really bad idea. So putting VMTs in a static section is usually not a good idea.

A declaration like the one above defines the variable *classname*._VMT_. In Section 12.9, you will see that you need this name when initializing object variables. The class declaration automatically defines the *classname*._VMT_ symbol as an external static variable. The declaration above just provides the actual definition for this external symbol.

The declaration of a VMT uses a somewhat strange syntax because you aren't actually declaring a new symbol with this declaration; you're simply supplying the data for a symbol that you previously declared implicitly by defining a class. That is, the class declaration defines the static table variable *classname*._VMT_; all you're doing with the VMT declaration is telling HLA to emit the actual data for the table. If, for some reason, you would like to refer to this table using a name other than *classname*._VMT_, HLA does allow you to prefix the declaration above with a variable name. For example:

```
readonly
    myVMT: VMT( classname );
```

In this declaration, myVMT is an alias of *classname*._VMT_. As a general rule, you should avoid using aliases in a program because they make the program more difficult to read and understand. Therefore, it is unlikely that you would ever need to use this type of declaration.

As with any other global static variable, there should be only one instance of a virtual method table for a given class in a program. The best place to put the VMT declaration is in the same source file as the class's method, iterator, and procedure code (assuming they all appear in a single file). This way you will automatically link in the virtual method table whenever you link in the routines for a given class.

## 12.8.2 Object Representation with Inheritance

Up to this point, the discussion of the implementation of class objects has ignored the possibility of inheritance. Inheritance affects the memory representation of an object only by adding fields that are not explicitly stated in the class declaration.

Adding inherited fields from a *base class* to another class must be done carefully. Remember, an important attribute of a class that inherits fields from a base class is that you can use a pointer to the base class to access the inherited fields from that base class, even if the pointer contains the address of some other class (that inherits the fields from the base class). As an example, consider the following classes:

```
type
    tBaseClass: class
        var
            i:uns32;
            j:uns32;
            r:real32;

        method mBase;
    endclass;

    tChildClassA: class inherits( tBaseClass )
        var
            c:char;
            b:boolean;
            w:word;

        method mA;
    endclass;

    tChildClassB: class inherits( tBaseClass )
        var
            d:dword;
            c:char;
            a:byte[3];

    endclass;
```

Because both tChildClassA and tChildClassB inherit the fields of tBaseClass, these two child classes include the i, j, and r fields as well as their own specific fields. Furthermore, whenever you have a pointer variable whose base type

is tBaseClass, it is legal to load this pointer with the address of any child class
of tBaseClass; therefore, it is perfectly reasonable to load such a pointer with
the address of a tChildClassA or tChildClassB variable. For example:

```
var
    B1:  tBaseClass;
    CA:  tChildClassA;
    CB:  tChildClassB;
    ptr: pointer to tBaseClass;
        .
        .
        .
    lea( ebx, B1 );
    mov( ebx, ptr );
    << Use ptr >>
        .
        .
        .
    lea( eax, CA );
    mov( ebx, ptr );
    << Use ptr >>
        .
        .
        .
    lea( eax, CB );
    mov( eax, ptr );
    << Use ptr >>
```

Because ptr points at an object of type tBaseClass, you may legally (from a
semantic sense) access the i, j, and r fields of the object where ptr is pointing.
It is not legal to access the c, b, w, or d field of the tChildClassA or tChildClassB
objects because at any one given moment the program may not know exactly
what object type ptr references.

In order for inheritance to work properly, the i, j, and r fields must appear
at the same offsets in all child classes as they do in tBaseClass. This way, an
instruction of the form mov((type tBaseClass [ebx]).i, eax); will correctly
access the i field even if EBX points at an object of type tChildClassA or
tChildClassB. Figure 12-6 shows the layout of the child and base classes.

Note that the new fields in the two child classes bear no relation to one
another, even if they have the same name (for example, the c fields in the two
child classes do not lie at the same offset). Although the two child classes
share the fields they inherit from their common base class, any new fields they
add are unique and separate. Two fields in different classes share the same
offset only by coincidence if those fields are not inherited from a common
base class.

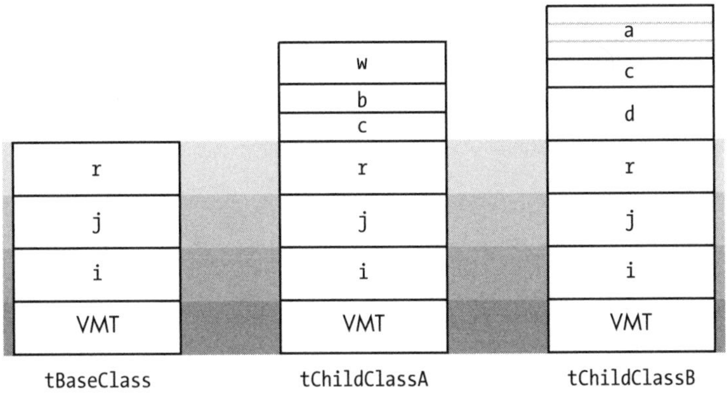

Derived (child) classes locate their inherited fields at the same offsets as those fields in the base class.

Figure 12-6: Layout of base and child class objects in memory

All classes (even those that aren't related to one another) place the pointer to the virtual method table at offset 0 within the object. There is a single virtual method table associated with each class in a program; even classes that inherit fields from some base class have a virtual method table that is (generally) different than the base class's table. Figure 12-7 shows how objects of type tBaseClass, tChildClassA, and tChildClassB point at their specific virtual method tables.

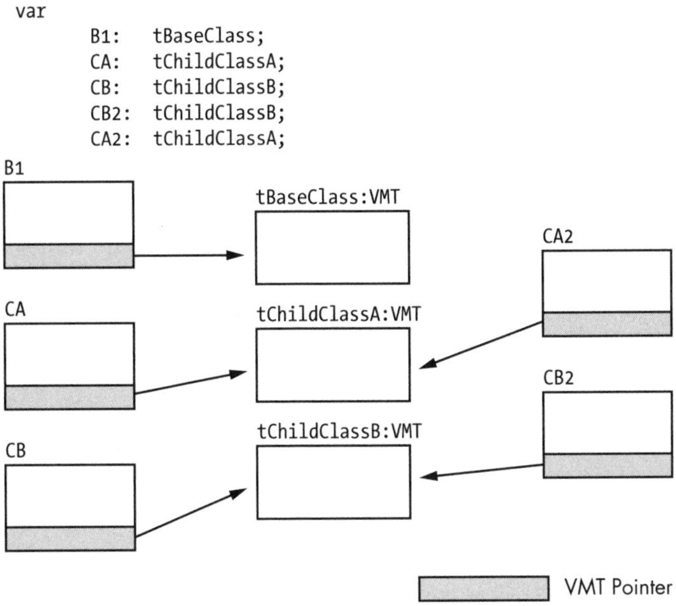

```
var
        B1:     tBaseClass;
        CA:     tChildClassA;
        CB:     tChildClassB;
        CB2:    tChildClassB;
        CA2:    tChildClassA;
```

Figure 12-7: Virtual method table references from objects

A virtual method table is nothing more than an array of pointers to the methods and iterators associated with a class. The address of the first method or iterator that appears in a class is at offset 0, the address of the second appears at offset 4, and so on. You can determine the offset value for a given iterator or method by using the @offset function. If you want to call a method directly (using 80x86 syntax rather than HLA's high-level syntax), you could use code like the following:

```
var
    sc: tBaseClass;

        .
        .
        .

    lea( esi, sc );     // Get the address of the object (& VMT).
    mov( [esi], edi );  // Put address of VMT into edi.
    call( (type dword [edi+@offset( tBaseClass.mBase )] );
```

Of course, if the method has any parameters, you must push them onto the stack before executing the code above. Don't forget when making direct calls to a method, you must load ESI with the address of the object. Any field references within the method will probably depend on ESI containing this address. The choice of EDI to contain the VMT address is nearly arbitrary. Unless you're doing something tricky (like using EDI to obtain runtime type information), you could use any register you please here. As a general rule, you should use EDI when simulating class method calls because this is the convention that HLA employs, and most programmers will expect this usage.

Whenever a child class inherits fields from some base class, the child class's virtual method table also inherits entries from the base class's table. For example, the virtual method table for class tBaseClass contains only a single entry—a pointer to method tBaseClass.mBase. The virtual method table for class tChildClassA contains two entries: a pointer to tBaseClass.mBase and tChildClassA.mA. Because tChildClassB doesn't define any new methods or iterators, tChildClassB's virtual method table contains only a single entry, a pointer to the tBaseClass.mBase method. Note that tChildClassB's virtual method table is identical to tBaseclass's table. Nevertheless, HLA produces two distinct virtual method tables. This is a critical fact that we will make use of a little later. Figure 12-8 shows the relationship between these virtual method tables.

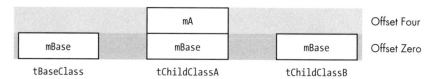

Figure 12-8: Virtual method tables for inherited classes

Although the virtual method table pointer always appears at offset 0 in an object (and, therefore, you can access the pointer using the address expression [ESI] if ESI points at an object), HLA actually inserts a symbol into the symbol table so you may refer to the virtual method table pointer symbolically. The symbol _pVMT_ (pointer to virtual method table) provides this capability. So a more readable way to access the pointer (as in the previous code example) is:

```
lea( esi, sc );
mov( (type tBaseClass [esi])._pVMT_, edi );
call( (type dword [edi+@offset( tBaseClass.mBase )] );
```

If you need to access the virtual method table directly, there are a couple of ways to do this. Whenever you declare a class object, HLA automatically includes a field named _VMT_ as part of that class. _VMT_ is a static array of double-word objects. Therefore, you may refer to the virtual method table using an identifier of the form *classname*._VMT_. Generally, you shouldn't access the virtual method table directly, but as you'll see shortly, there are some good reasons why you need to know the address of this object in memory.

## 12.9 Constructors and Object Initialization

If you've tried to get a little ahead of the game and write a program that uses objects prior to this point, you've probably discovered that the program inexplicably crashes whenever you attempt to run it. We've covered a lot of material in this chapter thus far, but you are still missing one crucial piece of information—how to properly initialize objects prior to use. This section will put the final piece into the puzzle and allow you to begin writing programs that use classes.

Consider the following object declaration and code fragment:

```
var
    bc: tBaseClass;
        .
        .
        .
    bc.mBase();
```

Remember that variables you declare in the var section are uninitialized at runtime. Therefore, when the program containing these statements gets around to executing bc.mBase, it executes the three-statement sequence you've seen several times already:

```
lea( esi, bc);
mov( [esi], edi );
call( (type dword [edi+@offset( tBaseClass.mBase )] );
```

The problem with this sequence is that it loads EDI with an undefined value assuming you haven't previously initialized the bc object. Because EDI contains a garbage value, attempting to call a subroutine at address [EDI+@offset(tBaseClass.mBase)] will likely crash the system. Therefore, before using an object, you must initialize the _pVMT_ field with the address of that object's virtual method table. One easy way to do this is with the following statement:

```
mov( &tBaseClass._VMT_, bc._pVMT_ );
```

Always remember, before using an object, be sure to initialize the virtu method table pointer for that object.

Although you must initialize the virtual method table pointer for all objec you use, this may not be the only field you need to initialize in those object Each specific class may have its own application-specific initialization. Althoug the initialization may vary by class, you need to perform the same initializa- tion on each object of a specific class that you use. If you ever create more than a single object from a given class, it is probably a good idea to create a pr cedure to do this initialization for you. This is such a common operation tha object-oriented programmers have given these initialization procedures a special name: *constructors*.

Some object-oriented languages (e.g., C++) use a special syntax to declar a constructor. Others (e.g., Delphi) simply use existing procedure declara- tions to define a constructor. One advantage to employing a special syntax that the language knows when you define a constructor and can automatical generate code to call that constructor for you (whenever you declare an object). Languages like Delphi require that you explicitly call the constructo this can be a minor inconvenience and a source of defects in your program HLA does not use a special syntax to declare constructors: you define constru tors using standard class procedures. Thus, you will need to explicitly call th constructors in your program; however, you'll see an easy method for auto- mating this in Section 12.11.

Perhaps the most important fact you must remember is that *constructor. must be class procedures.* You must not define constructors as methods. The reason is quite simple: one of the tasks of the constructor is to initialize the pointer to the virtual method table, and you cannot call a class method or ite ator until after you've initialized the VMT pointer. Because class procedures don't use the virtual method table, you can call a class procedure prior to in tializing the VMT pointer for an object.

By convention, HLA programmers use the name create for the class co structor. There is no requirement that you use this name, but by doing so yo will make your programs easier to read and follow by other programmers.

As you may recall, you can call a class procedure via an object referenc or a class reference. For example, if clsProc is a class procedure of class tClas and Obj is an object of type tClass, then the following two class procedure invocations are both legal.

```
tClass.clsProc();
Obj.clsProc();
```

There is a big difference between these two calls. The first one calls clsProc with ESI containing 0 (NULL), while the second invocation loads the address of Obj into ESI before the call. We can use this fact to determine within a method the particular calling mechanism.

### 12.9.1  Dynamic Object Allocation Within the Constructor

As it turns out, most programs allocate objects dynamically using mem.alloc and refer to those objects indirectly using pointers. This adds one more step to the initialization process—allocating storage for the object. The constructor is the perfect place to allocate this storage. Because you probably won't need to allocate all objects dynamically, you'll need two types of constructors: one that allocates storage and then initializes the object, and another that simply initializes an object that already has storage.

Another constructor convention is to merge these two constructors into a single constructor and differentiate the type of constructor call by the value in ESI. On entry into the class's create procedure, the program checks the value in ESI to see if it contains NULL (0). If so, the constructor calls mem.alloc to allocate storage for the object and returns a pointer to the object in ESI. If ESI does not contain NULL upon entry into the procedure, then the constructor assumes that ESI points at a valid object and skips over the memory allocation statements. At the very least, a constructor initializes the pointer to the virtual method table; therefore, the minimalist constructor will look like the following:

```
procedure tBaseClass.create; @nodisplay;
begin create;

  if( ESI = 0 ) then

      push( eax );      // mem.alloc returns its result here, so save it.
      mem.alloc( @size( tBaseClass ));
      mov( eax, esi );  // Put pointer into esi.
      pop( eax );

  endif;

  // Initialize the pointer to the VMT:
  // Remember, "this" is shorthand for "(type tBaseClass [esi])".

  mov( &tBaseClass._VMT_, this._pVMT_ );

  // Other class initialization would go here.

end create;
```

After you write a constructor like the preceding, you choose an appropriate calling mechanism based on whether your object's storage is already allocated. For preallocated objects (such as those you've declared in var, static, or storage sections[7] or those you've previously allocated storage for via mem.alloc), you simply load the address of the object into ESI and call the constructor. For those objects you declare as a variable, this is very easy; just call the appropriate create constructor:

```
var
        bc0: tBaseClass;
        bcp: pointer to tBaseClass;
             .
             .
             .
        bc0.create();  // Initializes preallocated bc0 object.
             .
             .
             .
        // Allocate storage for bcp object.

        mem.alloc( @size( tBaseClass ));
        mov( eax, bcp );
             .
             .
             .
        bcp.create();  // Initializes preallocated bcp object.
```

Note that although bcp is a pointer to a tBaseClass object, the create method does not automatically allocate storage for this object. The program already allocated the storage earlier. Therefore, when the program calls bcp.create, it loads ESI with the address contained within bcp; because this is not NULL, the tBaseClass.create procedure does not allocate storage for a new object. By the way, the call to bcp.create emits the following sequence of machine instructions:

```
        mov( bcp, esi );
        call tBaseClass.create;
```

Until now, the code examples for a class procedure call always began with an lea instruction. This is because all the examples to this point have used object variables rather than pointers to object variables. Remember, a class procedure (method) call passes the address of the object in the ESI register. For object variables HLA emits an lea instruction to obtain this address. For pointers to objects, however, the actual object address is the *value* of the pointer variable; therefore, to load the address of the object into ESI, HLA emits a mov instruction that copies the value of the pointer into the ESI register.

In the preceding example, the program preallocates the storage for an object prior to calling the object constructor. While there are several reasons for preallocating object storage (for example, you're creating a dynamic array

---

[7]You generally do not declare objects in readonly sections because you cannot initialize them.

of objects), you can achieve most simple object allocations like the one above by calling a standard create procedure (such as one that allocates storage for an object if ESI contains NULL). The following example demonstrates this:

```
var
    bcp2: pointer to tBaseClass;
        .
        .
        .
    tBaseClass.create(); // Calls create with esi=NULL.
    mov( esi, bcp2 );    // Save pointer to new class object in bcp2.
```

Remember, a call to a tBaseClass.create constructor returns a pointer to the new object in the ESI register. It is the caller's responsibility to save the pointer this function returns into the appropriate pointer variable; the constructor does not automatically do this for you. Likewise, it is the caller's responsibility to free the storage associated with this object when the application has finished using the object (see the discussion of destructors in Section 12.10).

## 12.9.2 Constructors and Inheritance

Constructors for derived (child) classes that inherit fields from a base class represent a special case. Each class must have its own constructor but needs the ability to call the base class constructor. This section explains the reasons for this and how to do it.

A derived class inherits the create procedure from its base class. However, you must override this procedure in a derived class because the derived class probably requires more storage than the base class, and therefore you will probably need to use a different call to mem.alloc to allocate storage for a dynamic object. Hence, it is very unusual for a derived class not to override the definition of the create procedure.

However, overriding a base class's create procedure has problems of its own. When you override the base class's create procedure, you take the full responsibility of initializing the (entire) object, including all the initialization required by the base class. At the very least, this involves putting duplicate code in the overridden procedure to handle the initialization usually done by the base class constructor. In addition to making your program larger (by duplicating code already present in the base class constructor), this also violates information-hiding principles because the derived class must be aware of all the fields in the base class (including those that are logically private to the base class). What we need here is the ability to call a base class's constructor from within the derived class's constructor and let that call do the lower-level initialization of the base class's fields. Fortunately, this is an easy thing to do in HLA.

Consider the following class declarations (which do things the hard way

```
type
    tBase: class
        var
            i:uns32;
            j:int32;

        procedure create(); @returns( "esi" );
    endclass;

    tDerived: class inherits( tBase );
        var
            r: real64;
        override procedure create(); @returns( "esi" );
    endclass;

    procedure tBase.create; @nodisplay;
    begin create;

        if( esi = 0 ) then

            push( eax );
            mov( mem.alloc( @size( tBase )), esi );
            pop( eax );

        endif;
        mov( &tBase._VMT_, this._pVMT_ );
        mov( 0, this.i );
        mov( -1, this.j );

    end create;

    procedure tDerived.create; @nodisplay;
    begin create;

        if( esi = 0 ) then

            push( eax );
            mov( mem.alloc( @size( tDerived )), esi );
            pop( eax );

        endif;

        // Initialize the VMT pointer for this object:

        mov( &tDerived._VMT_, this._pVMT_ );

        // Initialize the "r" field of this particular object:

    fldz();
    fstp( this.r );
```

```
// Duplicate the initialization required by tBase.create:

mov( 0, this.i );
mov( -1, this.j );

end create;
```

Let's take a closer look at the tDerived.create procedure above. Like a conventional constructor, it begins by checking ESI and allocates storage for a new object if ESI contains NULL. Note that the size of a tDerived object includes the size required by the inherited fields, so this properly allocates the necessary storage for all fields in a tDerived object.

Next, the tDerived.create procedure initializes the VMT pointer field of the object. Remember, each class has its own virtual method table and, specifically, derived classes do not use the virtual method table of their base class. Therefore, this constructor must initialize the _pVMT_ field with the address of the tDerived virtual method table.

After initializing the virtual method table pointer, the tDerived constructor initializes the value of the r field to 0.0 (remember, fldz loads 0 onto the FPU stack). This concludes the tDerived-specific initialization.

The remaining instructions in tDerived.create are the problem. These statements duplicate some of the code appearing in the tBase.create procedure. The problem with code duplication becomes apparent when you decide to modify the initial values of these fields; if you've duplicated the initialization code in derived classes, you will need to change the initialization code in more than one create procedure. More often than not, however, this results in defects in the derived class create procedures, especially if those derived classes appear in different source files than the base class.

Another problem with burying base class initialization in derived class constructors is the violation of the information-hiding principle. Some fields of the base class may be *logically private*. Although HLA does not explicitly support the concept of public and private fields in a class (as, say, C++ does), well-disciplined programmers will still partition the fields as private or public and then use the private fields only in class routines belonging to that class. Initializing these private fields in derived classes is not acceptable to such programmers. Doing so will make it very difficult to change the definition and implementation of some base class at a later date.

Fortunately, HLA provides an easy mechanism for calling the inherited constructor within a derived class's constructor. All you have to do is call the base constructor using the class name syntax; for example, you could call tBase.create directly from within tDerived.create. By calling the base class constructor, your derived class constructors can initialize the base class fields without worrying about the exact implementation (or initial values) of the base class.

Unfortunately, there are two types of initialization that every (conventional) constructor does that will affect the way you call a base class constructor: All conventional constructors allocate memory for the class if ESI contains 0, and all conventional constructors initialize the VMT pointer. Fortunately, it is very easy to deal with these two problems.

The memory required by an object of some base class is usually less than the memory required for an object of a class you derive from that base class (because the derived classes usually add more fields). Therefore, you cannot allow the base class constructor to allocate the storage when you call it from inside the derived class's constructor. You can easily solve this problem by checking ESI within the derived class constructor and allocating any necessary storage for the object *before* calling the base class constructor.

The second problem is the initialization of the VMT pointer. When you call the base class's constructor, it will initialize the VMT pointer with the address of the base class's virtual method table. A derived class object's _pVMT_ field however, must point at the virtual method table for the derived class. Calling the base class constructor will always initialize the _pVMT_ field with the wrong pointer. To properly initialize the _pVMT_ field with the appropriate value, the derived class constructor must store the address of the derived class's virtual method table into the _pVMT_ field *after* the call to the base class constructor (so that it overwrites the value written by the base class constructor).

The tDerived.create constructor, rewritten to call the tBase.create constructors, follows:

```
procedure tDerived.create; @nodisplay;
begin create;

    if( esi = 0 ) then

        push( eax );
        mov( mem.alloc( @size( tDerived )), esi );
        pop( eax );

    endif;

    // Call the base class constructor to do any initialization
    // needed by the base class. Note that this call must follow
    // the object allocation code above (so esi will always contain
    // a pointer to an object at this point and tBase.create will
    // never allocate storage).

    (type tBase [esi]).create();

    // Initialize the VMT pointer for this object. This code
    // must always follow the call to the base class constructor
    // because the base class constructor also initializes this
    // field and we don't want the initial value supplied by
    // tBase.create.

    mov( &tDerived._VMT_, this._pVMT_ );

    // Initialize the "r" field of this particular object:
```

```
        fldz();
        fstp( this.r );

    end create;
```

This solution solves all the above concerns with derived class constructors. Note that the call to the base constructor uses the syntax (type tBase [esi]).create(); rather than tBase.create();. The problem with calling tBase.create directly is that it will load NULL into ESI and overwrite the pointer to the storage allocated in tDerived.create. The scheme above uses the existing value in ESI when calling tBase.create.

### 12.9.3  Constructor Parameters and Procedure Overloading

None of the constructor examples to this point have had any parameters. However, there is nothing special about constructors that prevents the use of parameters. Constructors are procedures; therefore, you can specify any number and any type of parameters you choose. You can use these parameter values to initialize certain fields or control how the constructor initializes the fields. Of course, you may use constructor parameters for any purpose you'd use parameters for in any other procedure. In fact, about the only issue you need concern yourself with is the use of parameters whenever you have a derived class. This section deals with those issues.

The first, and probably most important, problem with parameters in derived class constructors actually applies to all overridden procedures and methods: The parameter list of an overridden routine must exactly match the parameter list of the corresponding routine in the base class. In fact, HLA doesn't even give you the chance to violate this rule because override routine prototypes don't allow parameter list declarations: They automatically inherit the parameter list of the base routine. Therefore, you cannot use a special parameter list in the constructor prototype for one class and a different parameter list for the constructors appearing in base or derived classes. Sometimes it would be nice if this weren't the case, but there are some sound and logical reasons why HLA does not support this.[8]

HLA supports a special overloads declaration that lets you call one of several different procedures, methods, or iterators using a single identifier (with the number of types of parameters specifying which function to call). This would allow you, for example, to create multiple constructors for a given class (or derived class) and invoke the desired constructor using a matching parameter list for that constructor. Interested readers should consult the chapter on procedures in the HLA documentation for more details concerning the overloads declaration.

---

[8] Calling virtual methods and iterators would be a real problem because you don't really know which routine a pointer references. Therefore, you couldn't know the proper parameter list. While the problems with procedures aren't quite as drastic, there are some subtle problems that could creep into your code if base or derived classes allowed overridden procedures with different parameter lists.

## 12.10 Destructors

A *destructor* is a class routine that cleans up an object once a program finish using that object. As for constructors, HLA does not provide a special synt for creating destructors, nor does HLA automatically call a destructor. Unli constructors, a destructor is usually a method rather than a procedure (becau virtual destructors make a lot of sense, whereas virtual constructors do not

A typical destructor might close any files opened by the object, free th memory allocated during the use of the object, and, finally, free the objec itself if it was created dynamically. The destructor also handles any other cleanup chores the object may require before it ceases to exist.

By convention, most HLA programmers name their destructors destro About the only code that most destructors have in common is the code to fr the storage associated with the object. The following destructor demonstrat how to do this:

```
procedure tBase.destroy; @nodisplay;
begin destroy;

    push( eax );   // isInHeap uses this.

    // Place any other cleanup code here.
    // The code to free dynamic objects should always appear last
    // in the destructor.

        /************/

    // The following code assumes that esi still contains the address
    // of the object.

    if( mem.isInHeap( esi )) then

        free( esi);

    endif;
    pop( eax );

end destroy;
```

The HLA Standard Library routine mem.isInHeap returns true if its para eter is an address that mem.alloc returned. Therefore, this code automatica frees the storage associated with the object if the program originally allocate storage for the object by calling mem.alloc. Obviously, on return from this method call, ESI will no longer point at a legal object in memory if you alle cated it dynamically. Note that this code will not affect the value in ESI no will it modify the object if the object wasn't one you've previously allocated v a call to mem.alloc.

# 12.11  HLA's _initialize_ and _finalize_ Strings

Although HLA does not automatically call constructors and destructors associated with your classes, HLA does provide a mechanism whereby you can force HLA to automatically emit these calls: by using the _initialize_ and _finalize_ compile-time string variables (i.e., val constants) that HLA automatically declares in every procedure.

Whenever you write a procedure, iterator, or method, HLA automatically declares several local symbols in that routine. Two such symbols are _initialize_ and _finalize_. HLA declares these symbols as follows:

---

```
val
    _initialize_: string := "";
    _finalize_: string := "";
```

---

HLA emits the _initialize_ string as text at the very beginning of the routine's body, that is, immediately after the routine's begin clause.[9] Similarly, HLA emits the _finalize_ string at the very end of the routine's body, just before the end clause. This is comparable to the following:

---

```
procedure SomeProc;
    << declarations >>
begin SomeProc;

    @text( _initialize_ );

        << Procedure body >>

    @text( _finalize_ );

end SomeProc;
```

---

Because _initialize_ and _finalize_ initially contain the empty string, these expansions have no effect on the code that HLA generates unless you explicitly modify the value of _initialize_ prior to the begin clause or you modify _finalize_ prior to the end clause of the procedure. So if you modify either of these string objects to contain a machine instruction, HLA will compile that instruction at the beginning or end of the procedure. The following example demonstrates how to use this technique:

---

```
procedure SomeProc;
    ?_initialize_ := "mov( 0, eax );";
    ?_finalize_  := "stdout.put( eax );";
begin SomeProc;

    // HLA emits "mov( 0, eax );" here in response to the _initialize_
    // string constant.
```

---

[9] If the routine automatically emits code to construct the activation record, HLA emits _initialize_'s text after the code that builds the activation record.

```
    add( 5, eax );

    // HLA emits "stdout.put( eax );" here.

end SomeProc;
```

Of course, these examples don't save you much. It would be easier to type the actual statements at the beginning and end of the procedure than to assign a string containing these statements to the _initialize_ and _finalize_ compile-time variables. However, if we could automate the assignment of some string to these variables, so that we don't have to explicitly assign them in each procedure, then this feature might be useful. In a moment, you'll see how we can automate the assignment of values to the _initialize_ and _finalize_ strings. For the time being, consider the case where we load the name of a constructor into the _initialize_ string and we load the name of a destructor in to the _finalize_ string. By doing this, the routine will "automatically" call the constructor and destructor for that particular object.

The previous example has a minor problem. If we can automate the assignment of some value to _initialize_ or _finalize_, what happens if these variables already contain some value? For example, suppose we have two objects we use in a routine, and the first one loads the name of its constructor into the _initialize_ string; what happens when the second object attempts to do the same thing? The solution is simple: Don't directly assign any string to the _initialize_ or _finalize_ compile-time variables; instead, always concatenate your strings to the end of the existing string in these variables. The following is a modification to the above example that demonstrates how to do this.

```
procedure SomeProc;
    ?_initialize_ := _initialize_  + "mov( 0, eax );";
    ?_finalize_  := _finalize_  + "stdout.put( eax );";
begin SomeProc;

    // HLA emits "mov( 0, eax );" here in response to the _initialize_
    // string constant.

    add( 5, eax );

    // HLA emits "stdout.put( eax );" here.

end SomeProc;
```

When you assign values to the _initialize_ and _finalize_ strings, HLA guarantees that the _initialize_ sequence will execute upon entry into the routine. Sadly, the same is not true for the _finalize_ string upon exit. HLA simply emits the code for the _finalize_ string at the end of the routine, immediately before the code that cleans up the activation record and returns. Unfortunately, "falling off the end of the routine" is not the only way that you could return from that routine. You could explicitly return from somewhere in the middle of the code by executing a ret instruction. Because HLA emits the _finalize_ string only at the very end of the routine, returning from that routine in this manner bypasses the _finalize_ code. Unfortunately, other than manually emitting the _finalize_ code, there is nothing you can do about this.[10] Fortunately, this mechanism for exiting a routine is completely under your control. If you never exit a routine except by "falling off the end," then you won't have to worry about this problem (note that you can use the exit control structure to transfer control to the end of a routine if you really want to return from that routine from somewhere in the middle of the code).

Another way to prematurely exit a routine, over which, unfortunately, you don't have any control, is by raising an exception. Your routine could call some other routine (e.g., a Standard Library routine) that raises an exception and then transfers control immediately to whomever called your routine. Fortunately, you can easily trap and handle exceptions by putting a try..endtry block in your procedure. Here is an example that demonstrates this:

```
procedure SomeProc;
    << Declarations that modify _initialize_ and _finalize_ >>
begin SomeProc;

    << HLA emits the code for the _initialize_ string here. >>

    try   // Catch any exceptions that occur:

        << Procedure body goes here. >>

    anyexception

        push( eax );            // Save the exception #.
        @text( _finalize_ );    // Execute the _finalize_ code here.
        pop( eax );             // Restore the exception #.
        raise( eax );           // Reraise the exception.

    endtry;

    << HLA automatically emits the _finalize_ code here. >>

end SomeProc;
```

Although the previous code handles some problems that exist with _finalize_, by no means does it handle every possible case. Always be on the lookout for ways your program could inadvertently exit a routine without executing the code found in the _finalize_ string. You should explicitly expand _finalize_ if you encounter such a situation.

There is one important place you can get into trouble with respect to exceptions: within the code the routine emits for the _initialize_ string. If you modify the _initialize_ string so that it contains a constructor call and the execution of that constructor raises an exception, this will probably force an exit from that routine without executing the corresponding _finalize_ code. You could bury the try..endtry statement directly into the _initialize_ and

---

[10] Note that you can manually emit the _finalize_ code using the statement @text( _finalize_ );.

_finalize_ strings, but this approach has several problems, not the least of whi⟨
is the fact that one of the first constructors you call might raise an exceptic⟨
that transfers control to the exception handler that calls the destructors fo⟨
all objects in that routine (including those objects whose constructors you
have yet to call). Although no single solution that handles all problems exis⟨
probably the best approach is to put a try..endtry block within each constr⟨
tor call if it is possible for that constructor to raise some exception that i⟨
possible to handle (that is, doesn't require the immediate termination o⟨
the program).

Thus far this discussion of _initialize_ and _finalize_ has failed to addre⟨
one important point: Why use this feature to implement the "automatic" c⟨
ing of constructors and destructors, because it apparently involves more wo⟨
than simply calling the constructors and destructors directly? Clearly there
must be a way to automate the assignment of the _initialize_ and _finalize⟨
strings or this section wouldn't exist. The way to accomplish this is by using
macro to define the class type. So now it's time to take a look at another HL⟨
feature that makes it possible to automate this activity: the forward keyword⟨

You've seen how to use the forward reserved word to create procedure
prototypes (see the discussion in Section 5.9); it turns out that you can decla⟨
forward const, val, type, and variable declarations as well. The syntax for su⟨
declarations takes the following form:

```
ForwardSymbolName: forward( undefinedID );
```

This declaration is completely equivalent to the following:

```
?undefinedID: text := "ForwardSymbolName";
```

Especially note that this expansion does not actually define the symbol⟨
ForwardSymbolName. It just converts this symbol to a string and assigns this strir⟨
to the specified text object undefinedID.

Now you're probably wondering how something like the above is equiv⟨
lent to a forward declaration. The truth is, it isn't. However, forward declaratio⟨
let you create macros that simulate type names by allowing you to defer th⟨
actual declaration of an object's type until some later point in the code.
Consider the following example:

```
type
    myClass: class
        var
            i:int32;

        procedure create; @returns( "esi" );
            procedure destroy;
        endclass;
```

```
#macro _myClass: varID;
    forward( varID );
    ?_initialize_ := _initialize_ + @string:varID + ".create(); ";
    ?_finalize_ := _finalize_ + @string:varID + ".destroy(); ";
    varID: myClass
#endmacro;
```

Note, and this is very important, that a semicolon does not follow the varID: myClass declaration at the end of this macro. You'll find out why this semicolon is missing in a little while.

If you have the above class and macro declarations in your program, you can now declare variables of type _myClass that automatically invoke the constructor and destructor upon entry and exit of the routine containing the variable declarations. To see how, take a look at the following procedure shell:

```
procedure HasmyClassObject;
var
      mco: _myClass;
begin HasmyClassObject;

    << Do stuff with mco here. >>

end HasmyClassObject;
```

Because _myClass is a macro, the procedure above expands to the following text during compilation:

```
procedure HasmyClassObject;
var
      mco:                    // Expansion of the _myClass macro:
        forward( _0103_ );  // _0103_ symbol is an HLA-supplied text
                            // symbol that expands to "mco".

    ?_initialize_ := _initialize_ + "mco" + ".create(); ";
    ?_finalize_ := _finalize_ + "mco" + ".destroy(); ";
    mco: myClass;

begin HasmyClassObject;

    mco.create();  // Expansion of the _initialize_ string.

    << Do stuff with mco here. >>

    mco.destroy(); // Expansion of the _finalize_ string.

end HasmyClassObject;
```

You might notice that a semicolon appears after the mco: myClass decl‍a‍tion in the example above. This semicolon is not actually a part of the mac‍instead it is the semicolon that follows the mco: _myClass; declaration in th‍original code.

If you want to create an array of objects, you could legally declare tha‍array as follows:

```
var
    mcoArray: _myClass[10];
```

Because the last statement in the _myClass macro doesn't end with a se‍colon, the declaration above will expand to something like the following (almost correct) code:

```
mcoArray:                       // Expansion of the _myClass macro:
    forward( _0103_ ); // _0103_ symbol is an HLA-supplied text
                                // symbol that expands to "mcoArray".

?_initialize_  :=  _initialize_ + "mcoArray" + ".create(); ";
?_finalize_    :=  _finalize_ + "mcoArray" + ".Destroy(); ";
mcoArray: myClass[10];
```

The only problem with this expansion is that it calls the constructor o‍for the first object of the array. There are several ways to solve this proble‍one is to append a macro name to the end of _initialize_ and _finalize_ rath‍than the constructor name. That macro would check the object's name (mcoArray in this example) to determine if it is an array. If so, that macro cou‍expand to a loop that calls the constructor for each element of the array.

Another solution to this problem is to use a macro parameter to specify t‍dimensions for arrays of myClass. This scheme is easier to implement than t‍one above, but it does have the drawback of requiring a different syntax f‍declaring object arrays (you have to use parentheses rather than square brackets around the array dimension).

The forward directive is quite powerful and lets you achieve all kinds o‍tricks. However, there are a few problems of which you should be aware. Fir‍because HLA emits the _initialize_ and _finalize_ code transparently, you‍can be easily confused if there are any errors in the code appearing within‍these strings. If you start getting error messages associated with the begin o‍end statements in a routine, you might want to take a look at the _initializ‍and _finalize_ strings within that routine. The best defense here is to alwa‍append very simple statements to these strings so that you reduce the likel‍hood of an error.

Fundamentally, HLA doesn't support automatic constructor and destr‍tor calls. This section has presented several tricks to attempt to automate t‍calls to these routines. However, the automation isn't perfect and, indeed, t‍aforementioned problems with the _finalize_ strings limit the applicability‍this approach. The mechanism this section presents is probably fine for simp‍

classes and simple programs. One piece of advice is probably worth following: If your code is complex or correctness is critical, it's probably a good idea to explicitly call the constructors and destructors manually.

## 12.12 Abstract Methods

An *abstract base class* is one that exists solely to supply a set of common fields to its derived classes. You never declare variables whose type is an abstract base class; you always use one of the derived classes. The purpose of an abstract base class is to provide a template for creating other classes, nothing more. As it turns out, the only difference in syntax between a standard base class and an abstract base class is the presence of at least one *abstract method* declaration. An abstract method is a special method that does not have an actual implementation in the abstract base class. Any attempt to call that method will raise an exception. If you're wondering what possible good an abstract method could be, keep on reading.

Suppose you want to create a set of classes to hold numeric values. One class could represent unsigned integers, another class could represent signed integers, a third could implement BCD values, and a fourth could support real64 values. While you could create four separate classes that function independently of one another, doing so passes up an opportunity to make this set of classes more convenient to use. To understand why, consider the following possible class declarations:

```
type
    uint: class
        var
            TheValue: dword;

        method put;
        << Other methods for this class >>
    endclass;

    sint: class
        var
            TheValue: dword;

        method put;
        << Other methods for this class >>
    endclass;

    r64: class
        var
            TheValue: real64;

        method put;
        << Other methods for this class >>
    endclass;
```

The implementation of these classes is not unreasonable. They have fields for the data and they have a put method (which, presumably, writes the data to the standard output device). They probably have other methods and procedures to implement various operations on the data. There are, however, two problems with these classes, one minor and one major, both occurring because these classes do not inherit any fields from a common base class.

The first problem, which is relatively minor, is that you have to repeat the declaration of several common fields in these classes. For example, the put method declaration appears in each of these classes.[11] This duplication of effort results in a harder-to-maintain program because it doesn't encourage you to use a common name for a common function since it's easy to use a different name in each of the classes.

A bigger problem with this approach is that it is not generic. That is, you can't create a generic pointer to a "numeric" object and perform operations like addition, subtraction, and output on that value (regardless of the underlying numeric representation).

We can easily solve these two problems by turning the previous class declarations into a set of derived classes. The following code demonstrates an easy way to do this:

```
type
     numeric: class
          method put;
          << Other common methods shared by all the classes >>
     endclass;

     uint: class inherits( numeric )
          var
               TheValue: dword;

          override method put;
          << Other methods for this class >>
     endclass;

     sint: class inherits( numeric )
          var
               TheValue: dword;

          override method put;
          << Other methods for this class >>
     endclass;

     r64: class inherits( numeric )
          var
               TheValue: real64;
```

---

[11] Note, by the way, that TheValue is not a common field because this field has a different type the r64 class.

```
        override method put;
        << Other methods for this class >>
endclass;
```

This scheme solves both the problems. First, by inheriting the put method from numeric, this code encourages the derived classes to always use the name *put*, thereby making the program easier to maintain. Second, because this example uses derived classes, it's possible to create a pointer to the numeric type and load this pointer with the address of a uint, sint, or r64 object. That pointer can invoke the methods found in the numeric class to do functions like addition, subtraction, or numeric output. Therefore, the application that uses this pointer doesn't need to know the exact data type; it deals with numeric values only in a generic fashion.

One problem with this scheme is that it's possible to declare and use variables of type numeric. Unfortunately, such numeric variables don't have the ability to represent any type of number (notice that the data storage for the numeric fields actually appears in the derived classes). Worse, because you've declared the put method in the numeric class, you actually have to write some code to implement that method even though you should never really call it; the actual implementation should occur only in the derived classes. While you could write a dummy method that prints an error message (or, better yet, raises an exception), there shouldn't be any need to write "dummy" procedures like this. Fortunately, there is no reason to do so—if you use *abstract* methods.

The abstract keyword, when it follows a method declaration, tells HLA that you are not going to provide an implementation of the method for this class. Instead, it is the responsibility of all derived classes to provide a concrete implementation for the abstract method. HLA will raise an exception if you attempt to call an abstract method directly. The following is the modification to the numeric class to convert put to an abstract method:

```
type
    numeric: class
        method put; abstract;
        << Other common methods shared by all the classes >>
    endclass;
```

An abstract base class is a class that has at least one abstract method. Note that you don't have to make all methods abstract in an abstract base class; it is perfectly legal to declare some standard methods (and, of course, provide their implementation) within the abstract base class.

Abstract method declarations provide a mechanism by which a base class can specify some generic methods that the derived classes must implement. In theory, all derived classes must provide concrete implementations of all abstract methods, or those derived classes are themselves abstract base classes. In practice, it's possible to bend the rules a little and use abstract methods for a slightly different purpose.

A little earlier, you read that you should never create variables whose type is an abstract base class. If you attempt to execute an abstract method, the program would immediately raise an exception to complain about this illegal method call. In practice, you actually can declare variables of an abstract base type and get away with this as long as you don't call any abstract methods in that class.

## 12.13 Runtime Type Information

When working with an object variable (as opposed to a pointer to an object) the type of that object is obvious: It's the variable's declared type. Therefore, at both compile time and runtime the program knows the type of the object. When working with pointers to objects you cannot, in the general case, determine the type of an object a pointer references. However, at runtime it is possible to determine the object's actual type. This section discusses how to detect the underlying object's type and how to use this information.

If you have a pointer to an object and that pointer's type is some base class, at runtime the pointer could point at an object of the base class or any derived type. At compile time it is not possible to determine the exact type of an object at any instant. To see why, consider the following short example:

```
ReturnSomeObject(); // Returns a pointer to some class in esi.
mov( esi, ptrToObject );
```

The routine *ReturnSomeObject* returns a pointer to an object in ESI. This could be the address of some base class object or a derived class object. At compile time there is no way for the program to know what type of object the function returns. For example, *ReturnSomeObject* could ask the user what value to return so the exact type could not be determined until the program actually runs and the user makes a selection.

In a perfectly designed program, there probably is no need to know a generic object's actual type. After all, the whole purpose of object-oriented programming and inheritance is to produce general programs that work with lots of different objects without having to make substantial changes to the program. In the real world, however, programs may not have a perfect design and sometimes it's nice to know the exact object type a pointer references. Runtime type information, or RTTI, gives you the capability of determining an object's type at runtime, even if you are referencing that object using a pointer to some base class of that object.

Perhaps the most fundamental RTTI operation you need is the ability to ask if a pointer contains the address of some specific object type. Many object-oriented languages (e.g., Delphi) provide an is operator that provides this functionality. is is a boolean operator that returns true if its left operand (a pointer) points at an object whose type matches the right operand (which must be a type identifier). The typical syntax is generally the following:

```
ObjectPointerOrVar is ClassType
```

This operator returns true if the variable is of the specified class; it returns false otherwise. Here is a typical use of this operator (in the Delphi language):

```
if( ptrToNumeric is uint ) then begin
   .
   .
   .
end;
```

It's actually quite simple to implement this functionality in HLA. As you may recall, each class is given its own virtual method table. Whenever you create an object, you must initialize the pointer to the virtual method table with the address of that class's virtual method table. Therefore, the VMT pointer field of all objects of a given class type contains the same pointer value, and this pointer value is different from the VMT pointer field of all other classes. We can use this fact to see if an object is some specific type. The following code demonstrates how to implement the Delphi statement above in HLA:

```
mov( ptrToNumeric, esi );
if( (type uint [esi])._pVMT_ = &uint._VMT_ ) then
   .
   .
   .
endif;
```

This if statement simply compares the object's _pVMT_ field (the pointer to the virtual method table) against the address of the desired classes' virtual method table. If they are equal, then the *ptrToNumeric* variable points at an object of type uint.

Within the body of a class method or iterator, there is a slightly easier way to see if the object is a certain class. Remember, upon entry into a method or an iterator, the EDI register contains the address of the virtual method table. Therefore, assuming you haven't modified EDI's value, you can easily test to see if the method or iterator is a specific class type using an if statement like the following:

```
if( edi = &uint._VMT_ ) then
   .
   .
   .
endif;
```

Remember, however, that EDI will contain a pointer to the virtual method table only when you call a class method. This is not the case when calling a class procedure.

## 12.14  Calling Base Class Methods

In the section on constructors you saw that it is possible to call an ancestor class's procedure within the derived class's overridden procedure. To do this all you need to do is to invoke the procedure using the call (type *classname* [esi]).*procedureName*( *parameters* );. On occasion you may want to do this same operation with a class's methods as well as its procedures (that is, have an overridden method call the corresponding base class method in order to do some computation you'd rather not repeat in the derived class's method). Unfortunately, HLA does not let you directly call methods as it does procedures. You will need to use an indirect mechanism to achieve this; specifically you will have to call the method using the address in the base class's virtual method table. This section describes how to do this.

Whenever your program calls a method it does so indirectly, using the address found in the virtual method table for the method's class. The virtual method table is nothing more than an array of 32-bit pointers, with each entry containing the address of one of that class's methods. So to call a method, all you need is the index into this array (or, more properly, the offset into the array) of the address of the method you wish to call. The HLA compile-time function @offset comes to the rescue: It will return the offset into the virtual method table of the method whose name you supply as a parameter. Combined with the call instruction, you can easily call any method associated with a class. Here's an example of how you would do this:

```
type
     myCls: class
           .
           .
           .
           method m;
           .
           .
           .
     endclass;
           .
           .
           .
     call( myCls._VMT_[ @offset( myCls.m )]);
```

The call instruction above calls the method whose address appears at the specified entry in the virtual method table for *myCls*. The @offset function call returns the offset (i.e., index times 4) of the address of *myCls*.m within the virtual method table. Hence, this code indirectly calls the m method by using the virtual method table entry for m.

There is one major drawback to calling methods using this scheme: You don't get to use the high-level syntax for procedure/method calls. Instead, you must use the low-level call instruction. In the example above, this isn't much of an issue because the m procedure doesn't have any parameters. If it did have parameters, you would have to manually push those parameters onto the stack yourself. Fortunately, you'll rarely need to call ancestor class methods from a derived class, so this won't be much of an issue in real-world programs.

## 12.15 For More Information

The HLA reference manual at *http://webster.cs.ucr.edu/* or *http://www.artofasm.com/* contains additional information about HLA's class implementation. Check out this document for additional low-level implementation features. This chapter hasn't really attempted to teach the object-oriented programming paradigm. See a generic text on object-oriented design for more details about this subject.

# ASCII CHARACTER SET

| Binary | Hex | Decimal | Character |
|---|---|---|---|
| 0000_0000 | 00 | 0 | NUL |
| 0000_0001 | 01 | 1 | CTRL A |
| 0000_0010 | 02 | 2 | CTRL B |
| 0000_0011 | 03 | 3 | CTRL C |
| 0000_0100 | 04 | 4 | CTRL D |
| 0000_0101 | 05 | 5 | CTRL E |
| 0000_0110 | 06 | 6 | CTRL F |
| 0000_0111 | 07 | 7 | bell |
| 0000_1000 | 08 | 8 | backspace |
| 0000_1001 | 09 | 9 | TAB |
| 0000_1010 | 0A | 10 | line feed |
| 0000_1011 | 0B | 11 | CTRL K |
| 0000_1100 | 0C | 12 | form feed |
| 0000_1101 | 0D | 13 | RETURN |
| 0000_1110 | 0E | 14 | CTRL N |
| 0000_1111 | 0F | 15 | CTRL O |
| 0001_0000 | 10 | 16 | CTRL P |
| 0001_0001 | 11 | 17 | CTRL Q |
| 0001_0010 | 12 | 18 | CTRL R |
| 0001_0011 | 13 | 19 | CTRL S |
| 0001_0100 | 14 | 20 | CTRL T |

| Binary | Hex | Decimal | Character |
|--------|-----|---------|-----------|
| 0001_0101 | 15 | 21 | CTRL U |
| 0001_0110 | 16 | 22 | CTRL V |
| 0001_0111 | 17 | 23 | CTRL W |
| 0001_1000 | 18 | 24 | CTRL X |
| 0001_1001 | 19 | 25 | CTRL Y |
| 0001_1010 | 1A | 26 | CTRL Z |
| 0001_1011 | 1B | 27 | CTRL [ |
| 0001_1100 | 1C | 28 | CTRL \ |
| 0001_1101 | 1D | 29 | ESC |
| 0001_1110 | 1E | 30 | CTRL ^ |
| 0001_1111 | 1F | 31 | CTRL _ |
| 0010_0000 | 20 | 32 | space |
| 0010_0001 | 21 | 33 | ! |
| 0010_0010 | 22 | 34 | " |
| 0010_0011 | 23 | 35 | # |
| 0010_0100 | 24 | 36 | $ |
| 0010_0101 | 25 | 37 | % |
| 0010_0110 | 26 | 38 | & |
| 0010_0111 | 27 | 39 | ' |
| 0010_1000 | 28 | 40 | ( |
| 0010_1001 | 29 | 41 | ) |
| 0010_1010 | 2A | 42 | * |
| 0010_1011 | 2B | 43 | + |
| 0010_1100 | 2C | 44 | , |
| 0010_1101 | 2D | 45 | - |
| 0010_1110 | 2E | 46 | . |
| 0010_1111 | 2F | 47 | / |
| 0011_0000 | 30 | 48 | 0 |
| 0011_0001 | 31 | 49 | 1 |
| 0011_0010 | 32 | 50 | 2 |
| 0011_0011 | 33 | 51 | 3 |
| 0011_0100 | 34 | 52 | 4 |
| 0011_0101 | 35 | 53 | 5 |
| 0011_0110 | 36 | 54 | 6 |
| 0011_0111 | 37 | 55 | 7 |
| 0011_1000 | 38 | 56 | 8 |
| 0011_1001 | 39 | 57 | 9 |
| 0011_1010 | 3A | 58 | : |
| 0011_1011 | 3B | 59 | ; |
| 0011_1100 | 3C | 60 | < |
| 0011_1101 | 3D | 61 | = |

| Binary | Hex | Decimal | Character |
|--------|-----|---------|-----------|
| 0011_1110 | 3E | 62 | > |
| 0011_1111 | 3F | 63 | ? |
| 0100_0000 | 40 | 64 | @ |
| 0100_0001 | 41 | 65 | A |
| 0100_0010 | 42 | 66 | B |
| 0100_0011 | 43 | 67 | C |
| 0100_0100 | 44 | 68 | D |
| 0100_0101 | 45 | 69 | E |
| 0100_0110 | 46 | 70 | F |
| 0100_0111 | 47 | 71 | G |
| 0100_1000 | 48 | 72 | H |
| 0100_1001 | 49 | 73 | I |
| 0100_1010 | 4A | 74 | J |
| 0100_1011 | 4B | 75 | K |
| 0100_1100 | 4C | 76 | L |
| 0100_1101 | 4D | 77 | M |
| 0100_1110 | 4E | 78 | N |
| 0100_1111 | 4F | 79 | O |
| 0101_0000 | 50 | 80 | P |
| 0101_0001 | 51 | 81 | Q |
| 0101_0010 | 52 | 82 | R |
| 0101_0011 | 53 | 83 | S |
| 0101_0100 | 54 | 84 | T |
| 0101_0101 | 55 | 85 | U |
| 0101_0110 | 56 | 86 | V |
| 0101_0111 | 57 | 87 | W |
| 0101_1000 | 58 | 88 | X |
| 0101_1001 | 59 | 89 | Y |
| 0101_1010 | 5A | 90 | Z |
| 0101_1011 | 5B | 91 | [ |
| 0101_1100 | 5C | 92 | \ |
| 0101_1101 | 5D | 93 | ] |
| 0101_1110 | 5E | 94 | ^ |
| 0101_1111 | 5F | 95 | _ |
| 0110_0000 | 60 | 96 | ` |
| 0110_0001 | 61 | 97 | a |
| 0110_0010 | 62 | 98 | b |
| 0110_0011 | 63 | 99 | c |
| 0110_0100 | 64 | 100 | d |
| 0110_0101 | 65 | 101 | e |
| 0110_0110 | 66 | 102 | f |

| Binary | Hex | Decimal | Character |
|--------|-----|---------|-----------|
| 0110_0111 | 67 | 103 | g |
| 0110_1000 | 68 | 104 | h |
| 0110_1001 | 69 | 105 | i |
| 0110_1010 | 6A | 106 | j |
| 0110_1011 | 6B | 107 | k |
| 0110_1100 | 6C | 108 | l |
| 0110_1101 | 6D | 109 | m |
| 0110_1110 | 6E | 110 | n |
| 0110_1111 | 6F | 111 | o |
| 0111_0000 | 70 | 112 | p |
| 0111_0001 | 71 | 113 | q |
| 0111_0010 | 72 | 114 | r |
| 0111_0011 | 73 | 115 | s |
| 0111_0100 | 74 | 116 | t |
| 0111_0101 | 75 | 117 | u |
| 0111_0110 | 76 | 118 | v |
| 0111_0111 | 77 | 119 | w |
| 0111_1000 | 78 | 120 | x |
| 0111_1001 | 79 | 121 | y |
| 0111_1010 | 7A | 122 | z |
| 0111_1011 | 7B | 123 | { |
| 0111_1100 | 7C | 124 | | |
| 0111_1101 | 7D | 125 | } |
| 0111_1110 | 7E | 126 | ~ |
| 0111_1111 | 7F | 127 | |

# INDEX

bx, 9
Byte, 60
byte compile-time function, 559
Byte strings, 633
Bytes, 58

## C

C integer types, 478
C programming language, 478
C/C++ switch statement, 451
Cache, 12
Call indirect, 329
call instruction, 255–256, 288
Callee/caller register
      preservation, 259
Calling base class methods, 698
Carriage return character, 34
Carry flag, 10, 358, 418
    and, or, and xor instruction
      effect, 605
    as a bit accumulator, 609
Case
    insensitive comparison, 207
    labels (noncontiguous), 450
    neutral identifiers, 2
case statement, 423, 442
cbw instruction, 77
cdq instruction, 77
Central processing unit (CPU), 8
ch, 9
Change sign (floating point), 399
Changing the value of a val
      object, 173
char
    compile-time function, 559
    data type, 106
Character
    classification compile-time
      functions, 561
    constants, 165
    data type, 101
    literal constants, 105, 165
    strings, 185
Character sets, 209
    expressions, 212
    implementation, 210
    operators, 213

Choosing an alignment value for
      variables, 131
cl (register), 9
    in rotate operations, 84
    in shl instruction, 81
Classes
    class implementation in
      HLA, 654
    classes and objects, 651
    information hiding, 683
    procedures vs. methods, 663
clc instruction, 88, 609
cld instruction, 88
cli instruction, 88
Clipping (saturation), 80
cmc instruction, 88, 609
cmp instruction, 357
cmps string instruction, 644
cmpsb instruction, 634
cmpsd instruction, 634
cmpsw instruction, 634
Coalescing bit strings, 612
Code sections, 120
Coercion, 111, 133
Column-major ordering, 225, 228
Command-line compiler, 5
Comments, 7
Commutative operators, 374–375
Comparing
    bits, 601
    dates, 88
    floating-point numbers, 92
    a register to zero, 365
    registers with signed integer
      values, 136
    strings, 206–207, 633, 645
Comparison operators in a con-
      stant expression, 169
Comparisons
    dates, 88
    floating point, 92, 386
    unsigned, 363
Compile-time
    conversion of text objects, 564
    decisions, 565
    expressions and operators, 555
    functions, 148, 558. *See also*
      Compile-time functions

Negation
    of boolean variables in an if
        statement, 429
    floating-point, 399
    of large values, 502
Negative numbers, 72
Nested array constants, 231
Nesting record definitions, 239
Nesting try..endtry statements, 43
new memory allocation operator
        (C++ or Pascal), 147
New style procedure
        declarations, 287
Newline constant, 33
newln, 35
Nibbles, 58, 59
nl (newline) constant, 3, 33, 168
Noncommutative binary
        operators, 375
Normalized floating-point numbers,
        95, 388
not in operator, 19
not instruction, 70, 376, 601
not operation, 67, 69
NUL character, 187, 306, 518
NULL, 120
Numbering systems, 54
Numbers, unsigned, 72
Numeric
    compile-time functions, 561
    output field width, 35
    representation, 65

# O

Object
    constructors, 677
    in HLA, 657
    implementation, 668
    initialization, 677
    memory allocation, 679
    pointers (generic objects), 662
    representation with
        inheritance, 673
Object-oriented programming, 651
    benefits, 652
    general principles, 652
One's complement numbering
        system, 73

Operands, mixed size, 530
Operations
    and, 605
    on binary numbers, 70
    not, 67, 69
    or, 67, 68, 376, 605
    rotation, 80
    shift arithmetic right, 83
    shifts, 80
    xor, 67, 69, 376, 605
Operator precedence, 23, 370
    in compile-time expressions, 5
Operators
    in, 19
    logical, 170
    not in, 19
    type, 134
Opposite condition jump, 420
Options
    @align, 657
    @cdecl, 657
    @noalignstack, 288, 297, 657
    @nodisplay, 288, 657
    @noframe, 288, 291, 657
    @nostorage, 124, 186
    @pascal, 657
    @returns, 280, 657
    @stdcall, 657
    @use, 317, 324, 657
Optional parameters in a macro
        expansion, 581
or instruction, 70, 376, 601, 605
or operation, 67, 68
Output field width, 35
Outputting values in HLA, 3, 137
Overflow exception (FPU), 384
Overflow flag, 10, 156, 159, 358, 4
    and the and, or, and xor
        instructions, 605
    testing, 156, 159

# P

Packed
    arrays of bit strings, 615
    data, 85
    decimal arithmetic, 537
Packing and unpacking bit
        strings, 609

Unsigned division, 355–356
Unsigned multiplication,
    352–353, 488
Unsigned numbers, 72
Unsigned variable declarations, 75
Unstructured code, 441
until statement, 17
Untyped reference parameters, 334

## V

val
    declarations, 160
    fields in a class, 656
    section, 172
    val object modificiation, 173
    value parameter
        specification, 272
Value parameters, 269, 310
Values, inputting in an HLA
    program, 7
var
    declarations, 125
    pass-by-reference
        parameters, 273
Variable alignment, 131
Variable declarations, 75
Variable number of parameters in a
    macro, 579
Variable option, @nostorage, 124, 186
Variable-length parameters, 306
Variant types, 247
Vars (_vars_) constant in a
    procedure, 300
Virtual method table pointer
    initialization, 678
Virtual method tables, 671. *See
    also* VMT
Virtual methods in a class, 661

VMT
    declaration, 672
    initialization, 678
    record structure, 671
    virtual method tables, 671
Von Neumann Architecture, 8

## W

while statement, 17, 24, 456, 457
word compile-time function, 559
Word strings, 633
Words, 58, 61
Writing compile-time
    programs, 592

## X

xlat instruction, 540
xor instruction, 70, 376, 601,
    604, 605
xor operation, 67, 69

## Y

Y2K, 87

## Z

Zero divide exception (FPU), 384
Zero extension, 356
Zero flag, 10, 358, 418, 606
    setting after a multiprecision o
        503
    settings after mul and imul
        instructions, 353
Zero-terminating byte (in HLA
    strings), 188
Zero-terminated strings, 186
zstring data type, 186

**The Electronic Frontier Foundation** (EFF) is the leading organization defending civil liberties in the digital world. We defend free speech on the Internet, fight illegal surveillance, promote the rights of innovators to develop new digital technologies, and work to ensure that the rights and freedoms we enjoy are enhanced — rather than eroded — as our use of technology grows.

EFF.ORG

ELECTRONIC FRONTIER FOUNDATION

Protecting Rights and Promoting Freedom on the Electronic Frontier

# THE ART OF DEBUGGING WITH GDB, DDD, AND ECLIPSE

*by* NORMAN MATLOFF *and* PETER JAY SALZMAN

*The Art of Debugging with GDB, DDD, and Eclipse* illustrates the use of three the most popular debugging tools on Linux/Unix platforms: GDB, DDL and Eclipse. In addition to offering specific advice for debugging with e; tool, authors Norm Matloff and Pete Salzman cover general strategies fo improving the process of finding and fixing coding errors, including ho inspect variables and data structures, understand segmentation faults an core dumps, and figure out why your program crashes or throws excepti You'll also learn how to use features like catchpoints, convenience varia and artificial arrays and become familiar with ways to avoid common del ging pitfalls.

SEPTEMBER 2008, 280 PP., $39.95
ISBN 978-1-59327-174-9

# HACKING, 2ND EDITION
## The Art of Exploitation

*by* JON ERICKSON

While many security books merely show how to run existing exploits, *Ha ing: The Art of Exploitation* was the first book to explain how exploits actua work—and how readers can develop and implement their own. In this al new second edition, author Jon Erickson uses practical examples to illust the fundamentals of serious hacking. You'll learn about key concepts un lying common exploits, such as programming errors, assembly language, working, shellcode, cryptography, and more. And the bundled Linux Live provides an easy-to-use, hands-on learning environment. This edition ha: been extensively updated and expanded, including a new introduction to complex, low-level workings of computers.

FEBRUARY 2008, 488 PP. W/CD, $49.95
ISBN 978-1-59327-144-2

# GRAY HAT PYTHON
## Python Programming for Hackers and Reverse Engineers

*by* JUSTIN SEITZ

*Gray Hat Python* explains how to complete various hacking tasks with Pyth which is fast becoming the programming language of choice for hackers reverse engineers, and software testers. Author Justin Seitz explains the c cepts behind hacking tools like debuggers, Trojans, fuzzers, and emulato He then goes on to explain how to harness existing Python-based securit tools, and build new ones when the pre-built ones just won't cut it. The be teaches readers how to automate tedious reversing and security tasks, sni secure traffic out of an encrypted web browser session, use PyDBG, Immu Debugger, Sulley, IDAPython, PyEMU, and more.

APRIL 2009, 216 PP., $39.95
ISBN 978-1-59347-192-3

# E IDA PRO BOOK, 2ND EDITION

### nofficial Guide to the World's Most Popular Disassembler

HRIS EAGLE

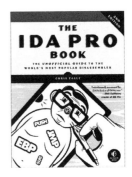

ed by the creator of IDA Pro as the "long-awaited" and "information-
ed" guide to IDA, *The IDA Pro Book* covers everything from the very first
s with IDA to advanced automation techniques. You'll learn to identify
wn library routines and how to extend IDA to support new processors
filetypes, making disassembly possible for new or obscure architectures.
second edition of *The IDA Pro Book* has been completely updated and
ed to cover the new features and cross-platform interface of IDA Pro 6.0.
er additions include expanded coverage of the IDA Pro Debugger,
Python, and the IDA Pro SDK.

2011, 672 PP., $69.95
978-1-59327-289-0

# TOTOOLS

### ctioner's Guide to GNU Autoconf, Automake, and Libtool

HN CALCOTE

*tools* is the first book to offer programmers a tutorial-based guide to
Autotools, a group of utilities that lets developers easily create software
is portable across many Unix-based operating systems. Beginning with a
ussion of high-level concepts, author John Calcote first gives readers an
view of many different use-cases and examples, then moves into more
anced details, like using the M4 Macro Processor with Autoconf, extend-
the framework provided by Automake, building Java and C# sources, and
e. The book teaches readers how to structure and organize open source
ware, master the Autotools framework and functional project configura-
scripts, use extensions to Autoconf, convert an existing open source
ect from a custom build system to an Autotools build system, and write
own Autotools macros.

PP., $44.95
978-1-59327-206-7

NE:
420.7240 OR
863.9900
NDAY THROUGH FRIDAY,
M. TO 5 P.M. (PST)

EMAIL:
SALES@NOSTARCH.COM

WEB:
WWW.NOSTARCH.COM

*The Art of Assembly Language, 2nd Edition* is set in New Baskerville, Futura, TheSansMonoCondensed, and Dogma.

This book was printed and bound by Sheridan Books, Inc. in Chelsea, Michigan. The paper is 60# Finch Offset, which is certified by the Forest Stewardship Council (FSC). The book uses a layflat binding, which allows it to lie flat when open.

# UPDATES

Visit *http://www.nostarch.com/assembly2.htm* for updates, errata, and other information.